GOTHIC ARCHITECTURE
IN ENGLAND

LICHFIELD CATHEDRAL FROM S.W.

GOTHIC ARCHITECTURE IN ENGLAND

AN ANALYSIS OF THE ORIGIN & DEVELOPMENT OF ENGLISH CHURCH ARCHITECTURE FROM THE NORMAN CONQUEST TO THE DISSOLUTION OF THE MONASTERIES

BY

FRANCIS BOND,

M.A., LINCOLN COLLEGE, OXFORD;
Fellow of the Geological Society, London;
Honorary Associate of the Royal Institute of British Architects

WITH 1254 ILLUSTRATIONS, COMPRISING 785 PHOTOGRAPHS, SKETCHES, AND MEASURED DRAWINGS, AND 469 PLANS, SECTIONS, DIAGRAMS, AND MOLDINGS

LONDON
B. T. BATSFORD, 94 HIGH HOLBORN
1906

Printed at THE DARIEN PRESS, *Edinburgh.*

PREFACE.

In the preparation of this work full use has been made of the materials which have accumulated, both English and foreign. In all important cases an attempt has been made to render due acknowledgment. A list of the sources which have been drawn upon most freely will be found on page viii.; reference is made to many others in footnotes in the course of the book. But, in addition, the writer has to acknowledge the ready assistance of many friends who have obtained information or verified data for him on the spot. As to the illustrations he is under special obligation to members of the architectural profession for the ready and generous assistance they have given. The difficulty has been to select from the valuable material placed at his disposal.

For plans, sketches, moldings, or measured drawings his acknowledgments are due to Mr Maurice B. Adams, F.R.I.B.A.; the Committee of the Architectural Association Sketch Book; Mr H. J. Austin; Messrs G. Bell & Son; Mr W. H. Bidlake, M.A.; Mr J. Bilson, F.S.A.; the Council of the Cambridge Antiquarian Society; the Delegates of the Clarendon Press, Oxford; the Rev. Canon Church, M.A.; the Rev. R. Corrie Castle; Mr J. J. Creswell, A.R.I.B.A.; Mr Reginald Fowler; Mr G. Frisch, A.R.I.B.A.; Mr S. K. Greenslade, A.R.I.B.A.; Lord Grimthorpe; Mr T. G. Jackson, R.A.; Mr Montague Rhodes James, LITT.D.; Mr C. Henman, A.R.I.B.A.; Mr Gerald C. Horsley; Mr A. H. Kersey, F.R.I.B.A.; Mr J. Langham; Mr John Murray; Mr J. T. Micklethwaite, F.S.A.; Mr J. Norton; Mr A. Y. Nutt; Mr H. A. Paley, A.R.I.B.A.; Mr Roland W. Paul, F.S.A.; Mr H. Phibbs; Professor Beresford Pite, F.R.I.B.A.; Mr E. S. Prior, M.A.; Mr H. A. Prothero, M.A.; Mr Harbottle Reed; the Council of the Royal Institute of British Architects; Mr J. Oldrid Scott, F.S.A.; Mr C. Wontner Smith, A.R.I.B.A.; Professor Elsey Smith, M.A.; the Committee of the Society of Antiquaries; Mr Charles Spooner; Mr Russell Sturgis, M.A., PH.D.; Mr Sydney Vacher, A.R.I.B.A.; Mr H. D. Walker; Mr F. S. Waller, F.R.I.B.A.; Mr W. G. Watkins, A.R.I.B.A.; Mr W. S. Weatherley, F.R.I.B.A.; Mr A. Needham Wilson, A.R.I.B.A.; as well as to others with whom it has been found impossible to communicate.

A large number of photographs has been placed at his disposal; and though they necessarily lose in reproduction by mechanical process, the results show how excellent in many cases were the originals. He is indebted for the use of photographs to Dr F. J. Allen; Rev. W. Tuzo Alston; Mr W. G. Bannister; Mr R. H. Barker; Mr F. Bligh Bond, F.R.I.B.A.; Mr R. P. Brereton, M.A.; Dr Oscar Clark; Mr J. S. Collings; Mr W. Davidson; Messrs Dawkes & Partridge; Mr J. P. Freeman; Mr S. Gardner; Mr J. Pattison Gibson; Mr Donald Gooding; Rev. T. Gough; Mr E. Gunn, A.R.I.B.A.; Mr C. C. Hodges; Mr G. H. Lovegrove; Rev. T. Perkins; Dr H. W. Pigeon; Rev. H. Bedford Pim; Mr Alan Potter; Rev. G. W. Saunders; Mr F. R. Taylor; Mr G. H. Tyndall; Mr E. H. Walker; Mr E. W. M. Wonnacott, F.S.I.

As the preparation of the work advanced, the importance of liberality of illustration became increasingly apparent. It is only right to acknowledge the readiness with which Mr Batsford seconded the author in his wish to widen the scope of the book and to bring it out in worthy form. Special acknowledgment is due to Mr Harry Batsford; his interest in the subject and acquaintance with architectural literature made his assistance of great value. The whole of the moldings, diagrams, plans, and sections have been drawn by Mr L. R. Stains. Sections are drawn to a uniform scale; the plans of the parish churches, and that of St Gall, are drawn to half the scale of those of the greater churches. The text has had the advantage of the revision and criticism of Mr John Bilson, from whose sound and accurate scholarship the writer has benefited at all stages of its preparation. Various portions of the proofs have been revised by Mr T. D. Atkinson, M.A.; Mr S. B. Beale, A.R.I.B.A.; Mr Harold Brakspear, F.S.A.; Mr R. P. Brereton, M.A.; Mr J. N. Comper; Mr J. J. Cresswell, A.R.I.B.A.; Rev. R. A. Davis; Mr C. H. Grinling, M.A.; Mr E. M. Hick; Mr W. H. St John Hope, M.A.; Mr G. H. Lovegrove; Mr R. Phené Spiers, F.S.A.; and Mr E. W. M. Wonnacott, F.S.I., to all of whom the writer is indebted for suggestions and criticisms of much value. Not seldom, however, he has ventured to disregard their advice, and has remained of the same opinion still; for all the shortcomings of the text, therefore, he alone is responsible. Valuable assistance has been rendered by Rev. R. A. Davis in the preparation of the index.

The student and archæologist will find in Chapter XLII. a dated list of English buildings arranged in alphabetical order. Such a list

should be of great service to all who are interested in the history of
English architecture.   The preparation of this list has involved much
labour; but it is obvious that the first draft of such a chronology
cannot be free from imperfections and inaccuracies.   The writer will
welcome any corrections or additions to it.

To the architectural student it is hoped that the twenty-eight
sheets of moldings will be found specially valuable.   In the largest
collection hitherto published, that by Mr Paley, the moldings are very
minute and crowded together, nor are they to the same scale; yet
it makes all the difference whether, for instance, a capital and arch
come from a piscina or a pier arcade; several species of moldings are
omitted altogether, *e.g.* those of vaulting ribs, basement courses, doorways and windows; and of those which are illustrated the locality from
which they come is in many cases not indicated.

Of the other collections, that in Sharpe's *Architectural Parallels*
is of great value, but it is contained in an expensive book long out of
print; nor does it illustrate any moldings later than the fourteenth
century; that in Sharpe's *Mouldings of the Six Periods of British
Architecture* extends up to the Reformation, but was never finished.
The present collection gives a conspectus of English moldings from
the middle of the twelfth to the middle of the sixteenth century; they
are drawn boldly and clearly; they are to the same scale; the locality,
as far as possible, of each is given; molds of ribs, basement courses,
doorways and windows have been included; and three sheets have
been added of the plans of piers, as well of the greater churches as of
the parish churches.   It has been attempted, moreover, to show the
correlation of cognate members.   A sheet has been prepared to show
the relation of the pier on the one hand to the base and plinth, on the
other to the abacus or capital and arch.   In the same way illustrations have been inserted to show the relation of the arch to the jambs
of doorways and windows.   These architectural members are not
complete in themselves; each is part of a group, and should not only
be beautiful in itself, but should fit the position it occupies as a
member of that group or whole.   The co-ordination of the various
members of the pier and arch has hardly ever been systematically
illustrated except in Messrs Johnson and Kersey's valuable *Churches
of the Nene Valley*, to the authors of which special acknowledgment
is due.   The various members have not always been illustrated on the
same sheet.   To facilitate reference, however, all the illustrations,
including the moldings, have been indexed alphabetically (709-738).
In many cases also it will be found that a photograph has purposely

been given as well as a drawing, *e.g.* of the foliated capital of West Walton. The index to the illustrations, therefore, should constantly be consulted. In the same way a vault is often shown both in perspective and in plan, *e.g.* that of the choir of Oxford Cathedral (331); as also the piers, *e.g.* that of the nave of Norwich Cathedral (238 and 659). It may be added that the photographic representation of vaults on plan has not hitherto been attempted in an architectural treatise (see 327-334), and it is believed that this will greatly clear up the intricacies of rib construction. In many later vaults, indeed, *e.g.* that of the nave of St George's, Windsor (330, 332), the construction is utterly unintelligible as the vault is usually seen, *i.e.* in perspective. In conclusion, the writer begs the student to believe that no collection of moldings will absolve him from the task, as delightful as it is indispensable, of drawing them for himself *in situ*.

THE FOLLOWING ARE THE TITLES OF AUTHORITIES QUOTED SUMMARILY
IN THE COURSE OF THE TEXT.

ANDERSON, W. J., and R. PHENÉ SPIERS. *The Architecture of Greece and Rome.* London, 1902.

ARCHITECTURAL PUBLICATION SOCIETY. *Dictionary of Architecture.* 7 vols. London, 1849 to 1892.

Architecture and Building, Dictionary of. Edited by Russell Sturgis. 3 vols. New York, 1901.

BARRY, E. *Lectures on Architecture.* 1881.

BELL. *Series of English Cathedrals.* London, 1896-1904.

BECKETT, Sir E. *Book on Building.* 2nd edition. London, 1880.

BILLINGS, R. W. *Carlisle Cathedral.* London, 1840.

—— *Durham Cathedral.* London, 1843.

—— *Kettering Church.* London, 1843.

—— *Temple Church.* London, 1838.

BILSON, JOHN. *The Beginnings of Gothic Architecture.* Journal of the Royal Institute of British Architects. March 11 and 25, April 15, 1899, and May 10, 1902.

—— *Chapter House of Beverley Minster.* Archæologia, liv. 425.

—— *On the Recent Discoveries at the East End of the Cathedral Church of Durham.* Archæological Journal, liii. 1-18.

—— *Beverley Minster.* Architectural Review, iii., 197-204 and 250-259.

BLOXAM, M. H. *Gothic Ecclesiastical Architecture.* 11th edition. 3 vols. London, 1882.

BOND, FRANCIS. *English Cathedrals Illustrated.* 3rd edition. London, 1903.

BOND, FRANCIS. *On the Comparative Value of Documentary and Architectural Evidence in establishing the Chronology of the English Cathedrals.* Journal of the Royal Institute of British Architects. November 21, 1898.

—— *Classification of Romanesque Architecture.* Journal of Royal Institute of British Architects. April 22, 1901.

BOWMAN, H., and CROWTHER, J. S. *Churches of the Middle Ages.* 2 vols. London, 1850.

BOYLE, J. R. *Holy Trinity Church, Hull.* Hull, 1890.

BRAKSPEAR, HAROLD. *Hayles Abbey Church.* Archæological Journal, lviii. 350-357.

—— *On the First Church at Furness.* Transactions of the Lancashire and Cheshire Antiquarian Society, xviii.

—— *Lacock Abbey Church.* Archæological Journal, lvii. 1-9.

—— *Lacock Abbey.* Archæologia, lvii. 125-158.

—— *Burnham Abbey.* Archæological Journal, lx. 294-317.

—— *Waverley Abbey.* Surrey Archæological Society, 1905.

—— *Beaulieu Abbey.* Archæological Journal. 1906.

BRANDON, R. and J. A. *Analysis of Gothick Architecture.* 2 vols. London, 1847.

—— *Open Timber Roofs of the Middle Ages.* London, 1849.

—— *Parish Churches.* London, 1848.

BRITTON, JOHN. *Architectural Antiquities of Great Britain.* 5 vols. Lond., 1807-1835.

—— *Cathedral Antiquities of Great Britain.* 6 vols. London, 1814-1835.

BROWN, G. BALDWIN. *From Schola to Cathedral.* London, 1886.

—— *The Arts in Early England.* 2 vols. London, 1903.

BROWNE, WILLIS. *Survey of the Cathedrals of York, Durham, &c.* 1727.

BRUTAILS, J. A. *L'archéologie du moyen âge et ses méthodes.* Paris, 1900.

BUCKLER, GEORGE. *Twenty-two Churches of Essex.* London, 1856.

"BUILDER," THE. *Cathedrals of England and Wales.* London, 1894.

BUTLER, W. *Measured Drawings of Christ Church, Dublin.* 1874.

—— *Christ Church, Dublin.* London, 1901.

BUTTERFIELD, W. *Shottesbrooke Church.* London, 1844.

CARPENTER, R. H. *Sherborne Abbey Church.* Journal of the Royal Institute of British Architects. March 19, 1877.

CARTER, J. *Ancient Architecture of England.* London, 1795.

—— *Plans and Drawings published by the Society of Antiquaries,* 1807.

CATTANEO, R. *L'architecture en Italie du VIe au XIe siècle.* Traduction par M. le Monnier. Venise, 1890.

CAUMONT, A. DE. *Abécédaire, ou Rudiments d'archéologie.* 3 vols. 1858-1862.

CAVELER, W. *Specimens of Gothic Architecture.* 2nd edition. London, 1839.

—— *Warmington Church.* London, 1850.

CHOISY, A. *Histoire de l'Architecture.* 2 vols. Paris, 1899.

—— *L'art de bâtir chez les Romains.* Paris, 1873.

—— *L'art de bâtir chez les Byzantins.* Paris, 1893.

CHRISTIAN, E. *Skelton Church, Yorkshire.* London, 1846.

Churches of the Archdeaconry of Northampton. Oxford, 1849.

COLLING, J. K. *Details of Gothic Architecture.* 2 vols. London. 1856.

—— *Gothic Ornaments.* 2 vols. London, 1850.

—— *English Mediæval Foliage.* London, 1874.

COLSON, J. B. *Reparations of the Roof of Winchester Nave in 1896.* Winchester, 1899.

CONDER, E. L. *Long Melford Church.* London, 1887.

COX, Rev. J. C., LL.D., *Churches of Derbyshire.* 4 vols. London, 1875-1879.

Cox, Rev. J. C., and Sergeantson, Rev. R. M. *Church of the Holy Sepulchre, North-ampton.* Northampton, 1897.

Craddock, Thomas. *Peterborough Cathedral.* Peterborough, 1874.

Cresy, E. *Stone Church, Kent.* London, N.D.

Dartein, F. de. *L'architecture lombarde.* 1865-1882.

Dehio and von Bezold. *Die Kirchliche Baukunst des Abendlandes.* 2 vols., text; 601 plates. Stuttgart, 1884-1901.

Dollman, F. T. *Church of St Mary Overie, Southwark.* London, 1881.

—— *Analysis of Ancient Domestic Architecture.* 2 vols. London, 1861.

Enlart, Camille. *Origines françaises de l'architecture gothique en Italie.* Paris, 1894.

—— *Manuel d'archéologie française.* Vol. I. *Architecture religieuse.* Paris, 1902. Vol. II. *Architecture civile et militaire.* 1904. (Unless otherwise specified, the refer-ences in the text are to Vol. I.)

Fen and Marshland Churches. Wisbech, N.D.

Fergusson, J. *History of Architecture in all Countries.* 2 vols. 3rd edition. Edited by R. Phené Spiers. London, 1893.

Ferrey, B. *Christ Church, Hants.* London, 1834.

Freeman, Archdeacon. *Architectural History of Exeter Cathedral.* 2nd edition. Exeter, 1888.

Freeman, E. A. *Window Tracery.* Oxford, 1851.

Garbett, E. L. *Principles of Design in Architecture.* 7th edition. London, 1891.

Gardner, J. Starkie. *Ironwork.* London, 1893.

Godwin, E. W. *Bristol Cathedral.* Archæological Journal. Vol. 20.

Greenwell, Canon W. *Durham Cathedral.* 4th edition. Durham, 1892.

Grimthorpe, Edmund, Lord. *St Alban's Cathedral and its Restoration.* 2nd edition. St Albans, 1893.

Hadfield, J. *Ecclesiastical, Castellated, and Domestic Architecture in Essex.* London, 1848.

Hodges, C. C. *Hexham Abbey.* London, 1888.

—— *Blyth Priory Church.* 1881.

Hope, W. H. St John. *Alnwick Abbey* (White Canons). Yorkshire Archæological Journal. 1887.

—— *Canterbury, St Pancras.* Archæologia Cantiana. Vol. 25.

—— *Canterbury, Inventories of Christ Church* (with J. W. Legg). London, 1902.

—— *Castle Acre Priory* (Cluniac). Norfolk and Norwich Archæological Society. 1894.

—— *Dale Abbey* (White Canons). Derbyshire Archæological Society, i. 100, and ii. 128.

—— *Fountains Abbey* (Cistercian). Yorkshire Archæological Journal, xv. 269-402. 1900.

—— *Furness Abbey* (Cistercian). Transactions of Cumberland and Westmorland Archæological Society. Vol. xvi.

—— *Notes on the Abbey Church of Glastonbury.* Archæological Journal, lxi. 185-196. 1904.

—— *Gloucester Abbey* (Benedictine). Records of Gloucester Cathedral, iii. 1.

—— *Hulne* (White Friars). Archæological Journal. 1890.

—— *Lewes Priory* (Cluniac). Archæological Journal, xl.

—— *Architectural History of the Cathedral, Church, and Monastery of Rochester.* London, 1900.

HOPE, W. H. ST JOHN. *St Agatha's Abbey, Richmond* (White Canons). Yorkshire Archæological Journal, x. 117-158. 1887.

—— *St Radigund's Priory* (White Canons). Archæologia Cantiana, xiv. 140.

—— *Watton Abbey* (Gilbertine). Archæological Journal, lviii. 1.

—— *West Langdon* (White Canons). Archæologia Cantiana, xv. 59.

HUBSCH, H. *Monuments de l'architecture chrétienne.* Paris, 1866.

JOHNSON, J. *Reliques of Ancient English Architecture.* London, N.D.

JOHNSON, R. J. *Specimens of Early French Architecture.* London, 1864.

KING, T. H. *Study Book of Mediæval Architecture and Art.* 4 vols. London, 1858.

LASTEYRIE, Comte ROBERT DE. *Discours sur les origines de l'architecture gothique.* Caen, 1901.

—— *Crypte de St Martin, Tours.* Memoires de l'academie des inscriptions et belles lettres. Tome xxxiv., Part I. Paris, 1891.

LETHABY, W. R. *Mediæval Art.* London, 1904.

LIVETT, Rev. G. M. *Southwell Minster.* Southwell, 1883.

LONGMAN, W. *St Paul's Cathedral.* London, 1873.

MICKLETHWAITE, J. T. *Westminster Abbey.* Arch. Journal. Vol. 51.

MURRAY. *Cathedrals of England and Wales.* 8 vols. London, 1861-1873.

NEALE, J. *St Alban's Abbey.* London, 1877.

Nene Valley, Churches of. Edited by E. Sharpe, J. Johnson, and A. H. Kersey. London, 1880.

PALEY, F. A. *Manual of Gothic Moldings.* 4th edition. London, 1877.

—— *Manual of Gothic Architecture.* London, 1846.

PARKER, J. H. *Glossary of Gothic Architecture.* 5th edition. 3 vols. Oxford, 1850.

—— *Guide to Architectural Antiquities in the Neighbourhood of Oxford.* Oxford, 1846.

—— *Great Haseley Church, Oxon.* Oxford, 1840.

—— *Dorchester Church, Oxon.* Oxford, 1845.

PETIT, Rev. J. L. *Remarks on Church Architecture.* London. 2 vols. 1841.

—— *Boxgrove Priory.* Chichester, 1861.

POTTER, JOSEPH. *Tintern, Buildwas, and Wenlock Abbeys.* London, 1849.

PRIOR, E. S. *History of Gothic Art in England.* London, 1900.

PUGIN, A. *Specimens of Gothic Architecture.* 2 vols. London, 1821.

PUGIN, A. and A. W. *Examples of Gothic Architecture.* 3 vols. London, 1838-1840.

PUGIN, A. W. *True Principles of Pointed or Christian Architecture.* London, 1841.

—— *Chancel Screens and Rood Lofts.* London, 1851.

REEVE, J. A. *Fountains Abbey.* London, 1892.

RICKMAN, T. *Styles of Architecture in England.* 7th edition. London, 1881.

RUPRICH-ROBERT. *L'architecture normande aux XIe et XIIe siècles en Normandie et en Angleterre.* 2 vols. Paris, N.D.

RUSKIN, J. *Seven Lamps of Architecture.* 3rd edition. Orpington, 1891.

SAINT-PAUL, ANTHYME. *Viollet-le-Duc, ses travaux d'art et son système archéologique.* 2nd edition. Paris, 1881.

—— *Histoire monumentale de la France.* 4th edition. Paris, 1895.

SCOTT, Sir G. G. *Gleanings from Westminster Abbey.* 2nd edition. Oxford, 1863.

—— *Lectures on the Rise and Development of Mediæval Architecture.* 2 vols. London, 1879.

SCOTT, G. G. (Jun.). *Essay on the History of English Church Architecture.* London, 1881.

SHARPE, EDMUND. *Architectural Parallels in the Twelfth and Thirteenth Centuries, selected from Abbey Churches.* London, 1848.
—— *Supplement to ditto, containing full-sized moldings.* London, 1848.
—— *Mouldings of the Six Periods of British Architecture.* 3 parts. London, 1871.
—— *Decorated Window Tracery in England.* 2 vols. London, 1849.
—— *Lincoln Excursion of Architectural Association.* London, 1871.
—— *Architecture of the Cistercians.* Journal of the Royal Institute of British Architects. June 19, 1871.
—— *Ornamentation of the Transitional Period.* London, 1876.
—— *New Shoreham Church, Sussex.* Chichester, 1861.
—— *Seven Periods of English Architecture.* 3rd edition. London, 1888.

SKETCH-BOOKS. *Architectural Association.* 32 vols. 1867-1904.
—— *Abbey Square.* 3 vols. 1872.
—— *John o' Gaunt.* 3 vols. 1874-1879.
—— *Spring Gardens.* 8 vols. 1866-1890.
STATHAM, H. H. *Architecture for General Readers.* London, 1895.
STEWART, Rev. D. J. *Architectural History of Ely Cathedral.* London, 1868.
—— *Architectural History of Norwich Cathedral and Cloister.* Archæological Journal. Vol. 32.
STOKES, MARGARET. *Early Christian Architecture in Ireland.* London, 1878.
—— *Early Christian Art in Ireland.* 2 vols. London, 1887.

VIOLLET-LE-DUC. *Dictionnaire raisonné de l'architecture française du XIe au XVIe siècle.* 10 vols. Paris, 1858-1868.

WALCOTT, Rev. M. E. C. *Church and Conventual Arrangement.* London, 1861.
WALLER, F. S. *Gloucester Cathedral.* 1856.
WEALE. *Quarterly Papers on Architecture.* 4 vols. 1844-1845.
WHEWELL, Rev. W. *Notes on German Churches and Normandy.* Cambridge, 1835.
WICKES, C. *Spires and Towers of England.* 3 vols. London, 1853.
WILLIS, Rev. R. *Architecture of the Middle Ages, especially of Italy.* Cambridge, 1835.
—— *Canterbury Cathedral.* 1845.
—— *Chichester Cathedral.* Chichester. 1861.
—— *York Minster.* Archæological Institute. York volume, 1846.
—— *Worcester Cathedral.* Archæological Journal. Vol. 20.
—— *Worcester Monastery.* Archæological Journal. Vol. 20.
—— *Winchester Cathedral.* Archæological Institute. Winchester volume, 1846.
—— *Lichfield Cathedral.* Archæological Journal. Vol. 18.
—— *Facsimile of the Sketch Book of Wilars de Honecort.* 1859.
—— *On the Construction of the Vaults of the Middle Ages.* Transactions of the Royal Institute of British Architects. Vol. I., Part II. 1842.
—— *Architectural History of Glastonbury Abbey.* Cambridge, 1866.
—— *Architectural Nomenclature of the Middle Ages.* Cambridge, 1844.
—— and J. W. CLARKE, M.A. *Architectural History of the University of Cambridge.* Cambridge, 1886.

Yorkshire Churches. Leeds, 1844.

WINTERS, W. *Waltham Abbey.* Waltham, 1888.

TABLE OF CONTENTS.

xiv   CONTENTS.

UCTION.

English race two make unchallenged
literature and our mediæval archi-
here be said ; its triumphs are still
latter it is not so. Painting, music,
by thousands. The new symphony
respectful audience and admiration ;
rged on every second-rate painting or
re. There never was a time of such
-art of architecture. It was not always
literature, little painting, little play-
architecture. Everybody loved it, or
fifteenth century every village mason
enter could crown it with a hammer-
ays, Lord Bacon, Lord Burghley, the
France, were students of architecture ;
the planning and design of hall and
ish literature and English architecture,
ied the palaces of Palladio and Michael
s the proportions of the orders. A
y equipment of the gentleman. Lord
, the paternity of which belonged to
chitects, before the English aristocracy
n the destruction of the pheasant and
the fox.

Nowadays architecture is outside the precincts of culture. Educated people know little and care less about architecture. Classic and Renaissance, Romanesque and Gothic, are naught to them ; their ignorance is naked and unashamed. In this general neglect mediæval architecture beyond all is immersed. For a brief period indeed interest in this supreme artistic achievement of our race was revived by Britton, Pugin, Petit, and Willis, greatest of all. That interest was not to endure.

Nowadays the students of our national architecture are few. It is surprising that there are any in the face of the discouragements which their study meets. At the older universities tens of thousands of pounds are expended every year to encourage the study of classical literature, mathematics, history, or science ; not a penny on architecture. Neither at Oxford nor at Cambridge is there a single professorship, lectureship, scholarship, or fellowship in English mediæval architecture. France and Germany have several able periodicals devoted exclusively to the subject of mediæval architecture ; we have not one. Government subventions support a great museum of mediæval art in the Trocadero at Paris ; we have at South Kensington a few casts, and those chiefly of foreign Renaissance work, mixed up with pitchers and jugs and fiddles and furniture. At the annual exhibition of the Royal Academy one small room is deemed enough for the drawings of the architects. Year by year we have exhibitions of the potsherds of Rome and Greece and Egypt; not of our own mediæval art. Immense sums are spent in excavating civilisations in far-away countries with which we have little concern ; our own Byland, Rievaulx, Glastonbury remain lost beneath the soil.

For this apathy and neglect there must be a reason ; probably there is more than one. In the first place architecture, if it is to be studied to the best advantage, must be studied, like botany and geology, *in situ*. But such study is open to few. Hexham and Dore, Norwich and St David's are far sundered. Yet these and countless others must be visited in any thoroughgoing survey of English mediæval architecture. Next to actual inspection of the buildings, the best thing is to study them in illustrations. Hitherto, however, it has not been possible, except to the few, to study them even in this form. There are indeed comparatively few mediæval buildings of the first rank which have not been illustrated in measured drawings. But what private person could afford to become the possessor of the tomes, many of them rare, costly, and bulky, in which they are to be found: Bowman and Crowther's *Churches of the Middle Ages*, Brandon's *Analysis* and *Open Timber Roofs*, Britton's *Architectural Antiquities* and *English Cathedrals*, Caveler's *Specimens*, Colling's *Details, Gothic Ornaments*, and *English Mediæval Foliage*, Hadfield's *Essex*, Johnson and Kersey's *Nene Valley Churches*, Pugin's *Examples* and *Specimens*, Sharpe's *Architectural Parallels*, Professor Willis' invaluable papers, scattered about in the Transactions of various provincial societies, the Architectural Association *Sketch Book* (32 vols.), the *Spring Gardens Sketch Book* (8 vols.), the *John o' Gaunt Sketch Book* (3 vols.), the *Abbey Square Sketch Book* (3 vols), Neale's *St Alban's*, Hodges' *Hexham*, Reeve's *Fountains*, and a host of other monographs. These, in default of personal visits to each church, are the sources to which the architectural student must resort. Such a collection, however, is entirely out of reach except to residents in London. This difficulty of access to adequate illustrations may well explain, to some extent at any rate, the unpopularity of the study of mediæval architecture. It has been unpopular because the apparatus for its proper study has not been available. To the writer, therefore, the first thing to be done, to advance the study of mediæval architecture, seemed to be to provide copious illustrations. Fortunately two circumstances combine to make this possible, even in the compass of a single volume to do this in a fairly adequate manner. One is that the copyrights of many large and costly works have run out, and it has become possible to reproduce from them illustrations long out of print. The second is the facility of illustration given by modern photographic processes. It has been the writer's pleasant task to visit nearly every important church in England, camera in hand, and he has had abundant aid from his brother photographers. But for photography an illustrated volume so copious in examples would have been out of the question. With its aid, it has been possible to include 20 whole-page collotypes, 785 reproductions of photographs, sketches, and measured drawings, in addition to 469 further illustrations which are arranged on 12 pages of plans, 2 pages of sections, 8 pages of diagrams, and 28 pages of moldings. A great book is a great evil; but not, it is to be hoped the reader will think, a great picture-book.

A yet graver reason it may be for the failure of mediæval architecture to arrest and retain the attention of the modern student is the fragmentary and disconnected presentation of the subject which has been usual. Open any of the text-books from Rickman downwards and try to obtain a consecutive and complete treatment of any one of the chief features of the mediæval church—its plan, its vault, the abutments of the vault, the drainage of the roofs, the fenestration—what do we find? Perhaps we would like to know about the principles of construction of the vault. On this we get a few isolated scraps of information under "Norman," followed by details about doorways and buttresses and windows and capitals and things in general. The few scraps of information about Norman vaults are lost in this *olla podrida.* When we have forgotten all about them, we get perchance some information about "Early English" vaulting. This in turn is overlaid by layer upon layer of other miscellaneous matter. And so on to the end. No subject can be understood nor can any subject interest, when treated in such desultory fashion. There seemed to the writer, therefore, to be room for a connected analysis of mediæval architecture. In this, first of all, should come the subject of planning—a subject of primary importance, which however has usually been omitted altogether. Secondly should come the important matter of the vault and its supports. Of great importance also is the question of abutment; it is one thing to put up a vault, it is another to induce it to stay up. This includes the whole machinery of buttresses, pinnacles, and flying buttresses. Then there is the drainage question. How is the rain to be kept from damaging roof and wall? This includes the corbel-table and dripping eaves, and the later contrivances of gutter, gargoyle, parapet, and battlement; also the protection of wall, window, and doorway by basement course, string, dripstone, and hood-mold. Then there is the whole question of lighting, and the development of window tracery as controlled by the exigencies of stained glass; and many other subjects, each needing separate treatment, such as the capital and the base, the triforium and the clerestory, the doorway and the porch, the roof, the tower and the spire. On every one of these a separate treatise seems to be demanded; not necessarily lengthy, but consecutive in treatment, and as far as space allows, complete. It is precisely to such a collection of short treatises on mediæval planning and building construction that Part II., the bulk of the work, is devoted. (See Table of Contents, xiii, xiv, xv.)

The fragmentary treatment of mediæval architecture which has prevailed so long is probably due mainly to the influence of Rickman's work. Just as Linnæus taught the botanical student to arrange his plants in orders, genera, and species, so Rickman taught his followers to classify their churches in architectural periods. Linnæus' methods long prevailed; and while they prevailed, botany was a dull science. Later on, botanists arose who taught how plants grew, and botany at once became a fascinating study. Architecture had not the good fortune of botany; it has remained a classificatory science. No wonder, then, that it has been found void of life and interest.

Nor is that the only objection to a mere classificatory treatment. It is bad enough that it devitalises the subject of interest; it is worse still if the classification is itself unsound. And that is so. We have been told for nearly a century that there are four periods of English mediæval architecture: Norman, Early English, Decorated, and Perpendicular. But there is no such thing; the famous four periods are mere figments of the imagination. Take a subject of primary and fundamental importance: that of the planning of the greater churches; there are not four, but only two periods of planning; of which the first, the period of the three parallel eastern apses and of the periapsidal plan, ends with the twelfth century, while all the later plans were in use by that time. Or take vaulting as the criterion. Then the periods become five: that of the groined vault, the ribbed vault whether quadripartite or sexpartite, the vault with tiercerons and ridge ribs, the lierne vault, and the fan vault; the periods are not four but five, and do not coincide with the traditional Norman, Early English, Decorated, and Perpendicular. If the very important matter of abutment be taken as a criterion, we are equally in difficulty. All the main methods of abutment had come into use by A.D. 1200; in the Early English, Decorated, and Perpendicular periods no important novelty as to methods of abutment is introduced. Only to one, and that quite a subordinate member of the building, does the antiquated terminology fairly apply, viz., to the fenestration; and even here it is badly chosen and inaccurate, and was very properly revised and corrected by Mr Edmund Sharpe.*

The whole classification, moreover, is mischievous as well as baseless. The novice is led to believe that architecture stopped at the end of each of the four periods, turned over a new leaf, and began again *de novo*. Nay further, that there is in each of the four periods some inward and spiritual significance, which, could it be discerned, would give us the keynote or character of the whole architecture of the time. But it is just as easy to argue about the deep moral and spiritual significance of the two planning or abutment periods as about that of the traditional four; and just as futile. The greatest objection of all, however, to this cutting up of architectural history into periods is that it obscures the essential unity of the development of the building art. Professor Freeman ever protested against the demarcation of ancient and modern History. Equally important is it to emphasise the unity of architectural art, and to protest against its being cut up into arbitrary sections. Architecture is one, not many. Every so-called style was a transition from that which preceded it, and a transition to that which was its successor. "From Roman to Renaissance the history of architecture is an uninterrupted series of transitions; it is quite time that we studied the art of the Middle Ages in the fashion in which we study the

---

* For Rickman's Norman, Early English, Decorated, and Perpendicular, Mr Sharpe substituted Norman, Transitional, Lancet, Geometrical, Curvilinear, Rectilinear.

development of a living being, which from infancy passes to age by a series of insensible transformations, without its being possible from one day to another to say where infancy or youth ceases or where age begins." *

In the present volume, therefore, the traditional classification into periods has been abandoned,† except that in Chapters II., IV., V., and VI., the characteristics of the so-called Norman, Early English, Decorated, and Perpendicular periods are enumerated.

It follows from what has been said above that it is here attempted to introduce into the subject of English mediæval architecture that evolutionary method of treatment which has been so fertile of results in every branch of knowledge to which it has been applied. The book is an attempt not to classify, but to work out processes of development. Evolution, whether in architecture or in anything else, was not a flux of blind and unmotived change. For every change there was a reason. What that reason was it may perhaps now in many cases be impossible to discover. We cannot look through the eyes of the old builders. We may think we see what they were about; but we merely think, we do not know; we are in the region of conjecture, and conjecture is hazardous. But are we therefore to discard conjecture? It is not discarded from modern science. The naturalist does not know that the colours of insect or of bird are due to protective or sexual reasons; this is but a hypothesis, *i.e.* a conjecture of his. So too in architecture hypothesis is not to be discarded, provided that it explains the phenomena, and that the cause it assigns is a *vera causa* and is adequate to produce the effect. The writer, therefore, has not shrunk from the suggestion of causative relations. Nothing is more interesting than the search for the hidden cause; nor should the investigator be deterred even if at times his discovery prove but a mare's nest.

From the adoption of an evolutionary method of treatment yet one more consequence flows. It is that the evolution should be traced back, not half-way, but if possible to the fountainhead; in other words the question of origins should be dealt with. English mediæval architecture has been presented too often as a sort of architectural Melchizedek, or as if it sprang forth full-grown like some Pallas from the teeming head of Zeus, in the last half of the eleventh century, in Caen or Canterbury. But the Norman offshoot of the great Romanesque stock had its roots in a distant past. Its history goes back to the earliest days of church building in newly Christianised Rome, to the first years of the fourth century. That history indeed, from the fourth to the eleventh century, is dark and dubious. But that the Romanesque and Gothic minsters are the offspring of the early Christian basilicas there can be no doubt, however difficult it may be at present to establish each step of the pedigree. Throughout the book, therefore, reference has been made, where reasonable evidence exists, to the origin and history of mediæval architecture not only in our own country but throughout Gaul, Germany, and Italy in the Dark Ages. The statements made are in many cases far from pretending to certainty; but by the references which have been given to authorities the reader is put in a position to test for

* Viollet-le-Duc.

† The French archæologists have long discarded the arbitrary divisions of De Caumont and others.

himself the validity of the conclusions presented. English architectural history will lose nothing if it ceases to be so insular. To the Romanesque architecture of Normandy in particular much attention has been given; in the great abbeys of that country we have the incunabula of the English abbey church and cathedral.

Nor has the writer hesitated to describe developments which are to be found in the Gothic of France, but which were not reached here. French writers do not fail to include in their architectural treatises an account of those features, such as the open timber roof, the lierne and fan vault, which were developed here only, or reached here the highest stage of development. Similarly it seemed desirable not to conclude the discussion, for example, of the treatment of the triforium without some account of the "transparent" triforium of the Ile de France. Wherever possible, the comparative method of investigation has been adopted, at any rate as regards the most important of the schools of mediæval architecture; those of the Ile de France and England.

Many shortcomings there are, and must necessarily be, in this or in any attempt to deal with the vast subject of English mediæval architecture. It is true that measured drawings of most of the greater churches are to be found scattered here and there in the various Sketch-Books; in the *Builder, Building News, Architect, British Architect, Builder's Journal;* and in such collections as those of Bowman and Crowther, Brandon, Colling, the Churches of the Nene Valley, and various monographs. But very few scientific descriptions of churches, with complete apparatus of measurements, plans, sections, elevations, details, moldings, and critical text have hitherto been published.

Again, a writer on the mediæval architecture of France or Germany has a vast corpus of facts ready to his hand in the archæological literature of that country; in England the Transactions of the provincial societies, though they were founded mainly for the study of mediæval architecture, are largely devoted to non-architectural subjects.* Their proper task—that of analysing, describing, and classifying the churches of each district—has with a few noteworthy exceptions, made exceedingly little progress. The want of accurate classified information and the lack of an index to measured drawings have made and must make the preparation of any work on English architecture difficult and incomplete; errors must needs occur in battalions. The author will be grateful for any corrections, suggestions, or criticisms addressed to him through the publisher.

* Among recent papers may be mentioned one, " On the Ceremonial of the Toda Dairy ;" an interesting topic, but *qu'allait-il faire dans cette galère ?*

GOTHIC ARCHITECTURE.

PART I.

THE ORIGIN AND DEVELOPMENT OF THE MEDIÆVAL CHURCH ARCHITECTURE OF ENGLAND.

CHAPTER I.

Architecture Defined—Basilican and Byzantine Architecture—Romanesque Architecture —Schools of Romanesque—Gothic Architecture Defined—Relation of Gothic to Romanesque.

DEFINITION OF ARCHITECTURE.—The art of Architecture has been defined very variously. It was defined by Mr Garbett * as "the art of well building ; in other words, of giving to a building all the perfection of which it is capable." Mr Ruskin † defined it as "the art which so disposes and adorns the edifices raised by man, for whatever uses, that the sight of them may contribute to his mental health, power, and pleasure." In the American *Dictionary of Architecture and Building* (1901) it is defined as "the art of building with some elaboration and skilled labour " ; and, in a more limited sense, as "the modification of the structure, form, and colour of houses, churches, and civic buildings, by means of which they become interesting as works of fine art." But it can hardly be held that there is one art of making things well, and another of making them badly. There is not one art of making clothes that fit and another art of making misfits. One and the same art makes flower-pots for the gardener and Worcester ware for the connoisseur. So it is with Architecture. It is simply "the art of building." ‡ *Good* architecture is indeed the art of building beautifully and expressively ; and *bad* architecture is the reverse. But architecture is the art of building in general.

This seems clear enough. But as a matter of fact the definition contains an ambiguity in the use of the term " building." In the erection of every edifice the work necessarily falls into two parts. There is the actual putting together of the materials by manual labour and machinery so as to form roofs, supports,

---

* *Principles of Design*, 1.   † *Seven Lamps*, 13.

‡ So Viollet-le-Duc (*Architecture*, i. 116), who defines architecture as "*l'art de bâtir.*" So also Mr Barr Ferree, for whose discussion of the current definitions see the *Architectural Record*, i. 199.

A

and abutments. There is also the preliminary process of planning and designing the buildings, and, it may be, of making drawings, whether rough sketches, or drawings to scale or full size, as well as that of superintendence. Now these two operations, the preliminary and the subsequent one, may be carried on by the same individual, or they may not. If a modern builder is erecting a terrace of small tenements, he may conduct both operations himself; he may plan and design the terrace, superintend the actual building of it, and take part in the work with his own hands. In such a case he is both architect and builder. And what is sometimes done nowadays by a modern builder was no doubt at all periods occasionally done by builders. We may be sure that in the fifteenth century many a village builder was capable of planning and designing a new aisle or chancel as well as of putting it up. In such a case, as in that of the modern builder quoted above, he was, in the modern and restricted sense of the terms, both architect and builder. But when a large and important building is erected nowadays, one and the same man does not undertake both divisions of the work; one part of the work is handed over to one man, the other part to another; in modern parlance the first is the architect, the second the builder. And we may be sure that at all periods when any great building was erected, there was a similar division of functions. When the Parthenon was built, or Santa Sophia, or Amiens Cathedral or Salisbury, even if the architect had gone through the "shops," as the British engineer still does, he would have too much to do with planning, design, drawings, and superintendence, to work at the buildings to any considerable extent with his own hands. The more he used his hands, the less time he would have to use his brains. To be accurate, therefore, we must not, except in comparatively small and unimportant work, define "architecture" as "the art of building," but as "the art of planning, designing, and drawing buildings, and of directing the execution thereof." *

Another difficulty has been raised as to whether Architecture should be classed with the Fine or the Industrial Arts; i.e. whether it belongs to the category in which are found Painting, Sculpture, Music and Imaginative, Literature; or whether it ranks with the Industrial Arts. The difficulty arises from the fact that there is really a third category intermediate between the Fine and the Industrial Arts. No one would contend, except by way of paradox, that farming and cookery are anything but Industrial Arts. But

---

* How far the mediæval *magister operis* was builder as well as architect has long been a *quæstio vexata*. See *Notes on the Superintendents of English Buildings in the Middle Ages*, by Wyatt Papworth, *Journal of R.I.B.A.*, xxxviii.; *On the Hope of English Architecture*, by W. H. White, *Journal of R.I.B.A.*, December 1874; *Architects and Master Workmen*, by J. J. Stevenson, *Journal of R.I.B.A.*, January 1875; *Die Romanische und Gotische Baukunst*, by Max Hasak, Stuttgart; Mr T. G. Jackson, in *Builder*, 10th April 1897; Enlart's *Manuel*, i. 62; Choisy's *History*, ii. 518 and 256; Anthyme St Paul's *Hist. Monumentale*, 293; Viollet-le-Duc, *Dictionnaire*, iv. 198; *The Basis of Gothic Architecture*, by Mr E. S. Prior, in *Builder*, 23rd February 1901; *Education in Building*, by Professor Lethaby, in *Journal of R.I.B.A.*, 17th June 1901; and his *Mediæval Art*, 255. On Mediæval Working Drawings, see article by Mr Burges in *Journal of R.I.B.A.*, xxxviii.; article on "Drawing" in *The Dictionary of Architecture*, issued by the Architectural Publication Society; list of mediæval drawings in *Journal of R.I.B.A.*, 25th November 1858; and in Lethaby's *Mediæval Art*, 260; West, in *Journal of R.I.B.A.*, 1874, 38; Viollet-le-Duc, *Dictionnaire*, ix. 197; Enlart's *Manuel*, i. 65.

Apse of Basilica of S. Clemente, Rome.

it is different when we turn to what are called the Applied Arts or the Decorative Arts. These arts are, in the main, utilitarian ; nevertheless their products may to some extent be beautiful and expressive; in the case of the jeweller, sometimes to a very considerable extent. It is true that if the jeweller make a clock or watch, his main object is utilitarian; but if he make some purely useless article, such as a ring or necklace, his occupation becomes a Fine Art. So it is with the architect or builder. When he is providing shelter, which is a utilitarian occupation, and the primary function of Architecture, his art to that extent is an Industrial Art. But if he provide shelter in the fashion in which it is provided in Westminster Hall or Westminster Abbey Church, his work ranks among the Fine Arts; without ceasing, however, to be an Industrial Art. When, however, he is building a Triumphal Arch, a Nelson's Column, an Eleanor Cross, his Architecture becomes a Fine Art, pure and simple. For a Fine Art, pure and simple, is one which has no connection with material utility and use.

EARLY CHRISTIAN ARCHITECTURE.—What we are concerned with here is the Church Architecture which was done in England between the Norman Conquest and the Dissolution of the Monasteries in the sixteenth century ; the earlier part of which goes by the name of Romanesque or Anglo-Norman or Norman, while the latter part is called Gothic. Church Architecture had a very long history before the Norman style reached these islands in the eleventh century. What Mr Pugin designated Christian Architecture began on a large scale at the commencement of the fourth century of our era, in the reign of Constantine. Almost at once it diverged in two opposite directions. One half of Christendom used the Greek, the other the Latin liturgy. The Greek Christians developed their churches on the lines of such buildings in Rome as the Pantheon, S. Stefano Rotondo, and the like ; producing that great style of domed churches, which, because centred at Constantinople (whose Greek name was Byzantium), goes by the name of *Byzantine* Architecture. Its origin and history would be far clearer if it were called East Roman. It is an architecture in which Roman methods of construction were worked out by Hellenistic craftsmen.

But those who used the Latin liturgy, *i.e.* Western Christendom, erected churches of vast dimensions—indeed OLD ST PETER'S (147) and St Paul's *extra muros*, Rome, had areas of about 100,000 feet—but quite simple in structure.* These Early Christian churches are called Basilicas, and the style is the *Basilican;* what the French archæologists call the *Latin* style.† It is neither Byzantine nor Romanesque, but a style with quite distinct characteristics of its own. Up to the ninth century it may be said to have had the field entirely to itself in the greater churches of Western Christendom. It persisted, in its own country at any rate, here and there throughout the whole Romanesque‡ period and well into the Gothic days.

* In section they are practically the same as ELY nave (34.1).

† See article on *Latin* style by W. P. P. Longfellow in the American *Dictionary of Architecture and Building.*

‡ Pisa Cathedral, S. Ambrogio, Milan, and St Mark's, Venice, may well have been building together ; the first is Basilican, the second Romanesque, the third Byzantine.

ROMANESQUE ARCHITECTURE.*—The last part of the sixth, the seventh, and the eighth centuries were the worst times probably ever known in Western Europe; they were emphatically the Dark Ages. The Roman Empire of the West had sunk beneath the barbarian hordes; it was not till the redistribution of Europe into nationalities, till Charlemagne arose, late in the ninth century, that civilisation lifted its head again, and a new architecture became possible. To the ninth century may be attributed the elaborate planning of the monastery of ST GALL (194); the eastern parts of S. Ambrogio, Milan, and the ambulatory of ST MARTIN, TOURS (192.3). This new style is called *Romanesque.*† It is a term by no means easy to define. Quicherat's well-known definition is that Romanesque architecture is that which has ceased to be Roman, though it still retains much that is Roman; and which is not yet Gothic, though it has already something Gothic about it. The definition is an attractive one, but is really but little helpful; it is to explain "*obscurum per obscurius.*" To understand it we must first know what Roman and what Gothic architecture is. The same objection applies to M. Anthyme St Paul's definition; that it is " Roman architecture purified and developed to suit the needs of the Catholic liturgy and the genius of each of the peoples who employed it from the ninth to the thirteenth century"; we want to know what he means by Roman architecture. Turn to Viollet-le-Duc (*Dictionnaire,* iv. 60) and all becomes clear. The Roman work of which Romanesque is the offspring is just one particular sort of Roman work; that of the Basilica. "Le problème que les architectes de l'époque *romane* (= Romanesque) s'étaient donné à résoudre était celui-ci : élever des voûtes sur la basilique antique;" *i.e.* put shortly, the Romanesque problem was that of vaulting a basilica. Romanesque architecture is the art of building vaulted basilicas. And by a basilica we mean what is basilican both in plan and elevation; in plan, as having nave and aisles; in elevation, as having aisle wall, lean-to roof, and clerestory wall containing windows. This then was the problem of problems of the Western builders from the ninth century onward; to vault an aisled church without destroying its clerestory lighting.

ROMANESQUE SCHOOLS.—This problem could be solved, and was solved perfectly in more than one way; nowhere probably till late in the eleventh century. One solution was to ceil the nave with barrel vaults resting on clerestory walls pierced with windows. This was the solution of the two schools of Burgundy and Provence. A second was to ceil the nave with a row of domes; a method peculiar to Le Puy Cathedral and St Hilaire, Poitiers. A third was to ceil the nave with intersecting vaults; groined vaults, as at Speyer; ribbed vaults, as at Durham.‡ It was the last solution which resulted in Gothic

---

* The term "Romanesque" was first proposed by Mr Gunn; and was adopted by Dr Whewell in his *Notes on German Churches,* 1835.

† The application of the term varies greatly. Many apply it, with Mr Fergusson (i. 411), to all Christian Architecture, except Byzantine, done in Western Europe, before Gothic; *i.e.* all the work between the fourth and the latter part of the twelfth century. Such an application, which would designate the fourth century basilicas of Rome and the sixth century ones of Ravenna as Romanesque, is confusing in the extreme, and should be discarded.

‡ In the above no account has been taken of the schools which evaded one of the conditions of the problem, by omitting either the aisles or the clerestory lighting. On the whole subject see *Classification of Romanesque,* and table on page 13.

architecture. The Burgundian and Provençal solutions with barrel vaults, and that of Le Puy with domes, proved unfruitful ; nothing came of them. The third solution, however, is of the utmost importance. This solution was worked out in several countries, more or less independently ; in particular, in Lombardy, Germany, and Normandy. From Normandy it was borrowed by England. In Germany, at Speyer, the high vault was groined. In Lombardy, *e.g.* at S. Ambrogio, Milan ; in Germany, *e.g.* at Worms ; in Normandy, *e.g.* at LESSAY (319) ; in England, *e.g.* at DURHAM (8) ; the high vault had diagonal ribs.

But at this point a difficulty arises. Such churches as EXETER (9) and Amiens Cathedrals also come within the definition. Both are aisled churches with clerestory lighting ; both are vaulted with diagonal ribs. Yet Exeter and Amiens are as undoubtedly Gothic as S. Ambrogio, Milan ; Worms ; Speyer ; Lessay and Durham are undoubtedly Romanesque. What then is it which constitutes the one set of churches Romanesque, but the other set Gothic ?

GOTHIC ARCHITECTURE.—The answers given to this question are extraordinarily diverse. The term "Gothic" occurs much before the seventeenth century.* Those who invented it were quite clear as to what they meant. They meant that it was something barbarous, because non-classical. Some believed that it was actually invented by the Goths and Vandals who overthrew the Roman Empire. "Then," says Vasari, "arose new architects who after the manner of their barbarous nations erected buildings in that style which we call Gothic." So also Evelyn says that "the ancient Greek and Roman architecture answered all the perfections required in a faultless and accomplished building" ; and that the Goths and Vandals demolished these, and "introduced in their stead a certain fantastical and licentious manner of building ; congestions of heavy, dark, melancholy, monkish piles, without any just proportion, use, or beauty" ; utterly devoid of all "true and just symmetry, regular proportion, union, and disposition." †

We may now turn to definitions expressed, as they ought to be, in constructional terms. The first is extracted from various statements, not very definite, of Viollet-le-Duc ; the substance of which is, that Gothic architecture is the art of erecting buildings in which the outward thrusts of the vaults are neutralised by the inward thrusts of the flying buttresses. The objection to it is that the thrusts of the vaults are far more powerful than the thrusts of any of the flying buttresses, and cannot be neutralised by them (see 378).

The next is an attractive one ; it is that of M. Anthyme St Paul ; viz. that Gothic construction is the result of the fusion, in one and the same vault, of diagonal ribs and pointed arches, abutted, when necessary, by flying buttresses. To this it may be objected, first that no mention is made of buttresses, which are of primary, whereas flying buttresses are only of secondary importance ; also that the pointed arch is not of primary importance. Exeter Cathedral

* See references in Paley's *Gothic Architecture*, 16, and Lethaby's *Med. Art*, 135.

† Mr Ruskin's definition may be inserted as a curiosity. "Our final definition of Gothic," he says, "is Foliated architecture, which uses the pointed arch for the roof proper, and the gable for the roof-mask" (*Stones of Venice*, ii. 222). By "foliated architecture" he explains that he means that in which the arches (other than bearing arches and pointed arcading) are cusped ; and the apertures foliated.

might be rebuilt with every arch semicircular, yet its construction might remain Gothic.

To M. Enlart * also the diagonal ribs and flying buttresses appear to be

Durham Nave from S.E.

essential elements, though the latter are but organs of transmission ; the real work of stopping the thrusts of the vault being passed on to the buttresses ;

* *Manuel*, 435-442.

moreover many buildings, undoubtedly Gothic, have no flying buttresses at all ; *e.g.* Poitiers and BRISTOL (35.4) Cathedrals. He recognises, however, that the pointed arch is non-essential. On the ground that the pointed arch is freely employed in Romanesque construction half a century before the Gothic period, he says, "*Cet élément doit être éliminé de la définition du style gothique.*" To the vault with diagonal ribs and the flying buttress he adds, " *une ornamentation toute nouvelle, puisée, non plus dans les traditions, mais dans l'étude directe de la nature ;* " a statement hardly true of the foliated capitals and scrolls of the early Gothic

Exeter Nave from West.

of England, if they be derived, as suggested below (420), mainly from classical sources.

On one point at any rate we may agree ; viz. that the one thing of primary importance is the vault. Flying buttresses, buttresses, pinnacles, pointed arches, would none of them be there, were it not for the vault. The pointing of the arches facilitates its construction (322); the buttresses, flying buttresses, and pinnacles are the machinery by which its thrusts are neutralised. Now in vaults with diagonal ribs one peculiarity is universally found. They are not constructed like barrel vaults ; they have not a continuous thrust along the whole length of the walls on which they rest. This very fact brings an immensely powerful, because concentrated, thrust against certain points of the wall.   At these points it is necessary to strengthen the wall.

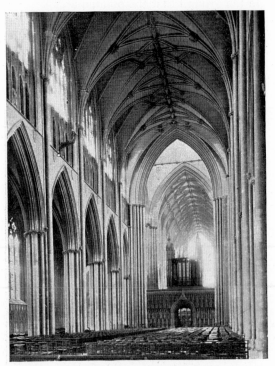

York Nave from S.W.

It is just at this point that we part company with such Romanesque as that of Durham and Lessay.   Compare them with Exeter or Amiens.   The aisles of all four have vaults with diagonal ribs, giving intermittent and concentrated outward pressures.   How are these pressures met?   In the first two, by thickness of wall; in the second two, by buttresses.   In Durham and Lessay intermittent pressures are stopped, unscientifically, to the great waste of material, by continuous abutment; at Exeter and Amiens, scientifically, to the great economy of material, by intermittent abutment.   This then is the difference between our Romanesque and our Gothic, between Durham and Exeter; a difference of abutment.   So we may frame a final definition of our Romanesque and Gothic architecture.   Anglo-Norman Romanesque is the art of erecting aisled and clerestoried buildings whose vaults have groins or intersecting ribs and the thrusts of whose vaults are stopped by walls.   English Gothic architecture is the art of erecting aisled and clerestoried buildings with vaults whose ribs intersect * and whose thrusts are wholly or mainly stopped, directly or indirectly, by buttresses.   The second definition excludes Durham nave, though it has a vault with intersecting ribs, flying buttresses, and pointed transverse arches in the vault; on the ground that the abutment is by thickness of wall, not by projection of buttress.

One difficulty remains.   It is that in many churches which no one would think of calling anything but Gothic, e.g. Salisbury, the thrusts of the vault are not wholly stopped by buttresses, but partly by the wall.   If we insist that the buttress shall do all the work, and that the wall shall be reduced to a mere pier, we shall have to exclude nearly all the Gothic work of England—Salisbury Chapter House and GLOUCESTER CHOIR (35.5) would be exceptions—and much of that of the Continent; and confine Gothic architecture to a few examples in the style of the Ile de France.   A definition so restricted carries with it its own condemnation.

* It is best not to introduce "diagonal" ribs into the definition; for some of our later vaults have no diagonals, e.g., the high vault of Winchester nave.

It remains to see whether the definition given above is of sufficiently general application. First, it applies to such buildings as the TEMPLE CHOIR (35.1), ceiled with vaults which produce opposing thrusts; the diagonal ribs and buttresses are there, though not the flying buttresses. Secondly, there are diagonal ribs and buttresses in buildings without aisles or clerestories, such as Ely Lady Chapel and the Sainte Chapelle, Paris; though no flying buttresses. To include this second class we may curtail our definition; making it read, "Gothic architecture is the art of erecting buildings with vaults whose ribs intersect and whose thrusts are stopped by buttresses."

York, N. transept.

But there is a still larger set of buildings to which we cannot deny the term Gothic; but which have wooden roofs, not vaults; viz. the vast majority of the parish churches; and here and there cathedral work; *e.g.* YORK MINSTER (10) and Carlisle Choir. These have no stone vaults, and therefore no thrusts. The only thing left of our definition is the buttress. They all have buttresses. Revise the definition once more, and we may include Carlisle Choir and the rest. It now reads, "Gothic architecture is the art of erecting buttressed buildings." So it turns out after all that the universal element in Gothic is not the vault with intersecting ribs, but the buttress.

One case remains to be put. What is to be said of the Eleanor Crosses or of such a monument as the canopied tomb of Archbishop Grey in York transept? The Eleanor Crosses present no difficulties, if we alter the definition to "Gothic architecture is the art of building with the aid of buttresses"; for all the Eleanor Crosses have buttresses. There are no buttresses, however, in Archbishop Grey's Monument.* There are, however, trefoiled arches richly molded, triangular pediments above them, capitals with stalked conventional foliage, conventional leaf scrolls and crockets, water-holding bases, moldings generally of peculiar design; all characteristic of Gothic and not of Romanesque architecture; the monument is unquestionably Gothic. In its widest sense, therefore, Gothic architecture is the art of erecting buildings whose vaults possess intersecting ribs and the thrusts of whose vaults are wholly or largely, directly or indirectly, stopped by buttresses; and also of doing work which possesses the chief characteristics of buildings so constructed.

* Nor round Clymping Church.

As we have enlarged the definition of Gothic, so we must enlarge that of Romanesque. The majority of our greater Romanesque churches, *e.g.* Peterborough nave, have no high vaults; a few, *e.g.* Carlisle nave, have not even aisle vaults. Nevertheless, there is such a large amount of Romanesque about them that they must be called Romanesque, not Basilican. *E.g.* in Carlisle nave there is a clerestory passage and inner arcade; the pier arches are in recessed orders; the cylindrical piers are of unclassical proportions; the bases and strings are unclassical; there are scalloped capitals; from the abaci rise roofing shafts; there are shafts in the jambs of windows; there is a corbel table. A nave which has so many of the characteristics which we find in such a church as Durham must be classified with Durham as Romanesque. Therefore the definition may be enlarged as follows: Anglo-Norman Romanesque architecture is the art of erecting buildings whose vaults are groined or have diagonal ribs, and the thrusts of whose vaults are stopped by walls, not by buttresses; and it is also the art of doing work which possesses the chief characteristics of buildings so constructed.

From what has been said above it will be clear that the difficulty of establishing a line of demarcation between Anglo-Norman Romanesque and Gothic is very great. The connection between the two is of the most intimate nature. It is difficult to exclude the nave of Durham from Gothic, without excluding at the same time those of Wells and Salisbury. It follows that the idea that Gothic is an individual and independent style is fallacious. Our Romanesque and our Gothic are not two styles but one style. Gothic is perfected Romanesque; Romanesque is Gothic not fully developed, not carried structurally to its logical conclusion. This was recognised long ago by Mr Petit:* "The Romanesque of Normandy, and still more of England, is essentially Gothic; not indeed fully developed, but quite sufficiently so to mark its direct and inevitable tendency." So also M. Enlart: "L'architecture gothique n'est que la perfectionnement de celle qu'on appelle romane." M. Anthyme St Paul takes the same view:† "If, from an artistic point of view, Romanesque and Gothic seem to be, and indeed are, two distinct arts, historically they are one and the same art; two phases of the same existence. Gothic is not superposed on Romanesque; has not supplanted or stifled it; on the contrary, it is its supreme result; the last stage in its development; its apogee, consummation and accomplishment." So also Comte de Lasteyrie‡ says: "Gothic architecture did not

---

* *Church Architecture,* i. 93.

† "*On Viollet-le-Duc*," 123.

‡ On the following page the main systems of high vaults are shown tabularly. The perfected systems are those which include aisles, clerestory lighting, high vaults, and aisle vaults. Peterborough has aisles, clerestory lighting, and aisle vaults, but no high vault. The Périgueux churches have high vaults and clerestory lighting, but no aisles. Notre Dame, Poitiers, and Issoire have aisles, aisle vaults, and high vaults, but no clerestory lighting. All the rest, *i.e.* the four perfected types of Romanesque, have aisles, clerestory lighting, aisle vaults, and high vaults. To the four perfected types may be added the abbey church of Tournus, which is *sui generis*. In this the barrel vaults of the nave were set transversely as in the aisles of FOUNTAINS (101) nave and London Bridge. To the imperfect types may be added certain Syrian churches with flat stone ceilings and aisles, but no clerestory lighting, *e.g.* Tafka, see 285. The curious church of Loches near Tours may be mentioned: two bays of its unaisled nave are roofed with spires.

arise from a reaction against the principles of Romanesque ; on the contrary it is the natural development of those principles ; the logical consequence of the germ-idea of the Romanesque builders, of protecting the naves of their churches by vaults of stone " (*Discours*, 17).

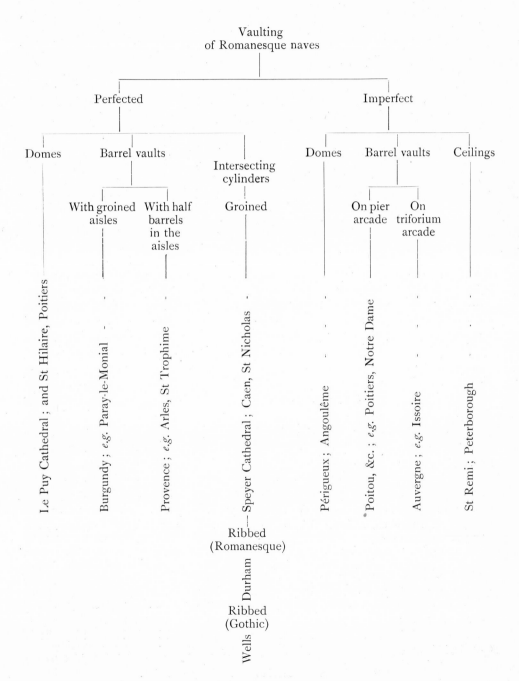

CHAPTER II.

CHARACTERISTICS OF THE ROMANESQUE ARCHITECTURE OF ENGLAND

FROM 1050 TO *c.* 1200.

Anglo-Saxon Architecture—Number of Norman Churches—Size of the Norman Churches —Planning—Vaulting—Masonry—Foundations—Internal Elevation—External Elevation—Clerestory — Abutment — Buttresses — Arches—Piers—Abacus—Capital—Base—Roof Drainage—Ground Courses—Strings—Windows—Doorways—Towers—Ornament.

NUMBER OF CHURCHES.—The history of Primitive Romanesque or Anglo-Saxon or Pre-Conquest architecture in England is referred to only incidentally in this volume; a full account of it has been given recently in *The Arts in Early England* by Professor G. Baldwin Brown. It was a backward member of the great Romanesque family; and was cut off untimely by the advent from Normandy of another branch of the same family, which had there reached a far higher stage of development. For a whole century the history of English architecture is mainly the history of the development of the Romanesque of Normandy. The history commences with the building of Westminster Abbey by Edward the Confessor, which was commenced in 1050, sufficient of the eastern part of the work being complete in 1065 to allow a consecration to take place. The Romanesque of Normandy, therefore, had already found its way into this country before the Norman Conquest. But after the Conquest the progress it made far surpassed anything that had been done in its mother country. Within a century the land was covered with churches, great and small. There was hardly one of the greater Anglo-Saxon churches which was not rebuilt,* and a great number of churches, entirely new, were erected. The resources of the Norman bishops and abbots were of course vast; conquered England had been divided up in largess; some of the grantees, ecclesiastics as well as laymen, counted their manors by hundreds. Nevertheless when one remembers that the whole population of the country was less than half of that of the present metropolis (4½ millions), the bulk of building done seems incredibly great. Very many of the churches then built have perished from the face of the earth; but even if a list be confined to those which remain wholly or in part, or which have been rebuilt in Gothic, it is an astonishing record of the labour and the piety of the scanty popu-

* Hexham nave seems to be a solitary exception.

ST. ALBANS, NAVE FROM S.W.

lation of England in the eleventh and twelfth centuries.*   Imagine all those churches enumerated below, and many other great churches like Cirencester and Coventry and Leicester, crowded into one-half of the present metropolis, together with the vast number of parish churches rebuilt throughout Norman England, and some idea may be formed of the enormous bulk of church building which followed the Conquest.

SIZE OF CHURCHES.—Moreover the churches built from 1050 to 1200 were not only exceedingly numerous, but very many were also amazing in scale, far surpassing the very largest churches of their mother country, Normandy ; † so large indeed that even in Gothic days nothing was set out on so vast a scale. To the very last some of the proudest Gothic minsters remained content with the dimensions that had been laid down in the eleventh century ; with the naves of LINCOLN (151.1) and Winchester, the transept and nave of CANTERBURY ‡ (149.3). Nowhere in Western Europe was there building in the eleventh century on the gigantic scale of the Romanesque of England.

PLANNING OF THE GREATER CHURCHES.—The width of the great Norman churches was conditioned only by the length of the tie-beams by which they were spanned (572).   Even when vaulting came into general use, the Romanesque widths were not exceeded.   The Norman naves of BURY (150.3), Peterborough, and Gloucester, have a span of 35 feet, a width rarely exceeded in Gothic days.

In length the greater churches were still more remarkable; except in the West of England; the greater part of the length being given to the nave, which at Ely and ST ALBANS (153.2) reached a length of thirteen bays, and

---

* Cathedrals of Benedictine Monks—*Canterbury, Durham, Ely, Norwich, Rochester, Winchester, Worcester.*
Churches of Benedictine Monks or Nuns—*Battle, Bath, Binham, Blyth, Bury St Edmunds, Chepstow, Chester St Werburgh, Colchester, Croyland, Glastonbury, Gloucester, Leominster, Lindisfarne, Malling, Malvern, Pershore, Peterborough, Ramsey, Reading, Romsey, St Albans, Selby, Sherborne, Shrewsbury, Tewkesbury, Thorney, Tutbury, Tynemouth, Westminster, Wymondham.*
Churches of Cluniac Monks—*Lewes, Castle Acre, Wenlock.*
Churches of Cistercian Monks—*Waverley, Buildwas, Fountains, Furness, Kirkstall, Louth, Rievaulx.*
Churches of Carthusian Monks—*Witham, London Charterhouse, Mount Grace.*
Churches of Premonstratensian Canons—*Bradsole, Easby.*
Churches of Gilbertine Canons—*Old Malton, Sempringham, Watton.*
Cathedral of Augustinian Canons—*Carlisle.*
Churches of Augustinian Canons—*Bourn, Bridlington, Brinkburn, Bristol, Bolton, Colchester St Botolph, Christ Church, Twynham, Dorchester, Dover, Dunstable, Kirkham, Kenilworth, Lanercost, Lilleshall, London St Bartholomew's, Llanthony, St Frideswide's, Oxford, St Saviour's, Southwark, Thornton, Waltham, Walsingham, Worksop.*
Cathedrals of Secular Canons—*Chichester, Exeter, Hereford, Lichfield, Lincoln, London, Old Sarum, Wells, York.*
Churches of Secular Canons—*Beverley, Chester St John's, Ripon, Southwell, Wimborne.*
† Mr Prior points out that the Abbaye-aux-hommes at Caen probably had originally an area of less than 30,000 feet.   But Norman Winchester and Old St Paul's occupied about 65,000 square feet ; while Bury St Edmunds had an area of 68,000 feet.   Cluny, the largest mediæval church of the West, had an area of but 54,000 square feet *c.* 1131.   *Gothic Art in England,* 34.
‡ Bath Abbey Church, rebuilt in the sixteenth century, occupies the site of the nave only of the Norman church.

at NORWICH (148.4) of fourteen.   The choirs varied in length from the two bays of Lincoln to the four of DURHAM (149.1); but by 1096 CANTERBURY (149.2) had set out a new choir of nine bays.   More accommodation being needed, instead of further prolongation of the church east or west, which would have given it a most unmanageable length, and would have been forbidden by the dimensions of most sites, cross arms (transepts) were set out ; at first at the junction of nave and choir ; afterwards, in the Canterbury of 1096, projecting also from the choir to north and south.   This second or eastern transept was, however, rare till Gothic days.   But every great church, without exception, had a central transept ; that of Bury St Edmunds was 234 feet long ; every great church was cruciform.

From each arm of the central transept there usually projected eastward one apsidal chapel, as at NORWICH (148.4) ; more rarely two, as at ST ALBANS (98).   At DURHAM (149.1) instead of an apse there is an eastern aisle to each arm of the transept.   Winchester and ELY (153.4) have a western as well as an eastern aisle.   Both have, or had, north and south galleries as well.

In nearly all the larger churches, so far as we can judge from surviving examples, it was usual for the nave to have a single aisle on each side.   Ripon built an unaisled nave c. 1170.

There was occasionally a highly developed western transept; as at BURY (150.3) and Ely.

Up to the middle of the twelfth century all the choirs of the greater churches ended in a semicircular apse, with the exceptions of Ely, Dover, Southwell, Sherborne, and Romsey.   All important choirs possessed aisles.*   But there were two entirely different ways of planning the choir aisles.   One was to terminate each aisle in a small apse parallel to the central apse of the choir ; e.g. DURHAM (149.1).   The other was to continue the choir aisle *round* the apse forming what is called an *ambulatory;* and to construct, leading out of it, apsidal chapels, usually three in number, pointing north-east, east, and south-east ; e.g. NORWICH (160).

A solitary exception to these two plans occurs at ROMSEY (151.3).   Here the ambulatory is rectangular instead of semicircular, and there were no chapels leading out of it, except one to the east ; cf. Hereford and LLANDAFF (164).

CISTERCIAN PLANNING.—But about the middle of the twelfth century another influence of Continental architecture has to be taken into account.   It is no longer that of the Romanesque of Normandy, but that of Burgundy ; the Romanesque amid which the monks of Cîteaux, Clairvaux, Pontigny had been bred.   Of all the churchmen of the twelfth century the Cistercians were the most influential; the greatest of them, St Bernard, practically ruled Western Europe.   Vast numbers of Cistercian abbeys were erected c. 1150.   So popular was the Order that in 1152 the Chapter-General at Cîteaux forbade the foundation of more abbeys; a rule broken several times subsequently.   In these abbeys, though compelled perforce to adopt mainly the indigenous methods of construction of each country, the planning was largely that of the mother abbeys in Burgundy : so much so that identity of plan prevails in churches as far apart as Kirkstall in Yorkshire, Maulbronn in Wurtemberg, Casamari in Italy, Fontenay in France.

* Lindisfarne, Melbourne, and others with unaisled choirs, are on a comparatively small scale.

Newhaven, Sussex.

In the early Cistercian churches in England the characteristic plan, *e.g.* at KIRKSTALL (152.4), has a short unaisled choir, a transept with a row of eastern chapels separated by solid walls; and an aisled nave, terminating sometimes in a narthex; and, originally, without a tower or with only a low tower at the crossing. Before the end of the century, however, more complex plans came into use among the Cistercians both of Burgundy and England.

PLANNING OF PARISH CHURCHES.—In the planning of the parish churches much more variety prevailed. In fact almost the only common feature they exhibit is that they always have a distinct architectural chancel. Unlike the greater churches, this chancel was more often rectangular than apsidal.

The simplest plan was that of the type of ADEL (220); composed of a nave and chancel; without aisles; without clerestory; without tower. Sometimes, as at Kirkburn, Yorkshire, there was a western tower.

A second is of the type of HADLEIGH (215.4) or NEWHAVEN (17); a tripartite church, composed of nave, choir and sanctuary, without aisles or clerestory; usually with a central tower over the choir.

A third is cruciform; without aisles or clerestory; with a central tower. Each arm of the transept may have an eastern apsidal chapel, as at North Newbald, Yorkshire.

A fourth has an aisled nave; an unaisled chancel; the nave usually has a clerestory, and a western tower; *e.g.* Steyning, Sutton St Mary, St Margaret at Cliffe.

A fifth has an aisled nave and clerestory, an aisled choir, a short unaisled presbytery, and a western tower; *e.g.* Northampton St Peter's.

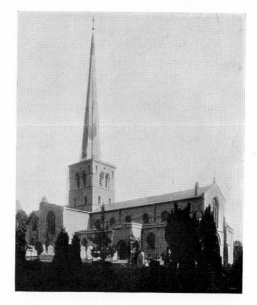

Hemel Hempstead.

A sixth is similar to the fourth; but with the addition of unaisled transepts, and with the tower central; *e.g.* HEMEL HEMPSTEAD, Hertford. This last, which is a town church, exhibits the highest development of parochial church planning reached in the twelfth century.

ROMANESQUE VAULTING.—When once the plan of a church had been settled—settled mainly by considerations of ritual—the rest of the task lay with the builder. With him the first thing to consider was how to roof over the area at his disposal: for the primary object of architecture is the provision of shelter. And a secondary object, insisted upon with astonishing persistence in the middle ages, was that the church, if large, should be fireproofed by building beneath the roof a stone ceiling or vault. In the smaller churches, except here and there in an unaisled chancel or beneath a tower, few attempts were made to build vaults. In the greater churches there are a few examples, *e.g.* the naves of

Carlisle and Rochester, where no vault was ever built even over the aisles.   And in the vast majority of the greater churches no vaults were built in the eleventh and twelfth centuries on the clerestory walls ; *i.e.* no "high" vaults.   They were simply ceiled, as some remain to this day ; *e.g.* Peterborough and ELY (57). The only examples of Romanesque high vaults remaining, wholly or in part, in aisled churches, are those of Durham, Lindisfarne, and St Cross, Winchester.

Various forms of vault were in use.   The barrel vault was employed in ST JOHN'S CHAPEL in the Tower of London (283); and by the Cistercians at Kirkstall and FOUNTAINS (101).   The half-barrel is in use at GLOUCESTER (282).   Semidomes were employed in many an apse ; *e.g.* CHECKENDON (21).   But the favourite vault in the eleventh century was the quadripartite groined vault.   All the Norman crypts were roofed with it ; and some of the aisles ; *e.g.* NORWICH (238).   It does not exist in any high vaults that remain in England.   Square, oblong, triangular, and trapezoidal spaces were all roofed by means of the groined vault.

For the quadripartite vault with groins there was soon substituted the quadripartite vault with ribs : first in DURHAM CHOIR (315), commenced in 1093.   In these ribbed vaults the transverse ribs were usually rectangular in outline and massive, while the diagonals were molded and were lighter.   All the ribs were much more massive than those in Gothic work.   The diagonal arches were rarely elliptical ; more often segmental or semicircular ; the transverse arches were usually stilted.   The pointed arch in a vault first appears in that of DURHAM NAVE (8).   The voussoirs were small, and consequently numerous.   Being filled in with rubble, both groined and ribbed vaults were very heavy, and required very massive supports.   Bosses were not employed till well on in the twelfth century, and they were of small projection.

MASONRY.—The vault and roof of the greater churches rest on aisle walls and clerestory walls ; and the clerestory walls rest on arches and piers.   All three—piers, arches and walls—were exceedingly massive.   All three were faced with ashlar ; this, however, was but skin deep ; the core was a mass of uncoursed rubble.   Of the various methods of construction that had been in use in ancient Rome one had employed faces of ashlar with a core of rubble laid in horizontal layers on a bed of mortar.*   This apparently was copied by the Romanesque builders both here and on the Continent ; with the exception that they employed much smaller blocks than those in Roman work.   Owing to the badness of the roads and the unbridged rivers, land transport was exceedingly difficult.   Water transport was employed, wherever possible.   Norwich and Peterborough Cathedrals are built of stone from the Barnack quarries in Northamptonshire ; that for Peterborough carried down the Nene ; that for Norwich down the Welland, then by sea, then up the Yare ; so also the abbeys of Ramsey, Croyland, Thorney, Ely, Bury St Edmunds ; and the churches at Stamford, Ketton, and Kettering.†   Caen stone was sent across sea to Chichester and other cathedrals.   Even at the end of the twelfth century, Christ Church, Dublin,‡ was built of Somerset Oolite.   Most of the stone used at Christ Church is of uniform scantlings of 2 ft. × 1 ft. × 1 ft.

* See Choisy's *Roman Building*, 17.   † *Assoc. Soc. Reports*, xxiii. 143.
‡ *Builder*, May 5, 1894, 350.

Checkendon Apse.

To lessen the cost of transport, the blocks were probably roughed out at the quarry. They were then dressed on the bench ; not worked in position, because to do so would have shaken the mortar beds. The capitals, however, seem frequently to have been set up in the rough, and carved afterwards.

Usually there is one stone for one member of a design ; *e.g.* there was one stone for the abacus, and one for the capital, till as late as the fourteenth century. It is exceptional to find a capital, like some of the crocket capitals in the Saint's Chapel at Canterbury, composed of two blocks superposed. Stone, owing to the cost of transport, was dear ; handicraft was cheap. Every bit of ashlar was utilised, whether to size or not. If a pattern, *e.g.* of zigzags, was to be carved round an arch, and one voussoir of the arch was broad, and another narrow, on each was carved a single zigzag ; though in the latter case it was too much cramped, and in the former spaced out too much.

The stones were usually of moderate size ; again owing to difficulties of transport ; it might be necessary to convey them for some distance by pack horse or cart. They average from about 1 foot square upwards : in early work they are usually rather square than oblong. They are smaller in early than in late work.

A toothed hammer or axe (*bretture*) was used in dressing the blocks ; and except in dressing shafts, was used with a diagonal stroke. These marks or *hatching* are often preserved where the block is a good freestone. In Normandy the hatching is less close in eleventh than in twelfth century work ; the teeth of the tool then used being further apart than later.* Both in Roman and in Anglo-Saxon work hatching occurs occasionally : *e.g.* in the Roman wall, Northumberland ; and in the Anglo-Saxon doorways of Kirkdale and Sherborne.†

The joints were usually thick, especially in early work. But in late work also, if a porous ‡ stone was employed, thick joints were necessary. As a rule, however, eleventh-century may be distinguished from twelfth-century masonry by the thickness of the joints. The difference is well seen in the north transept of Winchester ; where the portions with thick joints belong to the work

---

* Ruprich-Robert, i. 171.

† Mr Neale found that at St Albans the Norman work is axed ; the Transitional work is chiselled ; the Early English work is bolster-tooled ; the Decorated ashlar is claw-tooled ; the moldings scraped ; the Perpendicular finely scraped. *Journal of R.I.B.A.*, 1877, 80. Recent investigations of Mr E. S. Prior have shown that twelve different styles of masoncraft may be recognised in Chichester Cathedral between 1090 and *c.* 1450. (1.) Dressing with the pick, and with the axe diagonally, *c.* 1095. (2.) Dressing with the axe diagonally and coarsely, but obliterating the pick marks, *c.* 1120. (3.) Caen stone dressed with the axe diagonally and finely, *c.* 1180. (4.) Dressing with the axe diagonally ; shafts dressed vertically, *c.* 1195. (5.) Dressing with the axe diagonally (shafts vertically) and finely ; mixed with which is dressing with a claw chisel, the notches six to the inch, *c.* 1205. The same mixture of dressing is seen in St Hugh's work at Lincoln, *c.* 1200. (6.) Dressing with axe vertically to the bed. Diagonal axing also occurs in the vestry, *c.* 1210. (7.) Dressing with claw chisel with 9, 12, and 14 notches to the inch ; bosted always vertical to the bed, *c.* 1235. (8.) Dressing with claw chisel, of from 8 to 12 notches to the inch, not always vertical to the beds, but often irregular and crossing diagonally, *c.* 1260. (9.) Dressing finely with claw chisel, with notches 16 or 20 to the inch, often used as a drag, often crossing one another, *c.* 1290. (10.) Dressing finely dragged or diagonally clawed, *c.* 1335. (11.) Dressing diagonally chopped, *c.* 1420. (12.) Dressing dragged smooth, *c.* 1450. See *Proceedings of Harrow Architectural Club* for 1904.

‡ *Cf.* Brutails, 222.

commenced in 1079; while the portions with thin joints were built after the fall of the central tower in 1107.

Both walls and piers were exceedingly massive; *e.g.* the walls of Durham choir aisles have an average thickness of 7 feet. The tradition long survived in English Gothic of trusting rather to thickness of wall than to buttress, flying buttress, and pinnacle; the thirteenth-century clerestory wall of Salisbury is nearly 7 feet thick at the top.* Equally massive were the Romanesque piers. It has been calculated † that the major piers of the choir of DURHAM (659.1) occupy seventeen times as much space as the cylinders of the choir of CANTER-BURY (106), erected some eighty years later. But the tradition long survived of the massive Romanesque pier as well as of the thick Romanesque wall. Such piers as those of the choirs of WELLS (424.1), LICHFIELD (244), ST SAVIOUR'S, SOUTHWARK (521), have more of Romanesque stability than Gothic grace.

As we have seen, the substance of wall and pier was rubble and mortar. Everything depended on the quality of this mortar. It seems sometimes to have been excellent; *e.g.* in the Bishop's Palace at Winchester; ‡ at Worcester; and at Gloucester. When one recollects how Gloucester choir has been pulled about; how the Norman walls have been made to carry a tall Gothic clerestory and a heavy vault; and how an enormous Gothic central tower has been poised on the Norman piers of the crossing, it is plain that here at any rate the Norman masonry must have been good. At Binham, too, and elsewhere one may see great masses of Norman masonry hanging on still by the cohesion of the mortar, though their supports have collapsed or have been removed. But this was by no means always so; § *e.g.* at Hereford Mr Cottingham found in 1843 that the core of the piers of the central tower was composed of "broken stones, loam, and lime grouting"; so that the fourteenth-century tower superposed on them really had for support nothing but the thin shells of ashlar which enclosed the core. But this ashlar, not being well bonded and deeply headed into the rubble cores, had split and bulged; and the core itself was crushed to pieces for want of a proper proportion of lime in the mortar. In Old St Paul's, Sir Christopher Wren found that the piers of the nave were "only cased without, and that with small stones, not one greater than a Man's Burden; but within is nothing but a Core of small Rubbishstone and much Mortar, which easily crushes and yields to the weight." At St David's the cores of the walls of the central tower had disintegrated into dust; and when a hole was made, the core "began to pour out like an avalanche." Sir Gilbert Scott saw ten buckets of liquid cement poured into one hole. ‖ Nor was bad building unknown in Gothic days. In the west front of PETERBOROUGH (112) the mortar in the joints of the ashlar had crumbled into dust, and the blocks could be lifted from their positions by hand. In the south transept of

* On the other hand the aisle walls of Patrington, *c.* 1340, are only 2 feet 3 inches thick, though intended to carry a vault; those of the Temple Church, Bristol, are 1 foot 10½ inches.

† Prior, 34.

‡ See Willis' *Winchester*, 72; and E. Christian in *Journal of R.I.B.A.*, 1877, 151.

§ For the condition of the interior of the piers of Sherborne central tower see R. H. Carpenter in *Journal of R.I.B.A.*, 1877, 149.

‖ *Report to Dean and Chapter*, 1869.

YORK MINSTER (523) it was found in 1871 that the core of the clerestory walls had been made up of stone chippings without mortar. As late as 1323, after the fall of two Norman bays at the east end of the north side of the nave of St Albans, the cores of the new piers were built with such bad mortar that it was found recently that they had disintegrated into dust, and the whole weight of the superincumbent walls was carried by the casing of ashlar.

FOUNDATIONS.—Equally varied was the practice of the Romanesque builders with regard to foundations. They knew perfectly well what was the right thing to do ; sometimes they deliberately did the wrong. Frequently their foundations were both deep and broad. The foundations of the three eastern apses of Norman DURHAM (149.1) were carried down more than 14 feet, till the solid rock was reached. Those of the wall of the north choir aisle are so broad as to provide a footing both for the buttresses outside and the bases of the vaulting shafts within.* Lord Grimthorpe found that "the foundations of the piers of St Albans† are singularly large and strong." At Ely‡ the foundations of the thirteenth-century presbytery are about 6 feet deep and rest on the rock. But those of the Norman choir were only 4 feet 6 inches deep and did not go down to the rock. In the Lady Chapel of Glastonbury§ the foundations consist of a rubble wall 12 feet or more deep ; so that when a crypt was wanted in the fifteenth century, all that was necessary was to clear out the soil between the foundation walls. At York the first stone of the foundations of St Mary's Abbey ‖ was laid in 1271 at a depth of 9 feet. In places, however, the foundations were 24 or 26 feet deep.

Moreover the builders sometimes took the trouble to provide continuous foundations from pier to pier. Professor Willis¶ says that he "saw that at Lichfield, Ely, Hereford, and elsewhere, the ranges of piers were set on continuous foundations,** walls of rubble constructed with the greatest care." In Gothic work one of the best examples of good building construction is Lincoln nave; in this there are transverse walls underground from pier to wall, as well as longitudinal ones from pier to pier.

But the temptation to economise on the foundations was not always resisted. At Gloucester the north-west tower fell in 1170; "because of bad foundations," says Giraldus Cambrensis. At Croyland there is a bed of gravel underlying peat. The gravel is about 11 feet from the surface; but the peat was excavated for 6 feet only; and the foundations consist largely of layers of quarry dust. This culpable carelessness about foundations is not without parallels in Gothic work. The thirteenth-century Lady Chapel of Chester Cathedral has been found to have been built without foundations of any sort. Peterborough is especially noteworthy among our greater churches for insufficiency of foundations ; the

---

* Mr Bilson in *Archæological Journal*, liii. 8.
† The great care with which the foundations of St Albans were prepared is described in Buckler's *St Albans*, 35.
‡ See *Journal of R.I.B.A.*, Jan. 3, 1876, 70, 71, 79, 80 ; and Stewart's *Ely*, 20.
§ Willis' *Glastonbury*, 63.
‖ Rickman, 175.
¶ *Glastonbury*, 63.
** Continuous foundations are exposed to view at St Mary's Abbey, York.

Norman portions, the thirteenth-century west front, the eastern chapels of the fifteenth century were all built without proper foundation.*

INTERNAL ELEVATION.—Not only were the supports of the Romanesque churches exceedingly massive, but the walls were pierced with but few and small openings. Where in such a Gothic clerestory as that of SALISBURY (170) there would be three windows, or as at Exeter one broad window stretching from buttress to buttress, in a Romanesque church there was but one window, and that a small one. So with the aisles. In a Gothic church the voids preponderated over the solids; in a Romanesque church it was the very reverse; the building was almost wholly solid. This solidity, this monumental stability, is the special excellence and merit of Romanesque design. The lightness and grace that were already attained in large degree in ELY (57) and Peterborough are not half so impressive as the massive grandeur and gloom of the earlier work of WINCHESTER (261) and DURHAM (8).

Internally, all the great churches were three stories high. At the top was the clerestory wall; at the back of which was a single window in each bay, and in front of the window usually a triple arcade; e.g. ELY (273). At the bottom was the range of piers and arches—the pier arcade—separating the nave from the aisles. Between the pier arcade and the clerestory was the front wall of the triforium chamber, usually pierced with an arcade. The proportions of these three stories vary very considerably. They were largely controlled by the dispositions adopted for securing adequate light for the central aisle or nave. If the pier arcade was low, the light from the aisle windows was obstructed. Especially was this so, where there was a cloister roof outside one of the aisle walls; unless the aisle windows were set high in the wall, they would not clear the cloister roof. But if the aisle windows were set high, the piers and their arches must be lofty also. Where they were set high, an elevation resulted in which the pier arcade was lofty, and the triforium arcade comparatively small; e.g. GLOUCESTER NAVE (26). In such a design no windows were inserted at the back of the triforium, or at any rate, only small ones.

But an alternative method was much in favour. This was to raise the aisle wall, and to insert an entirely new row of windows in the upper part of it, which became a back wall to the triforium chamber. And as the light from these windows was wanted for the nave, there could be no solid wall in front of the triforium. Either the triforium chamber opened into the nave by one great arch, as at ST ALBANS (14); or if there were two arches, they were constructed lightly so as to obstruct the light as little as possible; e.g. ELY (57). In this design so much of the height of the interior was absorbed by the triforium arcade, that the pier arcade was usually low.

Besides the two above methods of designing a Romanesque interior, both more or less logical, there were illogical variants and compromises. Thus Durham has windows in the upper part of the aisle wall, but the triforium is low and is blocked by massive arches in front. On the other hand, Romsey has a tall triforium with a light open arcade, but no windows at the back of it. St

* This is the more remarkable as there is solid limestone rock a few feet below the foundations.

GLOUCESTER CATHEDRAL, NAVE FROM S.W.

Bartholomew's, Smithfield, has magnified its triforium at the expense of its pier arcade; though here also the triforium is a blind-story.

Another eccentric design is that which is seen in OXFORD CATHEDRAL (525), in which the containing arch of each bay of the triforium is continued down to the ground; with the result that what is a low three-storied is made to appear a tall two-storied interior.

Another curious design is that of St Botolph's Priory, Colchester, where again a three-storied is made to look like a two-storied elevation; but in this case by absorbing the triforium into the clerestory. Towards the end of the twelfth century this design reappears at ST DAVID'S (525).

In the Cistercian churches usually no windows were inserted in the triforium; and being consequently a blind-story, a solid wall was built in front of it; e.g. FOUNTAINS NAVE (101).

Walls which do not rest on pier arcades; e.g. the east wall of the south transept of NORWICH (168); are also usually divided into three stories, which may or may not be similarly proportioned to those of the aisled portions of the rest of the church.

EXTERNAL ELEVATION.— The usual elevation is one of two stories; aisle wall and clerestory. But if the triforium has windows, there are three stories, which, subdivided by strings, produce four stories at Ely, six at NORWICH (31).

Oxford Cathedral Choir.

Eastern Façade.—Of the churches ending eastward in three parallel apses we have no example complete. Peterborough retains the central apse, but has lost the side apses. Romsey retains the eastern side apses, but never had a central apse. The original form of our east ends may, however, be seen in Normandy: *e.g.* in ST GEORGE'S DE BOSCHERVILLE (160) and CÉRISY-LA-FORÊT (160). Of churches with the ambulatory plan and radiating chapels

Durham Cathedral.

we have good examples at NORWICH (148.4) and GLOUCESTER (135); though in both the eastern Norman Chapel was pulled down in the thirteenth century, to make room for a rectangular Lady Chapel. Good examples of rectangular east fronts survive at Darenth, Barfreston, and PATRIXBOURNE (218).

Of *West Fronts* the most important left are those of SOUTHWELL (520), Rochester, and Durham Cathedrals, and of Tewkesbury and Castle Acre; * but

* See Plate in Britton's *Arch Ant.*, iii.

they have been altered by the insertion of a big window in the centre of each. In Normandy, however, the west front of the Abbaye-aux-hommes remains almost as it was built. Fine west fronts remain in the parish churches of Castle Rising and Iffley.

Of the *Transept Fronts*, one, in a church of Monks or of Regular Canons, adjoined the dormitory and other buildings east of the cloister. Where these have been torn away, *e.g.* from the south transept of Ely, the result is necessarily an unsightly space of blank wall. But the elevation of the other transept is frequently one of much grandeur ; *e.g.* the north * transepts of Winchester, Ely, Peterborough ; and of NORWICH (31) ; finest of all.

CLERESTORY.—There was never but one window in each bay. At Southwell, by exception, the clerestory windows are circular. In the Cistercian churches, *e.g.* FOUNTAINS (101), and a few others, *e.g.* Leominster, there is no passage. Nearly always there is a passage in the thickness of the wall. In front of this usually there are three arches, of which the central one is the highest, *e.g.* ELY (57). Comparatively few parish churches had clerestories ; and then usually not till late in the twelfth century.

ABUTMENT SYSTEM.—We now come to the most difficult problem of the mediæval builders ; which was not how to erect a building, but how to keep it up. If a transverse section of one of the great Romanesque naves be examined, *e.g.* that of ELY NAVE (34.1) ; it will be seen that the nave † contains two high walls ("clerestory" or "nave walls") nearly 73 feet high, and two low walls ("aisle walls") nearly 50 feet high. What keeps them from falling over to north or south ? The nave walls have nothing whatever to keep them from inclining inwards except their vast weight, and the fact that they rest on adequate foundations. The aisle walls have nothing to prevent them from inclining outwards except buttresses of such slight projection as to be utterly inadequate for the purpose. Like the nave walls, they remain vertical simply because of their great weight and their good foundations. On the other hand, the lower half of the aisle walls is prevented from inclining inward by the loaded arches of the vault ; which thrust outward like a compressed spring. And in the same way the lower part of the high wall—in Ely about 28 feet out of 73 feet—is kept from inclining outwards by the thrust of the same vault, that of the aisles. And as the load on the arches of a Romanesque vault was very heavy—for they were filled in with a thick mass of rubble—the pressure brought to bear by the aisle vaults against the walls on either side was very considerable. So considerable was it that sometimes the aisle wall has been thrust *outwards*. And though the nave wall is loaded with an enormous weight of masonry, extending up to the top of the clerestory wall, it has been noted—*e.g.* by Sir Christopher Wren—that the pier arcade on which the nave wall rests has not infrequently received a considerable inclination *inwards*, owing to the thrust of the aisle vault. So valuable was the aisle vault in the construction of their larger churches that it is very rare to find the Romanesque builders omitting it. Indeed in churches of the first rank in England only two cases seem to occur ; viz. the naves of Rochester and

---

* The normal position for the cloister was to the south of the nave ; hence the principal transeptal façade was normally that of the north transept.

† The roof of the nave is omitted ; those of the aisles are shown in dotted lines.

Carlisle cathedrals : in the former of which, however, pilasters were built against the eastern part of the aisle wall, as supports for a vault which at first apparently was contemplated.

The weakest point of such a construction as that of Ely is that abutment is applied to the nave wall so low down. The first improvement on such a section is seen in CHICHESTER CHOIR (34.4), and DURHAM CHOIR (370). It consisted in building semicircular arches in the triforium chamber between the nave wall and the aisle wall. If this had been done at Ely, about 37 feet of the 73 feet of the nave wall would have got abutment, instead of only 28 feet.

Again, just as the aisle vault prevents the nave wall and the aisle wall from bulging towards one another, so a high vault over the nave, ever trying to expand between the two nave walls, prevents them from bulging inwardly. Such vaults were actually constructed at Durham ; where, in all probability, the high vaults of the nave were built between 1128 and 1133, and those of the transepts earlier still.

There can be no question as to the potency of the new ally. With a heavy vault between them, it was utterly impossible for the nave walls to incline inwards. The danger lay in the other direction. So far from being insufficient, the force exerted by the new agency was only too great. The high vault was always tending to thrust apart the clerestory walls. So much so that the high vault built over Durham choir, probably before 1104, collapsed early in the thirteenth century. Evidently the next thing to do was to provide a remedy to prevent the clerestory walls from bulging out. The remedy applied—once more at DURHAM (370)—in its day one of the most advanced churches of Western Europe in science of construction—was to build in the triforium chamber, not arches as in that of the choir, but flying buttresses. This made safe some two-thirds of the height of the nave wall. For the high vault, as may be seen on examining the photograph of the nave on page 8, does not spring from the top of the clerestory wall, but from a level considerably below it. So that it was unnecessary to provide abutment for the clerestory wall much above the springing level. This solution—that of Durham nave—is the one adopted even in much of our Gothic architecture ; e.g. at Wells, at Salisbury, at Tintern, even in Winchester nave in the remodelling commenced c. 1360. And where the high vault springs low down in the clerestory wall, it is entirely scientific and satisfactory.

If, however, it was desired that the high vault should spring at a higher point, then it was necessary to take the flying buttresses out of the triforium chamber, and to build them above, instead of beneath, the triforium roof. This it was left for the Gothic builders to do ; viz. in the choir of CANTERBURY (34.3), 1175 ; CHICHESTER (34.4), 1184 ; LINCOLN (34.5), 1192.

In the parish churches these difficulties of abutment very seldom presented themselves ; it was most exceptional for a parochial aisle to be vaulted.*

BUTTRESSES.—These were for the most part little more than decorative pilasters ; e.g. at STEYNING (359) ; and so late as 1175 in WELLS CHOIR (373).

---

* A fragment of the groined vault of the aisle remains at St Peter's, Canterbury.

Norwich North Transept.

But the Cistercians by the middle of the twelfth century were building effective buttresses of considerable projection at Fountains and KIRKSTALL (152.4).

ARCHES.—One of the special marks of mediæval architecture is that it is above all things an arcuated, not a trabeated style (257). It may be said that Greek architecture is a trabeated style pure and simple; that Græco-Roman work was a mixed style, partly trabeated, partly arcuated; but that Romanesque and Gothic are wholly * arcuated styles.

Up to about the middle of the twelfth century the semicircular arch was employed almost exclusively. Here and there a segmental or an elliptical arch occurred in the vaulting or in the heads of doorways. The pointed arch had indeed been introduced in Gloucester choir apses and DURHAM NAVE (8), and at Rochester; but chiefly in vaulting. In pier arcades the pointed arch was first employed by the Cistercians at FOUNTAINS (101) and Kirkstall, about the middle of the twelfth century. Some time elapsed, however, before it came into general use in doorways, windows and ornamental arcading. To the very end of the century conservative builders were still building their pier arches semicircular; not only in village churches such as SUTTON ST MARY (42), but a great cathedral as ST DAVID'S (525). In the last half of the century trefoiled arches also occur in doorways and wall arcading.

All the larger arches were built in recessed orders; not built like the BRIXWORTH ARCH (274), but as in page 272. At first the edge of each order was left square, as in the transept of WINCHESTER (261) (choir commenced 1079) and Blyth, founded in 1088.† But very soon, e.g. in Chichester choir, commenced c. 1088, either the edges were rounded off into roll moldings, or the faces were covered with carved ornament. But in the West country, which seems to have had its own school of Romanesque as well as of Gothic, it is very common to retain the plain square-edged arch, without molding or ornament, far into the twelfth century. Examples of unmolded and uncarved Romanesque arches are the pier arcades of Holy Cross, Shrewsbury, Malvern and Leominster naves, and St John's, Chester. The pier arches of the nave of TEWKESBURY (297), consecrated 1123, are but slightly molded. At Romsey, of the four orders of the pier arches of the nave, three are square-edged; only the outer one is carved with the chevron. At Hereford the arches are much carved; but little molded. In GLOUCESTER NAVE (313) and at Christ Church, Hants, the pier arches are molded; but the moldings are few and heavy. On the whole, the Romanesque of the West of England is characterised by the small progress made in molding the arch.

PIERS.—In the eleventh century cylindrical piers seldom occur, except in the West of England, as in the choirs of GLOUCESTER (294) and TEWKESBURY (165), where they are short and massive. As a rule either all the piers are compound, as at NORWICH (238); or compound piers alternate with cylinders, as at DURHAM (239). In the twelfth century cylinders alternate with octagons in PETERBOROUGH CHOIR (318); while in the West of England and Southwell nearly all the naves have cylinders; which, at GLOUCESTER (99) and TEWKES-

---

* Lintelled doorways are an exception.

† It is not necessary to take into account the square-edged arches of St Albans and of St Botolph's, Chichester. They were square-edged simply because they were built of bricks.

C

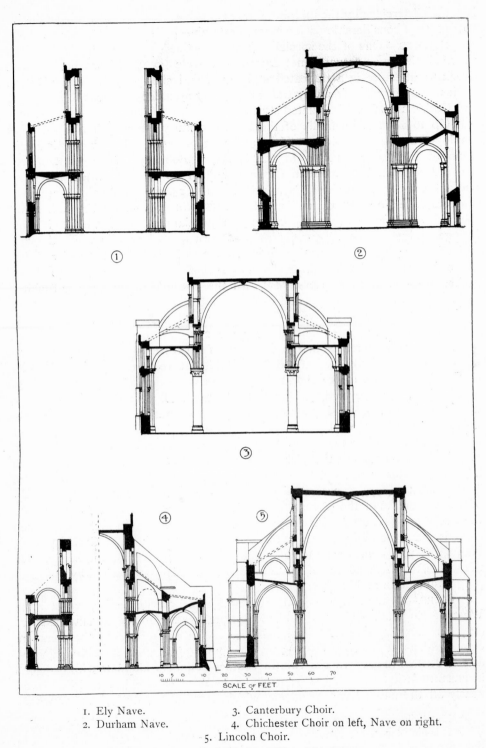

SCALE of FEET

1. Ely Nave.
2. Durham Nave.
3. Canterbury Choir.
4. Chichester Choir on left, Nave on right.
5. Lincoln Choir.

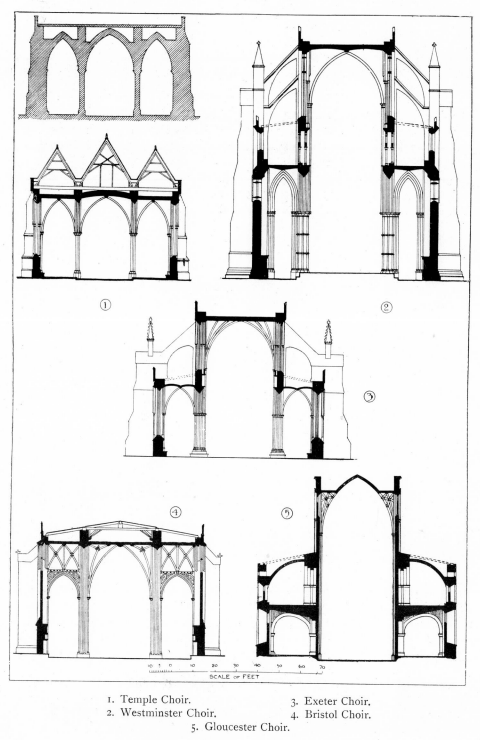

SCALE of FEET

1. Temple Choir.
2. Westminster Choir.
3. Exeter Choir.
4. Bristol Choir.
5. Gloucester Choir.

St Mary's, Guildford, North Apse.

BURY (297), are of enormous height and bulk. Where the compound pier is employed, it contains, in the best examples, *e.g.* DURHAM (659.1), a separate shaft or column for each order of the arch and for each rib of the vault.

In the aisled parish churches, few of which, if any, are earlier than the twelfth century, the pier is almost always a cylinder. NORTHAMPTON ST PETER'S (663.1) is an exception; in this compound piers and banded columns are employed.

ABACUS—The Norman abacus is always square-edged. Its under surface is usually a straight chamfer, as at YOULGREAVE (421.4); or a hollow chamfer, as at CANTERBURY (417.7). In plan it is usually square; but the cylinders of GLOUCESTER CHOIR (99) have circular abaci and capitals; another peculiarity of West of England Romanesque. At DURHAM (239) and Buildwas cylindrical piers have octagonal abaci. Abaci logically subdivided appear as early as the eleventh century in ELY TRANSEPT (506).

CAPITALS.—There is a great variety of Romanesque capitals. Imitations of debased Roman versions of the Corinthian and Composite capital are frequent, especially in the eleventh century. At first the band of acanthus is usually omitted; in the twelfth century it is attempted; *e.g.* at CANTERBURY (417.7). These Corinthianesque capitals survive to the very end of the twelfth century. The most common of the Norman capitals is the cubical or cushion cap; *e.g.* CANTERBURY (430). At Peterborough hardly anything else occurs. Usually it is a little scalloped. When much scalloped or coniferous, it is usually late; *e.g.* in the apse of ST MARY, GUILDFORD (36). In the last quarter of the century, the incurved cone is frequent in the West of England work; *e.g.* ST DAVID'S (412.5). Another capital which persists to the end of the twelfth century is that with interlacings; *e.g.* ELY (412.1). In the last quarter of the century attempts are made here and there to render naturalistic foliage. The water-leaf cap is very characteristic of the period *c.* 1165 to *c.* 1190; *e.g.* WALSOKEN (417.2).

BASE.—The Norman base is at first quite insignificant; altogether disproportionate to the great spread of the capital. Its moldings are usually of the simplest and rudest. Little attention was paid to the base till well on in the twelfth century; when a variant of the Attic base was adopted, with flattened lower roll. The plinth was either square; or if the pier was compound, separate rectangular plinths were provided for the shafts and columns of the pier; *e.g.* DURHAM (659.1). The "spur" ornament may occur, where the plinth is square; *e.g.* NORTHAMPTON (663.1).

ROOF DRAINAGE.—The roofs had a fairly steep pitch; as is shown by the weatherings on TEWKESBURY TOWER (390). The upper courses of the walls, except at Ely, projected on corbels or corbel arches, and the roof coverings again projected beyond these; *e.g.* SOUTHWELL TRANSEPT (390). For this system of "dripping eaves" the Cistercians substituted gutter, gargoyle, and parapet at FOUNTAINS (385.6), Kirkstall, Roche, and Byland.

GROUND COURSES.—At first the importance of protecting the foot of the wall from drip and splash was little recognised. Round the base of the twelfth-century work at Hereford, however, a basement course, semicircular in section, exists. About the middle of the century the Cistercians built basement courses at FOUNTAINS (679.1) and Kirkstall of considerable height and projection.

STRING COURSES.—On the other hand, strings were employed from the first in great numbers; not only to shelter the walls from drip, but merely ornamentally. Owing to the great amount of wall space in the Romanesque churches, strings were of great decorative importance. In the strings, carving was employed as well as molding.

WINDOWS.—The balustered window, being unsuited for glazing, was confined to towers; the baluster was generally set near the outer face of the wall. The usual window was oblong and round-arched; set near the outer face of the wall, and much splayed internally. In the jambs were frequently set decorative shafts. The clerestory window of the greater churches was usually ornamented with an inner arcade; *e.g.* ELY (57). With the exception of a solitary example at ROMSEY (457.2), there is no grouping of aisle or clerestory windows till GLASTONBURY LADY CHAPEL, 1186 (465). On the other hand, circular windows were highly developed; *e.g.* PATRIXBOURNE (218).

DOORWAYS.—The oldest type of doorway is that at ELY (39), with lintel and tympanum. More often these are omitted, as at SEMPRINGHAM (40). The arch of the doorway is almost always semicircular till late in the twelfth century. There are no double doorways.* The arch of the doorway is constructed in recessed orders; of which at Malmesbury there are eight. More room for orders was got sometimes by thickening the wall in the neighbourhood of the doorway. Norman porches survive, some of two stories; *e.g.* at Southwell and SHERBORNE (576). Nor are Norman doors lacking, with the original iron work; *e.g.* SEMPRINGHAM (40).

TOWERS.—All the greater churches seem to have had a central tower, except EXETER (377), whose towers were placed at the ends of the transepts. The normal group was one central and two western towers. Sometimes, as at ELY (587), there was but one western tower; sometimes, as at Tewkesbury, there was none. None of the greater Norman towers seem to have been octagonal; they were square. The central towers were meant to be lanterns. Not only have they windows, but they have elaborate arcades round the inner wall, intended to be seen from the floor of the church. Sometimes a central tower barely rises above the roofs; *e.g.* at Winchester; more often it rises to a considerable altitude, as at TEWKESBURY (390), St Albans, Norwich, Castor, Sandwich, St Lawrence. Internally, as well as externally, the towers are usually much ornamented with arcading. Probably they were roofed with low square spires. In flint districts the towers of the parish churches were often circular.

NORMAN ORNAMENT.

Of the Romanesque schools of sculpture the most skilful seem to have been those of Toulouse, Provence, Northern Spain, Poitou and Burgundy. The Normans were among the most backward; and through lack of skill had to

---

* Abroad these are very common; *e.g.* magnificent double doorways lead from the cloister into the transept of Tarragona Cathedral, and from the narthex into the nave of Vézelay.

confine themselves largely to geometrical work, simple and easy of execution. The decorative stock-in-trade of the Normans in the eleventh century, with which they started us in England after the Conquest, was composed of *billet*,

Ely, Western Processional Doorway of Nave.

square or round; *damiers*, patterns like a chessboard; *stars; imbrications*, or shingle; *interlacings; chevron*, or zigzag; *torsades*, or cable; *palmettes*, honey-suckle, or anthemion; and *rinceaux*, or scrolls of foliage.* All the above occur

* Ruprich-Robert, 124.

also in the twelfth century both in Normandy and England, and in much greater profusion.

The *billet* is more common in the eleventh, the chevron in the twelfth century; *e.g.* the earliest parts of Ely have the billet; but it also occurs in Canterbury choir in 1175, in Lincoln south-east transept in 1192. The billet may be square, as at St Augustine's, Canterbury; or round, as in Binham Priory.

The *chevron* is used with great profusion in the twelfth century; *e.g.* in the western doorway and windows of IFFLEY (574); in the window of ST JAMES', BRISTOL (516); in the pier-arches of WALTHAM (521) and STEYNING (273); in the ribs of DURHAM VAULT (8). In later work of this century it is often studded with "pearls," or otherwise enriched; it may be inverted; and in late examples it may be much undercut. The chevron is an almost exact reproduction of devices found on ancient Roman stones; *e.g.* on the fine altar recently discovered at Lanchester * in Durham. Late examples are seen at ST DAVID'S (412.5); in the north porch of Wells; in Glastonbury Lady Chapel; highly undercut, with a roll beneath it, in the north transept chapel of Tewkesbury, *c.* 1230; and in the doorway of Stone Church.† It survives in archivolts in Cyprus and Sicily till the fourteenth and fifteenth centuries. For examples see above.

SCALE OF FEET.

Sempringham.

The *saw-tooth* ornament is common in early work; with teeth first of an obtuse, later often of acute angle.

The *star* ornament is found in Roman work, *e.g.* on the Lanchester altar; it occurs in Ernulph's work at Canterbury; at Romsey; Stringham, Norfolk; Herringfleet, Suffolk; Upton, Gloucester, and elsewhere.

The *nail-head*, being easy of execution, was a great favourite; *e.g.* Ely. A band of nail-head was often employed in the first half of the thirteenth century in capitals; *e.g.* at KETTON (440.2); compare the buttress of ST PATRICK, DUBLIN (354).

* *Builder*, Dec. 28, 1895, 474.

† Cresy illustrates it in page 6, and gives reasons for believing that it belonged to an earlier doorway.

The *pellet* or "stud" might be circular; either flat, as at Stoneleigh, or forming a boss, as at Iffley and Crickfont. Or it might be a lozenge, as at Essendine.

The *patera* or *medallion* is a large flat, circular disc, often containing foliage or figures; *e.g.* at LLANDAFF (580) and HALES (575).

The *fret* or key or embattled ornament is a most ancient decorative form; common in Arabia, China, South America; Greek, Roman and Byzantine work.* Good examples occur in the doorways of Middle Rasen and Kirkstall.

Imbrications or shingle or scale work is also a very ancient motive; more common in Normandy than England; it occurs in Westminster Hall and on Castor tower.

Interlacings are common in England before the Conquest, and after *c.* 1090; but are somewhat rare between 1066 and 1090.† Good examples occur at Castor, *c.* 1124; IFFLEY (256); NORTHAMPTON ST PETER'S (415.6); SHOBDON (415.3). Canon Taylor held that the Irish scribes imported them into the Continent; Professor Boyd Dawkins that they originated with the Franks; being found in great numbers on Germanic sword-hilts, brooches, buckles, &c., as early as the fifth century. But they are common in Byzantine work, especially in the eighth century; and very common indeed on Roman sarcophagi and especially in the Roman mosaic pavements which were executed all over the Empire. They occur in Armenia, Hungary, Styria, Wallachia, Mycenæ, Chaldæa, Assyria, the Canarese or west coast of India; in fact, wherever the traditions of plaiting basket work decoratively have survived.

Interlacing snakes occur on an eighth century bas-relief on the wall of the old Cathedral of Athens;‡ on the jamb slabs of the Anglo-Saxon doorway of Monkwearmouth; in Norman doorways at Kilpeck; on a fourteenth-century capital at Oakham; and elsewhere.

The *bead and roll* occurs in the slype of the south transept of St Albans, in the doorway of HALES (575), and in ST LEONARD'S PRIORY, Stamford, where it produces a curious molding (705.3). It is common in Greek and Roman work; and is probably motived by a child's necklace.§

A *double cone* occurs at Stoneleigh, Warwickshire.

The *chain* occurs in St William's Chapel, York, and in the vaulting of St Peter in the East, Oxford; the dedication of which may have been to St Peter *in vinculis*.

The *cable* is frequent and effective, especially at Southwell over the arches of the crossing. Sometimes it occurs in bases.

The *nebule* is used instead of corbels beneath the eaves of SOUTHWELL (390) and Binham.

Beak-heads and *cat-heads* are common in the twelfth century; *e.g.* in the west doorways of IFFLEY (574) and BARTON-LE-STREET (427). Wolf-heads occur over the pier arches of Bayeux nave.

Pearls are very common in Norman leafage and ornament; *e.g.* in NORTHAMPTON ST PETER (415.6). They have been supposed to be reminiscent

---

* Barry's *Lectures*, 101.   † J. T. Irvine in *Journal of Arch. Assoc.*, 48, 26.
‡ Cattaneo, 77, Fig. 19.   § See Statham's *Architecture for General Readers*, 152.

of the ornament (dots of ink) in the Irish missals. But they are particularly common in Poitou, Berri, and Burgundy ; and in Scandinavian wood-carving.

The *palmette*, honeysuckle, or anthemion, is common in Greek, Roman and Byzantine work ; especially in Corinthian and Composite capitals ; so also in Norman work ; *e.g.* at TILNEY (423.4).

Rinceaux or leaf-scrolls were very common in Greek, Roman and Byzantine work. They are much used in Norman work, especially in capitals ; and had much to do with the origin of the conventional stalky leaved capital of early Gothic (429). See BARTON-LE-STREET (427); ELY (430); NEW SHOREHAM (430).

Sutton St Mary.

Roses were common in the ' lacunaria" or Roman ceilings, and in Corinthian capitals. They occur in the south doorway of IFFLEY (577).

Reminiscences of Classical Mythology occur ; *e.g.* Centaurs ; the Sagittarius ; Sirens ; Mermaids. The stock illustrations of animals are taken from the Bestiaires.* The signs of the zodiac, the works of the months, the virtues and vices all find representation, first in Romanesque, and afterwards in Gothic sculpture.

DURATION OF THE ROMANESQUE STYLE.—We saw that the first building in the Anglo-Norman variety of Romanesque was the abbey church of Westminster, commenced in 1050. It does not follow that all the world set to work immediately to build to Anglo-Norman design. There have always been Radicals and Conservatives in architecture, as in politics. For another generation or two, well into the twelfth century, we may be sure that many people went on building in Anglo-Saxon fashion. Similarly, when all the world had adopted the Anglo-Norman style, they would not give it up simultaneously. The greater churches would be the first to abandon it for Gothic: but even among these the progress was far from being at a uniform rate. The naves of St David's and Wells were building

* On Ecclesiastical Zoology see Evans' *Animal Symbolism in Ecclesiastical Architecture ;* and the article on " Physiologus " in the *Encyclopædia Britannica.*

simultaneously *c.* 1190; the nave of St David's is almost as Romanesque as St Botolph's, Colchester, founded in 1102; while Wells nave is in many respects as Gothic as the choir of Lincoln Minster. At no time and in no style was the progress uniform in different parts of the country; *e.g.* the choir of St Bartholomew's, Smithfield, commenced in 1123, is not so advanced as the Norwich choir of 1096 or the Durham choir of 1093. Still slower would the rate of progress be in the villages; a fact which has always to be borne in mind in estimating the date of a village church. In village churches rude and archaic work is not necessarily a proof of an early date. If we judged by the rude and archaic exterior and interior of TOWYN CHURCH (458) we should unhesitatingly assign it to the eleventh century; but it might well be that the new current of Romanesque did not strike the remote coast of Merionethshire till well into the twelfth century. SUTTON ST MARY (42) was not begun till after 1180. On the whole, we may conclude that Romanesque work was still being done in the smaller churches, here and there, till the end of the twelfth century. In the greater churches we may take it that Gothic architecture came into being not later than *c.* 1175, with the commencement of the choir of Wells Cathedral by Bishop Reginald de Bohun; that of Canterbury under the direction of William of Sens; and those of Roche, Byland, RIPON (102), and York. In France the choir of St Denis was commenced in 1140; that of Notre Dame, Paris, in 1163.

By Mr Sharpe the work done *c.* 1145 to *c.* 1190 has been designated TRANSITIONAL; by Mr Brandon SEMI-NORMAN. But in the first half of it the presence of pointed arches, *e.g.* at Fountains and Kirkstall, is not a sufficient ground for admitting them to the fellowship of Gothic; they are churches in which much more reliance is placed on thickness of wall than on projection of buttress. Nor on the other hand, because of the retention here and there of the semicircular arch, are well-buttressed buildings, such as Canterbury choir, to be denied the name of Gothic.

CHAPTER III.

CHARACTERISTICS OF ENGLISH GOTHIC ARCHITECTURE.

Monastic *v.* Secular Gothic—Admixtures of Romanesque—Procedure in Rebuilding—
Length, Span, Height, Area of English Churches—Proportions—Abutment—
Skeleton Construction—Economy of Material—Lightness of Construction—Importance of Stained Glass—Reasons for Height of Gothic Churches—The Vertical
and Horizontal Line.

IN the Anglo-Norman architecture of the eleventh and twelfth centuries the first
landmark is Edward the Confessor's Church at Westminster. The second is the
commencement of the building of Cistercian churches *c.* 1140 ; in what has been
called the Transitional, Semi-Norman, or Pointed Norman style. More than one
hundred Cistercian abbeys were founded between 1125 and the end of the century.
Of the Cistercian churches remaining the oldest appear to be Fountains, Kirkstall,
and Furness. Only a quarter of a century separated these from the Gothic
architecture of Canterbury, Wells, Roche, Byland, and Ripon.

Up to *c.* 1175 the lion's share of the work had been done by the Monks and
the Canons Regular. In the eleventh and twelfth centuries the monastic orders
were the progressives and the reformers in the Church. Much energy had
been shown even before the Norman Conquest, *e.g.* by Dunstan, in expelling
Secular Canons from their churches, and in replacing them by monks. But
gradually the Secular Canons reformed themselves, and regained their influence ;
the proof of which is to be seen in the great amount of Gothic architecture to be
put to their credit. If we take as a test the cases where whole Romanesque
churches were pulled down and rebuilt, not under stress of fire or storm or
because of collapse of masonry, we shall find that the Secular Canons were much
the more thoroughgoing in Gothic building. To them is to be credited the rebuilding of the cathedrals at Wells ; Lincoln ;* Salisbury ; Lichfield ; Exeter ; York ;
Ripon and BEVERLEY (176) Minsters ; and Howden. On the other hand, the
Benedictine monks rebuilt Whitby, Westminster, St Mary's, York, and Bath ;
the latter not till the sixteenth century. The Cistercian abbeys were but
partially rebuilt, some not at all. The Augustinian Canons † rebuilt St Saviour's,
Southwark.

* Portions of the Norman west front were incorporated at Lincoln ; at Exeter the transeptal
towers were retained ; York retains a Romanesque crypt ; Ripon allowed some Romanesque
work to remain south of the choir.

† The Canons Regular, of whom the Augustinians were the most important order in
England, lived a common life in a cloister under a Rule (*regula*) ; and differed little from the
monks, except that none of them were laymen, and that they were attached to a cathedral or
other collegiate church.

LINCOLN CATHEDRAL, FROM N.E.

The comparison is largely in favour of the Secular Canons. If it is true that we owe the majority of our Romanesque churches to the Regular orders, it is equally true that the Secular Canons took the leading part in the development of English Gothic.

The number of English churches of the first rank built or rebuilt wholly in Gothic is not great. What is rare here is quite common in France. The number of cathedral, abbey and collegiate churches without admixture of Romanesque in the Domaine Royale and Champagne is very large.*

In some of our greater churches the *mélange* of styles is something extraordinary. At Hereford, Chichester, St Albans, Wimborne, every variety and subvariety of our mediæval architecture may be seen in juxtaposition in one building. As a rule, an English cathedral is not a study in harmonies, but in contrasts. Most often it is a contrast of a Romanesque nave and a Gothic choir ; as in Ely and Hereford cathedrals ; sometimes one transept is Romanesque, the other Gothic ; as in Hereford and Chester Cathedrals ; or a Romanesque transept contrasts with a Gothic choir and nave, as in Winchester Cathedral ; or a Romanesque choir has a Gothic retrochoir, as at Peter-

Ely Lantern.

borough, Durham and Chichester ; or the eastern bays of the nave are Romanesque ; the western Gothic, as at Romsey ; Gloucester ; Shrewsbury ; or the reverse

* The following list, necessarily imperfect, will give some idea of the extent to which Romanesque was retained in our more important churches :—

A. Binham, Blyth, Bolton, Boxgrove, Bury, Canterbury C., Canterbury St Augustine, Carlisle C., Castle Acre, Chepstow, Chester C., Chichester C., Christ Church, Hants, Colchester St Botolph, Dorchester, Durham C., Ely C., Gloucester C., Hereford C., Leominster, Lindisfarne, London Old St Paul's and St Bartholomew's, Malling, Malvern, New Shoreham, Norwich C., Pershore, Peterborough, Ramsey, Rochester, Romsey, St Albans, Selby, Shrewsbury, Southwell, Tewkesbury, Thorney, Tutbury, Tynemouth, Waltham, Wimborne, Winchester C., Worcester C., Wymondham ; the above contain work earlier than 1150.

B. Buildwas, Cartmel, Chester St John's, Dore, Dunstable, Fountains, Furness, Kirkstall, Temple Church, London, Malmesbury, Oxford St Frideswide's, Wimborne, Winchester St Cross ; the above contain work *c.* 1150 to *c.* 1200.

is the case, as at Rochester.   Sometimes early is in juxtaposition to late Gothic; as at WELLS (127), Lincoln, Lichfield, Canterbury, York.   Sometimes the substructure is Romanesque, the superstructure Gothic; as in Selby nave; St John's, Chester; and in the naves of Rochester and Malmesbury; OXFORD CHOIR (27).   Sometimes the church was poor ; and do all it could, the work went on very slowly ; in the naves of Selby and Binham there is a difference of date and a difference of style almost in every bay.   More heterogeneous churches and more picturesque churches cannot be imagined ; as delightful to the artist as to the archæologist.

What has been said of the greater is largely true of the smaller churches also.   As a rule, an English parish church was not pulled down and rebuilt *de novo ;* the old church frequently remains inside,* forming the nucleus round which all the later additions have crystallised ; *e.g.* at St Mary's, Guildford ; where all that is left of the original building is the central tower.   The chief exception is that in districts where the farmers were making large profits from their wool, and the weavers and merchants from their woollen cloth, *e.g.* Norfolk, Suffolk, and Somerset, frequently the churches were wholly rebuilt ; the chancel often in the fourteenth, and the nave in the fifteenth century ; leaving no trace of the original church.

Romanesque largely survived in England, while in the Domaine Royale and Champagne most of it disappeared.   The output of Norman building here in the eleventh and twelfth centuries had been enormous ; and at the end of the latter century it must still have been in good repair.   The very number and grandeur of our Romanesque churches may have saved them from being promptly rebuilt in Gothic.

The substitution of Gothic for Romanesque was a long and slow process in most of the greater English churches.   Some, like Selby, Chester St John's, Binham, Romsey, at the end of the twelfth century, had Romanesque naves still incomplete; and finished them in Gothic.   More often, however, the nave was complete ; and the new Gothic was first employed at the east end of the church. At Norwich nothing was done but to substitute a rectangular Lady Chapel for the eastern apsidal chapel.   At Chichester, Ely, Durham, St David's, and Hereford, the eastern limb was prolonged or extended.   In very many cases a clean sweep was made of all work east of the crossing ; so that Romanesque choirs are now rare with us ; *e.g.* Winchester, Worcester, Southwell, Boxgrove, Fountains, Pershore, Carlisle, in the thirteenth century ; Selby, mainly in the fourteenth ; Malvern and Christ Church, Hants, in the fifteenth and sixteenth centuries.   Not only a new choir, but a new central transept also was built at Hexham, Rochester, Rievaulx, in the thirteenth, and at Bristol in the fourteenth century.   At St Albans in the thirteenth ; at Shrewsbury and Waltham Abbeys in the fourteenth ; at Gloucester in the fifteenth century, a beginning was made of rebuilding the Norman naves from the west end.   At Rochester a commencement was made at the east end.

A less drastic method was adopted at Gloucester and Tewkesbury ; an example copied at Winchester and Norwich in the fourteenth, at Sherborne and Malvern in the fifteenth century.   It was not to pull down the old Norman work, but merely to put a new face on it ; to give it a Gothic veneer.   At TEWKESBURY

---

* Last to disappear generally were the responds of the chancel arch.

Gloucester Choir, N.E. Angle.

(165) the recasting was of a more drastic character than at GLOUCESTER (135). At Tewkesbury the ambulatory plan is still there, and the Norman cylindrical piers, somewhat heightened ; but the Norman triforium and clerestory were removed. At Gloucester the clerestory was removed ; but the vaulted upper aisle was left, to give abutment to the new lierne vault of the choir. At WINCHESTER (90, 342) and Sherborne Abbey, piers, arches and thick clerestory wall were all left, but transformed into Gothic guise. The piers in Winchester nave are the original Norman ones, with the moldings * modified ; while the vaulting shafts are the Norman roof shafts unaltered.

Sometimes the rebuilding was continued till the whole church became Gothic. In some few cases the works were carried on with considerable rapidity ; and in these the result is a uniformity and regularity of style in which a Frenchman sees nothing remarkable, but which at once strikes one of ourselves as something exceptional. Lincoln (as it was c. 1250), SALISBURY (170), St Saviour's Southwark, and Exeter, were each built in about half a century. Other churches, built wholly in Gothic, but Gothic extending over long periods of time, are Canterbury Cathedral, Lichfield, Beverley Minster, and Westminster. In the last two the later is assimilated to the early work, so that in these two there is remarkable unity and uniformity of design.

In several cases, when the original Anglo-Norman cathedral had been wholly rebuilt in Gothic, another period of Gothic building set in later, by way of extension of the eastern limb ; in the last half of the thirteenth century at LINCOLN (151.1) and Old St Paul's ; in the first half of the fourteenth century at Wells, Lichfield, Glastonbury, Carlisle.

Still more extensive was the Gothic work done at York. Here there was first, a Norman cathedral. Then the choir was rebuilt, 1154-1181 ; the transepts 1247-1260 ; the nave 1291-1345 ; making the whole cathedral Gothic. Then once more the works recommenced, the choir of 1154-1181 was pulled down and the present presbytery and choir were built, 1367-c. 1400 ; and the three towers c. 1400-1474.

As we have seen above, almost always the short Norman choirs were either rebuilt or lengthened ; and the Gothic choirs themselves were sometimes lengthened a second time. The result of this was that the greater Gothic churches are remarkable for the great length of their eastern limb ; differing in this respect completely from their Norman predecessors, where the excess of length is to be found in the nave ; e.g. at ST ALBANS (153.2), Winchester,† ELY (153.4), Peterborough, NORWICH (148.4).

In total length we can show churches, with their long Romanesque naves and long Gothic choirs, surpassing the largest mediæval churches of Europe.

				Feet.					Feet.
Old St Paul's	-	-	-	586	Milan	-	-	-	475
Winchester	-	-	-	530	Florence	-	-	-	475
St Albans	-	-	-	520	Amiens	-	-	-	435
Ely	-	-	-	517	Rouen C.	-	-	-	435
Canterbury	-	-	-	514	Reims	-	-	-	430
Westminster	-	-	-	505	Cologne	-	-	-	427

* The diagram on page 659 shows the Norman pier as remodelled.
† Winchester nave was longer still before its remodelling by Wykeham and his successors.

In the spans of their naves they are surpassed by many.

	Feet.		Feet.
King's C. C.	45½	Gerona	73
York	45	Toulouse	63
Ripon	40	Perpignan	60
Boston	40	Albi	58
Ely	39	Milan	56
Lincoln	39	Seville	56
Canterbury choir	39	Florence	55
Glastonbury	38	Reims	48
Old St Paul's	36	Amiens	46

In internal height * they fall far short of their Continental brethren; some being exceptionally low; *e.g.* Lichfield, 57 feet; Chichester, 61 feet; Beverley, Wells, Gloucester, 67 feet; Worcester, 68 feet; Exeter, 69 feet.

	Feet.		Feet.
Old St Paul's nave	103	Cologne	155
Westminster	103	Beauvais	150
York choir	102	Bologna, S. Petronio	150
Gloucester choir	86	Amiens	144
Salisbury	84	Bourges	117
Lincoln nave	82	Chartres	106
Peterborough	81	Strasburg	101
Canterbury nave	80	Toledo	100
Winchester	78	Leon	100

In area also they have many superiors on the Continent.

	Sq. feet.		Sq. feet.
Old St Paul's	72,460	Seville	150,000
York	63,800	Milan	92,600
Lincoln	57,200	Saragossa	80,000
Bury	56,270	Amiens	70,000
Winchester	53,480	Cluny	66,000
Glastonbury	48,000	Toledo	66,000
Ely	46,000	Cologne	65,800
Westminster	46,000	Florence	65,700
Durham †	44,400	Bologna, S. Petronio	65,000
Salisbury	43,515	Chartres	65,000
Canterbury	43,215	Reims	65,000
Peterborough	41,090	Bourges	59,000

Much has been written on the subject of the proportions of the Gothic churches here and abroad; *e.g.* the assumption being that the interiors were proportioned according to the ratio of the sides of equilateral or of isosceles triangles, as the case might be. No two of these theories agree; nor are they based on uniform systems of measurement.‡ In this, as in all matters, practical considerations may fairly be assumed to have come first with the builders. The

---

* These measurements give the height up to the apex of the vault. The lengths, breadths, and heights given in the above tables are internal measurements.

† Durham occupies nearly an acre. The boundary line of Salisbury, following the angles made by the buttresses and other projecting parts, is nearly half a mile.

‡ Moreover, the new work was frequently erected on the old foundations, *e.g.* the nave and central transept of Canterbury. " It is vain to look, as many have done, for any general doctrines of proportion in work so conducted" (Lethaby, *Med. Art*, 169).

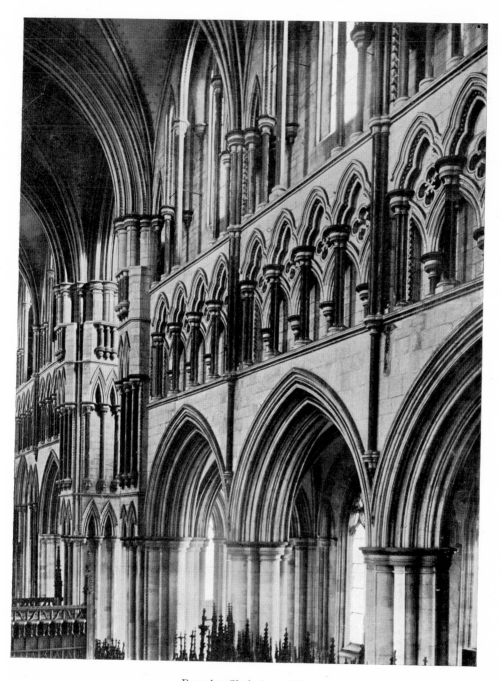

Beverley Choir from S.E.

span of the nave could not be expanded at will; it was confined within certain limits by the difficulties and cost attending roofs of exceptional span. Again, in determining the height of the nave, the first thing to take into account was the amount of light desired; this regulated the height of the aisle window and of the clerestory window; consequently, of the pier arcade and the clerestory wall. Again, there was the question of borrowing light from the triforium chamber; if that was desired, the height assigned to the triforium had to be considerable. On the other hand, if no light was desired from this source, the height of the triforium could be greatly diminished. As for the length of each limb, that again could not be determined by geometrical ratios. Its length depended mainly on considerations of ritual; on the number of monks or canons attached to the church; and on the number of altared chapels desired. It often happened that the length of a church was curtailed by some obstacle; by a highroad or a foot-path, or the city wall. Thus the east end of the presbytery of OXFORD CATHEDRAL (152.3) extended up to the city wall; and there was no room to the east for a Lady Chapel; it was therefore placed to the south. The Lady Chapel of Gloucester and the chancel of Walpole St Peter's were built over rights-of-way; in these two instances curtailment was avoided by building a vaulted subway. This may have been the case at Hythe also. But, of course, the most weighty factor was the amount of money at the disposal of the monks or canons. Given funds and spaciousness of site, the number of bays in a nave, choir or transept could be multiplied till, as at BURY (150.3), there was a nave of 296 feet, or, as at Old St Paul's, a transept of 293 feet and a choir of 224 feet. In England, at any rate, the ratio of height to span varies so greatly, that certainly it cannot be predicated of the builders that they had any abstract scheme of ratios in their heads. The following table shows the height and span of some of the more important vaulted churches*—

	Span.	Height.	Ratio.		Span.	Height.	Ratio.
Tewkesbury nave -	33	58	1.8	Noyon - - -	—	—	2 07
Gloucester nave -	34	68	2	Laon - - -	—	—	2.21
Exeter nave - -	34	69	. 2	Chartres - - -	46	106	2.3
Lichfield nave	28	57	2	Bourges - - -	46	117	2.5
Wells nave - -	32	67	2.1	St Sernin, Toulouse			
Lincoln nave - -	39	82	2.1	(Romanesque) -	—	—	2.59
Winchester nave -	32	78	2.4	Toledo - - -	38	100	2.6
Gloucester choir -	33	86	2.6	Amiens - -	46	144	3.1
Beverley choir -	26	67	2.6	Leon - - -	31	100	3.2
Salisbury nave -	32	84	2.7	Beauvais - - -	45	150	3.3
Norwich choir -	28	83	2.9	Conques(Romanesque) —		—	3.45
Westminster nave -	35	103	2.9	Cologne - - -	41	155	3.8
				St Trophime, Arles			
				(Romanesque) -	—	—	4.2

On nothing does the effectiveness of an interior depend so much as on the ratio of height to span. In the naves of GLOUCESTER (26), TEWKESBURY (297), EXETER (9), and Lincoln the vault is crushingly low. There can be no question that the most successful vaulted interiors we possess are those

* The dimensions given in this and the preceding tables must be accepted as only approximate: of many churches the measurements are not trustworthy.

of the naves of Westminster, Salisbury, Beverley, and Winchester. Where height and span are also properly correlated with length, as in the naves of WINCHESTER (342) and WESTMINSTER (63), there an English interior is seen at its very best.

But there is yet another factor which has very great weight. What it is, may be seen by examining the naves of LICHFIELD (523) and Wells. They are quite sufficiently long; but their height is only about twice their span. Yet they do not look low; as do the naves of EXETER (9) and Lincoln, which also are only about half as broad as they are high. The reason for this is that we have taken into account only the breadth of the nave. But the breadth of each of the bays of which the nave is composed is also an important factor. The following table shows the ratio of the breadth to the height of the bay in a few examples. It will be seen how great is the difference of bay proportion in such interiors as those of Westminster * and Exeter.

	Breadth of Bay.	Height of Bay.	Ratio.
Exeter nave - - - -	20	63	3.1
Lichfield nave - - -	$16\frac{1}{2}$	57	3.5
Lincoln presbytery - -	21	74	3.5
Wells nave - - - -	16	68	4
Westminster choir - - -	18	100	5.5

Yet another factor is treatment of the vaulting shaft. Where it rises from the pavement, as at Lichfield, the apparent height of the bay is enhanced; but the church looks lower where as at Exeter and Lincoln presbytery it starts from a corbel at some intermediate point.

Of all our interiors, perhaps that of WINCHESTER NAVE (342) is most successful. If we take 2 as the unit, then if the breadth of each of its twelve bays is 2; the span of the nave is $2\frac{2}{3}$; the height of the vault and of each bay is $6\frac{1}{2}$; the length of the nave is $22\frac{2}{3}$. It is to be noted that it retains massive Norman vaulting shafts descending to the pavement.

So much for the dimensions and proportions of the greater churches. Another factor of enormous importance is the character of the methods of abutment employed.

ABUTMENT.—Of systems of abutment to Gothic clerestories we may distinguish four. The first is that which was first employed in DURHAM NAVE (34.2), and which was contemplated at NORWICH (371). In this the clerestory walls are abutted low down by flying buttresses concealed beneath the aisle roof. The second is seen in CANTERBURY CHOIR (34.3), commenced 1175. Here there is retained the arch spanning the triforium chamber, which was employed in DURHAM CHOIR (370); except that it is segmental instead of semicircular. But in addition a flying buttress emerges, for the first time, into the open air. It is constructed in very timid fashion, just crawling along above the triforium roof; unornamented; regarded, plainly, as nothing more than a builder's expedient. In LINCOLN CHOIR (34.5), commenced 1192, precisely the same system is adopted as in Canterbury choir; except that the arch in the

---

* WESTMINSTER CHOIR and LINCOLN PRESBYTERY, illustrated on pages 55 and 56, may be taken as average specimens of a French and an English internal elevation.

triforium chamber is pointed. The third system is seen in CHICHESTER NAVE (34.4), which was vaulted in the last years of the twelfth century. Here also, as at Canterbury, flying buttresses are displayed in the open air; but they are heavy and clumsy. Plainly they are no copies of Canterbury work, but just the flying buttresses of Durham nave built out of doors. Similar flying buttresses, equally massive and plain, are seen at NEW SHOREHAM and BOXGROVE (373). But down below, in the section on the right, page 344, may be seen a second flying buttress, helping to support the aisle roof. Here then we have a double set of flying buttresses, one above, the other beneath the triforium roof. The fourth system is that in which all abutment inside the triforium chamber is discarded, and in which, as at EXETER (35.3), the flying buttress is displayed in the open air. The fifth appears at WESTMINSTER (35.2) c. 1245; and earlier still in Ely presbytery c. 1234. In both these churches the thrusts of the high vaults are stopped by two flying buttresses in superposition, both of them above the aisle roofs. In the Gothic architecture of England two of the five systems remained in employment, viz., the first and the fourth; with an ever-increasing tendency to employ the fourth. In France, in the Gothic of the Domaine Royale, the fourth and fifth systems chiefly were employed. Owing to the vastly greater height of their clerestories, the first three systems would have been ineffectual.

SKELETON CONSTRUCTION. — From the character of the Gothic vault and from the employment of the buttress there flowed consequences which entirely transformed the face of Gothic architecture. Owing to the fact that in a Gothic vault the ribs only descend to the wall opposite the piers, it follows that, while the parts of the wall to which they do descend are exposed to an enormous bursting pressure, the whole of

SCALE OF FEET

Westminster Choir.

ELEVATION

0 1 2 3 4 5 6 7 8 9 10 FEET

Lincoln Presbytery.

the space between the springs of the ribs—*i.e.* nearly the whole bay—is free from any such pressure. It follows that if the builder chooses to omit the wall space between each pair of buttresses, he can do so, provided that he builds a relieving arch across from buttress to buttress to carry the parapet and roof. And where the wall was, he can have glass. To a large extent, therefore, Gothic architecture meant the substitution of voids for solids and window for wall. The difference between the Romanesque and the Gothic construction may be seen by comparing ELY NAVE (57), LINCOLN PRESBYTERY (56), and WESTMINSTER NAVE (55).

At Ely the distance from window to window in the clerestory is about 13 feet; and the whole breadth of each bay is solid wall, except a window 4 feet across. In Lincoln presbytery the clerestory window occupies 12 feet out of a total breadth of $23\frac{1}{2}$ feet; leaving $11\frac{1}{2}$ feet of solid wall; the voids and solids nearly balancing. But at Westminster the clerestory window occupies as much as 10 feet in a bay of a total breadth of 18 feet; leaving 8 feet of solid wall; so that the voids outbalance the solids. Ely may be taken as an average specimen of late Romanesque construction; Lincoln presbytery of English Gothic; Westminster approaches the construction of the Ile de France. The French churches go far beyond Westminster in the attenuation of the clerestory wall. In Amiens nave the windows of the clerestory are more than three times as broad as the strips of clerestory wall; which are also narrower than the piers down below between nave and aisles. In the nave of St Denis * (1231 to 1280) the piers below are still broader than the strips of clerestory wall between the windows. While in Metz Cathedral * the piers between the nave and aisles are nearly twice as broad as those between the clerestory windows. Vast is the difference between such construction and that of Lincoln presbytery.

In such churches as Amiens, St Denis, EVREUX (539), the clerestory wall ceases to exist *qua* wall.† Really it has become the upper part of a pier: of one of the piers below between nave and aisles. In such examples the piers of the ground story do not stop, as they appear to do, at their capitals; each continues up, between the pier arches, between the bays of the triforium arcade, and between the bays of the clerestory, till it stops about one-third of the distance up the clerestory windows, as at Amiens and Metz; or half-way up, as at Beauvais and St Denis. Such a pier, which may be called the Vault pier, is at Beauvais nearly 140 feet high. How is it kept in position? The lower part of it, if it be a pier between the nave and aisle, is kept from moving to east or west by the arches which it supports. It cannot incline backward; because of the inward thrust of the vault of the aisle. Nor again can it incline forward, for it is weighted with its own upper portion, which is loaded with its share of vault and outer roof. In the triforium stage the arches of the triforium arcade act as straining arches. To oppose any movement forward or backward there is opposed the weight of its upper portion carrying its share of vault and outer roof. In the clerestory stage, it is pre-

* Elevations in Dehio, Plates 387, 388.

† See especially the longitudinal section of Gloucester choir on page 59.

SCALE OF 10 5 0 10 FEET

Ely Nave.

vented from moving to east or west by the arches of the windows, which act as straining arches. It cannot move forward because of the thrust of the high vault; it cannot move backward because of the flying buttress,* which acts as a stay, propped up on the top of the aisle buttress; which buttress is loaded with a pinnacle. All this complex mechanism is needed to keep such tall vault piers upright.

In England, as we have seen, even in the semi-French church of West-minster, usually we did not carry Gothic construction to such logical extremes; eliminating masonry till there remained nothing but a vault pier. It was not that we could not, but that we would not. Even in the thirteenth century the principle of the vault pier was thoroughly understood and properly applied in England. The construction of the Chapter House of Salisbury is precisely the same as that of the clerestories of Amiens, Beauvais, St Denis, Metz. In all five the wall between the windows is reduced to a pier; and the wall ribs of the vault serve also as the arches of the window. In GLOUCESTER CHOIR (59), finished c. 1350, a magnificent pier ascends uninterruptedly from the pavement to the spring of the arches of the clerestory window; a construction which was repeated, but with more timidity, in Henry the Seventh's Chapel, Westminster, Malvern, and Bath. But what was optional with us was a constructional necessity with the French builders. Even if they had wished, they could not have constructed their lofty churches in our English fashion, with retention of great breadths of clerestory wall. Look at a typical English Gothic elevation, such as that of LINCOLN PRESBYTERY (56). On a pier which is about $5\frac{1}{4}$ feet broad is balanced a mass of clerestory wall, which is no less than $11\frac{1}{2}$ feet broad. Such a pier is top heavy; the upper part is twice as broad as the lower. In the lofty French churches, to have poised such an enormous weight on the slender piers of the ground story, would have crushed them. Consequently the upper part of the vault pier, as we have seen, had to be made narrower, not broader, than the lower.

Other considerations no doubt had weight. The generative principle of Gothic architecture has been described, with considerable truth, as the economy of stone.† Labour was cheap, stone was dear. Stone was something precious; more like ivory than wood. Every care must be used to lessen the cube of stone. Any amount of labour might be expended on ornament; as little as possible on ashlar. The masons had grown up under this tradition. There was a premium on economy of ashlar. Nowhere is the result plainer than in the construction of the Gothic vault pier. It was an enormous saving in stone.

Such construction, of course, revolutionised Romanesque practice; which had been to rely wholly on walls for the stability of the vault. Now reliance was almost wholly on the pier with its paraphernalia of buttresses, flying buttresses, pinnacles. In the nave of a Gothic church in its final development all the windows might be taken away; also the end walls, the walls beneath the

---

* In Gloucester choir instead of flying buttresses there is a half barrel.

† "The most lavish expenditure of labour seems to have been considered no waste, if effecting the slightest saving of material" (Garbett's *Principles of Design*, 219). "Il fallait se suffire avec peu de matériaux; il fallait traiter la pierre comme une chose précieuse; tous les efforts devaient tendre à en limiter l'emploi; on devait bâtir avec le moins de matière." (Choisy's *Histoire*, ii. 526.)

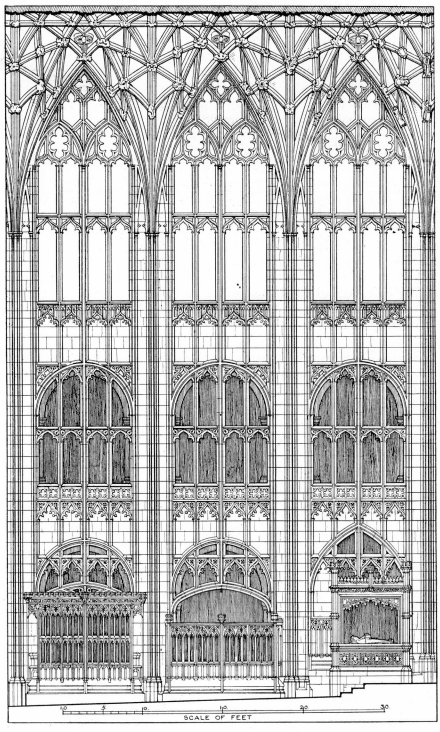

SCALE OF FEET

Gloucester Choir.

windows of the aisles and the clerestory, and the spandrils of the pier arcade :
it might be reduced to a mere skeleton, consisting of four rows of stone posts—
the inner two being the vault piers, the outer two the buttressed piers between the
aisle windows, connected by arches—and on these posts, with the winds of heaven
blowing through them, the vaults both of nave and aisles would still stand secure.
Like the half-timbered house, the Crystal Palace, or the American "sky-scraper,"
the constructional members are totally independent of the filling in.

With skeleton construction, moreover, another advance was made to the
more complete lighting of the mediæval churches. Every window, as in the clerestories of Amiens nave and Gloucester choir, could be widened till it occupied all
the whole space from one vault pier to the next. This was no small gain.

A church so constructed, with the voids so much in excess of the solids,
was very light in appearance. Its lightness of construction was still further
increased by the superiority of the masonry as compared with that of Romanesque. The walls could be, and were, made thin.* The piers themselves became
surprisingly slender in comparison with their Romanesque predecessors (659,
661). All this attenuation of the supports was again facilitated by the lightening of the later vaults ; for the web of these vaults was much thinner ; a shell
of ashlar being employed instead of heavy rubble ; nor was it covered with
a layer of concrete (304). The result was a wonderful church. A church
built logically with vault-pier construction presented an interior such as the
world had never seen or dreamt of. It was an " aerial immateriality "; something spiritual, incorporeal. In such an interior it all but seems that the load
might float away from the unsubstantial air or rather from the belt of coloured
light on which it rests. In a Romanesque minster like DURHAM (8) one
is impressed by the vast downward pressures that exist. Not so in the ethereal-
ised later Gothic. "Who, while viewing a stately tree in the pride of its growth,
ever thinks of its weight, or of the pressure of its boughs upon the stem ? It is
with its upward soaring that the mind is impressed ; and just so it is with the
interior of the Gothic cathedral. The perfection with which all the physical
forces are met has to the mind the effect, not merely that they are annihilated,
but that they are actually *reversed*." †

Nevertheless such construction may be deemed perhaps somewhat non-
architectural : a little out of consonance with the material employed ; masonry
being made almost as pliant and ductile in design as if it were metal. The great
Gothic churches are of stable construction—have they not stood for hundreds of
years ?—but however much the intellect appreciates the unseen balance of forces
by which their stability is assured, the eye desiderates something more ; solidity
as well as stability : and this in its later phases the Gothic preponderance of
voids fails to give. "In works of a monumental character which are designed
to last for centuries, the strict economy of material, which is sometimes deemed
necessary in engineering works, is not advisable ; because mass, solidity and
durability are of the very essence of their architectural character." ‡

* In late Gothic, *e.g.* in the Coventry churches and in the choir of ST MARY REDCLIFFE
(525), the clerestory wall was made thinner than the pier arches which supported it.
  † Scott's *Lectures*, ii. 189 ; *cf.* Ruskin's *Seven Lamps*, 64.
  ‡ Fergusson's *History*, i. 15.

This unsubstantiality of skeleton construction was, however, largely counter-acted by opacity of glass. How essential to Gothic design is stained glass may be seen by visiting any church which has now but white glass. Such a church seems but a collection of stone scaffolding. With stained glass, even if it be one great lantern, like KING'S COLLEGE CHAPEL, CAMBRIDGE (62), an apparent solidity is produced that reassures. "None would have made walls which are literally windows, unless strength of colour had come forward to simu-late strength of substance." * Nothing in the whole history of architecture is so unsatisfactory as an Amiens glazed in white glass; nothing so delightful as that same church filled with stained glass, provided that the glass be good.

ALTITUDE AND VERTICALITY OF GOTHIC.—In a Gothic as compared with a Romanesque church or part of a church there is usually a considerable increase of height; e.g. at Norwich the nave, which retains its Norman clerestory, is 69½ feet high; the choir, which has a Gothic clerestory, is 83½ feet high. A similar difference between the height of nave and choir obtains at Gloucester. The parts that rise are the pier arcade and the clerestory; the triforium tends to diminish in height, as its roof is flattened more and more. The primary reason for the greater height of Gothic pier arcade and clerestory is a practical one; it is due to the desire to have taller windows and more light. It would be useless to make the aisle windows taller if the pier arcade remained low. Tallness of pier arcade is as necessary as tallness of clerestory, if more abundant light is to be had.

Of the two chief factors in the dimensions of an interior, breadth and height, the former is the master-factor; the breadth governs the height; e.g. if an English church is to have a nave of 32 feet span, as at Salisbury and Winchester, each aisle may have a span of about 16 feet. And if the aisle windows are to be sufficiently tall, the aisle should be about 40 feet high; which should be the height of the pier arcade also. Now a satisfactory elevation is one that allots one-half of the total height of the interior to the pier arcade, one-sixth to the triforium, and one-third to the clerestory; therefore if the pier arcade has a height of 40 feet, the triforium arcade will occupy about 13 feet, the clerestory about 27 feet, and the total height to the top of the clerestory will be 80 feet; externally, the ridge of the roof will be about 108 feet high. This corresponds pretty closely with the distribution of the three vertical stories of Salisbury, which is 84 feet high, and of WINCHESTER NAVE (90), which is 78 feet high. In such an elevation, the height both of the nave and of the aisles is about two and a half times their span.†

But in the Ile de France the builders, in fixing the height of the churches, by no means allowed themselves to be curtailed by the fenestration. Amiens, with a nave of 46 feet span, would, if built with the average English proportions, have an internal height of 114 feet; as a matter of fact, the height is 144 feet. In Amiens the height of the nave and aisles is respectively nearly three times their span. Light enough could have been gained without running up the aisles and nave to such great heights. Partly from ambitions of masoncraft, partly

* Rensselaer's *English Cathedrals*, 431.
† The above dimensions are of course merely an imaginary example; there are many deviations from such a standard as this.

from exalted ideas of design, the boundaries of the material were far outpassed. The result was a series of buildings surpassing all the other works of man ; in which the builders reached forward to and attained not merely the beautiful, but the sublime. Nowhere does one feel so much the greatness and the insignificance of man. Man who built these towering vaults is crushed and overwhelmed by his own work.

To a large extent verticality is the dominant note of Gothic architecture ; horizontality of Romanesque. All the vertical lines that were present in the Romanesque building are present in the Gothic ; but they are all elongated owing to the greater height of the building. The piers of Durham give important vertical lines ; but there is a great difference between these and the vault piers of GLOUCESTER CHOIR (59) rising into the clerestory 66 feet from the pavement. So with the vaulting shafts ; they shared in the general uplifting of the interior. The pointing, too, of every semicircular arch carried the eye upwards. The articulation of the piers into shafts and columns and the disuse of the Romanesque cylinder immensely multiplied the number of vertical lines. So also did the multiplication of window mullions. On the other hand the space from buttress to buttress being occupied with windows, there was less room for the horizontal line either inside or outside the buildings. Bands, too, which checked the upward flow of the shafting, were for the most part abandoned. From the summit of the vaulting shafts, as at EXETER (9), whole sheaves of ribs ran upwards to the ridge of the vault. Externally, the vertical line was still more pronounced ; in the great projection of the buttress ; in the substitution of the pinnacle for the gablet ; above all, in the upward growth of the spire.

Nevertheless, it is possible to overemphasise the verticality of Gothic architecture. What the builders took away with one hand, they put back with the other. If they added tiercerons to diagonal and transverse ribs, they also added horizontal ridge ribs. If they articulated the vaulting shaft, they usually cut it short at a corbel. If more and more they disused the string, they more and more filled their windows with transoms. If they added the pinnacle, they substituted for the corbel table the far more emphatic horizontality of the pierced or embattled parapet. Whole districts gave themselves up to tower design, and eschewed the spire. So then we may say, with more justice, that Gothic is not the embodiment of verticality alone, but rather the just balance of the two conflicting principles of the vertical and the horizontal line.

INTERIOR OF KING'S COLLEGE CHAPEL, CAMBRIDGE, LOOKING WEST.

Westminster.

CHAPTER IV.

CHARACTERISTICS OF ENGLISH GOTHIC
FROM *c.* 1170 TO *c.* 1315.

Planning—Internal Elevation—East Front—Transept Front—West Front—Vaulting—
Piers—Ornament.

PLANNING.—By the end of the twelfth century * the planning of the greater churches had been revolutionised. Three new systems of church planning had come into use ; differing from one another ; but all agreeing in breaking away completely from Romanesque tradition. No more churches were built with parallel side apses, like those of ST MARY'S, GUILDFORD (36); a belated example of this class. Equally the Norwich plan, with semicircular apse, ambulatory and tangential chapels, went out of use ; except at Westminster in the thirteenth and Tewkesbury in the fourteenth century, where it was revived with polygonal apses. No more semicircular apses were built after those on the east sides of the choir transepts of Canterbury and LINCOLN (66). All the great churches, however, remained cruciform, and most had aisled naves. The Norman western transept was repeated at LINCOLN (151.1) and Peterborough. The eastern transept of Canterbury was much copied in this period ; *e.g.* at LINCOLN (66), Rochester, Worcester, SALISBURY (170), BEVERLEY (176). Of the transepts some were without aisles ; some had an eastern aisle ; few had western as well as eastern aisles ; none had return aisles, except the north-eastern transept of Lincoln.† Some of the eastern transepts were as lofty as the choir ; *e.g.* at Beverley, Worcester, and Salisbury ; others were as low as the aisles ; *e.g.* at Southwell and Exeter. So also if there was an eastern chapel, it might be low, as at Chichester and SALISBURY (170); or of the full height of the choir, as at Rochester, Worcester, BEVERLEY (176).‡ At FOUNTAINS (150.2) and Durham the choir transept was built at the eastern extremity of the church. Of eastern limbs three types came into use about the same time ; that of OXFORD CATHEDRAL (152.3), 1154-1180, with aisled choir and unaisled sanctuary ; that of ST CROSS, WINCHESTER (104) (probably not earlier than 1160), New Shoreham (probably *c.* 1175); and JERVAULX

---

* The period *c.* 1170 to *c.* 1315 corresponds roughly with the Early English and Early Decorated of Rickman, Bloxam, and Parker ; and with the Late Transitional, Lancet, and Geometrical periods of Sharpe.

† The south-eastern transept of Lincoln seems to have been remodelled in the thirteenth century.

‡ When tall, it sometimes formed the presbytery.

E

S.K.G
Sept 1891.

Lincoln Minster, S.E. Transept.

(153.3), in which both choir and presbytery are completely aisled; and that of Chichester, *c.* 1170, with retrochoir and rectangular eastern chapel.* Many Norman choirs were found too small and were pulled down and rebuilt in Gothic.† In several cases, as at Lincoln, this was the prelude to the rebuilding in Gothic of the whole church.

Little change occurs in the planning of the parish churches till the second half of the thirteenth century. All the Norman forms of plan remain in use. The simple forms of plan, however, tend to be replaced by the more complex forms, as transepts and aisles come more into use. Aisles are still narrow and low; and clerestories rare. It was not till the second half of the thirteenth century that the aisles became broad, as at St Martin's, Leicester, and Warmington; or lofty, separated from the nave by tall, slender, graceful piers, as in HOWDEN NAVE (546), HEDON (544) and Stone.

INTERNAL ELEVATION.—As in the Romanesque churches, so in our early Gothic work all the greater churches internally were three stories high; ground story, triforium arcade, and clerestory. And all the various Romanesque dispositions still survived. In ELY PRESBYTERY (526) and in WESTMINSTER (379) the triforium still retains windows in its back wall; giving an exterior three stories high. This arrangement is, however, rare in Gothic. The curious design of the Augustinians of OXFORD (27) and Dunstable is repeated by the Benedictines of GLASTONBURY (536), but with pointed arches. Then this design also disappears. The tall triforium arcade of Romsey, St Bartholomew's, Smithfield—illogical in design because the triforium has no windows at the back—is repeated in the early Gothic of Hexham and WHITBY (114), and later in YORK TRANSEPT (523), and the north side of the nave of BRIDLINGTON (125). More often, however, the height of the triforium is reduced by flattening its roof more or less. The space thus gained was sometimes given to the clerestory; as in the south side of BRIDLINGTON NAVE (125), and in Guisborough choir;‡ and Exeter; or the height of the piers was increased, as the choirs of CANTERBURY (106), Salisbury, and BEVERLEY (51).

In the Cistercian churches, however, the design of Fountains and Kirkstall naves survives, here and there, as late as TINTERN (524), 1269-1287. But a much more common and a more important elevation is that in which the jambs of the clerestory window are carried down to the string of the triforium; *e.g.* ST DAVID'S (525); Dore; Southwell and PERSHORE choirs (75); and the south side of BRIDLINGTON NAVE (125). The most advanced specimen of this treatment is the nave of YORK (10), the foundation stone of which was laid in 1291. Here not only the jambs, but all the four mullions of the clerestory windows, descend to the triforium string.

The parish churches for the most part are still without a clerestory, and the

---

* The Chichester plan occurs also at Dore and Glastonbury, but without the eastern Lady Chapel.

† *E.g.* Ripon; York; Wells; Lincoln; Lichfield; Salisbury; St Paul's; Beverley; Southwell; Hexham; Southwark; Rochester; Worcester; Whitby; Boxgrove; Chester Cathedral; Pershore; Rievaulx; Fountains; Carlisle; and after *c.* 1250 Lincoln, Tintern, Thornton, Exeter, Guisborough.

‡ Illustrated in Sharpe's *Arch. Parallels*, Plate 70.

internal elevation is of one story, even in the great church of Yarmouth. Where a clerestory occurs, in the first half of the century, its windows are often set in an arcade of pointed arches ; *e.g.* at Darlington, Great Grimsby,* Elm, and West Walton. In the last half of the century low clerestories become more common ; their windows are often small circles. The naves of HOWDEN (546) and HEDON (544) show the clerestory window rising to a considerable height. Where the parish church has a clerestory, the internal elevation is one of two stories.

EAST FRONT.—Of the east fronts of the thirteenth century several distinct types survive. 1. At DORE (182) there is a rectangular ambulatory, but not a projecting eastern chapel. St Saviour's, Southwark, is similar ; and originally perhaps Winchester, before the Perpendicular Lady Chapel was added. 2. At SALISBURY (170), Chester Cathedral, Hereford in the first half of the century, and at Chichester, Exeter, St David's and St Albans in the second half, a low Lady Chapel forms the eastern termination. 3. At Tynemouth, BEVERLEY (176), and SOUTHWELL (359), the choir ends at full height in a short unaisled presbytery or Lady Chapel. 4. At Whitby, Rievaulx, BOXGROVE (373), ELY † (464), in the first half of the century, both choir and aisles are carried at full height to the east : as they were in the second half at LINCOLN (177), Tintern, Ripon, and Guisborough. The east fronts of the chapels of Ely Palace, London, and MERTON COLLEGE, OXFORD (473), also belong to the last years of the thirteenth century. 5. At FOUNTAINS (150) and Durham the churches terminate to the east in an eastern transept, with nine altars. 6. WESTMINSTER (63) adopts the polygonal apse of French Gothic.

TRANSEPT FRONTS.—To the twelfth century belong the transept fronts of Ripon and Canterbury ; as well as those of the eastern transepts of LINCOLN (66). To the first half of the thirteenth century belong the north tran- septs of LINCOLN (69) and Hedon ; four transepts of SALISBURY (170) and four of BEVERLEY (176) ; two of Whitby and Rievaulx ; two of York — differing entirely in design—the north transept of Rochester ; and later in the century those of Tintern. As these fronts were often seen in conjunction with the sides of the transepts, they often followed the dispositions of the latter ; ‡ *e.g.* at Hedon § and in the east transepts of Worcester the sides of the transept contain two rows of windows ; and beneath the bottom row is blank wall. In the north elevation, therefore, at Hedon there is a doorway, at Worcester a blank wall ; two triplets of lancets superposed, corresponding to the rows of lateral windows ; and a third graduated triplet of lancets in the gable. This is the logical eleva- tion for an unaisled transept ; viz. one of four stories. On the other hand, if the transept have aisles, then on its flanks there may be (1) wall beneath aisle windows ; (2) aisle windows ; (3) aisle roof, which gives a half gable at the end of the transept ; (4) clerestory windows. The normal elevation for such a transept is one of five stories. This logical disposition obtains in all the

---

* Illustrated in *Building News*, March 21, 1875.

† The eastern terminations of the aisles have been ruined by conversion into chantry chapels by Bishops Alcock and West.

‡ So also in Norman transepts ; *e.g.* Winchester and Norwich.

§ Illustrated in *Builder*, Dec. 17, 1887.

Lincoln North Transept.

transept fronts of SALISBURY (170); in each there is (1) wall, with or without doorway; (2) a triplet or quintet of lancets; (3) a band of arcading or
of low windows; (4) another triplet or quintet of lancets; (5) the gable containing graduated lancets or a rose window. To this type belongs the noble
north façade of Westminster. It is five stories high; the great rose is placed in
the fourth story instead of the gable; and as the chief entrance to the church
is from the north, there are three lofty doorways. But when it was thought fit,
such logical dispositions were disregarded; e.g. in the central transepts of
BEVERLEY (176) and the south transept of York the logical arrangement was
disturbed in order to get more headway for doors; while in all the Beverley
transepts, quite illogically, the gables were cut up into two stories by a string.
The Whitby elevation also is illogical. The greatest revolution, however, was
in the north transept of YORK (11). Here the three central stories were consolidated into one; and this one great central story was filled with five enormous lancets, all of the same height, the famous Five Sisters. A little later
this elevation of three stories was adopted at Tintern Abbey; except that for a
quintet of lancets there was substituted a tall traceried window of six lights;
and in the north transept of Hereford.

In the east transept of Canterbury; and the central transepts of LINCOLN
(69), Whitby, and Beverley; and in the south transept of York and the north
transept of Westminster circular windows are employed.

WEST FRONT.—Of the artistic problems which came before the mediæval
builder for solution none seem to have presented such great difficulties as the
composition of the grand façade of the greater churches. When a civic building
was designed, e.g. the Cloth Hall of Ypres,* which is 440 feet long, no one
dreamt of making one end of it the grand façade. But this is exactly what
the church architect, for ritualistic reasons, everywhere was compelled to do.
Otherwise he might have made what is now a side of the church the principal
façade; a façade which in many cases would have exceeded 500 feet in length.
In the centre of this might have been placed the main entrance; emphasised,
perhaps, as at Ypres, by a great central tower. Two minor towers, to the far
east and west, might have brought together the wings. But to restrict to a
breadth of some 80 feet the grand façade of a church 500 feet long, and with
transepts spreading out perhaps 200 feet, was to make an adequate solution
almost impossible.

Nevertheless an adequate solution was found. This was to give to the
façade in height what could not be given in breadth. Such a façade was familiar
to the builders in Normandy in the eleventh century; and was reproduced
at SOUTHWELL (520), DURHAM (28), LINCOLN (592), and elsewhere. Early in
the thirteenth century it is seen at Ripon; and at the very end of the century
at LICHFIELD (frontispiece). Still greater is the adequacy of the façade if
the towers have spires; as at Lichfield, and formerly at Lincoln and Ripon.
And if, behind and between these, there is a central spire, so lofty that this also
enters into the grouping of the west front, as at Lichfield, and formerly at
Lincoln and Ripon, then, narrow as is the façade, it is adequate even for a
church so vastly long and broad as Lincoln.

* Illustrated in Fergusson, ii. 201.

This fine type of design was still further strengthened by setting the western towers clear of the aisles instead of in a line with them.   At Lichfield the

Howden West Front.

towers project but slightly to north and south; but at WELLS (154.3) they are quite clear.

For the success of the twin tower façade, however, it is indispensable that the towers shall be towers all the way to the ground.   The towers must be wholly independent of the central façade: as they are in the Abbaye-aux-Hommes, Caen; Castle Acre, and Southwell. The distinction between the central and the lateral façades is strongly emphasised at Bayeux and Beverley Minster, and with magnificent effect. In this respect the western towers of Durham and Ripon show some timidity; at Wells and Lichfield the towers are lost in the façade; both at Lincoln and Peterborough their bases are masked from view by a later façade.

The towered façade, however, was perhaps an architectural extravagance; one of the few instances in Gothic architecture of work done mainly for effect.* For this reason, perhaps, and because of its cost, it was adopted in comparatively few churches. Another design was borrowed from the Norman churches which could be turned to religious account. At Ely and Castle Acre, and originally at Hereford, the façade had included a screen wall ornamented with band upon band of arcadings of semicircles, intersecting semicircles, pointed and trefoiled arches. These arcades were built more deeply recessed; and in each recess was placed a statue. Such a statued screen, an open-air reredos or iconostasis, was defensible on religious grounds. It taught Scripture History and the Legends of the Saints.† Such a great rectangular wall was not designed merely as a façade, and is not to be criticised as a façade. The criticism which it does provoke is that it was ill advised to put sculpture at heights where its meaning was indistinguishable, and where it is exposed to the inclemency of our English climate. Lincoln, Wells, Salisbury adopted this reredos type of façade in the first half of the thirteenth century. At the very end of the century it reappears, for the last time, at Lichfield; but with a couple of steeples perched on the top of it. After this it disappears from English architecture.

The simplest method of disposing of the difficulty with the grand façade was to recognise frankly that the west front was *not* the grand façade; and to cease to try to make it one. This was the sensible method adopted in far the most churches. The west front was designed in them in the same simple fashion as the north and south fronts of the transepts. Possibly Cistercian precedent had considerable weight; for no Cistercian church had either western towers or the screen-wall façade. So the simple type of west front greatly preponderated. It occurred in the first half of the thirteenth century at Wenlock; Whitby; Bolton; St Saviour's, Southwark; Romsey; BINHAM (471); in the second half at HOWDEN (72); and frequently in later work. It is the same as the west front of a parish church which has no western tower; for distinctness we may call this third type of western façade the parochial. The history of the design of the parochial façade is the same as that of the transept façade. At first it is cut up into four or five stories; as at Bolton and Byland. Then, in the west front of Romsey, the central tiers of windows are consolidated into one gigantic triplet of graduated lancets; and the number of stories is reduced to three. But little, if at all later, is the west front of BINHAM (471); here

---

* One western tower might be useful as a campanile. But bells were often placed in the central tower; *e.g.* LINCOLN (328). The western towers, however, have constructional value; see pages 381 and 598.

† The French preferred to teach them in the statued archivolts of their doorways; and they were taught both by French and English in the stained glass windows.

it seems to have been intended to have superposed rows of lancets, as at Ripon; but a single great window of bar tracery was preferred.   Other three story façades are those of Valle Crucis and Tintern.

At Peterborough, as at Lincoln, there are two façades.   The inner façade was built at the end of the twelfth century; and was to have flanking towers (as at Wells) of which one only has been completed.   The outer façade was built a generation later and is still broader.

VAULTING.—None of the Gothic vaults are groined; * all are ribbed.   But there are considerable differences between the ribbed vaults, *e.g.* of DURHAM AISLE (315) and NAVE (8); and those, *e.g.* of NEW SHOREHAM (313) and CHICHESTER (313).   In the first place, the filling-in of the latter is of ashlar, and is much less heavy.   Rubble "filling-in," however, was frequently retained, *e.g.* in LICHFIELD NAVE (313).   The ribs became much less massive; and were composed of longer blocks.   It ceased to be customary to make the transverse thicker than the diagonal ribs.   At ROCHE (675) they differ much; while at BYLAND (675), which can be but little if any later, they are of the same profile.   The rectangular is gradually replaced by a triangular profile; the Gothic moldings being executed more and more on the chamfer plane: *e.g.* contrast the ribs of WHITBY CHOIR (675.12) with that of LINCOLN GALILEE (677.3).   The lower portion of the ribs ceases to be built independently; being constructed in solid springers.   Sexpartite vaulting received encouragement from Canterbury choir; but quadripartite vaulting was always the more common, and finally superseded sexpartite.   Additional ribs were added in LINCOLN CHOIR

Tooth Ornament.

(327), commenced 1192; and to give abutment to these a new rib, the longitudinal ridge rib, was invented.   Other intermediate ribs, or *tiercerons*, were added in LINCOLN NAVE (327), *c.* 1230; and to abut these, transverse as well as longitudinal ridge ribs, were employed.   At Ripon, Hexham, WHITBY (114), Carlisle, the tradition of the Norman ceiling survived, and no high vaults were built.

PIERS.—In the greater churches three types of pier were in use in the earlier part of the period.   The first is the western pier; usually short and massive; not employing marble; but encircled with slender shafts of freestone, arranged in triplets; *e.g.* in WELLS (209), LICHFIELD (244); a late example is PERSHORE CHOIR (75).   The second is the southern pier; usually tall and graceful; encircled by slender detached shafts of marble; banded with annulets of marble or bronze; *e.g.* CHICHESTER RETROCHOIR (245), ELY PRESBYTERY (247); late examples are Winchester chancel and Wells retrochoir.   The third is the northern pier, which discards slender shafts, and is made up of a cluster of stout columns, which are generally of freestone.   Some or all of these columns are usually pointed in section; *e.g.* ROCHE (661.2) and BYLAND

* Throughout the volume the term "groined" is confined to vaults which do not possess ribs.

Pershore Choir from S.W.

(661.3). The clustered column is sometimes found where the southern or western type of pier might be expected; *e.g.* ST SAVIOUR'S, SOUTHWARK (521); ST ALBANS NAVE (14); EXETER (241).

ORNAMENT.—The *tooth ornament* had enormous* vogue in the thirteenth century; *e.g.* at SKELTON and WARMINGTON (78 and 578); partly because of its effectiveness, partly because it was easy to execute; as is shown in the diagram on page 74. It had its origin in the Norman *nail-head*.† It is one of the few ornaments without a classical pedigree. An early example of it occurs in the labels of the aisle windows of the west front of Rochester, which is probably 1125 to 1137.‡ It occurs, fully developed, 1131-1133, at Terouanne in the North of France.§ It occurs in the west doorways of Lessay Abbey (316), and of Davington Priory; the latter was founded in 1153; also in the so-called Baptistery at Canterbury, *c.* 1160; ‖ in doorways at Stillingfleet and Brinkburn; and in the sanctuary arch of Compton; and among Norman moldings in the north doorway of St Margaret at Cliffe. It occurs as a string at the back of the pier arches of Steyning. It is used profusely at Canterbury in the work of 1175-1184. It is very rare after the thirteenth century; but an example occurs in the moldings of a Tudor arch at Lichfield,¶ and an imitation of it in another at Congresbury Vicarage. It was common in Continental Gothic also; *e.g.* in Italy at Perugia, Terni, and Verona;** and is very common in Spanish Romanesque; *e.g.* in Tarragona cloister. It is still a favourite in Cyprus.†† Usually this ornament is designed as a pyramid of four leaves; but at Salisbury it consists of only two leaves; *i.e.* a *half* pyramid; the treatment at Binham ‡‡ and West Walton ‡‡ is similar. In late and rich work scrolls of foliage are carved on each face of the pyramid; *e.g.* the north doorway of Lichfield and west front of Dunstable.

Crockets are said to be derived from the volutes of the Corinthian or Composite capital (425) But our earliest examples are mere incurved hooks, resembling the pastoral staff of a bishop; and corresponding to the earliest *knobby* type of stalk foliage, *e.g.* in St Hugh's work at LINCOLN (249) and all round the orders and down the jambs of the west doorway of Strata Florida. These hooks were soon foliated or otherwise ornamented; *e.g.* at Wells and Salisbury;§§ the south porch of the west front of St Albans and Lincoln presbytery.‖‖

Some of the earliest crockets occur at the back of shafts; *e.g.* in St Hugh's work at Lincoln and the west porch of St Albans; soon they are placed between the shafts. From the middle of the thirteenth century their chief use is to run up the straight gables of canopies; but they are found in many other positions; *e.g.* on the flying buttresses of ST MARY REDCLIFFE, BRISTOL (376); on the hood-molds of doorways, *e.g.* CLEY (85); and of windows, *e.g.* Louth spire and WREXHAM tower (609); on gables, as at LOUTH (397); on canopies, as in HOWDEN CHAPTER HOUSE (137); on spires, as at LOUTH (611).

---

* Nowhere more than in the Lincoln galilee, which "bristles with tooth ornament, like a cavern of crystals"; 5355 examples occur in this porch.

† Sharpe's *Nene Valley*, 4.   ‡ Hope's *Rochester*, 33.

§ Illustrated in Enlart's *Manuel*, i. 354.   ‖ Willis' *Canterbury*, 82, note.

¶ Petit's *Church Architecture*, i. 215.   ** Willis' *Middle Ages*, 196.

†† Enlart's *Manuel*, 354, 1.   ‡‡ See Colling's *Details*, i., E.E., Plates 22 and 24.

§§ Illustrated in Bloxam, 179.   ‖‖ Colling's *Gothic Ornaments*, i., Plates 56 and 21.

FRONT ELEVATION

SECTION THRO THE CENTRE

SECTION OF MOULDING. A

PLAN

SCALE OF ⌊⌋ 12 6 0 1 2 3 4 5 6 7 8 9 10 11 12 FEET

Skelton Porch.

For the remaining members of churches of this period, Chapters XV. to XLI. may be consulted. For *arches* see especially page 279 ; for *buttresses* and *pinnacles,* pages 358 and 363 ; for *flying buttresses,* page 371 ; for *corbel tables, parapets,* pages 392, 393 ; for *strings, hood-molds, dripstones,* and *basement courses,* page 406 ; for *foliated capitals,* page 429 ; for *molded capitals,* page 442 ; for *bases, plinth, griffe,* page 451 ; for *windows* and *tracery,* page 460 ; for *roofs,* page 559 ; for *doorways,* page 579 ; for *towers,* page 597 ; for *spires,* page 617. See also pages 105-126.

CHAPTER V.

CHARACTERISTICS OF ENGLISH GOTHIC
FROM *c.* 1300 TO *c.* 1350.

Planning—Internal Elevation—East Front—West Front—Vaulting—Piers—Ornament.

PLANNING.—No new plans were adopted in the greater churches.* The Salisbury plan was repeated at Milton Abbas, WELLS (154.3), and Ottery St Mary.
The aisled choir, with unaisled presbytery, reappears at Bristol ; and at Lichfield
an aisled presbytery with a tall unaisled Lady Chapel is built. At Howden,
SELBY (86), and CARLISLE (128) aisles are built to the full length eastward of
the eastern limb. Eastern transepts are again built ; at Bayham and Wells.
The rebuilding of choirs had been carried on with such vigour in the thirteenth
century that not much remained to do. However the choirs of Lichfield, Wells,
and Carlisle were lengthened ; and those of Howden, Selby, and Bristol were
rebuilt.

In the parish churches all the plans in use in the twelfth were retained in
the fourteenth century. Penton Mewsey, Hampshire, has unaisled nave and
chancel. Leckhampton, Gloucester, had unaisled nave, towered choir and
sanctuary. Shottesbrooke is cruciform, without aisles. BOSTON (222), Holbeach, Hingham have aisled nave and unaisled chancel. The last is by far
the most common plan of the parish church to the end of the Gothic period. In
large churches, however, the cruciform plan was still in vogue ; *e.g.* at Tideswell,
Nantwich, and Snettisham, where the nave is aisled ; at Patrington, where both
nave and transept have aisles on each side ; at HULL (96), where there are
full-length aisles to the chancel as well as to the nave. Many chancels are
rebuilt ; and aisles are rebuilt broader and loftier.

INTERNAL ELEVATION.—In the fourteenth century the internal elevation,
as before, in the greater church is one of three stories. One belated example
occurs of a tall triforium with windows at the back ; viz. in ELY CHOIR (522).
This, however, was so designed in order to assimilate it to the presbytery, with
which it is in juxtaposition to the east. In the naves of Beverley, Worcester, and
Westminster Abbey, triforium arcades occur of moderate elevation ; in all cases
to be in harmony with earlier work with which they are in juxtaposition. But,
more commonly, the precedent of Pershore and Southwell is followed ; and the
jambs of the clerestory window are brought down to the triforium string ; as in
Chester nave and TEWKESBURY CHOIR (165). Sometimes the design of York

---

* The first half of the fourteenth century corresponds roughly to the Late Decorated period
of Rickman, Bloxam and Parker ; and the years 1315-1360 to the Curvilinear period of Sharpe.

Hull Chancel.

F

nave or the south side of Bridlington nave is adopted; and the wall passage
is protected by a parapet; *e.g.* in the choirs of Lichfield and SELBY (390).
At WELLS (127) the front of the triforium of the choir of 1175 and that of
the fourteenth-century presbytery were alike masked by rows of niches. To the
eye all these latter interiors, viz. at Chester, Tewkesbury, Lichfield, Selby, Wells,
have the appearance of being but two stories high.

In the larger aisled parish churches the precedent of Howden and Hedon is
adopted generally; most of them have clerestories, and the elevation is one of
two stories. PATRINGTON (133) is an exception. Towards the end of the
period, however, above all in the chancel of HULL (81, 474), the clerestory
window grows vastly both in height and breadth. And before the century is
over, two windows may be found in each bay of the clerestory; *e.g.* at BOSTON
(222) and Holbeach; as previously at HOWDEN (546).

EAST FRONT.—1. In the fourteenth century the Salisbury type of east front
is revived at WELLS (602) and at Ottery St Mary; by the latter in imitation
of Exeter. At Lichfield the choir is lengthened and a lofty Lady Chapel is
added. 2. At Tewkesbury the semicircular apse and chapels of the choir are
made polygonal. 3. But the characteristic east front now is rectangular; with
aisles as long as the choir, and the latter carried up in three stories. Of this there
are magnificent examples at Selby; Hull; CARLISLE (128); and Howden.*

WEST FRONTS.—The chief west fronts of the fourteenth century are
Howden, Exeter, and York. HOWDEN (72) and Exeter † are both of the
parochial type. At YORK (82) the lateral façades are blended with the central
one, to the great detriment of the towers: as at Wells and Lichfield, the west
front is really a single complete façade with a pair of towers perched on the top
unrelated to it.

Beautiful façades of this period are seen in many parish churches; especially
in Mid-Lincolnshire.

VAULTING.—The simpler forms of quadripartite vaulting were still retained;
especially in the North of England; *e.g.* Beverley nave; Howden choir; Guisborough; and also in the choir of Milton Abbas, Dorset. But in the South and
West a new rib, the lierne, was highly developed, and led to combinations of the
utmost complexity; *e.g.* in TEWKESBURY NAVE and CHOIR (332, 330).‡

In BRISTOL CATHEDRAL (329) skeleton vaulting is much employed.

Owing to the multiplicity of ribs in some of these vaults the filling-in consisted of "panels," instead of coursed ashlar.

In Selby choir a wooden vault was substituted for the stone vault originally intended. In BRIDLINGTON (125) and Howden naves no high vaults
were built; nor in the south transept of St Werburgh, Chester; nor in the
retrochoir of St Albans Cathedral. On the other hand, the churches of St Mary
Redcliffe, Bristol; Ottery St Mary, and Patrington were vaulted, wholly or in part.

PIERS.—The fourteenth century is marked by the disappearance both of the

---

* A restoration of the east front of Howden is given in Sharpe's *Arch. Parallels*, Plate 86.

† Exeter façade has been greatly altered by subsequent additions.

‡ Lierne vaults occur in Tewkesbury nave and choir; Bristol Cathedral choir and the
south transept of St Mary Redcliffe; WELLS CHOIR (332) and LADY CHAPEL (325); Malmesbury
nave; Ottery St Mary; ELY CHOIR (329) and Lady Chapel, Nantwich chancel and transept.

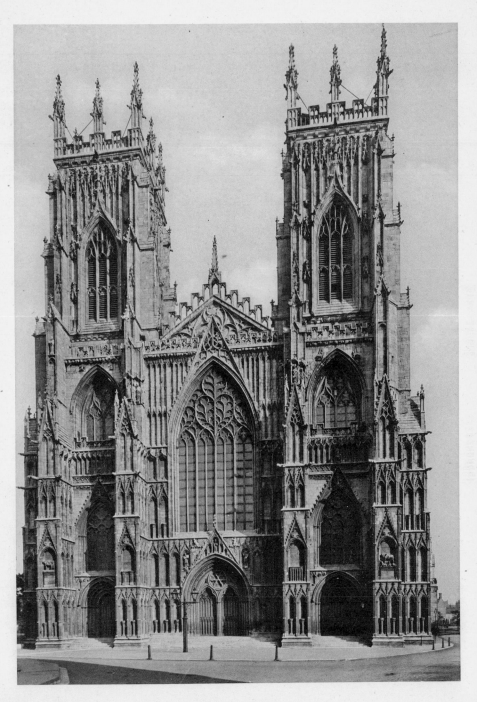

YORK MINSTER, WEST FRONT.

Western triple * shafts of freestone and the Southern detached and banded shafts of marble. Instead of these the Northern type of pier prevails ; viz. a cluster of engaged columns; *e.g.* in the choirs of Milton Abbas, SELBY (390), and Howden; the naves of York, St Albans, and Worcester ; ELY CHOIR (251); and Chester south transept. But at BRISTOL (661.11)† a completely new form of pier is devised.

ORNAMENT.—The *ball-flower* is just as characteristic of the first half of the fourteenth century as is the tooth ornament of the thirteenth. It has been supposed by some to be the trollius or globe-flower ; by others to be derived from a hawk's bell‡ ; by others to be a horse-bell, in that the thong as well as the bells is sometimes represented.§ It is found, however, in late Norman work, side by side with the pellet ; and so may be taken to be but a survival of this Norman ornament. ‖

In France also it first occurs solid, then pierced with lobes, in the twelfth and thirteenth centuries ; *e.g.* in the balustrade of the towers of Notre Dame, Paris.¶ During the course of the thirteenth century it was abandoned in France. In England it has been said to be confined almost wholly to the reign of Edward II. (1307-1327). But it occurs in the hollow architrave moldings of the arches of the thirteenth-century clerestory of Beverley Minster ** ; and in the west front of Salisbury. Late examples are seen, *c.* 1380, in the west doorway of St Mary's, Beverley ; and in the late Gothic porch of Worlingworth, Suffolk. It is used with the greatest profusion in the Western counties ; *e.g.* St Catharine's Chapel, Ledbury ; Hereford central tower ; GLOUCESTER (360), south aisle of nave ; in every window and doorway of Badgeworth, Gloucestershire. At Gloucester †† a horizontal line drawn across the head of an aisle window, just above the spring of the arch, cuts no fewer than thirty-two ranks of the ball-flower, sixteen within and sixteen without. ‡‡

The *four-leaved* flower, composed of four leaves arranged so as to form a square, is particularly common in cornices, *e.g.* at GRANTHAM and ENSHAM (385). It occurs at all periods, but has specialised forms in each ; *e.g.* on a Norman arch of Northampton St Peter's ; *c.* 1291 in the Eleanor Crosses ; in the fourteenth century at St Stephen's Chapel, Westminster ; and is very common in all the later Gothic ; both in stone and wood work.

By the end of the thirteenth century *crockets* cease to be incurved, and the foliage becomes naturalistic; *e.g.* in Southwell chapter house and Exeter reredos;§§ or the leaves are more conventionalised as at Bridlington and Guisborough and Selby;‖‖ in either case they are given an undulating ogee curve, which in the work of 1315-1350 is strongly emphasised ; *e.g.* in Selby choir, the Percy tomb at BEVERLEY (269), and ELY LADY CHAPEL (269).

---

* Except in Wells presbytery. † See pages 242 and 255.
‡ *Glossary*, 53. § Scott's *Essay*.
‖ A solid ball-flower and a fluted pellet occur together at Lincoln ; illustrated in Parker's *Manual of Gothic Mouldings*, page 14.
¶ Illustrated in Viollet-le-Duc, *Architecture*, ii. 243, 6. ** Bloxam, 178.
†† Murray's *Cathedrals—Gloucester*, 18.
‡‡ For other examples of the ball-flower see illustrations on pages 474.4 and 587.
§§ Colling's *Gothic Ornaments*, i., Plate 14, and *Mediæval Foliage*, Plate 56.
‖‖ For Bridlington, Guisborough, and Selby see Sharpe's *Arch. Parallels*, Plate 115.

The word *diaper* ("d'Ypres or dyaper") was originally applied to cloth worked in square patterns, which was produced at Ypres. It was common on great festivals to hang the walls of the interiors with tapestry; and this may have led to diaper work in stone. But rude diaper work or trellis occurs in Ernulph's work at Canterbury, 1096, and Rochester, 1114; and in Grosstête's work at Lincoln (1235-1253). The spandrils of the Norman triforium of Rochester nave were covered with rude foliated patterns, about the middle of the twelfth century. In Gothic it is used in the greatest profusion in the triforium of WESTMINSTER (119) and *c.* 1290 in the Eleanor Cross at Geddington. Diaper work was in special favour in the fourteenth century; *e.g.* in SOUTHWELL SCREEN (179); and in that of the south-east transept of Lincoln, where it takes the form of expanded lilies.

Leverington Church Porch.

Niches occur late in the eleventh century in Remigius' west front at Lincoln; late in the twelfth century all round Barfreston Church;* and in the thirteenth century on a vast scale in the west fronts of Lincoln, Wells, Salisbury, and Lichfield. In the second half of thirteenth century they are generally surmounted by a straight-sided hood-mold;† as in the west front of Wells, the interior of the nave and chapter house of York, the buttresses of GUISBOROUGH (354) and the west window of HOWDEN (72). For this triangular hood-mold the fourteenth century frequently substituted an ogee hood-mold; or used them in alternation. The ogee hood-mold, moreover, may bend forward and retreat; as in the arcading of ELY LADY CHAPEL (269). The niche with ogee canopy may be considered the characteristic feature of fourteenth-century design;

* Illustrated in Britton's *Arch. Ant.*, iv.

† The monument of Aymer de Valence (*c.* 1325) in Westminster is a late example of this.

SCALE OF 12 9 6 3 0   1   2   3   4   5   6 FEET

Cley, Norfolk.

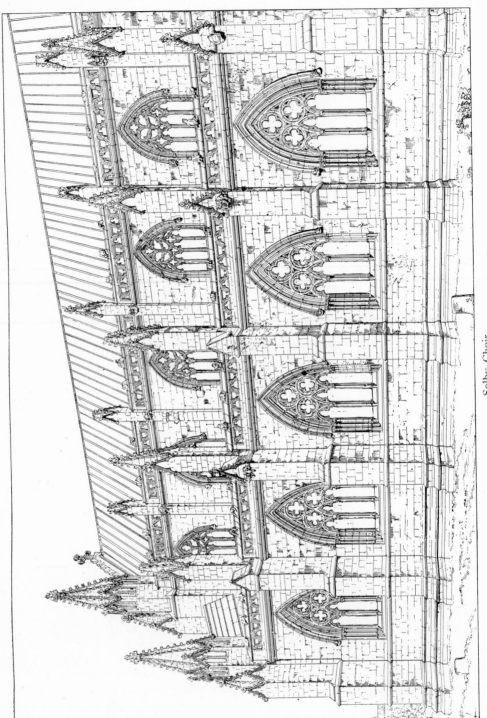

Selby Choir.

it is used in vast profusion in the west front of Lichfield Cathedral, the ruined east front of Howden, and the interiors of the presbyteries of WELLS (127) and Lichfield. So complex and beautiful was the elaboration of the niche that it usurped the interest which should have been retained for the statue it was designed to enshrine. It is as if some school of artists had spent their main effort not on their pictures but on their picture frames. It appears in arcading; as in the aisle walls of Beverley nave, and under the west towers of LINCOLN (269); in the screen of wood or stone, as at SOUTHWELL (179); in the reredos, as at CHRIST CHURCH, HAMPSHIRE (180); in the canopy of a monument, a piscina, a stoup, or sedilia; or in the wall recess of a tomb; on the font, the chest, the memorial brass; even in the pinnacle, as in HOWDEN NAVE (72), Lincoln nave, and Boston.* To some extent there was a geographical difference in the design of the canopies of niches. To the north and east they were more often solid; e.g. the Percy tomb at BEVERLEY (269); the arcading of the Ely Lady Chapel; the sedilia and Easter sepulchres of Hawton, Navenby, and Heckington. In the south and west light open spire-work was preferred. It was appropriate for wood, and had been used all over England in the wooden canopies above stalls. It was equally unsuitable for stone; nevertheless it was greatly in favour; e.g. the sedilia of Exeter and Ottery St Mary; the Exeter throne; the tomb of Edward II. at GLOUCESTER (294); that of Sir Hugh Despenser (1349) and Sir Guy Bryan (1380) at Tewkesbury; and the Durham reredos, which is south country work; made of clunch, and shipped from London to Durham † via Newcastle, in 1372-1380.‡

For other characteristics of a fourteenth-century church, see Chapters XV. to XLI. For *arches*, see 279; for *buttresses* and *pinnacles*, 358, 363; for *flying buttresses*, 377; for *parapets* and *battlements*, 396; for *strings, hood-molds, drip-stones*, and *basement courses*, 406; for *foliated capitals*, 436; for *molded capitals*, 443; for *base* and *plinth*, 452; for *window tracery*, 479; for *roofs*, 558; for *doorways*, 579; for *towers*, 608; for *spires*, 617. Also see 126-134.

---

* Illustrated in Prior, 404.

† Greenwell's *Durham*, 71. The Selby sedilia are also probably of the same London make.

‡ For a full account of the treatment of the niche see Prior, 381-404.

CHAPTER VI.

CHARACTERISTICS OF ENGLISH GOTHIC
FROM *c.* 1330 TO 1538.

Planning—Internal Elevation—East Front—West Front—Vaulting—Piers—Ornament.

PLANNING.—Only three important choirs of the greater churches were rebuilt ; viz. York, commenced 1361 ; BATH (373), commenced *c.* 1500 ; both with aisles of the full length of the choir ; and Christ Church, Hampshire ; where an aisled choir with unaisled Lady Chapel was commenced *c.* 1400. None of the three exhibit any novelty in planning.*

In the parish churches the normal type is that with aisled nave and unaisled chancel. Some few churches, however, continued their aisles to the full length of the chancel ; *e.g.* Louth, GRESFORD (214). Others, *e.g.* ST NICHOLAS, LYNN (214) ; North Walsham ; ST STEPHEN'S, NORWICH (228), identical in plan with Louth, differed from it in omitting the chancel arch. But the cruciform plan is never abandoned ; *e.g.* St Mary Redcliffe, Bristol ; TERRINGTON ST CLEMENT (92).

INTERNAL ELEVATION.—In this period all the varieties of triforium treatment are reduced to one. The triforium arcade, whether tall or short, disappears altogether. At Malvern the triforium chamber is masked with a blank wall, as in the early work of Fountains and Kirkstall. At Bath is the same arrangement ; but the blank wall is less conspicuous ; for the triforium roof is so much flattened that little height is left for the wall in front. Elsewhere the precedent of York nave is followed. The triforium is closed from the nave by a blank wall, to the bottom of which descend the mullions of the clerestory window, which are allowed sometimes, as in GLOUCESTER CHOIR (59), to descend to the hood-molds of the pier arcade. This mullioned wall appears in front of the triforium in Gloucester choir (1337 to *c.* 1350) ; and in the last half of the same century in the naves of WINCHESTER (342) and CANTERBURY (90) ; in the south transept of St Mary Redcliffe, Bristol ; and in York choir. In the fifteenth and sixteenth centuries it is seen in the choir and nave of ST MARY REDCLIFFE (525) ; in the choir of Christ Church, Hants ; and in Sherborne ; in ST GEORGE'S, WINDSOR (330) ; and in Henry the Seventh's Chapel at Westminster.

Probably the example set in Gloucester choir had most weight in spreading

---

* The period *c.* 1330 to 1538 corresponds roughly with the Perpendicular or Rectilinear period of Rickman, Bloxam, Parker, and Sharpe, except that it also includes the work at Gloucester, between 1330 and 1360, which their chronology excludes.

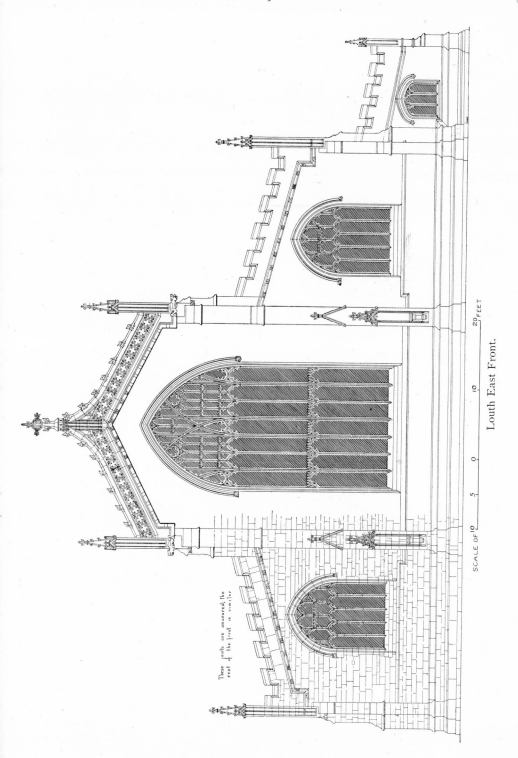

These joints are measured, the rest of the front is similar

SCALE OF 10 5 0 10 20 FEET

Louth East Front.

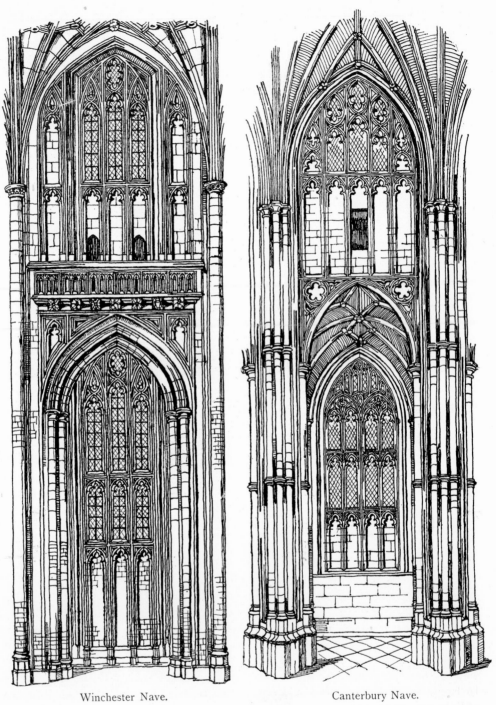

Winchester Nave.   Canterbury Nave.

this design. In the Gloucester choir such a design was almost compulsory ; it was necessary to hide away the great semicircular arches of the lower and upper aisles by panelling them over with the mullions of the clerestory windows (135).

When designed, as in Gloucester choir, in conjunction with vault piers, this design gives one the impression, and no doubt was intended to give the impression, that the interior is one of a single story. Unity was the ideal of late Gothic design, and nowhere was that ideal realised so completely as in the choir of Gloucester. Similarly, at CHIPPING NORTON (548), the interior is of one story.

EAST FRONT.—In the fifteenth century a high Lady Chapel and aisled choir are built at Christ Church, Hants ; and less lofty Lady Chapels at GLOUCESTER (132); St Mary Redcliffe, Bristol ; and Malvern ; the last has been destroyed. To the latter part of the fourteenth century belongs the east front of York ; to the fifteenth century that of LOUTH (89); to the sixteenth century that of BATH (373); in all three the aisles are as long as the choir, and the latter is carried up full height.

WEST FRONT.—Of the towered west front there are three examples ; Bridlington, which is a patchwork of various dates ; Canterbury, of which the northwestern tower was Norman till the " restoration " of 1834 ; and BEVERLEY MINSTER (599), which, with the exception of Peterborough, which is *sui generis*, has the most successful western façade in England ; the towers are not absorbed by the façade, but are towers all the way to the ground.

The parochial west front becomes more and more common in the greater churches. It appears at Winchester, Malvern, Gloucester, WINDSOR (492), Bath. At Winchester and Gloucester it was even substituted for a towered façade. In the parish churches, in this as in all periods, the west front is mainly occupied by a western tower. Fine façades occur at Maidstone ; HULL (96) ; BEVERLEY ST MARY'S (366) ; Yatton ; Crewkerne ; TERRINGTON ST CLEMENT'S (92).

In the late Gothic façades the normal elevation is one of three stories ; *e.g.* at Winchester, Canterbury, Beverley Minster ; the third story being that of the gable. But the roofs were flattened more and more ; in addition, the west window might have a four-centred arch. In such a façade there would practically be no gable, and the elevation would be one of two stories only ; the doorway story and the window story ; *e.g.* Gloucester, Bath, BEVERLEY ST MARY'S (366), HULL (96), WINDSOR (492). Even with roofs of steep pitch, the elevation is sometimes of two stories only ; *e.g.* at TERRINGTON ST CLEMENT'S (92).

In all the western façades, from first to last, there was a rivalry between the central doorway and the central window. In France, by moderating the size of the central west window, which was often a rose, a loftier doorway could be had beneath. Still further to increase the importance of this doorway, it was often surmounted with a triangular gable, which in Auxerre Cathedral is filled with open tracery and allowed to rise high up in front of the window. Thus the doorway becomes, as it should be, an imposing and influential member of the façade In England nothing was too precious to sacrifice to bigness of window, to floods of light and acreage of stained glass.*

* In Beverley Minster the west window is so tall that its head is cut off by the vaulting of the nave.

Terrington St Clement's.

VAULTING.—It was in this period that the most magnificent of all our vaults were built.*   In the first place, Fan vaulting came into use; probably its earliest application being in GLOUCESTER CLOISTER (344); afterwards it was employed in high vaults; *e.g.* SHERBORNE (346), KING'S COLLEGE CHAPEL (62); and HENRY THE SEVENTH'S CHAPEL, WESTMINSTER (348).   Lierne vaults, however, were in even greater favour; *e.g.* Bristol, St Mary Redcliffe;

Hull Nave.

Canterbury, Black Prince's Chantry, nave, and St Michael's Chapel; Christ Church, Hampshire, choir and Lady Chapel; ELY, Bishop West's Chapel (334); GLOUCESTER, south transept (306), choir (334), north transept, west bays of nave, and Lady Chapel; HEREFORD (333), south transept; NORWICH (330), all the high vaults; OXFORD, the Divinity School (331) and the Cathedral

* One must not forget, however, the TEWKESBURY VAULTS (330), which are exceedingly beautiful.

choir (331); WINCHESTER NAVE (342); and all the high vaults of ST GEORGE'S, WINDSOR (332).

High vaults were projected at Malvern, but not carried out. Those of York are of wood.

PIERS.—Three varieties of Perpendicular piers may be distinguished. 1. Occasionally the cluster of columns survives; *e.g.* in York choir, where the design is but a fourteenth-century version of that of the nave. 2. More often the columns become less prominent and the central mass more so, and some of the shafts are reduced to "beads"; *e.g.* at CIRENCESTER (448); the nave of St Mary, Oxford; St Mary Redcliffe, Bristol; Bath; ST GEORGE'S, WINDSOR (255); Christ Church, Hants; Malvern choir; Gloucester west nave. 3. In all these cases the pier is symmetrical; and two, four, eight or more shafts are retained. But in Sherborne choir and in HENRY THE SEVENTH'S CHAPEL, WESTMINSTER ABBEY, the piers are entirely unsymmetrical masses, their form being wholly regulated by their functions. The first step in this direction had been taken at BRISTOL (661.11) in 1298.

In the smaller parish churches there was no scope for complexity of plan in the piers. At all periods they may be found circular or octagonal. A cluster of four columns was also very common; it appears even in the sixteenth-century nave of Ripon Minster.

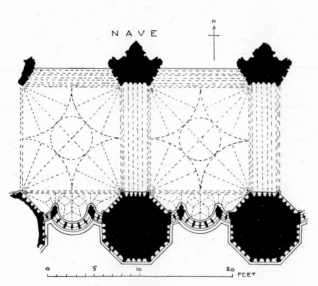

Aisle of Henry the Seventh's Chapel, Westminster.

ORNAMENT.—In late Gothic design the window was all important, and its tracery overspread the church; *e.g.* in GLOUCESTER CHOIR (47); thus reducing very largely the amount of foliated ornament. What foliage was employed was usually of bulbous or undulatory character, and highly conventionalised. Hard square forms or lozenges are characteristic. Square leaves and four leaves arranged in a square are most common in cornices. Stone diaper was abandoned; but painted diaper occurs; *e.g.* in Bishop Beckington's tomb at Wells (1464). The vine and strawberry leaf were favourite forms of leafage. The rose is common in late work; *e.g.* KING'S COLLEGE CHAPEL (473), with the portcullis of Henry VII. Shields, heraldic emblems, and grotesque animals are all common. Foliated bosses are frequent in the richer roofs; *e.g.* Sall, Tenterden, NEW WALSINGHAM (570). A cornice of vine leaves and tendrils is exceedingly common in the cornices of screens; it is usually crested with the Tudor flower. Angels are used in capitals and roofs; *e.g.* in the pier arcade of St Mary Magdalene, Taunton. The symbols of the

Kettering Western Doorway.

Passion are frequently represented on fonts; also on the ceiling of Winchester presbytery: a capital with the passion flower occurs at TIVERTON (437.6).

After *c.* 1350 CROCKETS lose much of the undulating outline of Decorated foliage ; they are usually conventionalised, and become stiff and square ; *e.g.* St Mary, Bury.*

For other characteristics of a late Gothic church, see Chapters VIII. to XLI. For *arches*, see 280 ; for *buttresses* and *pinnacles*, 361, 364 ; for *flying buttresses*, 377 ; for *parapets* and *battlements*, 396, 398 ; for *strings, hood-molds, dripstones, and basement courses*, 406 ; for *foliated capitals*, 438 ; for *molded capitals*, 444 ; for *base* and *plinth*, 453 ; for *window tracery*, 491 ; for *roofs*, 562 ; for *doorways* 579 ; for *towers*, 608 ; for *spires*, 622.   See also 133-142.

* Illustrated in Colling's *Mediæval Foliage*, 56.

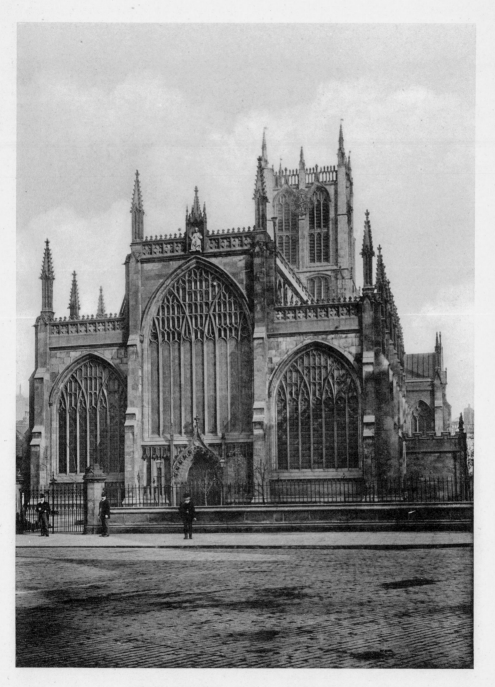

HOLY TRINITY, HULL, WEST FRONT.

CHAPTER VII.

A CHRONOLOGICAL DESCRIPTION OF THE CHIEF ENGLISH CHURCHES.

[NOTE.—Except where documentary and architectural evidence coincide, the dates in this chapter are to be regarded as merely conjectural approximations ; see note on page 638. For references to the documentary evidence see pages 638 to 657.]

1050—1150.

XI. CENTURY: THIRD QUARTER (*Edward the Confessor, Harold, William I.*).— WESTMINSTER ABBEY, begun 1050. Lanfranc's CANTERBURY, begun 1070.

XI. CENTURY: FOURTH QUARTER (*William I.*, 10th year, to *William II.*, last year).—BLYTH, founded 1088. BURY ; part finished in 1095. Ernulph's CANTER- BURY, begun 1095. CANTERBURY, ST AUGUSTINE ; CASTLE ACRE, founded before 1089 or in 1090. CHICHESTER, begun 1091. CHESTER, ST JOHN'S, begun 1067 to 1095. CHESTER CATHEDRAL (St Werburgh), refounded in 1093. CHRIST CHURCH, Hampshire, begun *c.* 1099. DURHAM, begun 1093. ELY, *c.* 1090. GLOUCESTER, begun 1089. HEREFORD, begun 1079-1095. LASTINGHAM, 1078-1088. LEWES, founded 1077. LINCOLN, consecrated 1092. LONDON, ST JOHN'S CHAPEL IN TOWER, *c.* 1080. LONDON, OLD ST PAUL'S, 1087. MALLING NUNNERY, 1077-1108. MALVERN, begun *c.* 1084. NORWICH, begun 1096. ROCHESTER, begun 1077-1108. ST ALBANS, begun 1077. SELBY, begun 1097. SHREWSBURY ABBEY, begun 1083. TEWKESBURY, choir entered in 1102. THORNEY, 1085-1108. TUTBURY, founded 1080. WINCHESTER CATHEDRAL, begun 1079. WORCESTER, begun 1084.

XII. CENTURY: FIRST QUARTER (*Henry I.*, 1st year to 26th year).—BINHAM, re-endowed 1101-1106. BURY, gateway, 1121-1130. CARLISLE, after 1101. COL- CHESTER, ST BOTOLPH, founded 1102. EXETER CATHEDRAL, towers, 1112-1136. LEOMINSTER, consecrated 1130. LINDISFARNE, partly finished before 1128. LONDON, ST BARTHOLOMEW'S, begun 1123. PETERBOROUGH, begun 1117 or 1118. READING, founded 1121. ROMSEY, *c.* 1120. SHERBORNE, begun 1107. SOUTHWELL, begun 1108-1114. WALTHAM ABBEY, nave, *c.* 1120. WYMONDHAM, founded before 1107.

XII. CENTURY: SECOND QUARTER (*Henry I.*, 26th year, to *Stephen*, 16th year). —CHEPSTOW. DEVIZES, ST JOHN and ST MARY, before 1139. DOVER, ST MARTIN'S PRIORY, begun 1131-1139. DUNFERMLINE, probably soon after 1124. NEW SHOREHAM, nave, *c.* 1130.

THE history of the Norman branch of Romanesque architecture in England commences with the building of Westminster Abbey in 1050 by Edward the Confessor. His church was of great importance to Anglo-Norman design ; for it was the first example in this country of the periapsidal plan (164), derived probably from St Martin de Tours, and anticipating Cluny by thirty-nine years ;

G

a plan which was reproduced at Gloucester in 1089 and at Norwich in 1096.   Of
the earliest churches after the Conquest, Lanfranc's Canterbury was but of
moderate dimensions, being closely modelled on the Abbaye-aux-Hommes at
Caen and CÉRISY-LA-FORÊT (148.3) both in plan and elevation.   The choir of
the former was rebuilt in Gothic; and the western bays of the nave of Cérisy
have been destroyed; but from one or the other we can form a fair idea of what
Canterbury Cathedral was like, as rebuilt by Lanfranc.*

But the Anglo-Norman was far from being a mere servile imitation of the
Norman Romanesque, either in plan or structure.   Many of our churches were
on a far grander scale than the Romanesque churches of Normandy; even such
early examples as BURY ST EDMUNDS (1070) (150.3), ST ALBANS (1077) (153.2)
Winchester (1079), Ely (1083), Old St Paul's (1087); especially remarkable was
the vast length of the naves of the above.   Some, moreover, *e.g.* Winchester, Ely,
Old St Paul's, had western as well as eastern aisles to their transept; a great

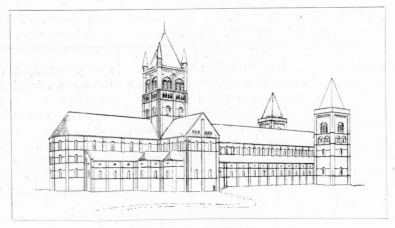

St Albans in the Twelfth Century.

advance on the eastern apse or apses of the transepts of Normandy.   As early as
1096, CANTERBURY (149.2) set the example of a vast prolongation of the choir
also, and in addition built an eastern transept.   And in due course BURY ST
EDMUNDS (150.3), Ely, and Peterborough provided themselves with vast and
complex western transepts.   A still greater revolution in planning is seen at
Dover, Sherborne, Southwell, Ely, in which the eastern termination of the
choir was square; and at ROMSEY (151.3), begun before 1120, where not only
was the choir rectangular, but it was encircled by a rectangular ambulatory
projecting from which was an eastern chapel.   These were the greatest innovations in planning.   In construction the primacy rests easily with Durham.
Durham was designed for vaults with diagonal ribs as early as 1093; and high
vaults with diagonal ribs seem to have been constructed over the whole
cathedral before 1133 (8).   To receive the springs of these ribbed vaults piers
and abaci were built of logical design (659.1); and to abut the high vaults

* See interior of the ABBAYE-AUX-HOMMES (319); plan of CÉRISY (148); exterior (160);
interior of choir (161); of transept (199); and of nave (521).

flying buttresses were built in the triforium chamber of the nave. To

facilitate the vaulting, every transverse arch of the nave was pointed. It would be difficult to find another church in Western Europe, at the end of the eleventh century, which had advanced so far as Durham on the way to Gothic.*

Nevertheless it is not to be supposed that every Anglo - Norman Church advanced as far as the Durham of 1093-1133. Even to the middle of the twelfth century or later Durham seems to have remained unsurpassed. For the progress of architectural art is not uniform; it is not like the steady progress of the steamship. Rather it is as in a yacht race, where first one boat and then another catches a breeze and forges ahead, while others it may be are becalmed and stationary. Peterborough Cathedral was commenced late; not before 1117 or 1118; but the improvements of Ernulph's Canterbury and Durham are largely ignored. It had the old-fashioned plan with three parallel eastern apses; it had neither the ambulatory nor the elongated choir nor the

Gloucester, North Aisle of Nave.

eastern transept of Canterbury; nor the high vaults and pointed transverse arches of Durham. Still more retrograde is St Bartholomew's, Smithfield; begun 1123;

* For DURHAM see 149.1, 34, 306, 315, 8, 308, 239, 370, 28, 659.1.

where there are no preparations for high vaults and where the aisle vaults are without ribs. Still slower to innovate was the Anglo-Norman builder in the villages; *e.g.* the church of SUTTON ST MARY, Lincolnshire (42), a thoroughly Romanesque design, was not commenced till after 1180.*

Not only did English Romanesque advance at different rates; but in distant districts, dissevered by trackless forests and unbridged rivers, it tended to form divergent local schools. Thus the West built its churches less vast in scale, with naves considerably shorter, with less amplification of central transept, and without western annexes, and exhibited a preference for the ambulatory rather than the three parallel eastern apses. So also instead of the compound pier, or of alternation of compound pier and cylinder, or cylinder and octagon, it preferred rows of simple cylinders, short and stout, as in GLOUCESTER CHOIR (294), or immensely tall, as in GLOUCESTER NAVE (26). Of these piers the capitals were often no more than imposts, and the bases were of the most archaic character. The recessed orders of the arches often remained square-edged, with little molding or carving, if any (276). Durham, again, forms a school of its own, with its connections, Lindisfarne, Warkworth, Dunfermline, Selby, and WALTHAM (521). The school, however, that claimed most adherents was the South-Eastern, with its elongated naves, at NORWICH (148.4), ELY (153.4), BURY (150.3), Peterborough, ST ALBANS (153.2), Old St Paul's, Chichester. It may be that this elongation of the nave is due to the precedent set by CÉRISY (148.3).

1150—1175.

XII. CENTURY: THIRD QUARTER (*Stephen*, 16th year, to *Henry II.*, 22nd year).—BOLTON PRIORY, begun *c.* 1151. BRINKBURN, *c.* 1170. BUILDWAS, *c.* 1148. BYLAND, the monks entered, 1177. DUNSTABLE, nave, *c.* 1160. DURHAM, galilee, *c.* 1175. ELY, upper parts of west transept and infirmary, and ST MARY'S CHURCH, *c.* 1170. FOUNTAINS, begun *c.* 1135. FURNESS, after 1148. KIRKSTALL, *c.* 1152. LANERCOST, consecrated 1169. [MALMESBURY, probably *c.* 1150. OXFORD CATHEDRAL, 1154-1180. ROCHE, *c.* 1165. STAMFORD, ST LEONARD'S PRIORY. STRATA FLORIDA, 1166-1203. WIMBORNE, central tower and part of nave. WINCHESTER, ST CROSS, *c.* 1160 *seq.* WORCESTER, west bays of nave, *c.* 1170. YORK, part of crypt, 1154-1181.

THIS forms the early part of the period to which Mr Sharpe gave the name Transitional Norman or Transitional.† It is the period of transition from Romanesque to Gothic. By Mr Brandon it was called Semi-Norman; by others Pointed Norman. Mr Sharpe regarded it as having lasted from *c.* 1145

---

* In this church all the walls have been raised; and what were originally clerestory windows are now openings looking into the aisle.

† Owing to lack of documentary evidence as to the date of many of the churches it has been found impossible to arrange and discuss them in strict chronological sequence. They have been arranged, therefore, in this chapter in periods of twenty-five years.

to *c.* 1190. *It is characterised*, he says, *by the simultaneous use in the same building of semicircular and pointed arches.* But here again there were retrogressive builders, who admitted no pointed arches at all into their churches ; *e.g.* Dunstable nave and OXFORD CATHEDRAL CHOIR (27) ; the latter is 1154-1180. Even so late as 1180 the Cathedral of St David's was designed with all its pier arches semicircular. More often, however, to facilitate the

Fountains Nave from S.E.

vaulting of the aisles (322), the arches of the pier arcade are pointed. These pointed pier arches are at first very obtuse ; *e.g.* in Fountains nave and in Furness, Kirkstall, Buildwas, all Cistercian ; MALMESBURY (522), Benedictine ; and the Hospital Church of St Cross, Winchester. More acutely pointed, but covered with Romanesque ornament, are the west transepts of Ely and Peterborough, the latter probably 1177-1193. Still more advanced towards Gothic are

Ripon Choir.

Brinkburn, Lanercost, RIPON * (102), Roche, and Byland ; though they are all without high vaults. In Durham galilee† the arches are semicircular and covered with chevron ; and there is no vault ; but the design is so light and graceful that it has more of the Gothic in it than the Romanesque. The most advanced of all are St Cross, Winchester, probably not begun before 1160, and the Cistercian abbey of Roche. Both had high vaults, which at St Cross still remain. In other respects St Cross is thoroughly Romanesque, relying for stability entirely on immense thickness of wall and pier ; it has neither flying buttresses nor transverse arches in the triforium chamber.‡ Indeed St Cross is less advanced than the nave of Durham ; the chief difference being that at St Cross the pointed arch is employed in the arches of the crossing and the pier arcade, and in the wall ribs and the diagonals as well as in the transverse arches of the vault.

In the Cistercian churches more progress is made. A distinct tendency is seen to buttress rather than to thicken the walls.§ But, in accordance with Burgundian tradition, there was a distrust in these abbeys of the flying buttress, which therefore remained undeveloped. The drainage of the walls was improved by heightening the corbel-table, so as to form a parapet masking a gutter behind (385) ; and by amplifying the basement course, as at Kirkstall and FOUNTAINS (679.1). Owing to the injunctions of the founders of the Cistercian Order and especially of St Bernard, sculptured ornament was discouraged ; one result of which was to increase the employment of moldings. For the compound pier, cylinder, or octagon a cluster of columns was often substituted, as at ROCHE (661.2). Scalloped, coniferous, and water-leaf capitals and corbels were especially common in the Cistercian churches. Masonry improved most of all, the Cistercians laying great stress on sound construction, and often working at the masonry with their own hands. The triforium was almost always walled in, and the clerestory passage was infrequent. Stone towers and bells were forbidden by the statutes of the Chapter-General. The walls were left plain ; not covered with arcading. Corbels were used wherever possible instead of vaulting shafts or roofing shafts. There was an almost total absence of colour, whether in pictures, wall-paintings, mosaic pavements, or glass. Cistercian architecture may be fairly described as a combination of ascetic ardour, temperate good sense, straightforward procedure, and practical utility. ‖

None of the Cistercian churches were of the vast scale of Bury, Lewes, or Old St Paul's. Instead of the western transept they had occasionally a small lean-to western porch ; they had no long choir or eastern transept ; nor had any central transept a western aisle. On the eastern side the transept, as at KIRK-STALL (152.4), had an aisle divided into chapels. The presbytery was usually

* The greater part of the work of Lanercost, Roche, Byland, Ripon, and the Transitional choir of York was probably done after 1170, and belongs rather to the period 1175-1200.

† Originally the piers of the Durham galilee consisted of but two marble shafts.

‡ Section in Dehio, Plate 148.

§ See plan of Kirkstall (152) ; and buttress of Kirkstall chapter house (359).

‖ On Cistercian architecture see Dehio, i., book ii., c. xiii. ; and Anthyme St Paul in Enlart's *Gothic in Italy*, 224-228.

short and without aisles, and it was usually rectangular. Byland had also a
rectangular ambulatory, as, later on, had Dore.

Such an unaisled rectangular presbytery as that of Cistercian Kirkstall was
of course a complete breaking away * from the traditions of Anglo-Norman
planning, whether with three parallel eastern apses or with semicircular ambulatory. But others beside the Cistercians were innovating in planning. At
OXFORD (152.3) the Augustinian Canons built an aisled choir and unaisled
rectangular presbytery. At ST CROSS, WINCHESTER (215.8), a further step
was taken ; the rectangular presbytery being aisled as well as the choir.

In one point all the three new types of plan, those of Kirkstall, Oxford, and

St Cross, Winchester, from S.E.

St Cross, agreed ; their presbyteries were all rectangular. Through the influence of these plans, especially of those of the numerous Cistercian churches
built at this time, the apsidal presbytery of the Continent, with rare exceptions,
disappeared from English architecture. The English became differentiated from
the Continental presbytery by being square-ended.

One more innovation of the utmost importance was made at ST CROSS.
This was that the roof of the presbytery was continued to its eastern termination in undiminished height. At St Cross was reached the plan and eastern

* It was of course a reproduction of the simplest type of Burgundian plan ; probably that
of the Clairvaux Church of St Bernard.

termination which remained in fashion till the very end of English Gothic architecture, till York Minster and Bath Abbey.

On the whole, the third quarter of the twelfth century was an epoch fertile in change and improvement, except as regards the important matter of vaulting; and for much of the improvement the builders of the new Cistercian abbeys may fairly claim the credit. Their influence was greatest where their abbeys were most numerous, viz., in the North of England.

1175—1200.

XII. CENTURY: FOURTH QUARTER (*Henry II.*, 22nd year; *Richard I.;* to *John*, 2nd year).—BISHOP AUCKLAND, hall, *c.* 1190. CANTERBURY, choir, 1175-1178. SAINT'S CHAPEL and CORONA, 1179-1184. CARTMEL, founded 1188. CHICHESTER, retrochoir, &c., 1186-1199. DARLINGTON CHURCH, *c.* 1192. DEEPING, ST JAMES, *c.* 1180. DORE, choir, *c.* 1190. DUBLIN, CHRIST CHURCH, after 1171. GLASTONBURY, LADY CHAPEL, dedicated 1186; choir of ABBEY CHURCH, commenced 1184. HARTLEPOOL, *c.* 1188. HEREFORD, east transept, 1186-1199. JEDBURGH, *c.* 1175—*c.* 1190. JERVAULX, *c.* 1170—*c.* 1190. LINCOLN, choir and eastern transept, begun 1192. LLANDAFF, *c.* 1190. LLANIDLOES, work of *c.* 1180 from Cwm Hir. LLANTHONY. LONDON, nave of TEMPLE CHURCH, consecrated 1185. NEW SHOREHAM, choir, *c.* 1175—*c.* 1210. OAKHAM, hall of CASTLE, 1165-1191. OLD MALTON, *c.* 1180. PETERBOROUGH, clerestory of nave, west bays of nave, and west transept, 1177-1193. ST DAVID'S, begun 1180. SELBY, parts of west nave, west front, and porch. ST RADEGUND'S, 1191. SHREWSBURY, ST MARY'S, nave, *c.* 1180. WELLS, 1174-1191. WENLOCK, *c.* 1190. WITHAM, 1176-1186.

THE last quarter of the twelfth, like the last quarter of the eleventh century, was a momentous period in English mediæval architecture; the latter completed the structural development of English Romanesque, the former that of English Gothic. The former is usually assumed to commence with the building of St Hugh's choir at Lincoln in 1192. Really, however, the first complete Gothic of England commences with the choir not of Lincoln, but of Wells, as begun by Reginald Fitz Bohun, who was Bishop from 1174 to 1191.

As in our Romanesque, so in our early Gothic, three distinct schools may be recognised: the Western, the Northern, and the Southern. The claims of the Western school have only recently been recognised. In reality not only was it the first to start, but its geographical extension was the most considerable of all, and its output the greatest. In England, Whitchurch Canonicorum, Witham, Glastonbury, WELLS (209), DORE CHOIR (182), the eastern transept of Hereford, the western bays of Worcester nave, Wenlock, the nave of ST MARY'S, SHREWSBURY (521), Lilleshall, and the original Gothic choirs of LICHFIELD (244) and Chester; in Wales, Llandaff and Cwm Hir; in Ireland, Christ Church, Dublin, all belonged to this school. It was in the West of England that the art of Gothic vaulting was first mastered; first, so far as we know, at Worcester; and it was in the West, first apparently at Wells, that every arch was pointed and the semicircular arch was exterminated. At the neighbouring abbey church of

Canterbury Choir.

Glastonbury, begun in 1184, the vaults of the Lady Chapel were thoroughly Gothic in character. At Glastonbury and Dore choirs were planned with rectangular ambulatories, but without the eastern Lady Chapel of Romsey. The Western sculptors were far ahead of the rest of England; at Wells the craftsman's hand can be seen gaining in cunning, capital by capital, till foliated capitals and scrolls of conventional foliage were produced that remained unsurpassed to the last days of English Gothic.* Of this work the earliest is probably that at Worcester. It is earlier in character than the dated work either at Wells or Glastonbury; and can hardly be placed later, therefore, than c. 1170.†

In the desolate regions of Northern England the output was smaller. Byland was completed, or nearly so; it was complex in plan, but had no high vault. The greatest progress is to be seen in the Cistercian abbey church of Roche, which may have been commenced c. 1165. It seems to have been vaulted throughout; and alone of the northern churches compares with the advanced architecture of St Cross, Winchester, New Shoreham,‡ Wells, and Glastonbury. The works in Selby nave slowly advanced. To this period probably belongs the completion of the choir of York

* See 412.6, 424.1.2.3.

† For the Western pier, see 245; for the arch-molds, 279; for the capitals, 422, 412, 424.

‡ Certain resemblances between New Shoreham and Hartlepool are pointed out by Rev. J. F. Hodgson in *Arch. Aeliana*, xvii. 201.

Sens.

St Thomas' Chapel, Canterbury.

Minster (rebuilt in the fourteenth century), and of the choir and transept of Ripon. Jervaulx built a new church planned like that of St Cross. Important churches were erected at Hartlepool and Darlington; to the same school belong the churches of Holy Trinity, Micklegate, York; and Nun Monkton. Possibly Hexham choir was commenced.

In Southern England little was done that can be called Gothic; but this is of great historic importance. NEW SHOREHAM CHOIR (373), *c.* 1175, is the first in the South of England to exhibit the St Cross plan on a large scale; internally, however, in spite of a pointed pier arcade and well-molded arches, its ground story is of massive and Romanesque character. The great work in the South of England was the rebuilding of CANTERBURY CHOIR (149.3) after the fire of 1174. The architect selected by the monks was a Frenchman, William of Sens; and he gave them a French design: one modelled to a large extent on that of his own cathedral at SENS * (107). Here then we have a disturbing factor of the first magnitude in the steady development of Anglo-Norman architecture, and it becomes important to consider what was precisely the extent of the Continental innovations introduced by William of Sens at Canterbury.

As regards the plan, the circular chapel of the Holy Trinity † is directly copied from Sens Cathedral. The internal elevation of the choir, with its tall pier arcade and low triforium, is reminiscent of Sens. The vaulting is sexpartite, as at Sens. Norman sexpartite vaulting exists in the chancel of Tickencote, Rutland, but that of Canterbury is probably copied from Sens. The vaulting shafts, both at CANTERBURY and SENS (106, 107), are alternately massive and slender. Most of the vaulting shafts rest on the abaci at Canterbury, as do the more slender shafts at Sens. In both churches the transverse arches of the aisle vault are semicircular, and are much broader than the diagonals; whereas at Worcester and Wells both are pointed, and differ little in dimensions. The side cells of the high vault at Canterbury are round arched, as originally were those at Sens.‡ Many of the pointed pier arches, *e.g.* in the Chapel of St Thomas and in the crypt, are much stilted; also they have plain rectangular soffits, as in the twelfth century Gothic of France. The absence or insignificance of the hood-mold over these arches is also a French characteristic. Piers composed simply of a couple of columns put side by side are very rare elsewhere, but are found in Sens choir and the Chapel of St Thomas, Canterbury. The magnificent Corinthian and Composite capitals (428) are French; so also are the crocket capitals of the Chapel of St Thomas. The lancet windows are much less slender than the normal lancets of England.§ The great circular windows of the eastern transept, undivided except by iron bars, resemble those of Notre Dame de Dijon.‖ The buttresses have immense

---

* Sens Cathedral is commonly said to have been commenced in 1140; but little of the existing church appears to belong to this period. The main structure of the choir is probably that which was consecrated in 1167, and can be but little anterior to Notre Dame, Paris, commenced 1163.

† It was built to enshrine the crown (*corona*) of the skull of St Thomas.

‡ Scott's *Lectures*, i. 94, 96.

§ Broad lancets occur at Wells and Glastonbury; but not earlier than those of Canterbury.

‖ Illustrated in Viollet-le-Duc, *Architecture*, iv. 132.

projection in comparison with their English predecessors or contemporaries. For the first time the flying buttresses emerge from beneath the aisle roofs into the open air, and are of light French construction; very unlike those built soon after at Chichester and New Shoreham. The French had a long start in Gothic architecture; St Denis, Noyon, Notre Dame, Paris, St Martin des Champs, St Germer, as well as Sens, were all well advanced before Canterbury choir was commenced. No wonder that it is so reminiscent of the advanced architectural art of Northern France.

The next important work in the South of England was the building of the retrochoir of CHICHESTER (34.4) and the vaulting of the whole church after the fire of 1187. The plan of Chichester, with rectangular ambulatory and projecting rectangular Lady Chapel, and its vaulting of the highly advanced character of that of Worcester and Wells, clearly connect it with the Gothic of the West of England, and not with Canterbury. Of all the French features in Canterbury choir enumerated above, hardly one reappears at Chichester, unless it be the crocket capitals (245) proportioned in depth to the diameter of the shafts or columns.

The last and greatest work of the period is that of St Hugh at LINCOLN (151.1); viz. the apse, which has been removed; the north-eastern and south-eastern transepts, with their western adjuncts; the choir; and a single bay of the eastern aisle of the great transept adjoining either side of the choir.* The design of St Hugh's architect is full of originality and even of eccentricity. But it is impossible to deny that it is largely indebted to the new work at Canterbury, finished in 1184. Both plans include an eastern transept (149.3, 66); both these transepts have to the east two pairs of semicircular apses (a survival of Romanesque). In both the vault springs at the mid height of the triforium. In both distrust of the flying buttress is shown by the construction of pointed arches spanning the triforium chamber (34). Both at Lincoln and in the Chapel of St Thomas at Canterbury intermediate buttresses are inserted in the centre of each bay between each pair of lancet windows. In both the circular molded abacus is found; at Canterbury in the crypt; in Lincoln almost universally. Romanesque billet occurs in the ribs of the vault of the Chapel of St Thomas, Canterbury, and in the south-eastern transept of Lincoln. Marble shafting is used profusely in both churches. The corner piers of St Hugh's transepts closely resemble those in the same position at CANTERBURY (523). The design of the choir piers of Lincoln, each faced with a single vaulting shaft descending to the pavement,† occurs sporadically both in the choir and on the east side of the eastern transepts of Canterbury.‡ The proportioning of the depth of the capitals of the pier arcade to their supports appears at Lincoln and Chichester as well as at Canterbury. The light flying buttresses, displayed in the open air, are reminiscent of Canterbury (112). The buttresses have much projection. It is plain that the obligation of the Lincoln to the Canterbury design is great. It is equally plain that the

---

* The apses of the eastern transepts and the remainder of the great transept were probably taken in hand c. 1205.

† The lower parts of the vaulting shafts were cut away when the stalls were inserted.

‡ See 111; and Britton's *Canterbury*, Plates 11 and 19.

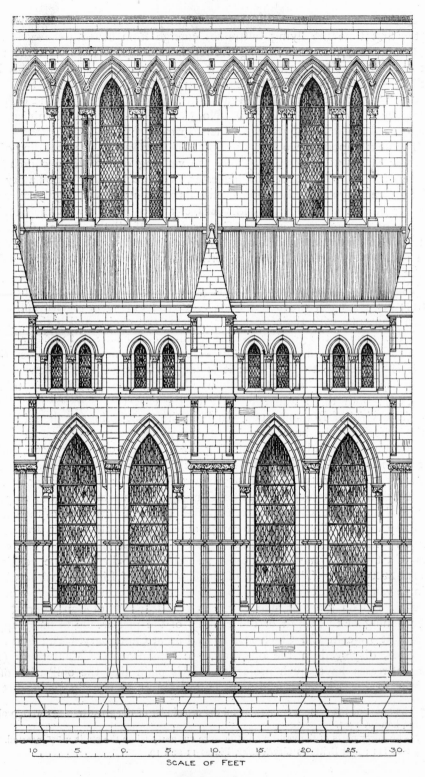

SCALE OF FEET

Lincoln Choir.

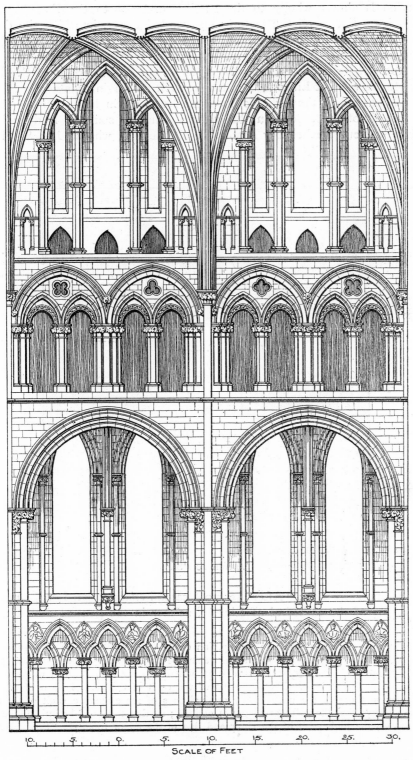

SCALE OF FEET

Lincoln Choir.

obligation is almost wholly to the English and not to the French part of that design. For of all the features enumerated above, in which the designs of the Lincoln and Canterbury choirs agree, only the last two, the designs of the buttresses and flying buttresses,* are characteristically French; they form much too slender a basis for theorising as to the French origin of the design of St Hugh's work at Lincoln. Even were such an origin granted for Lincoln, it would not hold for the early Gothic of the North of England; still less for the vast amount of work done in the western counties, some of it done before William of Sens reached our shores. Viollet-le-Duc, who studied St Hugh's

Lincoln from S.E.

work on the spot, says: " After the most careful examination I could not find in any part of the cathedral of Lincoln, neither in the general design, nor in

        * It is a curious fact that Lincoln choir seems to have been designed with less reference to Canterbury than we now see it. In the opinion of Sir G. G. Scott neither the intermediate buttresses, nor the flying buttresses, nor the transverse arches in the triforium formed part of the original design. But they must have been added very soon afterwards; when the high vault of the choir was built. The rib-molds of the vault of the central span of the choir are similar to those of the undoubtedly original ones of the sexpartite vault of the minor transepts, except that the tooth ornament is omitted; so that there can be little difference of date between the high vault of the choir and that of the minor transepts. See *Assoc. Soc. Reports*, xii. 190 note and 191.

PETERBOROUGH CATHEDRAL, WEST FRONT.

any part of the system of architecture adopted, nor in the details of ornament, any trace of the French school of the twelfth century, so plainly characteristic of the cathedrals of Paris, Noyon, Senlis, Chartres, Sens, or even Rouen. On the exterior the choir is thoroughly English. . . . The vaults have not at all the same construction as the French vaults of the end of the twelfth century. Arch-moldings slender and deeply undercut, abacus round, the tooth ornament —do not at all resemble the ornaments which we find at Paris, Sens, St Denis, &c. . . . Nowhere in France do we find between 1190 and 1200 pillars similar to the corner pillars of the eastern transepts of LINCOLN (249), with the crockets placed between the shafts; nowhere in France do we find crockets carved like these; nowhere shafts with hexagonal concave section; nowhere capitals or abacus similar to those of these pillars. . . . The construction is English; the profiles of the moldings are English; the ornaments are English; the execution of the work belongs to the English school of workmen of the beginning of the thirteenth century."

1200—1225.

XIII. CENTURY: FIRST QUARTER (*John*, 2nd year, to *Henry III.*, 10th year).— BOLTON PRIORY, aisle and west front. ELY, galilee, 1198-1215. FOUNTAINS, choir, 1208—*c.* 1220. HEXHAM, choir, *c.* 1180—*c.* 1210; transepts, *c.* 1215—*c.* 1230. LICHFIELD, choir, finished in 1211; south transept, *c.* 1220. LINCOLN MINSTER, great transept and nave. PETERBOROUGH, west front. RIEVAULX, transept rebuilt, *c.* 1210. ROCHESTER, presbytery and east transept, begun *c.* 1200; choir finished, 1227. ROMSEY, west nave and west front, *c.* 1220. ST ALBANS, John de Cella's porches, 1195-1205; Trumpington's work, 1214-1235. ST SAVIOUR'S, SOUTHWARK, 1213-1238. SALISBURY, begun 1220. SELBY, upper nave, *c.* 1190—*c.* 1220. TYNEMOUTH, choir, *c.* 1200. VALLE CRUCIS, founded *c.* 1200. WELLS, west front, 1218-1239. WHITBY, choir and transept. WINCHESTER CATHEDRAL, retrochoir begun *c.* 1202. WORCESTER, retrochoir, 1202-1218.

THE building of Lincoln choir, 1192-1200, was followed by a vast output of the new Gothic. In some cases, however, the work was of retrograde character; the ceilings of Anglo-Norman work being yet retained; as in Hexham, Tynemouth, and WHITBY choirs (114), and the western bays of the nave of ST ALBANS (14). In the last the piers were of massive and Romanesque character. At ST SAVIOUR'S, SOUTHWARK (521), also, there is little of Gothic economy of material; the piers are short and heavy, the arches low and the walls thick, as in the school of Wells. Nor was the flying buttress, employed at Canterbury, Chichester, and Lincoln, received with much favour. Hexham, Tynemouth, Whitby, dispensing with high vaults, did not require it. Rochester choir was designed throughout so as to dispense with it. At Worcester and Salisbury* it was hidden beneath the aisle roofs, as it had been at Wells. Only in the transept and nave of LINCOLN (112, 115), NEW SHOREHAM,

* Those now seen at Salisbury are later additions.

H

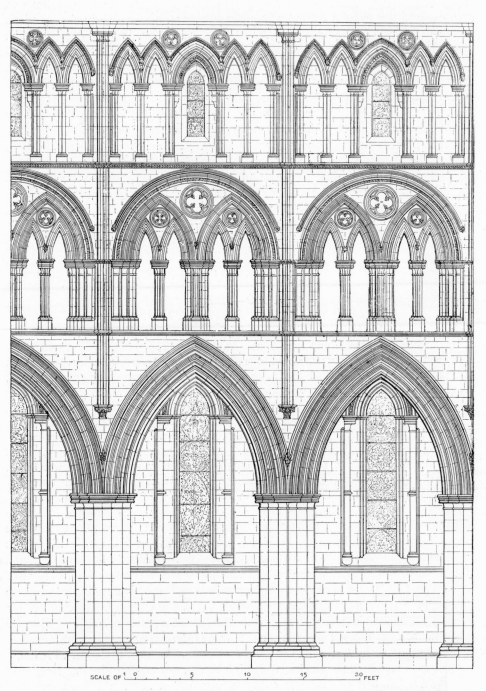

SCALE OF | 0   5   10   15   20 FEET

Whitby Choir.

Lincoln Nave.

Sussex (373), and perhaps in Rievaulx transept and Fountains choir, is it employed. The most striking feature is the sudden decline of the vigorous school of the West, which in the preceding period had had by far the largest output. The works at Wells, Glastonbury, Lichfield, and Chester choirs, and Christ Church, Dublin, were completed or continued; but no new work was commenced wholly in the Western style. The dominant influence now was probably that of Lincoln choir. The most important advances were those made in vaulting in LINCOLN NAVE (327). In the North, the most important work was the rebuilding of the transept and choir of Fountains and Rievaulx. In the South, the rectangular ambulatory was expanded into a retrochoir at Winchester; St Saviour's, Southwark; and SALISBURY (154.2); and in addition was carried in undiminished height eastwards at Rochester and Worcester. The St Cross and New Shoreham type of choir was adopted in the North at Hexham and Whitby. In this period also were designed the façades of St Albans, PETERBOROUGH (112), Wells,* Bolton, Romsey; and the galilee of Ely Cathedral.† The most important work of all was SALISBURY CATHEDRAL (170), commenced in the same year as Amiens, 1220.

1225—1250.

XIII. CENTURY : SECOND QUARTER (*Henry III.*, 10th to 35th year).—BEVERLEY MINSTER, choir and transepts, *c.* 1225—*c.* 1245. BINHAM, west front, 1226-1244. BRISTOL, Elder Lady Chapel. BOXGROVE, *c.* 1235. CARLISLE, choir. DUBLIN, CHRIST CHURCH, nave finished in 1235. DUBLIN, ST PATRICK'S. DUNSTABLE, west front. DURHAM, east transept, 1242—*c.* 1280. ELY, presbytery, 1235-1252. EXETER, chapter house, 1224-1244. FOUNTAINS, eastern transept, *c.* 1220-1247. GLOUCESTER, vault of east nave, 1243. HEREFORD, Lady Chapel. LICHFIELD, north transept, chapter house and vestibule. LINCOLN, nave and chapter house. LONDON, Temple choir finished 1240. NETLEY, begun 1239. OXFORD, chapter house. RIEVAULX, choir. RIPON, west front, *c.* 1233. ROCHESTER, north transept, *c.* 1240-1255. SOUTHWELL, choir begun before 1233. WORCESTER, choir begun 1224. YORK, south transept, 1230—*c.* 1241.

THE disastrous reign of John (1199-1216), during part of which the kingdom had been under an Interdict (1207-1211), had doubtless greatly checked the advance of the new Gothic. On his death architectural activity revived, and the reign of his successor, Henry III., was productive of an enormous amount of work; but on the whole marking but little advance on that of the preceding period, or even on that of Lincoln choir. By this time the vault entered into

---

* Mr W. H. St John Hope points out that the commencement of the west front of Wells may be fixed by the grant of sixty great oaks in 1220, and of thirty more in 1225 ; in each case *ad rogum faciendum, i.e.*, to make a lime-kiln ; the first thing done when great works were to be commenced.

† The Ely galilee is assigned by Sir G. G. Scott (*Lectures*, i. 127) to Bishop Eustace, 1195-1214. Professor Willis considered this date too early.

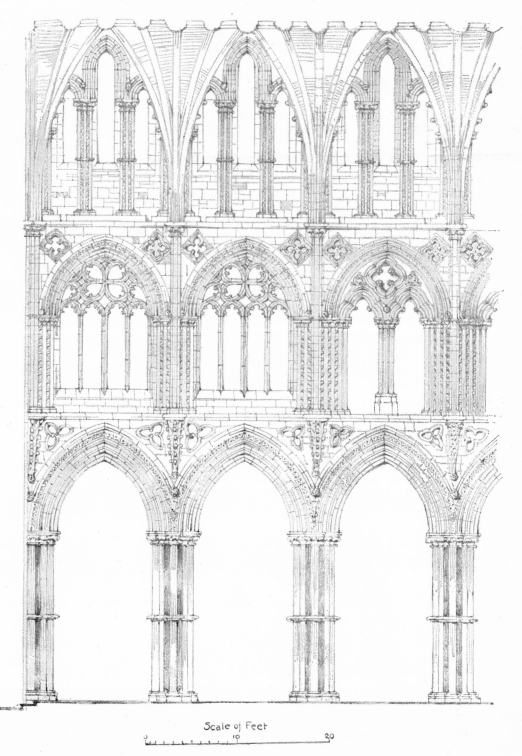

Scale of Feet

0   10   20

Ely Presbytery.

the design of nearly all the greater churches. The chief exceptions were Carlisle choir (burnt in 1292); Lichfield transept (not vaulted till the fifteenth century); and YORK TRANSEPT (523); where there are the springers of a stone vault, which, however, was constructed in wood. The external flying buttress, however, of Lincoln choir made few converts; only in BOXGROVE (373), LINCOLN NAVE (115) and BEVERLEY MINSTER (176) is it external. These are the three most advanced works of the period; LINCOLN NAVE (327) far ahead of all in its rib-system; BEVERLEY CHOIR (51) remarkable for the high spring of its vaults; BOXGROVE quite unique (318). During this period the works at Lincoln probably included the completion of the nave, chapter house, galilee, and part of the west front; Rochester built its north transept; Worcester and Rievaulx their choirs; ELY its presbytery (117); Fountains its eastern transept; Christ Church, Dublin, its nave; Salisbury was in a fair way to completion; and inspired the design for St Patrick, Dublin; Durham commenced its eastern transept; the choir of the TEMPLE CHURCH, LONDON (462), was finished in 1240; the Cistercian church of NETLEY (471) was commenced in 1239; and the western façades of LINCOLN (592), Ripon, BINHAM (471), Dunstable were erected wholly or in part.

The plans of the choirs of SALISBURY (154.2) and ELY (153.4) represent the two types which remained in use at all subsequent periods. A variant of the former is that of SOUTHWELL (152.2). The only innovation, which was not repeated, was at FOUNTAINS (150.2) and Durham, where the eastern transept was built at the east end, and not athwart the choir. The most striking change to the eye is that traceried windows commence; at Binham, Netley, Old St Paul's, and WESTMINSTER (63).

What is specially remarkable about the architecture of the first half of the thirteenth century is the perfection of the work even in the smallest village churches in some districts, e.g. Northants and South Lincolnshire; the same artistic fitness of design, the same faultless execution and delicacy of treatment is to be seen in them as in the largest cathedral and the noblest conventual church.*

1250—1275.

XIII. CENTURY: THIRD QUARTER (*Henry III.*, 35th year, to *Edward I.*, 4th year).—CHICHESTER, St Edmund's Chapel, 1245-1253. EXETER, eastern chapels and retrochoir commenced, *c.* 1270. HEREFORD, choir clerestory, *c.* 1250; north transept, *c.* 1260. LINCOLN, presbytery, 1256-1280. LICHFIELD, nave. ST ALBANS, choir clerestory begun 1257; retrochoir, 1260-1326. SALISBURY, upper portions, finished 1266; chapter house and cloister, 1263-1284. TINTERN, parts, 1269-1288. WESTMINSTER ABBEY, choir, transept, and four eastern bays of nave, 1245-1269; chapter house finished, *c.* 1253.

PARTLY because of the disturbed state of the kingdom, partly, perhaps, because the preceding quarter of the century had been so productive, there remains a much smaller amount of work done between 1250 and 1275: but what there is, is of the

* Sharpe's *Nene Valley*, 13; and *Lincoln Excursion*, 50.

Wells Chapter House.

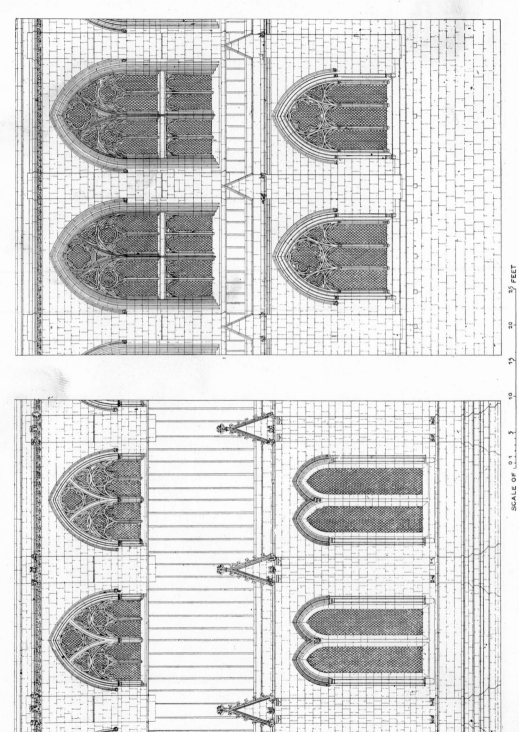

Bridlington Nave : South Side.

Bridlington Nave : North Side.

SCALE OF 0 1 5 10 15 20 25 FEET

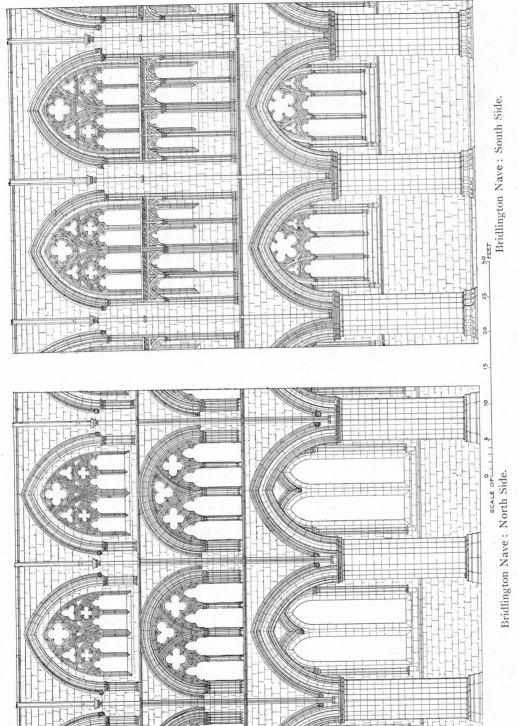

Bridlington Nave : South Side.

SCALE OF FEET

Bridlington Nave : North Side.

1300—1325.

XIV. CENTURY: FIRST QUARTER (*Edward I.*, 29th year, to *Edward II.*, 19th year).—BOSTON, tower, begun 1309. BRISTOL, cathedral choir, 1298-1332. CANTERBURY, St Augustine's gateway, 1309. EXETER, choir, 1291-1307. GLOUCESTER, south aisle of nave, 1318-1329. LICHFIELD, Lady Chapel, begun 1310. MILTON ABBAS, choir and south transept. NORWICH, chapel of charnel house, 1310-1325. OXFORD, St Mary's spire. ST ALBANS, shrine, 1302-1308. WELLS, chapter house, *c.* 1310. WINCHELSEA CHURCH, *c.* 1310. WORCESTER, east bays of north nave, 1317-1324. YORK, chapter house, *c.* 1300.

IN this period Worcester rebuilt much of the Norman part of its nave; GLOUCESTER (360) the south aisle of its nave; Milton Abbas its choir and south transept. Lichfield Lady Chapel and WELLS CHAPTER HOUSE (123) were nearly completed. York also built a chapter house.* York nave and Exeter choir were finished. By far the most progressive work is to be found in the choir of BRISTOL CATHEDRAL (329), where signs of the coming revolution in English architecture may already be detected.

The greatest achievement of the period is its lierne vaulting, which seems to have originated in the polygonal chapter houses; *e.g.* of Lincoln, York, Wells.

The noble churches of Orford and Winchelsea appear to belong to this period, and, like Bristol choir, are of highly advanced type.

1325—1350.

XIV. CENTURY: SECOND QUARTER (*Edward II.*, 19th year, to *Edward III.*, 24th year).—BATTLE, gateway, 1339. BEVERLEY MINSTER, nave, *c.* 1320-1349. BOLTON PRIORY, choir. BRISTOL, St Mary Redcliffe, south transept. BURY, gateway, 1327. CARLISLE, east front. CARTMEL, east aisle of presbytery. CHESTER CATHEDRAL, south transept. ELY, Lady Chapel, choir, and Prior Crauden's Chapel, begun 1321; octagon, begun 1323. EXETER, nave, 1308-1350. GLASTONBURY, choir prolonged, 1341-1374. GLOUCESTER, south transept, 1331-1337; choir, 1337—*c.* 1350. HOWDEN, choir. HULL, chancel. LICHFIELD, presbytery and south-west spire. MALMESBURY, remodelling of nave. NANTWICH, chancel, 1327-1333. OTTERY ST MARY, begun 1337. OXFORD CATHEDRAL, Latin Chapel, before 1355. PATRINGTON. PETERBOROUGH, south-west spire. SALISBURY, spire. SELBY, choir. TEWKESBURY, choir remodelled. WELLS CATHEDRAL, Lady Chapel, presbytery and retrochoir; central tower heightened. WORCESTER, nave and tower completed.

ENGLAND'S greatness and prosperity under Edward III. are reflected in her architecture. The first twenty-four years of his reign were marked by one of the most momentous outbursts of building activity in the records of English history.

* It may be that York chapter house belongs to the preceding period.

The fourth quarters of the eleventh and twelfth centuries; the second quarters of the thirteenth and fourteenth centuries are the great building periods of our mediæval architecture.   In the last, 1325-1350, were laid, broad and deep the

Wells Presbytery from West.

foundations of all our later Gothic.   At this period too the art of architectural composition reached a level that never afterwards was surpassed.   The lateral elevation of SELBY CHOIR (86), the poetic façade of CARLISLE (128), the solid dignity of the east front of Selby, the grouping of the masses of Ottery St Mary and PATRINGTON (612), the tower composition of ST MICHAEL, COVENTRY (635), show how consummate was fourteenth-century design. Above all, there was a delight in erecting great spires; the south-west spires of PETERBOROUGH (112) and LICHFIELD (*Frontispiece*); those of SALISBURY (170), Grantham, St Mary, Stamford, KETTON (621), Shottesbrooke, Snettisham, Heckington, and many another, belong to this prolific twenty-five years.

Of the greater work, the naves of EXETER (9) and Beverley Minster are assimilated to early work; and the choir of SELBY (86) is the completion of work laid out in the thirteenth century. At MALMESBURY (375) the nave, at TEWKESBURY (165) the choir are remodelled in the style of the period. The great southern transept of Chester Cathedral was commenced in this period, but not completed till later. Carlisle and Glastonbury both slightly lengthened their eastern limbs. Lichfield built a new presbytery and largely remodelled its choir; but the work was greatly damaged in the sieges of 1643. The two great examples of the rich, decorated work of the period left to us are the retrochoir and presbytery of WELLS (127) and the Lady Chapel, octagon, and choir of ELY (522). But here again, both in Ely choir and Wells presbytery, the design was largely fettered by the fact that it had to be in harmony with earlier work with which it came into juxta-position to the east or west; we have not a single interior of the first rank in which the designer had a free hand. This it may be that has so long disguised the essential unity of the Late Decorated style of Edward the Third's reign in England and the great later style of France, the so-called Flamboyant, which is nothing but our English Decorated carried to its logical issue. Yet just as surely as the Romanesque architecture of the eleventh and twelfth centuries of England is the imported and naturalised Romanesque of Normandy, so surely the Flamboyant architecture of the fifteenth and sixteenth centuries in France is the imported and naturalised Late Decorated architecture of England.[*] Our architectural debt to William of Normandy we repaid during our long occupation of France in the fourteenth century by the loan of our Late Decorated architecture. That century to much of France was a period of the utmost misery. Just when our own Gothic was winning its most brilliant triumphs at Hull, BOSTON (222), Howden, Selby, Beverley, Carlisle, Lichfield, Wells, Ely, France had to pass through the ordeal of the English Wars, La Jacquerie, the Black Death, the alienation of the Duchy of Burgundy, and the troubles in Flanders.[†] For a whole hundred years the English Wars went on. French Gothic architecture was practically annihilated. Her thirteenth-century style ceased to be; and died without an heir. In many districts of France hardly a single important church was erected in the fourteenth century.[‡]

[*] It is not intended to deny the considerable extent of Flemish influence in French Flamboyant ; *e.g.* in the church of Brou-en-Bresse ; and it must be admitted that, whatever the extent of the foreign elements admitted by France into her later Gothic, she gave them a development all her own, characterised by native harmony and elegance.

[†] Gonse, 261.

[‡] " Il faut dire que nous n'avons pas en France un seul grand édifice complet d'architecture religieuse du quatorzième siècle " (Viollet-le-Duc, *Architecture*, iv. 207, note).

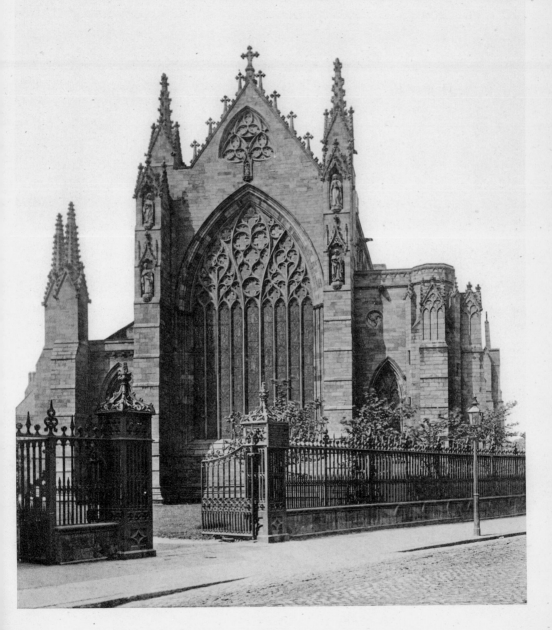

CARLISLE CATHEDRAL, EAST FRONT.

The history of the period is written plain in many a French cathedral; Sens, Beauvais, Limoges, Auxerre, Amiens, Troyes, Senlis, Séez; where the choir and nave are of the twelfth or thirteenth century, the transepts of the fifteenth.

Boston, South Doorway of Nave

There is a great interval of time between these two building periods; an interval so long that there was time for the great traditions of French craftsmanship largely to die out; so that when the foreigner at last was expelled from her soil,

I

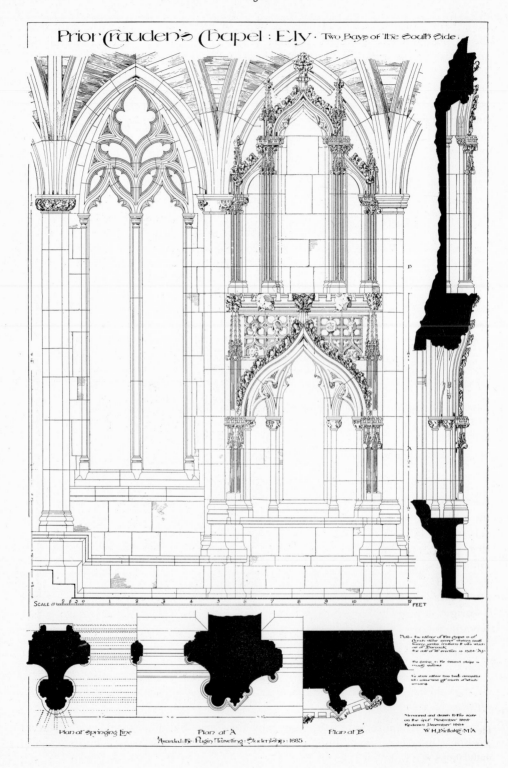

Prior Crauden's Chapel : Ely · Two Bays of the South Side ·

Plan at Springing Line   Plan at A   Plan at B

Awarded the Pugin Travelling Studentship 1885.

and France again was free, she had to make copious drafts on the art of England and of Flanders.* Then once more, but not till the fifteenth century,† with the aid of England and Flanders, she suddenly commenced to build in Flamboyant fashion. The complicated vaults of GLOUCESTER (334) with ridge ribs, tiercerons and liernes; the absorption of the triforium at Lichfield and WELLS (127); the molded piers of Bristol choir; the logical responds of GLOUCESTER SOUTH TRANSEPT (495); the bulbous, undulatory foliage of the capitals, corbels, crockets, finials, spandrels of ELY LADY CHAPEL (269); the flowing tracery of MERTON COLLEGE VESTRY (480); Prior Crauden's Chapel at ELY (130); the BEVERLEY REREDOS (486) and the BOSTON DOORS (129); the ogee hood-molds of doorway and window, the presence of the ogee arch and the ogee curve in leafage and molding — everywhere curve echoed by countercurve ‡—all this was welcomed in France, and received a yet more graceful French dress. Strongest of all, as was to be expected from its origin, was the new Flam-

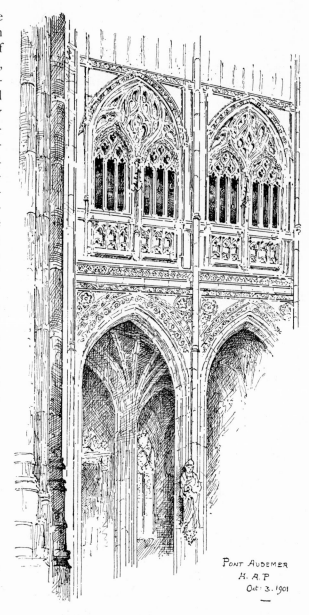

PONT AUDEMER
H. A. P
Oct. 3. 1901
—

boyant in the North of France, e.g. PONT AUDEMER, and Flanders, where it flourished amazingly, and in turn sent forth missionaries to Antwerp,

* On the obligations of France to Flemish art, see Enlart's *Manuel*, 587.

† With the solitary exception of a chapel of 1373 in Amiens Cathedral. Enlart's *Manuel*, i. 588.

‡ "There is no part of the ornamental portions of Heckington Church, the contours or profiles of which do not exhibit the ogee or wave form, both in outline and section" (Sharpe's *Lincoln Excursion*, 81). So Enlart, *Manuel*, 464, says that Flamboyant is a style "où les ondulations sont multipliées systématiquement."

Dordrecht, Milan, Cintra, and Luz.*   A highly specialised late school of French Gothic is that of Brittany, which, architecturally, would seem during the fifteenth century to have been influenced by Western England.†   Up to the present the influence of England on French Flamboyant has been but sparingly admitted. M. Anthyme St Paul indeed recognises that part of St Severin, Paris, is in the English style.‡   But it has been reserved for M. Camille Enlart § to state definitely the dependence of the fifteenth-century architecture of France on that of the fourteenth century of England.

"Il a été dit, tome premier, pages 586 et suivantes, que le style flamboyant s'est introduit en France pendant la guerre de Cent ans. On peut dire plus. Ce style est un produit de l'occupation anglaise ; en effet, les tracés en accolade, les remplages à soufflets et mouchettes, les crochets de feuillages extrêmement frisés, et les chapiteaux compris comme des frisés, existent en Angleterre dès le commencement du quatorzième siècle ; la grande fenêtre de façade de la cathédrale d'York, la chapelle de la Vierge d'Ely, à Beverley le tombeau (of Lady Eleanor Fitz-Alan) presentent ces particularités ; le vestiaire de Merton College à Oxford a des fenêtres à remplages flamboyants ; et, dès le treizième siècle les cathédrales de Durham (transept oriental) et de Lincoln (nef) montrent des tracés de voûtes, qui chez nous sont propres au quinzième siècle ; la voûte à liernes et à tiercerons et la voûte à tiercerons sans les ogives. Au quinzième siècle l'architecture anglaise s'écarta du style flamboyant ; mais elle en avait fourni depuis cent ans et plus tous les éléments à la France ; qui de ces éléments a composé un style un peu différent, mais dont l'origine n'est pas douteuse pour qui considère les dates, le nombre et l'importance des emprunts, et l'époque de création du style, qui est précisément celle de l'occupation anglaise. Avant donc qu'une guerre heureuse nous donnât le style de la Renaissance, une guerre malheureuse nous avait valu le style qu'il devait remplacer."

In the period 1325-1350 a second leading feature was the glorification of the parish church. At all periods indeed noble parish churches had been built ; *e.g.* in the twelfth century the churches of Northampton St Peter's, Whaplode, St Margaret at Cliffe, Hartlepool, Warmington ; in the thirteenth century West Walton, Skelton, Stone ; but it was the exception to build a church *de novo ;* seldom did the resources of the parish allow more than to build annexes to the original building. But under Edward III. people were prosperous ; the farmers got a good price for their wool, the weavers and merchants for their cloth. Now it became more common than it had ever been before to rebuild the whole church, leaving not a trace of the old. In whole districts, especially in Lincoln-shire, the churches were rebuilt at this time. And very noble churches they are ; lofty, spacious, and spired ; yielding no whit in composition or in beauty of detail to abbey church, collegiate or cathedral. Such are Heckington, Pembridge, Boston, HOLBEACH, PATRINGTON (opposite), Cley, Snettisham, Hingham, Tides-well, Shottesbrooke, Nantwich ; the south transept of St Mary Redcliffe, Bristol,

---

* Enlart's *Manuel*, 587, note.

† Prior, *Gothic Art*, 332 ; who instances St Pol, Quimper, Treguier, Folgoet, Lamballe, and the Kreizker. So also Choisy, *Histoire*, ii. 508, admits that at St Pol de Leon "l'imitation est évidente."

‡ *Histoire Monumentale*, 208.

§ In page 12 of the Introduction to the second volume of his *Manuel d'Archéologie*, 1904.

GLOUCESTER CATHEDRAL FROM S.E.

and the chancel of Holy Trinity, Hull.* Two of the most advanced in type are the great town churches of Boston and Hull. In both the pier arcades † are tall and stately, as if they were cathedrals ; and owing to excellence of masonry are built with the minimum of material. BOSTON (222) leads the way in the insertion of double windows in each bay of the clerestory. HULL (81) is the first realisation of the stone-lantern type of church which was to be the ideal of English Gothic for two whole centuries.‡ Of village churches, in spaciousness and height, and in beauty of proportion, the noble church of SNETTISHAM (481) is almost unrivalled. Nor is the minor work in the parish churches any less beautiful. Ely, Beverley, St David's, have nothing more consummate in design to show than the Sedilia and Easter Sepulchres of the village churches

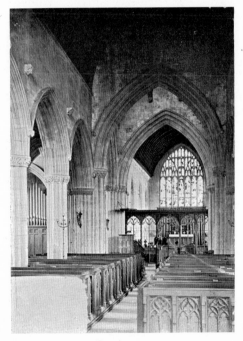 

Patrington.   Holbeach.

of Heckington, Navenby, and Hawton. A curious feature about many of the finest churches, *e.g.* Heckington, is that the interior is bare and barn-like, except for the fittings ; whereas on the exterior the utmost richness of detail is lavished.§

But the history of this great period does not end here. As has been pointed out by M. Enlart above, though between 1325 and 1349 we had worked out a

* The churches of this period are admirably illustrated in Bowman and Crowther's *Churches of the Middle Ages*.

† On the rise of the pier arcades see Sharpe's *Lincoln Excursion*, 131.

‡ Just as Hull was the most advanced, so Patrington, with low massive piers and with clerestory omitted, was one of the most retrogressive churches of this period. A comparison of these two neighbouring churches shows the fallacy of supposing that dissimilarity of design necessarily argues difference of date.

§ *Cf.* Sharpe's *Lincoln Excursion*, 80.

style so beautiful that it was adopted by France, and remained in vogue there till the very last days of French Gothic, nevertheless in England we had hardly developed it when we threw it aside for something else. This was the architecture of GLOUCESTER ; there elaborated in south transept (495) and choir, between *c.* 1331 and *c.* 1350, when it was adopted at Winchester, Canterbury, and York, speedily overran England, superseded Late Decorated design, and became our one and only style till the very last days of English Gothic architecture. This is the famous Perpendicular or Rectilinear style.

The supreme importance of Gloucester in the history of the later Gothic has never been adequately recognised. She turned the current of English architecture in a wholly new direction. But for Gloucester English Decorated work might well have developed into a Flamboyant as rich and fanciful as that of France. But to the remotest corners of the land, to cathedral, abbey church, collegiate and parish church, there was brought the influence of Gloucester by countless pilgrims returning from the shrine of Edward the Second in her choir. In the first place, she set the greater churches the fashion, which had long prevailed in the parish churches, of remodelling rather than rebuilding. At GLOUCESTER (135) Norman choir and transept were not pulled down to the ground to be rebuilt ; but only the clerestory. A similar treatment, more or less conservative, was adopted in Malmesbury nave, Tewkesbury choir, Winchester nave, Malvern, Norwich choir, Sherborne, OXFORD CATHEDRAL (27). Throughout England the new stained glass of GLOUCESTER (47) was adopted. Throughout England big aisle and end windows were inserted, and tall clerestories were erected to hold it. Everywhere the tracery of the windows became, as at Gloucester, rectilinear ; and the whole church was brought into harmony by spreading rectilinear panelling over wall, buttress, battlement, tower, even over the fan vaulting. Gloucester taught SHERBORNE (576) how to dispense with flying buttresses in her vaulted nave. GLOUCESTER exhibited the uttermost exuberance of lierne vaulting (496). Gloucester transept brought every rib of the vaulting into the organism of the pier. GLOUCESTER CHOIR (59) converted clerestory wall into clerestory piers ; and on this skeleton construction poised her lierne vaults midway amid the painted glass—an audacity of construction which to the very end of English Gothic remained unrivalled. All these great things were wrought in Gloucester by the middle of the fourteenth century.*

1350—1375.

XIV. CENTURY: THIRD QUARTER (*Edward III.*, 24th to 49th year).—CANTERBURY, Black Prince's Chantry, 1370-1379. EDINGTON CHURCH, 1352-1361. GLOUCESTER, north transept, 1368-1373. NORWICH, clerestory of choir, after 1361. WESTMINSTER, west nave, 1350-1422. WINCHESTER, presbytery, Edington's work, 1345-1366. YORK, presbytery, 1361-1370.

IN 1349-50 the prosperity of England and the brilliant art of Ely and Gloucester received a sudden check on the advent of the Black Death or Asiatic plague.

---

* On the superiority of the Gloucester mason, see Willis' *Vaulting*, 57.

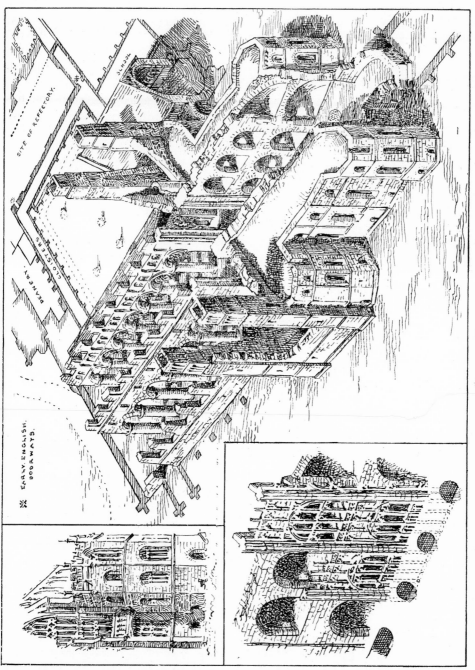

Norman Gloucester.

Unfinished work was everywhere stopped ; and for a whole generation little new work was begun. And when the country had somewhat recovered from the decimation of the population, then there began the long miserable Wars of the Roses. Not till Tudor days were there assured peace and prosperity again in England. There was no such halcyon period for architecture as the first half of Edward the Third's reign till Henry the Seventh assumed the crown in 1485. Yet in this long period—1349 to 1485—much was done ; but far more in the parish and town churches than in cathedral or abbey. Cathedral and abbey were grand enough already, and there were quite enough cathedrals and abbeys. To the monks' church especially the hearts of men had grown cold ; it was to found collegiate churches, as at Higham Ferrers and Maidstone ; colleges, as at Winchester and New College, Oxford; parish churches and chantry chapels, that religious enthusiasm turned in the later days. Just as in the last, so in the present and subsequent period, the wealth that accrued in any particular district, especially in the wool trade, took monumental expression in new, lofty, and spacious parish churches ; above all, in Norfolk, Suffolk, and Somerset ; of which however, as a rule, not more than the chancel was completed till the fifteenth century.

At WESTMINSTER (63) the work of building the nave was resumed. Gloucester finished remodelling her north transept. Her next great triumph was the invention of fan vaulting, employed in the eastern walk of her cloister (344). At Edington Church in Wiltshire the new Gothic is seen perhaps for the first time outside Gloucester (1352-1361). It is employed in the presbytery of YORK (199) ; the design of which is based on that of the nave. At Canterbury is built the Black Prince's Chantry Chapel, 1370-1379.

1375—1400.

XIV. CENTURY : FOURTH QUARTER (*Edward III.*, 49th year, to *Richard II.*, 23rd year).—BEVERLEY, west front and towers, *c.* 1380—*c.* 1430 ; CANTERBURY, nave, *c.* 1379—*c.* 1400 ; cloister, 1397-1412. COVENTRY, ST MICHAEL'S, tower finished 1394. ELY PORTA, 1397. GLOUCESTER, cloister, 1351-1412. HOWDEN, chapter house, 1380-1407. NORTH WALSHAM, after 1381. OXFORD, NEW COLLEGE, 1380-1386. ST ALBANS, gatehouse, 1349-1396. THORNTON, gatehouse, 1382-1388. WELLS, south-western tower, after 1386. WESTMINSTER HALL, 1397-1399. WINCHESTER COLLEGE, 1387-1393. WINCHESTER, cathedral nave, 1371—*c.* 1460. WYMONDHAM, central tower, 1390-1409. YORK, choir, *c.* 1380—*c.* 1400.

THE chief works of this period were the remodelling of Winchester nave and the rebuilding of York choir. The great churches of North Walsham, Maidstone All Saints', Warwick, and TERRINGTON ST CLEMENT'S (92) were built. In two churches, Etchingham and Wymington, there are brasses stating that the founder of the former church died in 1387, of the latter in 1391.

SCALE OF | 0   1   2   3 FEET

Howden Chapter House.

Yet both churches are almost wholly of the style of 1325-1350; proving that not every one was willing to accept at once the new style of Gloucester. At North Walsham both the east end, and the porch, which was built before 1405,* are mainly of the earlier style.

1400—1425.

XV. CENTURY: FIRST QUARTER (*Henry IV.*, 1st year; *Henry V.;* to *Henry VI.*, 4th year).—CARLISLE, north transept, 1401. CHRIST CHURCH, Hampshire, Lady Chapel, *c.* 1400. GLOUCESTER, south porch, west nave and west front, 1421-1437. LYNN, ST NICHOLAS, 1413-1418. MANCHESTER CATHEDRAL, after 1422. OXFORD, MERTON, transept, finished 1424. WINCHESTER, chapel in cloister, 1420. YORK, central tower, *c.* 1400—*c.* 1423.

THE work at Gloucester still went on. She finished the fan vaulting of the cloister, built a new west front and south porch, and remodelled the two western bays of the nave. Christ Church, Hampshire, starts to rebuild the whole of the eastern limb, commencing with the Lady Chapel. The noble parish church of Bury St Mary and the Chapel of ST NICHOLAS, LYNN (214), are fifteenth-century versions of those of Boston and Holbeach. Fotheringhay is a thoroughgoing specimen of the lantern type of church; roofed in wood, but with clerestory piers strengthened by flying buttresses.

1425—1450.

XV. CENTURY: SECOND QUARTER (*Henry VI.*, 4th to 29th year).—BRISTOL, ST MARY REDCLIFFE. CAMBRIDGE, King's College Chapel is commenced in 1446. CANTERBURY, St Michael's Chapel, finished 1439. CROWLAND, north-western tower. ETON COLLEGE CHAPEL, begun 1441. OXFORD, ALL SOULS', 1438-1442. SHER-BORNE, choir, 1436-1459. WELLS, north-western tower, after 1424. WIMBORNE, western tower, 1448-1464. WYMONDHAM, north aisle, 1432-1445. YORK, south-western tower, 1433-1447.

AT Canterbury St Michael's or Warrior's Chapel is built with a lierne vault as tangled as that of Gloucester. SHERBORNE remodelled her choir; covering it with fan vaults (376). The two Royal Chapels of Eton College and of KING'S COLLEGE, CAMBRIDGE (62), were commenced; but neither made much headway in these troubled times. Blythburgh and Tattershall are characteristic parish churches. St Mary Redcliffe, Bristol, carries on throughout the transformation commenced in the south transept; with its cruciform plan, and nave, transept, choir, and aisles vaulted throughout, it has a cathedral-like air very unusual in an English parish church.

* *Norfolk A.S.*, v. 341.

Louth from N.E.

1450—1475.

XV. CENTURY: THIRD QUARTER (*Henry VI.*, 29th year, to *Edward IV.*, 15th year).—BRISTOL CATHEDRAL, central tower, *c.* 1450—*c.* 1470. CANTERBURY, Lady Chapel, 1448-1455. DURHAM, central tower, *c.* 1470. GLOUCESTER, central tower, 1450-1460; Lady Chapel, 1457-1498. MALVERN, choir begun *c.* 1450. OXFORD, Divinity School, 1445-1480. YORK, north-western tower, 1470-1474.

GLOUCESTER (132) erects its central tower and commences its Lady Chapel, a veritable glass-house; Malvern choir is remodelled; at Canterbury is built the Lady Chapel or Dean's Chapel with fan vaulting; OXFORD elaborates lierne vaulting yet further in the Divinity School (331).

1475—1500.

XV. CENTURY: FOURTH QUARTER (*Edward IV.*, 15th year; *Edward V.*; *Richard III.* to *Henry VII.*, 16th year).—ELY, Alcock's Chapel, 1488. FOUNTAINS, tower, 1494-1526. OXFORD CATHEDRAL, choir vault, 1478-1503. PETERBOROUGH, eastern chapels, 1438-1471, and 1496-1528. SHERBORNE, nave, 1475-1504. WINCHESTER, Lady Chapel, 1487-1500. WINDSOR, St George's, 1481-1537.

SHERBORNE NAVE (346) and OXFORD CATHEDRAL CHOIR (27) are remodelled; the former covered with fan vaulting, the latter with lierne vaults. The eastern chapels of Peterborough and that of Bishop Alcock at Ely are completed; both with fan vaults. Another Royal Chapel, ST GEORGE'S, WINDSOR (330), is begun. Rotherham, LONG MELFORD (547), and Fairford are characteristic parish churches. Long Melford has the lantern type developed to the uttermost limit. Fairford retains practically the whole of its original painted glass. Painted glass has by this time passed wholly away from the Gloucester type; is heavily painted, enamelled and opaque, and betrays Flemish influence.

1500—1525.

XVI. CENTURY: FIRST QUARTER (*Henry VII.*, 16th year, to *Henry VIII.*, 17th year).—BATH, 1500-1616. BOLTON PRIORY, west front, begun 1520. CAMBRIDGE, King's College Chapel, 1508-1515, begun 1446. CAMBRIDGE, Trinity College gateway, 1518-1535. CANTERBURY, Christ Church gateway, 1517. HEREFORD, north porch, *c.* 1520. LOUTH, spire, 1501-1515. OXFORD, Magdalen tower, finished 1505. OXFORD, Corpus Christi College, 1516-1520. RIPON, aisles of nave, begun 1502 or 1503. ROCHESTER, Lady Chapel, *c.* 1512. WESTMINSTER, Henry the Seventh's Chapel, 1500-1512. WINCHESTER, presbytery, 1500-1528.

WITH the Tudors came peace, wealth, and prosperity, and a richness of architectural detail that vies even with the Flamboyant of France. BATH

(373) showed its confidence in the stability of the new *régime* by commencing to rebuild its abbey church ; Bolton Priory began a new western façade.
The Ripon Canons added aisles to their nave.   Rochester built a Lady Chapel.
The Royal Chapel of KING'S COLLEGE, CAMBRIDGE (62) was now taken in
hand in earnest, and was brought to completion in 1508-1515.   The most
gorgeous of all Royal Chapels, except perhaps that of Batalha in Portugal, was
built at Westminster, as the Chantry Chapel of Henry VII.   Magnificent naves
were erected in the churches of Cirencester and St Mary's, Oxford ; LOUTH
(139) built its spire ; to this period belong most of the towers of Somerset,*
e.g. St Mary Magdalen, TAUNTON (595).

1525—1550.

XVI. CENTURY: SECOND QUARTER (*Henry VIII.*, 17th year, to *Edward VI.*,
5th year).—BANGOR, nave, 1532.   ELY, West's Chapel, 1534.   WYMONDHAM, south
aisle, 1534.

BUT the days of Gothic were numbered ; the storm was about to burst ; not
only the old religion but the old art of England were to succumb to its fury ;
Catholicism was to yield to Protestantism ; Gothic to Renaissance art.   So little
more Gothic was done.   Lavenham built a magnificent Gothic porch *c.* 1529 ;
at ELY (143) was built Bishop West's Chantry Chapel, precursor of the
Renaissance.†   The greater monasteries were dissolved in 1538.

SEVENTEENTH CENTURY.

XVII. CENTURY.—LEEDS, St John, consecrated 1634.   LOW HAM, before 1624.
OXFORD, WADHAM COLLEGE, 1610-1613; fan vault of staircase of CHRIST CHURCH
HALL, 1640.   STANTON HAROLD CHURCH, Leicestershire, 1653.

HERE and there Gothic lingered on ; especially in " that home of lost causes,
and forsaken beliefs, and unpopular names, and impossible loyalties," the
University of Oxford.   It is astonishing to find the exquisite Gothic design of
the fan-vaulted staircase of the hall of CHRIST CHURCH, OXFORD (348), so late
as 1640.

---

* On the distinctive characteristics and artistic qualities of Tudor work see Scott's
Essay, 176, 186 : " I regard the Tudor style as the most original and able thing that the
English have achieved in art.   It was really the discovery of new and quite unlooked-for capa-
bility in pointed architecture."   See also Freeman's *History of Architecture*, 394, 395 ; and
Statham's *Architecture for General Readers*, 317.

† The mixture of Gothic and Renaissance, which is well seen in Bishop West's Chapel, is
illustrated by Mr Gotch in chapter ii. of *Early Renaissance Architecture in England*.   For similar
work in France, where it is much more abundant, see Enlart's *Manuel*, vol. i., chapter vi.

Ely, Bishop West's Chapel.

PART II.

AN ANALYSIS OF THE MEDIÆVAL CHURCH ARCHITECTURE OF ENGLAND.

———

CHAPTER VIII.

Early Christian Basilicas—Apsidal *v*. Rectangular Choirs.

EARLY CHRISTIAN BASILICAS.—Both in Eastern and Western Christendom, the history of architecture begins in Rome; in architecture, as in law, all roads lead to Rome. In quite early days, before the recognition of Christianity by the State, Christian churches were built in Rome, at any rate in the suburbs. Eusebius tells us * that in the year 260 A.D. the Emperor Gallienus ordered the restitution to the Christians of churches at Rome, already forty in number. None of these survive. Two venerable monuments, however, of the third century survive, at least in part. It was a custom at Rome, both with Pagans and Christians, to erect a small building, which goes by the name of Schola, over the graves of the members of a burial club or of persons of wealth. In this little lodge-room commemorative banquets were held. The practice grew common; indeed, too common. In A.D. 384 St Augustine complains that it had become a practice to go drinking from schola to schola, "honouring martyrs." Of these scholæ two remain; one above the catacombs of Soter, the other above those of Callixtus. It was in the latter that the Bishop of Rome, Sixtus II., was murdered by a mob in 258; when the building was razed nearly to the ground. In the year 320 it was restored by Constantine, who added a vaulted roof and façade. Then it became a church, and was dedicated jointly to Bishop Sixtus and the martyred maiden, Cæcilia, who lies buried in a chamber of the catacomb beneath. It was long a place of pilgrimage; but ultimately shared the neglect into which the catacombs fell generally, and fifty years ago was a wine-cellar. Now once more, since 1882, it is a church; the Church of Sixtus and Cæcilia.†

When, however, the Emperor himself, Constantine, became a Christian, Christianity had no need any longer to lurk in the back streets and suburbs, and to build exteriors as unobtrusive as possible, such as are to this day those of the

---

* *Ecclesiastical History*, vii. 13. A church at Nicomedia was destroyed in the persecution of Diocletian; it must therefore have been built before the end of the third century. Lethaby's *Mediæval Art*, 16.

† See Lanciani's *Pagan and Christian Rome;* and Baldwin Brown's *From Schola to Cathedral.*

Coptic churches in the Mohammedan environment of Cairo ; and accommodation was provided on a vast scale for the new cult. At first Pagan buildings were largely utilised. Every Pagan building which was capable of giving shelter to a congregation was transformed, at some time or other, into a church. Smaller edifices, like temples and mausoleums, were adapted bodily to their new office ; while the larger ones, such as thermæ, theatres, circuses, and barracks, were occupied in part only.* S. Adriano was the Senate House of Diocletian. S. Andrea was the Basilica of Junius Bassus. And several of the smaller temples became churches : *e.g.*—

SS. Cosmo e Damiano	-	-	-	Temple of Sacra Urbs.
SS. Sergius e Bacchus	-	-	-	„ Concord.
S. Maria in Cosmedin	-	-	-	„ Ceres.
S. Nicola in Carcere	-	-	-	„ Piety.
S. Stefano Rotondo	-	-	-	„ Mater Matuta.†

S. Lorenzo e Damaso, built in 370 in the stable-yard of the Factio Prasina. ‡

Such buildings, however, must from the first have been inconvenient for the ritual of the new religion ; and churches, many of them of great dimensions, were built in the reign of the first Christian Emperor, Constantine, A.D. 312 to 337 ; and during the course of the fourth century. Several survive, at any rate in part ; repaired indeed and remodelled again and again ; but still sufficiently intact to show what was the plan of the first great Christian churches. To this period belong basilicas at Bethlehem (part of the nave) ; and at Orléansville, in North Africa. To the latter, which is in ruins, is attributed the date A.D. 325.§ At Rome were built churches vast in scale. Of these the five most important were S. John Lateran, *Omnium urbis et orbis Ecclesiarum Mater et Caput ;* S. Peter ; S. MARIA MAGGIORE (148.2) ; S. Paul extra muros ; and S. Lorenzo extra muros. The above form the five patriarchal basilicas.‖ The old basilica of S. Peter was removed at the end of the fifteenth century to make room for the present Renaissance cathedral. The basilica of S. Paul was enlarged and its orientation was reversed in 388. It was burnt down in 1823, but has been restored mainly on the original lines. S. Maria Maggiore was built 352-356. Constantine helped with his own hands in digging the foundations of S. John Lateran. He is said to have founded S. Lorenzo *c.* 330 ; it may be a century later.

These and many other great basilicas¶ in Rome were familiar to all Christian

---

* Lanciani's *Pagan and Christian Rome,* 160.
† Or it may have been a Macellum, *i.e.* a market hall.
‡ Lanciani's *Ancient Rome.* See also Eusebius, *Hist. Eccles.,* 4, 24 ; and Sozomen, *Hist. Eccles.,* 7, 15.
§ Plan in Fergusson, 1, 510. Cattaneo, 82, holds that the sculpture of the altar belongs to the second half of the seventh century.

‖ " Paulus, Virgo, Petrus, Laurentius atque Johannes ;
    Hi patriarchatus nomen in Urbe tenent."

¶ Sta. Sabina, built about 430, is probably the most complete and least altered of the early basilicas.

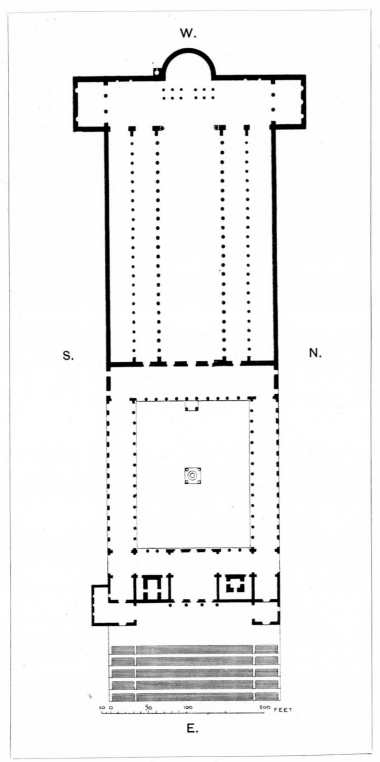

W.

S.

N.

10 0   50   100   200 FEET

E.

Old St Peter's, Rome.

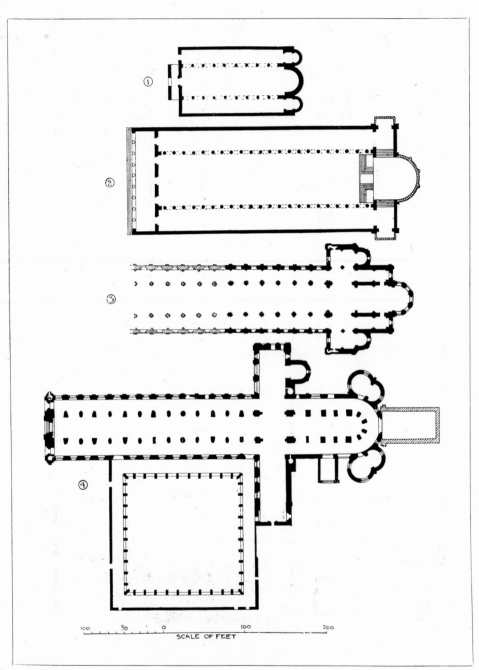

SCALE OF FEET

1. Torcello.
2. S. Maria Maggiore, Rome.
3. Cérisy.
4. Norwich.

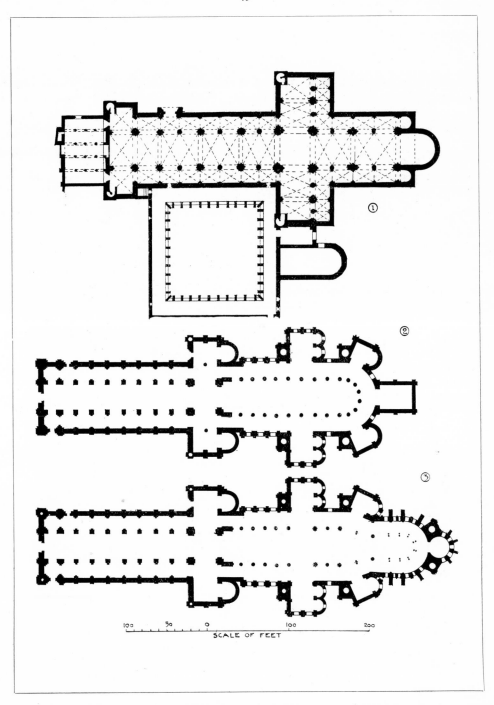

1. Durham, *c.* 1180.   2. Canterbury in 1130.   3. Canterbury in 1184.

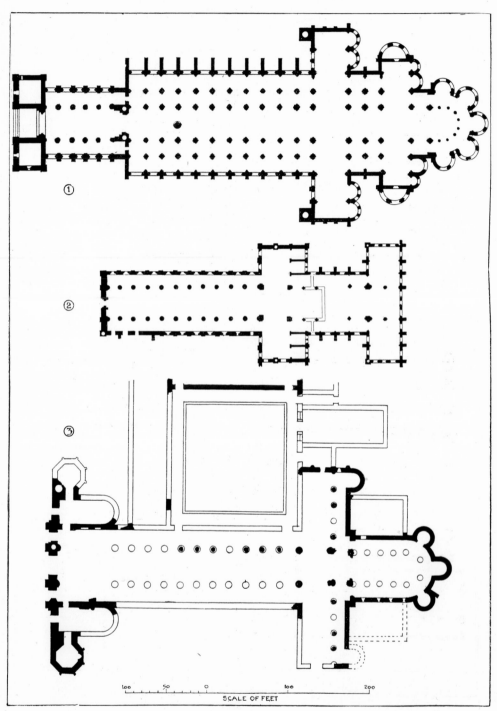

1. Cluny.   2. Fountains.   3. Bury St Edmunds.

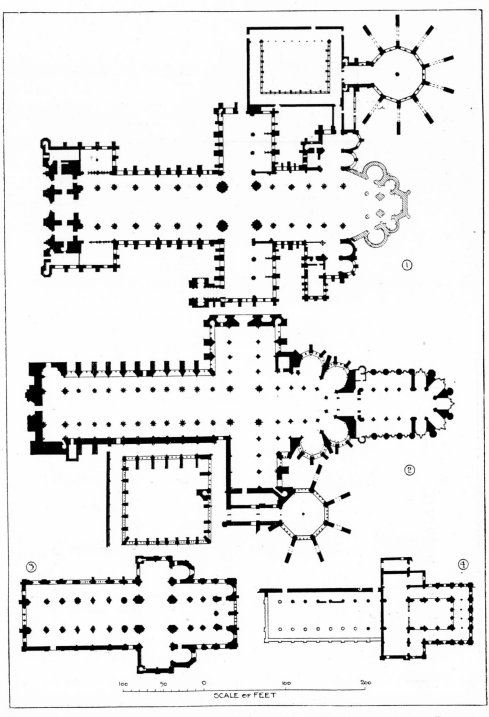

SCALE OF FEET

1. Lincoln, *c.* 1250.　　　2. Westminster.　　　3. Romsey.　　　4. Dore.

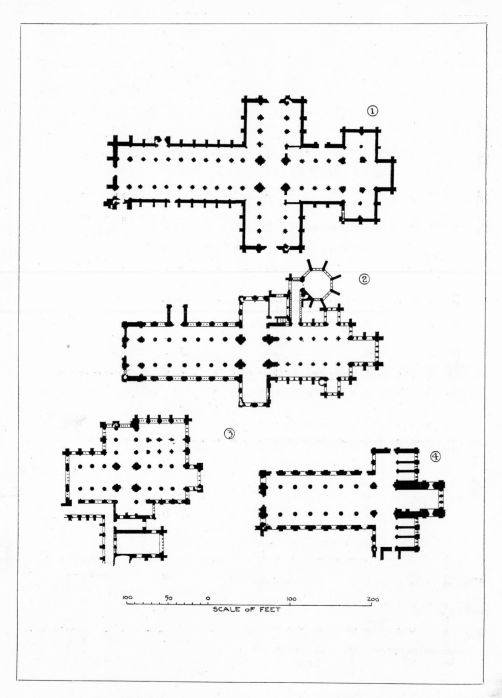

SCALE OF FEET

1. Beverley Minster, *c.* 1400.   3. Oxford Cathedral.
2. Southwell.   4. Kirkstall.

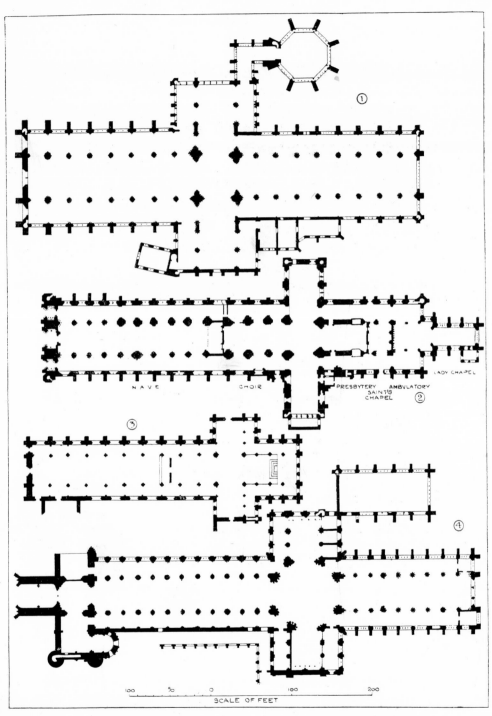

NAVE CHOIR PRESBYTERY AMBVLATORY

SAINT'S
CHAPEL

LADY CHAPEL

① ② ③ ④

100 50 0 100 200

SCALE OF FEET

1. York Minster.　　　3. Jervaulx.
2. St Albans.　　　　4. Ely.

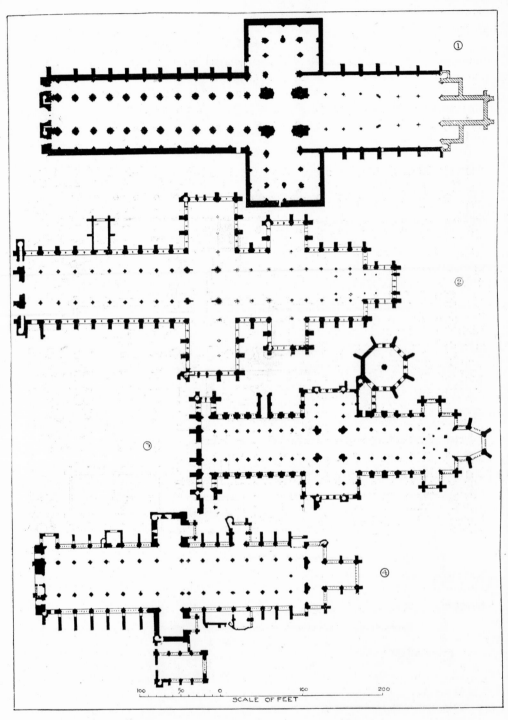

SCALE OF FEET

1. Winchester Cathedral.   2. Salisbury.   3. Wells.   4. Exeter.

people.* Thousands and hundreds of thousands of pilgrims visited Rome while all the five patriarchal basilicas were still standing. Their fame went out to the ends of the earth. Bede tells us that when Northern England was barely emerging from heathendom, Benedic Biscop journeyed to Gaul and to Rome for masons and for fittings for the church which he built at Monkwearmouth ; this was in 675. Bishop Wilfrid also, about the same date, when he built important minsters at Ripon and Hexham,† sought his inspiration at Rome. Hardly any other type of great church but the basilican was built in Western Christendom till S. Ambrogio was commenced at Milan between 824 and 859. To this type

S. Agnese, Rome.

belongs the magnificent group of basilicas at Ravenna, which are of the sixth century : to which period also belongs the remarkable façade of St Saviour,

* The heavenly temple described in the Book of Revelation, chaps. iv. to xxi., is but an idealised Christian basilica ; and the ritual an idealisation of early Christian rites. In the apse is the throne of the Bishop ; in the hemicycle the seats of his presbyters, as at Torcello and Norwich (iv. 2, 4). In front of him is the altar (viii. 3) ; and beneath the altar is the confessionary, containing the relics of martyrs (vi. 9). The "sea of glass" is tesselated pavement (iv. 6) ; in front of the church is the *atrium* or *narthex*. (See Scott's *Essay*, 29.)

† He would hardly have constructed crypts both at Hexham and Ripon but for Italian influence. It is probable that the Ripon crypt was orientated to the west, as originally many of the basilicas at Rome. See Mr J. T. Micklethwaite, quoted in Walbran's *Guide to Ripon*, 18th edition, page 39.

Spoleto.* Even when the Romanesque style was in full development, and indeed in Gothic days too, as late as the fourteenth century, the basilican type of church still found adherents, especially in Italy, its mother-country.

Of the basilican plan the characteristic features are (1) that the church consists of nave and aisles, and that the roof of the nave is raised high above those of the side aisles so as to admit of clerestory windows above the aisle roofs; (2) that the nave terminates in a semicircular sanctuary or apse; (3) that no choir is interposed between nave and apse, *e.g.* ROME S. AGNESE (155).

Some of these churches, constructed in the early days, had double aisles on either side of the nave. Such were the basilicas of ST PETER (147) and St Paul at Rome. And this peculiarity was copied in the Romanesque churches of the end of the eleventh century at Cluny; St Martin de Tours; La Charité; S. Sernin de Toulouse; S. Rémi de Reims; Ripoli in Catalonia; S. Abbondio, Como; S. Hilaire, Poitiers; Souvigny; Gannat, north of Auvergne; though in the three last the inner and outer aisles are of different date. This plan is repeated in Early French Gothic in the cathedrals of Paris, Bourges, and Meaux; at Beaumont-sur-Oise (late twelfth century) and at Lagny, *c.* 1250; and, later, at Troyes, Cologne, Milan, and elsewhere. In England one cathedral, Chichester, and several churches have two or more aisles on each side; but this has usually come about by the accretion of chantry or other chapels. In Scotland the ruined cathedral of Elgin seems to have had a nave set out in the thirteenth century with double aisles.

Hales, Exterior of Apse.

To the east the basilica ended in a semicircular apse. This apse may have existed in larger Anglo-Saxon buildings; but all their larger churches have perished. In their smaller churches, *e.g.* St Pancras, Canterbury; Reculvers; Brixworth; Worth; it certainly existed, but was less common than the rectangular east end. In Norman days nearly all the larger Norman churches, both in Normandy and England, from *c.* 1040 to *c.* 1140, seem to have had an apse.

* Cattaneo, 146.

But, as time went on, the Normans were Anglicised; they sank into and were absorbed into the immensely preponderating population of Anglo-Saxon and Celtic origin in the midst of which their lives were cast: they became naturalised Englishmen. The process, indeed, of naturalisation was long retarded by the vastness of the possessions held by our early kings in what is now France; but it was always growing in force and was never arrested. The English language, the English institutions, and the English law emerged into strength; and in church planning the English oblong type of chancel more and more superseded the apse with its long and hallowed pedigree stretching back to the fourth-century basilicas of early Christian Rome. We may indeed speculate that the fact that the apsidal chancel was largely associated with a foreign priest-hood, foreign bishops, and foreign masters was not calculated to endear it to English minds. In any case, from the middle of the twelfth century, the tendency was, more and more, to build new chancels rectangular, and to square those that had been apsidal; e.g. MELBOURNE (213).

It is to be noted, moreover, that though the greater presbyteries, both in Normandy and England, were very generally apsidal, yet, at any rate in England, some few seem to have been rectangular; viz. Dover; Southwell; Sherborne, and ELY (153). Moreover, the presbyteries of Hereford, Llandaff, and ROMSEY (151) were rectangular, though east of all of them there was probably an ambulatory, with an apse or parallel apses projecting east from it. Here and there, more-over, there were rectangular eastern chapels, e.g. at Canterbury and Rochester. Such examples—and there may have been many of them in the numerous Norman choirs remodelled or rebuilt in Gothic days—as well as the numerous rectangular chancels of parish churches, must have tended to familiarise the eye with the rectangular eastern form.

But, apparently, it was reserved for an alien and Continental influence to administer the *coup de grâce* to the apsidal type of choir. This was the advent in England from Burgundy of the Cistercians and of Cistercian planning. During the twelfth century Cistercian influence was predominant throughout the whole Catholic world, from Scotland to Sicily, from Scandinavia to Spain. By this puritanical order the utmost simplicity of planning, as of ritual, was uniformly enforced when the first great group of Cistercian abbeys was built in England; e.g. Fountains, c. 1135; Buildwas, c. 1148; Furness, c. 1148; Kirk-stall, c. 1152; Louth, Lincolnshire, founded 1139; Roche, c. 1165; Jervaulx, c. 1180; Netley, 1239; Tintern, 1269; all of which accordingly have rectangular chancels. And when an ambulatory was built east of the choir at Byland, c. 1170, and Dore, c. 1200, the east end still remained square. In nearly all our Cistercian churches the original plan of the Burgundian abbey church of Clair-vaux was followed. It was exceptional to copy, as at Croxden, c. 1188, and Beaulieu, c. 1221, both Cistercian, the apse and ambulatory of the second Clairvaux and Pontigny. Reinforced by the example of these great builders, we English threw off the yoke of the foreign plan. The Sens plan indeed arrived and found realisation at Canterbury in 1175; but it made proselytes nowhere; and the Ile de France plan, with polygonal instead of semicircular apse, arrived in 1245, and gave us the chevet of WESTMINSTER (151.2), but with English emendations.*   And in 1192 St Hugh's architect had given us a curious polygonal apse at LINCOLN (151.1), only to be destroyed in 1256.   In the fourteenth century Tewkesbury built a polygonal apse, probably on Norman foundations.   A few minor examples may be seen in parish churches ; *e.g.* Madley, Herefordshire ; fourteenth century.   These, however, were the last expiring efforts to retain the apse.   What had been the predominant type of east end both before and after the Conquest, in our smaller churches, but which in Norman days had been superseded by the apse in the larger churches, had become, as it was to continue to the end, the characteristic eastern termination of the English church.†

* For these see Sir G. G. Scott's *Gleanings*, 23.

† Enlart's *Manuel*, 483, 485, gives lists of numerous French churches with square east end ; chiefly small parish churches ; it is particularly common in Normandy, Burgundy, Champagne, and the south-west.

CHAPTER IX.

PLANS OF THE EASTERN LIMB OF THE GREATER CHURCHES.

FIRST PLAN : TYPE, NORMAN DURHAM : THREE PARALLEL EASTERN
APSES ; OR VARIANTS THEREOF.

WE have now to consider the planning of the aisles of the choir. At first, in basilicas of the simple type of S. Maria Maggiore, or S. Maria in Cosmedin, Rome, the central apse projected clear of the aisles, which were square-ended. But this simple plan seems soon to have been complicated by the need of a sacristy and a library ; in the earliest basilicas room may have been found for these near the entrance, as at Old St Peter's, Rome, where there was a building arranged like a little basilica, to the left of the narthex.* But it was more convenient to have them nearer the high altar. And so Paulinus of Nola, who died in 431, describes on the right of the apse a sacristy where the bread and wine and the church plate and the vestments are kept—

> " Hic locus est veneranda penus qua conditur, et qua
> Promitur alma sacri pompa ministerii ; "

and on the left the library—

> " Hic poterit residens sacris intendere libris." †

The same arrangements occur in the sixth century in the churches of S. John the Evangelist and S. Vitale, Ravenna ; ‡ in the fifth and sixth century in Central Syria : e.g. Tourmanin and St Simeon Stylites ; § three parallel eastern apses are found. A recent discovery at Hispalis proves that the central apse contained the episcopal chair ; the one on the right the church plate ; the one on the left the library.‖ From the Eastern Church the triple eastern apse passed to Rome : an early example, perhaps, is seen at S. Maria in Cosmedin, which was re-modelled for the Greeks who had been exiled by the Iconoclasts of Con-stantinople. Pope Adrian is described as " tres absides in ea constituens " ; this was in 872. A still earlier example at Rome is that of S. Maria in Domnica,

---

* Cattaneo, 60.

† Scott's *Essay*, 81. The basilican church of the monastery of St Catherine at Sinai, which is undoubtedly of the time of Justinian, has apse and side chambers. Lethaby's *Mediæval Art*, 60.

‡ The basilica at Bethlehem has three parallel eastern apses. These are held by De Vogüé, R. de Fleury, and Kraus to be Constantinian. Professor Lethaby (*Med. Art*, 58) thinks that they are later than Constantine, and may be anterior to Justinian.

§ Illustrated in Scott's *Essay*, 62.   ‖ Lanciani's *Ancient Rome*, 187.

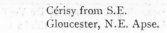

Cérisy from S.E. St George's de Boscherville from E.
Gloucester, N.E. Apse. Norwich, S.E. Apse.

Wells from East.

Peterborough N. Transept.

Cérisy Choir.

Castle Rising.
St Margaret's, Lynn.

St David's.
Sudbury St Peter.

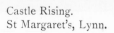

817-824.* The central apse of TORCELLO CATHEDRAL (148.1) is dated by Cattaneo *c*. 650 ; the absiodoles *c*. 864.

From these basilicas the plan passed to the earliest Romanesque churches. It appears in the ninth century at ST GALL (194), and in the oldest work of S. Ambrogio, Milan, A.D. 824-859; again, *c*. 850, in the same city, at S. Vincento in prato ; and again at Alliata, near Monza, A.D. 881.† In France it appears in Carlovingian work at Germigny-les-Prés, consecrated 806 ; and at St Généroux, which also may be of the ninth century. When we come to the great churches of Normandy in the eleventh century, the triple apse or some modification of it is the invariable arrangement.‡ (1.) Three parallel apses occur in the eleventh century at Guibray and the Abbaye-aux-Dames at Caen.§ (2.) The semidomes, however, of such little side apses are much easier to roof with wood, if they are squared externally ; and this is often done. So that while the central apse is semicircular externally and internally, the side apses may be semicircular internally, but externally rectangular. This arrangement is characteristic of the Romanesque churches of the Como district ; *e.g.* S. Abbondio. In Normandy it occurs in the eleventh century at Lessay ; St Gabriel ; St Nicolas, Caen ; St George's de Boscherville ; and in the transept apses of the Abbaye-aux-Hommes. ‖ (3.) But when the apses of the aisles had been squared externally, it was not a long step to square them internally also. And so we get a central apse flanked by aisles squared within and without. In Normandy this plan occurs at CÉRISY-LA-FORÊT (148.3), which may have been set out in the eleventh century ; and on the eastern frontier of Normandy at Gournay, where the work is probably of similar date.¶

This, then, was the normal plan of eastern limb which the Norman builders brought over to England at the Conquest : a central apse flanked (1) by absiodoles, (2) which might be rectangular externally, or (3) by square-ended aisles. In England, unfortunately, the greater part of the eastern limbs of the large Norman churches have disappeared. Either they were pulled down, as at Lincoln, to be rebuilt on a more magnificent scale in Gothic ; or, where the church was served by monks, the parishioners at the Dissolution retained for their use only the nave, as at Binham, Leominster, Wymondham ; and the choir fell into ruin, was pulled down, and disappeared. Nevertheless, excavations have made clear the eastern terminations of several of the large Norman choirs.

Peterborough retains the central apse ; the foundations of semicircular lateral apses exist underground. At DURHAM (149.1) the foundations of three parallel eastern apses have been found. In both cases the lateral apses were semicircular within, square without ; so also probably at Selby.** The same arrange-

---

* Plans in Cattaneo, Figs. 80 and 90.   † Cattaneo, Figs. 123 and 128.

‡ It must be borne in mind, however, that several of the east ends have been destroyed, or have been replaced in Gothic ; some of those may not have possessed the triple parallel eastern apses. Rouen Cathedral has a periapsidal plan of Gothic date, which may perhaps be a survival of a similar Romanesque plan.

§ Ruprich-Robert, i., Plates 8, 9.   ‖ Ruprich-Robert, 60, 1, and Plates 8, 9, 93.

¶ Ruprich-Robert, Plate 54.

** Mr J. Bilson in *Archæological Journal*, liii. 8, on Durham apses ; and Mr C. C. Hodges in the *Archæological Journal*, liii. 1 *et seq.*, on Selby apses.

ment occurred at ST ALBANS (98),* St Mary's, York, Castle Acre,† and Exeter. At ROMSEY (151.3) lateral apses remain; these are semicircular within, rectangular without.   ST MARY'S, GUILDFORD (36), retains lateral apses, built in the last years of the twelfth century.

Both Lindisfarne and Melbourne originally had central apses; but they had no lateral apses, as their choirs were without aisles.

Not a single example remains entire.   If we wish to see the effect of the parallel apse plan, we must go to Normandy and visit CÉRISY-LA-FORÊT and ST GEORGE'S DE BOSCHERVILLE (160, 160); in both of which, however, the aisles are square-ended externally, while at Cérisy they are also square internally, except in the triforium, where they are semicircular.

Two important variants remain to be noticed.   One is that in which the aisles end in semicircular apses, but the presbytery is rectangular.   Ely‡ presbytery, originally intended to be apsidal, was made rectangular between 1103 and 1106.   The other three are Sherborne,§ begun 1107; Southwell,‖ between 1108 and 1114; St Martin's Priory, Dover,¶ between 1131 and 1139.**   The other variant is seen at Hereford, LLANDAFF (580), and ROMSEY (151.3).   In these the presbytery is rectangular, but it opens by a semicircular arch or arches into an aisle or ambulatory running north and south.   This ambulatory survives at Romsey.   Romsey had also a central chapel or chapels, probably apsidal, projecting eastward from the centre of the ambulatory.   This was rebuilt in Gothic days.   Hereford †† and Llandaff may have had a similar plan.   This second variant is of the utmost importance, and is peculiar to the West of England school of Romanesque.

SECOND PLAN : TYPE, NORWICH CATHEDRAL ; SEMICIRCULAR AMBULATORY WITH RADIATING CHAPELS.

PERIAPSIDAL PLAN.—But another more complicated and improved type of planning was more common in England than that of the three parallel eastern apses.   In this the central eastern apse was encircled by a semicircular aisle, which is called the *ambulatory*.‡‡   Of this we may distinguish three species— (1) The ambulatory with tangential chapels; (2) the ambulatory without chapels; (3) variants of the above.

By far the most common type is that in which chapels radiate to the north-

* The late Lord Grimthorpe's *Guide to St Albans*, 5 ; and Buckler's *St Albans*.

† For the plan of Castle Acre see paper by Mr W. H. St John Hope in *Norfolk and Norwich Arch. Soc.*, 1894.

‡ Willis, in Stewart's *Ely*, gives plan of the discoveries in Ely choir.

§ Carpenter in *Journal of R.I.B.A.*, March 1877.

‖ E. Christian in *Journal of British Archæological Association*, January 1853.

¶ Rev. Dr Plumptre in *Arch. Cantiana*, vol. iv., has plan of Dover Priory.

** Bristol also is said, by Mr E. W. Godwin, to have had a square-ended choir, but this is merely a conjecture.   *Archæol. Journal*, xx. 47.

†† Mr A. Moore, Hereford, sends the following extract from the *Hereford Journal* of June 13, 1863 :—"At the commencement of the present restoration the foundations of the original apsidal (or semicircular) terminations of the choir and its aisles were discovered."

‡‡ No ambulatory with tangential chapels is older than *c.* 900 A.D.   Lenoir, *Architecture monastique*, ii. 35 ; Viollet-le-Duc, *Architecture*, ii. 456 ; and Comte Robert de Lasteyrie's *Monograph on St Martin de Tours*.

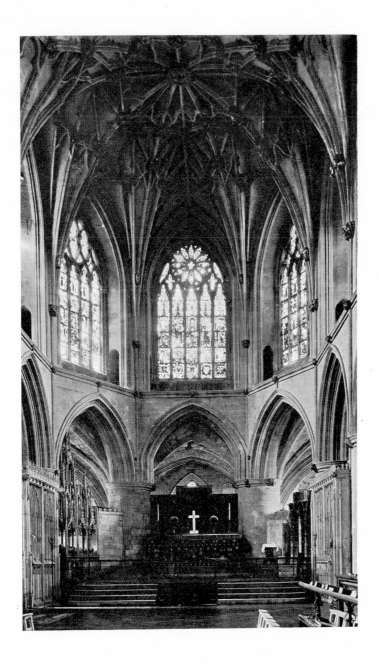

Tewkesbury Choir.

east, east, and south-east. The usual number of these radiating chapels is three. Lewes, a Cluniac abbey, as remodelled soon after 1100, had five of these chapels, probably copying the arrangements of CLUNY (150.1). Not one of these choirs survives entire. GLOUCESTER (135) and NORWICH (160) have retained their north-east and south-east chapels, but in either case the eastern chapel was demolished and rebuilt much larger as a Lady Chapel, which also at NORWICH (148.4) has disappeared. At GLOUCESTER (192.1), however, the original eastern termination is seen perfectly in the crypt. At CANTERBURY CATHEDRAL, in Ernulph's choir, 1096-1107 (149.2), there were three chapels, of which the eastern one was square; tangential chapels, those of St Anselm and St Andrew, still survive. Diggings have shown that the periapsidal plan existed at St Augustine, Canterbury, which had an apse of seven bays;* also at the collegiate church of St Martin-le-Grand, Dover. So it did at Tynemouth, and Bury St Edmunds;† in the present cathedral of Chester;‡ at Leominster;§ and at Battle and Pershore.‖ From the present form of the choir of TEWKES-BURY (165), and from its proximity to Gloucester, Pershore, Leominster, and Worcester, it is probable that this church also had the same plan. All but one of the above were Benedictine churches, and Canterbury and Norwich were Benedictine cathedrals; Lewes was Cluniac. The same plan was also adopted by Secular Canons at Chichester;¶ and by Cistercian monks at Croxden. The Benedictine abbey of Reading had central apse and ambulatory; it is uncertain whether there were radiating chapels.

Of the second type of plan, viz. without radiating chapels, there are few undoubted examples. Edward the Confessor's Benedictine church at Westminster had central apse and ambulatory; so far no chapels have been discovered. Lichfield Cathedral, built by Secular Canons, had central apse and ambulatory, but no chapels have yet been found.** The same is the disposition of St Bartholomew's, Smithfield.†† But an ambulatory without radiating chapels is so rare in Romanesque that these three examples should be regarded as doubtful.

Thirdly, variations are played on the periapsidal plan. At Worcester Cathedral, as the remains of the CRYPT (192.2) show, there was central apse and ambulatory; but instead of radiating chapels‡‡ the choir was flanked by elongated chapels projecting eastward from the transepts. This was the plan of the Abbaye-aux-Dames at Caen, except that in that church there was no ambulatory; so also of the Cistercian church of Vaux-le-Cernay (1128); and probably of Cluny before the rebuilding of 1082. Winchester possessed apse and ambulatory; but the side chapels were not set tangentially, but due east, parallel to an eastern chapel; as is well seen in the CRYPT (192.5). This is a sort of blend of the plan with three parallel eastern apses and that with apse and ambulatory.

In plan the normal type of the tangential chapel is semicircular. But at

* See paper by Mr St John Hope in *Archæologia Cantiana*, xxv.
† Paper by Dr M. R. James in *Camb. Antiq. Society's Octavo*, xxviii.
‡ Sir G. G. Scott in *Chester Architect. and Archæol. Soc. Journal*, iii. 169.
§ *Arch. Journal*, 10, 111.   ‖ Scott's *Gleanings*, 19.
¶ See Willis' plan and evidence in monograph on Chichester.
** *See* Mr Hope's plans in *Builder*, Feb. 7, 1891.
†† Plan in *Architectural Review*, i. 1, 22.
‡‡ If radiating chapels exist, they are blocked up, and have still to be found.

GLOUCESTER (192.1) the chapels are pentagonal; while at NORWICH (148.4), each is composed of part of a small circle, serving as choir, and part of a large circle, serving as nave. At CANTERBURY (149.2) the north-east and south-east chapels are oblong, but with eastern apses.

Cluny.

Whence came these apses with circumambient aisles in Ernulph's Canterbury; St Augustine's, Canterbury; Norwich; Gloucester; Bury St Edmunds; Leominster; Battle; Tewkesbury; Pershore; Chichester; Lewes; Lichfield; Worcester; St Bartholomew's, Smithfield; Winchester; St Werburgh, Chester; St John's in the Tower of London, and the Norman abbey of Westminster? Hardly from Normandy; for "till Fécamp, A.D. 1082, there was no 'Rond-Point' in Normandy; and Fécamp remained without imitators for at least a century."* Nor again is the ambulatory characteristic of the Romanesque schools of Lombardy, Germany, Provence, or Périgueux. Three schools employ it most; those of (1) Burgundy, (2) Poitou, (3) Auvergne and Toulouse.† It is difficult to connect historically eleventh-century England with Auvergne and Toulouse. In Burgundy the periapsidal plan is characteristic; especially in the great

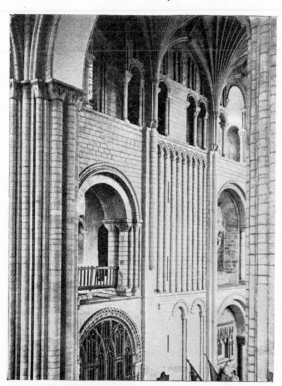

Norwich, East Side of South Transept.

* A. St Paul in Planat's *Encyclopédie*, vi. 23. Enlart quotes, however, the substructures of the cathedral of Evreux, where there was a consecration in 1072 (*Manuel*, 227). Avranches may be added.

† See paper by the author on Classification of Romanesque in the *R.I.B.A. Journal*, 3, viii. 12, p. 282.

churches of the Cluniac Order. CLUNY (168), the largest Romanesque church in Christendom, had this plan. So has its daughter church, Paray-le-Monial, which was dedicated in 1104. La Charité, another Cluniac church, which originally had three parallel eastern apses, received an ambulatory in the twelfth century.* The same transformation of a triapsal into a periapsidal choir occurred at Tournus and Vignory; and in England at Lewes; all early in the twelfth century. The choir of St Etienne, Nevers, a great church which architecturally is on the frontier of Burgundy and Auvergne, has an ambulatory; it was begun in 1063, but was not consecrated till 1099. It were natural to suppose that the grand church of CLUNY (150.1) would be the leading influence in England in the eleventh century. But, in the first place, the Cluniac Order was never strong in England; and nearly all our periapsidal churches were Benedictine. (2.) Chronology forbids the supposition. The ambulatory of Cluny was not commenced till 1089; but that of Winchester was begun in 1079, that of Worcester in 1084, of Gloucester in 1089; while the little chapel in the Tower of London is *c.* 1080; and Edward the Confessor's abbey church at Westminster, consecrated in 1065, had an ambulatory; for a contemporary writer † says that the "*ambitus ipsius aedis duplici lapidum arcu clauditur.*"‡ The bases of three of the piers of this *duplex lapidum arcus, i.e.* apse and ambulatory, exist below the pavement of the present sanctuary; and one of them may be seen, by means of a trap-door, to the north of the high altar.§ So far as dates go, therefore, it would be more reasonable to derive the ambulatory of Cluny from that of Westminster than that of Westminster from that of Cluny.

The truth is, both are derived from one common source; and that source is to be found in one of the most important abbey churches in mediæval Europe, a special resort of pilgrims, ST MARTIN, TOURS (192.3). Excavations made in 1860 have shown that the great double ambulatory and radiating chapels—a work of the thirteenth century, destroyed at the French Revolution—were an amplification of an earlier eastern limb, built between 997 and 1014, which consisted of a choir of two bays and an apse of five bays, surrounded by a single ambulatory and five radiating chapels.‖ Immediately following this, in all probability, was the work at Notre Dame de la Coûture, Le Mans, where to a ninth-century aisleless choir and apse, similar to that shown in the plan of ST GALL (194), were added an ambulatory and five radiating chapels. This was built in the time of Abbot Gauzberts, 990-1007; who came from Tours, and had been a great builder there. Close on this follow S. Remi at Reims, *c.* 1005; St Savin, between 1020 and 1030; St Hilaire de Poitiers, consecrated 1049; Notre Dame du Pré, Le Mans, remodelled *c.* 1050; St Sernin de Toulouse, whose choir was consecrated in 1096: all great pilgrim-churches. And so we arrive at the unexpected con-

---

* Dehio, Plate 120, 2, and 121, 3.
† Quoted in full in Scott's *Essay*, 131, note.
‡ See plan by Mr Micklethwaite in *Builder*, Jan. 6, 1894.
§ This base is figured in the *Builder, loc. cit.*
‖ *Bulletin Monumental*, vol. 40, 147. Dehio, text, i. 267; and Comte de Lasteyrie's monograph on the excavations, in the *Mémoires de l'Academie des Inscriptions et Belles-lettres*, Paris, 1891.

clusion that the great majority of our Norman churches are probably not Norman in their planning, but hail from St Martin de Tours.

The convenience and superiority of the periapsidal as compared with the triapsal plan must have been from the first manifest. The fact that it occurs first in the great pilgrim-churches of Western France may point to its origin. The triapsal plan meant danger to life and limb on days of crowded pilgrimages. But, with an ambulatory, the pilgrims could proceed up one choir aisle, pass behind and round the apse, and down the other choir aisle, without having to retrace their steps. It was equally convenient in processions, especially the great Sunday Procession,* when the monks had to circumambulate the church in order to asperge every altar before the supreme Mass of the week.† Moreover, three or five altars which before, probably, had cumbered the nave, could now be placed in the new radiating chapels of the ambulatory. And the ambulatory afforded the necessary access to them. Again, each apsidal chapel could be treated as a sanctuary to be entered only by the officiating priest and his attendants, and the ambulatory provided the necessary nave for the worshippers. At GLOUCESTER (135),‡ indeed, the three radiating apses of the ambulatory of the choir, as well as the two eastern apses of the transept, were built three stories high; one in the crypt, one on the ground-floor, and one in the upper aisle. And, for access to these, three ambulatories were constructed in a similar position; the uppermost ambulatory being open to the choir, floored, lighted by windows at the back, and approached by broad staircases. So very convenient were these arrangements found at Gloucester, that they were allowed to remain almost intact even when the central apse was made square, c. 1350; the ambulatory of the upper aisle reappearing in the so-called Whispering Gallery.

In France the periapsidal plan subsisted to the end. The five choir-chapels of St Martin de Tours, St Savin, Cluny, St Sernin de Toulouse, St Jago de Compostella, amplify into the seven apsidal chapels of Amiens, Beauvais, Cologne, and that masterpiece of French Gothic, Le Mans. But because arches curving on plan are difficult to construct, the semicircular apses and absiodoles of Romanesque became polygonal in Gothic.

These then were the two characteristic plans of the greater Romanesque churches in England; either (1) three parallel eastern apses, or some variant of these; or (2) an ambulatory, almost always with radiating chapels. These two plans held the field to the almost total exclusion of all others for about a century after the Norman Conquest. The one important exception is that of ROMSEY (151.3), and perhaps Hereford, Llandaff, and Sarum.

---

* For the route of the Sunday Procession see Hope's *Rochester*, 217.

† In the account, quoted in Willis' *Canterbury*, 61, of the rebuilding of Canterbury choir in 1180, the monk Gervase expressly says that "the master preserved as much as he could the breadth of the passage outside the choir on account of the processions which were there frequently passing."

‡ In the illustration of Gloucester Cathedral (160), the three tiers of windows in each absiodole correspond to the three superposed chapels.

SALISBURY CATHEDRAL FROM N.E.

THIRD PLAN: TYPE, SALISBURY CATHEDRAL: RECTANGULAR AMBULATORY;
SOMETIMES WITHOUT, MORE OFTEN WITH A LOW RECTANGULAR
EASTERN CHAPEL.

Both the above plans—that with the parallel eastern apses, and that with
the semicircular ambulatory—were, as we have seen, direct importations from
the Continent. The next plan, which came into use mainly in the last half of
the twelfth century, is of twofold origin. In the early Gothic of the North of
England it is of Cistercian, i.e. of Burgundian origin. The plan of Byland
Abbey is plainly but a simplified version of such a Cistercian plan as that
in the Sketch Book of Villard de Honnecourt; or those of Ebrach, Lilien-
feld, Arnsburg, Riddagshausen.*

But in the South of England it appears in the Benedictine nunnery church
of ROMSEY (151.3), quite early in the twelfth century; too early for any Cistercian
influence. Romsey was built not later than 1120. Here the high choir was
given a square east end, but the ground-story of this was pierced with two
arches. Behind these was built a processional aisle or ambulatory connecting the
north and south aisles of the choir, and from the ambulatory projected an eastern
chapel or chapels. The new eastern aisle may be regarded as the rectangular
equivalent of the semicircular ambulatories which were exceptionally numerous
in the abbey churches of the West of England; e.g. Worcester, Pershore,
Leominster, Gloucester, Tewkesbury. The Romsey plan may have existed
also at Hereford, Llandaff, and Old Sarum, which William of Malmesbury
tells us was built anew by his contemporary, Roger, Bishop of Salisbury; i.e.
between 1115 and 1139.† It is quite clear that the rectangular ambulatory
was adopted at Wells Cathedral, c. 1180; and at Glastonbury,‡ after the fire of
1184. Another early adoption of the Romsey plan is in the choir of Lichfield
as built c. 1190. From its plan, as well as from the moldings and capitals,
this choir clearly belongs to the West of England School of Gothic. Lichfield,
like Romsey, had two arches from the choir to the ambulatory.§

In Cistercian work it occurs twice: at Byland, in Yorkshire, to which
the monks removed from Stocking in 1177; and at DORE (182), in Hereford,
where the eastern termination of the choir seems to have been remodelled c.
1200. Dore choir is practically a reduced version of that of Ebrach, consecrated
1178. The Cistercian churches in Europe were so commonly built from plans
inspired by the mother-abbey at Cîteaux or by its daughter churches, that it
is hardly safe to regard the plan of DORE (151.4) as derived from that of Romsey.

Two more doubtful cases occur in Yorkshire. In the choir of York, as
rebuilt by Archbishop Roger, 1154 to 1181, it has been conjectured‖ that
there was a rectangular ambulatory. If so, this may have been the case also

* Dehio, Plate 193 (Byland); 191, 195.
† A plan of it is given in Prior, 67; the evidence for it is not strong.
‡ There is no evidence as to the existence of a projecting eastern chapel at Wells. Mr
James Parker in his paper in the *Somerset Arch. Proceedings*, vol. xxvi., gives a plan of
Glastonbury east end; in 1190 it was exactly the same as that of DORE (151.4). Willis
assumed that Glastonbury had a projecting eastern chapel. Mr W. H. St John Hope has
recently proved by excavations at Glastonbury that there was no eastern chapel in 1190.
§ See Mr St John Hope's plans in *Builder Cathedrals*. ‖ Willis' *York*, 11.

with his choir at Ripon; the east end of which, however, had to be rebuilt at the close of the thirteenth century.

At Romsey, Byland, and Wells there was but one eastern aisle. The next improvement was to increase the number to two, as at Dore and Glastonbury. At Dore there are remains of five altars against the eastern wall, and of low walls cutting up the easternmost of the two aisles into so many chapels.* The westernmost aisle was employed as ambulatory or processional path. The next improvement was that of Bishop de Lucy at WINCHESTER, 1202 (154.1), viz. to construct three eastern aisles with three chapels east of them; thus providing plenty of space for worshippers to attend the services at the eastern altars; as well as room for processions. At St Saviour's, Southwark,† 1213-1238, which was connected with Winchester, similarly three eastern aisles were provided, but without the three eastern chapels of Winchester.

The Romsey eastern chapel as well as the rectangular ambulatory soon inspired imitation. At Chichester the Secular Canons had finished a rectangular eastern chapel before 1175. After the fire of 1187, for the Norman ambulatory and its radiating chapels two eastern aisles were substituted; and at the end of the thirteenth century the Lady Chapel was prolonged still further. At Hereford, *c.* 1190, the Norman ambulatory appears to have been raised and vaulted, eastern aisles added, and the Norman eastern chapel replaced by a square one; this chapel was still further prolonged *c.* 1230, and forms the present Lady Chapel (464).

Finally, all these experiments were summed up in the beautifully symmetrical plan of SALISBURY (154.2); with triple eastern arch, two eastern aisles, and projecting Lady Chapel. St Patrick's Cathedral, Dublin, finished in 1235, is the same in plan as Salisbury; except that the choir has but one arch in the eastern wall and one eastern aisle. The choir of Milton Abbas, Dorset, 1290 to 1300, had three eastern arches, an aisle or aisles, and a Lady Chapel. EXETER, *c.* 1280 (154.4), was satisfied with two eastern arches, one aisle, and Lady Chapel. ST ALBANS (153.2) has three eastern arches, three eastern aisles, and Lady Chapel. WELLS, *c.* 1340 (154.3), presents the plan in its most attractive form; with piers, arches, and vaults set so as to produce fairy-like vistas and perspectives. Ottery St Mary, also of the fourteenth century, is a reduced copy of Exeter. The great parish church of St Mary Redcliffe, Bristol, was remodelled, *c.* 1442, very much on the lines of Ottery St Mary.‡

The geographical distribution of the Salisbury plan is remarkable. It is

---

* Piers and capitals from Dore retrochoir are illustrated on page 422.

† Later on a projecting Lady Chapel was added; this was destroyed to make room for the south approach to London Bridge.

‡ It is often assumed that every eastern chapel was intended as a Lady Chapel. This is not certain in all cases; especially in early examples, such as at Romsey and Winchester. For it was not till Pope Innocent III. and St Bernard urged increased veneration of the Blessed Virgin that Lady Chapels rose to importance, and finally received such great augmentation in scale and splendour, as at Peterborough and Ely. Even then it was not always thought desirable to dislodge the shrine of the local saint east of the high altar, and the new Lady Chapel was placed to the north of the choir as at Oxford, Wymondham, Llanthony, Bristol, Peterborough, Canterbury, Ely; or south of it, as at Rochester; or west, in the galilee, at Durham.

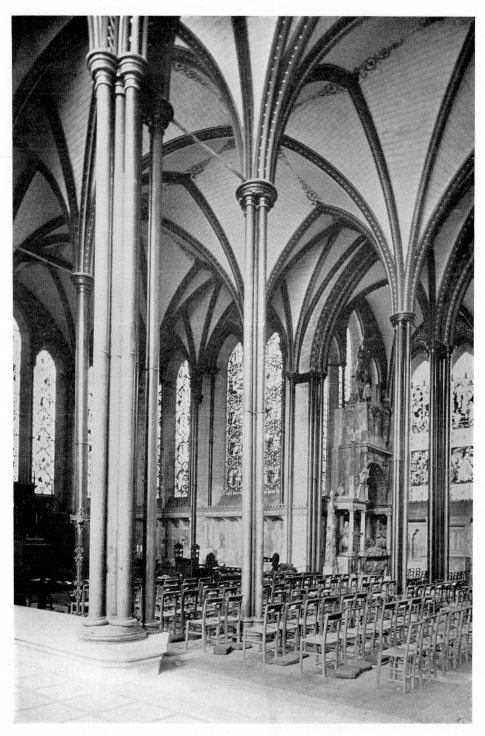

Salisbury Lady Chapel from N.W.

entirely confined to the South and West of England. In fact, it is one of the marks which differentiate the Southern from the Northern Gothic of England.*

It is to be regarded as a home-grown development of the Romsey plan; the first complete breaking away from Continental traditions of planning. It is a very beautiful plan. Internally, its shadowy recesses and broken lights add mystery and distance. Externally, Lady Chapel, Retrochoir, Choir, rising up in successive ranges, Alp behind Alp, leading up to, and culminating in the central spire, as at SALISBURY (170), group marvellously. It is a most worthy rival of the periapsidal plans of Amiens and Westminster; internally, it rivals them; externally, its superiority is beyond question.

SAME PLAN: TYPE, SOUTHWELL MINSTER; WITH HIGH RECTANGULAR UNAISLED PRESBYTERY OR LADY CHAPEL.

But neither was this beautiful type destined to endure, any more than that of the three parallel apses or the semicircular ambulatory. It was developed and perfected in the last half of the twelfth and the first half of the thirteenth century. After that, with the belated exceptions of Wells and Ottery St Mary in the fourteenth, and St Mary Redcliffe, Bristol, in the fifteenth century, it fell wholly out of use. It conquered for itself much of the South and the West of England; it failed to win over the Gothic of the North.

There must have been some inherent fault in the Salisbury plan. What was it? It may have been that the English mediæval builder had already begun to show his deep dislike of intricacy of planning. One practical consideration, however, may be suggested. The great churches of the eleventh, twelfth, and thirteenth centuries were exceedingly dark; there was often but one small window in each bay of the clerestory or aisle, and the walls were so thick that but little light could penetrate the gloom of the centre of nave or choir. What little light there was, was reduced to a minimum by the thickness and opacity of the stained glass. The chief source of light was through the end walls of the nave or transepts, as at PETERBOROUGH (161); or of the apse. With the ancient triapsal plan, as is well seen at CÉRISY-LA-FORÊT (161), the central apse of the choir was most effectively lighted by three tiers of windows, north, east, and south; but when an ambulatory was added, the light was usually reduced to that from the clerestory windows, which were too high up to be of much service.

The gloom of St Sernin, Toulouse, or St Etienne, Nevers, and even of Chartres, must be felt to be appreciated. To a practical builder like the Englishman, the bad lighting of Winchester and Salisbury, just at that spot where light was most essential—that all might follow with the eye each movement of the priest officiating at the Mass—may well have seemed an insuperable objection to either plan of choir.

A much simpler method, which at any rate ensured good lighting—for the light entered on three sides—was to construct a short unaisled oblong sanctuary immediately adjoining the central transept. It was a plan especially suitable to

---

* Unless the Ripon and York choirs of the twelfth century had projecting eastern chapels as well as rectangular ambulatories.

a monastic church in which the monks sat in the crossing and the eastern bays of the nave. And as it was a simple and easy solution of the lighting problem, it was adopted in very many of the large Cistercian churches ; *e.g.* in England at KIRKSTALL (152.4), Furness, Buildwas, and Roche, and no doubt in other Cistercian abbeys where, as at Rievaulx and Fountains, the choirs of the churches were afterwards enlarged and remodelled.* But, ritualistically, it was a retrogression ; it did not admit of processions, or of a continuous flow of pilgrims round the sanctuary. But as the Cistercians did not wish or expect to have a concourse of pilgrims in their sequestered churches, this probably seemed no disadvantage in their eyes. It was, however, a plan eminently suited for churches where the number of clergy was too small to admit of elaborate processional ritual ; and accordingly was, above all others, the normal plan of the parish churches. The vast majority of the village churches of England have unaisled chancels ; even such large churches as Gedney and Walpole St Peter's, and such important town churches as BOSTON (216.4). But such a plan was unsuitable for, and was seldom adopted, in the cathedral and larger collegiate churches.

Some churches, however, had already progressed beyond the simple plan of the unaisled chancel. In several churches built in the last half of the twelfth century, aisles were constructed to the western bay or bays of the chancel, leaving to the east an unaisled presbytery. This plan was much more convenient than that of Kirkstall ; for the unaisled presbytery with the high altar was excellently lighted. It was adopted by the Augustinian Canons of St Frideswide, OXFORD (152.3), 1154 to 1180 ;† and not much later by those of Lanercost Priory and Cartmel ; *c.* 1191 by the Premonstratensian Canons of St Radigund's Priory at Bradsole ; and *c.* 1190 by the Benedictines of Tynemouth. In the thirteenth century it was adopted by the Benedictines of Rochester and Worcester ; and by the Secular Canons of SOUTHWELL (152.2), BEVERLEY (152.1), and Wimborne ; in the fourteenth by the Augustinians of Bristol. The same plan was followed later at Lichfield and at Christ Church, Hants.‡

FOURTH PLAN : TYPE, YORK MINSTER : AISLED PARALLELOGRAM.

But a much simpler plan than either that of Salisbury or that of Oxford came into use simultaneously with those two plans, and in the end superseded both. Like them it originated in the last half of the twelfth century ; and originated, probably independently, in the South and North; in the South at St Cross and New Shoreham ; in the North at JERVAULX (153.3), Whitby, and Hexham. In these choirs, pillars and arches, clerestory windows, vault and roof ran in undiminished height without break from the central tower to the east end ;

* *Cf.* the plans of Fontenay, Casamari, Chiaravalle, Maulbronn, in Dehio, Plates 191-194. It was the most common of all the Cistercian plans ; and probably was the plan of the Clairvaux church in which St Bernard, the greatest man of the order, had worshipped.

† It is possible that this was the plan also of the church built by the Secular Canons of Wimborne early in the twelfth century. It may even have been the plan of Abbot Richard's presbytery at Ely in 1103.

‡ It should be noted that the unaisled member was not usually a presbytery. It was a Lady Chapel at Worcester, Lichfield, and elsewhere.

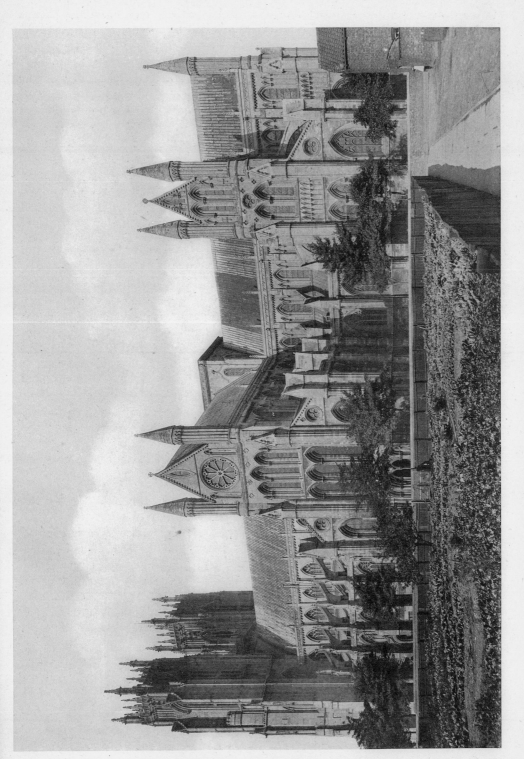

BEVERLEY MINSTER FROM SOUTH.

and choir was separated from presbytery, presbytery from Saint's Chapel, Saint's Chapel from ambulatory, ambulatory from Lady Chapel, merely by a series of screens, whether of stone or wood ; and the east wall was filled with as many windows as possible, as at ELY (464) ; or was made all window, as in Lincoln presbytery. This simple arrangement solved both the lighting and the ritualistic problems. It was the final and definitive solution of the English cathedral builder ;

Lincoln, East Front.

and was the full and final break with Continental tradition ; a plan which made the later English cathedral and abbey church utterly dissimilar both within and without to the interiors and exteriors of the Gothic of the Ile de France. Externally, it is a plan which has much grandeur ; a roof of the unbroken height of that of the choirs of Ely or Lincoln, some 160 feet long, is imposing in the highest degree ; internally, it is ruined by destruction of the screens.

M

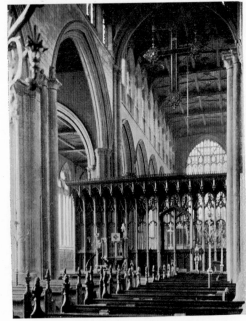

St Albans.   Rood Screen.
St Albans.   Reredos.

Lavenham.   Spring Pew.
Newark from S.W.

Like the Kirkstall and Oxford plans, it originated in the last half of the twelfth century. It is seen in the church attached to the Hospital of ST CROSS, Winchester (104), founded by Bishop Henry de Blois;* New Shoreham (*c.* 1175); Portsmouth (*c.* 1185); Boxgrove (*c.* 1235). But it was worked out on a far grander scale in the North, and probably independently of Southern Gothic, in the early years of the thirteenth century. Cistercian Byland had built a long choir, *c.* 1177, but with a rectangular ambulatory. Cistercian JERVAULX (153.3) and Benedictine Whitby followed with choirs without ambulatories. Early in the thirteenth century the Augustinian Canons of Hexham built a great choir of this plan. These were followed by the magnificent choir of Cistercian Rievaulx. All four choirs have full length aisles. The new plan soon re-appears in the Cistercian abbeys of the South of England, Netley, *c.* 1239, and Tintern, 1269; in the Benedictine Cathedral of ELY, *c.* 1235 (153.4); it produced the enormous choirs of Old St Paul's, London (dedicated in part in 1240), and the Angel choir of Lincoln, 1256, both of Secular Canons. The influence of the three choirs of Ely, Lincoln, and St Paul's must have been immense. We may add Thornton Abbey,† 1264; Ripon, Guisborough, and Selby (1280-1300); Howden and Carlisle, *c.* 1340; the magnificent choir of YORK (153.1), begun in 1361; and finally, Bath Abbey, *c.* 1500. The cruciform church of York, with full-length aisles on either side of nave, transepts and eastern limb, repre-sents the plan of the English cathedral in its complete and final form.

Southwell Choir from S.E.

SCREENS.

The number of screens which might occur in a church of the first rank was considerable. Of these the most important was the pulpitum. In the Early Christian basilicas there had been on either side an ambo or pulpit. Pairs of ambos are still retained in most of the Spanish cathedrals, *e.g.* Toledo and Burgos. In our mediæval churches the ambos were as it were connected by a broad platform, either end of which was used as an ambo for reading the Epistle and Gospel; sometimes it contained an altar; sometimes on it stood a pair of organs. This platform was reached by a staircase. The position of the pulpitum varied. If the stalls were in the nave, the solid pulpitum stood west of the stalls, and therefore some distance down the nave. The pulpitum remains in this position at Gloucester. But where the stalls were in the choir as in Lincoln and Southwell Minsters, Rochester, York, Ripon, Canterbury, the pulpitum was at the west end of the choir. The pulpitum had a central "quire door," leaving room for an altar on either side.

* The date of the Church of St Cross is uncertain; probably it belongs to the Bishop's later years; he was Bishop from 1129 to 1171.

† Plan in *A. A. Sketch Book,* 1872.

One bay west of the pulpitum, but this in monastic churches, was the rood screen. This also was surmounted by a platform or loft, in front of which stood the great Rood or Crucifix, with the attendant images of St Mary and St John. Sometimes the Rood rested on a separate beam, fixed a little above the loft.* Unlike the pulpitum, the rood screen had two side doors. This was for the two ranks of the Sunday procession. Between these doors was placed the altar of the laity, usually called the altar of the Holy Rood or of St Cross, or the Jesus

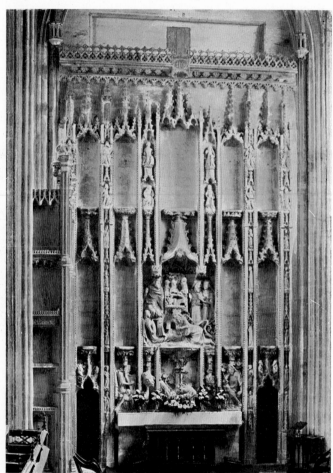

Christ Church, Hants.   Reredos.

altar. The rood screen still exists at ST ALBANS (178). The Jesus altar seems to have been protected by a wooden screen west of it, as at Dunstable.

East of the choir was the sanctuary or presbytery. At ST DAVID'S (162) is a low open screen of wood between choir and presbytery.†

At the east end of the presbytery was the high altar, behind which in later

---

* The sawn-off ends of the rood-beam may occasionally be seen. In the parish churches the rood-beam not infrequently remains ; *e.g.* at the east end of Knapton and Sall naves.

† There remain the supports of another at Michaelchurch, Hereford.

days there was often a reredos, which had two side doors in order to allow the priest to pass completely round the high altar while censing at High Mass. The reredos seems originally to have been low and inconspicuous, but in the fourteenth century at CHRIST CHURCH, Hants (180), and later at ST ALBANS (178), Winchester, and St Saviour's, Southwark, it became lofty and magnificent. The reredos or retablo is the special glory of the Spanish cathedrals.*

If there was a Saint's Chapel, as of St Alban at ST ALBANS (186), this also was fenced off to the east from the processional path and the eastern chapels by a screen, as it was to the west by the reredos of the high altar.

Finally, if there was an eastern Lady Chapel, this was separated from the processional path or ambulatory by a screen west of it, as at OTTERY ST MARY, Devon.

At YORK (153.1) the eastern limb consists of nine bays; which, counting from the east, were distributed as follows. The easternmost bay was the Lady Chapel. This was separated by a screen from the ambulatory, to which two bays were

assigned. The ambulatory was separated by a screen from the Saint's Chapel, that of St William of York, which occupied one bay. Then came the existing reredos screen east of the presbytery, which occupied two bays. West of the presbytery was the choir, occupying three bays, and screened off from the nave by the still existing pulpitum.

It should be added that the sides also of the choir and sanctuary were guarded with screens. In the parish churches, *e.g.* LYNN ST MARGARET (162), Collumpton,

Ottery St Mary, Lady Chapel.

SUDBURY ST PETER (162), these side or parclose screens were usually of oak. In the greater churches, as at Canterbury, Selby, Exeter, Winchester, they were often of stone.

None of the larger screens in England or in France are earlier than the thirteenth century; and from this Viollet-le-Duc drew the conclusion that the

---

* On the Reredos see paper by Mr T. Garner in *Assoc. Societies' Reports*, xvi. 136.

† See Willis' *York*, Plan 5. It should be noted that the screen at the entrance of a parochial chancel corresponds both to the pulpitum and the rood screen of the monastic churches; it often carried the rood, and was also used to put lights on. Many of these chancel screens survive; especially in East Anglia, Devon, and West Somerset, and the Welsh Border. Usually they are of oak, as at NEWARK (178); but occasionally of stone; *e.g.* at Compton Bassett, Wilts. (Illustrated in Weale's *Quarterly Papers*, vol. i.) On either side of the central door, if there were no aisles, there was an altar. Recesses for these side altars, one Norman, the other Early English, remain at CASTLE RISING (162). At Ranworth the painted wooden reredoses of the side altars remain. On the Devonshire screens, see Mr F. Bligh Bond's illustrated paper in *Transactions of Devonshire Association*, 1902. Some hundred and fifty screens remain in Devon.

thirteenth-century cathedral differed from the older monastic type in being laic;* in having no barrier between priest and layman; an idea which has

Abbey Dore from East.

been carried out in several modern French restorations. From the first, however, low screen walls doubtless surrounded choir and sanctuary. At Ely, indeed, the original Norman pulpitum forming the western termination of the choir was still standing in 1757.† It occupied the whole of the eastern-most bay of the present nave; so that there was one bay east of it before the construction of the present octagonal crossing. Moreover the monk Gervase, describing what he had seen before the fire of 1174 at Canter-bury, says that "at the base of the pillars was a wall of marble slabs; which, surrounding Ernulph's choir and presbytery (built 1096-1115), divided the church from its sides, which are called *alae*."

Chantry chapels, and later, family pews, *e.g.* that of the Spring family at LAVENHAM (178), were also screened off. The eastern bay of each aisle of the nave was almost always screened off as a chapel, with an altar of its own, which, in the unaisled church, had stood in each eastern corner of the nave.

* "Viollet-le-Duc tried to explain the appearance of Gothic by the substitution of laymen for monks in the direction of architectural work, by the triumph of the laic over the monastic spirit. It is a figment" (Comte de Lasteyrie, *Discours*, 14).

† Willis' *Canterbury*, 43; and Stewart's *Ely*, 43.

CHAPTER X.

PLANNING OF THE GREATER CHURCHES.

Ritualistic Divisions of Church—Length and Position of Choir—Saint's Chapel—
Eastern Transept—Crypt.

IT has been shown how the various ritualistic divisions of the church were marked off by screens. In the earlier work the architecture itself sometimes kept distinct the ritualistic divisions of the greater churches: as is well seen at Winchester and ST ALBANS (153.2). In the latter, first, from the west, comes the nave, occupying ten bays ; the tenth forming the sanctuary of the Jesus altar. The remaining bays of the nave, together with the crossing, formed the choir * of the monks. Then, east of the central tower, three bays formed the sanctuary of the high altar ; at the back of this is the great stone reredos. Behind this reredos is the Saint's Chapel or Feretory, containing the shrine of the great local saint ; that of St Alban at St Albans ; of St Swithin at Winchester ; of St Thomas the Martyr at Canterbury ; of St Cuthbert at Durham ; of St Werburgh at Chester.† Next comes the ambulatory. Beyond that, architecturally distinct, comes the projecting Lady Chapel.

These then were the divisions marked out either by stones and mortar or by screens in a great mediæval church. It remains to treat of each in order. First we will turn to the choir.

THE CHOIR.

In the earliest Christian churches, e.g. ST MARIA MAGGIORE (148.2), there were but two parts, a nave and sanctuary ; there was no architectural choir. The sanctuary occupied the apse, and the apse was joined immediately to the nave ; or, in the double-aisled basilicas of the fourth century, such as those of St Peter and of St Paul at Rome, to the transept ; there was no interposition of a choir between nave and apse. The choir was simply the east part of the nave, and was fenced off by low walls, usually of marble, carved or perforated with interlacing patterns, peacocks (the symbol of immortality), lions, doves, &c. Many specimens of these screen-walls remain, e.g. in S. Vitale, Ravenna, and Ancona Cathedral.‡ This arrangement is well seen in S. Clemente, Rome ; as rebuilt in 1108 with the material of the underground basilica demolished by the Norman, Robert Guiscard, in 1084.

* " Since the close of the seventeenth century *quire* has been fictitiously spelt *choir ;* but the spelling *quire* has never been altered in the English Prayer Book " (*New English Dictionary*).

† At St David's, Rochester, and Oxford Cathedrals, the shrines of the local saints were placed north of the choir.

‡ These walls were called *cancelli ;* hence our English word " chancel."

But in all the larger mediæval churches a choir is interposed between presbytery and nave.* Such a choir is clearly seen in the ninth-century plans of ST GALL (194), and of Notre Dame de la Couture, Mans.† In the earlier churches of Normandy, such as Bernay and CÉRISY (148.3), it is but short ; only two bays. St Stephen's, Caen ; Lanfranc's Canterbury ; Selby and Lincoln resembled Cérisy in having choirs of two bays. But the greater part of our eleventh-century cathedrals and abbeys set out choirs with more bays ; usually with four : e.g. BURY (150.3) ; St Augustine's, Canterbury ; DURHAM (149.1) ; Ely ; Peterborough ; St Albans ; WINCHESTER (192.5) ; NORWICH (148.4). And, as all the above were Benedictine, and the monks usually sat in the crossing or the eastern nave, the apsidal eastern limb of some four bays provided a very dignified presbytery ; occupied only by the high altar, and entered only by the priest and his attendants officiating at the Mass.

Lanfranc's choir at Canterbury, of two bays, was a very unworthy sanctuary of a church which was at once the chapel of a large Benedictine monastery and the church of an Archbishop and Primate. It was completed in 1077 ; but in 1096, only nineteen years after, Prior Ernulph commenced to build a new eastern limb (149.2), vast in scale, and with all the latest improvements in planning, such as were to be seen already at Gloucester and Cluny. It contained an apse and a choir of no less than nine bays ; and must have been at the time by far the longest choir in Western Christendom; even surpassing Cluny, whose enlarged and remodelled choir had been consecrated the previous year. The chief reason for this great eastern extension no doubt was that the monks were very much cramped in Lanfranc's short nave of nine bays. How short it was in comparison with other Norman naves in the South and East of England may be seen from the following table :—

Canterbury St Augustine's	-	11 bays	Ely -	-	-	-	13 bays
Peterborough	-	-	11 „	St Albans -	-	-	13 „
Bury	-	-	12 „	Norwich -	-	-	14 „
Winchester -	-	-	12 „				

while Bury, Ely, and Peterborough had western transepts in addition. It was impossible to extend Lanfranc's nave to the west ; for the new western towers were in the way; the only extension possible was eastward. Ernulph's vast choir of Canterbury, half choir proper, half sanctuary, turned the current of English planning. After this, with the exception of plans of foreign extraction, such as those of the earliest Cistercian churches, e.g. Kirkstall and the French plan of Westminster, the eastern limb of the English church was of vast length. The new position of the clergy east, instead of west, of the eastern arch of the central tower, was recommended not only by convenience of accommodation, but by the enhanced dignity which it gave to the monks and canons. Nevertheless there had been no alteration in the relative position of the clergy and the altar. In the earliest Christian churches the altar had been placed at the west end. The clergy, therefore, as at S. CLEMENTE, Rome (3), in order to face east, had to be seated west of the altar.

* A choir of one or more bays was not interposed in front of the apse till c. 900 (Quicherat and Comte Robert de Lasteyrie).
† Dehio, Plate 119, 7 and 7A.

When it became customary to place the altar at the east end, the clergy retained their seats west of the altar. The position of the altar was changed, not that of the clergy.

Hardly was Ernulph's choir rebuilt when Glastonbury built a choir of six bays (1186); to be enlarged to eight bays in the fourteenth century. Where the naves were exceptionally long, as at NORWICH (148.4), Peterborough, ELY (153.4), ST ALBANS (153.2); or where the choirs were short, as in the early Cistercian churches, the Benedictine abbeys of GLOUCESTER (135) and WEST-MINSTER (151.2), and the cathedrals of the Secular Canons of Chichester and Hereford, the stalls were allowed to remain in the east nave; or in the crossing and east nave; or else in the crossing and west choir. But in by far the greater number of churches, no matter by whom served, the stalls were placed in new choirs which were built in Gothic. This was especially so with Canons' churches. In the end we find nearly all the Canons, Secular or Regular, housed in new Gothic choirs: Augustinian Canons in the thirteenth century at Hexham, Southwark, Thornton, Carlisle, and Guisborough; in the fourteenth century at Bristol; in the fifteenth century at Christchurch; Secular Canons in the twelfth century at York; in the thirteenth century at Wells, Lincoln, Lichfield, Salisbury, St Paul's, Exeter; all seven cathedrals. In collegiate churches, the Secular Canons enlarged or built choirs in the twelfth century at Ripon; in the thirteenth at Beverley and Southwell; in the fourteenth at Howden. The example of the canons was largely followed by the monks also. Even the Cistercians built long Gothic choirs at Rievaulx, Fountains, and Tintern; and the Benedictines at Canterbury; Glastonbury; Rochester; Worcester; Whitby; Boxgrove; St Werburgh, Chester; Pershore; and Selby. Many others might be named. Enough have been enumerated to show how widespread was the tendency to remove the stalls eastward; a tendency which was to make the elongated eastern limb of the greater English churches so strikingly dissimilar to such plans as those of Amiens and Westminster, and to constitute one of the most marked differences between English and Continental Gothic architecture.

SAINT'S CHAPEL.

We have seen that it was at Canterbury in 1096 that the great prolongation of the eastern limb * commenced. Strangely enough, it was Canterbury that was to set an example of yet further prolongation eastward. For when the great

---

* There is much ambiguity about the terms *Choir* and *Presbytery.* Strictly speaking, the *Choir* is that part of the church where are the stalls of the clergy. (1) As these stalls may be in the east nave, *e.g.* at Westminster, it may occur that no part of the choir is in the eastern limb. (2) If the stalls are in the eastern limb, the choir will occupy its western bays; *i.e.* the space between the crossing and the sanctuary; *e.g.* at Canterbury. But (3) the term Choir is also used loosely of the whole of the eastern limb; including choir proper, sanctuary, retro-choir, &c.

The *Presbytery* (1) is the space between the choir and high altar. It was raised on steps, *gradus presbyterii;* and there were doors from it into the north and south aisles, *ostia presby-terii.* (2) But the term is also used loosely of all the space in an eastern limb between the choir and the eastern wall; *e.g.* at Ely, Lincoln, and York. (In non-collegiate churches the eastern limb is called the *Chancel,* the eastern portion of which is the presbytery or sanctuary.)

choir of nine bays built by Priors Ernulph and Conrad between 1096 and 1115
was burnt down, instead of its central eastern apse there were constructed four
more bays eastward. But this prolongation was not made for the same reason as
before. It was not to provide more accommodation for the monks; they had room
enough. It was to provide east of the high altar space for the shrine of the great
local saint, St Thomas the archbishop, martyred in 1170, and now the most famous
saint in Western Christendom. After the murder, following an ancient usage
which goes back as far as the burial of the bodies of the first Christian martyrs
in the catacombs of Rome, the archbishop's remains had been deposited below in
the crypt. But they were resorted to, for their miraculous powers, by thousands

Saint's Chapel, St Albans.

and tens of thousands of pilgrims. Ernulph's crypt was vast, and had escaped
damage by the fire; but even this great crypt was inadequate to accommodate
the multitudes who desired to pass round the shrine, to touch if it might be the
sacred relics, and to say one prayer before them. It was determined, therefore,
to remove the relics from the crypt, and to build a Saint's Chapel or Feretory
for them east of the high altar. Into this Saint's Chapel,* which at Canterbury
has usurped the name of the older Trinity Chapel, in which St Thomas had been
used to officiate, the body of the martyr was removed, and was deposited in a

---

* Mr St John Hope has shown that the so-called Trinity Chapel was the Chapel of St
Thomas, and that the Corona was the Trinity Chapel, and was designated "Trinity Chapel
ad coronam."

Pontigny.
Hereford.

Pontigny.
St David's.

magnificent shrine, amid a concourse of kings, princes, and ecclesiastical digni-
taries from all over Western Europe.   This shrine has utterly vanished ; but we
have considerable remains of others ; but, except at Westminster, of the pedestal
only.   The other shrines, which were usually of wood, were broken up in all cases
for their jewels, gold, and silver, by the commissioners of Henry VIII.   The
most important of these pedestals are those of St David at St David's, thirteenth
century ; of Edward the Confessor at Westminster, 1269 ; of Thomas Cantilupe at
HEREFORD (187) and St Frideswide at Oxford, both *c.* 1290 ; of St Alban at ST
ALBANS,* 1302-1308 (186); of St Etheldreda at Ely† and St Werburgh at Chester,
both *c.* 1340.   We may reconstruct, to some extent, the appearance of these
shrines by visiting PONTIGNY (187), between Sens and Auxerre, the largest
of the Cistercian churches in Europe.   Here there is a shrine to Edmund Rich,
Archbishop of Canterbury, who died near PONTIGNY (187) in 1240.   His body
began to work miracles, and he was canonised in 1246.   The shrine, a work of the
eighteenth century, stands considerably back from the high altar, and towers much
above it.   So must our English shrines have looked, elevated on high, behind and
above the high altar, conspicuous far down the church.   At the back of St Edmé's
shrine are the staircases by which the pilgrims ascend to and descend.   In
the shrine of ST DAVID (187) are holes through which the pilgrim could insert
a diseased limb for healing.   At Westminster a still more ancient Pagan and
Christian custom survived ; for in the shrine of Edward the Confessor‡ there
are niches in which the sick were left for the night in hope of cure.

From Canterbury the new fashion passed in a few years to Chichester ;
where, after a great fire, a retrochoir was added in 1186.   Here in later days
stood the shrine of St Richard (died 1253) ; a harper used to play and sing the
praises of the saint.§

EASTERN TRANSEPT.

Yet another change was made to increase the convenience of the eastern
limb.   It was the addition of an eastern or choir transept.   For the third time
it was Ernulph's CANTERBURY that led the way.   But (149.2) in Ernulph's
choir the pier-arches ran right across its entrances ; so that, internally, it was
a masked transept.‖   This peculiarity seems to connect it with the transeptal
basilicas of Rome, *e.g.* St Paul extra muros and Sta Prassede, rather than with
the eastern transepts of Cluny, St Benoît-sur-Loire, or Souvigny.   This eastern
transept of Ernulph was rebuilt by William of Sens in 1180, with the omission
of the pier and two arches which had previously masked each of its arms.   To
the east of each arm he built two semicircular apses.   His eastern transept was

* On the right of the photograph of the Saint's Chapel at St Albans is a glimpse of part of
the three narrow arches leading eastward to the ambulatory ; in the foreground is the pedestal
of St Alban's shrine ; to the left is the Watching-Loft ; and, above it, an arch leading into the
north aisle.
    † For this pedestal see Index of Illustrations.
    ‡ See article and illustrations by W. Burges in Scott's *Gleanings*, page 127.   In a woodcut
on page 136 a sick person is seen crawling into the pedestal of the Confessor's shrine.
    § Rev. T. Hugo.
    ‖ So also probably at Exeter ; see Professor Lethaby's plan of Norman Exeter in
Architectural Review, April 1903.

copied, apses and all, in St Hugh's choir at LINCOLN (151.1) in 1192. Simultaneously with Ernulph's work at Canterbury, there was going on a great remodelling of the eastern limb of Lewes,* 1091-1098. Lewes was a daughter-church of CLUNY (150.1), and copied not only the eastern transept with eastern apse, but also the five tangential chapels of Cluny; elsewhere English Romanesque was content with three. About 1200, eastern transepts were set out by the Benedictines of Rochester and Worcester, which show much similarity in the plan of the eastern limbs; and by Secular Canons in 1220 at SALISBURY (154.2), and a little later at BEVERLEY MINSTER (152.1). The Rochester plan also appears *c.* 1300 in the Premonstratensian church of Bayham, Sussex. In all these cases the transepts rose to the full height of the choir, and were invaluable both for internal and external effect. Internally they added shadowy recesses and half-seen, mysterious distances. Externally they were of the very greatest value in breaking up the exceptionally long, monotonous horizontal lines of the elongated choirs of English Gothic.

Elsewhere the choir transept took a humbler form; it was satisfied to be a projection to north and south, not of the choir, but of the choir aisles. Judging from the foundations in the crypt, something of the sort had been built by Archbishop Roger at YORK (199), *c.* 1160. And even when his choir was demolished and rebuilt, *c.* 1361, this secondary type of eastern transept was preserved, and adds immensely both to the external and internal effect of the long Perpendicular choir. So also at SOUTHWELL, *c.* 1230 (152.2), at EXETER, *c.* 1280 (154.4), and at WELLS, *c.* 1340 (154.3), low eastern transepts were thrown out from the aisles of the choirs.

Two noteworthy departures were made in the setting out of the new eastern transept. At FOUNTAINS † (150.2) it was placed not across the choir but to the extreme east of it. This disposition was copied a few years later at Durham. In both, the eastern transept goes by the name of the Chapel of the Nine Altars; a name which sufficiently explains its destination.

As we have seen, it was at St Benoît-sur-Loire, Cluny, and Souvigny that the eastern transept first appeared. It is strange that, with a few exceptions, such as Verdun, Besançon, and St Quentin, it found no welcome in the later Romanesque or in the Gothic of France. It appears sporadically elsewhere; *e.g.* at Nivelles, Ferrara, and Milan; and in the Liebfrauenkirchen at Trèves. But in the thirteenth-century Gothic of England it is one of the noblest and most characteristic features. Even in English Gothic, however, its reign was short. In its grandest form, at full height, it commences at Lincoln in 1192, and, with the exception of Bayham, ceases *c.* 1240.

What was the object of this choir transept? Probably, as the apses and aisles on the eastern side show, it was to provide more altared chapels; each apse or bay of the aisle serving as a choir, and the central space of the transept as a nave. At Rochester, however, the north transept was certainly appropriated from the first for the shrine of the local saint, a Scotch baker, William of Perth, who was murdered near Rochester in 1201, and buried in the

* See plan in Mr St John Hope's paper read to Royal Archæological Institute, Aug. 1, 1883.

† At Fountains it was finished in 1247.

cathedral "*miraculis choruscando*," "amid a coruscation of miracles." *   No
doubt the offerings at his shrine helped to pay for the great eastern extension at
Rochester.

THE CRYPT.

Beneath several of our choirs is a crypt.   The crypt has a long and venerable history, which goes back to the early days of Christianity at Rome.   Both the
Jew and the Christian were treated, on the whole, with much toleration at Rome ;
in spite of brief periods of persecution, such as that of Decius, 249 to 251 A.D.,
and that of Diocletian, 303 A.D.   They were allowed to form Burial Clubs, like
the Romans themselves ; they were at liberty to have cemeteries of their own ;
and to dispose of their dead as they thought fit.   The only restriction imposed
was that no one, Pagan, Jew, or Christian, might bury within the city.   Even
before the introduction of Christianity, the Jews had cemeteries in the catacombs
of the Roman suburbs.   The Christians followed the Jewish mode of burial, not
employing cremation, the general practice in Pagan Rome.   Now in the suburbs
of Rome there is a variety of volcanic deposits ; one of sand, which gives the
pozzolana pura, of which the famous Roman mortar was made ; another, the *tufa
litoide*, a very hard building stone ; a third, the *tufa granolare*, not so hard as
the last, nor so soft and crumbling as the first.   This stratum was worked just
as coal nowadays, or Caen stone.   Shafts were sunk, which afterwards served
both as staircases and air-holes ; and when the *tufa granolare* was reached, horizontal galleries were driven all round the area of the proposed cemetery ; and,
later, cross-galleries as well.   In the walls of these galleries, which were usually
only 2½ ft. to 3 ft. wide, were cut horizontal niches, much like the tiers of berths
in a ship's cabin ; each usually holding a single corpse.   Such a niche was called
a *locus ;* nowadays it is designated *loculus*.   In the case of richer people a solid
stone coffin was excavated out of the side of the gallery, closed with a horizontal
slab ; and an arch was hollowed out above it ; this is an *arcisolium*.   But in the
case of still more important personages, chambers, *cubicula*, were hewn out of the
rock at right angles to the gallery, arranged like the bedrooms leading out of an
hotel corridor.   Opposite the entrance of such a *cubiculum* was the rectangular
raised tomb ; a sarcophagus of solid rock, closed with a stone slab.   This slab or
mensa was used as an altar.   Prudentius, towards the end of the fourth century,
says, "The same table gives the Sacrament, and is the faithful guardian of the
bones of the martyr (Hippolytus) ; which it keeps laid up there in expectation of
the Eternal Judge, while it feeds the dwellers on the Tiber with holy food."   The
cubiculum or burial-chamber of such a martyr was called a *Confessio*, where lay
one who had confessed and given witness to his faith by his blood.†   It is
improbable that these *cubicula* were used for purpose of worship, except for the
Eucharistic service on each anniversary of the burial.   But from *c.* 350 the graves
of the martyrs in the catacombs received much attention.   The Bishops of Rome,
especially Damasus, had the more important graves marked by inscriptions,
improved the means of access, and constructed shafts to light and ventilate the

---

* Hope's *Rochester*, 40.

† The term "Martyrdom," applied to the north transept at Canterbury, is an exact
equivalent to "Confessio."

cubicula. For one or two centuries they were greatly frequented by pilgrims from all Christendom. St Jerome says that when he was a boy, *c.* 364 A.D., he used to go to the catacombs every Sunday, "to visit the tombs of the Apostles and martyrs, and to go into the *crypts* there excavated in the bowels of the earth."

What was done at Rome set a precedent for Christendom in general. At Rome the graves of the martyrs had not been dug in the surface soil, but deep down in a subterranean gallery. Outside Rome, therefore, where there was no subterranean gallery, churches, which possessed distinguished martyrs, built crypts, that should be reminiscent of the *cubiculum* or *confessio* of the Roman catacombs. There is an early example at Ravenna at S. Apollinare in Classe; A.D. 534. At first these were sometimes as deep sunk as the Roman "cubicula" themselves; *e.g.* at St Germain, Auxerre, and at Chartres Cathedral. Or, they they were but partly above ground, and were lighted by small windows placed in their side walls; *e.g.* Ernulph's crypt at Canterbury. Occasionally their floor was but little below the surface of the ground, as in the eastern crypt at Canterbury; or was even on a level with the pavement of the nave, as in S. Miniato, Florence. In these latter cases the crypt practically became a second or lower church; *e.g.* St Faith's, under Old St Paul's, London. Such a crypt, however, entailed a raised choir; hence it is that one ascends high flights of steps to such choirs as those of S. Miniato; Rochester; and Canterbury.*

That the connection of the mediæval crypt † with the early Christian "confessio" is no mere fancy is clear from the words of Edward the Chanter (quoted by the monk Gervase; see Willis' *Canterbury*), who expressly says that the crypt under the Anglo-Saxon Cathedral of Canterbury was copied from the Confessio of St Peter at Rome; "*ad instar confessionis Sancti Petri fabricata.*"

In our own country we have two examples undoubtedly of the seventh century; the crypts at Ripon and Hexham,‡ both built by Wilfrid between 671 and 678. Another, later than these, occurs at Wing, in Buckinghamshire; with an archaic barrel-vault, possibly added later. All three consist of a walled *cubiculum*, with a gallery round; not on one side only, as in a Roman catacomb. Originally, probably, they had separate entrances and exits § on either side of the chancel arch. Later still, but yet Anglo-Saxon, is the pillared crypt of Repton; from which it is but a short transition to the eleventh-century Norman crypts of Lastingham, WINCHESTER (192.5), WORCESTER (192.2), Rochester, GLOUCESTER (192.1); CANTERBURY (193); which latter was again lengthened after the fire of 1174; and to the twelfth-century crypts of St Peter in the East, Oxford; and York Minster. ‖

With such a long pedigree, Roman, Gaulish, and Anglo-Saxon, it is a little

---

* S. Apollinare in Classe had a crypt and raised choir from the sixth century.

† St Jerome used the terms "crypt" and "catacombs" as synonymous in the passage quoted above.

‡ On the Anglo-Saxon crypts see Baldwin Brown's *Arts in Early England*, ii. 263 *seq.*

§ *Cf.* the crypts of St Peter in the East, Oxford; and Madley.

‖ The latter is of various dates; some of it built with re-used material. See plan in *Builder Cathedrals*.

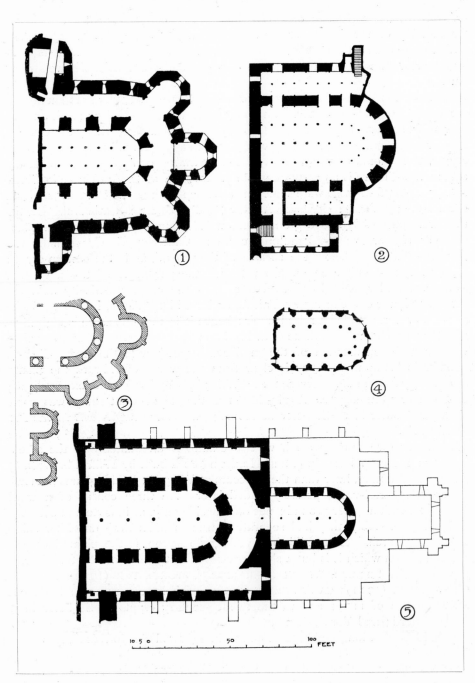

CRYPTS.

1. Gloucester.   4. St John's Chapel, Tower of London.
2. Worcester.   3. St Martin de Tours.   5. Winchester.

surprising that the crypt did not come into still more general use. Most of our churches, however, whether great or small, have no crypt and never had. It might be thought that it was where there were no relics buried of a famous local saint that the crypt was omitted. But in many churches where the local saint, *e.g.* St Etheldreda, St Cuthbert, St Alban, was held in the highest repute, there was never a crypt. Nor does the objection to building deep down in a watery soil explain the omission ; for the cathedrals of Ely, Durham, St Albans all stand high ; whereas the crypt of Winchester Cathedral is below the level

Canterbury Crypt.

of the neighbouring stream. It may be that the omission and disuse of the crypt were largely due to Cluniac example.*

In the end, probably because the number of pilgrims to the more noted shrines, *e.g.* to that of St Thomas the Martyr at Canterbury, passed beyond what even the very largest crypts could contain, the more important shrines were removed from the crypt and placed on the pavement of the presbytery, behind and above the high altar ; in such a position as is seen in PONTIGNY (187). Thus at Canterbury the body of St Thomas was translated to the chapel above in 1220, after lying in the crypt for fifty years. So in France Abbot Suger had

* Dehio remarks that the omission of the crypt was especially characteristic of the Cluniac churches.

translated the body of St Denis and his two companions in 1144 from the crypt of St Denis. The crypts, therefore, deserted by the great saints, lost their value, and no more were built; except in later days the crypt of the present St Paul's, destined to receive the remains of great generals and admirals.

In addition to the above there were others of quite different purpose. Some were merely constructional; *e.g.* in France at Bourges the east end of the cathedral, and at Madley * in Herefordshire the fourteenth-century east end of the church, were built on steep declivities; and the substructures necessarily took the form of crypts. Moreover, it was not uncommon to excavate an Ossuary or Golgotha. One remains at Norwich, a little west of the cathedral; formerly there was one north of Worcester Cathedral; the crypt at Hereford may be a Golgotha. That at Hythe till lately was filled with bones. Both at Hythe, however, and at Wimborne Minster, the crypt may be but a subway to give communication between the choir aisles without crossing the sanctuary.

* But here no doubt, as often elsewhere, a crypt, constructional in origin, was utilised for ritualistic purposes.

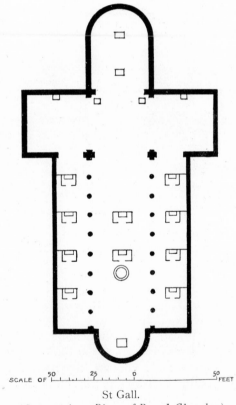

SCALE OF 50 25 0   50 FEET

St Gall.
(*Same scale as Plans of Parish Churches.*)

Chapter XI.

THE CENTRAL TRANSEPT.

Early Transepts—Position and Object of Central Transept—Enlargement of Transept.

ALL the greater churches in Normandy and England, and many of the smaller,* seem to have been cruciform ; *i.e.* the nave and choir, which ran east and west, were crossed by another arm running north and south ; the intersection of the four arms is what is called the "crossing." † The "crossing" is generally covered with a central tower. This sometimes was low ; *e.g.* Winchester Cathedral ; but often rose to a great height, and was richly ornamented ; *e.g.* at St Albans, Tewkesbury, Castor, Norwich. The question naturally arises, " Was the central tower anterior to the transept, or the transept to the central tower ? " It has been argued that the four walls of a central tower rest on four arches, which again, in the larger churches, rest not on solid walls, but on piers. Now these arches, loaded with the weight of the tower walls, exercise enormous thrusts. To the west and east these thrusts are met by the walls or by the piers and arches on either side of nave and choir. But to the north and south they would have no abutment if there were no transept. It therefore would seem that the transept is but a structural necessity due to the pre-existence of a central tower.

Chronologically, the very reverse is the case. Transepts occur many centuries before central towers. They appear in all the double-aisled basilicas of Rome in the fourth century of our era. The basilica at SILCHESTER (215.1), ‡ which is very much like a church in plan, has a transept ; it cannot be later than the end of the Roman occupation of Britain. There still exist in Syria the remains of the immense cruciform church of St Simeon Stylites,§ built between 459 and 560. At Como, beneath the present eleventh-century church of St Abbondio, ‖ there have been found the complete foundations of a church with an apse attached almost directly to the transept ; it is held to be of the fifth century. At St Denis, as at Como, the church was originally a *crux com-*

---

* *E.g.* our Pre-Conquest churches of Deerhurst ; Worth ; and St Mary's in Dover Castle ; and such Norman churches as North Newbald, Yorkshire ; St Martha's Chapel, Guildford ; Melbourne ; St John, Devizes ; Hemel Hempstead.

† The term " transept " is used indifferently either of the whole arm or of the part which projects from the crossing, north or south. In French the former is termed " transept," the latter " croisillon."

‡ The plan of Jataghan, an early Christian church in Asia Minor, is very similar to that of Silchester. It is shown in Lethaby's *Mediæval Art*, 25. Compare also the plan of S. Maria Antiqua in the Roman Forum.

§ Plan in Scott's *Essay*, 60.

‖ See De Dartein, 312 ; Beito's monograph, Milan, 1868 ; and plan in Dehio, Plate 66.

missa, not a Latin cross, *crux immissa ; i.e.* as in the Constantinian basilicas, the apse was attached directly to the transept without the interposition of a choir : this Viollet-le-Duc assigns to the sixth century ; * Professor Baldwin Brown gives the date of 628.† In the sixth century the church which Namatius caused to be built at Clermont had a transept ; so also the predecessor of St Germain-des-Prés, and of St Martin de Tours,‡ which belong to the same period. The Spanish church of St John de Bonos, Palencia, has two small square transeptal projections opening opposite the east bay of the nave arcade ; it has an inscription set up in 661. In the ninth century the transept begins to be common ; *e.g.* in the plan of ST GALL (194) ; at Hersfeld ;§ at St Généroux ; where, as in our Pre-Conquest churches, the transepts are lower than the nave. Instances of small Anglo-Saxon transepts are given above ; and it is clear from the descriptions that have come down to us that some at any rate of their greater churches had central towers and transepts ; *e.g.* the church of Ramsey is described as having two towers, one western, the other " in the centre of the square, standing upon four columns connected by arches stretching from *ala* to *ala, i.e.* from transept to transept." This was written in the last half of the tenth century.‖ In France and Italy, however, transepts are exceedingly rare till the eleventh century. They seem to be a special mark of the German and Anglo-Saxon schools of Primitive Romanesque.

When, however, transepts were introduced, there arose at once a difficulty in the roofing of the church, where the span-roof of the transepts met the span-roofs of nave and choir ; a difficulty which was all the greater when the transepts and their roofs were lower than the nave and choir. The simplest remedy was to raise low walls on the four arches of the crossing, and to run all four roofs up to these four walls. This, then, is suggested¶ as the origin of the central tower ; and at the same time as the reason why, at first, in Norman churches at any rate, it was so low.

In England transepts were the rule from the first in the greater Norman churches. Their length was out of all proportion to the needs of northern and southern abutment to a central tower. Some of the internal lengths ** are :—

St Albans	-	175 feet.	Winchester	-	209 feet.
Ely	-	185 ,,	York	-	222 ,,
Peterborough	-	185 ,,	Lincoln	-	223 ,,
Reading	-	190 ,,	Bury	-	234 ,,
Glastonbury	-	192 ,,	Old St Paul's	-	300 ,,

In France, on the other hand, the transepts of some of the largest cathedrals do not exceed 150 feet ; *e.g.* Paris and Reims. And even at Amiens, where the transept is prolonged to nearly 200 feet, it projects but little beyond nave and choir, owing to the fact that the choir has double aisles and a ring of buttress-chapels, while the nave has a single aisle and buttress-

---

* Plan in Dehio, 42.   † *Builder*, Nov. 9, 1895.
‡ Enlart's *Manuel*, 122.   § Dehio, Plate 42.
‖ Scott's *Lectures*, ii. 33.   ¶ Enlart's *Manuel*, 123.
** Beckett, 376.

chapels. It is indeed owing to the utilisation * of the buttresses to form the side walls of chapels that the French Gothic cathedrals are able to dispense with the elongation of the transept, thus gaining great compactness in plan. These cathedrals are broader and far loftier than our own ; their vaults are proportionally far heavier ; and the thrusts of the vaults, transmitted over the aisle roofs by flying buttresses, have to be stopped by buttresses of excessive projection. Given such long thin buttresses, it was a short step to roof over each pair, providing thus an altared chapel. To such a scheme the comparatively small English buttresses did not so readily lend themselves. But there were as many saints to worship in England as in France, and as much need therefore of the multiplication of altared chapels. Not being able to utilise his buttresses,† the Englishman turned to his transepts, already much elongated, in order to find room for additional chapels. These he prolonged still further to north and south. The eastern sides of the long English transepts thus became fringed by a row of altared chapels. As late as St Mary Redcliffe, Bristol, this was the ritualistic use of the transept ; there it was built to hold four altars, two in each arm ; to St Catherine, St George, St Blaise, and All Souls.‡

For each one of the altars a sanctuary was needed ; the main body of the transepts serving as a nave where the worshippers stood or knelt. At first the sanctuary took the form of a little eastward-pointing apse. Usually there was one apse in each arm of the transept ; as at Notre Dame du Pré, Le Mans ; and Cérisy. This was the usual arrangement in England ; e.g. at Melbourne, GLOUCESTER (135) ; ROMSEY (151.3) ; Chichester ; Chester ; NORWICH (148.4) ; Lindisfarne ; Christ Church, Hants ; Tewkesbury ; Castle Acre ; Evesham. At Hereford the Norman south transept has a square sacristy instead of an apse. If the transept was long, there might be two apses in each arm, as at CLUNY (150.1) ; Canterbury, St Augustine's ; and ST ALBANS (98). But as early as 1079 WINCHESTER CATHEDRAL (154.1) was set out with an eastern aisle instead of eastern apses to its transepts ; and in 1083 ELY (153.4) ; and in 1093 DURHAM (149.1). This was a great improvement ; for in each of these three cathedrals it was now possible to get three eastern chapels instead of one or two apses in each arm of the transept. Peterborough, begun 1117, copied the Durham plan. This plan is characteristic also of the earlier Cistercian transepts here and

* In France the utilisation of the buttresses commenced with Notre Dame in 1290 : first, with the building of Saints' Chapels between the buttresses of the choir. Then, the shops which seem to have been allowed to be built and rented between the nave-buttresses were dislodged, and in their place family or chantry chapels were built : the whole range of chapels being finished to the west in 1320. The example of Notre Dame was followed in nearly all the northern Gothic cathedrals, except where the nave walls were exceptionally thick, as at Chartres and Reims ; or where the church was monastic, as St Ouen, Rouen. At Notre Dame, Paris ; Troyes ; and Amiens ; the chapels were added continuously, and according to a fixed and symmetrical plan. More often they were built intermittently, and different in area and design, as at Bourges.

† They were utilised, by exception, at Chichester, producing an additional outer aisle on either side of the nave. Cf. the chantries of Bishops Russell and Longland at Lincoln ; Bishop Audley's at Hereford ; and the chapels between the buttresses of Eton and KING'S COLLEGE chapels (199).

‡ Norris, 37.

abroad; * *e.g.* KIRKSTALL (152.4) and Roche; and of Ripon Minster (Secular Canons). In Gothic it was reproduced at LINCOLN (151.1), Whitby, Lichfield, Hereford (north transept), Selby, Howden. Such transepts, with eastern aisles only, are rare in France; nearly all the larger cathedrals have both eastern and western aisles. Lisieux, however, has eastern aisles only. A further step is seen at Winchester and Ely, where the Norman transepts have both eastern and western aisles. It is remarkable to find such complication of plan so early in Anglo-Norman work; it shows how very rapidly the builders on this side of the Channel left behind the precedents of the Normandy abbeys. Even in Gothic days but few of our abbeys or minsters indulged in the luxury of a double-aisled transept: Old St Paul's; the Cistercian Abbey of Byland, *c.* 1170; BEVERLEY (152.1) and YORK, *c.* 1240 (153.1); WESTMINSTER, 1245 (north arm only; 151.2); Chester, *c.* 1330 (south arm only) are the chief. It is found also in a few parochial or collegiate churches; *e.g.* Faversham; PATRINGTON (215.11); St Mary Redcliffe, Bristol. BURY (150.3) had both an eastern aisle and an apse in each transept arm. Glastonbury had two aisles,† both on the eastern side of the transept. The Gothic Cathedral of Rouen, which is curiously Romanesque in plan, has a double-aisled transept; and from each eastern aisle projects an elongated eastern apse. Where a western aisle was built to a transept, it could not have been very serviceable for worship. If the altar were placed to the west, there would be room for the congregation, but the altar would point in the wrong direction. If, on the other hand, the altar were placed under the arches between the western aisle and the transept, it would point correctly to the east, but there would be very little space for the congregation. In later days this western aisle was utilised to provide sacristies or vestries; as it does to this day in the south transepts of Peterborough and Ely and Winchester; and in the north transept of Wells.

Of all our transepts, those of Ely and WINCHESTER (154.1), built by two Norman brothers, were set out on the most magnificent scale. They not only had eastern and western, but return or end aisles as well. These existed also at CÉRISY (199); at St George's de Boscherville; at St Stephen and St Nicholas, Caen; and in Lanfranc's Canterbury. Gervase, the monk, lets us see the purpose of these north and south aisles in the transepts of Lanfranc's Canterbury. For he tells us that in the upper part of the eastern apse of the south transept there was the altar of All Saints; and in that of the north transept that of St Blasius. Thus the return aisle provided a means of access to these altars. Moreover, he says, the vault of the south aisle of the south transept carried an organ.‡ Another object may have been to provide continuous communication between the triforiums of the nave and choir.§ Winchester retains the original aisles; at ELY (506) they have been set back nearer to the end walls of the

---

* But in the early Cistercian churches, such as Kirkstall and Pontigny, there is no continuous aisle; the eastern chapels being completely separated by solid walls.

† The eastern of these was divided up, in Kirkstall fashion, into separate chapels.

‡ Willis' *Canterbury*, 39.

§ M. Besnard is of opinion that at St George's de Boscherville these transeptal galleries were employed for the exposition of relics, which were placed on a beam extending from the east to the west wall of the transept above the gallery (*Monographie de St George's de Boscherville*, 54).

York Choir.
Lincoln South Transept.

King's College Chapel.
Cérisy South Transept.

transepts. It is curious that a return aisle occurs also in the north arm of the eastern transept of Lincoln; and perhaps formerly in the south arm also. Even in Gothic days no further development of the transept obtained than that which had been reached at Winchester in 1079. Indeed many of the Gothic transepts were built on Norman foundations; and, as at Canterbury, remained aisleless, with merely the substitution of rectangular for apsidal eastern chapels.

Between the chapels of the transeptal aisles there were originally solid walls; such as still remain in the north transept of Ely, in the Cistercian transept of Kirkstall; later on, only low walls were employed; as at Abbey Dore and Lincoln; later still, they were usually separated merely by screens. Screens also were interposed between each chapel and the transept.

CHAPTER XII.

The Nave—Narthex—Galilee—Western Transept—Porch—Chantry Chapel.

As we have seen, the basilican prototype of the mediæval minster usually had aisles. Here and there, however, churches, even of great scale, were aisleless; e.g. the so-called basilica of Trèves,* which still stands. Of aisleless naves there were originally many in England; especially in the churches of the Secular and the Regular Canons. Of the former the nave built by Archbishop Roger at Ripon (1154-1181) was one of the most remarkable; it was 40 feet across; † but aisles were added in 1502. On the south or north side of the naves of the churches of the Regular Canons, on the other hand, there was a cloister; so that an aisle was only added on the opposite side of the nave to the cloister; e.g. at Brinkburn, Dorchester, Easby, Kirkham, Lanercost. Some naves, like those of Bayham and Lilleshall, remained without aisles to the last. The great peculiarity of the Anglo-Norman nave was the enormous length which it reached in such examples as Winchester, Norwich, Ely, Peterborough, and St Albans.

In front of some of the largest of the early Christian churches, such as OLD ST PETER'S (147) at Rome in the fourth century, and S. Sophia, Constantinople, in the sixth century, was a quadrangle with colonnaded walks on its four sides; what is called an *atrium*. It formed a grateful transition from the noise and glare of the streets and the outer world to the stillness and seclusion of the Christian church. In it were gathered together reminiscences of more than one type of building familiar to the early Christians. There was the great outer court of the Gentiles, which preceded Solomon's temple at Jerusalem. At Rome too, in front of such great secular basilicas as that of Trajan, there was often a square with covered colonnades all round. And in the great mansions of the Roman aristocracy, where ten generations of the Christians at Rome had worshipped, there was a threefold division; first, on entering, a court called the *atrium;* then, further in, another colonnaded court called the *peristyle;* and then the *tablinum*, where was probably placed the altar at their services.

Such a fore-court, however, to a church required an area of land costly and difficult to obtain in a great city. So the *atrium* survived but sporadically in Eastern and Western Christendom; e.g. at Novara and Parenzo (seventh century); in Salerno, c. 1077; in S. Clemente, Rome; S. Ambrogio, Milan; and the German monastery of Laach; all probably twelfth century. In England we have no example of it.

Where, however, it was impossible to find space for all the four

* It is not certain that this was originally a church.
† Illustrated in *Archæological Journal*, 31.

covered walks of an *atrium*, it was often possible to build the eastern walk in front of the main entrance to the church. This eastern walk we may call the *narthex*. The basilicas at Ravenna seem to have had usually a closed narthex : while those at Rome* were open to the west. But a mosaic in S. Apollinare Nuovo, Ravenna, shows an open narthex closed by curtains.

In the Burgundian churches, but not in England, the narthex was developed to an enormous extent ; in fact it became a great ante-church. It occurs in the archaic church of Gannat, and at the Benedictine abbey of Tournus ; both apparently early in the eleventh century ; and in the Benedictine abbey of Fleury or St Benôit-sur-Loire, commenced 1062. At Tournus and Fleury it is two stories high. Of all the Orders the Cluniac seems most to have favoured it ; it occurs at CLUNY (150.1), begun 1089 ; Vézelay ; Souvigny ; Paray-le-Monial : all Cluniac abbeys. There is an eleventh-century example at Romainmotier ; it occurs also in the Cathedral of Autun ; *c.* 1150. But at the great abbey-church of La Charité-sur-Loire, instead of an independent fore-church, the number of bays of the nave is simply increased to ten plus a western transept.† This Cluniac church affords a curious parallel to our long Benedictine naves at St Albans, Bury, Ely, Peterborough, Winchester, Norwich ; and it is possible that in them, as in La Charité, the excessive length of the nave is due to the fact that it was intended that its western bays should serve as a narthex.

Another survival of the narthex in England is to be found in the form of western porches ; some of which from the earliest times have been called *Galilees*. At DURHAM (149.1), Glastonbury,‡ ELY (153.4), and Snettisham, Norfolk, the galilee is to the west of the façade; at LINCOLN (151.1) it is west of the south transept. St Woolos, Newport, has a fore-church of earlier date than the church west of it. The western porch seems to be of the most venerable antiquity. It occurs at St Pancras, Canterbury ; South Elmham, Suffolk ; Ythanchester, Essex ; Monkwearmouth, Durham : all probably of the seventh century.§ And as at Ythanchester and Monkwearmouth the porch was afterwards raised to form a tower, it may be that in these western porches we have at least one of the origins of the western tower which is so common in Anglo-Saxon and English Gothic architecture.

With the Cistercians the fore-church was in much less favour than with the Cluniacs ; probably because their churches were purposely planted in most remote and sequestered sites, and there was little or no resort of pilgrims to them. So the narthex dwindles down with the early Cistercians to a low building west of the façade, covered by a lean-to roof. Remains of such a narthex exist at Fountains, Rievaulx, and Byland. At Byland it went by the

---

* *Cf.* the narthex of St Nicholas, Caen ; Ruprich-Robert, Plate 8.

† Nowadays the pier-arcade, triforium, and clerestory of the western part of this nave have been converted into house-fronts ; and the nave into a street.

‡ Willis (*Glastonbury*, 76, 78) quotes John Glaston as calling the east part of the Lady Chapel (St Joseph's Chapel) at Glastonbury the galilee. Willis says that there is no documentary evidence for calling the south porch of Lincoln a galilee. At Durham the galilee was a Lady Chapel.

§ See Mr Peers in *Archæological Journal*, December 1901.

name of Galilee. Fine examples of the Cistercian narthex survive in France at PONTIGNY (599); in Italy at Casamari and elsewhere.* The later Cistercian churches, *e.g.* Tintern, seem to have dispensed with the narthex altogether.

There was a curious revival of the narthex or vestibule in Post-Reformation days. In the Fen and Marshland churches of Norfolk and Lincolnshire much woodwork seems to have been introduced in the time of James I. and Charles I. Walpole St Mary, happily unrestored, retains a fine Jacobean screen separating off the western bay of the nave; as well as Jacobean font cover, open seats, pulpit, and chandelier. Terrington St Clement's retains much of the western screen.† It is noteworthy that Wren also in most of his London churches separated off a vestibule by means of an oak screen.

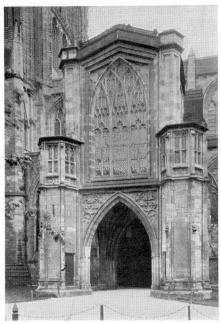

Hereford, N. Porch.

Melbourne from East.

WESTERN TRANSEPT.

Another form assumed by the "narthex" was the western transept. It occurs in the Romano-British basilica of Silchester; and in the seventh century at Brixworth. In our Romanesque and Gothic churches it may be seen in three forms. In the fine Norman church of MELBOURNE the aisles end as usual in a pair of western towers. These towers have a groined vault; and the space

* Illustrated in Enlart's *Gothic in Italy*, 43.

† Tilney All Saints' retains a Jacobean choir screen; that at Wiggenhall St Mary Magdalen has been brutally destroyed, like many others of this period, in a "restoration." Dore Abbey, Hereford, retains much of its Jacobean fittings. The best examples of all are Croscombe, Somerset, and St John's, Leeds.

between them also has a groined vault, the upper surface of which provides a gallery. The arrangement is curiously like that given by Mabillon, "*Duae turres sint in ecclesiae fronte statuta, et subter ipsas atrium ubi laici stare debent, ut non impediant processionem (monachorum).*" * A similar arrangement occurs in the two Caen † abbeys. A second plan was to build the two western towers not in a line with the aisles, but flanking them, and opening into them by lofty arches. This was the transept plan at the Norman priory of St Botolph, Colchester; at Ripon the towers originally flanked an aisleless nave ; and in the Transitional transept of Peterborough behind the thirteenth-century façade. It was planned at St Albans by John de Cella *c.* 1200, but never carried out. It is the plan of Bishop Jocelyn's transept at WELLS, *c.* 1220 (154.3). At

Llanbelig.

PETERBOROUGH (112), perhaps in rivalry with its neighbour Ely, three western porches of colossal height were built in Early Gothic in front of the Transitional western transept. The third plan is far more complex, and produces an interior of the very highest beauty. It survives in part at ELY (153.4); and in foundations at BURY (150.3).‡ That at Ely has an immense central arch to the west ; showing that it was intended in the twelfth century to be preceded by a great porch, perhaps even loftier than the present galilee. The magnificent vestibules of Ely and Bury were reproduced in Gothic at LINCOLN (151.1); save with the substitution of rectangular for apsidal chapels ; and a chapelled western transept is one of the noblest features in the planning of Wren's St Paul's.

The only other Romanesque province where the western transept is common is Germany ; where indeed it abounds : the flanking octagonal towers of Bury and Ely find analogues at Gernrode and Quedlinburg § in the tenth century and in many later examples. On the other hand, the simple Colchester plan with its flanking towers and the complexity and great projection of the Bury and Ely plans have little in common with the normal type of German western transept. There seems no reason for doubting that with us, as with Germany, it was an independent indigenous growth. In England the broad western transept, whether of the Wells or the Bury type, was built no more after the middle of the thirteenth century, with the exception of the seventeenth-century St Paul's. After that, the old type of Normandy, with two axial western towers, prevailed ;

---

* Dehio, i. 390.   † Ruprich-Robert, Plate 9.
‡ The western transept of Bury was 260 feet long.   § Plan 47, Dehio.

as at Chichester, Lichfield, and York ; or else even the towers were omitted, as at Exeter, Salisbury, Worcester, St David's ; giving a very unimpressive and parochial aspect to the main façade of many of our most important churches.

PORCHES.

In France we may perhaps regard the great cavernous western porches —three, as at Amiens and Reims ; five, as at Bourges and Bayeux—as lineal descendants also of the ancient narthex. Setting aside the projecting galilees of which we have spoken above (202), we have few analogues in England. There is a western porch at Chichester; added *c.* 1250; there are the superbly designed porches of John de Cella at St Albans, and the enormous triple portal of Peterborough. As a rule we did not care to develop the western doorways. The reason may be that our churches are all comparatively low ; to give the west doorways, therefore, any considerable elevation would be at the expense of the western windows. We needed western light badly in our English naves, especially in the twelfth and thirteenth century, and pre-ferred to develop the western window at the expense of the western doorway ; reaching in the end such a façade as that of ST GEORGE'S, WINDSOR (492). In France, on the other hand, the cathedral was frequently half as high again as in England ; and however much the doorways were developed, there was abundant space left for windows under the soaring vaults.

But there was ritualistic need of large porches in England as much as in France. Not being able to introduce them into the western façade except in the inartistic fashion of the Durham and Ely galilees, we built big porches in large numbers on the sides of the nave. So that the single big side porch in the end became as characteristic of the English church, whether cathedral, monastic, collegiate, or parochial, as great western porches, three or more, came to be of the French cathedral.

The porch was often two stories high, even in the twelfth century, as at Southwell, SHERBORNE (576), and Kelso. Sometimes the upper room contains a piscina, and therefore was used as a chapel ; sometimes, as at Southwell Minster, there is a chimney, and it was used as a dwelling-place for the sacristan,* or for a chantry-priest. After the Dissolution it was often used as a church library.

What was the precise use of these western adjuncts, whether narthex, galilee, western transept, or porch, it is now difficult to determine. No doubt it differed in different branches of the Catholic Church, and in different ages of the Church. But there must always have been a large number of functions which on the one side were of an ecclesiastical, on the other of a civil character ; *e.g.* the payments of tithes and rents : and for such functions an adjunct, half within, half without the sacred building, would have a natural suitability. Moreover, especially in early Christian days, special arrangements were made for the accommodation of the catechumens, who had as it were been but half initiated in the Christian rites. In the Cluniac churches the great narthex may have formed a waiting-room for pilgrims. Here, too, took place important ceremonies

---

* In 1294 Archbishop John Romanus of York ordered a sacrist to lie within the church of Southwell, to ring the bells at the appointed hours.

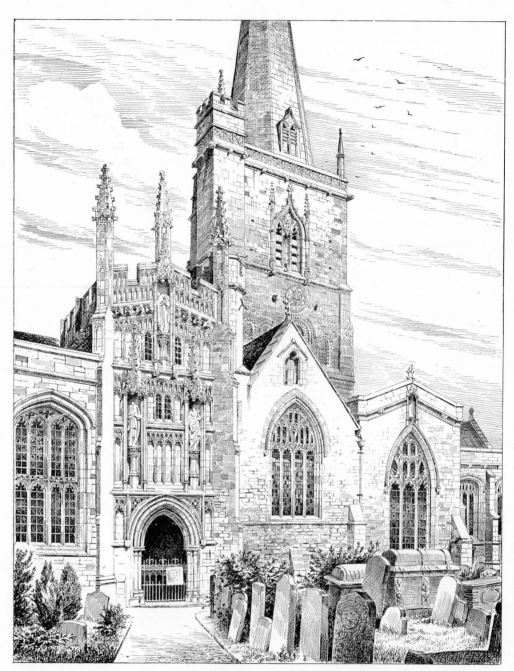

Burford, South Side.

on Palm Sunday ; the *Attollite portas* of Psalm xxiv. In some cases the abbot administered justice in his porch. Almsgiving took place here, and the rite of exorcism ; and part of the ceremonies of baptism, matrimony, and the churching of women. At Southwell the Pentecostals, or "Whitsun-farthings," were paid in the north porch.* Here too was placed the holy water stoup (204). At Dereham there are two external stoups in addition to one inside the porch.

Just as the "atrium" had dwindled down to the porch, so the great fountain in the centre of the "atrium" (which still exists at S. Sophia, Constantinople) dwindled down to the stoup. So also the early Christian practice of washing hands and face as well in the fountain has survived in the Mohammedan world ; but in Western Christendom dwindled to dipping the tip of the finger in the water of the stoup ; *e.g.* LLANBELIG (204).

COMPLEXITY OF THE MEDIÆVAL PLAN.

We are now able to see what a complex organism was the mediæval cathedral ; how manifold and diverse were the requirements prescribed to the architect by the ecclesiastical authorities ; and how able was the planning by which those requirements were satisfied. It was no longer the simple basilica of early Christian days, with its single altar to the one God. It was as if there had to be designed a temple for some great Polytheistic religion, with a crowd of deities all to be housed within one common roof. It was no longer for the Supreme Deity only churches were built ; but for an ever-growing multitude of Saints and Doctors of the Church. In earlier days it was thought enough sometimes to group several separate churches within one precinct ; such as the seven churches of Cashel, and those ten churches in the graveyard of Twyneham † which Bishop Flambard pulled down *c.* 1099 to make room for his Norman Christ Church. The next stage is seen in the ninth century at ST GALL (194) ; where all the churches are assembled under one roof, but in such a manner that all the aisles and nearly all the nave are blocked up with chapels ; congregational worship is impossible ; and the main body of the church is impervious to processions.‡ The next step, perhaps, is illustrated at ST ALBANS (14), where, as is shown by the paintings on the piers of the nave, altars were placed against the western side of each pier instead of in the centre of nave and aisles, as at St Gall. And this may be one reason for the enormous length of the naves of St Albans, Ely, Norwich, Peterborough, Bury ; that a

---

* Livett's *Southwell*, 11. On the whole subject see Lenoir's *Architecture Monastique*, ii. 73 ; and Thiers' *Sur les Porches*.

† Cart, Twyneham, Tiberius, D. VI.

‡ In the south aisle of St Gall, counting from the west, were the altars of St Agnes, St Sebastian, St Mauritius, and St Lawrence ; and in the north aisle those of St Cecilia, Holy Innocents, St Martin, and St Stephen. In the western apse of the nave was the altar of St Peter ; then the font ; then the altar of St John the Evangelist and St John the Baptist ; then that of the Crucified Saviour ; then in the western part of the eastern limb the high altar ; and in its eastern apse that of St Paul. On the east wall of the north transept was that of St Philip and St James ; and in the south transept that of St Andrew. Thus there were altogether fifteen altars, not including those in the crypt. At Chartres there were in the fourteenth century thirty-nine altars.

nave so elongated provided accommodation for an exceptionally large number of altared chapels. The next step is to remove these altars from the nave and its aisles to a chevet of chapels round the apsidal choir, as at St Martin de Tours and Norwich; to a central transept, as at Romsey and St Albans; to an eastern transept, as at Cluny and Canterbury; to a western transept, as at Bury and Ely; to an upper aisle, as in the five upper chapels of Gloucester choir and transept; leaving the nave free for the assembled laity, and the aisles un-encumbered for processions. Eastward of the nave, as we have seen, it became usual to provide an enclosed choir for the clergy and singers; east of the choir, a raised* sanctuary for the high altar. And when there was a famous local saint,

St Albans, Ramryge Chantry Chapel.

efficacious in answer to prayer, another great eastern annexe was added; both the great retrochoirs of Ely and Lincoln were but the glorified shrines, not in gold and silver, but in stone, of St Etheldreda or St Hugh. Then there was provision to be made more and more for a multitude of chantry chapels. One of the earliest was that at Lincoln Minster of Bishop Hugh of Wells, who died in 1235. In the thirteenth century they were few;† the greater number were founded in the fifteenth century. They were founded by kings and princes; *e.g.* Henry the Seventh's chantry chapel at Westminster; and that of his eldest son, Prince Arthur, in Worcester choir; by bishops, abbots, barons, commoners, and guilds; by any one who had the money to provide for the saying of masses for the repose of the soul of "himself and his parents and his relatives and his benefactors and of all the faithful dead."‡ Some two thousand chantries had been founded up to the time of Henry VIII.; when they were suppressed their income was found to be under £10,000 a year, which we may perhaps multiply by twelve to bring it to the present value of money. In a great church it was

* In England the sanctuary as a rule was but little raised, except of course where there was a crypt.

† The *Taxatio* records only two. In Yorkshire less than a dozen are recorded before the fourteenth century. Cutts' *Parish Priests*, 438.

‡ *Louth Records*, 163; "Chantry of Canon Thomas de Luda."

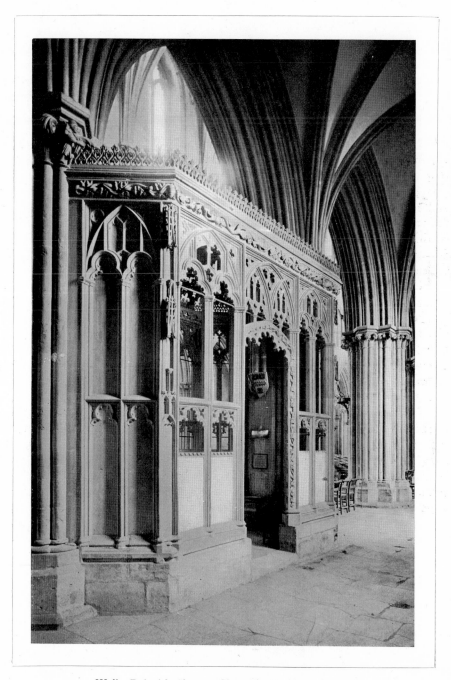

Wells, Bubwith Chantry Chapel in N. Aisle of Nave.

Wells, Bubwith Chantry Chapel in N. Aisle of Nave.

not difficult to find room for the combined tomb and chapel, what is often called
the "chantry";* which, in larger examples, consisted of a screened enclosure,
containing the tomb, the slab of which served as altar; in late examples, as in
Fox's chantry at Winchester, there might be also a vestry at the east end.
These were placed in great numbers under the arches separating the aisles from
the choir or nave; *e.g.* at WELLS (209) and ST ALBANS (208).   Owing to the
protection given by Fairfax, an old Winchester boy, the Cathedral of Winchester
retains an unusually fine set of chantries of its bishops; those of Edington and
Wykeham between the piers of the nave; those of Beaufort, Fox, and Gardiner
between the piers of the retrochoir and choir.   Frequently the eastern bay of
each choir aisle was turned into a chantry chapel; as by Bishops Alcock and
West at ELY (143).   At Durham the great family of the Nevilles was allowed
to screen off two whole bays of the south aisle of the nave as their chantry
chapel.   Sometimes, as at LINCOLN (112) and Eton and Windsor, chantries
were inserted between the buttresses.   Sometimes there was such an agglomeration of chantries that an additional aisle, or aisles, was produced, as at
Chichester Cathedral, Dorchester Priory, Manchester Collegiate Church.   All
this added greatly to the difficulty of planning the great mediæval churches.
But the problems and difficulties were triumphantly surmounted.   The mediæval
cathedral is a masterpiece of ingenious and scientific planning.   Complicated as
it is, there is no part but was necessary; and each part is situated where most
convenient for the requirements of ritual: there is no waste, no awkwardness of
spacing.   Every part had its use; and was in daily use.   The plan was as
utilitarian as it was magnificent.

* Strictly the term applies to the ecclesiastical foundation, not to the building.

CHAPTER XIII.

THE PLANNING OF THE PARISH CHURCH.

SO far we have spoken of the planning of the larger churches; cathedral, monastic, or collegiate. They were originally the offspring of the early Christian basilicas. It has often been assumed, therefore, that the humble village church also is again but the Italian basilica, cut down, curtailed, simplified in plan. The truth is the other way. The parochial church is really not so much a re- duction or simplification of a higher organism as an amplification of a very simple and lowly form of ecclesiastical architecture, gradually throwing out extensions, now here, now there, till in the end there is sometimes but little difference in plan between the parish church and the cathedral; as may be seen on comparing Patrington Church with York Minster; St Mary Redcliffe, Bristol, with Salisbury Cathedral; or Louth with Llandaff.

APSIDAL v. RECTANGULAR CHANCEL.

Of the Norman parish churches many were apsidal. The following retain *apses* at the end of the chancel: *—Berkshire*, Padworth, Finchamstead, Remen- ham; *Cambridge*, Iselham; *Cumberland*, Warthwick; *Derbyshire*, Steetley; *Essex*, Great Maplestead, Little Maplestead, East Ham, Haversfield, Hadleigh, Little Braxted, Langford, Copford; *Hampshire*, Nateley, Easton; *Hereford*, Kilpeck, Moccas, Pencombe, Peterchurch; *Hertfordshire*, Bengeo; *Kent*, Sutton, near Dover; *Norfolk*, Heckingham, South Runcton, Gillingham, Tritton, Hales; *Oxfordshire*, Checkendon, Woodcote, Swyncombe; *Suffolk*, Fritton, Dunwich; *Sussex*, Newhaven, Upper Waltham; *Warwickshire*, Bilston; *Wiltshire*, Manningford Bruce; *Yorkshire*, Feliskirk, Birkin, Lastingham; besides others in remote parts of England.

But, as in the smaller Anglo-Saxon, so in the smaller Norman churches of England, *rectangular chancels* are more common than apses; *e.g.* Avington, Berks; Adel, York; Barfreston, Darent, and PATRIXBOURNE (218), Kent.† The origin of this rectangular chancel is somewhat doubtful. We know that the greater part of England was not converted to Christianity by Augustine and the monks sent from Rome, but by Irish and Scotch missioners whose head- quarters were Lindisfarne, Iona, and Ireland. Now in Ireland the churches were of stone, and rectangular; none were apsidal. It has therefore been assumed that these missioners brought with them the lithic architecture of Celtic Christianity. But this is to ignore the fact that the Irish stone churches

* Parker's *Glossary*, 29.   † See list in Bloxam, 84.

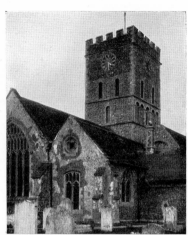

Leicester St Nicholas from S.W. St Lawrence from S.W.
Melbourne S. Choir. Louth from S.W.

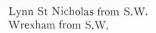

Lynn St Nicholas from S.W.
Wrexham from S.W.

Gresford from N.E.
Long Melford from S.W.

215

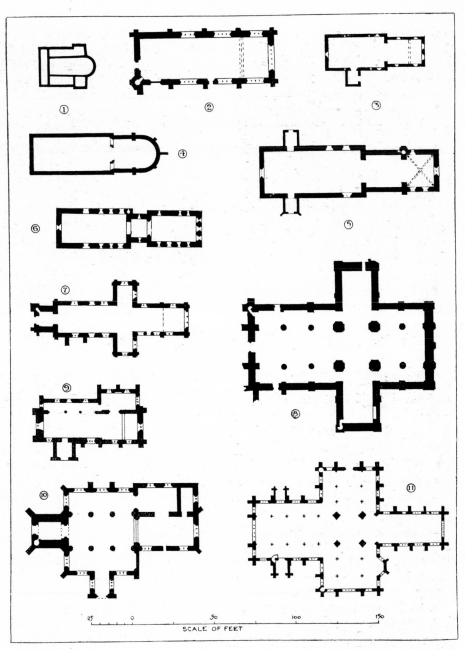

SCALE OF FEET

1. Silchester.
2. Temple Balsal.
3. Tangmere.
4. Hadleigh.
5. Cassington.
6. Bucknell.
7. Achurch.
8. St Cross, Winchester.
9. Howell.
10. North Mimms.
11. Patrington.

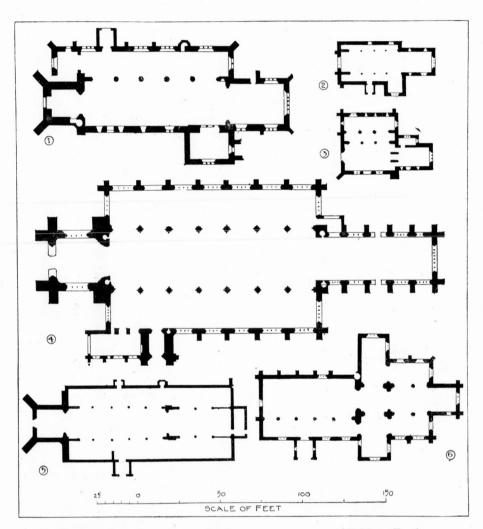

SCALE OF FEET

1. Westham, Sussex.   3. Baginton.   5. St Mary, Eastbourne.
2. Toot Baldon.   4. Boston.   6. Kidlington.

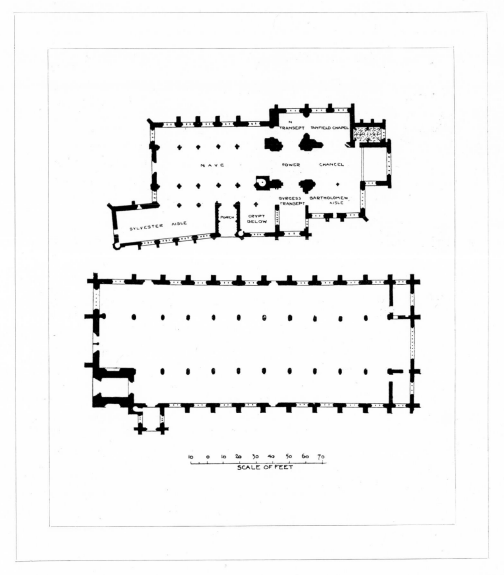

Burford.   St Nicholas, Lynn.

were of the rudest possible character in the seventh century and long after; little oblong sheds without aisles or chancel; without an arch; probably built without mortar.   How could a race, architecturally so backward, impose its building methods on a country which, even in the seventh century, as we read in the description of Hexham, by Wilfrid's own chaplain, Eddius, was able to build aisled churches, three stories high, with towers, crypts, galleries, and porticus? A race, which architecturally is on a higher plane, imposes its building methods on a race which is on a lower plane.   This was the case with the Normans when they came into contact with Anglo-Saxon architecture.   But when a race meets another in a more advanced stage of architectural development, its own architecture succumbs or makes but little headway.   This was the case with the Normans themselves when they came in contact with the advanced art, Byzantine or Saracenic, of Sicily and Southern Italy.   It is impossible then to believe

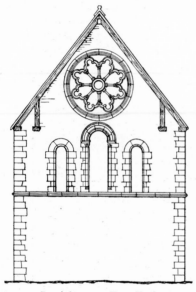
Patrixbourne, East End.

that the rude lithic architecture of Ireland * can have had any considerable influence on the far superior work of seventh-century England.

Simple constructional reasons are sufficient to explain the preference for the rectangular over the semicircular chancel.   In the first place, though the earliest Celtic churches in Ireland were of stone (perhaps because the Irish builders had not the tools for working wood), yet we read in Bede that when the first Celtic missioners landed in Lindisfarne, their first church was not of stone, but of wood.   Saxon records, from Bede downwards, contain abundant references to timber-built churches.   And the cases are very numerous in which an earlier structure of wood was rebuilt in stone, e.g. at York, Tynemouth, Chester-le-Street, Wilton, Lastingham.†   It is reasonable to suppose that in such instances the earlier plan might survive in the later structure.   Bede, too, speaks of building "*more Scottorum non de lapide*," which can only mean that the characteristic church, as planned by the first Celtic missioners in England, was of osiers or wood.   Again, he says,‡ that "*Naitanus, rex Pictorum, architectos sibi mitti petiit, qui juxta morem Romanorum ecclesiam de lapide ingenti facerent*,"§ which shows that stone-construction was exceptional on the north as well as on the south of the English Border; where, he says, it was a "*mos Britonibus insolitus*."   The first churches of the Celtic missioners in England, no

---

* It is not intended to deny that the Irish missioners did here and there build in stone. Bede describes the erection of a stone church in the south of Scotland, at Whitherne or *Stonehouse*, in Galloway.   Such churches would be of the archaic Irish type.

† Baldwin Brown in *Builder*, Dec. 21, 1895.   ‡ *Eccles. Hist.*, v., c. 22.

§ "Naitanus, king of the Picts, asked for architects to be sent to him (from Gaul), to build him a church of large stones after the manner of the Romans."

doubt, were constructed of osiers* plastered over with mud: a little later, these temporary oratories would be rebuilt in timber: ultimately, in stone. In these osier or timber churches, then, of the first Celtic missioners the origin of the rectangular chancel might be looked for.

But it is unnecessary to assume a Celtic origin. To build an apse would have been as unnatural to their converts as it was to the Celtic missioners. For the converts in England were Angles, Saxons, Jutes; and later on, Danes and Norwegians; and all these came from forest lands; and were shipwrights and carpenters by trade, not stone-masons; and well able to build substantial log-huts, such as those of the Norske bonder to this day. Of churches of this latter or timber type we have an example surviving in the Pre-Conquest church of Green-
stead, Essex. Now it would be difficult to build a log-chancel in the form of a semicircle; and just as easy to build it rectangular. Secondly, if a log-chancel were actually built apsidal, it would be difficult to cover it with a timber roof; though it is done at Worth and Brixworth. We may conclude that the churches of timber would invariably have rectangular chancels; and that this form, when hallowed, as in time it would be, by the associations of centuries, would become the natural and characteristic form for the chancel of the smaller, if not of the greater churches also, even when they were constructed in masonry. Thus we may explain the preference of the Anglo-Saxons for the rectangular form of chancel in spite of Continental tradition.

St Columba, Kells.

PLANNING OF PARISH CHURCHES.

The simplest form in which the church occurs is seen in the early churches of IRELAND. There it is just an oblong shed; no chancel; no chancel-arch. In England this form constitutes a chapel; not a church. It occurs, for instance, in St Cuthbert's Chapel at Lindisfarne; and in the Chapel of St Mary Magdalen

* Such a church long survived at Glastonbury; see Britton's *Arch. Ant.*, v. 96.

at Ripon and at Skirlaugh.*   It is but rarely seen in the smaller churches; *e.g.* at TEMPLE BALSAL, Warwick (215.2); which is rather a chapel than a church; built by the Knights Templars, and therefore anterior to the suppression of the Order in 1312

PLAN I.: UNAISLED NAVE AND CHANCEL.

The normal church, however, in Normandy † and in England has a distinct chancel, at any rate in early days.   The chancel may be square, as at TANGMERE (215.3); it may be polygonal, as at Brixworth and Wing; semicircular, as at HADLEIGH (215.4); but it is always there in our early churches.   The presence of some form of chancel and chancel-arch in England, long before it appears in

Adel from N.W.

Ireland, makes a Celtic origin for the English parish church impossible.   Of this *first* type of English church, without aisles, without clerestories, with or without towers, many examples are left us; such as the Pre-Conquest church of Corhampton;‡ Norman churches such as ADEL and Barfreston, which are square-ended, and Hadleigh, which is apsidal;§ Gothic churches, such as Elsfield and Tangmere (thirteenth century).   It should be noticed that though architecturally a church of this type divides into two parts, nave and chancel, nevertheless, ritualistically there is a triple division into nave, choir, and sanctuary; for the

* Plans and illustrations in *Churches of Yorkshire*.
† R. Robert, 57.   ‡ Illustrated in Rickman, fifth edition, xxxvii.
§ Buckler's *Churches of Essex*, 171, 4.

sanctuary is usually differentiated from the choir by having its floor at a higher level.*

SECOND PLAN: UNAISLED NAVE; CHOIR; PRESBYTERY.

A *second* type, however, is common, at any rate in early churches. In this a choir is interposed between the nave and the eastern limb; so that the division is no longer into nave and sanctuary, but into nave, choir, and sanctuary. It occurs in the Anglo-Saxon church of Brixworth, but with the addition of aisles to the nave; and in the unaisled Norman church of HADLEIGH, Essex (215.4). Frequently the central compartment, the choir proper, is covered with a central tower; *e.g.* in the Anglo-Saxon churches of Dunham Magna, Norfolk; St Mary's, Guildford; and Barton-on-Humber, as recent excavations have shown.† It is common in Norman churches, *e.g.* Stewkley;‡ St Andrew's; Cassington; Newhaven; in the last the sanctuary is apsidal. At BUCKNELL, Oxfordshire, the Norman towered choir remains; nave and sanctuary were remodelled later. At Iffley all is Norman, except that the sanctuary was lengthened in the thirteenth century. Leckhampton§ has a towered choir and sanctuary, both vaulted; built in the fourteenth century, yet Norman in plan. So also Fairford, Kempsford, Tong.

It is noteworthy that in many of the Norman churches with triple division the sanctuary is vaulted, whether it be apsidal or rectangular, as at CASSINGTON, Oxfordshire (215.5); Darent, Kent; Tickencote, Rutland; Compton Martin, Somerset; Stewkley, Buckingham. In the latter case there is a space

Bucknell.

between the sanctuary vault and the timber roof; and this seems to have been often utilised as a priest's room: as may be seen by the windows inserted in the gable to give light to it; *e.g.* St Peter in the East, Oxford; Stewkley; Darent.

---

* It is curious how closely the triple disposition of the Christian church reproduces that of the Jewish temple: (1) The Holy of Holies, entered only by the High Priest. There was the Ark, the resting-place of the Shekinah; where God was in visible presence. It was screened by a veil, *cf.* the Lenten Veil, the Iconostasis of the Greek Church, and the veiled Baldachinos above the High Altar in the Sanctuary of the ancient basilicas. (2) The Holy Place; entered only by the Priests; this corresponds with the choir of the Christian Church. (3) Next came the Court of the Israelites; accessible to Jews only, not to Gentiles; this corresponds to the Christian nave. (4) The outer court, or Court of the Gentiles; corresponding to the atrium; *e.g.* St Clemente, Rome. Moreover, the Jewish temple, like the earliest of the Christian basilicas, was orientated not to the east but to the west. (See Exodus xxvi. 27; and Scott's *Essay*, 64.)

† Illustrated in Baldwin Brown's *Arts in Early England*, ii. 210.

‡ Britton, ii. 2. § Illustrated in Brandon's *Parish Churches*, 65.

THIRD TYPE: CRUCIFORM.

As time went on, both the above types of church proved inadequate to accommodate an increased population, and to provide an adequate number of chapels. It was necessary to enlarge the church. To get this enlargement, two methods suggested themselves. One was to add aisles; this involved difficulties of construction, and at first was avoided. The other was to add transepts; this method had the additional recommendation that much more light could be obtained from the end walls of transepts than from the side walls of aisles. If the church consisted of nave, towered choir, and presbytery, as at Dunham Magna and Guildford, the obvious course would be to add transepts. The tower over the choir would be all the safer for having abutment to north and south in the form of transepts, as it already had to the east and west in the form of presbytery and nave. And for the cruciform shape thus given to the church there was abundant precedent. In the little church in the Romano-British town of SILCHESTER (215.1) there is a rudimentary transept of early Christian type. So also foundations of transeptal chapels may be seen in the very ancient church of St Pancras, Canterbury. Other Pre-Conquest examples exist or formerly existed at Deerhurst; Stanton Lacy, Salop; Repton; Stow; Norton, Durham; Worth, Sussex; St Mary in the Castle, Dover. Bradford-on-Avon has a north transept; and foundations of a southern one. And it is plain from numerous descriptions that transepts and a central tower were common enough in the greater Anglo-Saxon churches, now all gone. It is true that these cross-arms were, in the Anglo-Saxon churches, more of the character of transeptal chapels than of transepts; being usually lower and narrower than the nave; nevertheless they gave the church the cruciform outline. In Normandy and in England all the greater Romanesque churches had central tower and transepts. It was therefore but natural that in many of our earlier churches enlargement should take the form of transepts. And when churches were built *de novo*, the cruciform type, almost universal in the larger churches, and already introduced into some of the smaller ones, would here and there be adopted at any rate in churches of all but the humblest dimensions. Hence the plan of Barton Seagrave, North Hants, which has a south transept only, built as a chantry chapel; and of such cruciform churches as North Newbald and ACHURCH (215.7).

A different process of extension would lead to the same result, when applied to a church without a central tower. Here it would be easy to enlarge the church eastward by pulling down the sanctuary; building on its site a central tower; and projecting from the central tower transepts and a new sanctuary. This is the process through which ST NICHOLAS, LEICESTER (213), and Bakewell seem to have passed. By a similar change the aisled church of Sedgefield obtained transepts and a new chancel, *c.* 1290, some forty years after its rebuilding.*

Or thirdly, the easternmost bay of each aisle of the nave might be prolonged to north and south so as to form a transept; as at Weston.†

* If we accept the view of C. C. Hodges in *Archæologia Aeliana*, xvi. 389.
† Plan in *Fen and Marshland Churches*, vol. iii. Or it might be raised and perhaps partially prolonged also, so as to form the quasi-transept, characteristic of Herefordshire.

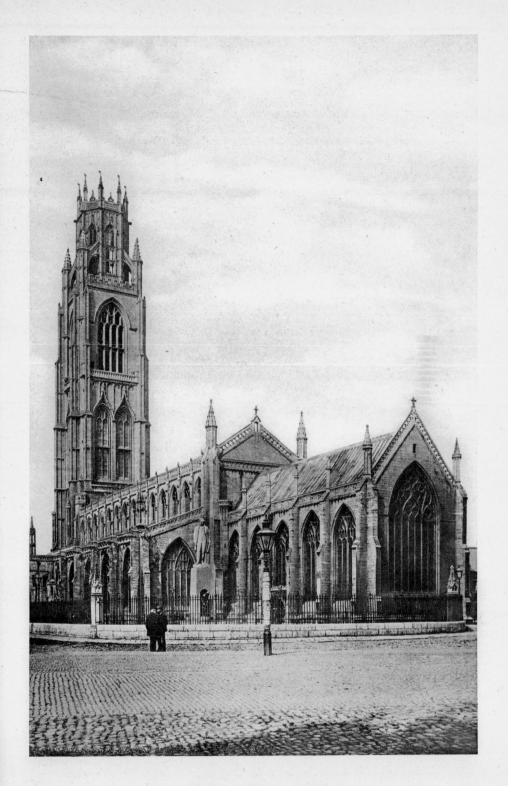

BOSTON CHURCH FROM S.E.

Such transepts, in whatever way they originated, were exceedingly convenient. They provided room for one or more chapels. And where a church was built *de novo* by a single benefactor, it seems to have been not unusual or him to reserve one transept as his chantry chapel ; *e.g.* the fourteenth-century church of Shottesbrooke was built by Sir William Tressell, who with his lady, Maud, is buried in the north transept.*

This fine church is without aisles. But transepts were added to, or built with, aisled naves as well. At PATRINGTON (215.11), built, like Shottesbrooke, *de novo*, *c.* 1330, the nave has aisles, and the transept has both eastern and western aisles ; so that, but for the absence of aisles to the chancel and of western towers, it is identical in plan with York Minster. A still grander and later example of the parochial use of the transeptal plan is to be seen at St Mary Redcliffe, Bristol.

The transeptal plan without aisles occurs at all epochs ; and not sporadically, but in quite large groups of churches here and there ; *e.g.* in North Wilts and the adjoining parts of Oxfordshire, Berks, and Bucks ; in South Somerset and West Dorset ; in Cornwall ; in West Sussex ; in Mid-Essex.† A fine example of the thirteenth century is the large church of Llan-badarn-fawr, just outside of Aberystwith. In later examples, of course, it occurs more often in conjunction with an aisled nave.

FOURTH TYPE: WITH AISLED NAVE.

Common, however, as the transeptal plan became, especially in the Norman churches of the twelfth century, it was in the end superseded in the vast majority of churches by a simpler type. This was a church with aisled nave, elongated chancel, and western tower. It may be regarded as simply a development of the second type, that of Anglo-Saxon Corhampton or Norman Adel. This is *the* type *par excellence* of the English parish church. There are thousands of churches, both great and small, so planned. Its most magnificent outcome is BOSTON CHURCH (216.4) ; which has an aisled nave 93 feet long.

In the early churches the aisles were often obtained in the simplest possible manner. Aisle walls were built ; windows were inserted in them ; a lean-to roof was put on ; then the walls of the old nave were pierced with arches, leaving big blocks of masonry between them to serve as piers ; as at ST NICHOLAS, LEICESTER (213) ; St Michael's, St Albans ; Ickham and Sturry, Kent ; Wing, Bucks ; Chobham, Surrey.

For the aisled nave there was abundant precedent. It was present in all the larger early Christian basilicas and in the Romano-British church at Silchester, and in the larger Anglo-Saxon and Norman churches. It existed even in many of the smaller Anglo-Saxon churches ; *e.g.* Reculvers, Wing, and Lydd ; and in some Norman parish churches ; *e.g.* TOWYN (458) ; Steyning ; Northampton St Peter ; St Margaret at Cliffe. And so, just as many a Guildford had enriched itself by the accretion of a Romanesque transept ; so many an Adel expanded by the addition of a basilican aisle. And, as we have said, many churches adopted both aisle and transept.

Sometimes, at first, it was but a single aisle that was added ; and here and

---

* Butterfield's *Shottesbrooke*.   † Prior, *Gothic Architecture*, 54.

there a church remains still with no more than a single aisle; *e.g.* EASTWOOD, Stanwick, and North Creake. More often there was built afterwards, or simultaneously, another aisle on the opposite side of the nave. The early aisles, *e.g* at TOOT BALDON, Oxon. (216.2), those built in the eleventh, twelfth, and thirteenth centuries, were usually narrow and low. They were therefore very frequently pulled down—sometimes more than once, as at Wakefield—and rebuilt broad and high. Or, beyond an original aisle was added another aisle, as at BAGINTON, Warwick (216.3), or more than one; giving the church, three, four, five, or even six aisles, as at Wisbech and Abingdon. Frequently, however, the newer outer aisles were really chantry chapels, belonging to private persons or families, and shut off from public use by screens; *e.g.* the outer south aisle at Collumpton is

Eastwood, Essex.

the chantry chapel of John Lane, Merchant; as appears from the inscription on his tomb therein (1510-1528). At Ludlow the whole of the south aisle and of the western part of the nave appears to be an agglomeration of various chantry chapels.* At Baginton, the outer aisle seems to be a chantry chapel founded in honour of St Thomas the Martyr, *c.* 1250, by Richard de Hertbull.†

In the great majority of the churches the aisles were roofed with lean-to roofs. Sometimes, however, instead of building an aisle, the nave was enlarged laterally by building another nave parallel to it; or two parallel naves were built contemporaneously. This plan occurs in early churches, and even so late as St John's, Leeds (1634). Sometimes, as at ST LAWRENCE, Thanet (213), and at Rye, in the last half of the twelfth century, three parallel naves were erected. In this way a very broad church could be got. It is a plan especially common in Kent and Sussex. But whether there were two or three parallel naves, each with its saddle roof, the plan was open to the objection that the gutter between any pair of saddle roofs, in the autumn became choked with leaves, in the winter with snow; and that at all times it was an unsatisfactory and risky method of carrying off the rainfall. So it remained exceptional.

Another method was to construct one saddle roof covering nave and aisles alike; as at Seaford, Sussex; and TOOT BALDON, near Oxford (225). This method of roofing was common in mediæval aisled barns; *e.g.* that of the Abbaye

* So also the south aisle of Dorchester Priory Church.
† Brandon's *Parish Churches*, 114.

d'Ardenne, near Caen. But the aisle walls, to be thus roofed, have to be kept very low ; little room is left for windows ; and the church is dark ; consequently this method had but little vogue.

Not only the nave received aisles, but the chancel was elongated. We have seen that nearly every cathedral had its Norman eastern limb re-built and lengthened, as at Lichfield, Lincoln, Wells, Exeter, York, Canterbury. The same process of elongation was applied to vast numbers of parish churches ; in Kent usually in the thirteenth century; elsewhere more often later. And so room was obtained in the chancel eastward for a spacious elevated presbytery, westward for the stalls of the clergy and choir. Norman chancels so en-larged are Iffley and MELBOURNE (213). In the latter, the curve of the truncated apse may still be seen outside.

Toot Baldon.

FIFTH TYPE: AISLED NAVE WITH RECTANGULAR CHANCEL PARTLY AISLED.

In one way or other, nearly all churches of any consequence were either built with aisled naves, or aisles were added to the nave subsequently. The next step is seen when the aisles begin to creep into the chancel.

At first the chancel aisle appears only in a rudimentary and imperfect form in the parish churches. One side of the chancel is aisled, the other is not. Or part of one side or of both sides have aisles. These additions of bits of aisle supplied chapels and sacristies ; both containing altars. The chancel of Hemel Hempstead consists of two vaulted bays ; to the north of the western of these is a vaulted chapel or sacristy; all this work, including the vaults, appears to belong to the third quarter of the twelfth century. At Higham Ferrers the chancel has a north aisle partly separated from it by a solid wall ; it is a Lady Chapel with a sacristy east of it. So also at North Mimms, Herts, the whole space north of the chancel is occupied by a chantry chapel and a sacristy; at Howell, Lincoln, by a chantry. At Worstead and Hingham, Norfolk, there is a sacristy north of the presbytery. At Barnwood, Gloucester, the whole space north of the chancel is occupied by a chapel of Norman date. At Marston, Beds, is a chantry south, and a sacristy north of the chancel. At Merstham, Surrey, the Early English choir is flanked by a Decorated chapel on one side, and a Perpendicular

P

chapel on the other; leaving a small projecting presbytery: *cf.* Outwell, Norfolk. At Solihull, Warwick, north of the presbytery is a vaulted sacristy, with a chantry above it; *c.* 1200.*

But, here and there, much earlier than is generally supposed, symmetrical aisles were built along the western bay or bays of the chancel. Examples occur in the first half of the twelfth century at Northampton St Peter; in the last half of the century at Walsoken in the Norfolk Marshland; at St Nicholas at Wade, and originally at St Lawrence, both in the Isle of Thanet. So again in the first half of the thirteenth century at West Walton, near Wisbech; and, later, at Herne, Kent, and KIDLINGTON, Oxon. (216.6). In the great churches of the later fourteenth and fifteenth centuries in East Anglia, a very favourite plan was to provide both nave and choir with aisles, but to build the presbytery of a single unaisled bay. Thus the presbytery could be lighted by a side window on either side; *e.g.* at Loddon, Blythburgh, Lowestoft, Southwold. At Covehithe these side windows rose to a vast height, and must have lighted the altar brilliantly.

SIXTH TYPE: WITH NAVE AND CHANCEL FULLY AISLED.

It was but a short step to continue these abbreviated aisles eastward to the full length of the chancel; and the plan of LOUTH (139) is reached. The full-length choir aisles which had been a special possession of the later great monastic churches, such as Rievaulx and Whitby, and of cathedrals such as Ely, Lincoln, York, were appropriated by the parochial builders; and their church became yet more dignified. This plan also seems to have been reached in the latter half of the twelfth century, *e.g.* at EASTBOURNE (216.5). It was naturally confined chiefly to large town-churches. LOUTH CHANCEL (213) is *c.* 1400 to 1445.†

The chancel of Burnham Overy, Norfolk, has a beautiful Early English aisle running along the whole of the south side of the chancel. Wimmington, Beds, which was built before 1391,‡ has full-length chancel-aisles; but they are partly separated from the chancel by solid walls.

SEVENTH TYPE: THE AISLED CHAPEL.

As we have seen, a constant characteristic of the English church was its division into nave and chancel. These were separated by a chancel-arch. But as time went on,§ the ritualistic distinction between the layman's nave and the chancel of the clerk and of the holy altar was emphasised still further by a screen. These screens constantly grew in magnitude and importance; *e.g.* that

* For plans of the above see Brandon's *Parish Churches;* Parker's *Churches of Northants;* Ringstead, 73. For Methley, where the Waterton chantry is flush with the chancel, see plan in *Churches of Yorkshire.*

† J. J. Creswell, *Associated Societies' Reports,* July 6, 1897.

‡ Brandon's *Parish Churches,* 94.

§ It should be noted that some screens at any rate existed in Norman times; *e.g.* in front of the upper story of the presbytery of Compton, Surrey.

of NEWARK (178). To get room for them the chancel-arch was built broader and broader, till, as at LOUTH (213), where, unfortunately, the screen has disappeared, and still more at NEWARK (178), there is internally little left of the transverse wall in which the chancel-arch is set ; while, externally, the distinction between nave and chancel almost ceases to exist. It was but a short step to remove the chancel-arch and its responds altogether, and the church was thrown into the shape of a great oblong aisled chapel.* In such a church, of course, a screen to delimit nave and chancel was indispensable.

We have called it " the aisled chapel " plan. And indeed an early and important example of it is at ST NICHOLAS, LYNN (217), which, though on a vast scale,† was nothing but a chapel-of-ease to the great Church of St Margaret's, and was originally debarred from the solemnisation of the rites of baptism and marriage. A long account might be given of the attempts of St Nicholas to get rid of its dependency on St Margaret.‡ At any rate, when it was rebuilt between 1413 and 1419,§ it would seem that the authorities of St Margaret insisted that even in plan St Nicholas should not be a church. And so it was built chapel-fashion with a chancel-screen instead of a chancel-arch.‖ But the new chapel was a glorious success, and many a church proper, when prejudice against adopting a chapel-plan had had time to evanesce, was built after the fashion of St Nicholas of Lynn. It was not, however, for nearly a century that this fine type of church, nearly always built with lofty and almost continuous clerestory windows,¶ came into general use. St Stephen's, Bristol, A.D. 1455, is an early example. It occurs in the village church of GRESFORD (214). Not far away is WREXHAM (214), which was originally of this type. But the Wrexham people seem to have been shocked at the absence of a chancel ; and so converted the east window into a chancel-arch (leaving the stumps of the tracery sticking out), and built a little chancel behind it. In London we have St Andrew Undershaft, Leadenhall Street, 1520-1532. At York there is St Michael's, 1535-1545. But the special habitat of this grand and final type of the English parish church is East Anglia. Three magnificent examples occur in St Andrew's, St Stephen's, and St Peter Mancroft, Norwich ; and, above all, at LONG MELFORD, Suffolk (214) ; all, however, have lost their screens. It should be noticed how gloriously lighted

* In churches with *unaisled* naves the screen naturally had been employed instead of the chancel-arch long before ; *e.g.* at Temple Balsal, which is before 1312 ; and at Ewerby, which is *c.* 1340. Almost all the churches of Cornwall omit the chancel-arch.

† It is internally 193 feet long by 81 feet wide ; and is divided into thirteen bays.

‡ See Monograph on St Nicholas by Mr E. M. Beloe.

§ A resolution of the Town Council, dated 1419, speaks of it as having been recently rebuilt by voluntary subscription.

‖ Unfortunately the chancel screen has been destroyed here, as in most churches of the aisled chapel type. From the interior of King's College Chapel, Cambridge, one can form an idea of the original aspect of these interiors.

¶ Still earlier is the plan of the great church at North Walsham, built after the destruction of the old church in the peasants' rising of 1381. The porch seems to be a later addition to the church, and contains the Royal Arms, in which the first quarter is ancient ; *i.e. semée de fleurs-de-lis ;* a bearing which was disused in 1405. This church therefore would seem to have been rebuilt, together with the porch, between 1381 and 1405. This early date is borne out by the flowing tracery of the eastern windows and of some of those of the porch.

were these "Tudor lanterns."; with a large window in every bay of the aisles,* and two in every bay of the clerestory; and a great east window, and a great west window; especially when, as at St Nicholas, Lynn, ST STEPHEN'S, NORWICH, TERRINGTON ST CLEMENT'S (92), and St John's, and many other churches in the Norfolk Marshland, the tower was built to the south-west or the north-west, so as not to obscure the great west window. The seventh type of plan, as it was the last, so was the grandest of all.

One further step might have been taken, and probably but for the collapse of church architecture at the Reformation would have been taken; that was to remove the aisles as well: it would have been to bring in the unaisled chapel type. This indeed had always been employed with frequency in smaller

Norwich St Stephen.   Norwich St Stephen.

churches; *e.g.* at Skirlaugh. Moreover, vast unaisled Lady Chapels, such as those of Peterborough and Ely, clearly pointed that way. KING'S COLLEGE CHAPEL, CAMBRIDGE (62), and Eton College Chapel are but versions of the Lady Chapels of Peterborough and Ely. Had this type come into general use, we should have had the logical outcome of that desire for simple and straight-forward planning which was ever at the heart of the English builder, whether he was building for monk or canon, for townsman or for villager.

South of the Loire, this Hall-type of church became exceedingly common; from Angers, where the cathedral was built (with transepts, however) *c.* 1150; south to the Mediterranean; leaving us the great Church of the Cordeliers,

* Long Melford actually has two windows in each bay of the aisles.

Toulouse,* and the magnificent Cathedral of Albi ; which has neither aisles nor transepts, but is simply one vast hall, 355 feet long.

With us the history of church planning ends with the great Chapel of King's College, Cambridge, one of the supreme glories of Christendom. Perverted as unpatriotic must the imagination be that can see decadence and debasement in this great monument of mediæval art. The three Royal Chapels, at Cambridge, Windsor and Westminster, with the East Anglian churches, present to us English Gothic planning at its very noblest and its best.

* Illustrated in Fergusson, ii. 70 ; recently burnt.

CHAPTER XIV.

THE BASILICAN COLUMN AND THE ROMANESQUE PIER.

Basilican Colonnades—The Basilican a Distinct Style—Why the Basilican Style Perished — Pre Conquest and Norman Piers — Origin of Compound Pier — Romanesque Piers—Vaulting Shafts—Cylindrical Piers.

THE history of the Christian Church practically commences in the fourth century with the great Christian basilicas built by Constantine and his successors (see 146). Unfortunately, however, for the early Christian architects, the great ages of Roman building had passed away. Nothing was ever done again greater than the Pantheon, erected by the Emperor Hadrian, greatest of all the Roman builders. One great building, indeed, commenced by Maxentius in the last years of the third century and finished by Constantine, rivalled the triumphs of the second century. This was the so-called Basilica of Maxentius or Constantine.* To what a depth of degradation Roman art had sunk is clear from the history of the triumphal arch of Constantine himself. Master though he was of a whole world, he could only get giallo antico columns of the yellow marble of Tunis for his arch by robbing that of his predecessor Trajan ; so it was also with the sculptures. And it was the methods of Constantine's arch, not the engineering triumphs of the Basilica of Constantine, that the Roman Christian copied ; not the genuine, indigenous arcuated building in brick and concrete, with the scientific disposition of thrust and abutment which the mediæval builders groped after all through the dark ages till the twelfth century, oblivious of the fact that in the Basilica of Constantine the problems that puzzled them were already solved ; but the Romano-Greek style, the style of the colonnade ; a style which shirked every engineering problem. But a colonnaded style requires a great wealth of columns. Those in the better days of Rome had not been built in drums as in the Parthenon, but were monoliths of rare marbles, of red granite and blue granite, of serpentines and breccias, of onyx and alabaster, and the yet more precious porphyry ; from Paros and Lesbos and Rhodes and Thasos and Euboea ; from Sicily and Spain ; from Tunis and the Atlas mountains ; from the islands of the Nile and Nubia ; from Phrygia, Cappadocia, and Persia : † picked for their beauty or their rarity ; quarried and transported at vast expense all over the Roman world ; hewn, it may be, above the precipices east of the upper Nile ; let down the mountain side by cable and capstan ; transported on rollers over the plain ; put on board barge or raft ; floated down the Nile ; transhipped from barge to sailing ship ; brought across the Mediterranean to Ostia ; put on barge again ; towed up the Tiber to

* It used to be called, wrongly, the Temple of Peace.

† See Corsi's list of Roman marbles in the *Builder*, March 9, 1889 ; and W. Brindley in *Builders' Journal*, Nov. 15, 1899.

Rome ; and then as Martial tells us in one of his epigrams, the corner houses of the narrow streets of old Rome had to be taken down to let them pass. Such magnificence of procedure was beyond the resources of the Christians ; even beyond the resources of the Christian Emperor. As it was with Constantine's Arch of Triumph, so it was with the early Christian churches ; it was easier to beg or buy and re-use than to cut and transport new columns. It is true that at S. Maria Maggiore, Rome, the magnificent ranges of white Ionic columns were cut for the positions they occupy, and there are other instances ; but they are exceptional. The usual practice was to collect as many marble columns, bases, capitals, strings, architraves, friezes, and cornices as could be got, and to piece them together as best might be. Thus at St Paul's *extra muros*, before the fire, there were thirty-two major columns ; of these sixteen were from some Pagan building, and the other sixteen had been cut to match. In Pelagius' work (*c.* 578)* in S. Lorenzo there are two columns of Hymettian marble and ten of *pavonazzetto;* ten of the capitals are Corinthian ; two are composed of greaves and bucklers and armour, plainly from some temple of Bellona or Mars ; above, hardly any two blocks of the entablature correspond either in design or in height. At S. Maria in Ara Coeli, where the colonnade may be sixth century, the melange is something extraordinary. Of the twenty-two columns eighteen are of Syenitic granite, two of fluted white marble, two of *cipollino* from Euboea. Bases and capitals vary still more ; some are perfect, some are truncated Corinthian capitals ; some are Composite, some Tuscan ; plinths and bases are of all sizes and design. Such was the church even in the metropolitan city of Western Christendom : like some tramp's suit of clothes ; coat begged from one man ; shirt stolen from another ; trousers a patchwork, pieced together from the remains of three separate scarecrows.

THE BASILICAN A DISTINCT STYLE.

But heterogeneous as were the materials of the Roman basilicas, when put together they produced interiors which were convenient for the collective worship of a great multitude, while as yet there was but one altar ; and they were well lighted, economical, and handsome. Few interiors in Christendom are more impressive than that of St Paul *extra muros* at Rome, as rebuilt.

What was done at Rome was imitated elsewhere. Constantine built at Bethlehem † a great double-aisled basilica. At Ravenna we have still surviving a magnificent group of basilicas of the sixth century. In Constantinople the traditions of the indigenous Roman building—that in brick and concrete—survived and were yet further developed ; and a new and grander style was evolved in the days of Justinian (sixth century), and produced S. Sophia and the Church of the Apostles. But even in Constantinople, the home of the Byzantine style and the domical church, basilicas also were built ; *e.g.* St John Studius.‡ To the same type belong Baquoza in Syria ;§ Orléansville in North Africa, and many others in the Byzantine dominions.

In Western Christendom the basilican church long prevailed with hardly a

---

* Cattaneo, 41, ascribes these columns to A.D. 325. † Plan in Fergusson, i. 419.
‡ Illustrated in Fergusson, i. 421. § Illustrated in De Vogüé.

rival.　In Germany many early naves of this type survive; *e.g.* Limburg (1030-1042); Hersfeld (1040); Alpirsbach (1100); to which may be added Constance (1052) and Schaffhausen (1052-1064) in German Switzerland.*　In France a good example is seen in the nave of St Genou (Indre), which may be early in the eleventh century;† and quite as early are the two bays of a basilica which now terminate the Gothic Cathedral of Nevers to the west.　In England the nearest approach we have to the columnar basilica is St Peter's, Northampton.‡

In Italy, its native country, the basilica naturally is very common.　We may mention Agliate, 881 (Cattaneo); Grado, ninth century (Rohan de Fleury); Como, S. Abbondio, consecrated 1095; Pisa Cathedral, commenced *c.* 1063 (Rohan de Fleury); Lucca, S. Frediano, 1112; and with pointed arches, in the thirteenth century, the cathedrals of Genoa and of Monreale, Sicily; and in the fourteenth century, Toscanella.　Even well on in the Renaissance period the Basilican type was still employed; *e.g.* the splendid Church of S. Annunziata, Genoa.§　A very high development of the basilica was reached at Pisa and Lucca, where it has been denominated sometimes Round-arched Gothic, sometimes Pisan Romanesque.　It is simply Basilican.　It is no more Gothic at Monreale than it is Romanesque in Pisa.　In Sicily, perhaps, its most notable triumphs were won.　When decorated, as at Monreale, with veneer of marble and mosaic, irradiated by a brilliant southern sun, it gave a glory of internal colour that vies even with Chartres and Le Mans.　As we have seen, its distribution was wide as Christendom, though it was more especially the heritage of the Western Church.　And it went on in use from the fourth to the fourteenth century.

WHY THE BASILICAN STYLE PERISHED.

Wide, however, as was the distribution of churches of Basilican style, that style was doomed to perish; it carried within it the seeds of its own dissolution. On the one hand it relied on a supply of columns which it had not wrought itself; on the other hand, even if obtainable, columns were unsuitable for the work the mediæval builder was planning to do.

Where possible, as at Rome, the columns were monoliths, often brought great distances. ‖　But the supply of monoliths failed, even in Rome itself.　No wonder; for whole families made a respectable living for many centuries by kilns built in the middle of the city, in which they burnt to lime the marbles of Imperial Rome.　Further afield, in our own remote country, for instance, monoliths of any considerable size would be still scarcer.　In any case the supply failed; and the monolithic column had to be built in drums or in small blocks.

Secondly, the column of classical proportions was too weak.　Three types of column had been in use in ancient Greece and Rome; Doric, Ionic, and

---

* Dehio, Plates 52, 55, 56.

† Enlart's *Manuel*, 424; for illustration of interior see Corroyer's *Architecture romane*, 177.

‡ Illustrated in R. Robert, ii. 67.　　　§ Illustrated in Fergusson's *Modern Architecture*.

‖ We hear of columns brought from Ravenna in the ninth century to Aix-la-Chapelle by Charlemagne.　Columns were brought to Venice for St Mark's in the eleventh century from all round the Mediterranean.　Some of the columns of rare marbles round the so-called Trinity Chapel at Canterbury must have been brought from some Mediterranean countries.

Corinthian. Of these the Roman Doric, with its variant, the Tuscan, seems seldom to have been employed in the Basilican churches. The columns were usually Corinthian ; much less frequently, as at S. Maria Maggiore, Ionic. Both the Ionic and the Corinthian column are slender and graceful, but by no means strong. They had not been designed to carry heavy weights. When, therefore, the early Christians put on a pair of columns an arch, and that arch bearing its share of clerestory wall and roof, they were giving the column work to do which it had not been designed to do. The load might indeed be lightened, as it was in the Byzantine basilicas—*e.g.* St John's Studius, Constantinople, and S. Lorenzo and S. AGNESE, Rome (155), in both of which Byzantine influence appears—by inserting an open arcade in the wall above the colonnade, but the columns had to be set very close together ; whether they carried an entablature (*i.e.* horizontal lintels or beams of stone), as at S. Lorenzo ; or arches,* as at St Paul *extra muros*. Set so closely, the long succession of columns and narrow arches produced a converging perspective, which, as later on in Romanesque and Gothic, increased the apparent length, and greatly added to the internal effect of the churches. On the other hand, such a close-set colonnade so obstructed the aisle that from it little of the service in the apse could be seen. So therefore, in spite of the beauty of the classical column with height nicely adjusted to diameter, partly because no more monoliths were available, and coursed columns were difficult to build, and when built not very handsome ; partly because the colonnades blocked the aisles ; most of all because the colonnades were unable to carry the heavy weights with which it was desired to load them ; some other form of support had to be devised. That form of support was found in the pier.†

Pre-Conquest and Norman Piers.

As regards our own country, it is clear that in the time of the Roman occupation colonnaded buildings were erected. The remains of one on a vast scale have recently been discovered in constructing a sewer at Lincoln.‡

---

* It is usually assumed that the first example of an arch resting direct on columns without the interposition of a piece of entablature is that of a gateway in Diocletian's palace at Spalato, late in the third century. But a wide arch so resting is seen at Atil in the Hauran, A.D. 151 ; and still earlier in the Propylæa at Damascus; illustrated in *Anderson and Spiers*, 167, 168. Also columns carrying an arch without intervening entablature occur at Pompeii.

† All through the book the term *pier* has been used in the generic sense of a "support" ; as one speaks of the "piers" of a bridge ; *i.e.* the masses of masonry on which the arches rest. A row of arches with their piers has been called a *pier-arcade*. The term *column* has been avoided except of a cylinder classical in its proportions ; *i.e.* with height and diameter correlated, or of a stout shaft forming part of a compound pier. A very broad, massive column has been designated a cylindrical pier or a cylinder. A very thin, attenuated column is spoken of as a *shaft*. A somewhat stout shaft partly sunk in the masonry of a compound pier is an *engaged column*. Shafts and columns are either *detached;* or *engaged*, *i.e.* "attached."

A *compound pier* is one which is made up of an assemblage of shafts or columns round a central mass, which may be circular, rectangular, or polygonal : *e.g.* the Norman piers of Durham and Peterborough ; the Gothic piers of Ely choir and Chichester presbytery. Or, it may be composed of a cluster of engaged columns, without any shafts ; *e.g.* those of Beverley Minster and Exeter Cathedral.

‡ Two of the bases of these immense columns are to be seen in a cellar.

To Anglo-Saxon days, probably,[*] belong the two columns, which originally formed part of the triple chancel-arch of Reculvers, and which now stand on the lawn to the north of Canterbury Cathedral. Two more, also in drums, have been placed in the porch of the Anglo-Saxon church of Repton. The vault of Repton crypt also is supported by four columns; these are monoliths. And there are examples in Northumberland,[†] where the columns may be Anglo-Saxon, or may be Roman columns re-used. No general use, however, of the column between nave and aisles in Anglo-Saxon churches can be substantiated. Had colonnades been in general use, fragments of columns, perhaps whole columns, would frequently be found on the site of Anglo-Saxon churches; which is not the case. We can hardly doubt that where aisles existed in the Anglo-Saxon churches, they were separated from the nave, not by a colonnade, but by a pier-arcade. At any rate, that is the case in the only aisled Anglo-Saxon churches which survive; those of Lydd, Brixworth, and Wing.[‡] The history of supports of our English churches begins then with the pier, not with the column.

The same is the case with the greater Norman churches of the eleventh century, whether in this country or in Normandy. Two forms of support are usually found in the eleventh century; either compound piers, as at Bernay[§] and Chichester; or an alternation of compound pier and cylindrical or octagonal pier, as at Jumièges, Durham, Peterborough; seldom cylinders[||] or octagons only. Plainly, here and in Normandy, the pier is as much the normal form of support as the column in Southern Christendom; perhaps because there were fewer Roman columnar buildings to rob in Northern Europe, or to suggest a church with colonnaded aisles.

ORIGIN OF COMPOUND PIER.

For the genesis of the compound pier we must go abroad. As has been pointed out, we have no Romano-British church, and but few Anglo-Saxon aisled churches surviving. Every one of the larger Anglo-Saxon churches was pulled down long ago,[¶] and most of the smaller ones, to be rebuilt in Romanesque or Gothic fashion. But, abroad, we can trace back the genesis and development of the pier, at any rate to the ninth century. Sometimes it replaces the column altogether. But sometimes the column makes a struggle. For instance, at S. Prassede, Rome, as built in the ninth century, all the supports were columns. But it was desired to introduce diaphragmatic roofing.[**] For this purpose it was necessary to build broad arches across the nave carrying a heavy load of masonry.[††] Columns were utterly inadequate to support such a

---

[*] See G. E. Fox in *Builder*, Oct. 27, 1900.   [†] Baldwin Brown, 8.

[‡] Plan of Wing in Scott's *Essay*, 44.   [§] Ruprich-Robert, Plate xi.

[||] There are short, massive cylinders in the choirs of GLOUCESTER (294) and TEWKES-BURY (165); both begun in the eleventh century.

[¶] The last to survive was the nave of Hexham. See C. C. Hodges' sumptuous monograph on Hexham Abbey.

[**] Every fourth clerestory window was blocked up by an arched stone principal of the roof, but may still be traced in the outer wall.

[††] As shown in Dehio, Plate 45.

load ; and accordingly every third column was replaced by a massive pier. Similarly the eleventh-century church of S. MINIATO, FLORENCE * and the twelfth-century church of S. Zeno, Verona, and the contemporary cathedral of Modena,† were built with a similar alternation of column and pier. In Normandy also and in Northern France roofs with arched stone principals were constructed here and there ; *e.g.* at Notre Dame du Pré, Le Mans;‡ at St George's de Boscherville ; § at Cérisy-la-Forêt.‖ The same form of roof may have been in use at the Abbaye-aux-Hommes at Caen. ¶

These diaphragmatic roofs, with arches carrying a gabled transverse wall, simplified the construction of the timber roof, for the purlins could rest directly
on the gables ; and moreover they divided it up in separate compartments ; so that if one compartment of the roof was burnt, the flames, owing to the party-walls, could not reach the adjoining compartments. As was natural, they were employed in the aisles also. The remains of such arches are to be seen over the aisles of St Peter's, Northampton ;** they are to be seen perfect at Chivy, near Laon, in the eleventh century ;†† they were intended at Thaon.‡‡ Enlart §§ cites twelve other examples of aisles with diaphragmatic roofs in Normandy, Brittany, and the north of France.

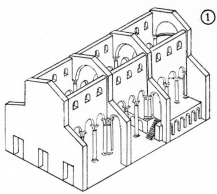

S. Miniato, Florence.

It is possible that in this system of roofing we see a constructional origin for the compound pier. In its simplest form, as at S. Eustorgio, Milan,‖‖ to the back of each pier there was added a pilaster facing another pilaster on the aisle wall. On these pairs of pilasters arches were built across each aisle, of which two still remain.¶¶ A similar example occurs in the tall oblong piers of STE.

---

* Illustrated in Norman Shaw's *Architectural Sketches*, Plate 47.
† Willis' *Middle Ages*, 89 ; and Dehio, Plate 66.
‡ Dehio, i. 286 ; and Enlart's *Manuel*, 264.
§ See perspective in Choisy, ii. 193.
‖ See Dehio, Plate 90 ; Enlart's *Manuel*, 264 ; St Paul in *Planat*, vi. 24 ; and R. Robert, Plate 72. Before the present vaults of lath and plaster were put up in 1868, R. Robert was able to see still *in situ* the three lowest voussoirs of one of the transverse arches of the nave.
¶ As shown in Dehio, Plate 87. It may have been intended, even if not carried out, in the transepts and nave of Durham. This may be suggested as an explanation of the roof-shafts, rendered objectless by the present vault, which run up in the end bays of the east sides of the Durham transepts. So also in the nave, the bottommost voussoirs of the great transverse arches of the vault are much broader than those above them. This must mean that broader transverse arches than the present ones were intended and were actually commenced ; arches strong enough to carry either arched stone principals or else a groined vault. (See section in Billing's *Durham*, Plate 15 ; and Bilson's *Beginnings*, 315, 26.) It should be noted that Modena Cathedral has gone through a similar series of changes to those suggested above for Durham. (See Willis' *Middle Ages*, 89 ; and Dehio, Plates 66 and 162.)
** See R. Robert, ii., Plate 67. †† Illustrated in Enlart's *Manuel*, 263.
‡‡ R. Robert, 136. §§ *Manuel*, 264.
‖‖ Tenth century, Cattaneo and Rivoira. ¶¶ Cattaneo, 245.

APHRODISIE, BÉZIERS, which appears to be of the tenth or early eleventh century; and in the church of Vaux-sous-Laon.

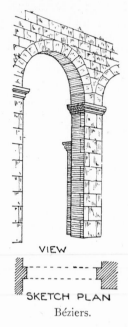

VIEW

SKETCH PLAN

Béziers.

The next step is seen at the dated Church of SS. FELIX AND FORTUNATUS, outside Vicenza (A.D. 985), where there are cased up in the walls columns alternating with compound piers. The latter are cruciform; they have pilasters to east and west, and engaged columns to north and south, as at S. Miniato, Florence, illustrated above. This is a great step in advance.* A further advance is seen in the primitive Romanesque church of S. Stefano, Bologna; where there is a square pier with four engaged columns. A yet further stage is seen at Jumièges,† and in our church of ST PETER'S, NORTHAMPTON (663.1), *c.* 1160; in the latter there is simply a cluster of four engaged columns. Each one of these has its own special work to do. The front column rises to the roof, and supported the tie-beam; the back column supported the diaphragmatic arch spanning the aisle. The pier-arches are in one order only; and the springing of each arch rests on an engaged column. The whole pier, therefore, is thoroughly logical and rational; each member of it has its own function; each has a different load.‡   A less logical pier is seen in the Norman church of St James, Bristol; it also consists of a cylinder with four columns attached.

In such examples as the above, it is plain that the compound pier is constructional in origin.

But possibly the idea of such construction was also suggested by the sight of actually existing Roman examples of it. For the compound pier was perfectly well known to the Romans. It occurs in the peristyle of a house at Pompeii; in the portico of the court of the Temple of the Sun at Palmyra; on the arch at Damas; in the Temple of Vespasian at Brescia; at Palatitza.§ In the Piscina Mirabile at Baiae,‖ the piers of the cistern are cruciform, there being pilasters on each of the four sides. Rectangular compound piers occur in the Roman baths at Bath. At Germigny, consecrated 806, antique shafts are

Vicenza.

* Illustrated in Cattaneo, 248.   † R. Robert, Plate 13.

‡ See section of St Peter's in R. Robert, ii. 67.   On the compound pier see Willis' *Middle Ages*, 90, *seq.*

§ De Dartein, ii. 467.

‖ Illustrated in Willis' *Middle Ages*, Plate v., 5, and text, 79.

applied to the piers;* as indeed was the constant practice in the Roman Thermæ. Compound piers or responds occur also in Anglo-Saxon, where they are probably an indication of late date ; e.g. in the tower arch of Sompting ; and at Bosham, Wareham, and Broughton.†

When, therefore, the Normans commenced to build their great churches in England, the compound pier had already a long pedigree. Their piers, however, were much more advanced than such as those of S. Miniato, Florence. This was partly because they had further developed the arch, and partly because they had learnt to vault the aisles. Both their arches and their vaults needed additional supports. Arches in the eleventh century were now generally double ; i.e. each arch was compounded of two independent arches, of which the upper— it is called the outer order of the arch—was broader than the lower—or inner order — and overlapped it. Such an arch required three supports at each springing on which to rest. At the junction of two arches, therefore, six columns or shafts were needed. Moreover, usually another shaft ran up the face of the pier—what is called a roofing shaft or a vaulting shaft—up to the wooden roof, or to the vault, if there was one, of the nave. This increased the number of supports to seven. But at the back of the pier there was a low transverse arch which spanned the aisle, and of which one end rested on a wall shaft or a wall pilaster, while the other required for its support a column attached to the pier. This raises the number of supports to eight. And it is just this pier, with four engaged columns and four detached shafts, which we find at Cérisy-la-Forêt ;‡ St Nicholas, Caen ; in the eastern bays of the nave of Lessay ; in the triforium of the Abbaye-aux-Hommes, in St George's de Boscherville, and in the west aisle of the north transept of ELY (659.2).§ In all these the outer order of the pier-arch is supported by shafts ; the other four supports are stout columns. Such a compound pier may be described as a pair of intersecting oblongs, with eight columns and shafts.

In the west aisle of the Norman NORTH TRANSEPT OF WINCHESTER ‖ (659.4), the number of supports is increased to ten. This is because shafts were added to carry the groins of the vault of the aisle. These are carried by a pilaster in the AISLE OF NORWICH NAVE (238).

In DURHAM CHOIR¶ (659.1) the number of supports rises to twelve. This is because the pier has on its north and south faces not single, but triple vaulting shafts.

---

* Enlart's *Manuel*, 177.   † Illustrated in Baldwin Brown's *Arts in Early England.*
‡ R. Robert, Plate 73.
§ But the eight supports might be utilised for other purposes ; e.g. in the Ely pier, 659.2 ; where d, d carry the inner orders and e, e the outer order of the pier-arches ; b carries the transverse arch and c, c the groins A, A of the aisle vault ; a is the roofing shaft of the central span of the transept. Plans of all these Norman piers in Bilson's *Beginnings*, 291, 306, 310.
‖ In 659.4, A, A are the groins of the aisle vault ; B, B, B, B are the outer orders and C, C the inner orders of the pier-arches ; a is a roofing shaft of the central span of the transept ; b supports D the transverse arch of one order of the aisle vault ; c, c support the groins of this vault ; d, d support the inner orders and e, e, e, e the outer orders of the pier-arches. See 261.
¶ In the pier of Durham choir, 659.1, d, d support the inner orders and e, e, e, e the outer orders of the pier-arches ; b supports the transverse arch and c, c the diagonal ribs of the aisle vault ; while a, f, f is a triple vaulting shaft rising nearly to the clerestory. See 306, 315.

Norwich Nave, North Aisle.   Peterborough Nave, South Aisle.

In the central transept of Lincoln and in the western bays of the nave of Worcester Cathedral, as at SENS (107) and Laon, there were also wall-ribs (*formerets*) round the clerestory windows. In RIPON CHOIR a vault of similar character seems to have been intended (102). For each of these wall-ribs two more vaulting shafts were required, raising the total of vaulting shafts to five,* and still further increasing the complication of the pier. Again, we have spoken of the pier-arches as constructed in two orders. But sometimes, as at St Albans and PETERBOROUGH, they were constructed in three orders; in this case two more supports on the east and two on the west side of the pier would be necessary to carry the additional outer order; an addition of four shafts. Again, the transverse arch spanning the aisle was usually built in two orders; this would necessitate two more shafts at the back of the pier.

So far we have spoken as if the supports devised for the orders of the pier-arch and the groins or ribs of the vaults were always either shafts or columns. This was not so; pilasters might be substituted for any or all of the shafts and columns. Thus, at ST ALBANS (659.5), where, owing to scarcity of freestone, the pier and arches are constructed with Roman brick from the ruins of the neighbouring Roman town of Verulamium, pilasters only are employed; as also at Autun,† and constantly in the Romanesque of Provence and Palestine.

It has been pointed out above that in the best examples, such as Durham

* There are five vaulting shafts in the western bays of Worcester nave.
† Illustrated in Viollet-le-Duc, *Architecture*, vii. 161.

choir, the composition of the pier is rigidly determined by its function as a group of supports. But strict logic was often disregarded either for practical or for æsthetic reasons. Thus at NORWICH (238), the pier-arches consist of two recessed orders; and the second pier (the one with the tablet) has, quite correctly, a single stout and ugly column to carry the broad inner order. But in the alternate piers, for this massive column three * shafts are substituted, making the pier less obstructive and less heavy in appearance. For the same reason each transverse arch of the vault of the aisle is supported not by one, but by two shafts.† For artistic reasons, also, there are four vaulting shafts in front of these piers, instead of three. Thus the alternate piers of NORWICH ‡ (659.7) come to consist of sixteen shafts and pilasters. In Gothic architecture this logic of the pier—*i.e.* the correlation of the articulation of the pier to the orders of the arch and to the ribs of the vaults of nave and aisle—is less often insisted upon. Usually, though not always, the builders were willing to correlate the members

Durham Nave, North Aisle.

of the pier with the orders of the arch; but much less frequently, at any rate in England, with the far-away vault of the nave. It became customary more and more to exclude the vaulting shafts from membership in the pier.

VAULTING SHAFTS.

In theory, indeed, where there is a vaulted nave, it is supposed that there should rise from the pavement in front of the pier a group of three shafts to support the transverse rib and the diagonal ribs of the high vault; and if the vault has wall-ribs, there should be a group of five. But we may observe that as a matter of fact the vaulting shafts do not really support the ribs of the vault at all.§ This is plain from the fact that in ruined churches vaulting shafts may be seen to have perished, but the vaults

* The photograph shows two of these shafts; but there are three.

† It should be noted that the diagonal groins or arrises of the vault are not supported by shafts as at Durham and Peterborough, but by pilasters.

‡ In the major pier of Norwich, 659.7, and 238, *d, d, d, d, d, d* carry the inner orders and *e, e, e, e* the outer orders of the pier-arches; *a, a* are roofing shafts of the nave; *b, b* carry the inner order and *c, c* the outer order of the transverse arch of two orders of the aisle vault. No separate shafts are provided for the groins of this vault.

§ So also Dehio, ii. 549.

remain perfectly safe without them. This is because the weight of the vault does not descend vertically as it appears to do ; but owing to the outer thrusts of the arches of the vault, passes out more or less laterally. Therefore, if we are to chop logic, the English Gothic builders were quite right, on scientific grounds, in refusing, as they usually did, to bring the vaulting shafts down to the pavement. It is true that there is great value in the latter treatment. It provides the strongest possible vertical lines ; as well as an emphatic line of demarcation between the respective bays of which an interior is composed. On the other hand, it is open to the practical objection that in a choir, if a group of vaulting shafts is placed in front of the piers, the choir is considerably narrowed thereby. So much was this felt at Lincoln, that when the present stalls were placed in St Hugh's choir, his vaulting shafts were chopped off from the piers. And it is open to the artistic objection that the group of vaulting shafts breaks in most ruthless fashion into the group of capitals which ought, but is unable, to encircle the pier. Examples of the retention of the vaulting shaft in the pier are Worcester nave, Rochester presbytery, ST SAVIOUR'S SOUTHWARK (521), YORK NAVE and CHOIR (10), Chester nave, Bath Abbey, and LICHFIELD NAVE (523), where great unity is given thereby to the triple horizontal division of each bay. So again, when WINCHESTER NAVE (342) was remodelled c. 1360, the Norman vaulting shaft was retained. Some ten years later CANTERBURY NAVE (90) copied Winchester ; but with the unfortunate addition of bands to the vaulting shafts, obstructing the upward flow of vertical line. At ST MARY REDCLIFFE, Bristol (525), c. 1442, the bands are omitted.

The more common Gothic treatment in England was to stop the vaulting shafts at or above the pier. Of all the methods adopted the worst is that adopted in the transept of PETERBOROUGH (161), at MALMESBURY (522), in Canterbury choir, in the nave of the Temple choir, and in the central transept of Lincoln ; in all of which the vaulting shafts rest on the abacus of the piers below. It is very common in French twelfth-century Gothic ; e.g. Notre Dame, Paris, and LAON (528). To the eye the abacus appears, and is, utterly inadequate to carry the weight of the vault ; and the vaulting shafts, perched on this thin slab, look painfully insecure. The most common English treatment is to insert a corbel at a little distance above the abacus ; as in the presbyteries of LINCOLN (56), ELY (117), and EXETER (241) ; where there are foliated corbels of extraordinary beauty. Sometimes the vaulting shaft is stopped at the sill of the triforium ; e.g. at New Shoreham ; ST DAVID'S (525) ; Hexham ; and Rievaulx choir. This is a less successful treatment ; it leaves a blank spandrel between the abacus and the sill of the triforium. This, however, was filled up at Guisborough and SELBY (390) by a statuette under a canopy. Worse still is Salisbury ; where the vaulting shaft is stopped about half-way up the triforium. Worst of all is WELLS NAVE (524) ; * where the vaulting shaft is stopped at the sill of the clerestory. In one way or other, the result usually was to exclude the vaulting shafts from membership in the pier. The builders thus obtained a freer hand, and were able to compose their piers with reference only to the orders of the arch and the ribs of the vault of the aisles.

* But see page 534.

Before long even this was felt to be a restraint and a bondage ; and both in France* and in England the strict subordination of the supports to the load was abandoned. Indeed, if we examine such a beautiful pier as that of Exeter, it is plain that so far from subordinating the columns of the pier to the orders of the arch, the very reverse is the case. The builder has designed the pier first, with sixteen columns ; and has then made the design of the arch follow that of the pier ; *e.g.* he has actually so grouped the moldings of his arch that he gets four sham orders instead of two genuine ones ; in order to make each of the latter correspond with the pair of columns beneath it. In this he has reverted to a very ancient practice (for not all the Romanesque builders were logicians first, artists afterwards) ; even as early as St Remi, Reims, in the tenth or eleventh

 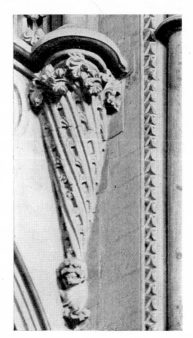

Exeter Choir.   Ely Presbytery.

century, to support arches of two orders, the builder erected a pier of fourteen clustered columns.† The fact is that in Gothic, now that the piers were built in good masonry, they had become so slender that there was no longer room for such an apparatus of shafts and columns as we saw at DURHAM‡ (659.1) and Norwich. Moreover, in England, the number of constructional ribs in the vault had been increased greatly by the addition of the *tiercerons ; e.g.* at Exeter ; and if all these, together with the wall-ribs, had to be found separate supports in the pier, there would be no end to its complication. In fact, logic had become impossible. Being sensible men, the builders recognised this, and made the best compromise they could between logic and art.§

* *E.g.* at Amiens.   † Illustrated in Viollet-le-Duc, *Architecture*, vii. 155.
‡ This pier occupies 160 square feet.   § Illogical piers are seen in HEDON NAVE (544).

Q

THE COMPOUND PIER IN LATE GOTHIC.

There was, however, here and there, a curious survival of strict logic as to pier-composition in the late Gothic of England, and still more of France. Indeed the logician bethought himself of yet further refinements. In the south transept of Gloucester a slender shaft, almost a "bead," with due capital and base, is provided for every rib of the high vault; viz. one transverse rib, two diagonals, two tiercerons, two liernes; as well as for the wall-ribs. Sometimes there is a desire that even the moldings of the vault-ribs should reappear down below in capital, shaft, and base. With us it produced such piers as those of the nave of ST GEORGE'S, WINDSOR (255). Very interesting it is to trace out the interdependence of load and support in such examples, and still more in such work as that of St Urbain, Troyes;[*] S. Severin, Paris; and S. Juan de los Reyes, Toledo.[†]   Ultra-logical, however, as such piers may be, their appeal is more to the intellect than to the eye: art is often sacrificed to logic; beauty of curve, alternation of high light and deep shadow may be lost; they are not to be compared for one moment with the illogical piers of the Ely presbytery or Exeter choir.

CYLINDRICAL PIERS.

So far we have spoken of the Romanesque compound pier and of its developments. In the eleventh century it was the prevailing form in all the larger Romanesque churches built here or in Normandy. In the twelfth century, on the other hand, there was a curious revival of the much older form, the column; but a column that no Greek could have looked at without a shudder; a column whose thickness was not regulated by artistical consideration of the fitting ratio of breadth to height, but by the weight of the load it had to carry; a column without any tapering upward, without any central entasis; without any flutes; with a mere impost for capital, as at GLOUCESTER (26), or with a capital unknown to or strangely changed from that of Ancient Greece. It is better to provide it with a new name at once, and call it a "cylindrical pier" or a "cylinder," not a "column."

The present geographical distribution of our Norman cylinders is a little curious: so many Norman minsters, however, have been rebuilt in Gothic, that it is impossible to speak with precision. At present Norman cylinders appear in the south at Colchester, St Botolph's; St Bartholomew's, Smithfield. In the Midlands they are seen at SOUTHWELL (520); MELBOURNE (203); Oxford; in the north at Carlisle and Dunfermline. But in the province of what later on was to be a distinct school of Western Gothic, the surviving examples are much more numerous; GLOUCESTER (294), TEWKESBURY (165), Malvern, SHREWSBURY (521), Hereford, Pershore, St David's, CHESTER ST JOHN'S (448.1). It is notable that these examples occur principally in naves, and that in all but the later examples, such as St Cross and St David's, it seems to have been intended that the nave should not have a vault.

At GLOUCESTER (26) and TEWKESBURY (297) the cylinders are of brobdingnagian proportions. Both are Benedictine churches; and because they have

---

* Choisy, ii. 350.   † Illustrated in Dehio, Plate 567.

a cloister on one side of the nave, the aisle windows have to be placed high in the wall to clear the cloister roof. By raising the piers and arches of the nave, it was possible to get into the aisle wall a taller window, and thus to improve the lighting both of aisle and nave. This may explain the extraordinary proportions of these piers.*

In our parish churches the cylinders, or their variant the octagonal pier, remained in constant use till the end of Gothic. This was simply because a more highly organised support was beyond the resources of most villages. But in our larger Gothic churches we abandoned it. The French, on the other hand, in the face of all the logic of construction, frequently employed the cylinder; not only round the apse, but flanking choir or nave; *e.g.* Rouen Cathedral. Indeed in their Flamboyant work, *e.g.* at St Lo and Montargis, it is one of the two most characteristic forms.†

ALTERNATION OF PIERS.—Frequently cylinders alternate with compound piers; *e.g.* in Lombardy in S. Stefano, Bologna; in Germany at Worms; in Normandy at Jumièges; in England at DURHAM (8), Castle Acre, Furness, and elsewhere. ‡

---

* Similar colossal piers occur early in the eleventh century at Tournus, on the Saône, which has a cloister south of the nave. Illustrated in *Classification of Romanesque*, 275.

† The other is that in which the moldings of the arch and vault are carried down the pier (242).

‡ On alternating supports see page 317.

CHAPTER XV.

GOTHIC PIERS.

The Western Pier—The Southern Pier—Shafts, Bands, Marble—The Northern Pier—
Clustered Columns—Ornamentation and Plan of Shafts.

IN English Gothic both forms of Romanesque pier were abandoned, or at any
rate totally transformed. The rectangular pier nearly surrounded by shafts, as
at Norwich, was composed altogether of columns and shafts, with its core
seldom visible. The cylinder was surrounded by shafts, and produced a second
type. In the first type the columns or shafts are *engaged ;* in the second they
are *detached.* Both were in use simultaneously for about a century. Of the

Beverley Minster.   Lichfield Choir.

piers with engaged columns or shafts there were two sorts ; those which were a
cluster of columns, and those which were encircled by triplets of shafts ; but they
agreed in eschewing marble, and in being constructed usually in courses of freestone, and not in monolithic blocks. The former we may call the Northern ;
the other the Western pier ; the pier with detached shafts, of the Canterbury
type, of which we have spoken above, we may call the Southern pier.

THE WESTERN PIER.

This is a pier very short and massive in proportion to its height, but which is prevented from looking heavy and squat by the exceptional amount of slender shafting encircling it. The special feature of the shafts is that they are arranged in groups of three ; and that they are constructed in coursed freestone. In the western bays of Worcester nave, which may be as early as 1170, all are of coursed freestone ; some are pear-shaped. The shafts are numerous and slender. At WELLS (209), c. 1175, the pier retains the Romanesque disposition of two intersecting oblongs, as in the typical pier shown in 661.4, but round these rect-

angular forms there are disposed eight triplets of shafts, twenty-four in all. Piers of the same type occur in St Cuthbert, Wells. In the piers of Cwm Hir, now at LLANIDLOES (552),* all traces of the rectangle have disappeared ; the pier is fully developed and consists of eight groups of triplets ; so also in PERSHORE (75) and LICHFIELD choirs (661.8).† In St Mary's, Shrewsbury, being a parish church, the piers are small and of early type ; a rectangle surrounded by four triplets.‡ LLANDAFF (424) has a simpler pier, consisting mainly of plain chamfers ; but still there are triplets of shafts attached instead of single columns. In the western piers of LICHFIELD CHOIR (244) the shafts are arranged in triplets. Of these the nave-piers are a variant (424.8). Similar triplets occur in the piers at the back of the high altar of Dore Abbey, Hereford. They occur again at Christ Church, Dublin. Their distribution is very remarkable. They are all to the west of a line drawn from Wells to Lichfield §

Chichester Retrochoir.

and Chester, and including Christ Church, Dublin ; which we know was built of Somersetshire oolite by masons from Bristol and Pembroke. In this western area the triple-shafted pier reigned almost alone from c. 1170 to c. 1200.

* See capitals of these piers (422).
† A curious parallel is seen in the fourteenth-century piers of S. Lorenz, Nuremberg ; which have eight triplets (Dehio, Plate 566).
‡ See capitals of these piers (424.7).
§ The Transitional piers of St Sepulchre's, Northampton, are an "outlier" (*Nene Valley*, Plate 16).

The Southern Pier; with Detached Shafts.

We will turn next to the pier with a cylinder for core, and round it disposed a number of shafts, some or all of which are detached.* The detached
shafts are seldom built in drums; but if the shaft be short it is a single block;
if long, it is composed of several blocks joined together. The use of monolithic
shafts was well known to the Romans; they were turned in the lathe.† Roman
monolithic shafts remain with the characteristic tapering and entasis. One
occurs *in situ* at Chester.‡ Two are re-used in the west doorway of St Woolos,
Newport. Others, with the marks of the turning-tool upon them, may be seen
in the museums of Leicester and Rouen. The Anglo-Saxons were expert in
turning baluster shafts in the lathe; and four of their monolithic columns remain
in Repton crypt. Monolithic shafts occur in the Norman work of Gundulph in
Rochester crypt, and of Ernulph in Canterbury crypt. They are very common
in Norman doorways and windows at all periods. Moreover, about the middle of
the twelfth century and onward, we have a large number of fonts, *e.g.* that in
Winchester nave, the bowls of which rest on a central cylinder surrounded by four
or eight shafts. This is precisely the plan of the Early Gothic piers of CHICHESTER
RETROCHOIR (245), Boxgrove, and St Thomas, Portsmouth. In these three
the shafts are very widely spaced from the central cylinder; on the other hand,
in the piers of Canterbury choir they are set close to the cylinder; it was the
latter precedent which most often found favour. The piers of ELY RETROCHOIR
(247), however, incline to the Chichester type.

The number of shafts in these piers varies greatly. Often, *e.g.* in Chichester
retrochoir and Salisbury nave, as at Chartres, there are but four; when these are
set close up to the internal cylinder, the effect is somewhat naked and unsatisfactory. More successful is the pier with eight spaced shafts, as at Ely.
In the choir of Westminster the piers have four shafts; in the nave, which was
built later, they have eight.§ Sometimes the number of detached shafts rose to
sixteen, as in the vestibule to the Chapter House of St Mary's, York; ‖ where the
central cylinder is surrounded by a ring of twelve detached shafts, with four
columns at the cardinal points of the pier outside the ring. At LINCOLN
(249) is a remarkable pier—all the more remarkable because it is so early—
it is part of St Hugh's work of 1192—at the junction of the choir with the
eastern transepts; it has eight shafts; of these four are circular, four are fluted
hexagons. Piers of surprising height and slenderness were erected by means
of these monolithic blocks; daringly beautiful are those of the north-west chapel
of Lincoln nave, and of SALISBURY LADY CHAPEL (173): the latter are nearly
30 feet high and carry a vault. Britton¶ points out that the central cylinders
of the Salisbury piers are composed of small square stones laid in mortar.
These must have settled considerably as they gradually got their load. If,
therefore, the shafts had been built at the same time as the cylinders, not

---

* This may be styled the Southern pier, because, though it occurs elsewhere, it is far more
common in the South of England.
† Enlart's *Manuel*, 328.   ‡ Baldwin Brown, 8 to 10.
§ In the western bays of Westminster nave, built later still, the shafts are engaged.
‖ Plan in Scott's *Lectures*, ii. 148.   ¶ *Salisbury*, 80.

Ely Retrochoir.

being able to settle so much, being monoliths, they would inevitably have been fractured. It is probable, however, that the shafts were not added till all settlement had ceased. We can still see, inside the western wall of St Alban's, bases, bands, and capitals prepared by John de Cella for the insertion of shafts; which, however, were never inserted. The same was the practice in France.* If we can trust Leland, the shafts of the choir of Worcester, built 1202-1240, were not added till the time of Bishop Giffard, 1268-1301.†

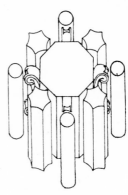

Lincoln, Eastern Transept.

We have spoken of the core of the central pier as a cylinder; and this was the most common form. But other forms, e.g. the octagon, were common. At Fountains Abbey, in STONE CHURCH (665.7), and in All Saints', Stamford, it is noteworthy that the builders have set their shafts round the special form of pier, which for its strength was adopted in some of the best of fourteenth-century Gothic of France; e.g. at St Urbain, Troyes.‡

BANDS.—The joints between the monoliths of which the longer shafts were composed were masked and strengthened by stone or marble bands (annulets). Usually the bands were solid. In the north transept of Tintern, however, they are pierced; so that the shaft passed through them; elsewhere at Tintern they are solid.§ The method of attaching the annulet to the central cylinder is shown in the diagram.‖ Some-

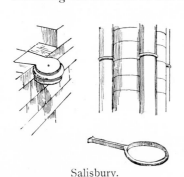

Salisbury.

times, however, as in the Salisbury pier, bands of copper or bronze¶ were employed; the method of attachment is shown in the diagram. Bands of stone occur occasionally abroad; e.g. at Noyon, Laon, Dol, Lausanne, Magdeburg. In England they usually disappear about 1280; but sometimes reappear in late work, as at Canterbury, Bath, Wrington, and Yatton. One of the earliest examples is the columns of St Peter's, Northampton, each of which consists of two monoliths, banded together.

MARBLE SHAFTS.—Not only is the employment of the pier with detached shafts far more common in England than abroad, but the further refinement, specially English, was added, that most often the shaft is constructed of marble: turned in the lathe. We have special mention of lathes in the account of the rebuilding of Canterbury choir by William of Sens, who, says

---

* Choisy, ii. 264.   † For examples of piers with detached shafts see 665.6, 7.
‡ For moldings of capital, band, and base see WEST WALTON (432).
§ T. Blashill's *Guide to Tintern*, 12.
‖ In early work the band is constructional; being a bondstone into which the detached shafts were socketed. But in the thirteenth-century work of the nave of All Saints', Stamford, there are decorative bands, running round the coursed work of the solid pier. *Nene Valley*, 14.
¶ On the bands of gilded brass which occur in Worcester retrochoir, but only where exceptional pressure had squeezed out the beds of the monoliths or flushed their edges, see Mr A. B. Pickney in *Journal of R.I.B.A.*, 27th April 1901, 300.

the monk Gervase, "*torneumata* ad lapides formandos fecit valde ingeniose." *
The marbles most commonly employed are formed of comminuted shells ; *e.g.*
those of Bethersden, Kent, used at Canterbury ; those found near Petworth,
Sussex ; and those found in the Isle of Purbeck, near Portland.   The last, being
of fine quality, and on the sea-board, was shipped in vast quantities wherever
there was water-carriage up the rivers ; up the Avon to Salisbury ; up the Ouse
to Ely ; up the Witham to Lincoln ; up the Humber and Hull to BEVERLEY
(51) ; up the Humber and Ouse to York ; up the Wear to Durham for the
galilee ; even across the sea and up the Liffey for St Patrick's Cathedral, Dublin.
Where there was a good local marble, that of course was usually substituted for
Purbeck ; Langport lias at Wells and Bristol ; Frosterley encrinital marble for the
eastern transept of Durham ; Yorkshire marbles for Fountains and Jervaulx.
The marble shaft is first found in general use in William of Sens' work at
Canterbury, begun 1175.   In the pier-arcade he uses the Purbeck shafts in
hesitating, tentative fashion.   One can see, as one walks from the eastern
transept eastward, that the material is a novel one, and that he is trying all sorts
of combinations of shafting to his cylinders and octagons ; in the triforium and
clerestory, however, it is employed with the greatest propriety and success.   But
the curious thing is that for this profusion of dark marbles against white freestone, which was to be the dominant note of most English Gothic for a century,
there was little precedent in the country from which he came.   A few piers shafted
with monoliths occur in the aisles of Notre Dame, and in two bays of the nave
of Laon ; † but they are too rare to have suggested the use of Purbeck on the
vast scale in which it is used at Canterbury.   Besides, we were employing
marble shafts in the galilee of Durham, *c.* 1160-1175 ; these were of Purbeck ;
a remarkable example of the great distance to which Purbeck marble was
exported.   Marbles also occur in piers and shafts in Jervaulx chapter house,
Pudsey's Hall at Auckland and at Hartlepool ; ‡ all *c.* 1190.   Plainly this
characteristic decoration of English Gothic is of English origin.

For detached shafts marbles were in employment chiefly from *c.* 1160 to *c.*
1300.   After this they appear in engaged shafts ; *e.g. c.* 1330 in the beautiful
piers of ELY CHOIR (251) and the back of BEVERLEY REREDOS (452), *c.* 1330.

POLYCHROMY.—The use of Purbeck marble is one of the few attempts on a
large scale at polychromy in mediæval art.§   In Auvergne polychromy was
popular ; *e.g.* at Le Puy ; brilliantly coloured stones being obtainable from the
extinct volcanoes in the neighbourhood.   But the nearest parallel to the attempts
of our thirteenth-century builders to make their church as it were studies in
pen and ink‖ is to be found in Northern Italy ; where may be seen a whole
cathedral, Siena, built in alternate stripes of black and white marble.   In
Verona red and white marbles are used alternately.   From this the Italians

---

* Willis' *Canterbury*.

† *c.* 1200, acc. to Viollet-le-Duc.   See Plate 66 in Johnson's *Early French Architecture*.

‡ Some of the Hartlepool piers have eight marble shafts.   This use, however, remained
characteristic of Southern piers.   In the Northern *pier-arcades* a different use prevailed.

§ There is a certain amount of polychromy also in the Norman work of Worcester ; in the
walls of Westminster choir, and throughout its high vault.   So also Ham Hill stone is alternated
with lias in Somerset.   Red ironstone is similarly used in the Midlands.

‖ "*Albo nigroque*" (*Metrical Life of St Hugh*).

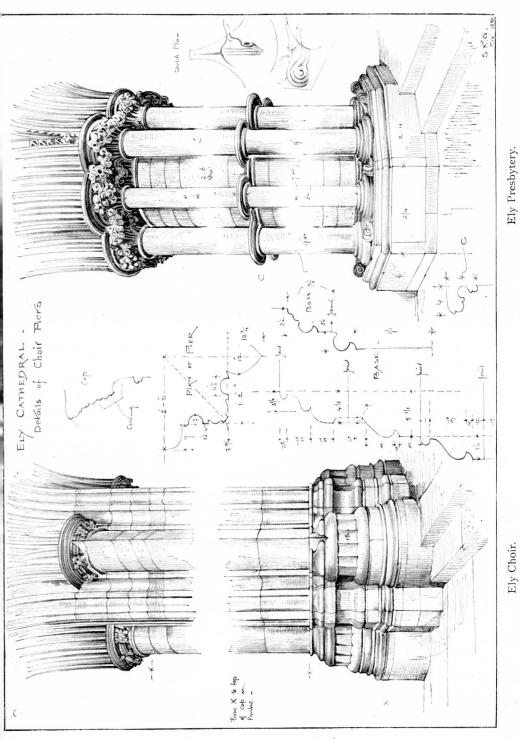

Ely Cathedral -
Details of Choir Piers

Sketch Plan

Cap
Caving

PLAN OF PIER

BASE

Ely Presbytery.

Ely Choir.

went on, as in the cathedral and its campanile at Florence, to panels of coloured marbles separated by mosaic borders ; about as artistic as "an elaborate Tunbridge work-box." *   In early work, indeed, in our own country, such as at Canterbury, we find a good deal of hesitancy in the use of the new material ; and at Rochester, *c.* 1200, some of the shafts have rather the appearance of glorified drain pipes.   But almost immediately the new marble shafting produced consummate design : the arcading of St Hugh's work at Lincoln ; of the porches of John de Cella at St Alban's ; of the galilee at Ely ; of Peterborough west front ; of the Lady Chapel of Salisbury ; of the unparalleled choir of Beverley.   And, with the aid of the lathe, marble was used, not only for cylinders and shafts, but for bases, capitals, and abaci.   And when Ely presbytery was built, the carvers had become so expert that foliated caps also were wrought of this intractable material.   It is interesting to note that at Christ Church, Dublin, the hundreds of Purbeck shafts employed are of a uniform length of 16¼ inches each.   Being brittle, they were probably sent in short lengths from Purbeck to lessen risk of breakage in sea-transit.   The uniformity of dimension of these shafts largely conditioned the builder's design.   He was not able to make his doors, windows, piers, &c., any height he chose ; each jamb or pier had to be so many multiples of 16¼ inches.†

DISUSE OF MARBLE.—We cannot but ask why a material which produced such splendid results was abandoned, as in the end it was.   It may have been that the quarries ceased to be able to furnish a supply of sufficient good marble. But this reason hardly seems adequate.   If the Purbeck quarries gave out, there were other quarries.   At any rate, other reasons may be adduced. When the shafts were put up, they were highly polished, and, to the mediæval eye, dazzlingly beautiful.   Geraldus Cambrensis,‡ speaking of St Hugh, says that "*Lincolniensem* beatae Virginis ecclesiam ex Pariis lapidibus marmoreisque columnis, alternatim et congrue dispositis, et tanquam picturis variis, albo nigroque, naturali tamen colorum varietate distinctis, incomparabiliter erigere curavit eximiam."   And the *Metrical Life of St Hugh*, speaking of the dancing lights of the polished shafts, says —

"Inde columellae quae sic cinxere columnas
Ut videantur ibi quandam celebrare choream ;"

and again he says that the surface of them

" Clara repercussis opponit visibus astra." §

This polish, however, does not last.   In the course of a century, if not before, the surface of the shafts, inside just as well as outside the church, probably began to peel and flake off in unsightly patches.   What had been the glory of the church became a spectacle of mouldering decay.   The very hardness of the surface was the cause of the mischief.   On a damp day the moisture in the air percolated into the porous freestone ; and on the next dry day was exuded again, without injury to the stone.   But on a damp day moisture collected in drops, and streamed down the cold impervious Purbeck marble ; till gradually the surface was disintegrated.   For one reason or other marble shafts went out of

* Willis' *Middle Ages*, 12.   † T. Drew, in *Builder*, May 5, 1894.
‡ *Vita S. Remigii*, vii. 97.   § " Dazzles the eyes like a mirror."

fashion; and the way was left clear for the rival form of pier; the clustered column.

THE NORTHERN PIER.

The Northern pier resembles the Western pier in one respect only, viz. that both are in courses of freestone. Instead of shafts, it employs columns; seldom more than eight. The examples are very numerous. They include piers at Kirkstall, Furness, Cartmel, Roche, Jervaulx, Ripon, Byland, Selby nave, Hartlepool, Darlington, Hexham, all *c.* 1150-1200; and but little later Whitby and Rievaulx. South of the Humber, New Shoreham has some clustered

columns (423); and in the western province Wenlock Abbey; late in the twelfth century. In the following century they occur out of their own area at St Saviour's, Southwark; in St Alban's nave (which was intended, however, by John de Cella to have piers encircled by Purbeck shafts); and at Netley and Tintern; which, being Cistercian, may have been influenced by the Yorkshire abbeys. In the Midlands they occur in Southwell* choir and at St James, Deeping. A special feature of this pier is that usually some or all of the columns are pointed; *e.g.* at ROCHE, BYLAND (661), and Beverley. Anything more majestic and at the same time elegant than the pier of BEVERLEY TRANSEPT (244) it is impossible to conceive. It has the grace of the Southern pier without its fragility and insincerity of construction; and one would certainly have expected that, of the three rival piers, this would be

Beverley St Mary, Nave.

the one to prevail. In the end it did prevail. But at first the victory was with its Southern rival.

CONQUESTS OF THE SOUTHERN PIER.

The first to disappear was the Western pier. After 1200 it is seldom seen again; but we may recognise it in the 1280 piers of EXETER (661.9), and in the fourteenth-century choir of WELLS (437). In the Western district the detached marble shafts of the Southern pier find their way into the west front of Wells, the very cradle of the Western School of Gothic; to the Lady

* Southwell was in the diocese of York, and so susceptible to Northern influence.

Capital

Label.

Base

Plan of Pier and Arch Mouldings

SCALE OF 12 6 0   1   2   3   4   5   6   7   8   9   10 FEET

Beverley St Mary, Chancel.

Chapel of St Patrick's, Dublin—the last reminiscent of the Lady Chapel of Salisbury—to the choir and retrochoir of Worcester; where the contrast between the Western Gothic of the western bays of the nave and the Southern Gothic of the eastern limb is particularly striking.

Equally sweeping were its conquests in the North. Southern influence has been recognised in the east transepts of Fountains and Durham.* In the Midlands it appears in Lincoln Minster; the lovely presbytery of ELY (117); and the unparalleled west front of PETERBOROUGH (112).

CLUSTERED COLUMNS.

But in the end, as we have said, the Purbeck fashion of the Southern Gothic passed away, c. 1300; Western Gothic had been long defunct; and the rest of the story of the English pier is that of the clustered column of the North.†

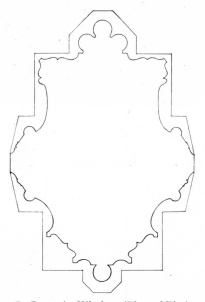

St George's, Windsor (Plan of Pier).

In Beverley transept, in Merton College, Oxford, and at Exeter the number of columns had risen to sixteen. For the rest of the story, with the exception of such ultra-logical piers as those of ST GEORGE'S, WINDSOR, the tendency was all in the direction of simplification. The sixteen columns of Exeter were very commonly reduced to four. A beautiful example is seen in the fourteenth-century choir of ELY (251), which, though it has four columns, is given eight bases; and moreover is worked in marble, that it may be in harmony with the piers of the presbytery to the east. The pier of four columns had, of course, been long with us; as far back as St Michael's, York, and ST PETER'S, NORTH-AMPTON (663.1). It is a pier of the simplest possible plan; merely four columns put together. There was, however, a decided difficulty as to how to treat the space between the columns. At SKELTON (663.3) c. 1245, the hollow is deeply undercut to get a black shadow; at HIGHAM FERRERS (663.4) there is a flabby hollow; at NORTHBOROUGH (663.5) a wedge; at MARKET DEEPING (663.2) the columns interpenetrate; all these are thirteenth-century work. In the fourteenth century, e.g. at BOTTISHAM (663.6), COGGESHALL (663.8), HEDON (544), and LONG MELFORD (663.9), the hollow is filled up with a small, illogical shaft. From the fourteenth century onward, by far the most common treatment is to leave between the columns a shallow hollow, called the "casement." But where the piers were

* By Mr C. C. Hodges in *Arch. Aeliana*, xvi. 382.
† Examples of clustered columns in the North of England are illustrated from Kirkstall, Roche, Byland, Bridlington, St Mary's York, and Guisborough, on 661.

very lofty and massive, a simple casement was not enough; and a double ogee ("bracket") might be added, as at LAVENHAM (663.7). At Cromer* a wave-molding is employed; and there are many other treatments; *e.g.* LONG MELFORD (665.12).†

ORNAMENTATION OF SHAFTS.

We may now turn to the decorative treatment of the column and shaft. The first thing to be noted is that Romanesque shafts are often carved;

Gothic shafts but seldom: the Gothic builders preferred the keel-molding or the fillet. The Durham School of Norman, *e.g.* at Durham, Selby, Dunfermline, Waltham, often incised their big cylinders with deep grooves;‡ sometimes the patterns ran spirally, as in CANTERBURY crypt (193), Lincoln west doorway, Pittington.§ Enriched shafts are seen at ST PETER'S, NORTHAMPTON, and IFFLEY; and in the doorway of SHOBDON (415.3).

Northampton St Peter.   Iffley.

PLAN OF SHAFTS.

In Norman work the shafts and columns are semicircular; nor was this form ever wholly abandoned; *e.g.* it is seen *c.* 1280 at EXETER (241); in fifteenth-century piers it is almost as common as in Norman. But from *c.* 1150 various other forms appear. One of the earliest is the pointed column or shaft; it is especially characteristic of the twelfth-century Gothic of the North. It appears, *e.g.* at ROCHE (661.2) and BYLAND (661.3); in the latter it alternates with the semicircular form. The next step was to emphasise the sharp edge ("arris") of the pointed column by hollowing the column a little on either side; this produces what is called the "pear-shaped molding." Frequently the sharp edge was cut off; producing a narrow "fillet." At GUISBOROUGH (661.6) the smaller columns have the "pear-shaped molding"; the larger have the "fillet." ‖ Towards the end of the thirteenth century the fillets often become broad; at Tideswell in the fourteenth century to an excessive extent; in the fifteenth century they are less common.

* *Glossary*, ii., Plate 153.

† For the final development of the compound pier in later Gothic, turn back to page 242.

‡ In the Cluniac Priory of Castle Acre, Norfolk, also the cylinders were grooved with spirals, lozenges, and frets (Mr W. H. St John Hope).

§ *Cf.* the remarkable columns of the ruined chancel of Orford, Suffolk. With these we may compare the spiral friezes of the column of Trajan at Rome.

‖ Filleted shafts are shown in SOUTHWELL CHOIR (448.2) and SHREWSBURY ABBEY (440.4).

CHAPTER XVI.

THE FORMS OF THE ARCH.

On Trabeated and Arcuated Construction—Semicircular, Stilted, Segmental, Horseshoe, Elliptical, Pointed, Four-centred, Foiled, and Ogee Arches.

TRABEATED AND ARCUATED STYLES.—In Greek architecture the voids between column and column, or between column and wall, were spanned by lintels; *i.e.* by horizontal beams of stone (Latin, *trabes*). The Greek, therefore, is a Trabeated style. From a constructional point of view it does not rank high; first, because long blocks were very costly; being but rarely found; and when found, difficult to extract; and if found and worked, costly to transport; and costly also to raise to their position; secondly, because Trabeated construction, except on quite a small scale, is to use stone for a purpose for which the nature of the material unfits it: to use it as if it were a tough material like an oak beam or an iron girder, whereas it is a granular material, and therefore incapable of supporting any serious strain. From stone post and lintel construction the Romans and Byzantines gradually freed themselves, and the mediæval architects freed themselves altogether: using stone only where its strength is greatest, that is, in resisting compression. With a moderate amount of pressure you may squeeze wood or iron out of shape; but not so with stone. When stone blocks

Skewback.

are used in an arch, they are in a state of compression; *i.e.* stone is used just in the way where its strength is at the greatest. Such a method of construction is called Arcuated. It is as scientific and practical as the Trabeated construction of the Greeks is the reverse. And as the arches are constructed in small blocks, which are to be obtained in abundance, are easy to quarry and work, and cheap to transport and to put in position, it is as cheap as it is scientific. Besides, in many districts, and in some whole countries, large blocks for lintels are not to be had at all; whereas small blocks, or clay hardened into bricks, are to be found everywhere; so that the application of Arcuated construction is universal and world-wide; whereas Trabeated construction is confined to a few favoured restricted districts.

MEMBERS OF THE ARCH.—Each wedge-shaped block of which an arch consists is called a *claveau* or *voussoir* (4 to 13 above). The central voussoir, if there is one, is called the *keystone* or *key* (French, *clef*) (9 above). Where several arches intersect in a vault, the keystone may become a *boss* or a *pendant* (302). A pointed arch sometimes has a keystone; but more often a straight joint, as

R

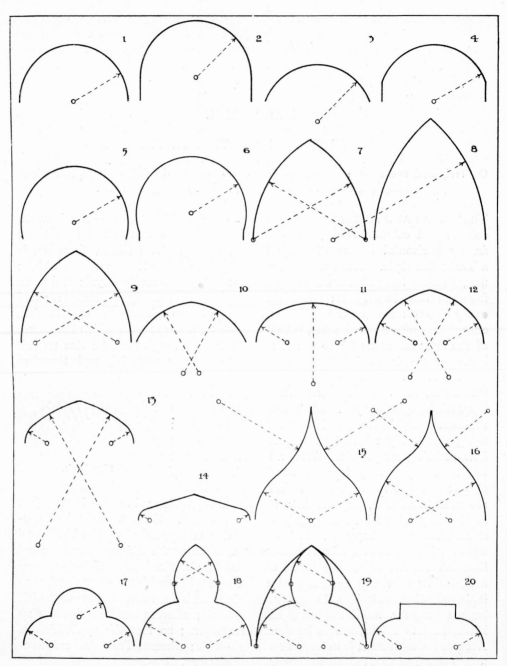

1. Semicircle.   2. Stilted Semicircle.   3. Segmental.   4. Stilted Segmental.
5. Horseshoe.   6. Stilted Horseshoe.   7. Pointed Equilateral.   8. Pointed Lancet.
9. Pointed Obtuse.   10. Pointed Segmental.   11. Three-Centred.   12. Four-Centred.
13. Four-Centred.   14. Quasi-Four-Centred. 15. Ogee.   16. Ogee.
17. Trefoiled.   18. Trefoiled.   19. Pointed Arch Trifoliated. 20. Shouldered Arch.

below. The lowest voussoirs are called *springers* (French, *sommier;* Old English, "sommer" or "summer"), 1, 2, 3, 15, 16, 17 in 257. The springers usually have one or both joints horizontal; and are said to be laid in *tas de charge* (302). The upper surface of the top springer, 3 or 15, against which the first voussoir of the real arch, 4 or 14 (in which *both* joints radiate) starts, is said to be *skew-backed.* The skewback is shown in 257 at X, Y.

The under surface of the arch, BD, is called its *intrados* or *soffit.* Its upper surface, AE, is its *extrados.* Mediæval arches are extradossed; but for decorative reasons some Roman and Renaissance arches were not; *e.g.* the upper surfaces of a Renaissance arch sometimes form a horizontal line: instead of forming a curve, and that curve the same curve as that of the intrados. If an arch is enclosed, or is imagined as being enclosed in a square, *e.g.* in the doorway of KETTERING (95), or WINCHESTER (261), then the spaces between the arch and that square are its *spandrels.*

FORMS OF ARCH.—In Rome and Western Europe (but not necessarily so in the East) the oldest and normal type of arch is the *Semicircular* (*arc en plein cintre*), 258.1. In this the centre is in the middle of the diameter. In 258.2, the arch does not start at the ends of the diameter, but at some distance above it; a vertical piece of masonry or *stilt* being interposed. (This differs from BX, DX in 257, in that the intrados is straight, not curved.) The centre is therefore at a point above the diameter. This is called a *Stilted* arch (*arc surhaussé*). Or, instead of taking a whole semicircle, we may select a curve that is less than a semicircle, and we shall have a much flatter arch, a segment of a circle (258.3), with its centre *below* the diameter. This is a *Segmental* arch (*arc surbaissé*). Or we may select a curve that is greater than a semicircle, and we shall have an arch with its centre

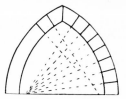

Radiating Joints.

above the diameter. This is the *Horseshoe* arch, 258.5 (*arc outrepassé* or *arc en fer à cheval*).

All the above four arches were struck each from one centre. The second class is struck from two. This arch is the *Pointed* (*arc aigu* or *arc brisé*). There are three chief varieties. The first is the *Equilateral* (*arc en tiers-point*). In this the two centres coincide with the ends of the diameter, 258.7. The second, more acutely pointed, is the *Lancet**(*lancette*), 258.8. In this the centres are on the line of the diameter, but *outside* it. The third is the *obtuse* or *Drop* arch (*arc en tiers-point surbaissé*), 258.9. In this the centres are still on the line of the diameter, but *inside.* Sometimes the arch is nearly straight-sided, as in Boxgrove clerestory and in Hereford north transept.

The third class consists of arches struck from three centres, as shown in 258.11. This is the three-centred or "basket-handle" arch (*arc en anse de panier*).

The fourth class consists of arches which are struck from four centres. The first variety is the *Four-centred* or Tudor arch from Bath (258.12); and from

* It is often asserted that the Lancet is characteristic of the first half, the Equilateral arch of the second half of the thirteenth century. But Sharpe points out that in the Nene valley (page 12) both forms occur indiscriminately throughout the whole of that century. In the clerestory of Bath Abbey the equilateral arch occurs at the beginning of the sixteenth century.

St George's, Windsor (258.13). The different way in which the curves are struck in these two examples should be noticed. In some examples, *e.g.* in the windows of the Divinity School, Oxford, the long curves are replaced by straight lines (258.14). In Jacobean Gothic both curves may be replaced by straight lines with a short curve at their junction.

Another variety of arch struck from three or four centres is the *Ogee* arch (*arc en accolade*), 258.15, 16. In this one or two of the centres are below, but the other two are above the arch. So that the two upper curves of the arch are concave, the two lower convex.

Foiled arches. These are arches with three or more lobes or leaves (Latin, *folia*). The simplest are the *Round-headed Trefoil* (258.17); the *Pointed Trefoil* (258.18); the *Square-headed Trefoil* (258.20); which also goes by the name of the *Shouldered* arch.* A *trifoliated* arch is a trefoiled arch enclosed in a

Tewkesbury Porch.

pointed arch, as in 258.19. A trefoiled arch is not enclosed in any other arch. Besides the trefoil there is the *cinque-foil* arch with five lobes or foils, and the *multifoiled* arch with several.

Again, the voussoirs may be all wedge-shaped; but the extrados and intrados composed not of curved but straight lines; this is a *Flat* arch (*plate bande*); it is in common modern use, instead of a lintel, over a window, door, or fireplace; it occurs over TEWKESBURY PORCH. Sometimes, to strengthen a flat, or even a curved arch, the voussoirs are notched or *joggled;* good instances occur at Kirkstall in the cellarer's lodgings; at Fountains over the big fireplace of the calefactory, 16 feet wide, of too great a span for a lintel; another survives over a fireplace in CONISBOROUGH KEEP (261).†

SEMICIRCULAR ARCH.—This arch is specially characteristic of Romanesque architecture. To us, perhaps, the pointed arch, from its association with Gothic architecture, seems the more beautiful. But of old the semicircular was the favourite form; as was natural; "for its type is ever before us in that of the apparent vault of heaven, and the horizon of the earth."‡ Certainly, when the pointed arch first came into use, it was unpleasing to eyes that had ever been accustomed to the older form; and though it was employed where it facilitated building construction; yet, wherever an arch was to be built for decorative purposes, it still usually remained semi-

---

* This is not an arch at all, but a lintel; it is very common in Carnarvon Castle.

† A coursed lintel occurs at the end of the third century in the Golden Gate of Diocletian's palace at Spalato, illustrated in Anderson and Spiers, 259.

‡ *Seven Lamps*, 189.

circular. A curious example of belated fondness for the older form is seen in the aisle windows of Glastonbury nave (A.D. 1184) which externally are pointed, but internally semicircular. The pointed arch is the arch *par excellence* of Gothic architecture; nevertheless, in early Gothic architecture, sometimes an arch was needed that was lower than a semicircle. Sometimes a very obtusely pointed arch, *i.e.* a SEGMENTAL POINTED ARCH, was employed; *e.g.* 258.10; or else a low segmental arch (258.3); but sometimes a semicircular arch. Gothic semicircular arches occur in the thirteenth century in the doorway of the transept of BEVERLEY (574); in the pier-arcades of St Gilles, Caen; and Woodford, North Hants: in the fourteenth century in

Winchester, N. Transept.   Conisborough.

the pier-arcade of Water Newton, Hants; and the doorway of Badgeworth, Gloucester; in the latter it is covered with ball-flower.*

STILTED ARCH.—By stilting, a narrow semicircular arch is enabled to rise to the same level as a broad arch. Where, therefore, broad and narrow arches come into juxtaposition, the eye is saved the pain of seeing the narrow arches rise to a lower level than the broader ones. There are three common cases of this. (1.) The arches between an apse and its ambulatory, *e.g.* at St Bartholomew's, Smithfield, are about half the span of those on either side of

* In the north-west of North Hants and in Rutland they are in some places as common as the pointed arch in the thirteenth and occasionally in the fourteenth century; *e.g.* in the pier-arcades of Bainton, Castor, Werrington, Garwell, Manton, Great Casterton, Preston, Seaton, Edith Weston, Clipsham, Barrowden; over two lancet lights, especially in belfries; *e.g.* Barnack, Etton, Tansor, Wadenhoe; and over doorways; *e.g.* Whitwell, Barrowden.—R. P. B.

the choir ; the former, therefore, are stilted ; *cf.* St Germer and La Charité   (2.)
The transepts are sometimes narrower than the nave or choir ; and its north and
south arches may be stilted, as at Malmesbury and SHERBORNE.* (3.) The pier-
arches are narrower than the diagonal arches of the aisle vault ; and to facilitate
vaulting (322) the former may be stilted, as at WINCHESTER (261).   At MEL-
BOURNE (203) the pier-arches are stilted, even though the aisles are not vaulted.

SEGMENTAL ARCHES.—These occur occasionally even in Norman work,
e.g. at Southwell there was little room under the window of the south transept,
and the doorway, therefore, has a segmental head.

HORSESHOE ARCHES.—Well-marked examples occur in Norman work,
but are rare ; *e.g.* Holywell Church, Oxford ; under the west towers of Southwell
Cathedral ; in the chancel-arch of Patrixbourne, Kent ; and a little later in the
west nave of Kilwinning Abbey.   They are not
uncommon in Norman ribbed vaults ; *e.g.* in
PETERBOROUGH AISLES (318).   They occur in
the aisled basilica of Dana,† near the Euphrates,
which has the inscription A.D. 540.   In Eastern
work the horseshoe arch is frequently not round-
headed, but acutely pointed.   This facilitates construction, as the upper and more difficult portion
of the arch or dome can then be constructed by
corbelling and without centering ; as in many
Indian domes.

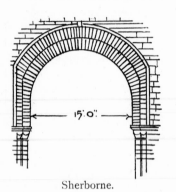

Sherborne.

ELLIPTICAL ARCHES.—It may be doubted
whether any true elliptical arches occur ; at any
rate otherwise than accidentally.   The *anse de panier* is sometimes called an
elliptical arch, but is really three-centred.   It is not likely that the mediæval
builders knew how to draw a true ellipse.   Sometimes, however, a vault has
given way somewhat ; its crown flattening, and its sides receding ; and thus
something like an ellipse is produced.   The following, among others, have been
cited as examples of elliptical arches ; the transverse arches of Vézelay nave
and Laach ;‡ the transepts of the Abbaye-aux-Dames and Montivilliers, and
Guéron apse ; § and the diagonals of Devizes St Mary and Dunstable. ‖

POINTED ARCH.—Though, as we shall see (314), in Durham transepts
our Romanesque architects, without the pointed arch, had solved triumphantly
in the first years of the twelfth century the greatest problem of the Middle
Ages, viz. how to vault throughout with stone a clerestoried church Basilican
in plan, yet the employment of the pointed arch greatly facilitated building
construction.   Next to the use of diagonal ribs and flying buttresses, it was
the greatest improvement introduced into mediæval architecture.

ORIGIN OF THE POINTED ARCH.—(1.) In discussing the origin of the
pointed arch and of that beautiful style with which it is associated, our authorities
almost break into poetry.   Stukeley in 1755 says " this pointed architecture and
its slender pillars are taken from the groves sacred to religion ; those verdant

---

* Illustrated in *R.I.B.A.*, 1877, 144.   † Illustrated in Scott's *Essay*, Plate 13.
‡ Petit's *Church Architecture*, i. 101.   § R. Robert, i. 169.
‖ Bilson's *Beginnings*, 308.

cathedrals of antiquity." "We were overshadowed," says Washington Irving,[*] " by lofty trees, with straight smooth trunks like stately columns ; and as the glancing rays of the sun shone through the transparent leaves, tinted with the many-coloured hues of autumn, I was reminded of the effect of sunshine among the stained windows and clustering columns of a Gothic cathedral. Indeed there is a grandeur and solemnity in some of our spacious forests of the west, that awakens in me the same feeling that I have experienced in those vast and venerable piles ; and the sound of the breeze sweeping through them supplies the deep breathings of the organ." (2.) For a long time the theory of Dr Milner, 1798, held the ground ; viz. that "the pointed arch arose from the intersection of semicircular arches." So it does at Southwell ; where the arcading of the north-west tower has the latter ; that of the south-west tower the former. But, unfortunately for this theory, just where in-tersecting semicircular arches were most employed, i.e. in Normandy and England, there the pointed arch is latest in making its appearance ; and where they are little employed, e.g. in Central and Southern France, there it appears. very early. (3.) Or Western Europe may have borrowed it from the East. It has been held that it may have travelled by an overland trade-route across Russia to Wisby, the great Hanseatic depot in the island of Gotland. But the Wisby churches, in which the pointed arch is used so largely, are now recognised not to be earlier than the middle of the twelfth century. (4.) On the other hand, it is possible that the pointed arch was borrowed from the East— perhaps through acquaintance with Saracenic work in Egypt and Sicily—by Southern France ; for it is there that it seems to make its first appearance ; and there not till the second half of the eleventh century. In Egypt the great mosque of Tulûn, built in 879, has pointed arcades ; so also the Nilometer in the island of Roda,[†] which is probably of 861. At Diarbekir in Armenia, two pointed arches crown a *Roman* colonnade, and may be contemporary with it ; also the great gateway of the palace of Ctesiphon (fifth century) is pointed.[‡] "The pointed arch is certainly found in the great aqueduct near Constantinople, and in one of the city cisterns ; both probably are of the age of Justinian. They are correctly illustrated in Miss Pardoe's *Bosphorus*." [§] The Roman bridge of Severus, illustrated in Hogarth's *Levant*, has pointed arches.

Of the antiquity then of the pointed arch in the East there can be no question : in many districts it is as much the normal form as is the semicircular in the Romanesque of Europe. But it does not follow that the latter *borrowed* it. Like the axe, it has probably been invented again and again as necessity arose. In countries where there was no timber or no tools to work it, the natives had to build shelters in stone, usually without mortar. Frequently the only way known of roofing these was to pile flat stones on one another, i.e. with horizontal beds, not with radiating joints, each course projecting a little further inward as the wall went up. Plainly these walls would topple in if a semi-circular roof had been attempted ; but they could be got to stand if the roof was built in the form of a pointed arch, at any rate if the arch was very acutely pointed. If a roof thus formed, i.e. by corbelling in, was constructed on a rect-

---

* *Tour on the Prairies*, 47.
‡ Enlart's *Manuel*, 293, 3.
† Mr Spiers in Fergusson, ii. 45.
§ Lethaby and Swainson's *Santa Sophia*, 220.

angular base, it would produce a pointed tunnel. If on a circular or oval base a pointed dome. People far apart in geography and in time, such as the Pre-Conquest Irish, and those who built the Treasury at Mycenæ and the Jaina domes in India, adopted perforce the pointed form, but as a condition of corbel-construction; no one borrowing from the other, but each driven to invent by necessity, the mother of invention. So again, several churches in Ireland, *e.g.* St Columba's, Kells, and Killaloe,* the latter probably *c.* 1007, have above the lower semicircular tunnel vault a pointed tunnel which also forms the external stone roof. This remarkable roof-system is not due to borrowing; but is the outcome of roof builders in a rainy climate without tools to work timber. And so it may have been with those who first used the pointed arch in the tunnel vaults and domes of Southern and Central France.

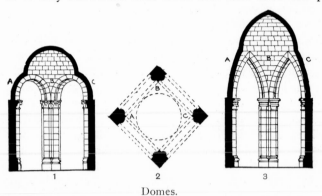

Domes.

VALUE OF THE POINTED ARCH.—More important than the question of the origin is the question of the value of the pointed arch. It is valuable in many ways. First, it is obvious that a flattish arch, *e.g.* the segmental arch in 258.3, cannot carry such a heavy load as an acute arch, *e.g.* the lancet arch in 258.8. So with other arches. Any form of pointed arch with the same span as a semicircular arch, but rising to a higher level, must be the stronger of the two. Secondly, a pointed arch has a more vertical, a less lateral, thrust than a semicircular one. This is pointed out by Samuel Ware in a paper in the *Archæologia* in 1814. Indeed, an arch may be so acutely pointed, that it has practically no thrust; the inward and outward pressures being exactly balanced.† This important property of the pointed arch was of enormous value in Romanesque districts such as Provence, Auvergne, and Burgundy, where it was customary to roof the naves with BARREL VAULTS (283). Indeed, when, in Provence and in Burgundy, the barrel vault rested on a wall pierced with clerestory windows, it was impossible to provide direct abutment against the continuous thrusts of these high tunnels, which necessarily therefore had to be pointed, *e.g.* at St Trophime, Arles, and Paray-le-Monial.‡ Again there were other Romanesque districts, *e.g.* in and round Périgueux, where the churches were roofed with stone domes as above. Here, as also at St Croix de Montmajour,§ to point the dome reduces the lateral thrust. In both these cases, as in the Irish churches, the introduction of the pointed arch was plainly due to an exigency of building construction. For the same reason, the diagonals as

---

* Illustrated in Fergusson, ii. 448.   † See Statham's *Architecture*, 91.
‡ See *Classification of Romanesque.*
§ To this the date A.D. 1019 used to be assigned, but it has been proved by M. Brutails, 196, 4, to be later.

well as the transverse arches of vaults were sometimes pointed ; *e.g.* at Wells. Thirdly, there is another reason which may have brought the pointed arch into use early in districts where domes were constructed on pendentives. It is that if the arches on which the dome ultimately rests are pointed, the pendentives between them will both be broader and more vertical, and consequently more stable ; as may be seen in the diagrams (264). Fourthly, over the barrel-vaulted naves of Southern France there seem originally to have been no outer roofs of wood. Masonry was added on the back of the vault till a straight slope on either side was obtained. Now if the diagrams be compared, it will be seen that while on the apex of a pointed barrel vault little masonry will be required, over the semicircular one a heavy load must be placed, and that just on the weakest part of it, its crown.* From the above considerations, it seems probable that it was in Southern and Central France that the pointed arch was first employed in Western Europe. Fifth, but the most valuable property of the pointed arch remains to be mentioned. It is that while the height of the semicircular arch was rigidly regulated by its span—the height must be just half the span, neither more nor less—the height of the pointed arch was independent of the span. It is, we may say, an elastic arch. Wherever, therefore, we may wish to retain the span unaltered, but to alter the height, we can effect this by employ-ing a pointed arch. And so all the old-fashioned shifts and dodges of stilted and horseshoe arches were superseded at once ; the entrances to narrow transepts, as at the Abbaye-aux-Dames, St Bartholomew's,† Smithfield, Oxford Cathedral, Bolton Priory, were given pointed arches ; while those of nave and choir remained

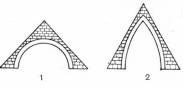

Barrel Vaults.

semicircular. So also the narrow arches of the apses ; as at La Charité, St Germer, Westminster, Tewkesbury. Still more valuable was the pointed arch in vaulting ; *e.g.* in vaulting an aisle the four narrow arches, *i.e.* the two trans-verse arches, the pier-arch, and the wall-arch were pointed ; while in most cases, for a long time, the two wide arches, the diagonals, remained semicircular. So again if three arches were required, the two side ones to be narrow and solid, the central one broad and pierced for a door, all three could be constructed of the same height by pointing the narrow lateral arches, but leaving the broad central arch semicircular ; as in Ketton façade and Selby north porch.

That the pointed arch came into English architecture for constructional and not for æsthetic reasons is plain from the fact that even when it had been adopted wherever it facilitated construction, in other cases, especially if it was merely a form of decoration, the semicircular arch was long used ; *e.g.* in doorways, which often had to be kept low not to interfere with a window above the semicircular arch long retained its ground. At New Shoreham, in spite of the advanced type of its vaults, piers, capitals, and moldings, the windows are round-headed, and there is semicircular arcading on the aisle walls. In Ripon

* See Petit's *Church Architecture*, i. 114.
† These are said to have been reconstructed (*Glossary*, 39, note).

choir, though internally the pointed arch forced itself into use for vaulting reasons, there is hardly a sign of it outside; except that narrow blank arches are pointed on either side of the clerestory windows. So abroad; no one from the exterior of Souillac would suspect that all the great arches and domes within were pointed. Even in the Durham galilee, all the arches remain semi-circular.

In the end, however, for the sake of harmony, pointed arches were used all over the church, whether constructionally necessary or not. But a good deal of difference of practice occurred as to what variety of pointed arch should be preferred. In the Ile de France the preference was rather for the equilateral arch; in the thirteenth-century work of England perhaps rather for the lancet. As regards this, construction is at war with æsthetics. It is obviously better to have obtuse arches, as in LINCOLN PRESBYTERY (56), in order to have fewer of the obstructive piers between nave and aisles; but there can be no doubt that a far more graceful elevation is obtained by the employment of a more acutely pointed arch, as at WESTMINSTER (55). Sir Gilbert Scott* remarks, that on comparing a series of pointed arches of different curve, the two which pleased him best, viz. the pier-arches of WESTMINSTER (258.8) and Wells, turned out on examination, the former to have exactly three, the latter two equilateral triangles in the height of each: so that beauty of curve here seems to rest on a geometrical ratio.

EARLY POINTED ARCHES.—Perhaps the two earliest examples we possess of the pointed arch are at Gloucester and Rochester. At Gloucester, com-menced 1089, the front compartment of the south-east apse is a pronounced oblong; and the wall-arches of its groined vault become pointed.† In Rochester nave, 1115-1130, the passage in the wall above the pier-arcade has a pointed head. But it is not till the middle of the twelfth century that the pointed arch enters into pier-arcades, to facilitate vaulting. The earliest example has been assumed to be Malmesbury nave, thought to be built by Roger of Salisbury, who died in 1139; but it is more likely work done some twenty years later. The pier-arches of Fountains nave are pointed: to the eastern bays of which Mr Reeve in his monograph assigns the date 1147-1150. In the opinion, however, of Mr Hope,‡ the nave was built between 1135 and 1147. Kirkstall was moved to its present site in 1152; and the pointed pier-arches of its nave may therefore be c. 1160. The pier-arches of Furness also are pointed; they were probably built when Furness became Cistercian in 1147. Fountains and Kirkstall also were Cistercian. And as the Cistercian mother abbeys in Burgundy exported Burgundian construction all over Europe,§ we shall probably be right in concluding that the introduction of the pointed arch into Yorkshire pier-arcades is due to designs or designers sent over from Cîteaux or Clairvaux. But though we were so slow to point our pier-arches, we had pointed the transverse arches of the high vault of Durham nave as early as 1128-1133.

FOUR-CENTRED ARCHES.—As the name implies, these arches are parts of four different circles. The position of the centres varies greatly, and with them

* *Gleanings*, 26.   † Illustrated in Bilson's *Beginnings*, 294.
‡ Paper in *Yorkshire Archæol. Journal*, vol. xv.   § See Enlart's *Gothic in Italy*.

the beauty of the arch. Perhaps the most usual position is for the upper and lower centres of each side of the arch to be in the same vertical line. It may happen, as in Winchester nave, that the lower curves on either side are parts of the same circle, and therefore are struck from one and the same centre; in which case the arch would more properly be called a four-curved, and three-centred, arch. As has been mentioned before, the long curves may be, if not straight lines, at any rate very nearly so. The four-centred arch has been considered peculiar to England; but it is common enough in Flanders at the same time as in England; a well-marked example occurs in the entrance to the sixteenth-century Hotel de Ville at Saumur.

As to the value of this arch, it may be regarded as the complement of the pointed arch. The latter answered admirably if an arch taller than a semicircle was wanted, without a change of span. But sometimes an arch lower than a semicircle was wanted, without a change of span. In this case three expedients presented themselves. A segmental arch (258.3) might be employed; as over Southwell doorway. Or a pointed segmental arch (258.10) might be used. But both of these give an ugly junction where they spring from the wall. The remedy was to round off the junction. If the springing of a segmental arch be rounded, a three-centred arch is produced; if the springing of a pointed segmental arch be rounded, we have a four-centred arch. The former was the form of arch favoured in late French Gothic; but it occurs occasionally with us, e.g. in Bishop Alcock's Chapel at Ely. The latter arch came more and more into favour with us from the fourteenth century. At first, as in Winchester nave, it is often considerably pointed; in later work it tends to become a very depressed arch, with its longer curves nearly, if not quite straight. At no period, however, did it wholly oust the pointed arch : least of all in pier-arches. Nevertheless pier-arches also, in late work, were sometimes four-centred; e.g., in Bath Abbey; St Stephen's, Norwich; KILKHAMPTON (568); sometimes they even occur in oak, as at Wingham.

There is an abnormally early example of four-centred pier-arches at Stanwick,* Northants, where "the hood-molds are so decidedly Early English that the arches cannot be later" (G. A. Poole).† Others of the thirteenth century are said to occur in the Lady Chapel of Oxford Cathedral, and in the doorway to the city schools at Bristol; also in the crypt of the Glastonbury Lady Chapel.

As to the *origin* of the four-centred arch, it is usual to say that it was arrived at by abstract mathematical considerations.‡ But as a matter of fact, the four-centred arches had long been presenting themselves, in more or less accidental fashion; e.g. when a curved brace was inserted beneath a tie-beam or collar, as at Knapton, Norwich St Andrew's, Leicester St Margaret, a four-centred form was originated. Again, it was not uncommon to " humour " the curves of the diagonal ribs of a vault at their foot, so that they might start

* Illustrated in *Nene Valley*, Plate 36.

† Inspection suggests that the hood-molds at Stanwick have been reset; and that the arches therefore are not thirteenth-century work.

‡ See Choisy's *History*, ii. 280 ; Viollet-le-Duc, *Architecture*, ix. 533 ; Willis' *Vaulting*, 25 *seq.* ; Garbett, 173.

at the same angle as the shorter transverse ribs, and not present the awkward collocation of curves seen in the aisles of Norwich and Peterborough and in the eastern crypt at CANTERBURY (334). But this straightening of the springing of a diagonal arch converts it at once from a pointed into a four-centred arch. Again, the rounding of the springing of a pointed segmental arch converts it into a depressed four-centred arch ; and this practice was of frequent occurrence ; *e.g.* in the great gateway of Wingfield, Suffolk, *c.* 1370, the outer archway is pointed segmental ; but the inner one, which is of the same date and character, is four-centred.

Whatever its origin, it greatly facilitated vaulting. Indeed, in fan vaults it disposes of all the difficulties of adjusting the curvatures of the ribs by allowing them all to be constructed of the same curvature.* And having found its way into the vaults, in the end it permeated the whole building. It is very useful in doorways ; for being so much lower than a pointed arch, it was not necessary to raise the windows, and consequently the whole wall of the church, to make room for the doorways beneath them. So also a window with a four-centred instead of a pointed head effected an economy of one or two feet of masonry all round the walls, both of the aisles and clerestory ; and great reduction of expense in constructing a large church. In some cases, even the pier-arches were constructed four-centred, for similar motives of economy ; *e.g.* at Bath. It is true that being so much flatter than a pointed arch, it was proportionately less adapted to carry the heavy load of a clerestory wall. But the fifteenth-century mason had become so scientific that he may well have felt that the weakness of the form of the arch was largely compensated for by the perfection of his masonry. Moreover the clerestory walls by this time had come to be nearly all glass, and the weight that fell on the pier-arches was reduced thereby. In any case, the great principle of harmony, which is the dominant note of late Gothic design, was offended by the juxtaposition of arches of different curves, and tended to eliminate the pointed form.

FOILED ARCH.—The remaining arches, viz. the foiled and the ogee, are not of constructional value, but decorative. The round-headed trefoiled arch is less common than the pointed. Examples of the former occur in Winchester Chapel, *c.* 1200 ; the triforium of CHESTER CHOIR (524) ; and the south doorway of St Michael's, Coventry. The cinquefoil is usually later than the trefoiled arch ; but it occurs in Wells façade ; another charming example is the aisle arcading of CARLISLE CHOIR (498) The early thirteenth century delighted in beautiful combinations of pointed and trefoil arcades ; *e.g.* the porches of St Albans and Ely ; the upper part of Ely façade and Durham west towers. The trefoiled arch appears first in doorways ; *e.g.* in Ely nave, *c.* 1150, and Ripon transept, *c.* 1170. It was not for nearly a century that the precedent set by cusped doorways led to cusping the arches of the window tracery.

OGEE ARCH.—As the upper curves of this arch (258) are reversed it cannot bear a heavy load, and so does not occur in pier-arches. It occurs, exceptionally, in doorways ; as at TENBY (580), and in the palace at St David's.† Ogee heads occur in windows, as not unfrequently in North Hants, *e.g.* at WILBY (270). Fine specimens of ogee arcading occur in the

---

* Willis' *Vaulting*, 43.   † Illustrated in Prior, 398.

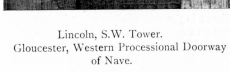

Beverley Minster, Percy Tomb.
Ely Lady Chapel.

Lincoln, S.W. Tower.
Gloucester, Western Processional Doorway
of Nave.

Wilby West Front.

PERCY TOMB, BEVERLEY (269), where even the cusps are ogees; and, in a more advanced form, beneath the western towers of LINCOLN (269). Finest of all are the ogee canopies in the LADY CHAPEL (269) and PRIOR CRAUDEN'S CHAPEL, ELY (130). Soon after 1300 ogee canopies almost wholly replace their predecessors, the straight-sided canopies of GUISBOROUGH (354) and HOWDEN (72).

Amongst the earliest specimens of ogee arches are those, both acute and depressed, of the Eleanor Cross, near Northampton: * the date of which, as shown by the executors' accounts, is between 1291 and 1294.† Not much later, probably, are the ogee dripstones over the windows of Lichfield Lady Chapel and Wells chapter house; and the ogee arches in the buttresses of Winchelsea. In France the ogee arch seems not to come into general use till late in the fourteenth century,‡ e.g. in the north chapel of Amiens Cathedral, c. 1373.§ In England it comes into general use, c. 1315. And when once introduced, there was a mania for it. Late English Decorated and French Flamboyant are simply a glorification of the ogee arch; the builders could not have enough of it: above all, in niches and window tracery.

* This cross has been much rebuilt. See *Proceedings of Society of Antiquaries*, 1903.

† Ogee arches occur in Prior Eastry's choir screen at Canterbury, 1304: illustrated in Caveler's *Specimens*, Plate 27. Other early examples are on the south side of Northfleet Church, Kent; in the east window of St Mary Stratford, Suffolk; in the piscina at Fyfield, Berkshire; and on the heads of the buttresses of Winchelsea choir.

‡ Viollet-le-Duc, *Architecture*, i. 9, and iv. 279.

§ The ogee arch makes its first appearance in France, but only as a very rare exception, in the last years of the thirteenth or the first years of the fourteenth century. Enlart's *Manuel*, 588.

"In its origin, it is, unquestionably, Oriental," says Mr G. G. Scott.* It is true that it is used in India on a vast scale in those domes which are constructed by corbelling. But in England it is not used constructionally at all, but only decoratively. Moreover, all the links are wanting which would be necessary to justify us in connecting our fourteenth-century ogees with those of India. A much simpler origin may suffice. It is that wherever in early geometrical window tracery, *c.* 1240-1290, a circle was set on two lancets, a reversed ogee arch is almost irresistibly suggested. Indeed it is often difficult to say that a reversed ogee was not really meant. If the other half of that figure be added, we have at once the reticulated patterns which appear so early in the fourteenth century ; *e.g.* in the vestry of MERTON COLLEGE, OXFORD (480.2, 487.5).

The ogee arch, like the pointed arch, may vary greatly in form : according to the character of the arch whose curve is reversed to give the upper part of the ogee, and according to the length assigned to the upper curve : *e.g.* in 258.16 the lower curves are parts of a pointed arch, and the upper curves are very short ; in 258.15 the lower curves are parts of a semicircle, and the upper curves are very long. Of all the various combinations attempted, perhaps the most successful are the very acutely pointed, and its opposite, the much-depressed ogee arch. The former is constructionally strong, as it approaches the vertical : it is a common and admirable feature of French Flamboyant window tracery.† In our fifteenth-century work the lower curve of the acute ogee arch is often so small as to be almost unnoticeable ; and sometimes it is suppressed altogether. This acute ogee arch with the lower curves omitted is particularly common in late canopies and tabernacle work ; *e.g.* the doorway leading into the cloister from the western bays of GLOUCESTER NAVE (269) ; the buttresses of ST NEOTS (356). On the other hand, the depressed ogee is so weak that it is more often executed in wood ; as in the doorway of the screen of ST MARGARET, LYNN (162). When it is executed in stone, it is usually placed beneath a pointed arch which acts as a relieving arch ; as in the tracery of the east windows of the aisles of Hull chancel.

* *Essays*, 126, *e.*
† Compare the Hedon window, 480.3.

Chapter XVII.

THE COMPOUND ARCH.

The Orders of the Arch—Recessing of the Orders—Sculpture on Arches—Arch-Molds.

COMPOUND ARCHES.—At first, *e.g.* in the early Christian basilicas and in much Norman work ; *e.g.* the aisles of LEICESTER ST NICHOLAS (213), the arches were simple, as in I.A below.   But if the arch needs to be unusually strong—say 6 feet thick—it is better to construct two independent arches, one on the top of the

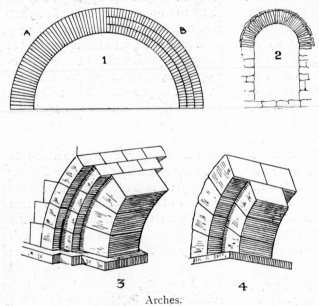

Arches.

other, each 3 feet thick. Or we may construct in three separate rings, as shown in the right in IB. Each of these sub-arches or rings of which the whole compound arch is composed is called an *order.** It is a safer form of arch than the simple arch. If anything happens to a part of the latter, the stability of the whole is involved. But in the compound arch even if one or two of its orders are fractured, the remaining orders or order may be able still to support the load.

Such a system of concentric arches or orders was employed by the Romans early in the sixth century B.C. in the Cloaca Maxima at Rome ; three occur where it enters the Tiber.   So also in the Anglo-Saxon church of BRIXWORTH (274), probably built in the eighth century, two concentric orders occur ; constructed of bricks from a neighbouring Roman station.   Another example occurs in the doorway of the Anglo-Saxon church of Clee.†   A pointed arch in two non-recessed orders occurs in the west doorway of Etchingham, Sussex.‡

* To ascertain of how many orders an arch is compounded, it is necessary to note carefully whether the joints fail to coincide; this is seen clearly in DURHAM TRANSEPT (8), and GLOUCESTER NORTH AISLE (99).

† Illustrated in Baldwin Brown, *Arts in Early England*, 164.

‡ At Dendera in Egypt, Professor Flinders Petrie found passages, 6 feet wide, covered with tunnel vaults of three rings of voussoirs, built in crude brick, and dating from 3500 B.C. Anderson and Spiers, 121.

Steyning.
New Shoreham.

Ely Transept.
Norwich Apse.

S

RECESSING OF THE ORDERS.—In the above compound arches the faces of the orders are in the same plane. But far more often the orders are successively recessed; *i.e.* the innermost sub-arch or order is narrow; the next above it is broader; the next is broader still, and so on; as in Figs. 3 and 4, page 272.

This principle of construction also was known to the Romans. It occurs in the Roman amphitheatre at Arles;* in the palace at Trèves in windows which have arches of three recessed orders; in S. Sophia, Constantinople, and S. Apollinare in Classe, Ravenna; both of the sixth century; in S. Pudenziana, Rome; probably of the eighth century. In France an early example is St Philbert de Grandlieu, which is assigned, doubtfully, to 815 A.D.†

Ickleton.   Brixworth.

It occurs in Anglo-Saxon work, *e.g.* in Yorkshire at Kirkdale and Kirk Hammerton.‡

The question now arises, why did the Romanesque and Gothic builders, practically universally, construct their compound arches, not in concentric, but in recessed orders? What was the special value of the latter? The following answer is often given. In early Norman work, and where ashlar was expensive, *e.g.* in the Isle of Thanet till late in the twelfth century, it was customary to build not only the walls and piers but the arches also with

* Illustrated in Petit's *Church Architecture*, i. 28.
† Enlart's *Manuel*, 178.   ‡ Illustrated in Baldwin Brown, 98.

a core of rubble : * *e.g.* the pier-arch of LEICESTER ST NICHOLAS (213). When an arch, however, was to be a compound one, then its construction was facilitated if the outer orders only were constructed with rubble cores, but the inner one in ashlar. And to economise ashlar, the inner order was made narrower than the orders above it. Such a method was undoubtedly often adopted : it is seen quite clearly in the tower arch of LEICESTER ST NICHOLAS (213), and in WHITBY choir. On the other hand, in early examples of the compound arch, the inner as well as the outer orders often have a rubble core : so that the explanation given above does not cover the whole ground. Moreover it does not meet the case of Roman recessed arches, constructed wholly in brick.

The true explanation probably lies in a fact which had the most profound influence in conditioning the methods of building construction not only among the mediæval builders but among Oriental, Roman and Byzantine builders also. It is impossible to study in M. Choisy's three classical works the methods of construction in use among the latter without being forced to the conclusion that the key to what seems to a modern builder the roundabout and eccentric practice so often pursued was nothing but the desire, or to speak more accurately, the necessity to economise centering and planks. Scaffolding poles no doubt were cheap and plentiful, as they are at present. But imagine a builder—Roman, Byzantine, Persian, Indian—let loose in a wood with nothing but a handsaw, perhaps with only axe and adze, with instructions to turn trees into planks. The fact is that the invention of the circular saw, and the application of water-power or steam-power to drive it, have revolutionised the methods of building construction. The methods of building construction now are such as to encourage the use of planks to the greatest possible extent; in the ancient and in the mediæval world it was just the reverse. It is only by constantly bearing in mind the excessive cost of wooden centering till modern

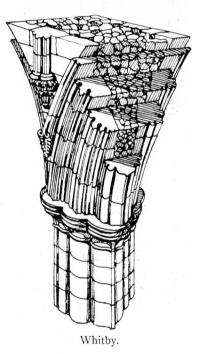

Whitby.

times that one can apprehend the rationale of what seem to us the abnormal forms of arch and vault and dome which M. Choisy has explained so lucidly. They are, each and all, the outward and visible sign of some non-modern method of construction conditioned by the necessity of building with the aid of as few planks as possible. So it was probably with the recessing of the orders of the arch. Look at the Norman arch (272.3). It consists of three orders.† Let us suppose that the wall to be carried by this compound

---

* It is noted by Professor Baldwin Brown that this method does not occur in Anglo-Saxon work.

† It is represented as constructed throughout in ashlar : generally the two upper orders would have rubble cores.

arch is 6 feet thick. If the arch had been constructed in three non-recessed orders, the innermost order would be 6 feet broad. Therefore, in order to construct this innermost order, it would be necessary to construct a temporary wooden arch (a "centre") 6 feet broad. Instead of that, a centre has been put together, say 2 feet broad. On this the first order, a narrow stone arch, is built; also 2 feet broad. On the back of that is built another stone arch, say 4 feet broad; on the back of that is built another, 6 feet broad. If that is not enough, order may be built round order, till there are as many as eight or more. The Gothic west doorway of Elgin Cathedral is in eight recessed orders. And all this without having to enlarge at all the original wooden centre of a breadth of 2 feet only. The economy of centering is enormous.*

Such, then, may be the origin of the recessing of the orders of the arch. Like almost everything else in mediæval architecture, though afterwards turned to decorative account, it was in its origin and in principle, nothing but a bit of engineering. The compound arch of WHITBY (275), with three recessed orders and a hood-mold, is nothing but the arches of Bernay and Jumièges beautified.

The principle thus introduced was of course applicable to all arches; not merely to the pier-arches, but to the arches of doorway, triforium, clerestory, window, and arcading. The side-walls of the Norman aisles were thick; and still thicker the end-walls. And it was in the openings in these, especially in the western doorways, that the Norman architects delighted in carrying the principle of the recessing of the orders to its furthest limits. Sometimes they even built the wall round the doorways exceptionally thick in order to get more orders for their doorways; not because there was any constructional need of them, but simply to increase the field for decoration. And even the small Norman windows were sometimes recessed, quite unnecessarily, in two or three orders.

MOLDINGS AND ORNAMENTS OF ARCHES. — In the earliest Norman arches; e.g. at Jumièges (c. 1040), the arches were square-edged: and thus they sometimes remained in Normandy till the very end of the century or later, e.g. at LESSAY and the ABBAYE-AUX-DAMES (319). In England also the unmolded arch was frequently employed. It seems to have been a special favourite in the greater Norman churches of the West and South of England; e.g. Chester Cathedral, Chester St John's, SHREWSBURY ABBEY (521), Leominster, Malvern, GLOUCESTER CHOIR (294), Chichester before it was remodelled after the fire of 1186, Winchester transept, Colchester St Botolph's, and St Albans; in the two latter it may have been conditioned by the employment of brick. It even occurs so late as c. 1170 in the transept of OXFORD CATHEDRAL (423.8).

As to the ornamentation of these square-edged arches, two methods were employed; sometimes one of the two exclusively; often both together, as in Steyning.† One was to carve the faces, and even, as in the central arch of STEYNING (273), the soffit or intrados of the arch; the other was to mold

* Cf. Garbett's *Principles of Design*, 202.

† It should be added that painted ornament was sometimes added; e.g. on the brick arches of the Norman tower at St Albans are painted sham voussoirs.

both face and soffit.   The former method became immensely popular in the first half of the twelfth century ; the various orders were smothered with a profusion of Romanesque ornament ; which, in Normandy and England, owing to our unskilfulness then as carvers, consisted chiefly of geometrical patterns.   In NEW SHOREHAM CHOIR (273), *c.* 1175, the ornament consists of scrolls of Romanesque leafage.   In late twelfth and in thirteenth century work the tooth-ornament is common.   But after this carving almost wholly ceases ; and molding is preferred.

One step to the molded arch was to chamfer off the square edges, as at SHREWSBURY ST MARY'S (424.7), where the inner order is chamfered and the outer molded.   The chamfered pier and the chamfered arch are specially characteristic of the late twelfth-century work at LLANDAFF (424.6).   And at all periods in the parish churches, simply because of the expense, the arch was as a rule chamfered, *e.g.* at Yarmouth ; and the pier was usually either a cylinder, or an octagon ; which is a chamfered cylinder.

But even so early as the ABBAYE-AUX-HOMMES (319) a small change was being made, which was destined to have the most momentous results.   It was the insertion of a small roll on the square edge of the arch ; a roll which was a near relative of the small shafts of Romanesque doorways, windows, and buttresses.   Just the same treatment is seen in TEWKESBURY NAVE (297). Reiterate these small rolls, and we have the moldings of the arches of the piers and triforium of NORWICH APSE (273) : in their multiplicity, delicacy, and refinement, unmistakable harbingers of such lovely moldings of the thirteenth century, as those of Ely and Durham, which are the special distinction of English mediæval art.

More often, however, the early moldings were bold and large : offsprings plainly enough of the jamb-shaft, as seen at ICKLETON (274).   In Bernay, *c.* 1140, the same heavy roll, resting on the same heavy shaft, is seen in the soffit of the pier-arches.   At Christ Church, Hants, the heavy rolls of the pier-arches "may almost be characterised as a mere continuation of the semi-columns from which they rise." *   Before the end of the eleventh century these massive rolls were coming into use in Northern and Eastern England, though in the west and south, as in Normandy, the square-edged arch was still preferred.   But in the end the molded arch superseded the unmolded in the south and west also ; *e.g.* in the pier-arch of the NORTH AISLE OF GLOUCESTER, seen at the foot of the illustration on page 313.

In the east, ELY (57) and Peterborough carried on the tradition of Norwich, with more vigour and less delicacy, and paved the way for Gothic moldings.

HOOD-MOLDS.—Above external arches, *e.g.* of doorways and windows, there is usually a narrow projecting hood to throw off the wet ; it is called a *dripstone* or *weather-mold*.   Inside the church a dripstone is of course unnecessary, and in the Ile de France is omitted ; but examples may be found elsewhere ; *e.g.* in the late Norman nave of Bayeux, at Graville, and at Vézelay.   But though unnecessary internally, its projection gives a beautiful shadow effect ; and serves to demarcate more distinctly the arch from its load.   Inside a building, it is called

* Ferrey's *Christ Church*, 42.

a *hood-mold*, not a dripstone. Both dripstones and hood-molds are often carried along horizontally as *strings ;* and their moldings are described under the head of "*Strings*" (404).

The omission of the hood-mold over the pier-arches is characteristic of late churches in EAST ANGLIA (552) and Somerset.

CHAMFERING.—Originally the orders of the arch were square-edged, and in the West of England sometimes remained so till late in the twelfth century, *e.g.* at St John's, Chester. It is probably because these sharp edges were often broken in transit or in working, that the practice of chamfering arose.

ARCH-MOLDS.—The history of these divides roughly into three periods : the first, that of the eleventh century up to *c.* 1160, when the molds employed are chiefly semicircular rolls and shallow, *i.e.* segmental, hollows. The second lasts till the end of the thirteenth century or a little later. In this period the roll may be pointed or have a keel or a fillet, or two or three fillets. The hollows generally form a semicircle or a segment larger than a semicircle, and the rolls are greatly undercut on either side, in order that, to the eye, they may seem not to be part of the arch behind them ; but detached from it just as much as shafts of dark Purbeck marble are detached from the core of a central cylinder. And under certain conditions of light, so black are the shadows of these undercut hollows, *e.g.* in the arch from CWM HIR (422.6), that the roll-molds really do seem to be detached. It may be said to be an attempt—and a successful attempt—to do in the arch by means of shadows what was done in the pier by means of dark marbles—to get as vivid a contrast between roll with high lights and black-shadowed hollows as is that of Purbeck marble shafts against a white limestone pier. In the third period, from the fourteenth century onward, the rolls tend to disappear from the arch, just as the shafts from the pier; and the hollows become "casements," broad and shallow; cut to hold, not one uniform blackness, but varying shades, grey white and black, or the reverse, according to the direction from which the light proceeds. The rolls were softened away almost entirely ; represented by a single undulation of surface (an *ogee*), or by two undulations separated by a quirk (a *double ogee* or *bracket*) ; the latter is well seen in ST MARY'S, BEVERLEY (253). In these arrangements in grey there is subtle and exquisite beauty ; perhaps because it is subtle, and so does not force itself on the observation, that our later Gothic system of molding has been held to be "degraded" and "debased," in comparison with the vivid contrasts of blackest black and whitest white which were the joy of the thirteenth-century mason.

Before studying or copying a suite of moldings, it is necessary first to ascertain what was the shape of the arch, with the exact dimensions of each member of it, before the moldings were sunk on it. If the arch is not later than *c.* 1260, the arch was probably built originally in square-edged recessed orders ; and the moldings were carved on the faces of these. After 1360, usually the square edges were previously chamfered off, and the moldings were then sunk in these chamfer planes. Between *c.* 1260 and *c.* 1360 both practices prevailed.

ARCH MOLDINGS, *c.* 1050—*c.* 1160.—Till about 1160 arch-molds consist, as a rule, of little more than suites of angle-rolls. The CHICHESTER (666.1) example is from the western bays of the nave, built after the fire of 1114. The arch at CASTLE HEDINGHAM (666.2) is said by Mr Hadfield to be between 1088 and 1107.

The examples from WARMINGTON and WALSOKEN (666, 667) belong to the early part; those from NEW SHOREHAM and BYLAND (667) to the latter part of the period of 1145 to 1190. Notice that at New Shoreham, though the hood-molds, A, A, are the same in section, and the arches are nearly if not quite contemporaneous, the arch on the right is quite different in type to the other; for all its rolls are pointed. Pointed shafts and pointed rolls are especially common in early Yorkshire Gothic; e.g. Byland. Note that both in New Shoreham and Byland (choir entered 1177) the rolls are already more numerous, and consequently have to be smaller. The New Shoreham capitals and arches are illustrated on pages 667 and 273.

ARCH MOLDINGS, c. 1190—c. 1245.—The example from WAWNE (666) shows a simply chamfered arch, carried by a cylindrical pier; these, from their economy of labour and skill occur at all periods in the smaller parish churches. The arch-mold from GRIMSBY (667.5), which probably belongs to the first years of the thirteenth century, is interesting as a survival of Romanesque molding. It has resemblances to that of the pier-arches of Peterborough nave, built about a century before. Little rectangular projections and curving horns are not uncommon; e.g. at West Walton church, Norfolk, where the rolls are either keeled or filleted. In the TEMPLE CHOIR (668.1), on the other hand (finished 1240), only one roll is filleted, viz. A. Note how greatly the rolls are undercut, showing the excellence at once of the stone and the mason. LINCOLN NAVE (668.2), c. 1120, is much more advanced; here all the rolls are filleted; and, what is very important, they are neither semicircular nor pointed. Perhaps the most exquisite moldings are those executed at the end of the period in Durham eastern transept.

ARCH MOLDINGS, c. 1245—c. 1315.—In such arches as those of the Temple and Ely, the hollows and rolls were so very numerous that they were necessarily very narrow. For a time they remain so. The arch in the TEMPLE CHOIR (668.3) is a glorification of yet another advance in type, viz. the roll and triple fillet. In this example also the necks of the rolls are perilously undercut; in fact the mason had been allowed too much play; he was executing in stone moldings which ought to have been confined to wood; he had become too clever. ST MARY'S, YORK (668.4), 1273-1295, is of early type, but this excessive under-cutting of the rolls has been restrained. The rolls, however, are still numerous and small. But in most of the later work of this century, the small delicate rolls and undercut hollows disappear, never to return. A bolder, more vigorous style comes in; the rolls are large, and the hollows are large and are comparatively little undercut. Moreover, as in LINCOLN PRESBYTERY (669), they are arranged, more often than before, in groups according with the orders of the arch; and the form of the filleted roll is varied with great freedom, as in TINTERN CHOIR (669) at A, A. And sometimes, as at Tintern, to facilitate the undercutting, the joint is placed in the hollow.

ARCH MOLDINGS, c. 1315—c. 1360.—In the WINCHELSEA ARCHES (669), which may be as early as 1310, the rolls are much broadened, and that at the expense of the hollows ; and either side of each roll forms an ogee or undulatory curve.   A vast change in the formation of moldings generally sets in about this time.   The roll and triple fillet is retained at B, B, B ; but with modifications.   The LEADENHAM ARCH (670) also retains the three fillets.   One of them is broad, usually a mark of late date ; the upper order has the wave-molding at B.   But at HELPRINGHAM (670) the side-fillets C, C, C, C, and the hollow of the Leadenham lower order have been softened away altogether ; so also with the hood-mold D ; so that *both* orders and the hood-mold also have wave-moldings. So also at NORTHBOROUGH (670) the two adjoining arches have the same characteristics of rolls with ogee curves.   At BOTTISHAM (671) a new characteristic appears ; two ogees meet at E, E, E, E, and produce a double ogee ("bracket").   In various forms this "bracket" remained in constant use to the end of Gothic architecture.   In the chancel of BEVERLEY ST MARY (670) we have an example later in date, but less advanced in type.

ARCH MOLDINGS AFTER 1360.—The moldings of the first half pass imperceptibly into those of the second half of the fourteenth century.   The nave of ST MARY'S, BEVERLEY (253), exhibits both the "bracket" and a narrow "casement."   This "casement" soon became broad and shallow ; and varying in contour according to its height above the line of vision, was to abide to the last ; it is a special characteristic of fifteenth and sixteenth century Gothic. CHELMSFORD (671) is a more advanced example ; the "casement" F is two-centred only ; and more complicated forms of the "bracket" occur.   Somewhat simpler molds are shown from the south side of ST MARY'S, OXFORD (671). All exhibit "casements" at F.

CHAPTER XVIII.

VAULTS WITHOUT DIAGONAL GROINS OR RIBS.

The Dome—The Semi-dome—The Barrel Vault—The Half Barrel—The Stone Ceiling—
The Span Roof of Stone.

As in the plan and the supports, so in the vaulting of the churches, the story begins with Rome. In ancient Rome, towards the end of the third century A.D., four methods of vaulting were in use—the dome ; the semi-dome ; the tunnel, wagon, barrel, or cradle vault ; and the groined vault. Of these the groined vault is of supreme importance ; it is one of the greatest inventions in the architectural history of mankind. It is the groined vault, reconstructed indeed by different methods, not the pointed arch or the flying buttress, which is the generative principle of Gothic architecture. We defer the detailed treatment of it till later.

THE DOME.—The dome is a vault of masonry, which, in its original form, as in the Roman Pantheon, was circular, and rested on all sides of the space to be covered. In the Pantheon the dome rests on a circular wall. A barrel vault rests on two sides of a rectangular space to be covered, and leaves two sides free. A groined vault rests only on the angles of the space to be covered, and leaves all four sides free. The dome and the barrel vault are of immemorial antiquity. In some districts men were compelled to build in stone or brick or mud because there was no wood—*e.g.* in Babylonia, as Strabo says ; in other districts because they had not the tools to work wood, *e.g.* Ireland—perhaps not having learnt to use iron or even bronze. In all such cases some form of dome or tunnel had to be devised for shelter. In Eastern Christendom the dome became the dominant factor in church design ; whether a single dome, as at St Sophia, Constantinople ; or a central dome encircled by other domes, as at St Mark's, Venice ; or a row of domes, as at Angoulême.* North of the Loire mediæval domes are exceedingly rare. In the early Norman abbey of Bernay the aisles are roofed with domes, which have usually been attributed to the eleventh century ; but from the precision of the masonry it is clear that they belong to the remodelling of the church in the time of Louis XVI. At Rucqueville † (Calvados) enough remains to show that there was originally a dome on pendentives ; but the capitals in this church are of Burgundian type, and show that the church is an "outlier." At Goring-on-Thames, ‡ under the tower is a Norman ribbed dome. § The courses are hori-

---

* The new Roman Catholic cathedral in Westminster reproduces the plan and domes of Angoulême.

† Ruprich-Robert, Plate v.　　　　　　　　‡ Illustrated in Scott's *Lectures*, ii. 170.

§ This is really a variant on the so-called *Cloistered* vault, or squared dome. See Scott's *Lectures, loc. cit.*

Gloucester, Upper Aisle of Choir.

Scarborough St Mary.   Scarborough St Mary.

zontal, but they stop at each rib, and start again at different levels on the other side; so that it is a compound of sections of four domes rather than one dome. Of domical ribbed vaults there are many instances, especially in France, *e.g.* all the Angevin vaults; but their courses are not horizontal with radiating joints, *i.e.* they are not of the form produced by the revolution of an arch round its own central vertical axis, and therefore are not domes.

THE SEMI-DOME.—But though we, with Northern France, lost the old Roman art of constructing domes, there never was a time when semi-domes could not be built. Hemicycles were common in the Roman Thermæ, palaces, and other large buildings, and were roofed with semi-domes. And throughout the whole of the Dark Ages, from the sixth century onwards, wherever an apse was erected, it was the rule to ceil it with a semi-dome of masonry. In Normandy in the eleventh century every apse was vaulted with a semi-dome (*cul de four*).[*]

In one of the earliest of our own Norman buildings, St John's Chapel in the Tower of London, the apse has a semi-dome. In village churches there remain several examples of semi-domes, *e.g.* CHECK-ENDON (21). Usually they are strengthened by ribs. When, however, the east end was squared, the semi-dome was no more of service, and went out of use.

THE BARREL VAULT. —This simple and ancient type of vault produced, south of the Loire, whole schools of Romanesque;[†] that of Poitou, with barrels

St John's Chapel, Tower of London.

resting on the pier-arches; that of Auvergne, with barrels resting on the triforium; that of Provence, with barrels resting on the clerestory walls, and with half-barrels in the aisles; and that of Burgundy, with similar barrels but with groined aisles. No such grand developments of the barrel vault were worked out in Normandy and England. Sometimes foreign influence—*e.g.* that of the Cistercians of Burgundy—imported the barrel vault; *e.g.* at Kirkstall Abbey the walled chapels of the transept are ceiled with pointed barrel vaults; at FOUNTAINS (101), also Cistercian, pointed barrels set transversely and resting on semicircular arches, were employed in the aisles of the nave.[‡] We have one very remarkable example of the use of the barrel vault—ST JOHN'S CHAPEL in the Tower of London (*c.* 1080). The chapel has both upper and lower

* Ruprich-Robert, i. 51.　　　　† For all these see *Classification of Romanesque*.
　‡ See plates in Sharpe's *Arch. Parallels;* and *cf.* Fontenay; and St Nicolas, Girgenti; illustrated in Enlart's *Gothic in Italy*, 75, 76, 247.

vaulted aisles; the nave and the upper aisles have barrel vaults; the lower aisles are groined. The barrel vault was in use in Anglo-Saxon days, *e.g.* in the crypts of Hexham and Ripon, which are undoubtedly of the seventh century; and in the porch of Monkwearmouth, which may be contemporaneous. The *slype*, or passage between a monastic cloister and the cemetery, often has a barrel vault; as in Oxford Cathedral. At Norwich, beneath the Bishop's Palace, is a barrel vault, 20 ft. in span. St Cormac's Chapel, Cashel, a specimen of the twelfth-century Romanesque of Ireland, has a barrel vault strengthened with transverse arches.* The chapter house of Reading Abbey had a barrel vault 42 ft. across: that of Gloucester has a pointed barrel of about 35

Abbotsbury.

ft. At ABBOTSBURY, Dorset, high on a hill above the sea, is St Catharine's Chapel, the roof of which is stone within and without: the internal roof is a pointed barrel; † so also is that of Bothwell in Scotland, ‡ with which may be compared the semicircular barrels of Roslyn Chapel. §

The barrel vault then left very few visible signs of its existence in English mediæval architecture.

THE HALF BARREL. —Of the barrel vault the demi-berceau is an important and valuable modification. If only one side of a barrel vault is built, it is called a half barrel or *demi-berceau;* it is simply one side of a barrel vault. In the Romanesque of Auvergne it was employed to vault the upper aisles, a whole barrel being employed to vault the nave. Then, the haunches of the nave barrel being filled up with solid masonry, it was easy to construct one solid roof of stone covering up both barrel and demi-berceau, as at Issoire.‖ But in the twelfth-century Romanesque of Provence a pointed barrel was set on the top of the clerestory wall, and the aisles were vaulted with half barrels in order to provide continuous abutment for the clerestory walls. Of the use of the half barrel we have one important example in England. In the upper aisle of GLOUCESTER CHOIR (282), on either side of the choir and originally round it to

* Illustrated in Scott's *Lectures*, ii. 23.
† Illustrated by J. D. Wyatt in *Building News*, 6th August 1880.
‡ Illustrated in Fergusson, ii. 435.
§ Illustrated in Fergusson, ii. 434.
‖ See *Classification of Romanesque*, 277, 278.

the east also, is a Norman half barrel strengthened with ribs. The same construction appears to have existed at Tewkesbury and Pershore.*

Exactly the same system occurs in the upper aisles of the nave of the Abbaye-aux-Hommes, Caen. This demi-berceau is held by Ruprich-Robert not to have been built till the seventeenth century, when the church was restored by the Benedictines with the greatest care and accuracy. But it seems very unlikely that at such a period they would have devised such an antiquated method of abutment as the demi-berceau; especially as the sexpartite vault of the nave requires intermittent, not continuous abutment. Probably what they did was to repair or rebuild the old demi-berceau of the eleventh century. If so, the Gloucester demi - berceau would probably be copied from that of Caen.

THE STONE CEILING. — We may here introduce two forms of roofs which might be designated semi-vaults; for they have in part, though not throughout, the arcuated construction of a genuine vault; more-over they are con-

Abbotsbury.

structed of masonry. These are stone ceilings and span roofs of stone.

The stone ceiling occurs in a rudimentary form in Roman ruins at Arles and Nîmes.† In Northern and Central Syria it gave rise to a distinct style, producing the buildings erected between A.D. 105, when Syria became a

* Scott's *Lectures*, i. 90.

† See Dr West in *Journal of R.I.B.A.*, November 1874, 32 ; and Anderson, *Greece and Rome*, 179.

Minchinhampton, South Transept.

Roman province, and *c.* 630, when these districts were deserted for ever on the approach of the Mohammedan invaders from Arabia. Of these the earliest dated buildings are of the time of Constantine—early fourth century. They have been fully described by De Vogüé.*

If we had to ceil an oblong room we might put beams across it, and on these beams put joists longitudinally. Being short of wood, the Syrian Christians erected transverse arches of stone instead of the beams, and on the haunches of these arches built up walls to form a horizontal bearing. The arches were

Minchinhampton, South Transept.

built 8 or 9 ft. apart, and then the distance from the top of each cross wall to the next was spanned by long blocks of basalt, which in those districts are plentiful. Of this method, which is only applicable where very long blocks of stone are to be had, we have no example.

THE SPAN ROOF OF STONE.—But where large flagstones were obtainable, it was not uncommon to construct porches of a series of arches set very close together ; on these it was easy to construct a substantial roof of flagstones. On

* *Syrie Centrale*, Paris. See also Scott's *Essay*, 54-62.

the south side of ST MARY'S, SCARBOROUGH (282), once a Cistercian priory, three chapels have been built in this fashion ; the roofs consist of overlapping flagstones. In the transept of MINCHINHAMPTON (287) the roof is of stone, and is supported by skeleton arches.* The room over Leverington porch is roofed in the same fashion.

* Mr Spiers mentions the Church of Montataire in Picardy, where the aisles have a roof of very steep pitch, consisting of long flagstones resting on arches nearly 10 ft. apart. *R.I.B.A.*, 1874, 3, 46. So also Willingham, Cambridge ; illustrated in Rickman's 7th edition, 218.

CHAPTER XIX.

GROINED VAULTS.

Object of Vaulting—Roman Groined Vaults—Romanesque Groined Vaults—Groined
Vaults in Crypts—Groined Vaults in Aisles—High Groined Vaults.

IT was, however, to none of the foregoing that the wonderful development
of vaulting is due in England and Northern France. It is due to the fact
that in the darkest ages the mediæval builders had never lost the tradition
how to construct another type of Roman vault—the groined vault. But before
we go further it may be well to ask what was the reason why there was such
a consuming anxiety from the eleventh century onwards to provide the
churches with the stone ceilings which we call vaults. We may also ask
why were the other Romanesque provinces of France anxious so early to
vault their churches, and why did the Normans and English postpone vaulting
so long. The answer generally given to the first question is that in the tenth
and eleventh centuries many churches had perished by accidental fires, some by
lightning, and that a very large number had had their roofs burnt off by the
Northmen all round Western Europe, Great Britain, and Ireland, wherever they
could get access by sea in their ships or up the rivers in their boats. The idea
is that the tenth century was marked by a sort of Norske *feu-de-joie* of the
churches of Western Christendom. The picture is dramatic ; but it must be
borne in mind that the Auvergne province, where vaulting seems to have been
developed very early, is wholly remote from Viking inroads ; and, secondly, it is
just in the districts which we know certainly were devastated by the Northmen,
Normandy itself and Northern France, just where the timber roofs had been
burnt, and where fireproof construction would have been most appreciated, that
vaulting was most backward. Perhaps humbler constructional reasons had
something to do with it. One people is a race of masons ; that may have
been so in Auvergne, where there are scores of miles of lava-streams from the
breached craters of the old volcanoes, providing in abundance the material, light
volcanic cinders (pumice and tufa), which is best adapted for vault construction.
Using these materials, the Auvergne builders were able early to construct churches
without any wood in them anywhere, with vault and roof all one, constructed of
solid stone. But the Normans and the Franks and the English were a race of
carpenters and shipwrights more than of masons. Those who could lay the keel
of a ship and bend up its ribs could invert the ribbed keel and make a roof of it.
It may therefore have been easier in Auvergne to build a stone roof than a timber
one ; in Normandy, England, and Northern France easier to construct a timber
roof than a vault. Nor did we in England ever lose our love for carpentering.
Nowhere else were such magnificent wooden roofs constructed. Indeed in the
North of England vaulting never made its footing sure : there the elaborate

T

lierne vaults and the fan vaults of the South seldom found their way ; the four-teenth-century vaults of Guisborough, Howden, and Beverley are of simple character ; and after these no high vaults of importance seem to have been con-structed.   York indeed and Selby prepared springers and pinnacles and flying buttresses for vaults of stone in the fourteenth century ; but in the end the carpenter had his way, and Selby choir and York transept, nave, and choir had to be content with vaults of wood.   Moreover the Gothic vault is but a thin shell, and requires a second roof of timber to shelter it from the weather.   Our old builders, being practical men, may well have objected to a roof which itself required to be roofed.   So the story of the English vault begins in Normandy

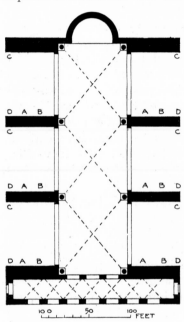

with the fact that though the builders vaulted the aisles, they omitted to put up a high* vault, *i.e.* to vault the central aisle or nave.   This is the position of things at Bernay Abbey, begun 1013-1017, and finished in part in 1050 ; and at Jumièges Abbey, begun 1040, and conse-crated in 1067.   Nor were either of the great Caen abbeys, or Cérisy, or St George's de Boscherville intended originally to have high vaults.   In many instances the builders hesi-tated ; hardly knew what they wanted ; de-signed the church for a vault, but ended by giving it merely a wooden roof, as at Ely and Peterborough.   But there is no sign of vault-ing shafts, or of any intention to vault, even in the twelfth century, in such important churches as Dunfermline, St Bartholomew, Smithfield, Malvern, Melbourne, Gloucester, Rochester, and Shrewsbury.   Even the Cister-cians, who came to England full of traditions of Burgundian vaulting, could not influence the Yorkshire people to put high vaults on the

Basilica of Maxentius.

naves of Fountains, Kirkstall, Furness, Byland ; nor would the Benedictines vault the naves of Whitby and Selby, or the Augustinian canons the choir of Hexham.

GROINED VAULTS.

But to return to the Roman groined vault.   It was constructed in mortar, in which stones were laid in horizontal layers.†   It was not a thin shell like the tunnel vaults of the Cluniac‡ churches or the ribbed vaults of Gothic architec-ture, but very thick and very heavy.   Being so thick and heavy, it was con-structed on arches of brick or tiles ; which, when the concrete had been built up on them, remained as permanent centres.   The under surface of the arches, as also of the concrete, was plastered over ; and then this under surface received a decorative treatment.   The arches were invisible when once the vault was

---

* This is a convenient term to distinguish the vault of a central from that of a side aisle.

† Choisy's *L'Art de bâtir chez les Romains*, 25.   ‡ *Classification of Romanesque*, 279.

finished. When once the concrete had set, the vault had little lateral thrust.*
But nevertheless the Roman builder provided a very large amount of abutment. His practice was the very reverse of that of the Gothic builders. He
liked to have an overplus of stability ; they were ever trying to find what was
the minimum to which supports and abutments might be reduced. Thus in the
BASILICA OF MAXENTIUS † (290) the plan shows enormous buttresses on
either side of the nave.‡ The dimensions of these vaults far transcended
anything that was attempted in mediæval times ; for each rectangular bay of
this nave had a span of 83 ft., and its diagonal groins a span of 117 ft. The
nave of Lincoln has a span of 39 ft. ; that of Amiens, 46 ft. ; Milan and Seville,
56 ft. Another vast groined hall, the *tepidarium* of the Baths of Diocletian,
forms the transept of the Church of S. Maria degli Angeli, Rome.

It was the massive Roman barrel vault which was copied by the Romanesque builders of France south of the Loire ; producing churches with
ponderous supports, and with high vaults of
barrel form. In the Gothic cathedral of Albi,
however, there is a genuine survival of the
Roman groined vault ;
it is built of brick,
with internal but-
tresses, and with mas-
sive groined vault
"holding together by
cohesion like an arti-
ficial monolith," with
ribs which are decorative, not constructional.§

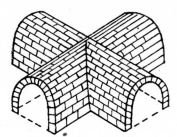

Roman Groined Vault.

A Roman groined vault consists of two intersecting semi-cylinders.‖ Or
imagine two drain-pipes to interpenetrate. It may have arisen more or
less accidentally ; imagine two corridors at right angles, of the same breadth
and height, both roofed with semicircular tunnels ; where they cross there
will be a groined vault. It is a case that must often have occurred in the
large mansions and underground reservoirs, and other public buildings of
Rome. Often one corridor would be smaller than the other, and its
tunnel vault at a lower level than that of the other. This is indeed the
case with most actually existing Roman vaults ; and there are a few examples

* On the homogeneous nature of the Roman vaults see Professor Middleton's *Ancient
Rome*, 2 vols., London, 1893. Objection has been taken to this theory, which certainly is con-
tradicted by Roman practice.

† In order to make the system of abutment clear, the screen walls from C to D have been
omitted ; as well as the arches from A to B which convert the three compartments on either
side of the nave into a continuous aisle.

‡ On the whole subject of Roman vaulting see the classic work of M. Choisy, *L'Art de
bâtir chez les Romains*.

§ Choisy's *Histoire*, 467, 510.

‖ This is only true in a general way. Some Roman, some Romanesque, and most Byzantine groined vaults are domical ; *i.e.* bulge upwards at the centre ; and are such as would be
produced by the intersection of two barrels or casks, not of two agricultural drain-pipes ; they
are intersecting barrel vaults, not intersecting tunnel vaults.

of it in Romanesque, *e.g.* in St Remi de Reims and St Benoît-sur-Loire.*
Usually in Roman work there are no transverse arches between the different
compartments of a groined vault; so also in the aisles of the nave and in the
crypts of the ABBAYE-AUX-DAMES, CAEN (293),† and Rochester; and the undercroft of Durham refectory.   But in Norman work far more often each bay of the
groined vault rests on a pair of massive square-edged transverse arches.   Early
examples are S. Vitale, Ravenna, sixth century; Aix-la-Chapelle, ninth century.
This is the normal form in which the vault appears from Roman times to the
eleventh century.

It is in the Romanesque crypts that the mediæval groined vault appears
earliest.   Even when the builders were afraid of vaulting anything else, they
usually vaulted the crypt.   In a crypt vaulting was easy; the crypt was low; the
pillars in it could be placed so as divide it up into numerous small compartments;
and each compartment could be kept square; and the vault did not need to be
very strong, as all that it carried was the pavement of the floor above.‡   A rude
attempt at a groined crypt may be seen in Wing Church.§   In the eighth
century it occurs in the crypt of the older cathedral at Brescia; in the ninth
century in those of St Vincent in Prato, Milan; of Alliata; and in two crypts
at Orléans.∥   The tradition preserved in the crypts also survived in the vaulting
of the little semicircular ambulatory of S. Stefano, Verona; and the eastern
bay of each aisle of Alliata; both probably ninth century; and both the nave
and the rectangular oratory of Cividale were vaulted even in the eighth century.

To the end of the eleventh century all the greater churches in Normandy
had groined vaults to their aisles, *e.g.* Bernay choir and Jumièges (in the latter
upper and lower aisles both have groined vaults); Cérisy, and the Abbaye-aux-
Hommes.¶   So also in the twelfth century at LESSAY (293), Blois, Poissy,
Pontigny; and the upper aisles of the choirs of St Germer and Vézelay: in the
latter at least as late as 1170; in some of the latter the builders were certainly
acquainted with the construction of ribbed vaults: yet constructed groined
vaults by preference in the aisles.   In England also in the eleventh century
the normal practice was to give the aisle a groined vault, *e.g.* at NORWICH (238).
And even till the middle of the twelfth century the same form still occurs
occasionally, *e.g.* in St Bartholomew's, Smithfield.

But, here and there, the builders took courage to construct high groined
vaults as well.   The photograph shows in the distance the semi-dome, and in the
foreground two oblong bays of the high vault over the aisled choir of ST
NICHOLAS, CAEN, *c.* 1080 (293),** with which that of St George's de Boscherville

* Choisy's *Histoire*, 151; and *Roman Construction*, 71.
† Illustrated in Scott's *Lectures*, ii. 157; and Hope's *Rochester*, Plate iii.
‡ See the western bays of the crypt of WORCESTER (192.2).
§ Seventh century, Micklethwaite; comparatively late, Baldwin-Brown.
∥ Cattaneo, 202, 231, 238, 250; and Enlart's *Manuel*, 166, 176, 184.
¶ The term *groined* vault is often used in a loose way of any intersecting vault, whether it
has diagonal ribs, or only diagonal groins, *i.e.* sharp edges or arrises.   It is convenient to
restrict it to the latter.   Throughout, therefore, when speaking of a *groined vault*, I mean an
unribbed intersecting vault.
** This church is now divided by floors, and used as a granary; the photograph is taken
from the top floor; the groined vault is seen in the foreground.

Abbaye-aux-Dames, Caen.
St Nicholas, Caen.

Lessay Abbey, Normandy.
Gloucester Choir Aisle.

may be compared. The choir of the Abbaye-aux-Dames is vaulted in the same way, except that the bays are nearly square; and that the high vault rests not on isolated piers, but on solid walls separating the choir from the aisles, as at Rochester, St Albans, and Cérisy. This vault may be earlier than that of St Nicholas, Caen.* The vast naves of the German Cathedral of Speyer and of the Burgundian Abbey of Vézelay received groined vaults; the former *c.* 1100, the latter probably after the fire of 1120. Any high groined vaults we may

Gloucester, North Ambulatory.

have had in England have disappeared. Sir G. Scott was of opinion that Hereford choir was designed for one.†

As the illustrations of Cérisy, Lessay, and Norwich show, the bays or severies of these aisle vaults were separated by massive unmolded semicircular arches. These arches were built first. Then on them a temporary vault of boarding was put together; what is called "centering"; the upper surface of the boarding was covered with a thin layer of mortar, and

* See Ruprich-Robert, i. 71 ; and Plans, i. 8, 9.
† See his restoration of it in *Building News*, August 9, 1878

on this was constructed the permanent vault of masonry. This masonry was mere rubble; packed together almost anyhow, without any attempt at regularity in the courses. When the mortar had set, the centering was removed and the lower surface of the vault was plastered over.* Usually the lower part of the groins is well marked, but towards the top they die away, leaving the summit of the vault a sort of flattish dome. In modern restorations these vaults have usually been plastered over neatly, and the groins have been carried up to the apex of the vault. These rubble vaults were of course very thick and very heavy; but if they were built with good mortar, which was not always the case, each bay would practically form one homogeneous block of concrete, with little if any lateral thrust. They required strong supports more than strong abutment; and therefore were well suited for Norman architecture, with its thick walls and piers, but shallow buttresses.

With these rude vaults the builders became exceedingly expert; they succeeded in vaulting not merely squares, or oblongs, as in the high vault of St Nicholas, Caen, but trapeziums and triangles, as in WINCHESTER CRYPT, c. 1080 (192.5), and in GLOUCESTER AMBULATORY (293). There are even hexagonal groined vaults in the eastern apses of Gloucester transept. Or sometimes, as in WORCESTER CRYPT (192.2), they covered the apse not with a semi-dome, but a series of triangular groined vaults. Or, in the ambulatories, they banished the trapezium by vaulting the bays alternately in squares and triangles.†

---

* Sometimes portions of the boarding stuck to the layer of mortar on their upper surface, and were left there. Fragments of the original centering may still be seen adhering to the mortar in Lastingham crypt and in the staircases of Rochester castle.

† This had been done in the sixth century at S. Vitale, Ravenna; in the ninth at Aix-la-Chapelle, and in S. Stefano, Verona.

CHAPTER XX.

CONSTRUCTION OF RIBBED VAULTS.

Vaults with Diagonal Ribs—Use of Ribs—Early Diagonal Ribs—Breadth of Ribs— Wall Ribs—Rib-molds—Voussoirs—*Tas-de-Charge*—Materials of Cells—Thickness of Web—Keystone, Boss—Pendant—Height of Spring.

WE have seen how very valuable the groined vault proved to be ; nevertheless it was very heavy, and needed massive and obstructive piers, and the groins were difficult to construct. So there was devised an immense improvement, which superseded the groined vault after a life of twelve centuries, and completely revolutionised the history of mediæval architecture. It was the substitution of ribs for the sharp edges of the groins. It had many good results ; some of them, no doubt, unforeseen by the inventors. First of all, it got rid of the special defect of the groined vault, the weakness of the diagonal groins.* But what was probably still more at the heart of the builders—it enabled them to construct the filling in with much less centering. Instead of building up the whole vault first of all in wood, a difficult, tedious, and expensive matter, the mason now first put up centres for the two diagonal arches and the two transverse arches, and built these in ashlar.† When the masonry of these arches was set, the four compartments (" cells") into which the vaulting bay ("severy") was now divided, could be vaulted one at a time. Instead of having to prepare centering for all four cells at once, he could employ it for one cell, take it down and employ it for another, and so on with the rest. And the centering required for vaulting each cell was of the simplest character, merely a set of planks of short lengths. When with these he had bridged the space from one of the diagonal ribs to one of the four outer arches, he could then fill in with rubble held together by mortar. But a further improvement was possible. It was that two planks should be so fastened together, that one would slide on the other ; forming a sort of extensible plank or templet ("cerce").‡ Thus the cerce, drawn out as it could be to any length required, might supersede planking altogether. No centering would be required at all for the " filling in " of the cells ; only for the construction of the arches (diagonals, transverse arch, and pier-arch) on which the cells rested. In those days, before steam and before circular saws, it was an important consideration to be able to economise in planks.

* *Cf.* Brutails, 98. † Ashlar is squared and dressed building stone.
‡ The "cerce" is illustrated on page 298.

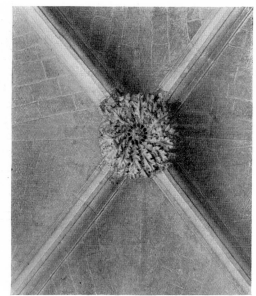

Gloucester West Nave.
Oxford Cathedral Choir.

Exeter Choir Aisle.
Tewkesbury Nave.

Another thing greatly desired by the Gothic builder was to lighten the vault, and to reduce the area of the thick piers with which the Norman naves were encumbered. This led the way to the light piers of Gothic, occupying sometimes only one-nineteenth of the area of such piers as those in DURHAM CHOIR (659.1). To effect this, all the mason had to do was to substitute a thin shell of worked stone for the thick mass of concrete of the groined vault. Indeed, if he wished to use the "cerce," * the vault could not be constructed at all in heavy concrete ; the "cerce" would not bear it. So on the upper surface of the "cerce," which had a segmental curve, a segmental arch was constructed, not in rubble, but in ashlar. Then the "cerce" was closed up, taken down, extended, set up again (one end resting on a diagonal and the other on an outer arch), and a second segmental arch was built on the first, and so on till the ridge of the cell was reached. Then, starting near the bottom † of the other half of the cell, the mason

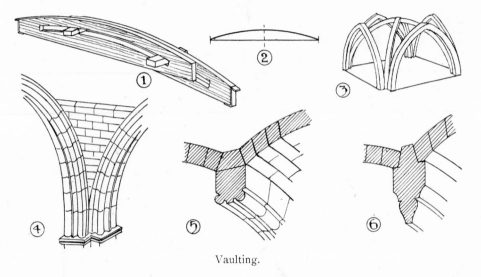

Vaulting.

worked upward till again he reached the ridge. Such work could only be done with worked blocks, not with rubble.

Another great advantage of ribs was that in a severy of several cells, each cell was independent of its neighbour. In the groined vault, if fracture occurred in any part of it, the safety of the whole vault was imperilled. But any cell in a ribbed vault might be fractured without necessary injury to the adjoining cells. Indeed, sometimes one cell was taken out, as in the high vault of SENS (107), and a cell of different shape substituted for it, in order to get room for a larger clerestory window. The cells of the vault of the south aisle of Chichester nave are similarly elevated to admit tall windows (see 34.4).

Still another advantage was that there was a very considerable amount of elasticity in the shell of such a vault. If, owing to pressures and strains, the

* We have no actual evidence that such a "cerce" was employed in mediæval construction : in large spans certainly it could not be used. Choisy's *Histoire*, ii. 274.

† The bottom courses, *e.g.* those shown in fig. 4, being vertical or nearly so, could be built without either "cerce" or centering.

diagonal arches of the vault were thrust apart a little,* the arched courses would sink ; if the diagonals were forced nearer together, the courses would rise ; and all this without necessarily causing the vault to fall.   In some French churches, *e.g.* in the collegiate church of St Quentin, the twisting and contortion of the vault surfaces is something extraordinary ; the vaults look most unpleasantly unsafe ; yet they have stood since the thirteenth century.   This elasticity was again further increased by the fact that the end vaulting stones (*voutains*) of the courses were not bonded into the arches on which they rested.   At first the courses of voutains passed over and rested on the backs of the arches (298.5).   In later work the arches were usually sunk ("rebated") to receive the voutain, or at least the lower part of its thickness (298.6).† Whichever method was adopted, the cells of the vault had a good deal of "play."   Sometimes, however, even in late vaults, the construction of the groined vault was retained, *i.e.* the cells were still built in rubble,‡ *e.g.* in Lichfield nave.   When this was the case, the under surface of the vault was plastered.   In modern restorations this plaster has often been removed, as at Lichfield.   But a vault so constructed has little elasticity ; and needs to be strengthened by other ribs in addition to the diagonals ; it is so strengthened at LICHFIELD (313).

Again, in a vault without ribs the eye has nothing to rest on but the webs ; and naturally, looking to them for beauty of curve, demands that their curves shall be true ; that the surfaces shall be portions of regular cylinders ; and notes with displeasure any deviation from regularity of surface.   But in a ribbed vault it is to the ribs that the gaze is directed, not at all to the surfaces ; unless they are exceptionally distorted, as at St Quentin.§   So long, therefore, as the ribs present agreeable curves to the eye, the builder may "play" with his surfaces ; and in Gothic he does so to a very large extent.   Many difficulties of Gothic vault construction are got rid of by a change of the direction of the vault surface, which escapes notice unless one goes out of the way to look for it. Thus, then, not in one but in many ways, the substitution of the rib for the groin was an immense advance.

BREADTH OF RIBS.—So much for the value of the rib.   Later on, its early and simple forms received an astonishing development.   But before we go on to speak of that, it may be well to describe more fully the construction of a bay or severy of an early ribbed vault.   In its simplest complete form it consists of two diagonal arches, AD, BC, and four outer arches, AB, BD, DC, CA.   Of the outer arches, BD is a pier-arch, the most massive of all.   AB, CD, are transverse arches spanning the aisle.   AC is the wall-arch (French *formeret*), with a window below it.   Compare 308.7, 298.3, and 313 (GLOUCESTER).

In early examples, *e.g.* in Canterbury choir, the transverse arches are usually much broader than the diagonals.   This is merely a "survival."   In the groined vault, as there were no diagonal arches, the whole of the weight of the vault was

---

* *E.g.* Hereford north transept.

† Scott's *Lectures*, ii. 194.

‡ Chichester and New Shoreham have early and beautiful examples of vaults accurately filled in with ashlar (313).

§ *E.g.* no one but an expert ever notices the frequent ploughshare vaulting in a Gothic clerestory (see page 311).

taken by the outer arches, which consequently had to be broad and strong, as in
NORWICH AISLE (238). But in a ribbed vault the diagonals carry most of the
weight.* This at first was not realised, *e.g.* in the aisle vault of DURHAM NAVE
(315); hence the unnecessary breadth of many early transverse arches. Later
on, both sets of arches are made of the same section. An early example of
the improved method is the aisle vault of the western bays of Worcester
nave † (*c.* 1170).

WALL RIBS.—Wall ribs are frequently absent in the early Gothic, both of
France and England. The eye distinctly requires them ; and the absence of
them is an artistic loss. Examples of wall ribs occur in the aisles of Aix-
la-Chapelle and S. Ambrogio, Milan ; the Norman groined aisles of Gloucester choir and Norwich ; the Norman ribbed aisle of Gloucester nave ; in
Glastonbury Lady Chapel; Wells Cathedral; NEW SHOREHAM and CHICHESTER
(313).

EARLY DIAGONAL RIBS.—The ribbed vaults of S. Ambrogio, Milan, are of
uncertain date. The damaged vault of the nave was repaired in 1196. Cattaneo
and Rivoira suggest *c.* 1050—*c.* 1100 for the construction of these vaults ; Comte
Robert de Lasteyrie puts them after 1100. In France early examples of diagonal
ribs occur at Quimperlé, Poitiers, St Gaudens, Moissac, St Guilhem du Désert,
St Gilles, Marseilles St Victor ; chiefly under towers. The chief early examples
in the Ile de France and Picardy are St Denis, 1140 ; Morienval, which may be
either before or after 1122 (Brutails, 213, 215) ; the ambulatory of St Martin-
des-Champs, *c.* 1130 to *c.* 1150; the aisle of St Etienne, Beauvais, *c.* 1115 to
c. 1125 ; Bellefontaine, after 1125. Enlart (*Manuel*, 440) is of opinion that in
1120 diagonal ribs had been in use but a short time in these districts ; this is
shown by "the clumsiness with which they were still employed." In England,
diagonal ribs appear in the eleventh century, viz. in the aisles of Durham choir,
which was built 1093 to 1099 (Bilson's *Beginnings*, 261 to 264). Early examples
of Gothic diagonal ribs are seen in the two western bays of the south aisle of
Worcester nave, *c.* 1170, where the wall arches and transverse arches are pointed
and are composed of a double roll ; in Glastonbury Lady Chapel, 1184-1186,
where also the wall arches and transverse arches are pointed ; as they are in the
round church of the Temple, dedicated 1185 ; and in the transept and nave of
Wells Cathedral. Earlier than any of these are the pointed arches of the vaults
of St Cross, Winchester. ‡

RIB-MOLDS.—As we have seen, *e.g.* at Lessay, Norwich, and Gloucester
choir, the earliest transverse arches were unmolded. But when diagonal ribs
were introduced in Durham choir aisles (*c.* 1093), pier-arches were often molded ;
indeed, in some cases, *e.g.* in the arches of Norwich apse and choir (1096)
(273), the moldings were already numerous, delicate, and refined. Therefore,
except now and then in crypts, *e.g.* Gloucester, or under towers, unmolded
diagonals do not occur. Nevertheless, for a long time, even in Gothic,
the rectangular outline of the ancient unmolded arches was preserved ; all

---

* Thus on page 675 the transverse and diagonal arches of ROCHE (1, 2) differ in section ;
but those of BYLAND (3) are the same.

† Prior, 91, adds Hereford east transept, Chester, and Llandaff.

‡ See quotation from Viollet-le-Duc, *Architecture*, 440 note.

the moldings being obtained by sinking hollows into ribs of rectangular section. Of the early molded ribs three species are most common. The first is a single roll; *e.g.* in the transverse ribs of KIRKSTALL NAVE (673.5) and the octopartite vault of CANTERBURY TREASURY (673.2). The second is a pair of rolls; as in the transverse arches of BUILDWAS CHAPTER HOUSE (673.10), GLOUCESTER (313) and Southwell nave aisles; and in Gothic, at Wells, Salisbury, Chichester, NEW SHOREHAM (313), and Lincoln. The hollow between these rolls is variously treated. A third arrangement is to set between the pair of rolls a third projecting roll; as at the ABBAYE-AUX-HOMMES (673.4) and BUILDWAS (673.11).

In all the above, and other such variants, the moldings are all inscribed in a rectangle. But, after a time, the rectangular was abandoned for the triangular form; as soon as it was seen that, for strength of rib, depth is more valuable than breadth (just as one lays iron girders on the flange, not on their side). In other words, instead of molding the faces and the soffit, the masons molded the chamfer planes; having cut the voussoirs of the ribs into a triangular shape before beginning to mold them. A good example of this is seen in LINCOLN GALILEE (677.3). In late vaulting the principle was sometimes carried further still, and triangular became what we may call "knife-edge" ribs, as in the lower story of the Old Convocation House at Oxford; Bishop Booth's Porch, Hereford; and Bishop West's Chantry at ELY (334).

Another reason for altering the quadrangular to the triangular form was that three, five, or more ribs had to descend to the same abacus; but if each rib was square, it was difficult to find room for them all.

Other alterations were mainly to gain various shadow effects. As in the diagonal rib of FURNESS (673.8), the rib became pointed in section; or a keel-molding was employed, as at HOWDEN (677.10); or a narrow fillet, as at RIEVAULX (675.14); or a broad fillet, as at JERVAULX (675.5). Sometimes the roll (or *bowtell*) had a double fillet, as at RIEVAULX (675.14); or even a triple fillet. Finally, all this alternation of roll and hollow was run into meagre undulatory curves and hollow chamfers, as in WELLS CLOSE (677.14).

It should be added, that as only one side of the wall ribs supports the webs, it is made smaller than the diagonal and transverse ribs; *e.g.* in the Norman aisle of GLOUCESTER NAVE (313); and at BYLAND, RIEVAULX, WHITBY (675).

Occasionally molded ribs are ornamented; *e.g.* in St Cross, Winchester, with zigzag; in St Peter in the East, Oxford, with chain ornament; in Lincoln south-east transept, with billet; in Canterbury choir and Lincoln galilee, with the tooth ornament; in the south aisle of Gloucester nave, with ball-flower.

VOUSSOIRS.—In early examples the ribs are composed of a large number of small blocks (*voussoirs*); in later work much longer blocks are employed. The length of the voussoirs may therefore be of value in determining the date of a vault. Thus the photographs of the vaults of the choir aisle of DURHAM, the choir of LESSAY, and the nave of the ABBAYE-AUX HOMMES (315) show that Norman ribs are composed of quite short blocks. In the north-east transept of Canterbury (*c.* 1175), which is 30 ft. wide, the transverse rib is made up of about a hundred voussoirs. In Westminster transept (*c.* 1245), the transverse rib above the solid springer contains thirteen or fourteen voussoirs; in the nave, which is much later, six only.*

TAS-DE-CHARGE.—Turning to the diagram 308.3, and the photograph of the vault of Chichester nave on page 313, it will be seen that five ribs—two diagonals CJ, GJ, one transverse arch DJ, and two walls ribs IJ and NJ—may all descend on to one capital or corbel J. So also five may descend on to D. But in 324.7 there are no less than thirteen ribs, all trying to find room on the capitals B and D. It was impossible to find room for them all; and so, in Gothic days, the lower parts (*springers*) of the groups of ribs were constructed in horizontal courses bonded to the wall: *i.e.* the courses of the lower part, the springers of the arches, were not arcuated at all; had not radiating joints: the arch proper only began where the springers ended. Such an arch is said to be built in TAS-DE-CHARGE: the lower part of its curve is merely corbelled out; it consists below of courses of horizontal blocks, each upper course projecting further forward than the course below it. It may extend upward to as much as one-third of the height of the vault.

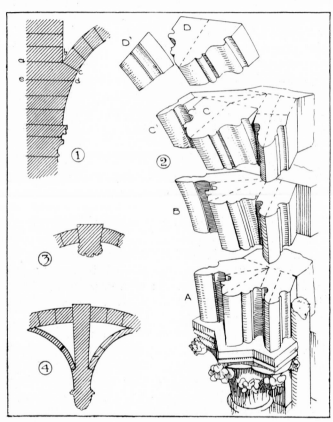

1, 2. *Tas-de-Charge.*
3. Keystone.   4. Pendant.

Many great advantages sprang from the construction of the springers in the solid. The weight from above was brought down on to horizontal blocks which could not slip, instead of being brought down to inclined voussoirs which might be forced out. In diagram 1 there are four horizontal springers (French *sommiers*) on which the weight descends. In diagram 2 there are three springers, A, B, C; in C radiating joints are seen from which three ribs are to spring—a broad transverse rib in the centre, a slender diagonal rib on either side. D shows the first voussoir of the transverse rib; D^1 that of either of

* Willis' *Middle Ages*, 6, 9.

the diagonals. Really *tas-de-charge* means continuing the pier so much upward ; *e.g.* in diagram 2 the pier does not really terminate as it appears to do at the capital beneath the sommier A, but at the top of the skewback C.* By a logical corollary, in later French Gothic, *e.g.* at St Lo, the capitals of the main piers are omitted altogether, as telling a false tale.

Another happy result is that since the haunches of the arches are executed in corbelling, the span of the real arches with radiating joints is much reduced ; and as it costs less to construct a narrow than a broad arch, owing to the reduction in centering, *tas-de-charge* effects considerable economy. In the transept of Westminster the real span of the vault arches is thus reduced by about one-sixth.†

As to the mode of execution, the easiest way would be to erect the springers in block, and then when the arches were built on them and had set, to work moldings downwards to correspond with the forms of the ribs above.‡ This may well have been a common practice. Professor Willis,§ however, proves that the molds of the springers were not worked *in situ* in the nave aisles of St Saviour's, Southwark, or in a late vault beneath Lanfranc's tower at Canterbury, both of which he saw in the course of demolition. In these the surfaces of the springers were covered with lines and profiles of moldings to enable the blocks to be cut to shape on the bench. Possibly the practice varied.

The use of *tas-de-charge* does not occur in England till towards the end of the twelfth century ; *e.g.* at Glastonbury, ‖ and in the central pillar of the guard-room of the Castle at Newcastle. In France it does not appear till the thirteenth century ; Soissons choir, finished in 1212, seems to be the first example of it ; it does not appear in Notre Dame, Paris, finished in 1220.¶

MATERIALS.—The cells of the vaults were constructed of rubble or of ashlar ; of a light stone if it could be had. Thus at Rome there were deposits of pumice and tufa from the neighbouring volcanoes ; these were used largely ; *e.g.* in the vaults of the Colosseum, and the Baths of Titus and Caracalla.** In the haunches of the vault, *e.g.* in the Temple of Minerva Medica, and the vaults of tombs, pots were often used. They were light, and they could be had for the fetching, for there was a mountainous dust-heap of old wine jars at Rome—the present Monte Testaccio. In England, when we could get it, *e.g.* in Kent and Gloucestershire, we used an aqueous tufa,†† a deposit of so-called petrifying

---

* Curiously enough, the real termination of the vaulting shaft in the clerestory of York presbytery is marked by a couple of little capitals set on either side of the top of the solid springers. (See int. elevation in Britton's *York*, Plate 24.)

† Willis' *Middle Ages*, 7. In Mr Pearson's church at West Croydon, the span is thus reduced from 22 ft. to 19 ft. (R. P. Spiers, *Architectural Drawing*).

‡ Scott's *Essay*, 180.   § *Vaulting*, 10, 11, 12.

‖ Illustrated in Willis' *Glastonbury*, 66.

¶ Enlart's *Manuel*, 506 ; and Choisy's *Histoire*, ii. 272, 274.

** Choisy's *L'Art de bâtir chez les Romains*, 96.

†† At Worcester the Lady Chapel is vaulted with rough lumps of tufa ; so also the two western bays of the nave. This tufa is found and is still used occasionally in the Stockton-on-Teme neighbourhood, some 15 miles to the west of Worcester. The rock is excessively soft when quarried, but hardens in the air. The Normans were fond of it in the West of England ; the church of Moccas, Hereford, is largely built of it (Mr A. B. Pickney).

springs issuing from limestone. It was not only light and tough, but gave a good hold to the mortar. The vault webs of Bredon porch and of Sherborne are or were of tufa ; and the vaults of Canterbury choir are, says Gervase, "*ex lapide et tofo levi.*" The webs of the vaults of Salisbury and of Canterbury cloisters and St Augustine's gateway,* Canterbury, are of chalk ; those of the fourteenth-century nave of Beverley are of brick.†

THICKNESS OF WEB.—Another way to reduce the weight of the vaults was to construct the webs in thin shells of cut stone or brick. Thus while the original rubble vault of the Abbaye-aux-Dames, taken down in the eighteenth century, was 12 in. thick, the vault of hollow tiles and Portland cement put up recently by Ruprich-Robert is only 6 in. thick.‡ Those of Chartres are nearly 11 in. thick : the result is seen in the extraordinary massiveness of the walls, buttresses, and flying buttresses of that great cathedral: a vast and unnecessary addition of expense. Many French Gothic vaults over naves, even in the twelfth century, are not more than 4 to 5 in. thick ; that of Notre Dame, Paris, an early example, is 6 in. The panels of the vault of Henry the Seventh's Chapel at Westminster were found by Mr Wonnacott to vary from $4\frac{1}{2}$ to 5 inches in thickness.

As regards the question of thickness, the builders show a certain amount of hesitation. The logic of the matter was, that if the vault webs were constructed in rubble, they ought to be thick. Again, if they were to be covered externally with tiles or with flagstones resting directly on their backs (*extrados*), they ought to be thick ; so also, if they were to be sheltered with a timber roof, but one resting on their extrados.§ But if the timber roof was to be quite independent of the vault, not touching it at all, then the thinner the vaults could be made, compatibly with stability, the better : a thin vault fireproofed the church just as well as a thick one. In practice, however, the builders were not always logical. They frequently added to the webs, on their extrados, a thick irregular course of rubble work, often covered with concrete ; *e.g.* in Winchester, Wells, Ely, Bristol Cathedral and St Mary Redcliffe, most of Westminster and Hereford, Sherborne crossing, Oxford Cathedral, and elsewhere. But in the west nave of Westminster and in the south transept and tower of Hereford the upper surfaces have no such covering ; and at Ely it was lately hacked away. In late work not only is this outer covering dispensed with, but a good deal of the surface of the blocks of the cells themselves was chipped away ; *e.g.* in the high vault of the nave of St George's, Windsor ; ‖ while in Henry the Seventh's Chapel at Westminster the whole of the outer surface is chipped off (347). Probably it was necessary to lighten the later vaults as much as possible, for they were far flatter than the earlier ones, and had much greater lateral thrust. The more the weight could be diminished, the less would be the thrust.

KEYSTONE, BOSS.—In an arch every one of the voussoirs of which it is composed is a keystone ; but the central voussoir, that at the apex of the arch,

---

* Caveler's *Specimens*, 36.   † Mr John Bilson in *Archit. Review*, xviii. 252.

‡ The high vaults (brick) of the nave of S. Ambrogio average 16 in. in thickness (Mr C. A. Cumming's *Architecture in Italy*, i. 105).

§ Choisy's *Histoire*, ii. 162.   ‖ Illustrated on page 341. See Willis' *Vaulting*, 9.

is generally called *the* keystone (French *clef*). In a pointed arch this central keystone is sometimes found, but usually the junction of the two curves of the arch is marked by a vertical joint. When diagonal arches, crossing one another, as in DURHAM AISLE (315), were first introduced, a difficulty arose because each diagonal could not have a keystone of its own. In some early examples, *e.g.* in the crypt of Gloucester, the eastern apse of the south transept of Tewkesbury, and Upton, Bucks, first one diagonal arch was set up complete; then the other in two halves, abutting awkwardly and obliquely against the first. Durham has keystones of unscientific form.* But in the repair of Winchester transept vaults after the fall of the central tower in 1107, there is one common keystone, which is "shouldered to receive the ribs, which abut against them with a joint at right angles to the direction of the rib." † Sculptured Norman keystones occur beneath Iffley tower and in the semi-dome of Kilpeck. In the eastern transept of Canterbury ‡ (*c.* 1180) there are bosses; but their arms are straight instead of being curved like the ribs.

The builders soon gave the boss increased dimensions. In Winchester nave there are keystones weighing about 2 tons.§ In lierne vaulting (340) bosses are especially necessary; for it is very difficult for the moldings of the obliquely set ribs of such a vault to form true intersections, or as it is termed "to mitre." Nevertheless the builders occasionally amused themselves by constructing elaborate "mitred" vaults without bosses; *e.g.* in the south transept of GLOUCESTER (306), and WEST'S CHANTRY, ELY (334).

Other uses also were found for bosses. Unusually large bosses with sculptured legends were placed over the spot where was the high altar or the shrine of some great saint; and from the boss we may be able to ascertain where formerly that shrine or altar stood; *e.g.* in Ely a very elaborate boss, representing the Coronation of the Virgin, points to the place where St Etheldreda's shrine stood, behind the high altar. Foliated bosses of the rarest beauty were common; albeit all their detail invisible except to a modern binocular; foliage changing from conventional to naturalistic, as at EXETER (297); from naturalistic to undulatory leafage, as in the BERKELEY CHAPEL (329), Bristol Cathedral; and finally to the square leaves of Perpendicular work. Or, in later work, coats of arms are on the bosses, and help, as in Winchester nave, to tell who provided the funds for the construction of the vault. In later work the carved boss and either the whole or the adjoining portions of the ribs were often painted and gilt.

Through the centre of the boss a hole was often pierced, through which a chain was passed. From the chain was suspended a lamp, or a censer, which on certain days was swung backward and forward, sending forth a "cloud" of incense.

PENDANT.—In Tudor work the boss is often greatly elongated, and is then called a pendant (302.4). In a transverse arch, as in the Divinity School and the high vault of OXFORD CATHEDRAL CHOIR (297, 331), more than one pendant may occur. Or between two adjacent pendants skeleton pointed

---

* Bilson's *Beginnings*, 299.   † Bilson's *Beginnings*, 301.
‡ A boss is a keystone bossed out for carving; a keystone not so decorated is not a boss.
§ Colson's *Winchester*, 22.

U

arches may be built up; with the result that, to the untrained eye, the vault appears to rest on the arches, and the arches on the end of the pendant, and the pendant on nothing at all (302.4). In Henry the Seventh's Chapel at Westminster there are two pendants in each transverse arch of the vault (347). It is the fashion to abuse these as unconstructional; but as a matter of fact each is an elongated voussoir of a transverse arch; and each is the foundation on and round which is built up with marvellous skill one of the inverted conoids or trumpets of the fan vault.

HEIGHT OF SPRING.—Much diversity exists as to the height at which the spring of the vault commences. Constructional and artistic considerations pull in opposite directions. The lower the spring, the safer the vault is, and the

Durham, S. Aisle of Choir.   Gloucester, S. Transept.

worse it looks. On the other hand, if the spring is very high up, the clerestory windows are unmasked; the vault itself is well lighted, its beauty can be seen; all heaviness disappears; as in GLOUCESTER CHOIR (59), it seems to float on the illumined air. But a vault set on narrow piers half-way up such vast clerestory windows as those of Gloucester and Norwich requires strong flying buttresses to take its thrusts; unless, as in SHERBORNE NAVE (346), it is a fan vault of pointed section; or as at GLOUCESTER, it is abutted by a half barrel vault below (35.5).

In TEWKESBURY NAVE (297) the vault actually springs from the abacus of the nave piers; the result is that the clerestory windows are almost wholly blocked, and the nave is gloomy in the extreme. In the monks' vault over the eastern bays of GLOUCESTER NAVE, c. 1220 (26), the vault springs from the sill of the triforium. In the Norman vaults of Durham choir, nave, and central transept ; in the choir vaults of CANTERBURY (106) ; in the thirteenth-century vaults of Lincoln choir, nave, central transept, presbytery ; and in Hythe chancel ; and in the fourteenth-century vaults of Pershore and Canterbury nave, the vault springs about midway in the triforium. At the end of the twelfth century in New Shoreham and Christ Church, Dublin ; in the thirteenth century in St Saviour's Southwark, Salisbury, Worcester choir, Hereford choir and north transept, ELY presbytery (117) and choir, Lichfield nave, and Exeter ; and in the fourteenth century in Winchester nave, the vault springs from the sill of the clerestory.*   Finally, the vault may spring from somewhere midway in the clerestory ; e.g. late in the twelfth century at Wells and Chichester ; in the thirteenth century at Rochester, BEVERLEY (51), Westminster ; in the fourteenth century in Gloucester choir, and in its imitators Sherborne and Norwich. Probably no part of mediæval design was, from an artistic point of view, of such overwhelming importance as the combination of towering clerestory and high-set vault.

* So it does at BOXGROVE (318), but is much stilted.

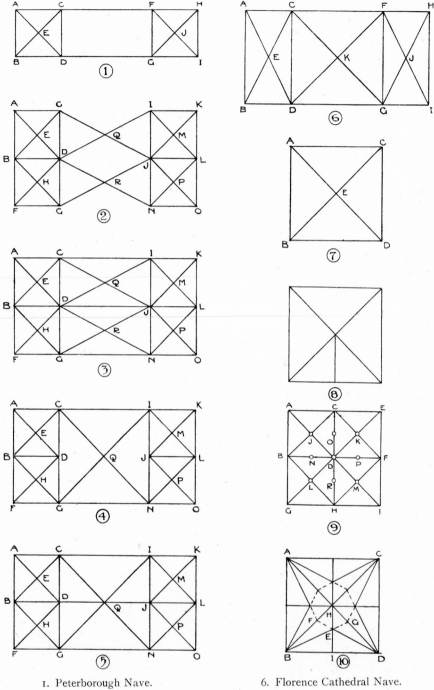

1. Peterborough Nave.
2. Durham Nave.
3. Lessay Choir.
4. Boxgrove Choir.
5. Canterbury Choir.

6. Florence Cathedral Nave.
7. Angers Cathedral Nave.
8. Lincoln Aisle of Nave.
9. Lincoln North-west Chapel.
10. Oxford Proscholium.

CHAPTER XXI.

VAULTS WITH DIAGONAL RIBS.

PART I.

Domed and Undomed Vaults—Vaults of Square and Oblong Severies.

DOMED AND UNDOMED VAULTING.—So much for the general principles of vault construction. We will now turn to their application in English and French hands : beginning with the groined vaults constructed by the Romans in the aisles of S. Sophia, Constantinople, and in S. Vitale, Ravenna ; which may be called Byzantine groined vaults. These are not composed, like the normal vault of Rome (see 291) of the intersection of two half cylinders, or two tunnel-vaulted corridors, with level ridges. In their construction the groins as well as the four outer arches are semicircular. The result is that since the semi-circular groins are wider than the outer arches, they are also necessarily loftier ; and consequently, the ridges of the vault are not level ; the vault is more or less domical. In the first diagram, supposing ABDC to be a square space covered with a vault, of which the groins AED and BEC are semi-circles, and the outer arches AGB, BHD, DIC, CFA, are also semi-circles, it follows that since the diagonal of any square is longer than its sides, E, which is the

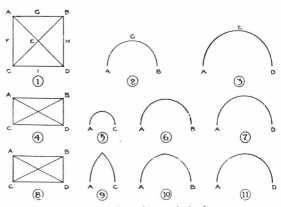

Forms of Severies and Arches.

apex of the two groins, must be higher than G, H, I, F, the apices of the four outer arches. Compare the arch on AB or on any one of the sides of the square with the arch on the diagonal AD or BC. It was this type of groined vault that was usually adopted in Lombardy, Germany, Burgundy, and Northern France, but seldom in Normandy and England. It was constructed at first with diagonal groins ; later, with diagonal ribs. It is a very good form of vault, for it has the merits of being stable and of being easy to construct. It is easy to construct ; for when all its arches are semicircles, they can be executed without full-sized drawings on the ground ; so even when some of them were pointed, the diagonals usually remained semicircular. Secondly, the more domical the cells are, the more support each course of the cell gets from the course below it. The flatter a vault surface is, the greater the difficulty in constructing it. Thirdly, just as a pointed arch has much less lateral thrust, and therefore requires less abutment than a semicircular or a segmental arch, so the more domical a vault is, the less is its thrust, and the less the abutment required. These are great advantages. One disadvantage is that since a domical vault is loftier than an undomed vault, the aisle or nave walls on either side of it have to be raised in proportion, and much time and material are wasted. This objection may have weighed with the Norman and English builders, and have caused their dislike of domical vaulting. We have indeed examples; *e.g.* at New Shoreham and the east side of Westminster cloisters; but they are not common. In France, east of Normandy, the early Gothic vaults, *e.g.* at St Denis, are usually excessively domical; later on, they are less so, but their ridges seldom become quite horizontal. As early as the twelfth century the diagonal as well as the outer arches were pointed in the aisles of St Cross, Winchester, in St Joseph's Chapel, Glastonbury, and in Wells Cathedral; the result being to make the vault domical, and at the same time to bring the thrusts down more vertically. Domical vaults of different types are shown in 325.6 and 321.

SQUARE SEVERIES.—In Normandy and England the type usually adopted was that of the vault with horizontal ridges (see 291). Now if this vault be studied, it will be seen that all the arches—the two diagonals, and the four outer arches— all start from the same level, and rise to the same level; and therefore both the ridges are horizontal. It follows that the diagonal arches are not semicircles. For we saw in 309.1, that if they were semicircles, they would rise much higher than the other arches, and the ridges would not be horizontal. Since the ridges are horizontal, it follows that the arches are of some other form than the semicircular. As a matter of fact they are half ellipses. So that by adopting the undomed rather than the domical type of groined vault, the builders had committed themselves to the adoption of the elliptical form of arch for the diagonals. But an ellipse is difficult to draw and difficult to execute. Probably in the eleventh century the builders could not draw an ellipse at all. Moreover, it is more difficult still to construct diagonal ribs of elliptical curve. So semi-elliptical diagonals are rare; they seem not to occur till the middle of the twelfth century. Examples* are Devizes St Mary and Dunstable Priory;† both probably *c.* 1150; in Normandy the transepts of the Abbaye-aux-Dames and of Montivilliers;‡ and Guéron apse; in the thirteenth century the choir of the Temple Church, London;§ the south and west sides of Westminster cloister and the passage leading into Dean's Yard.‖ Generally, however, the semi-ellipse was avoided. Some easier way had to be found out of the difficulty. The difficulty was that the diagonals were too tall and the transverse arches too low for horizontal ridges. Evidently the thing to do was to lower the tall diagonals or to raise the low outer arches, or to do both. This

---

* It should be noted that some of these occur in high vaults, not in vaulted aisles.
† Bilson's *Beginnings*, 308.   ‡ Ruprich-Robert, Plates 74 and 95.
§ Illustrated in Scott's *Lectures*, i. 119.   ‖ Garbett, 166, 167.

is precisely what was done in Norman England. For the semicircle in the diagonals the builders substituted the upper part of a semicircle; *i.e.* a segmental arch; the outer arches they raised on stilts. Segmental diagonals occur in the aisles of Durham, Winchester, Peterborough, Gloucester nave, Southwell, Lindisfarne, Selby, Warkworth; * all probably between 1093 and 1150. While beneath the transverse arches a few vertical courses of masonry were constructed; *i.e.* the arches were stilted; in the aisles of Durham, PETERBOROUGH (318), Romsey, Southwell, Lindisfarne, and others. Sometimes the "stilt" is not vertical, but incurved; making the arch more of a "horseshoe" than a stilted semicircle.

But all this was to break two of the principles of vault construction; one, that all the ribs of a vault should start from the same level, which the outer ribs no longer did; and secondly, that all the arches must be semicircular, which the diagonals no longer were. The penalty was that the webs would be no longer regularly cylindrical surfaces,† but would present irregular curves of surface. But having secured by these devices what they valued most—horizontal ridges—the builders did not trouble about the surface contour of the webs; they let it take its chance. So convenient in practice was this disregard of geometry found to be that the best Gothic of France and England constantly twisted its vault surfaces where there was the slightest convenience to be gained thereby. This was especially the case with the cell next to a window of an aisle or clerestory: this cell was often wide and very difficult to construct; but by disregarding the proper curve, and by constructing the lower part of it nearly vertical (298.4), that part of the cell, perhaps one-fourth, could be built without centering, each course resting securely on the course below it. Moreover, by pinching back the webs on either side of the window instead of letting them project forward at once more or less in front of it, the light

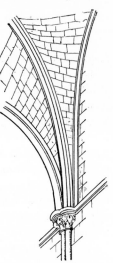

St Saviour's, South-
wark.

was less obstructed. In such a case, therefore, French and English alike disregarded regularity of web-surface in favour of facility of construction and improvement in lighting. This twisting of the surfaces is called *ploughshare* vaulting: examples are the high‡ vaults of Wells; ST SAVIOUR'S, SOUTHWARK; Salisbury; Westminster. But in Gothic, instead of stilting the ribs, they were often supplied with small upper shafts, from which they sprang, and not from the vaulting shafts; *e.g.* SENS (107).

OBLONG SEVERIES.—But we are anticipating matters. So far we have been speaking as if all vaults covered square spaces, as in 309.1. But oblong spaces also often had to be vaulted over. Then a still further difficulty

---

* Bilson's *Beginnings*, 299-307.

† Willis' *Middle Ages*, 74, says "the whole difficulty of vaulting a parallelogram with quadripartite vaulting resided in the assumed necessity of preserving the apex of the vaulting cells horizontal, and making their surfaces cylindrical throughout."

‡ It is in the high vaults that this occurs most; because it was more important to clear the clerestory windows of obstructions.

harassed the builders. Instead of semicircular arches rising to two different levels, as they did over a square, over an oblong they rose to three ; *e.g.* on the figure ABDC the two diagonals rise higher than the arches on AB and CD, and these again rise higher than those on AC and BD (309.4). So that now the builder had to humour three sets of arches instead of two, if he insisted on having horizontal ridges. Sometimes he was successful. The bays of the ribbed vaults of the Norman aisles of Durham, Southwell, and Kirkstall are all markedly oblong.

PART II.
HIGH VAULTS WITH DIAGONAL RIBS.

1. Durham—2. Lessay—3. Boxgrove—4. Lincoln Great Transept—5. Abbaye-aux-Dames—6. Florence Cathedral—7. Angers Cathedral.

As we have seen, here and there, as at St Nicholas, Caen, the builders had succeeded in constructing groined vaults, not merely over the aisles, but on the top of the lofty clerestory walls. What had been successful in the case of groined vaults had still to be attempted with vaults possessing diagonal ribs instead of groins. In the last years of the eleventh century this was the problem throughout Western Europe with all Romanesque builders, except those who had adopted the barrel vault or the dome to roof and fireproof their churches. The problem was solved not in one, but in many ways.

If we examine the plan of such a nave as that of NORWICH (148.4), it will be seen that if we divide each aisle into squares, the corresponding bays of the nave are necessarily oblongs ; the high vault consists of a number of oblong bays, and, as we have seen above, is consequently difficult to vault. In but too many cases the builders set to work not to overcome, but to shirk this difficulty. In PETERBOROUGH (308.1), as the diagram shows, they made things extremely easy by vaulting the aisles in squares, but covering the nave with merely a roof of wood. And that apparently * is what was done in all our large Norman naves except Durham and its copy, Lindisfarne. The naves of Peterborough, Ely, Binham, Carlisle, Chepstow, Chester St John's, Dunfermline, Leominster, London St Bartholomew's, Melbourne, Rochester, Romsey, St Albans, Selby, Shrewsbury, Southwell, Waltham, Wymondham, all had wooden ceilings and no high vaults. Not till Gothic days were high vaults constructed in the Norman naves of Chichester, Christchurch, Gloucester, Hereford, Norwich, Sherborne, Tewkesbury, Winchester. In Normandy also, and apparently throughout Northern France, *e.g.* St Germain des Prés, Paris, this unworthy solution seems to have been adopted generally ; although, as in the case of the Abbaye-aux-Hommes, Caen, the wooden roofs were often superseded during the course of the twelfth century by stone vaults.

FIRST SOLUTION.—To this survival of the wooden ceiling in so many of the Romanesque buildings of Normandy and England there seems to have been a conspicuous exception at Durham. Contemporary chroniclers tell us that Durham choir was commenced in 1093, and that in 1099 the work had been

* Almost all our greater Norman choirs have been rebuilt or remodelled : some of them, *e.g.* Gloucester and Hereford, may have been vaulted.

Lichfield W. Nave.
Chichester W. Nave.

Gloucester, North Aisle of Nave.
New Shoreham Choir.

extended as far as the nave ; that between 1099 and 1128 the nave had been built up *ad sui usque testudinem ;* and, lastly, that the church was finished between 1128 and 1133. It is contended that these dates cover both the aisle vaults and the high vaults of Durham. High vaults of early character (149.1, 8) remain over transepts and nave ; and the marks of the wall-cells of an earlier vault than the present one are plainly visible in the clerestory of the choir. Aisle vaults, still earlier in character (306, 315), remain in choir, transepts, and nave. The vaults of the choir aisles are the earliest, and are clearly part of the work of 1093 to 1099 ; for the masonry and moldings correspond in character with those of the pier-arcades of the choir ; and, for constructional reasons, the aisle vaults must, as usual, have been erected along with the main walls. The aisle vaults of Durham, therefore, are as early as 1093 to 1099. The next thing is to fix the date of the latest vault, the high vault of the nave. That may be fixed from what we know of the vault of the apse of the chapter house. This building, we are told by the chronicler, was finished between 1133 and 1140. Now, both as to the character of the chevron (zigzag) and the moldings, this vault is of more advanced type than the high vault of the nave. It follows that what was constructed in the cathedral between 1128 and 1133 was the high vault of the nave.* Moreover, as there is a regular sequence of change of profile and ornament in their ribs, we may arrange in chronological order all the vaults that remain, viz. (1) all the aisle vaults ; (2) the high vaults of the north transept; (3) those of the south transept ; (4) those of the nave ; (5) those of the chapter house ; all built between 1093 and 1140. Finally, as the original high vault of the choir was no doubt built *after* the aisle vault of the choir, and *before* the high vaults of the transepts and nave, it becomes probable that the original high vault of Durham choir was but little later than 1099. And as we know that the body of St Cuthbert, the patron saint, was translated in 1104 to the east end of the choir, the probability is that 1104 is the year in which the high vault of the choir, at any rate that portion of it above the shrine, was completed. It is of course to be borne in mind that the plan of the piers (659.1) shows that from the very first, *i.e.* from 1093, a choir-vault was intended.

After Durham, none of the aisled Norman churches remaining in England have high vaults built in the first half of the twelfth century, with the exception of the neighbouring church of Lindisfarne, *c.* 1125 ; where the whole church was vaulted. So many Norman churches, however, have been destroyed, especially the choirs, which were most likely to be vaulted, that this negative evidence has not much weight.

But though we cannot substantiate the existence of other high ribbed vaults over aisled buildings, except at Lindisfarne, in the first half of the twelfth century, they occur in considerable numbers over unaisled buildings, *e.g.* Kirkstall choir ; and the chancels of Warkworth, Hemel Hempstead, Stow, the two churches at Devizes, and others. Moreover, a vault, probably ribbed, was built in the nave of Lincoln between 1141 and 1148.

In Normandy, however, there is an example of a high ribbed vault, of even more advanced character than those of Durham, and not necessarily any later in date than the high vaults of Durham nave, viz. at Lessay. If a date

---

* The chronicler states that Bishop Flambard (who died in 1128), "*navem usque ad sui testudinem erexerat*"; and that in the next five years "*navis peracta est.*"

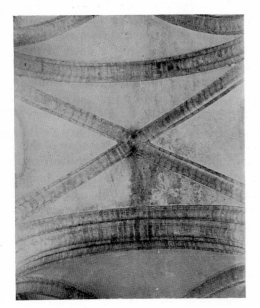
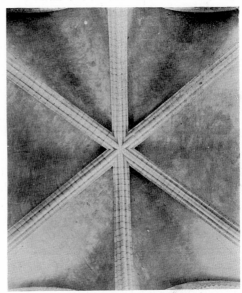

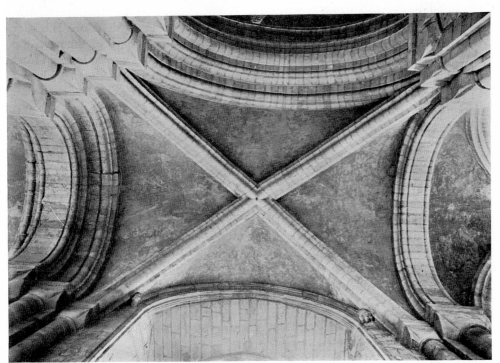

Lessay Choir.   Abbaye-aux-Hommes Nave.
Durham, S. Aisle of Choir.

early in the twelfth century can be substantiated for the Lessay vaults, it becomes easier to accept the dates above assigned to the vaults of Durham.

On the whole, the chronology of the Durham vaults, as given above, appears likely to receive increasing support.* If once the date of the choir aisle vaults (1093-1099) be admitted, there is no inherent difficulty about the dates of the high vaults. When once oblong severies had been vaulted with diagonal ribs in the aisles, there was no difference in principle in constructing similar vaults on the clerestory walls; the oblongs merely had to be placed side by side instead of end on. The height of the high vaults is no difficulty; for *c.* 1083 the clerestory of the choir of St Nicholas, Caen, was given a groined vault; a more difficult piece of construction than a ribbed one. The wide span of the high vaults of Durham also present little difficulty; for before 1140 the Norman builders had succeeded in vaulting the apse of the chapter house of Durham, which has an internal span of no less than 34 ft. 6 in.†

SECOND SOLUTION.—At Durham there was still one defect. Except in the single bays at the end of the transepts and nave, transverse arches were omitted between each pair of bays (see 149.1), a curious omission which occurs also in Magdeburg Cathedral,‡ A.D. 1209. At Lessay § the high vaults are arranged in single bays (308.3); all of which have diagonal ribs; those in the eastern part of the church are of the character illustrated in 315; in the west bays of the nave they are of less heavy profile. Now Lessay Abbey was begun in 1043; ‖ or according to others, in 1050 or 1064; the founder died in 1098, and was buried in the middle of the choir. The choir therefore is earlier than 1098. With the exception of the four westernmost bays of the nave, the church was not originally designed for a high vault. There appear to be at least five stages of work: (1) all except the west nave; (2) the vaults with heavy profile; (3) the west nave; (4) the vaults with lighter profile; (5) the west front. The west doorway has a band of tooth-ornament, but need not be later than *c.* 1150. The scalloped capital occurs in some of the western piers of the nave; but is not necessarily evidence of very late Norman date, for it appears in the earliest work of Norwich Cathedral; nor are the griffes. If we assume an interval of ten years between the different sets of work, this would give the date of *c.* 1140 for the lighter vault; *c.* 1130 for the west nave; *c.* 1120 for the heavier vault. Whatever be the exact dates it is undoubtedly a very remarkable and early example of ribbed vaulting. Here at Lessay, we have precisely the type of high vault which was employed in the early Gothic architecture both of the Ile de France and England; a complete solution of the great problem of the mediæval vault-builders.

* It is accepted by Professor Lethaby, *Mediæval Art*, 301.

† For the architectural and documentary evidence on which the above account of the Durham vaults is based, see the important papers by Mr John Bilson in the *Journal of the Royal Institute of British Architects*, Third Series, vi. 289, 345, and ix. 350.

‡ See plan in Dehio, Plate 447.

§ Lessay is a Benedictine Abbey Church at the foot of the Manche in Normandy. It is llustrated by Ruprich-Robert in Plates 89, 90; see also text 137, 138. His Plate 89 illustrates the *west* nave only. See 319, 315, 308, 293, 412.

‖ Anthyme St Paul in *Planat*, vi. 23. Ruprich-Robert, i. 282, gives "fin du 11ᵉ siècle," as the date of the Abbey, and thinks (ii. 10) that it was finished *c.* 1130. There was a consecration in 1178.

THIRD SOLUTION.—Other solutions, however, were obtained; all of them of considerable interest. One of the most important is that adopted in the ribbed vaults of S. Ambrogio, Milan. It is characteristic both of the Lombardic and the German school of Romanesque; and it was on these lines, *i.e.* with coupled bays and alternating supports, that the vast cathedrals of Worms and Mayence were vaulted, well on in the twelfth century.

We may suggest that it originated out of the diaphragmatic roof system; by which the churches, for roofing purposes, were crossed at every second or third bay by strong broad transverse arches carrying gables. An arch, so heavily weighted, required very massive supports; and these had to be piers, while the other supports might remain columns. Sometimes, as at S. Prassede, Rome, and S. MINIATO (235), Florence (eleventh century), the alternation of supports was pier, column, column, pier; in the end the customary arrangement was pier, column, pier. By far the greater number of the churches which adopted the alternation of supports had the latter disposition.* One solution, therefore, of the problem how to vault a church with alternating supports was to vault the nave in large squares, and the aisles in little squares (308.4). Each large square bay (or "severy"= "ciborium") of the vaulting rested on two major piers on either side of the nave; each little square severy of the vaulting rested on one major and one minor pier. This was a very neat solution. There were no oblongs; and the

---

* Several churches in and near Normandy have the alternating piers; *e.g.* Jumièges, 1040-1067, the earliest of all the large Norman churches except Bernay; the Abbaye-aux-Hommes; Graville; Notre Dame du Pré, Le Mans; and in French Transitional Gothic, Noyon and Laon. In England we have alternating supports at Durham, Selby, Waltham, Lindisfarne, Norwich, Ely, Boxgrove.

It has been asserted that Lanfranc, who was a native of Pavia, introduced from Lombardy the alternation of piers and columns into Normandy. But Jumièges was begun in 1040. Lanfranc did not arrive till *c.* 1042; and some years elapsed before he became powerful and influential. Before Lanfranc's time, William, abbot of Fécamp from 1010 to 1031, had great influence in Normandy; in his time forty new churches and monasteries are recorded to have been built. He was a Lombard. So also, a Lombard, born near Novara, "St William, abbot of S. Benigne, Dijon, was, at the end of the tenth century, the great restorer of the arts in Burgundy. He rebuilt his abbey in magnificent fashion. He brought his colony of monks, together with artists, from Lombardy in 996, according to the eleventh-century chronicler, Raoul Glaber. His abbey seems to have been the most ancient model of the style prevailing in the Mâconnais in the eleventh and twelfth centuries" (Virey, author of a valuable treatise on the Romanesque Diocese of Mâcon, 1892). But the difficulty arises that there seems to be no adequate evidence that any church in Lombardy with alternating supports is so ancient as the period either of William of Dijon or of William of Fécamp.

Ruprich-Robert was of opinion that in Normandy the alternating supports, the big open triforium, the windows at the back of it, the vaulted upper aisle, must have come from Lombardy; but not the masonry, nor the capitals (pages 54, 74, 84, 109, 115; so also Dehio, i. 286). On the other hand, the province of German Romanesque included the Netherlands, and that of Normandy extended up to the Netherlands; so that there may be a secondary influence of Lombardic work through its very important connection, the German Romanesque. On some minor resemblances between English and Lombardic Romanesque, see Colling, *Early Mediæval Foliage*, 20; and Petit's *Church Architecture*, 73, 75, 77. It may be added that while Norman is doubtless indebted to Lombardic or to German Romanesque, or to both, it is a moot question whether Lombardic is the parent of German, or German of Lombardic Romanesque.

Peterborough Choir Aisle.   Angers Cathedral Nave.

Boxgrove Choir.

Abbaye-aux-Hommes, Caen, Nave.
Lessay Abbey Nave.

Abbaye-aux-Dames, Caen, Nave.
Lessay Choir.

church was vaulted throughout. We have only one example of this vault system; the choir of BOXGROVE PRIORY, c. 1235 (308, 318). Here both nave and aisles are vaulted; but the nave vault rests on every other pier; while all the piers help to support the vaulting of the aisles. In such a plan, for every bay or severy in the nave there are two severies in the aisle.*

FOURTH SOLUTION.—A better solution suggested itself to the builders of Normandy (308.5). This, like the third, adopted the alternation of supports; but utilised them in a different way. Dividing the nave, as before, into squares, it utilised the minor piers also as supports of the nave vault, by constructing an additional intermediate transverse arch across the nave, from each minor pier, D, to the minor pier opposite, J. This was a distinct improvement, for each of the two cells CQG, IQN, was now divided into two; and it was easy to stretch planking across, e.g. from DQ to CQ and GQ, in filling in the cells. But the solution was imperfect; the cells CIQ, GNQ, were still much too large. However, this plan found great favour in Normandy; and from Normandy it was exported into France and into England. East of Normandy it is seen in Notre Dame, Paris; Laon; Senlis; Mantes; Sens; Beauvais; Bourges; Noyon nave; in Burgundy at Notre Dame de Dijon; Vézelay St Père; Pont sur Yonne; Chaumont; Rouvres; in Lausanne Cathedral, Switzerland; in Italy at Casamari; S. Galgano; S. Martino; St Francis Bologna; Certosa of Pavia;† not disappearing from Italy till the end of the fourteenth century. In Normandy probably it was adopted first at the ABBAYE-AUX-HOMMES, CAEN (315, 319); where the vaults may be between 1130 and 1160.‡ From Sens it was brought by the architect, William of Sens, to Canterbury, 1175; it occurs at Rochester, c. 1200; in Lincoln great transept, c. 1215; St Faith's Chapel, Westminster; Lincoln galilee; Durham east transept; Canterbury, St Augustine's gateway. § It appears to have been intended in the Norman nave of Norwich;‖ and of St David's.¶ Practically it disappears in England about the middle of the thirteenth century. A Norman sexpartite vault occurs in the chancel of Tickencote, Rutland; otherwise we might assume that our sexpartite vaults were copied from those of the choir of Canterbury.

If diagrams 6, 7, 4, be compared with diagram 5, 308, it will be seen that the high vault of Florence, Angers, and Boxgrove, and all the vaults in the various aisles, have only four cells in each severy; while Canterbury choir has six. The former is therefore called a quadripartite, the latter a sexpartite vault. The SKELETON of a sexpartite vault in diagram 321 shows on the left a pointed transverse arch AHB spanning the nave; on the right two small wall arches BFC, CED (above two clerestory windows); between them is the new intermediate transverse arch CGJ spanning the nave. As the diagonals are semi-circular, this particular vault is highly domical.

---

* Note that the flying buttresses (373) correspond to the bays of the nave, not of the aisles.

† Enlart's *Gothic in Italy*, 251.

‡ Note that the major and minor piers have respectively three vaulting shafts and one; and that the diagonal ribs are elliptical. In 315 note the large number of voussoirs in each arch.

§ This is a compromise between a sexpartite vault and a quadripartite one with a transverse ridge rib; illustrated in Caveler's *Specimens*.

‖ Ruprich-Robert, i. 144, and ii., Plate 91.   ¶ Scott's *Lectures*, i. 117, Plate 76.

FIFTH SOLUTION.—Of the sexpartite solution there is a variant (the fifth), which we may call the quasi-sexpartite : it looks sexpartite, but is not ; it seems to have six cells, but really only has four. It is well seen in the high vault of the ABBAYE-AUX-DAMES (319), as recently rebuilt. Like the true sexpartite vault, it has an intermediate arch. But this merely carries a wall ; whereas in the sexpartite vault below, it carries half a curved web on one side of it, and half on the other. In diagram 308.5, CDQ and GDQ are separate hollow cells, if the vault be sexpartite ; if it is quasi-sexpartite, CGQ is all one hollow cell, but with a partition wall DJ run up the centre. This wall is well seen in 319, on the left. The quasi-sexpartite vault is not found except in Normandy. It is an unscientific form ; the intermediate wall having no constructional value. This vault occurs at Bernières, St Gabriel, and Ouistreham ; a variant of it is seen in La Trinité, Angers. It does not occur in England.

SIXTH SOLUTION.—This was to divide the nave, not the aisles, into squares (308.6). Unfortunately the result was that the oblongs, which had been expelled from the nave, turned up again in the aisles. The contrast between the two forms of vault is exceedingly unpleasant ; but the Italians, who in Gothic architecture preferred engineering to art, continued to employ this form till late in the Gothic period ; *e.g.* S. Theodore, Pavia (1150-1180 ; *De Dartein*) ; Florence and Verona cathedrals ; S. Petronio, Bologna. This method was not adopted in England.

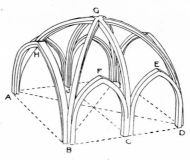

Sexpartite.

SEVENTH SOLUTION. — This was the drastic solution of the iconoclast who built the vaults of ANGERS CATHEDRAL, 1150 (318). He divided his nave into great squares, pulling down the aisles.* There were no oblongs to vex him then. We never carried out this plan on the magnificent scale of Angers Cathedral ; but we adopted it in smaller work ; *e.g.* in the Cistercian choir of Kirkstall. In France, however, Angers Cathedral produced a school ; and very large and noble Gothic churches in the South were designed on the hall plan, *i.e.* without aisles ; but with oblong instead of square bays ; *e.g.* St Vincent, Carcassonne, with a span of 69 ft. ; the nave of Gerona in Spain, with a span of 72 ft. ; the Church of the Cordeliers at Toulouse, now burnt to the ground ; † and the masterpiece of the style, Albi Cathedral.

POINTED ARCH IN VAULTING.—What is particularly remarkable about the high vault of DURHAM NAVE (8) is that its transverse arches are pointed. ‡ Next to the introduction of ribs instead of groins, it was the greatest improve-

---

* Originally Angers Cathedral had aisles. Afterwards the whole church was thrown into a single span. The same change took place in Notre Dame de Coûture, Le Mans ; in several of the churches of Zamora ; and probably in the nave of Bordeaux Cathedral. For the original plan of Angers Cathedral see Lethaby's *Med. Art*, 168.

† Illustrated in Fergusson, ii. 69, 70, 488.

‡ Other early examples are the west aisle of Peterborough transept ; Malmesbury ; St Cross, Winchester ; The Lady Chapel, Glastonbury ; and Wells Cathedral.

ment that was ever made in vault construction.   It removed at one stroke all
the difficulties which had been worrying the builders in their endeavours to
construct vaults with horizontal ridges, but *without* elliptical diagonals.   The
semicircular arch is non-elastic; its height is one-half of its span; cannot be
more.   But the height of a pointed arch is an elastic dimension.   Without
changing its span, we can make the arch as high as we please (258.7-10).
In other words, by employing pointed arches for the narrower spans of a vault,
we can make their ridges rise to just the same level as those of the semicircular diagonals, in spite of the wider span of the latter; so both the ridges
will be horizontal; *e.g.* in the sexpartite vault, figured on 321, it would have
been quite feasible to make all the six pointed outer arches more acutely
pointed still, till their apices were on a level with the central point of the vault;
then the ridges, instead of curving, would be horizontal.   It was a simple, but
a most scientific and successful way out of the difficulties that so long had
beset vault construction.   At first, however, and indeed for a long time in
Gothic architecture, though the outer arches were pointed, the diagonals remained semicircular.*   But, curiously enough, they are found pointed in some
of the earliest vaults; *e.g.* all those of St Cross, Winchester; and Wells
Cathedral; so also in the French cathedrals of Chartres and Reims.   The
result was to bring the thrusts down more vertically.   All four are churches
in which the massiveness of the construction argues an anxiety to secure an
overplus of stability more characteristic of Roman or Romanesque than of
Gothic architecture.

* A vault with the diagonals semicircular and the outer arches pointed is figured in 298.3.

CHAPTER XXII.

GOTHIC VAULTS.

Web Construction—Ridge Ribs—Tiercerons—Liernes—Fan Vaults.

WEB CONSTRUCTION.—We have seen how the builders, after much experimenting, arrived at the construction of quadripartite ribbed vaults. After this the history of the vault diverged in the schools of the Ile de France and England. This seems to have been largely due to a difference in mason-craft in the two countries. It was this. In France it was customary to construct each arched course, of which the web was composed, of voûtains of different sizes. In England* the mason constructed his web without troubling to cut the voûtains to shape. Let FEDB represent an oblong bay of a nave which it is required to vault (326.1). BAD is one of its four cells; in which BA, DA are diagonal ribs, BC, DC, transverse ribs. The dotted line AC represents the ridge of the cell. We have to vault BAD in two portions; first one half, then the other. We will take the half BAC. This half cell is shown separately in diagrams 2 and 3. BGH is a series of horizontal courses, built solid. It remains to vault the space above this BGH. First of all, we will fill up this space with a wooden vault of planks. We have two workmen, a Frenchman and an Englishman. Both are supplied with planks of the same width. First let us look at the Englishman's work (326.2). He cuts off as much of a plank as he wants, and rests one end of it on the diagonal BA and the other on the transverse rib BC; this is plank 1, 1. Then the same with plank 2, 2; and so on till he reaches the ridge. But at the ridge AC the planks do not make a straight joint. The Frenchman, on the other hand, in 326.3, alters the breadth of his planks, so that they are narrower towards the transverse rib and broader towards the diagonal. Then, when he has put them all on, he gets a straight joint at the ridge AC. Next, let us suppose each to be supplied, not with planks, but with blocks of stone ("voûtains"). Where each plank is shown in the diagram, he will have to build an arched† course of stones. The Frenchman treats each course as before; i.e. he shapes each voûtain on the scaffold by a few strokes of his tool, and makes one end of the course broader than the other. This takes trouble and time; but it results at the ridge in a clean straight joint. The Englishman's method is cheaper and more expeditious. He builds each course of the same breadth from end to end, and thus has

* "Le poseur (Anglais) pourra ainsi n'avoir à placer que des moellons également épais" (Viollet-le-Duc, _Architecture_, ix. 522 ; _cf._ iv. 108).

† The arched form of the course adds another complication, which need not be taken into account at present ; it is shown in 298.2.

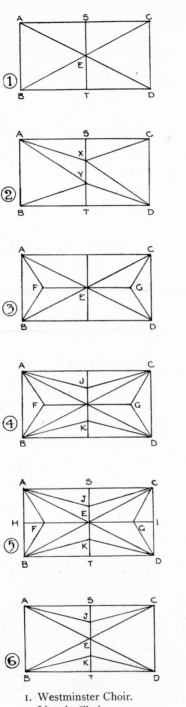

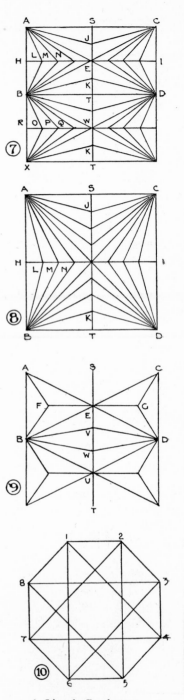

324

1. Westminster Choir.
2. Lincoln Choir.
3. Chester Chapter House.
4. Lincoln Nave.
5. Lichfield South Transept.

6. Lincoln Presbytery.
7. Exeter Nave.
8. Oxford Schools Tower.
9. Lichfield Nave.
10. Durham Kitchen.

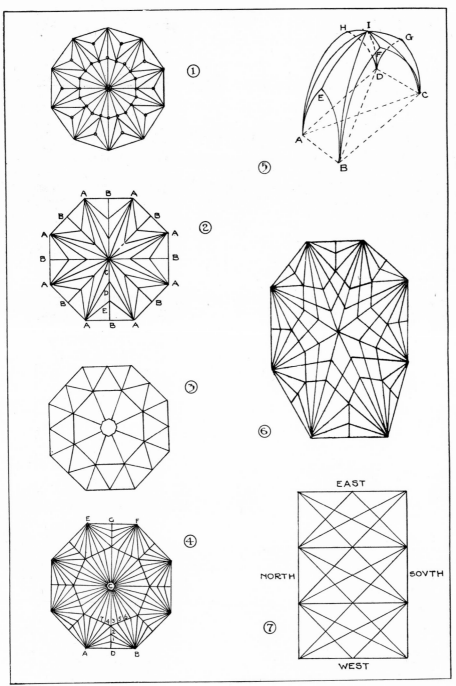

1. Lincoln Chapter House.
2. Southwell Chapter House.
3. Wells, Undercroft of Chapter House.
4. Wells Chapter House.
5. Oblong Severy with curved ridges.
6. Wells Lady Chapel.
7. Gloucester Choir.

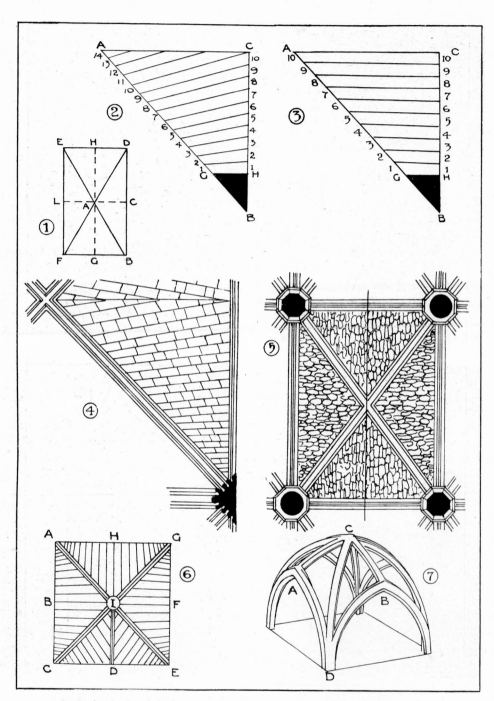

4. St Saviour's, Southwark.
5. Buildwas.

6. Westminster Cloister.
7. Square Severy with curved ridges.

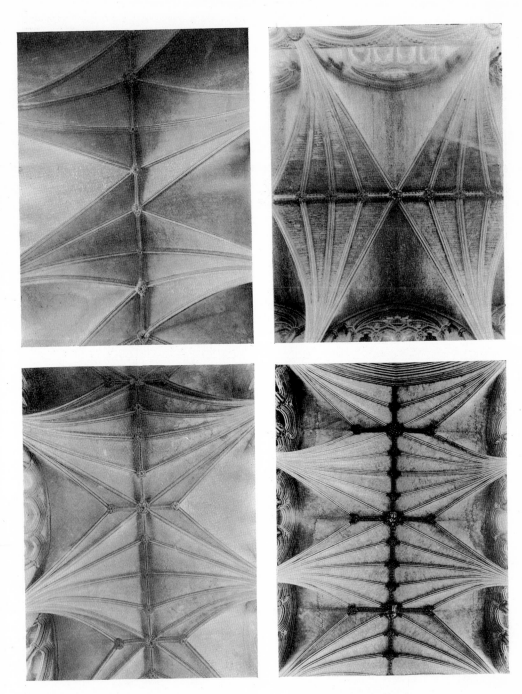

Lincoln Choir.
Lincoln Nave.

Lincoln Presbytery.
Ely Presbytery.

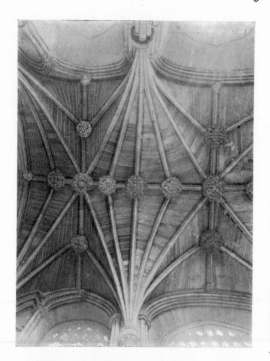

Lichfield S. Transept.
Lincoln S.W. Chapel.

Lincoln Central Tower.
St Hilaire, St Florent.

Bristol S. Aisle of Choir.
Bristol Berkeley Chapel.

Ely Choir.
Oxford Proscholium.

Norwich Nave.
Norwich Nave.

St George's, Windsor, Nave.
Tewkesbury Choir.

Oxford Divinity School.
Oxford Cathedral Choir.

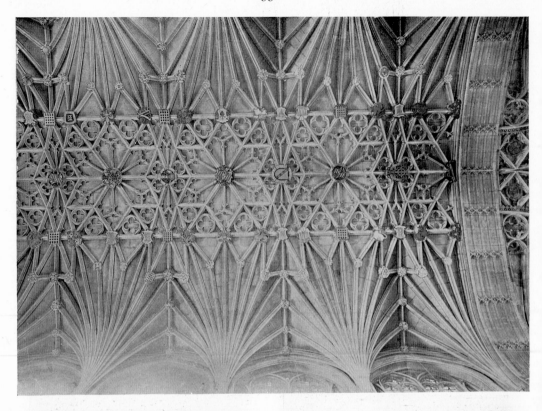

St George's, Windsor, Nave.

Wells Choir.   Tewkesbury Nave.

Hereford S. Transept.
Wells Lady Chapel.

Sherborne Nave.
King's College Chapel.

Ely, West's Chapel.
Canterbury Eastern Crypt.

Gloucester Choir.
Gloucester Lavatory.

not to shape his blocks, but he gets a ragged joint. As the two diagrams show, the French method divides the two ribs into an equal number of parts; while the English method divides them into an unequal number; here the diagonals have fourteen, the transverse ribs ten parts. Compare ST SAVIOUR'S (326.4), and CARLISLE CHOIR AISLE (498). The French method of filling in is found occasionally in England; e.g. in the Chapter House of BUILDWAS ABBEY, c. 1155 (326.5), where the filling in is of coursed rubble; in the Transitional aisle of Ripon transept; at NEW SHOREHAM and CHICHESTER (313); LINCOLN PRESBYTERY (327), and very frequently in late work. On the other hand the English method occurs now and then in France; e.g. in the cloister and crossing of Fontefroide Abbey; and in the aisles of Eu, Normandy.

RIDGE RIBS.—Let us imagine a vault at which a French and an English mason have been at work together, as in diagram 326.6. Plainly three webs were built by the Frenchman; the remaining web by the Englishman. The Englishman's ragged joint is not only unsightly, but less strong than the other. Therefore, partly to mask it, partly to strengthen it, a new rib was invented which is called the *ridge rib*, DI, with a number of saw-like teeth cut in its side to receive the ends of the top-courses of the web, where they abut on the ridge.* The first example we have is in the transept aisle of Ripon, c. 1170, where the ridge ribs are so slender that they can be but decorative; moreover, they are unnecessary, as the cells are filled in after the French fashion. Ridge ribs occur in the high vaults of Angers and Poitiers cathedrals, c. 1165; and, perhaps as early as 1130, at Airaines and Luchueux, Somme.† These slender unconstructional, decorative ribs form indeed one of the most striking features of the Plantagenet Gothic of Anjou (328). Constructional ridge ribs do not occur in England till Lincoln choir, which was commenced in 1192.‡ In the Ile de France and Picardy, and in the Burgundian Gothic exported to Italy, they are employed first to strengthen the vault of the crossing, because of its great span; e.g. of Fossanova, consecrated 1208; Casamari and Arbona in Italy; and of Amiens, c. 1265. There was indeed no structural need for them in the rest of the vaults, if constructed in the French manner.

Each compartment of a vault has ridges both ways; both across the church, and in the line of its axis; the former are called transverse, the latter longitudinal ridge ribs; the latter run the whole length of nave or choir and transept.

In a non-domical vault the transverse ridge-rib§ will be horizontal: in a domical vault it will curve downward at each side of each severy; i.e. if it occurs in a severy of a domical high vault, it will curve downwards both ways from the central boss of the vault to the tops of two opposite wall arches above the clerestory windows at H and F in 325.5. But it is just as feasible to make

* "Elles concourent au soutènement, et leur principale utilité est de former des couvrejoints pour masquer certains raccords défectueux d'appareil, au sommet des voûtains" (Enlart's *Manuel*, 39).

† Illustrated in Enlart's *Manuel*, 38.

‡ In the Chapter House of St George's de Boscherville, probably built between 1175 and 1200, is the commencement of a longitudinal ridge rib. See M. Besnard's monograph, 150.

§ The transverse ridge rib as shown on the plan of a vault must not be confused with the transverse ribs, which are parallel to it; nor the longitudinal ridge rib with the wall ribs which are parallel to it.

it curve up as to make it curve down. And sometimes the transverse ridge, and consequently the transverse ridge rib, *is* curved upward to allow a higher clerestory window to be inserted ; *e.g.* in the upper aisle of Notre Dame, Paris ;* at Norwich and DURHAM (306) in the south aisle of the nave ; and in the south outer aisle of CHICHESTER NAVE (34.4).

Artistically, the addition of the other ridge rib, the longitudinal one, running uninterruptedly from west door to eastern wall, and from one transept end to the other, is a very great improvement. It ties together the disconnected bays of an interior, and gives it a unity which no string-courses can effect. Without it such a church as Amiens or WELLS (524) or BOXGROVE (318) is like some invertebrate creature ; ribbed, but without a spine. What the strong fourteenth-century parapets do for the exteriors of Wells and Lincoln, that the longitudinal ridge rib does for interiors. Yet it was not till late, till the fifteenth century ; *e.g.* in Souvigny Abbey ;† that the French adopted this great artistic improvement ; and then they could only make a success of it by adopting also the English method of vaulting ; *i.e.* with horizontal ridges. For if the vault be domical, then in every severy the longitudinal ridge rib rises up from the summit of one transverse arch to the central boss and then plunges down to the summit of the next transverse arch ; then climbs to the next boss, descends, and so on. The result is, as may be seen in one or two of our early vaults, *e.g.* those of Lincoln great transept and its imitation in Southwell choir, and at St Riquier, a rib wobbling up and down distressingly all the way from the central tower to the end-wall window. In late vaults as many as three longitudinal ridge ribs occur ; *e.g.* in Gloucester west nave and choir ; TEWKESBURY NAVE (332) ; and ST GEORGE'S, WINDSOR (332).‡

INTERMEDIATE RIBS OR TIERCERONS.—The next, or perhaps a simultaneous step in advance, was to introduce an additional pair of ribs in each cell where they might be useful as intermediate supports to the ridge rib ; rising from the same capital as the diagonals, but not rising to the central boss where the diagonals intersect, but to some point between that boss and the summits of one of the four outer arches ; *i.e.* the two transverse and the two wall-arches (see 324). As we have seen, the English vault was much more flat-topped than the domical French vault, and accordingly more difficult to construct. By the addition of these extra pairs of ribs the span of each cell was reduced by one-half : and the centering required for the courses of the webs was greatly diminished.

The first attempt to reduce the distance from diagonal to diagonal was made in St Hugh's choir at LINCOLN (324.2 and 327). This is usually regarded as an architectural freak, without rhyme or reason ; really it is an ingenious attempt to provide additional permanent centering to make the web construction easier.§ It will be seen on reference to 324.2, that instead of dividing the longitudinal ridge rib, ST, into two halves at the centre, and con-

---

* Illustrated in Viollet-le-Duc, *Architecture*, ii. 289.   † Illustrated in Fergusson, ii. 170.
‡ Examples of this rib are illustrated in the naves of YORK (10) and EXETER (9). In WESTMINSTER CHOIR (324.1 and 63) there is a longitudinal, but not a transverse ridge rib.
§ So Prior, 95.

structing diagonal arches intersecting at that centre, diagonals have been omitted, and the ridge rib has been divided into three equal parts. Thus several of the cells of the vaults are much narrowed, and therefore their webs are easier to construct. But the solution is an imperfect one, for it still leaves two of the cells, AYB and CXD, too broad ; and for this reason probably this curious vault was never imitated.

The correct solution is seen in LICHFIELD SOUTH TRANSEPT (324.5 and 328). In this the longitudinal ridge rib, ST, in each severy is divided, not into three parts as in Lincoln choir, but into four, at the points J, E, K. At E the diagonals AD, BC intersect. From the two bottom corners of the severy, B and D, a new pair of ribs, BK, DK, is built up to the point K on the ridge rib. Similarly other pairs are built from A and C up to J. These new ribs, intermediate between the diagonal and outer ribs, are called *tiercerons*. In LINCOLN PRESBYTERY (324.6) the tiercerons occur in the east and west cells ; in CHESTER CHAPTER HOUSE (324.3) in the north and south cells ; in LINCOLN NAVE (324.4) and LICH- FIELD SOUTH TRANSEPT (324.5) in all four cells.

The practice varies. One reason for this is, that a severy oblong on plan, *e.g.* over a nave, requires different treatment from a severy square on plan, *e.g.* over an aisle. In 324.3, AEB and CED are broader cells than AEC and BED ; therefore sometimes, as in Chester chapter house, it is only in these broad cells that pairs of tiercerons, AF, FB and CG, GD are placed. In LINCOLN PRESBY- TERY (324.6), on the other hand, it is the narrow cells that receive pairs of tiercerons. In LINCOLN NAVE (324.4), LICHFIELD SOUTH TRANSEPT (324.5), and ELY PRESBYTERY (327), each of the four cells of the vault receives an additional pair of tiercerons ; in Lincoln nave and Chester chapter house trans- verse ridge ribs occur, but are abbreviated. The vault of LICHFIELD SOUTH TRANSEPT (324.5) is the same as that of Lincoln nave, except that the transverse ridge rib is not abbreviated, but is prolonged to the summits of the wall-arches H and I.

In 324.7 the complication increases ; for two cells contain one pair of tiercerons each, and the other two cells contain three pairs each. At Oxford the large square vault under the Schools Tower, and also the central compart- ment of that of the DIVINITY SCHOOL (324.8), have three pairs of tiercerons in each cell (331).

Then comes in another great improvement. For if the vault of the SOUTH TRANSEPT OF LICHFIELD (328) be examined—it is the same in plan as that of Westminster nave—it will be seen that the space from rib to rib is now so small that in the greater part of the vault it can be bridged over by single flat stones ; no arched courses being necessary. The difficulties of web-construction are not merely reduced, they are annihilated. The vault has become, or is on the verge of becoming, a *rib and panel* vault : a result little foreseen by Geoffry de Noiers when he designed Lincoln choir. When this was once realised, as it could not fail to be, that given plenty of ribs, the webs could be filled in with panels, more and more ribs were provided ; till the vault became nearly all rib. EXETER (324.7) is an example of this latter type ; with one pair of tiercerons east and west ; and three pairs north and south ; a most noble vault ; every rib doing definite work ; fastening down and clamping the bays

Y

like the lid of some ancient strong-box ; every curve guiding the eye upward to the horizontal ridge rib, and along it to furthest east and furthest west ; our very noblest achievement in ribbed vaulting. These vaults were designed, in EXETER CHOIR (9), as early as 1280.

Such are some of the main types of the quadripartite* vault with ridge ribs and tiercerons. But all sorts of variations occur. In LICHFIELD NAVE (324.9) the builder amused himself by omitting the transverse arches ; dividing the ridge EU into three equal parts instead of the usual four. It is an improved version of the vault of LINCOLN CHOIR (324.2).

With the aid of the new tiercerons the builders were able to obtain surprising results ; *e.g.* at Durham it was desired to vault the PRIOR'S KITCHEN, which is an octagon, but in such a way as to leave a hole in the centre of the

vault for the smoke to escape. This was done by transverse arches alone; without any tiercerons or diagonals. A transverse arch was thrown across from each corner to the opposite corner ; and the intersections of these eight transverse arches produced an octagonal central space, which was left open.† Or suppose that it is desired to vault a very large square or oblong space, with a central pillar at D. All that is necessary is to group together four simple

Durham Cathedral, Vault of the Prior's Kitchen.

quadripartite vaults: allowing the capital of the pillar D to rise to the same height, or thereabouts, as the capitals or corbels at A, B, G, H, I, F, E, C. Then the diagonals JD, LD, MD, KD, and the transverse ribs ND, RD, PD, OD, will descend on to the capital D of the central pillar ; and the remaining ribs will descend on to the capitals or corbels B, A, C, E, F, I, H, G. This is the plan of the N.W. CHAPEL OF LINCOLN NAVE (308.9). ‡ The S.W. CHAPEL (328) is precisely the same in plan: but there is no pillar at D. This is managed by not allowing the diagonals AJ, GL, IM, EK, and the transverse arches BN, CO, FP, HR, to begin to descend as before at the small bosses, but making them go on rising till they reach D, which now s no longer on the same level as A, B, G, H, &c., but at a much higher level,

---

* Note that it is still quadripartite ; it has only four cell-surfaces or webs, however much they are cut across by ridge ribs and tiercerons.

† Scott's *Lectures*, ii. 203.   ‡ Illustrated by Sir G. Scott in *Lectures*, ii. 198.

making the vault domical. Both these plans, *i.e.* with and without a central pier, occur in the vault of Glasgow crypt.* And it is obvious that, applying similar methods to cover an octagonal or polygonal space, we can produce a series of chapter houses; either with a central pier, as at LINCOLN (340), Westminster, Salisbury, WELLS (123); or without a central pier, and therefore highly domical, as at York, where the vault, however, is but of wood, and at Southwell, where it is of stone. The following is the plan of SOUTHWELL CHAPTER HOUSE (325.2). AA are diagonals; BB ridge ribs; AD, AE tiercerons. The former class of chapter houses may be descended from the twelfth-century chapter house of Worcester, which again may be but a development of the ribbed semi-dome of the apse in the crypt. The second class may perhaps be fathered on the Norman octopartite vault which covers the Treasury of Canterbury; both the above are *c.* 1160. In some cases, *e.g.* in vaulting a TOWER, AS AT LINCOLN (328) and York, where a central pillar is obviously impossible, the vault of the S.W. CHAPEL OF LINCOLN NAVE (328), just provides the model required. It will be noticed in the tower that a large hole has been left in the centre, *i.e.* round the point D, through which the bells could be drawn up (308.9).

Among other combinations may be mentioned Tripartite and Quinquepartite vaults. Tripartite vaults occur in the undercroft of WELLS CHAPTER HOUSE (325.3). Quinquepartite vaults, with five cells, are useful sometimes where the severy of an aisle is polygonal; or where there are two lancet windows in each bay, as in the aisles of LINCOLN (308.8), Salisbury, and Southwell. In the Salisbury aisle the vault in front is quadripartite; that at the back is quinquepartite. But there was practically hardly any limit to the combinations of ribs. Lincoln, in particular, was a vast laboratory of vault experiments in the thirteenth century.

RIDGE RIBS AND TIERCERONS.—It is sometimes asked whether the ridge rib or the tierceron appeared first. In Anjou, *e.g.* at ST HILAIRE, ST FLORENT (328), near Saumur, and in importations from Anjou, *e.g.* Airaines and Ripon transept, the ridge rib undoubtedly appeared first; and in these examples it is of no constructional use whatever; as the filling in is done in the French fashion with a straight joint at the ridge. But the solitary Ripon example created no school; and the ridge rib does not appear again with us till Lincoln choir, 1192. Here plainly it is brought in to form something for the ribs to abut on; because they do not meet in pairs and form arches (324.2). So again, wherever a pair of tiercerons is employed, they are not in the same plane and therefore do not form an arch: here again a ridge-rib is necessary.† On the other hand, a ridge rib is employed in WESTMINSTER CHOIR (324.1); here there are no tiercerons, but the filling in of the webs is done in the irregular English fashion, and a "cover-joint" at the ridge is desirable.‡ Ridge ribs, therefore, while purely decorative in Angevin vaulting,

---

* See Mr Watson's monograph on Glasgow Crypt.

† It will be noticed that the transverse ridge ribs are not always constructed across the whole span of the vault, as in LICHFIELD TRANSEPT (324.5); but only just so far as they are needed to provide abutment to the tiercerons; *e.g.* in CHESTER CHAPTER HOUSE and LINCOLN NAVE (324.3, 4).

‡ There is, however, no transverse ridge rib.

are constructional in English vaulting; either because they mask and strengthen irregular jointing, or because they give abutment to other ribs, or because they do both.

SKELETON VAULTING.—Sometimes a secondary rib system is constructed beneath the ordinary ribbing to give the vault additional support. This is especially common in Bristol Cathedral; the photographs are from the BERKELEY CHAPEL and the CHOIR AISLE (329); *cf.* Warwick chancel.

LIERNE RIBS.—At Exeter the builders might well have stopped. But the logic of vault construction urged them on yet further. If such a vault as that shown in 308.10 be examined, it will be seen that the tierceron DE is only obliquely abutted by the tierceron BE and the ridge-rib HI. It seems to call for abutment in the same plane. So a little strut, EF (French *lier*, to bind) was inserted, which provided the direct abutment required. In the same way, a lierne, EG, was inserted to abut BE; and so on, all the way round. This form of vault, the *Stellar*, became exceedingly popular in square compartments, *e.g.* in the OXFORD PROSCHOLIUM (329); under a tower, in the oriel of a window, in a cloister, or in a gateway. But probably what commended it much more than logic, was the prettiness of the patterns which were obtained, *e.g.* TEWKES-BURY CHOIR (330). And very soon all sorts of liernes were added, many of them not making even a pretence of being of constructional value. And not only liernes, but unconstructional ridge ribs as well; *e.g.* in the westernmost bay of Gloucester nave there are three longitudinal and three transverse ridge ribs. Triple ridge ribs occur also in GLOUCESTER CHOIR (334) and Lady Chapel, and in the naves of TEWKES-BURY (297) and ST GEORGE'S, WINDSOR (330). In GLOUCESTER (496), where most of the chief developments of later English Gothic art originated, lierne vaults of the most amazing complexity were constructed; that of the SOUTH TRANSEPT (306) before 1337, that of the CHOIR (334) before 1350. In spite of the rise of a rival type, the fan vault, the lierne vault remained in constant use till the extinction of Gothic architecture.

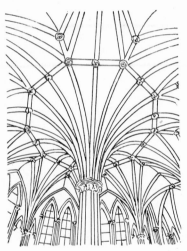

Lincoln Chapter House.

As to the name of the new rib, it is a very unfortunate one. For in the French of Philibert de l'Orme (sixteenth century) and in modern French architecture, a lierne is what we have called a ridge rib. However, the present English connotation of the term is too deeply rooted to be got rid of. Liernes may be defined as all those ribs which merely cross from rib to rib. They neither spring from an abacus, nor rise to the central boss.

The earliest example of the lierne ribs has been supposed to be that of the vault of LINCOLN CHAPTER HOUSE* (325.1), which can hardly be later than

* Mr W. C. Watkins and Mr John Allan, of Lincoln, have kindly supplied moldings of this vault.

c. 1230. Moldings occur in the nave of similar section to those of the ribs of this vault; so that the vault is contemporaneous with the chapter house itself, and is not a later addition. But the ribs which make up the inner decagon are really ridge ribs. The lierne rib proper seems not to come into general use till the beginning of the fourteenth century; *e.g.* St Stephen's crypt, Westminster; ELY CHOIR (329) and GLOUCESTER S. TRANSEPT (306), *c.* 1336. Other fine examples are the naves of WINCHESTER (342) and Canterbury; the OXFORD DIVINITY SCHOOL (331); and the CATHEDRAL CHOIR (331); all the high vaults of NORWICH (330); and of ST GEORGE'S, WINDSOR (330, 332). In this last they are often described erroneously as fan vaults; really they consist of two longitudinal sections of a lierne vault, separated by a segmental barrel vault.

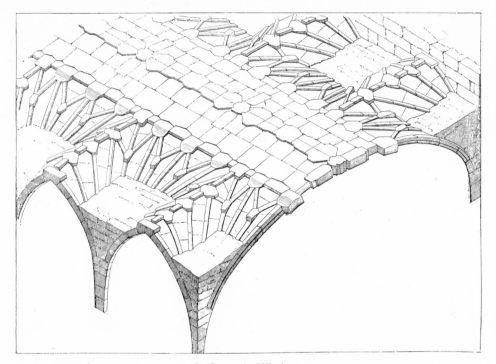

St George's, Windsor.

In the choir of Oxford Cathedral this disposition is reversed; for each severy contains a pair of segmental barrel vaults separated by a lierne vault. WELLS has a vault in the chapter house without liernes, and a very complex vault in the Lady Chapel (325.6). In Wells chapter house (325.4), AC, BC, EC, FC, are diagonal arches; tiercerons rise from A and B to 1 and 2; D3 is a ridge rib; 6, 5, 3, 4, 7, are also ridge ribs.

In the earlier and in the best examples, the main constructional ribs, the diagonals and tiercerons, are retained. But in some later examples, *e.g.* in WELLS CHOIR (332) and in Dreux transept, the whole construction of the vault is revolutionised. It ceases to be a ribbed vault at all; the ribs are merely surface carvings; the vault has become a group of purely geometrical forms, which are called conoids ; *i.e.* a solid form semicircular on plan, terminating in a point. A highly developed type of this kind of vault, the "Reticulated," is specially characteristic of the late Gothic of Germany.* It is a particularly objectionable type ; for its surface decoration has no connection whatever with the divisions of the bays below it. In France, fine examples of lierne vaulting occur in the Flamboyant churches of St Riquier, Montargis, Caen St Pierre, and Chaumont ; and in Rue Chapelle,† Somme. The late vaults of Spain, *e.g.* at Segovia, Zaragossa, Salamanca, S. Juan de los Reyes, Toledo, are magnificent, and alone may bear comparison with those of England. But, from first to last, even in such a simple type as ELY CHOIR (329), lierne vaults are vicious ; the liernes interrupt the flow of upward curve ; for the beauty of a vault it is essential that the ribbing should follow the lines of main strength. In such complex vaults as that of GLOUCESTER CHOIR (334), the rib system, to the eye, is simply a maddening chaos. Yet, on paper, it is simple enough. It ought to have remained on paper. Omitting, for simplicity, all non-essentials, its main structure, as seen in 325.7, is, that it has an additional set of diagonal arches spanning *two* bays ; and all the various sets of diagonals intersect one another, producing an astonishing medley of curves, but nevertheless leaving spaces for the heads of the clerestory windows. This vault is a panel vault rather than a ribbed vault.

It should be noticed that the symmetrical appearance of a vault plan on paper does not necessarily ensure that it will be symmetrical when seen in perspective on the surface of the vault, which is curved, not flat like the paper. The ribbing of the vault over the monument of Archbishop Stratford at Canterbury is symmetrical, as seen in perspective ; but drawn on paper is much distorted. The construction of such a vault argues great power of foreseeing the result of a design as seen in the solid. But, sometimes, as in WELLS CHOIR (332), a design is symmetrical on paper, unsymmetrical in execution, ‡ because account has not been taken of the concavity of the vault.

FAN VAULTING.—The same school of masons, that of Gloucester and Tewkesbury, which had given such an astonishing development to the lierne vault in those two abbey-churches, hit upon a still more advanced type of vault, the fan vault, perhaps to some extent accidentally. It was the custom to suspend over a corpse lying in state a pall supported by four posts. This velvet pall was translated into wood in the canopy which is still suspended over the tomb of the Black Prince at Canterbury ; and very soon it was translated into stone. Such a stone canopy occurs in Tewkesbury choir over the tomb of Sir Hugh Despenser, who died in 1349.§ Inside these stone canopies it was customary to carve on a diminutive scale an imitation of the elaborate vaults of the day. But in this canopy, to save himself the trouble of carving a multiplicity of tiny ribs branching up from one abacus, the mason simply carved a plain half funnel, and then *painted* the ribs on it. In the Trinity Chapel, however, which was probably erected after the death of Edward, Lord Despenser, in 1375, the half funnels or fans are decorated with real ribs of stone. Following such examples, it was but

* See illustration in Dehio, ii. 571.
† Illustrated in Enlart's *Manuel*, 598.   ‡ Willis' *Vaulting*, 39.
§ This tomb is illustrated in the *Spring Gardens Sketch Book*, vol. vi., Plates 29, 30, 31.

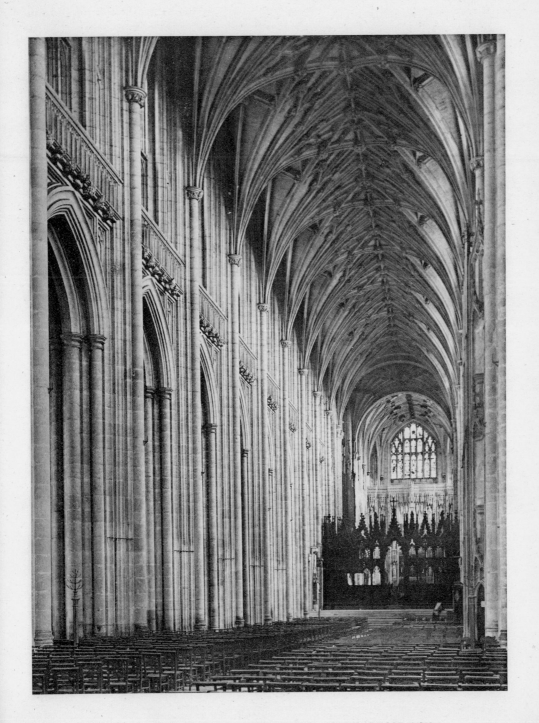

WINCHESTER CATHEDRAL, NAVE FROM S.W.

a short step for Abbot Horton of Gloucester (1351-1377) to put a fan vault over the portion of the east walk of the cloister which he built—viz. from the nave to the door of the chapter house.

In the Tewkesbury monument we have but a suggestion of fan vaulting. Apart from any such suggestion, however, the fan vault had become inevitable. For a long time, without noticing it, the builders had been working towards an inverted conoid as the form of the lower courses of their sheaves of ribs. In the early vaults, e.g. in Peterborough aisle, and the EASTERN CRYPT OF CANTERBURY (334), the springing of the vaults has decidedly an ugly appearance, because the long diagonal ribs leave the abacus at a different angle to that of the short transverse ribs. Various expedients were adopted to remedy this; e.g. the diagonal might be made to spring further back on the abacus, or the transverse rib spring further forward; or the true curve of the ribs was tampered with.* Now the more successful these and such-like expedients were, the more the springing of the vault approached the form of an inverted conoid. The spandrel of the vault, which had at first been rectangular as in 344.1, had reached the form shown in 344.2, and was then far on the way to the semicircular spandrel of fan vaulting (344.3).

A more scientific origin, however, is usually claimed for the fan vault. Each fan is held to be due to the revolution of a *four-centred* arch half-way round its vertical axis. Hitherto each rib had been half a pointed, semicircular, or segmental arch; and therefore had a simple curve. Now each rib, it is said, had come to be half of a four-centred arch, and therefore was a two-centred rib; its curve was a compound of two curves. Each of the new ribs consisted of two curves; the lower curve, rising from the abacus, very short; the upper curve very long (see 258). These two-curve ribs were made of different lengths, but of precisely the same curve. It follows that if the whole of the sheaf or group of ribs, where it rises from the abacus, have the same curve, the sheaf will be semicircular in plan; in fact it will be like the lower part of a trumpet. In 344.4, from ALL SOULS', OXFORD, the two-centred form of the ribs is clearly seen on the left. But there is a serious objection to this theory. It is that the earliest fan vault of importance, that of Gloucester cloister, is not constructed with four-centred, but with pointed arches; as also is that of Sherborne nave. It would seem, therefore, that though the four-centred arch facilitated the construction of fan vaults, it did not suggest them. We may add that to think that theorising about mathematics or geometry led the old men to improvements in building construction is to look at past times through modern spectacles. Building was not taught in those days in polytechnics or science and art classes; the masons learnt to improve by making blunders and having to correct them.†

As we have seen, in such examples as the lierne vault of HEREFORD SOUTH TRANSEPT (333), the builders had approximated so closely to the form of the conoids of the new vault, that fan vaulting resulted inevitably. But the two types of vault are distinct. In the lierne vault the ribs which rise from the

---

* See diagrams in Willis' *Vaulting*, 65, showing the differing plans of the spandrels of the vaults in Norwich cloister, executed at different periods.

† *Cf.* Brutails, 3; Prior, 88.

abacus are of different lengths, and do not terminate in horizontal lines. But in a fan vault they are all crossed by horizontal lines, and each piece of rib between these lines is of the same length. And the solid spandrel of the fan vault is an inverted conoid; whereas that of the lierne vault only approximates to that form.*

It is usually said that the fan vaults are confined to England. Examples, however, occur in the Baltic lands.

Various combinations of the conoid may be arranged; whole circular conoids or quadrants, or semicircles, *e.g.* all along a corridor, such as the walks of GLOUCESTER CLOISTER (344) or LAVATORY (334), or Peterborough retrochoir, we may arrange on either side a series of semicircular conoids, meeting one

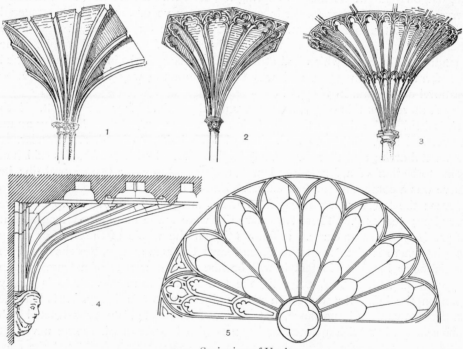

1, 2, 3. Springing of Vaults.
4. All Souls', Oxford.   5. Westminster South Transept Window.

another in the centre; to the eye the effect will be that of a series of pairs of semicircular corbels, each pair carrying a small section of stone ceiling. Or, as in the passage leading into the gardens of St John's College, Oxford, we may have a small quadrant in each corner, and a very large spandrel. In the Dean's Chapel, Canterbury, there is a quadrant, semicircle, quadrant, on each side. In the Central or Bell Harry Tower of Canterbury four quadrants and four semicircles are arranged alternately. Across Henry the Seventh's Chapel at Westminster are semicircle, circle, circle, semicircle. In the very late STAIRCASE OF CHRIST CHURCH, OXFORD, 1640 (348) the space to be vaulted

* The high vaults of Oxford Cathedral and St George's, Windsor, and that of the Divinity School, Oxford, are frequently, but incorrectly, described as fan vaults.

GLOUCESTER CATHEDRAL, THE CLOISTERS.

is treated as if it were a square chapter house; the centre having a tall column carrying a whole conoid, while round the walls are arranged quadrants and half conoids projecting forward till they meet the central conoid. It is just the vault of Canterbury central tower plus a central pier carrying a conoid.

The treatment of the spandrel between the fans varies. In Gloucester cloister it is flat. More often it is slightly arched; it is necessarily so, when, as at SHERBORNE (333), the ribs do not stop at the horizontal rim of the fan, but are continued into the spandrel. It would be feasible to erect a little dome over the space between the fans. Sometimes there is a large boss, as in the Salisbury chantry at Christ Church, Hants. Or, as in Bishop Alcock's chantry at Ely, the boss may be enlarged into a long pendant, which weights and steadies the vault. If the pendants are very long and heavy, they may be constructed as hollow tabernacles, as in OXFORD cathedral choir (297).

The construction of the fans also varies. Sometimes the space between the ribs is filled by panels, except where the tracery requires to be sunk out of larger stones; e.g. at SHERBORNE * (346). Sometimes, even in the earliest fan vaults of Gloucester cloister, the vault is all rib; what seems to be a panel is really part of one of the ribs on either side. It was found to be less trouble to cut a thickish block to be rib and panel at once than to cut rib and panel separately. When they are cut separately, the joints run alongside the ribs. When they are cut out of the solid, the joints run down the centre of the web; e.g. in GLOUCESTER CLOISTER (344). Or, thirdly, in Henry the Seventh's Chapel at WESTMINSTER (347), the vault, as may be seen by examining the back of it, is all panel, no ribs at all; except decorative ribs carved on its under surface. Most often, the first and second systems are combined; the broader spaces being closed by panels; while, in the narrower, rib and panel are carved out of the solid; e.g. in the eastern chapels of Peterborough.

As for the decorative system of such a vault as that of Henry the Seventh's Chapel, the artist had a free hand. What he did, however, was to reproduce on his conoids the familiar tracery of a window of rectilinear type. And so it came about, by a strange reverse of fortune, that the vault, which hitherto had been the dominant member of a Gothic building, marshalling its obedient array of piers, bases, capitals, buttresses, flying buttresses, and pinnacles, in the last days of Gothic fell under the subjugation of the window. In Tudor days it was the window that was the dominant note. The church was, and was meant to be, a Lantern church. Rectilinear window tracery had descended from the lofty clerestories of GLOUCESTER CHOIR (59) and WINCHESTER NAVE (90), and had panelled triforium and pier-arcade and walls; had passed outside, as in the Beauchamp Chapel, Warwick, to panel buttress and wall and battlement alike; had panelled great towers at Evesham, Boston, Wrexham. Its last triumph was to panel the fan vault. It was but to acknowledge facts. The craftsman in glass had been a more important person than the mason for a century or more.

A remarkable feature about the fan vault is that it has little thrust. At SHERBORNE (376) the choir was vaulted first, and flying buttresses were erected. But in vaulting the nave they were omitted; the vault merely being given a more

---

* Carpenter in *Journal of R.I.B.A.*, 1877, 145.

acutely pointed section (576). Still more daring is the southern outer aisle or chantry of Collumpton Church (1510-1528); where, on the north side, the fan vault rests on the piers between the two aisles. The inner aisle and nave are unvaulted; so that there is no counter-thrust. In Cirencester an *inner* aisle has a fan vault, although both the central aisle of the choir and the outer aisle have wooden roofs. Unfortunately, Gothic architecture came to an end before the builders had realised the full value of the new construction, enabling them to dispense straightway with the cumbersome apparatus of external stone scaffolding which had been the curse of mediæval building. One sees, however, timidity and hesitation in adopting such a revolutionary step as the abolition of the flying buttress. All Saints', Maidstone, which was practically complete in 1395, was planned with broad and lofty aisles to the nave, and narrow and low ones to the

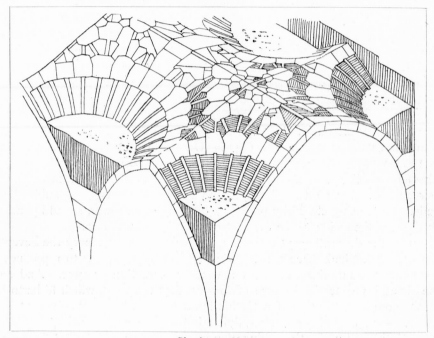

Sherborne Nave.

choir. The choir aisles were designed for a fan vault. But the time was not ripe for the adoption in Kent of the West of England improvement; and the choir aisles were raised and covered with a wooden roof. So, at Rochester, a nave of three bays was added to the Lady Chapel, in just the same position as the Collumpton chantry: but the intention of covering it with a fan vault was abandoned; probably it was regarded as too risky, as two sides of the chapel were open arches.* Double the Oxford staircase (348); provide two central piers and two conoids instead of one of each, and we have the original Rochester design. Another sign of distrust is the construction of massive transverse arches, as at KING'S COLLEGE CHAPEL, CAMBRIDGE, 1512-1515 (62), passing up the centre of each half conoid and spanning the nave.

* See Hope's *Rochester*, 87.

The suggestion of these transverse arches seems to have come from Oxford, where they were employed in two superb lierne vaults of novel character.   The first is that of the DIVINITY SCHOOL (331), begun *c.* 1445 and finished *c.* 1480.   It is a long and very broad room.   The obvious way to vault it was to divide it into nave and aisles, as here shown, and then to ceil these with three vaults; *e.g.* as in the choir of the Temple Church.   But the eight piers would have been obstructive ; moreover there would have been no credit to be got for merely repeating what had been done before in scores of churches.   Imagine, however, that it had actually been vaulted in three divisions of nearly equal height ; and that each of the piers carried a capital.   Would it be possible to retain the capitals, while withdrawing the piers, without bringing the three vaults down ?

Divinity School.

What would a modern contractor do if he were asked to leave the vaults of the Temple choir (35.1) standing, while withdrawing the supports ?   Obviously, from A in one wall to E in the opposite wall, he would insert an iron girder ; and if this girder passed under the capitals of the piers I, J, he could then take away the piers.   So with the other piers.   What a modern contractor

Henry the Seventh's Chapel.

would do with iron girders, that the Oxford builder did with strong transverse arches of stone.   The pendants of each transverse arch, which represent the imaginary capitals, are but two of the voussoirs of the arch, greatly elongated. This beautiful novelty was imitated soon after in the vault of the CATHEDRAL

CHOIR, *c.* 1478-1503 (331, 297); where each compartment of the high vault is similarly divided into nave and aisles; the latter ceiled with segmental tunnel vaults, the former with a lierne (stellar) vault. Compared with the complex loveliness of such a vault, the monotonous uniformity of fan-design is tame indeed.

In one great fan vault, however, that of Henry the Seventh's Chapel at WESTMINSTER (347), by developing further the Oxford improvement, the builder was enabled to break away entirely from the somewhat monotonous repetitions of the fan vaults of Sherborne, Bath, and King's College, Cambridge. This famous vault, the masterpiece of English masonry, the wonder of foreign lands, is but the lierne vault of the Divinity School with certain modifications. First, it is executed in fans. Secondly, from the bottom of each of the two pendants in

Staircase of Hall of Christ Church, Oxford.

each transverse arch is built up a complete circular conoid. Thirdly, each transverse arch passes *through* the vault, and consequently its upper portion, as may be seen in 347, is invisible from below; so that from below the astonishing effect is produced of inverted conoids resting on pendants, which themselves rest on nothing but the unsubstantial air. Fourthly, as is seen in 347, the vault is purely a panel one : constructional ribs do not exist in it.* And so, in the most amazing way, all in a moment the history of the English vault has been revolutionised. It began in the far-away eleventh century, as a vault all web, and no ribs. In the aisles of Durham, in 1093, diagonal ribs were added; at Lincoln more ribs still; ridge ribs and tiercerons. More and more the ribs multi-

* So also there are no ribs on the extrados of the fan vault of Wells central tower ; nor on the central part of the vault of the nave of ST GEORGE'S, WINDSOR (341).

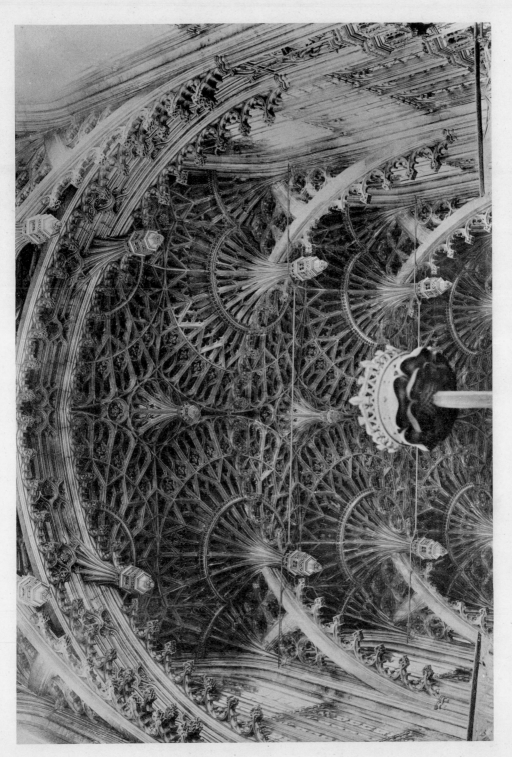

HENRY VII. CHAPEL, WESTMINSTER, FAN VAULTING.

plied ; more and more close-set the rib structure became, till a single flat panel was enough to bridge the rib openings.   Then, in Gloucester cloister, even the panel disappeared ; the vault became one solid mass of ribs.   Finally, in the moment of its triumph, the rib is struck down ; and the vault becomes a thin shell of panels ; the most consummate achievement of the masonry of the Middle Ages ; put together with as unerring science and precision as the parts of a steam-engine or an astronomical instrument.*

* Truly, if vault construction is the be-all and end of Gothic architecture, it is not with any foreign country, but with England, that the artistic supremacy in mediæval architecture rests. From first to last—in the vaults of Durham nave, of Lincoln, of Exeter, of the choir of Oxford Cathedral, of Henry the Seventh's Chapel at Westminster—we were the envy of less happier lands.   We English are too modest in claiming our artistic dues.

CHAPTER XXIII.

PART I.

THE BUTTRESS.

Functions, Dimensions, and Origin of the Buttress—The Columnar Buttress—The Pilaster Strip—Gothic Buttress—The Diagonal Buttresses—Stages of Buttress—Omission of Buttress—Internal Buttresses.

A BUTTRESS is a thickening of a wall at intervals by projecting masonry. It has economical, constructional, and decorative value. A wall of 4 feet in thickness, with buttresses projecting 3 feet, is much stronger and far cheaper than a wall of 6 feet thick without buttresses.* Moreover, the wall may help to carry a wooden roof; and the tendency of the roof to spread and to force the wall out has to be guarded against by buttresses applied to the walls where the rafters may bring down pressure. And if the wall be pierced with windows, especially if they be large windows, so that the wall perhaps is nearly all glass, as in the Tudor Lantern churches, all the more is there need of strong buttressing. Yet more is it needed if the roof is composed of arches loaded with masonry —*i.e.* a vault.

If indeed the vault be an unribbed barrel vault, like that in St John's Chapel in the TOWER OF LONDON (283), the thrust of the vault is exerted against the whole length of the wall, and continuous abutment is required; intermittent abutment would be inadequate; it is necessary to thicken the whole wall. But if the vault be composed of a series of arches carrying flagstones, as at MINCHINHAMPTON (287), then only intermittent abutment will be needed. The usual vault, however, is not a barrel, but one with intersecting groins or intersecting diagonal ribs. Therefore at certain points; *e.g.* in 308.3, at the point B, half of the pressure of the vault of the aisle is brought down by the diagonal BE, and the outer arches BD, AB; and similarly half of the pressure of the adjoining vault. In the same way, in 324.7, the pressure is brought down to the point B by the diagonals EB, WB, the transverse rib TB, and the tiercerons LB, MB, NB, OB, PB, QB, and the wall ribs HB, RB. At these points, D or B, therefore, great pressure is brought against the wall, and very strong buttresses are needed to withstand it. On the other hand, between the points from which the ribs of the vault spring; *e.g.* between BA and BX in 324.7, there is little pressure, and the intervening wall may be replaced, if desired, by mullioned

---

* Pugin's *True Principles*, 3.

windows. This, then, is the main use of the buttress in mediæval architecture; to provide resistance at intervals, and not continuously.*

The dimensions or mass required for a buttress will depend on several considerations. A tall wall will need more abutment than a low one; a thin wall than a thick one; a badly built wall of rubble more than a well-built wall of ashlar. Again, the greater the amount of glass, the greater must be the mass of the abutment; and if there be inside the wall a vault, yet more strength must be given to the buttress. Again, a vault which springs high up on the wall requires more abutment than one which, as in GLOUCESTER NAVE (26) or HEREFORD LADY CHAPEL (464), springs low down. A vault which is of flattish curve, like that of WINDSOR (341) or Ely Lady Chapel, has greater lateral pressure than an acutely pointed vault, like that of Wells, which has diagonal as well as transverse ribs pointed. No mathematical theory can take into account all these and other differences; and it was doubtless purely by empirical methods that the old builders estimated the height, breadth, projection, and shape required for their buttresses.†

Roman buttresses occur in the apses of the Temple of Minerva Medica at Rome; in S. Vitale, Ravenna, and S. Lorenzo, Milan, both sixth century, according to Rivoira; in S. Ambrogio, Milan, and the Baptistery of Biella, ninth century. In Syria buttresses are frequent from the fifth century. Africa had churches from the fourth century with vaulted aisles and buttresses. In our own country, the churches of Ythanchester (Essex); Canterbury St Martin and St Pancras; and the apses of Brixworth and Wing, all of which are ascribed to the seventh century, have buttresses. They do not taper upwards; and at Ythanchester and St Martin's have sloping heads of brick in horizontal courses. At Ythanchester they project 2 feet.‡ But after that date the Anglo-Saxon buttresses are merely pilaster strips. Plainly the Roman buttress went out of use in England, and had to be reinvented in the twelfth century. We must resist the temptation to derive from the Roman buttress that of English Romanesque and Gothic.

Frequently in Northern Italy, e.g. S. Abbondio, Como; and in France south of the Loire; the column is elongated and made to serve as a buttress, especially to an apse. It is highly decorative, but almost wholly useless. It occurs in Normandy in the apse of St Gabriel. We have a few examples; the Norman tower of Northampton St Peter's has three columns at each angle; Norman examples occur in the aisle of Ely and in the clerestory of Peterborough; Transitional in Leicester St Mary's. It is rare in Gothic; but occurs in the Ely galilee.

The Norman buttress is descended not from the Roman buttress, but from the Roman pilaster strip, employed in S. Apollinare in Classe, Ravenna, in the sixth century, in Rome at S. Balbina A.D. 600; and S. Pudentiana, eighth century. This pilaster strip in turn may be the descendant of the classical pilaster, employed instead of a column to carry an entablature. In our Anglo-Saxon work it seems to be a mark of late date; e.g. at Barnack, Bradford-on-

---

* See also the illustrations of the naves of NORWICH and WINDSOR (330, 332).

† See Viollet-le-Duc, *Architecture*, iv. 63, for suggested method.

‡ Peers in *Archæological Journal*, vol. 58, p. 431.

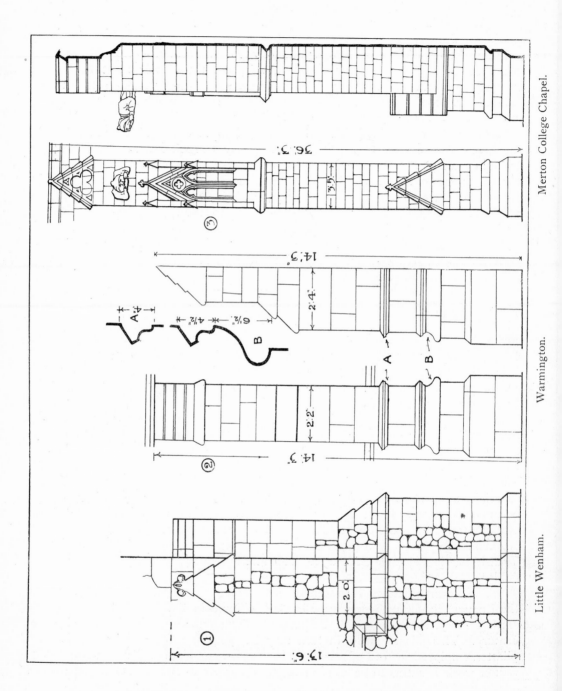

Merton College Chapel.

Warmington.

Little Wenham.

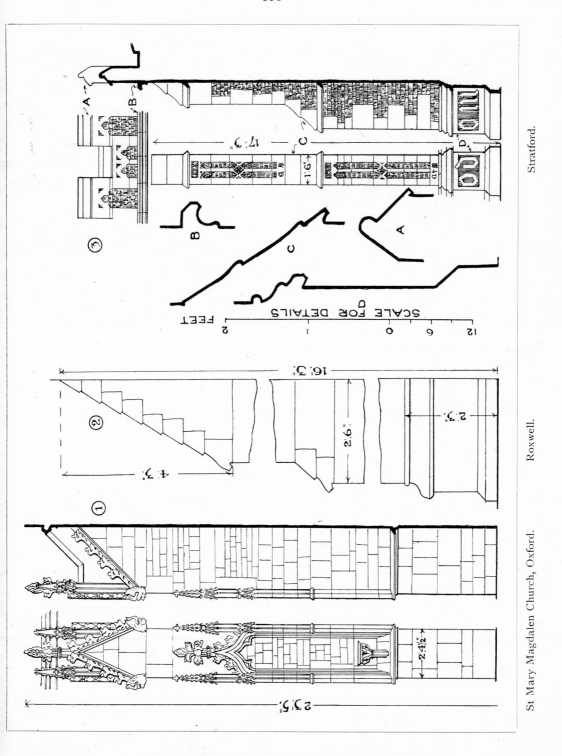

St Mary Magdalen Church, Oxford.

Roxwell.

Stratford.

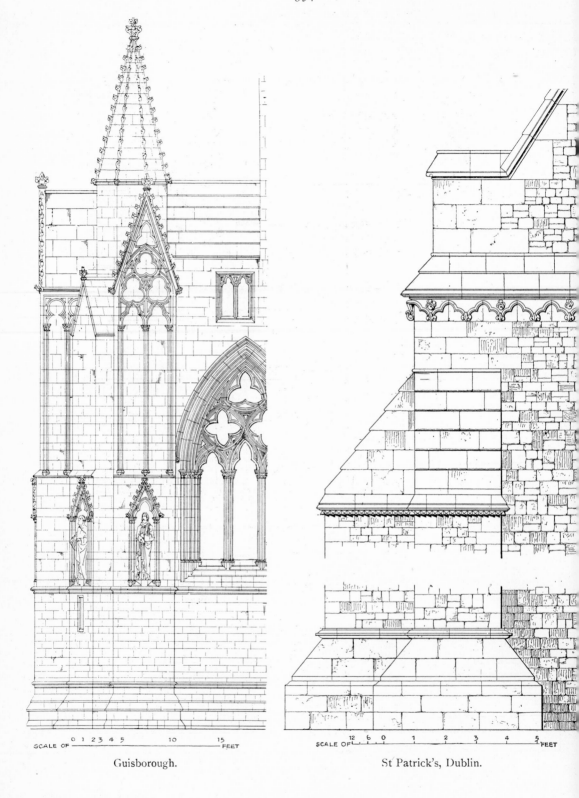

Guisborough.

St Patrick's, Dublin.

SCALE OF 0 1 2 3 4 5 10 15 FEET

SCALE OF 12 6 0 1 2 3 4 5 FEET

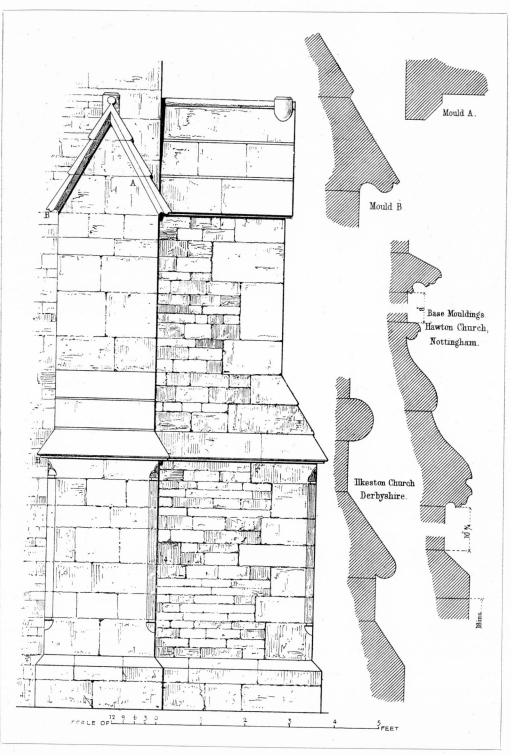

Mould A.

Mould B.

Base Mouldings.
Hawton Church,
Nottingham.

Ilkeston Church
Derbyshire.

Pucklechurch.

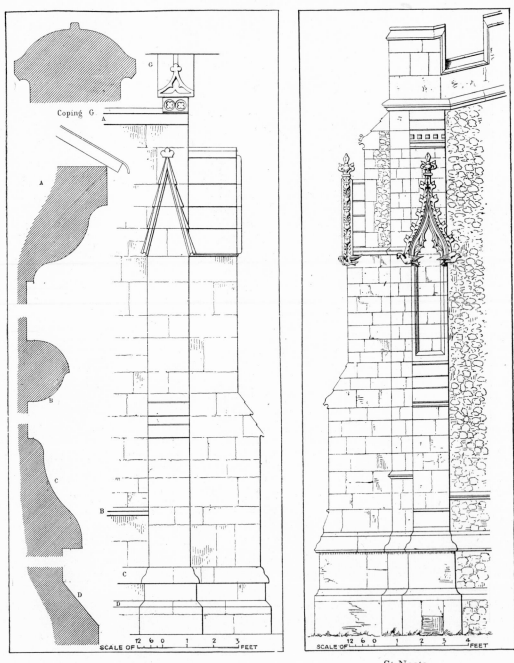

Coping G

A

B

C

D

G

A

B

C

D

SCALE OF 12 6 0 1 2 3 FEET

Austrey.

SCALE OF 12 6 0 1 2 3 4 FEET

St Neots.

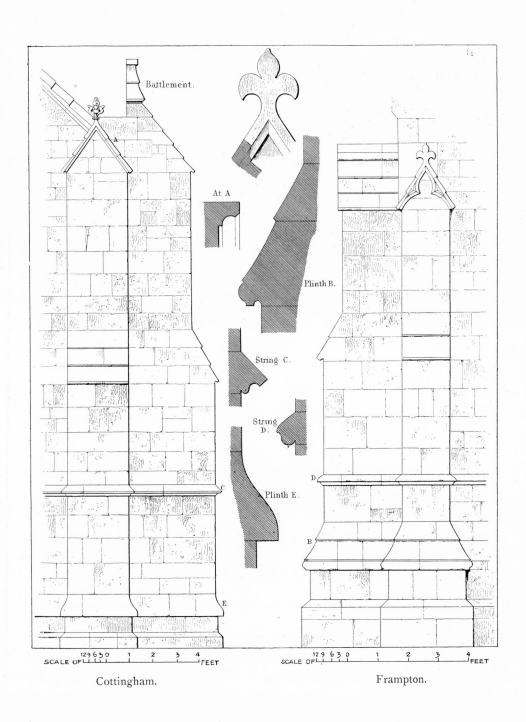

Battlement.

At A

Plinth B.

String C.

String
D.

Plinth E.

SCALE OF 129 6 3 0 1 2 3 4 FEET

SCALE OF 129 6 3 0 1 2 3 4 FEET

Cottingham.

Frampton.

Avon, Earl's Barton, Sompting. It is common in the eleventh-century work of Normandy and England ; *e.g.* STEYNING (359).

These pilaster strips, rising only to the eaves or short of the eaves, when attached to the massive walls of Norman architecture, can have little constructional value. Artistically they give relief and intermittent shadows to the flat surface of an unbroken wall ; they serve also to define externally the limits of the bays into which the interior is divided. But when the walls are thin and are built of rubble, as in most Anglo-Saxon work and in some Norman, *e.g.* the aisles of Carlisle and Rochester, they have a real constructional value ; for they act as binding-courses to stiffen the wall. In no case are they of use as buttresses. It is to be noticed that where ashlar was scarce, or had to be imported, *e.g.* from Caen, the windows are sometimes set not in the walls, but in the buttresses, as at Old Shoreham, to economise the imported stone.

Soon, however, the pilaster strip, instead of being broad and thin, became square, as at Birkin ; and in such Transitional work as Glastonbury Chapel is converted into a buttress. The next step is to give it more depth than breadth ; as in KIRKSTALL CHAPTER HOUSE, *c.* 1160 (359). A good many village churches retain this simple squat buttress in the thirteenth century, not divided into retreating stages. It occurs at Pembridge in the fourteenth century.

To decorate the Norman buttress, slender shafts, with cap and base, were sometimes attached at each angle ; *e.g.* outside NORWICH TRANSEPT, *c.* 1096 (31) ; in Rochester nave ; and outside LINCOLN CHOIR and TRANSEPTS (66, 484). Very effective, too, is the sharp chamfer of LINCOLN NAVE (115), as if cut with a knife ; imitated in SOUTHWELL CHOIR (opposite). This chamfering of the edges of the buttress is common in the thirteenth century. A few examples occur later. Another note that distinguishes Romanesque from Gothic buttresses is that the former never terminate in a gable. But the special distinction of the late Transitional and Gothic buttresses is that they are usually divided into stages, each drawn back more than the stage next below ; so that the buttress as a whole tapers upward. In the first half of the thirteenth century the aisle-buttress often has but two stages,* as at ST PATRICK'S, DUBLIN (354), LITTLE WENHAM (352) ; later, three stages are more common ; but there was no period at which the buttress of two stages was not employed, *e.g.* AUSTREY (356).

Of the buttresses of the period 1245 to 1315, a good example is seen at WARMINGTON, *c.* 1260 (352) ; and richer ones at MERTON COLLEGE CHAPEL, OXFORD (352), GUISBOROUGH CHOIR (354), and GLOUCESTER NAVE (360), where the niche has the characteristic straight-sided gable.

Later differ from Early Gothic buttresses in that the moldings may contain undulatory ogee curves ; and that where a niche is introduced it usually has an ogee arch for head, and crockets of bulbous foliage, as at ST NEOTS (356) and ST MARY MAGDALEN CHURCH, OXFORD (353). It must be remembered, however, that plain unmolded set-offs may occur in any period ; *e.g.* at HINGHAM, 1316-1359 (489); GIMINGHAM (576); PETERBOROUGH (365), depriving us of a valuable criterion of date. Usually the later buttress is marked by the imposing molded

---

* Salisbury, however, and others have three.

Steyning.
Southwell Choir.

Kirkstall Chapter House.
Hedon Nave.

basement courses of the period carried round its foot; *e.g.* at HAWTON (355) and FRAMPTON (357). Many of the fourteenth-century buttresses are singularly simple and sober in design; *e.g* HEDON (359); this was the golden age of composition; when the best men anxiously avoided the crying sin of Gothic over-elaboration and exuberance of ornament. Hence, while some buttresses

Gloucester, S. Aisle of Nave.

of the period, *e.g.* those of the nave of Beverley Minster, are rich in the extreme, many, such as those of SELBY CHOIR (86), Madley, and Patrington, are kept studiously simple, that all the ornamentation may be concentrated at one zone, and that the uppermost—in the parapet and pinnacle. It is the same feeling that supplied the pinnacled spires of PATRINGTON and OXFORD

ST MARY'S (634, 631) with a plain tower as basement and foil. Viollet-le-Duc notes the same tendency to sobriety and restraint in the fourteenth-century buttress of France.

The later buttresses differ but little from those of the fourteenth century, except that they tend to become thinner (and therefore to project further), *e.g.* in the Divinity School, Oxford, and KING'S COLLEGE CHAPEL, CAMBRIDGE (199), in order to leave as much room as possible for the great windows of the period. In the richer examples the presence of panelling or of a very acutely pointed incurved canopy, as at Aylsham, is significant. Examples are ROX-WELL, *c.* 1400 (353); STRATFORD, SUFFOLK (353); LAVENHAM (576); the inserted buttresses at Aylsham, Norfolk, and PETERBOROUGH RETROCHOIR (365).

At the angles of a church, or of its tower or porch, it was usual to place a couple of buttresses at right angles to one another; and this disposition was never wholly abandoned. But from the fourteenth century it was also common to employ one buttress only at the angle, but to set it diagonally, as in TERRINGTON ST CLEMENT'S tower, aisle, and porch (92). The angle buttress, set diagonally, may occasionally be found even in the thirteenth century; *e.g.* in the tower of Pole-brook Church;* also at Warmington and Morton Pinkney. In France it is employed

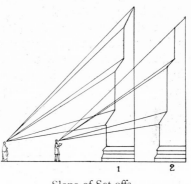

Slope of Set-offs.

almost invariably from the beginning of the fifteenth century, but hardly ever till then.†

As we saw above (358), the early buttresses usually rose vertically, undivided into stages, as in 367.1. But as the thrust passes diagonally downwards to the point B, the masonry which occupies the triangle BDA seemed, to a large extent, unnecessary. In 367.2, it is supposed to have been removed. In such a buttress, however, it would be necessary to protect the joints from the infiltration of rain all the way from D to B. It is better construction, therefore, to construct as much of the buttress as possible in vertical stages, uniting its different stages by short slopes (" set-offs ") DH, FG, which can be protected from the weather. This is an artistic as well as a practical improvement; and involves the use of but little more masonry.

THE ANGLE OF SLOPE of these weatherings or set-offs varies according to the distance from the eye. A set-off high up slopes much more than one near to the ground. The higher the buttress, the steeper will be its upper set-offs (see above). If this is not attended to, parts of the upper stages of the buttress will be hidden by the too flat set-off, and to the eye the buttress will lose in height. Nevertheless, at Netley Abbey, the lower set-offs are steeper than the upper; this may be scientifically correct, because the line of pressure tends to become more and more vertical as it approaches the ground. ‡

* Illustrated in Rickman, 142.   † Choisy's *Histoire*, ii. 298. *Cf.* page 131.
‡ Sharpe's *Parallels*, Plate 44.

In Anglo-Saxon churches, except in some of seventh-century date, buttresses are dispensed with; so also in several of our Norman churches, *e.g.* Abinger, Gillingham, Kippax; and in Normandy, Thaon. They are absent even in Northampton St Peter's, though the aisle is crossed by transverse arches (236); and in the unaisled choir of Creully, Normandy, though it has a quadripartite vault of two bays, the side walls have no buttresses. At Ensham, near Oxford, the fourteenth-century choir has no buttresses; but its walls are 3 feet thick. Some towers also, *e.g.* Southfleet and Barnwell, are without buttresses, and many churches in chalk districts, *e.g.* Tangmere, Sussex, where freestone had to be brought from a distance.

In Roman construction, *e.g.* in the BASILICA OF MAXENTIUS (290), the outer walls, instead of being set inside, were set *outside* the buttresses. Thus the buttresses became internal instead of external. Much additional space was thus gained, simply and cheaply. And when the buttresses were pierced with arches, as in the Basilica of Maxentius and the Cordeliers' Church at Toulouse, a continuous aisle was obtained. This improvement we seldom adopted in England;[*] probably because our buttresses had much less projection than those of France, and hardly lent themselves to such a treatment.

PART II.

THE PINNACLE.

Pinnacles may be divided into two classes: those which rest on the flanking buttresses of the side walls of a church, whether aisle-walls or clerestory walls; and those which are set over the angle where two walls meet; *e.g.* at the corners of a nave, a tower, a polygonal chapter house.

CORNER PINNACLES.—The latter were employed on a large scale from the first. Norman or Semi-Norman pinnacles occur at the corners of Peterborough choir; at Oxford St Peter's, where they are circular; at BREDON and BISHOP'S CLEEVE (363), where they are square; in Rochester west front, where they are octagonal; in GLASTONBURY LADY CHAPEL (465); over Southwell porch. In the thirteenth century a shafted octagon is a favourite form; *e.g.* in LINCOLN EASTERN (66) and CENTRAL (69) TRANSEPTS and PRESBYTERY (177), and SALISBURY (458). In the east end of GUISBOROUGH (354) is a massive combination of gables and pinnacle; in the west end of Howden the pinnacles become tabernacles of open work. The eastern pinnacles of SELBY (86) are reminiscent of those of HOWDEN (72) and Guisborough. Fine pinnacles crown the angles of Canterbury central transept, LOUTH STEEPLE (611), WREXHAM TOWER (609), ST GEORGE'S, WINDSOR (492), and BEVERLEY ST MARY (366).

FLANKING PINNACLES.—Though, as we have seen, the pinnacle was employed early to weight the angles of a building, it is a curious fact that both

---

[*] Except in KING'S COLLEGE CHAPEL, CAMBRIDGE (199).

here and in France it was long before it was recognised that it was of value in weighting the lateral buttresses also ; indeed, of exceptional value, where there are flying buttresses. Great cathedrals, like Bourges, with tier upon tier of flying buttresses, had at first no pinnacles. The early practice was to give a flanking buttress no finial except a saddle-back roof to keep the rain out of the joints. This then was the first step towards the pinnacle ; a mere gable ; *e.g.* in Whitby choir, in York transept, and the chapel of MERTON COLLEGE, OXFORD (473). But in LINCOLN CHOIR and NAVE (115), and still more in SOUTHWELL CHOIR (359), it begins to be recognised that the gable may be more than a roof-covering ; it may be enlarged and heightened so much as to act as a weight also. The diagram below shows this use of it. C is supposed to be an arched spring (which we may imagine to be loaded above, just as the arches of a vault are loaded by the masonry of the cells), with a thrust equivalent to 12 in each direction. W is a wall and B its buttress. WB together have an inert resistance of 10 ; therefore C will push over WB. But if on B we put A whose weight is equivalent to

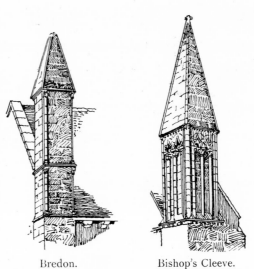

Bredon.　　　　　　Bishop's Cleeve.

3, A and WB together have a strength of 13, and are able to stop the outward thrust of C. The addition of the pinnacle to the flanks of churches was one of the few contributions made by Gothic to the art of mediæval building construction. Almost everything else was invented in Romanesque days ; for the most part Gothic art had but to develop and make beautiful what Romanesque genius had invented.

Before the fourteenth century, pinnacles on flanking buttresses are rare. Perhaps the earliest were those (now disappeared) which formerly crowned the curious polygonal buttresses of the aisle added to Chichester nave.* At WESTMINSTER (379) the pinnacles are restorations ; but probably they reproduce pinnacles of 1245 ; which the builders would hardly fail to introduce in imitation of Amiens, which had pinnacles *c.* 1230. At the end of the century flanking pinnacles appear in EXETER CHOIR (377), where they are square with crocketed edges. At the beginning of the fourteenth century they appear in YORK NAVE (366), SELBY CHOIR (86), MALMESBURY NAVE (375), and in the chapter houses of Southwell, Wells, Lincoln, and York.

In the fourteenth century the pinnacle received considerable development in minor work ; such as the spire-like open-work of the canopied monument of Edward II. at GLOUCESTER (294), of that of Sir Hugh Despenser at Tewkes-

---

* Illustrated in Willis's *Chichester*, Plate 3.

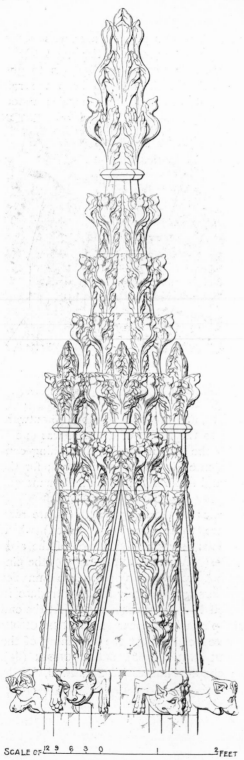

SCALE OF ⟨12 9 6 3 0⟩ 1 2 FEET

Heckington.

bury, and of the Exeter sedilia. The characteristic design in minor work of the fourteenth century in the north and east was more solid and massive; *e.g.* the PERCY TOMB (269), and the Ely Lady Chapel arcade. Having therefore such a decorative origin, the fourteenth century pinnacles passed without any transition into compositions of exuberant beauty—triangular gable, ogee niche, crocketed finial all blending into consummate design even in village churches; *e.g.* at HECKINGTON. In SELBY and ELY CHOIRS (86, 365), and in the ruined choir of Howden, the pinnacles are square. In Lichfield choir they are crocketed octagons. In the fourteenth-century clerestory of Lincoln nave, and at Boston, the front of each pinnacle contains a niche; very beautiful must both have looked when the range of arched pinnacles was peopled with angels, on guard round the sacred walls. Most frequently the pinnacle consists of a spirelet rising out of a cluster of gables, as in the CHOIR OF ELY (365) and YORK NAVE and CHOIR (366).

In late Gothic the pinnacle loses in variety and interest: the tall, thin spike of York choir is only too common. In minor work, and sometimes elsewhere; *e.g.* in the tower of St Neots and in YORK EASTERN TRANSEPT (199), a slender spike sometimes sticks up from the buttress; it may be called the "spear-head" pinnacle. It is usually set diagonally; as in the PORCH OF BEVERLEY ST MARY (365). These pinnacles look painfully unsafe. In Tudor days a few interesting variants occur. Ogee cupolas are not infrequent; as in Winchester choir, Henry the Seventh's Chapel at WESTMINSTER (378), WREXHAM TOWER (609), and King's

Ely Choir.
Peterborough Retrochoir.

Beverley St Mary.
Lavenham Nave.

York Minster from S.E.
Beverley St Mary from W.

College Chapel, Cambridge. Sometimes the pinnacles are flat-topped; to carry statuettes of saints ; as in Norwich choir and PETERBOROUGH RETRO-CHOIR (365); or of angels, as in Blythburgh nave and Sall chancel ; or of birds and beasts rampant, wrought in iron, as originally in St George's Chapel, Windsor. On some late towers, *e.g.* TAUNTON ST MARY'S (607) and GLOUCESTER CATHE-DRAL (132), the pinnacle is a square steeple of open-work divided into as many stages as there are stories in the tower.

So far we have spoken of the constructional value of the pinnacle in weighting a flanking or a corner buttress. But if a parapet or battle-ment is light and open, the pinnacle is of much service in securing it to the wall, as at SELBY (86). It can hardly be maintained, how-ever, that at TIVERTON (390) the pinnacle is anything but a bit of constructed decora-tion.

Sometimes the presence of a range of pinnacles, such as those of the aisles of SELBY CHOIR (86) or of YORK NAVE, is a sign of an intention, never carried out, to construct a vault of stone with flying buttresses thereto. Both at Selby and York in the end the vaults were put up in wood. Outside the clerestory of Selby choir and York nave there may still be seen the "tushes";

i.e. the projecting courses on which the heads of flying buttresses were to rest.

From a constructional point of view, pinnacles, being tall detached masses of masonry, are no improvement on the gablets of Lincoln and Southwell choir.* For they are exceptionally exposed to the weather ; and indeed in many cases have perished and have had to be renewed again and again. Artistically, too, the row of sharp spikes gives a restless, fussy look to many late exteriors ; far better seems the simple unbroken flow of horizontal line of early thirteenth-century work.

It was perhaps because the pinnacled buttress was felt to be bad con-struction that the gabled buttress was employed late in the thirteenth century ; *e.g.* in Tintern ; Lichfield nave ; Hereford north transept ; Howden nave ; Merton Chapel, Oxford ; Bridlington nave ; Lincoln presbytery ; and in the fourteenth century in the choirs of Guisborough, Carlisle, and Beverley St Mary. And in some examples, *e.g.* at HEDON (359), HOWDEN (72), and HAWTON (483), the very construction of the buttress was modified, so that no pinnacle should be required.† If the following diagram be examined, it will be seen that the triangle of masonry BDA in 1 is omitted in 2, giving the buttress a tapering form. But it is evident that, if retained, it will act as a weight on the lower part of the buttress just in the same way as a pinnacle. There was, as a matter of fact, from about the middle to the end of the thirteenth century, *e.g.* in the Saint Chapelle at Paris and that at St Germer, a frequent reversion to the upright type of buttress which had prevailed in Romanesque.

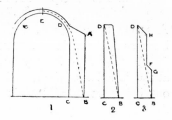

In England it occurs in Hedon nave, and on a large scale in the north transept of HEREFORD (587), and the Lady Chapel of LICHFIELD (369); where the contrast of the choir with, and the Lady Chapel without pinnacles, is very striking. Another motive for the vertical type of buttress would be that the drippings from the gurgoyle above, as at Hedon, would be projected further from the face of the buttress if it were vertical or nearly so, than if it were built in retreating stages. And in a town church like Notre Dame de Dijon, built in a narrow street, the vertical buttress blocked up the street less. Also the superficial area of the church was reduced, and with it the cost of the site.

The chief justification of the importance given to the late Gothic pinnacles is that the walls were so much weakened by the enormous breadth of the windows that the buttressed piers between the windows needed to be reinforced as much as possible ; hence the array of pinnacles on the naves not only of KING'S COLLEGE CHAPEL (199), where the vault within calls for exceptional abutment, but of HULL (474) and LOUTH (139), where all the roofs are of wood.

* Both at SOUTHWELL (359) and at MALMESBURY (375) the lowering of the pitch of the high roofs has projected the pinnacle against the sky-line ; which was never intended.

† In the second diagram, BD should be an unbroken line ; BA, AD should be dotted lines.

CHAPTER XXIV.

PART I.

THE FLYING BUTTRESS.

Definition—Need, Value, and Origin of the Flying Buttress—Internal and External
Flying Buttresses—Substitutes—Curve, Inclination, Mass, and Spring of Flying
Buttress—Clerestory Buttress—Pinnacle—Design of the Flying Buttress—Flying
Buttresses Superposed or in Two Flights—Function of Flying Buttress.

A FLYING buttress, as usually constructed, is a half arch springing from the
buttress of the aisle wall, and abutting the clerestory wall.

The need of it may be seen on examining LICHFIELD CATHEDRAL (369)
at the junction of the unaisled Lady Chapel with the aisled choir.   Even without being weighted by pinnacles, the projecting buttresses effectually stop the
thrusts of the vault of the Lady Chapel.   But the aisled choir also has a high vault
whose thrusts must be stopped.   A carpenter might have kept the clerestory wall
from being forced out by putting up a beam sloping from the top of the aisle
buttress to the clerestory wall.   What a carpenter would do with a beam, the
builder has done by a stone bar carried by an arch.   Both the arch and the bar
act as stays ; but the bar more than the arch ; the main function of the latter is
to carry the straight bar.   It is very rare to find the bar omitted, as in CANTER-
BURY CHOIR (34.3), Hereford choir, and Fotheringhay,* where the flying buttress
is all arch.   On the other hand, in St Urbain de Troyes,† the central voussoir
of the arch is also the central stone of the bar ; and to that extent this flying
buttress is more of a bar than an arch.

The flying buttress, however, is not confined to clerestory walls within which
is a vault of masonry.   In Winchester choir, remodelled by Bishop Fox, 1500-
1528, there are elaborate flying buttresses, though the vault is of wood ;
perhaps, as at York and Selby, the original intention had been to vault it
in stone.   So there are in the parish church of Fotheringhay, although it
has a roof of wood, and an elevation of but 40 feet.   The vast hammerbeam
roof of Westminster Hall‡ also has flying buttresses.   On the side of Worstead
Church and of TERRINGTON ST CLEMENT (92) is a single flying buttress,
set where a pier has settled outwardly.   At Rye and Tewkesbury are flying
buttresses set against a wall, just as a farmer sets a prop against a haystack,

* Illustrated in *Glossary*, i., Plate 43.   † Illustrated in Viollet-le-Duc, *Architecture*, i. 76.
‡ Illustrated in Pugin's *Specimens*, i. 32.

where the wall has bulged out. At Glastonbury, instead of building inside the cloister obstructive buttresses outside the wall of the vaulted aisle of the nave, flying buttresses were constructed in the fifteenth century over the roof of the cloister; flying buttresses are used in a similar position in Exeter and CHESTER Cathedrals (522).

As to the origin of the flying buttress, it has been held* that it may have been suggested by a half-barrel roofing an aisle. Imagine a ribbed half-barrel such as that in the upper aisle of GLOUCESTER CHOIR (282); retain the ribs, but omit the half-barrel, and we have a series of flying buttresses. But where the flying buttress was employed early, *i.e.* in England and Normandy, half-barrels are exceedingly rare. And secondly, where they are exceedingly common, *e.g.* in the upper aisles of the Romanesque churches of Auvergne, the flying buttress appears exceedingly late. So far as Normandy and England are concerned, a much more probable origin of the flying buttress is to be found in the transverse arches which crossed the triforium of several of our vaulted churches. Semicircular arches still span the triforium of DURHAM CHOIR (370), begun 1093. At CHICHESTER (34.4) they seem to have been removed when the cathedral was re-roofed and vaulted and

Lichfield from S.E.

provided with flying buttresses after the great fire of 1186. The ragged ends of the old arches of the work of 1091 still remain in the triforium chamber. Similarly transverse arches, but not semicircular ones, appear in the triforium of the choir of CANTERBURY, *c.* 1175 (34.3); and of LINCOLN CHOIR, *c.* 1192 (34.5).† Both at Chichester and Durham the arrangement apparently was felt to be unsatisfactory, for the transverse arch abutted the clerestory wall far too low down to

* Viollet-le-Duc, *Architecture*, i. 61.

† So also in Bayeux choir; at Narbonne and Bari, and in the transepts of St Pierre-sur-Dives and St Quentin.

enable it to resist the thrust of the vault. At CHICHESTER (34.4) the transverse arches were removed, and were rebuilt as shown in the section on the right. At DURHAM (34.2), when the nave was built (it was finished in 1133), instead of the semicircular arches employed in the choir, the builders built half arches, which are still standing, and are shown below. Still earlier, in the triforium of Norwich choir, begun in 1096, arrangements were made for flying buttresses beneath the roof.* Along both sides of the triforium chamber of nave and choir and apse are supporting shafts; short ones along the wall, tall ones at the back of the arcade of the triforium.† Internal Romanesque flying buttresses occur also at the Abbaye-aux-Dames; and c. 1150, in the upper aisle of St

Durham Choir Triforium.
Durham Nave Triforium.

Germer near Beauvais; at St Gabriel‡ (Calvados); and Creil,§ near Paris. All these are genuine flying buttresses; and plainly they were developed by the Anglo-Norman builders at a very early period. For the invention of the flying buttress—which next to that of diagonal ribs was the most important invention in Western mediæval architecture—the rival claimants are Norwich, Durham nave, and the Abbaye-aux-Dames.‖ Of the last, unfortunately, the chronology cannot be fixed definitely. Durham choir was commenced in 1093; Norwich choir in 1096. At the end of the eleventh century, the builders of England and Normandy had made great advances towards the development of Gothic

---

* In the west end of the choir triforium it almost looks as if flying buttresses were actually built: if so, they were probably taken down when the choir received external flying buttresses, *i.e.* 1472-1499.

† They are shown as a restoration in Ruprich-Robert, ii., Plate 92.

‡ Illustrated in Ruprich-Robert, ii., Plate 80.   § Illustrated in Enlart's *Manuel*, 449.

‖ The pier-arcade and upper parts of the Abbaye-aux-Dames do not belong to the eleventh-century work.

architecture; and of the two countries England was ahead, having developed diagonal ribs and flying buttresses as well; whereas the vaults of Normandy did not get either till the twelfth century was well advanced. Only in one point was England behind the times; viz. in the employment of the pointed arch.

It must be noted that though the internal flying buttresses, *e.g.* of Wells choir, were put there for the purpose of abutment just as much as the external flying buttresses of WELLS PRESBYTERY (373), yet it is quite probable that another object than that of abutment was also present in the builders' minds. This was to provide support for the purlins (563) of the lean-to roof of the aisle. In the case indeed of CHICHESTER NAVE (34.4) it cannot be doubted that one object of the employment of the lower flying buttress was to facilitate the roofing of the aisles.

The next step was apparently taken earlier in France than in England and Normandy. It was to construct the flying buttress, not beneath the aisle roof, but above it, in the open air. From one point of view, it was an improvement. For it enabled abutment to be given to the clerestory wall at a much higher level; and therefore put

Norwich Nave Triforium.

it in the power of the builders to construct much taller clerestory windows, and proportionately to improve the lighting of the church. From an artistic point of view, at any rate when used in superposition and in double flights, as at Le Mans and WESTMINSTER (379), it almost wholly hides from view the building round which it is placed; most especially is this disability felt round the east end of an apsidal choir. And from the point of view of a practical builder, the external flying buttress has grave defects. It is difficult to construct, requiring lofty and expensive scaffolding. And when the aisle roof has been put on, a flying buttress high above it is difficult to repair. Worst of all, this stone stay, on which the stability and the very existence of the whole building depends, now that it has been brought out of doors from the shelter of the aisle roof, is exposed to all the mischances of the weather; to rain, and frost, and storm. To the English builder, who was nothing if not practical, these objections may have seemed grave; and for nearly a century the English flying buttress remained concealed beneath the aisle roof, as it was built in Durham nave. It was not till Canterbury choir was rebuilt, and then probably only because the architect, William, was a Frenchman (from Sens, 1175-1178), that it emerged from inside the triforium. Even at Canterbury it only just crawls along close to the aisle roof, almost unseen from below. And the builders have shown their distrust of it by inserting a transverse arch in the triforium below it (34.3). Next we come to CHICHESTER (313),* where high vaults were constructed after the fire of 1186 (34.4). Here the flying buttress is much more advanced in type than at Canterbury; but, like its imitators and neighbours at NEW SHOREHAM and BOXGROVE, is heavy and ungainly. On examining the section of Chichester, on the right, it will be seen that here, as at Canterbury, the builders had not much faith in their new ally; and have supplemented it by another flying buttress concealed beneath the aisle roof.† In France, on the other hand, flying buttresses had been constructed in the open air long ago. Those of the St Denis of 1140 have disappeared; but that church was so light in construction that it is hardly conceivable that its clerestory walls could have stood without the support of flying buttresses. Those of Poissy may be c. 1135; and Poissy very soon after inspired Sens. Examples of the last half of the twelfth century occur at St Germain les Prés, Paris; St Remi choir, Reims; Notre Dame, Chalons-sur-Marne; S. Quiriace, Provins; Langres, Paris, Mantes, Senlis, Noyon cathedrals; and the churches of Domont and Ebrueil.‡ By the thirteenth century the flying buttress had become the trade-mark of the Gothic of the Domaine Royale; no church in this style, whether in France, Spain, Italy, Cyprus, was complete without it.

As we have seen, the English builders were by no means in a hurry to construct flying buttresses out of doors. And even when it had come into common employment in current Gothic, there was frequently evinced an anxiety to avoid it. In the twelfth century external flying buttresses were dispensed with at Durham, Lindisfarne, St Cross, and Wells; in the thirteenth century at Rochester (except one north of the choir); in Worcester choir;§ in Salisbury (except those which were added when the steeple was built); in SOUTHWELL CHOIR (400) (the present ones are c. 1355); in Gloucester nave; at Dore Abbey; at Tintern (except over the aisle of the north transept, which was not finished till the middle of the fourteenth century); while in Rievaulx the flying buttresses which existed were so low and slight that the builder evidently trusted for his abutment to other means. In the fourteenth century the very lofty clerestory of Gloucester has no flying buttresses although its windows are of vast size; nor has the neighbouring nave of Tewkesbury. In the fifteenth century the fan-vaults of the choir of Sherborne have flying buttresses, but not those of the nave: so also the lierne vaults of Norwich choir have flying buttresses, but not those of the nave. Finally, they are dispensed with in the lierne vault of Oxford Cathedral choir. Rather than employ such a dangerous ally, the builders had resort to all sorts of expedients. The most drastic alternative was to construct the vault not in stone, but in wood. In the North of England dislike of the external flying buttress seems to have been particularly strong. In Selby choir, and on the north side of York nave, the builders had

---

* There were flying buttresses on either side of the choir of St Radegund, Bradsole; arranged as at Rievaulx. See Plan by Mr W. H. St John Hope in *Archæologia Cantiana*, xiv. 147. The Bradsole work was commenced in or soon after 1191.

† A similar disposition occurs in the choir of the Abbaye-aux-Hommes.

‡ Gonse, 41.

§ It is possible that the present external flying buttresses of Worcester choir were substituted in the fourteenth century for internal ones.

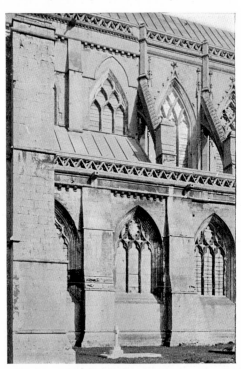

New Shoreham.
Wells Choir.

Boxgrove.
Bath Choir.

actually constructed pinnacles (86, 366) to weight the feet of flying buttresses; nevertheless they altered their minds; no flying buttresses were built, and both were vaulted in wood. Sometimes, as in the twelfth century, in Durham nave and Wells; in the thirteenth, at Salisbury and York transept; in the fourteenth, in Winchester nave; the flying buttresses are concealed beneath the aisle roof.* Sometimes, the clerestory wall being Norman, as in the naves of St Cross, Norwich, Blyth, Gloucester, Tewkesbury, Oxford, Sherborne, is so exceedingly thick that it takes the thrusts of the vault quite safely. Or, though Gothic, as at Salisbury, it is built nearly seven feet thick at the top, with the same object. Or the pier below is made unusually thick and massive, in order to carry a strong clerestory buttress,† as at WELLS (373). Or the vault is made to spring from a very low level (see 306); from the capital of the pier at TEWKESBURY (297); or but little above it, as at Blyth. Or the thrust is brought down as vertically as possible, by pointing the diagonal ribs of the vault, as at Wells; or by constructing the vault as a pointed barrel, as in GLOUCESTER CHOIR (35.5); or by accepting the abutment of an ancient demi-berceau (282), as in the same choir. It is indeed only the scientific combination of pointed barrel and demi-berceau that allows the existence of that splendid clerestory and vault. Again, in SHERBORNE NAVE (346) account was taken of the smallness of the thrust of a fan-vault of pointed section to dispense with flying buttresses. Finally, in Bristol choir a totally different force was called to aid; that of opposing thrusts (see 381). All these vaults stand safe; a monument to the engineering skill of English builders, determined to secure Gothic architecture without Gothic flying buttresses.

For a time mistakes were made in the construction of the flying buttress. Some of the earliest had arches which were quadrants of circles. But, obviously, the greater the curve of the arch, the more likely is it under the pressure of the vault to buckle up in the middle. What is wanted is as flat an arch as possible. So the later flying buttresses, e.g. in Malmesbury and BATH (373), are much depressed.

Again, the early buttresses, e.g. at BOXGROVE (373), were not tilted up enough. The result was that it was difficult to construct buttresses and pinnacles substantial enough to resist the strong lateral thrusts transmitted to them by the flying buttresses; it will be seen how excessively massive are buttress and pinnacle at NEW SHOREHAM (373). Still worse was it in many of the flying buttresses of the twelfth century in France; e.g. those of St Remi, Reims.‡ But in later examples, e.g. MALMESBURY (375) and BATH § (373), it is remarkable at what an acute angle the flying buttress is set. ‖

* In Italy also there are internal flying buttresses; these, however, are not arches but solid walls; built upon the transverse arches which span the aisles, and reaching, at S. Ambrogio, Milan, up to the roof boarding; and at S. Michele, Pavia, one or two feet above it.

† Such a buttress is in what is called "false bearing" (*porte-à-faux*). See the sections of Canterbury, Lincoln, Westminster, Exeter, and Gloucester (34, 35).

‡ Illustrated in Viollet-le-Duc, *Architecture*, i. 62.

§ So also when Ely presbytery was remodelled, the flying buttresses were given a much sharper slope; for the original flying buttresses, being too flat, had pushed the buttresses out of the perpendicular. See illustration 365, and Stewart's *Ely*, p. 80, and section in Plate 4.

‖ So also at Bourges, Semur-en-Auxois, Notre Dame de Dijon, and Pontigny choir.

Again, too much masonry was employed in the earlier examples. CANTER-BURY CHOIR (34.3) is an exception ; but there the flying buttress is reinforced by a transverse arch beneath. At Chichester, Boxgrove, and New Shoreham the flying buttresses are excessively massive and heavy. But it must be noticed that at Boxgrove, owing to the peculiar system of vaulting (see 320), each severy of the high vault is twice as broad as usual, and therefore an exceptionally powerful thrust has to be dealt with. We may surmise from the analogous

disposition of the buttresses at New Shoreham, that there a similar vault system was planned, though not carried out. The lightness of such flying buttresses as those of Lincoln choir (34.5) comes on one as a surprise, considering that the vaults of New Shoreham and Lincoln choirs are contemporaneous work.* In this we may surmise the influence of Canterbury choir; followed by Lincoln not only in lightening the flying buttresses, but in reinforcing them by transverse arches in the triforium chamber.†

By the time the choirs of Canterbury and New Shoreham were built, the French had learnt to construct light and elegant flying buttresses.

Malmesbury.

The fact that our earliest examples are so massive and ugly, or so unusual in type, tends to show that those who built them had little acquaintance with what was going on in France, or at any rate did not imitate the French work.

* But their unusual lightness supports the opinion of Sir Gilbert Scott and Professor Lethaby that the vault and flying buttresses of Lincoln choir were added later (see 112).

† In France also the earlier flying buttresses often exceeded in massiveness ; e.g. Pontigny ; Notre Dame, Chalons-sur-Marne ; Ourscamps. Later they sometimes exhibit astonishing tenuity ; e.g. at Narbonne, and above all, at St Urbain de Troyes.

Instead of avoiding the mistakes which the French by 1175 had corrected, we insisted on making the mistakes for ourselves, and the corrections for ourselves. The development of the flying buttress here seems to be mainly independent of its development in France.

Another point that seems to have troubled the builders was to settle to what height on the clerestory wall the flying buttress should be tilted up. One cannot see a thrust ; and even now mathematics cannot tell us where exactly the thrust is concentrated. The matter had to be settled empirically. Sometimes the head of the flying buttress was set exactly opposite to the spring of the ribs of the vault inside ; that was found to be too low. In some French examples, on the other hand, the flying buttress was set too high ; so that, as at Evreux, it has been necessary to pull down vault and flying buttresses, and give the vault abutment lower down.* Really, the thrust is felt most at some point

Sherborne Choir.   St Mary Redcliffe.

between the spring of the ribs and half-way up the vault ; but the exact situation of that point varies in every vault. Only practical experience, correcting itself by the study of failures, enabled the old builders to get their flying buttresses right.

One expedient, and a very successful one, was very commonly adopted, to meet the difficulty of estimating the height of flying buttress required. It was to build a stout buttress outside the clerestory wall, and to set the head of the flying buttress against this, not against the wall.† It is well seen in CANTER-BURY CHOIR and WELLS PRESBYTERY (34.3, 373). In this way the flying buttress gets a grip of the whole height of the clerestory wall, and the thrust of the vault can hardly escape it. On this point the Lincoln builders differed from the common practice ; first they built the eastern transept with tall clerestory buttress ; then choir and nave with one half size ; then the presbytery with none at all : going from bad to worse.

* See Ruprich-Robert, i. 140, on the abutments at the Abbaye-aux-Dames.
† For examples of clerestory buttresses see the sections on 34, 35.

At BOXGROVE (373), as in the apse of Reims St Remi, the upper surface is flat. This is objectionable, because the rain finds its way into the joints. At NEW SHOREHAM (373) there is a double slope or coping, which sheds the rain, and at the same time improves the appearance of the flying buttress. In WELLS PRESBYTERY (373), in addition, each stone of the outer surface is cut so as to overlap the one beneath ; protecting the joints still better. And if the coping be molded, the flying buttress becomes something more than the piece of brute engineering which it had been at Boxgrove. Occasionally one more change was made ; its upper surface was channelled that it might serve as an aqueduct, as at SOUTHWELL * (400).

Exeter S. Choir.

At BOXGROVE (373) the buttress has to stop, unaided, the pressure transmitted to it by the flying buttress. But, in later examples, the buttress is generally weighted by a pinnacle. Sometimes this pinnacle is placed, as at Amiens and EXETER, close to the outer face of the buttress. But the flying buttress is liable to burst up at its haunches ; and therefore, more correctly, the pinnacle is often placed close to the inner face of the buttress, or even resting partially on the flying buttress in *porte-à-faux* or "false-bearing." *Cf.* NEW SHOREHAM (373), NORWICH CHOIR (160), and MALMESBURY (375).†

Beyond molding the coping, the builders, as in the choir of EXETER, usually left the flying buttress plain. Often even moldings were omitted, that there might be less access given to rain and frost. In Winchester presbytery, however, and the transept of ST MARY REDCLIFFE, BRISTOL (376), a row of crockets runs along the upper surface of the flying buttresses ; and in this and several late examples, *e.g.* SHERBORNE (376), Windsor, Bath, the upper spandrel of the flying buttress is pierced, and is filled with tracery.

Frequently also late spires were connected with their corner pinnacles by ornamental flying buttresses. It is remarkable how unsuccessful almost all are. Some are thin and flimsy ; some have a weak compound curve ; *e.g.* Patrington and St Michael, Coventry. LOUTH (139) has the one success ; a flying buttress far surpassing both in strength and grace any attempted elsewhere. It consists of an arch cusped beneath ; the arch carries vertical balusters ; the balusters carry a first bar ; tracery on this bar carries a second bar, which again is crocketed. The only other flying buttresses which will compare with

---

* So also the thirteenth-century flying buttresses of Burgos are utilised as aqueducts.

† At Ely, when the presbytery was remodelled, the pinnacles were set back three feet nearer to the clerestory wall.

the highly decorative flying buttresses of France, *e.g.* at Eu and Abbeville, are those of Henry the Seventh's Chapel at WESTMINSTER (378). Here an arch carries a first bar; the bar carries tracery, the tracery a second arch; and this second arch a third; but this third arch is inverted. The object of this inversion, which occurs often in late French Gothic, as at Alençon,* is to stop the tendency of the flying buttress to rise at its haunches.

We have seen above that the precise point where the thrust of the vault should be met could not be ascertained with exactness; and that this difficulty was met by the addition of a clerestory buttress. But in the lofty French churches, and in Westminster, the loftiest vaulted church in England, it was met in another and very ingenious way; viz. by superposing two or three flying buttresses, which held firm the clerestory buttress at two or three points, and effectually steadied it against the outward thrust of the vault. An early example is seen at CHICHESTER (34.4), where one flying buttress is concealed by the aisle roof, while the other is built in the open air. In those bays of Ely presbytery, *c.* 1240, which have not been re-modelled, two flying buttresses are superposed. WESTMINSTER (35.2), following French precedent, has super-posed flying buttresses; two over the aisle roof; and three over the roof of the cloister; which in this example corresponds to the outer aisle of a double-aisled choir such as that of Le Mans or Beauvais.

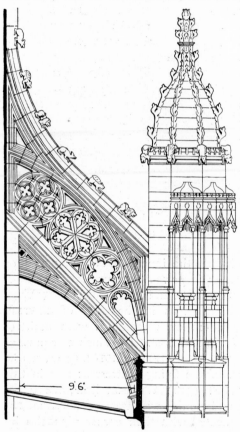

In Westminster cloister it will be seen that the flying buttress does not pass at one flight all the distance from the cloister buttress to the clerestory wall, but in two flights; the piers between the aisle and the cloister being raised to such a height that they support the foot of the upper flying but-

Henry the Seventh's Chapel, Westminster.

tress and the head of the lower one. This intermediate pier is weighted by a pinnacle. Flying buttresses of two flights occur also in Roslyn Chapel.† In France many choirs and some naves have double aisles, and this disposition is very commonly employed. It existed originally in Notre Dame, Paris; but afterwards for two flights of flying buttresses there was substituted a single flying buttress of the vast span of 50 feet.

The function of the flying buttress has been much misunderstood. It

---

* Choisy, ii. 305.   † Illustrated in Britton's *Architectural Antiquities*, vol. iii.

has been held that the flying buttress exercises a powerful *inward* thrust; that in a Gothic aisled nave, for instance, the outward thrust of the high vault is neutralised by the inward thrust of the flying buttress; so that the lofty pier, pressed on one side by the high vault, and on the other by the flying buttress, cannot budge an inch to north or south. This cannot be so. It

Westminster Nave and South Transept.

is true, of course, that the arcuated vault has an outward thrust. But a flying buttress has little inward or upward thrust. Yet it has been supposed to be able to deliver a counter-thrust; as if it were a sort of hydraulic ram, set in motion by some hidden force, and always pushing inward at the clerestory wall. It is true, indeed, that if the flying buttress be set almost horizontally, as at St Remi, Reims, Notre Dame de Châlons-sur-Marne, Canterbury choir, New Shoreham, and certain other examples of twelfth-century Gothic, the weight of the upper part of the flying buttress will press against the clerestory wall. And if the flying buttress be heavily loaded with masonry, as were some of the early examples, *e.g.* at New Shoreham, at Boxgrove, at St Martin, Laon, the pressure against the wall will be considerably increased. But if we look at the buildings of the thirteenth century—the culminating period of Gothic engineering—we shall find that the flying buttress is set much more vertically—*e.g.* at Bath—and is often of exceedingly light construction—*e.g.* at St Urbain, Troyes—and that in these thirteenth-century flying buttresses the inward pressure is practically a negligible quantity. Think of a ladder set up against a window. If it be set up at a considerable angle it will certainly break the glass, more especially if the ladder be a heavy one. If it be set up nearly vertically, it will, perhaps, not break the glass. The former case is that of such flying buttresses as those of New Shoreham, Chichester, and Boxgrove; the latter of such as Sherborne and St Urbain de Troyes.

But the main function of the flying buttress is not to originate thrusts itself. What it was meant to do, and does effectively, is to *transmit* thrusts. Apart from the comparatively slight pressure which the weight of its upper part exerts against a clerestory wall, the function of a flying buttress is mainly that of a stay. Of its two components, the bar above and the arch beneath, it is the former which is of primary importance. The primary function of the arch is, not to transmit, still less to produce thrusts, but simply to support the bar. That the inward thrust of the later flying buttresses, if it exist at all, must be but inconsiderable, is evident from the fact that the flying buttresses at Melrose have not pushed in the clerestory walls, although the high vault has fallen.

Quite as remarkable as the engineering skill which invented the flying buttress was the artistic instinct that beautified it. What can there be in building "construction that is *à priori* more unpromising, as a subject for architectural treatment, than a shore of masonry, built up on the outside of a wall to prevent it from being thrust out by the pressure from within? I do not know what the modern architect would do as an artist if as a constructor he found it necessary to employ such a member. In the absence of applicable precedents he would be apt to conclude that so ugly an appendage to his building would not do to show, and to conceal it behind a screen-wall nicely decorated with pilasters.* But the builders upon whom the use of this member was imposed, not having enjoyed the advantage of a classical education, saw nothing for it but to exhibit the shore and to try to make it presentable by making it expressive of its function. Their early efforts were so 'uncouth' that the modern architect, if he had seen the work at this stage, would have been confirmed in his conclusion that the shore was architecturally intractable. The mediæval builders kept at work at it, master after master, and generation after generation, until at last they made it speak. Made it speak? They made it sing, and there it is, a new architectural form, an integral part of the most complicated and most complete organism ever produced by man, the Gothic cathedral."†

* As Sir Christopher Wren did at St Paul's.
† Montgomery Schuyler in *Architectural Record*, iv. 1, 11

PART II.

OPPOSING THRUSTS.

So far we have dealt with two cases of abutment. The first is that of the Lady Chapel of LICHFIELD (369), where the outward pressure of the loaded arches of the vault is stopped by the inert resistance of the buttresses. The second is that of the presbytery of Lichfield, where the outward thrusts are transmitted by flying buttresses to the aisle buttresses, by whose inert resistance they are stopped. But there is a third method of parrying a thrust. It is to bring to bear an opposing thrust. Suppose that a stream is crossed by a bridge of three arches of equal span. Here the two outward thrusts of the central arch are exactly neutralised by the inward thrusts of the two outer arches. The same is the case with the range of arches on either side of an aisled nave. All the way down the nave there are thrusts and counter-thrusts neutralising one another, except in the case of two arches, the western-most and the easternmost. As to these, the outer thrust of the westernmost arch is stopped by a big buttress built on to the west front in the axis of the pier-arcade; or else by a western tower. But in a cruciform church, the thrust of the easternmost arches is exerted, about midway up, against the western piers of the crossing. This is therefore a very dangerous point in a mediæval church; and at this point many churches gave way; *e.g.* Winchester, Lincoln, Chichester, Ely. Various remedies—none quite satisfactory—were employed to parry this danger. One was to weight the four piers of the crossing by a tower; another was to construct a solid stone screen between the two eastern piers of the crossing, as at York, Canterbury, Ripon; another was to build horizontal stone * girders ("strainer-arches") across from pier to pier, as at Salisbury, Canterbury, Rushden; † or else a St Andrew's cross, as at Wells, and originally at Glastonbury, where the grooves of the cross may still be seen in the piers of the crossing.

Another weak point is that the inward thrust of the aisle-vault, *e.g.* EF, has nothing to stop it adequately, unless the pier be made excessively thick, as *e.g.* in NORWICH (238). It is true that the pier is loaded by the whole weight of the triforium and clerestory wall, and even by a pinnacle B in addition (382.1). Nevertheless, as Sir Christopher Wren observed, many of these piers incline inward; showing that the inner thrust of the aisle-vault is not fully stopped by the weights superimposed on the pier. If, however, we look again, it is seen that there is a thrust CD from the high vault of the nave which runs in the opposite direction to that, EF, of the aisle-vault. Obviously, if we could bring these thrusts into proximity, CD might be employed to neutralise EF. And if so, the happy result would follow, moreover, that we could then dispense with the flying buttress G.

How is it to be done? We cannot lower the nave, so as to get the thrusts of its vault lower down. But we can raise the aisle, as in Fig. 2; and then the

---

* Or a "strainer-beam," as at Pembridge.
† Illustrated in *Churches of Northants*, 181.

thrust AB will partially neutralise the thrust CD, even without the aid of the pinnacle E. But plainly the thrust A of the wider and heavier vault will push the pier outward in defiance of the thrust CD; from this point of view, therefore, the weighting pinnacle E is essential.*

The above is a case of the opposition of unequal thrusts. But if we follow the precedent of the bridge over the stream, and establish an opposition of equal thrusts, then there will be no need of the pinnacle E. To do so, however, the nave and its aisles, like the three arches of the bridge, must be of equal height and equal span. There will be no need then, nor any place, for flying buttresses. However, since the aisles now rise as high as the nave, there can be no clerestory lighting. All the side-light must be derived from the aisle windows. But since, *ex hypothesi*, we have made the aisles as lofty as the nave, there is room in the aisle-walls for very tall windows; and the church will be flooded with light as if it had a clerestory; as may be seen in the TEMPLE CHOIR (35.1). Thus without injuring the lighting of the church, we have got rid of our dangerous

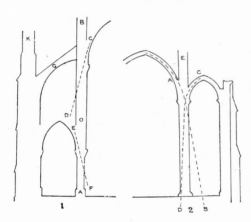

ally, the flying buttress. Practically, what we have built is not a nave and aisles; but three parallel naves.

And, of course, the system is just as applicable to two parallel naves as to three;† as is seen in the highest grandeur in the vaulted church of the Jacobins at Toulouse. In the last half of the twelfth and in the thirteenth century it is the special mark of one of the most highly individualised schools of French Gothic, the Plantagenet style of Anjou; examples of which are Poitiers Cathedral, begun 1163, the Hospital of St Jean, and the Church of St Serge, Angers. It is also a special characteristic of much German Gothic; *e.g.* Marburg, Wetzlar, Minden, Soest, Landshut, Thorn, Munster.

In England an early and important example is the choir of the TEMPLE CHURCH (35.1), London, finished in 1240. Here the three transverse arches, though of the same height, are not of the same span; their haunches accordingly are heavily loaded. And both here and in Bristol choir each pier receives a vertical load of masonry. In the Temple choir each of the three naves has its own gabled roof. This leaves between the three roofs two gutters running the whole length of the choir. Infiltration may occur from these; and they may be choked with snow. At BRISTOL (35.4) all three naves are spanned with a single roof, giving a much superior drainage system.

A similar system to that of the Temple choir is sometimes adopted where two or more aisles are built on one side of a clerestoried nave, as in Oxford

---

* *Cf.* the system of Romanesque high aisles in Poitou, *Classification of Romanesque*, 277.

† In many districts, *e.g.* in Kent and Sussex, the system of double or triple nave is common in parish churches; *e.g.* at Wingham, Kent, and ST LAWRENCE (213) in the Isle of Thanet, in preference to nave and aisles.

Cathedral choir. So again, the retrochoir of Winchester,* *c.* 1200, consists of three, that of St Saviour's, Southwark, of four naves, side by side, of equal height. At SALISBURY (154, 458, 173), the builder has amused himself by dividing the narrow Lady Chapel into three naves; and although all three have one span-roof in common, he has built three eastern gables instead of one, to draw attention to the disposition of the interior.

In other cases also, where it was desired to keep the vault low, instead of vaulting an apartment hall-fashion, it was divided into two naves: *e.g.* at Fountains the undercroft west of the cloister originally carried the dormitory of the lay brethren; and was divided into two avenues instead of one. So also over Fountains chapter house was the dormitory of the monks; the chapter house was kept low, therefore, by being divided into three avenues. But even when the building was a lofty refectory, the monks never designed it with a clerestoried nave. If it was large, it was divided into two naves, as at Fountains, or three; and sufficient light was obtained from windows in the side and end walls. We cannot help concluding that the clerestoried nave, with its appanage of flying buttresses, was looked upon as a necessary evil, at any rate in this country, and was seldom adopted where adequate height, breadth, and light could be obtained in a simpler way.

* Illustrated in Dehio, Plate 601.

Chapter XXV.

THE DRAINAGE OF THE ROOFS.

External Roofs—Corbel-Tables—Cornices—Parapets—Battlements—Gargoyles—Spouts.

External Roofs.

As we saw above, the enemy which the mediæval builders had most to dread was fire. To this they opposed their system of vaults; and by the presence of the peculiar form of vault that was affected from the twelfth century onward— the vault with diagonal ribs—the whole construction and the whole aspect of the church, internal and external, was dominated. But there was another enemy, which did not come to the attack with the momentary fury of a conflagration, but which yet was so unremitting, subtle, and destructive in its operations, that it was quite as formidable as fire; this was rain and snow. This peril too had to be provided against; and the provisions against the destructive action of snow and rain, assisted by frost, profoundly modified the external aspect of the churches.

In the vast structures of ancient Rome, the groined vaults were never sheltered by an external roof of wood, but either by plates of metal or by large tiles; or else they were simply coated with fine cement. In the Baths of Caracalla, the valleys between the groins were filled up with cement so as to form a level pavement; this was covered by a mosaic of coloured marbles, forming a magnificent terrace. In S. Maria degli Angeli, originally a portion of the Baths of Diocletian, and elsewhere, the external is precisely the same as the internal disposition of the groined vaults, the hollows between the groins forming excellent valleys for the rain to run down.*

These Roman vaults, whether groined, barrel, or domical, were enormously thick and massive; and though they were copied, with their absence of pro- tective roofs, in the Romanesque of the middle and centre of France,† they were replaced in Burgundian Romanesque by barrel vaults, and in Northern Gothic by intersecting ribbed vaults so thin as to be but mere shells in comparison with the massive vaults of Auvergne, Provence, and ancient Rome. Such thin light shells were quite incapable of bearing the load of superposed masonry forming the external slopes of the vault; and if they had been capable, the thrusts of a groined vault so loaded would have been increased beyond all reasonable power of resistance. Therefore, both in the light barrel vaults of Cluny (1089-1095), and

---

* See Choisy's *Roman Building*. The same system prevailed originally in several of the earlier Spanish cathedrals; traces of the old roofing-system are still visible here and there.

† See *Classification of Romanesque*, 276 *seq.*

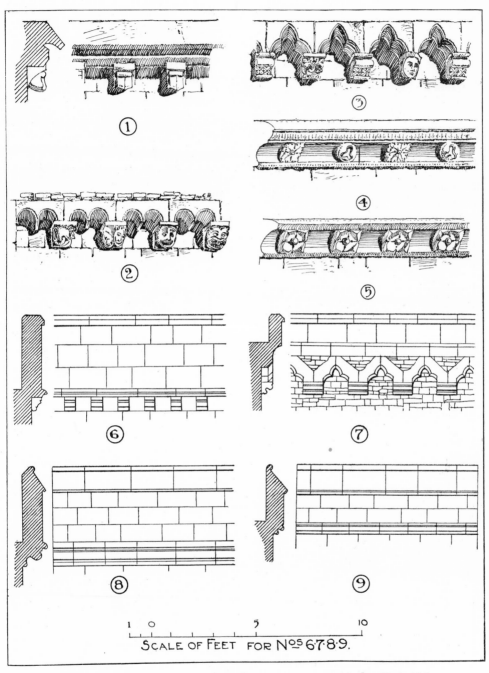

SCALE OF FEET FOR Nos 6·7·8·9.

1. West Walton.
2. Romsey.
3. Romsey.
4. Grantham.
5. Ensham.
6. Fountains Nave.
7. Netley Choir Aisle.
8. St Mary's, York.
9. Bridlington N. Aisle.

2 B

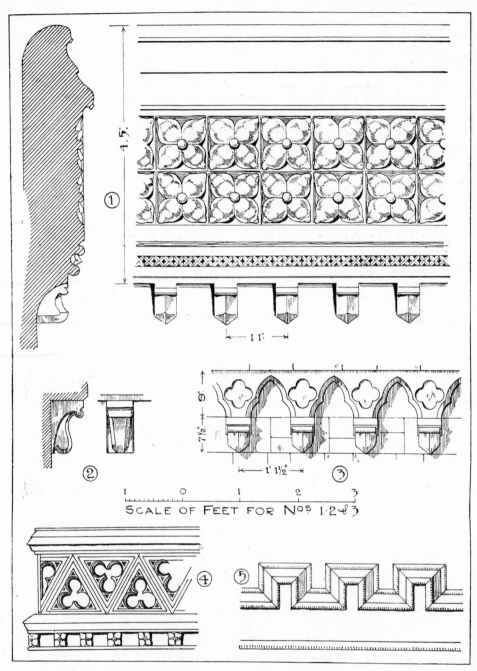

1. Beverley Minster.
2. St Mary, Scarborough.
3. Warmington Spire.
4. St Mary Redcliffe, Bristol.
5. Westminster, St Erasmus Chapel.

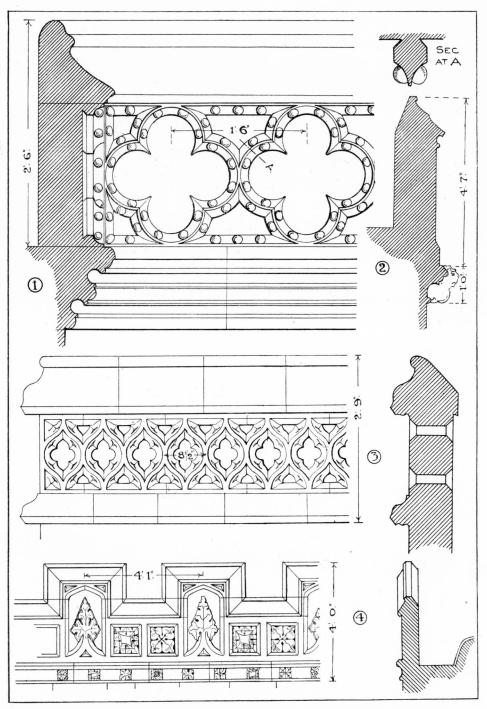

1. St Mary, Beverley.
2. New College, Oxford.
3. Bishopstone.
4. Lavenham.

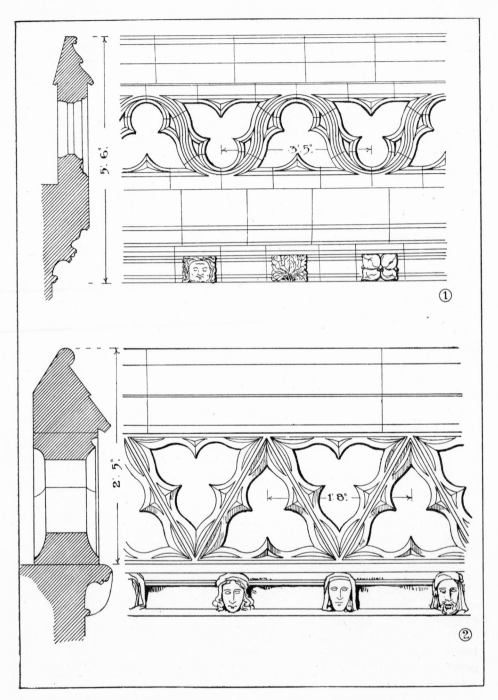

1. Heckington.   2. Winchelsea.

in all the Gothic architecture of France and England, the protective covering of the vault had necessarily to take the form of an independent roof.*

In the Romanesque churches the wooden roofs, in all probability, were usually covered with tiles. But there are records of the use of metal also. The great and wealthy pilgrim-church of St Martin de Tours was famous for roofs of tin. Lead was in frequent employment from the earliest times. Wilfrid is said by Eddius to have roofed York Minster *c. 669*, "*artifiose plumbo puro tegens*." When Ernulph's choir at Canterbury (1093-1130) was burnt down, Gervase tells us that the sheet-lead melted; in 1706 two large glue-pots were filled with lead picked out of the joints in the pavement of Ernulph's choir.† Gervase also tells us that William the Englishman covered the roofs of the choir-aisles of Canterbury with lead in 1184. But probably the most common material was tiles; or in stone districts, flat stone slates. In wood districts shingles were commonly used. Imitations of these in stone are common in the Gothic spires of Normandy; *e.g.* Vernouillet.

The greater the amount of rain and the greater the amount of snow, the sharper it is desirable to make the pitch of the roofs. Thus the Greek and Roman temple with its comparatively low-pitched roof gives way to a high-pitched roof in the Early Gothic of England and France; while, in Norway, with its heavy snowfall, the roofs, *e.g.* at Borgund, are made excessively steep; the snow must be got rid of at once, before it consolidate and its weight break down the roof. A second consideration is the nature of the material which is used as a roof-covering. If covering of tiles or stone slabs or shingle or thatch is employed, it is usual to give the roof a high pitch; as with these materials it is desirable that the rain should drain off rapidly. But sheets of lead, alternately expanding and contracting under the heat of day and the cold of night, tear themselves from their fastenings unless the roof be considerably flattened. (To minimise this, *e.g.* in covering timber spires with lead, the strips of lead are often set diagonally.) And as lead came into greater use as a roof-covering in later Gothic, probably because of the increasing exploitation of lead-mines and its greater cheapness, the tendency of English Gothic was to lower the pitch of the roofs ever more and more. It is curious that in France the tendency was the very reverse; from the beginning of the eleventh on to the sixteenth century French roofs became more and more acute; especially in Northern France; where it is not rare to see gables that have been heightened again and again, each time that the roof has been reconstructed.‡ In England, on the other hand, we see almost everywhere weatherings on the towers showing that originally there was a roof, sometimes more than one, of sharp pitch, before the existing low-pitched roof was constructed; *e.g.* Pershore and TEWKESBURY (390). There are indeed few exteriors which have not lost much of their beauty from their roofs being of a lower pitch than they used to be; but generally the weather-mold remains to show the original pitch; *e.g.* in 391

* For such a roof, one of timber independent of the vault, there was a sixth-century precedent at Ravenna. There the vaults were sometimes constructed of hollow pots; *e.g.* the dome of S. Vitale; and in such cases it was necessary to protect them with an independent wooden roof.

† Willis' *Canterbury*, 108.   ‡ Enlart's *Manuel*, 50.

Tewkesbury from W.
Southwell Transept and Choir.

Selby Choir.
Tiverton.

ABC shows the original steep roof. In time the ends of the rafters BA, BC, decayed. Sometimes, instead of replacing these decayed timbers, it was thought sufficient to cut off a foot or two from the ends of the old rafters. Thus the rafters, being shortened, only reach to D, and the roof is lowered. Then the ends decay again, and the sooner, now that the rafters are old; another piece is cut off, and the roof sinks to E. But this is not all. Supposing ABC to be a gable with a lofty window in it; the window will probably be decapitated when the roof and gable are lowered to D; certainly, when they are lowered to E. This was often the case, till recent restorations; e.g. the east windows of Dorchester Abbey Church,* and at Great Haseley; † it is still so at Whaplode.

In general our English roofs, till about the end of the thirteenth century, had a pitch from about 45° to 50°. Exceptionally sharp, and exceptionally effective, is the steep pitch of the roofs of Lincoln Minster. Here there is a consummate harmony between the high-pitched roof and the acute lancets of windows and arcade. Still more so, where, as at Salisbury, and originally at Lincoln, the lancet window leads the eye up to the acute span-roof, and the high-pitched roof to a soaring spire. Thus in Late Gothic the French preserved, and we often lost, the two great excellences of a mediæval exterior; the high gable and the high-pitched roof. The later English church only too often became, to the eye, four walls with a hole in the middle; little or no roof was visible at all: e.g. the fourteenth-century naves of York and HULL (96), contrasting with the earlier transepts, which have high-pitched roofs; St George's, Windsor; King's College Chapel, Cambridge; and hundreds of parish churches. The culminating skyline of the roof was gone. Nevertheless the eye was not satisfied without some emphatic upward termination of the wall; and this was provided by the greater elaboration of the later battlement and parapet. The pinnacle too, which had originally been constructional in function, now frequently was used merely decoratively, to distract attention, with the aid of parapet and battlement, from the fact that the roof has disappeared. The elaboration of these late wall crestings is well seen in York choir, Peterborough eastern chapels, Lavenham, Tiverton chantry, King's College Chapel, Cambridge (365, 199), and in Henry the Seventh's Chapel, Westminster. Of these we may perhaps fairly say, that though the roof has disappeared, its absence is hardly felt.

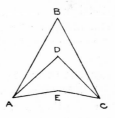

CORBEL-TABLE.

When it has been decided what relation the slope of the roof shall bear to the amount of rain and snow on the one hand, and the properties of the roofing material on the other, there still remains the important question how to get rid of the drainage from the roof with the minimum of injury to the walls, window-tracery, and doorways. If the rain be allowed to drip down the walls, the surface will soon disintegrate, peel, and decay. This has

* Illustrated in Parker's *Dorchester*, 104, 105.
† Illustrated in Parker's *Gothic Churches near Oxford*, 12, 13.

to be prevented by all means. One remedy is to make the roof overhang the walls as far as possible. If the roof is one of thatch, as still in many churches of East Anglia, the overhanging thatch, with deep shadows below, provides a pleasing and adequate protection. But in very many churches in the same district, covered with lead, *e.g.* Martham, Wiggenhall St Mary the Virgin, Worsted, NORWICH ST STEPHEN'S (228), the rafters project beyond the wall, and sheets of lead overhang the rafters; following no doubt the precedent of the indigenous thatched roof of reeds. Elsewhere, usually, the two or three upper courses of the wall are made to project beyond the lower ones; forming what is called a " table " or a " cornice." The blocks composing the lower course of such a table require supports. These supports take the form either of projecting stones in the wall ("corbels"), or of arches. The former are the more common in English Romanesque; the latter in the Romanesque of Lombardy and Germany. Of the table with a horizontal base, Jumièges, Cérisy, Lessay, Caen St Nicholas, the Abbaye-aux-Dames, in Normandy, and in England NORWICH APSE (160), STEYNING (359), WEST WALTON (385.1), ST MARY'S, SCARBOROUGH (386.2), WELLS (373), and BEVERLEY MINSTER* (386.1), furnish examples. Usually, but not always, the corbel is placed beneath each joint of the base-course of the table. The origin of the corbel-table has been sought in the projection of the tie-beams of a wooden roof beyond the walls; in some districts, *e.g.* Auvergne, the decoration of the corbel is evidently motived by shavings of wood.† But corbel-tables were in use in ancient Rome and in Ravenna; *e.g.* in the mausoleum of Galla Placidia.‡ And no doubt they were invented over and over again, wherever the need was felt of giving the tiles the greatest possible projection beyond the face of a wall.

Secondly, as in the Basilica of Junius Bassus,§ the projecting table may rest on small arches. And the arches may either be supported by corbels or by pilasters. The arches in Romanesque work are usually semicircular, and in Early Gothic trefoiled; *e.g.* at ROMSEY (385.2, 3), under the broach spire of WARMINGTON (386.3), Ely façade, Carlisle Cathedral, Lincoln presbytery, BOXGROVE (373). In the Norman work of Winchester and Ely the arches of the corbel-table are segmental. Or the lower end of the corbels of the arches may be rounded; producing a flow of curve called the *nebule; e.g.* at Peterborough; SOUTHWELL transept (390).

Thirdly, where bricks only are employed, the necessary projection may be obtained as at St Albans, ‖ by causing each upper course of the table to project somewhat beyond the lower course. If stone be employed, the same method may be employed; but the stone courses admit of moldings, as at Shottesbrooke.

Fourthly, the arches supporting the table may rest not on corbels, but on pilasters; as in the transepts of Tewkesbury.¶

* The Beverley cornice no longer carries the roof.
† See Viollet-le-Duc, *Architecture*, illustrated in iv. 309.
‡ Dehio, Plate 31, 8. § Dehio, Plate 31, 11.
‖ A similar treatment occurs in the mausoleum of Galla Placidia, at Ravenna.
¶ A similar arrangement occurs *c.* 410 in the Baptistery of St Orso at Ravenna; and in the fifth or sixth century in the Syrian church of St Simeon Stylites. Illustrated in Scott's *Essay*, 62.

A late example of this system of *dripping eaves* is that of Shottesbrooke Church; where the rain has dripped from the eaves since 1337 till quite recently, without serious injury to the flint facing of the walls. In France, too, dripping eaves are found throughout the whole Gothic period, where economy had to be studied.* Indeed, the preference for the open-air system of drainage is a rational one. It is a great advantage to have all parts of the drainage-system visible and accessible; whereas leakage in a gutter or a spout may go on for months without being detected, and may do irreparable mischief to the masonry. It provides no troughs for snow or leaves or dirt to accumulate, blocking up the drainage. It is true that drip from eaves soon ruins the face of masonry if it is of a freestone easily disintegrated by frost; but if it is of a hard stone, *e.g.* like the flint facing of Shottesbrooke, the mischief done is practically inappreciable.

PARAPET.

Nevertheless, the system has practical disadvantages. In the first place, in the case of a clerestoried church, if the roofs be of tiles, then in the case of heavy rainfall, the rain falling on to the tiles of the aisle-roofs from the height of the central roofs will certainly find its way through the aisle-roof and ruin any vault beneath it. And masses of snow slipping from the central roofs on to the lower roofs, in their fall will injure, if they do not break them down. So will slates or tiles or sheets of lead dislodged from the high roofs. In a town where the church rises from a street or square, these flying missiles are dangerous to life and limb. Moreover, repairs of the slightest damage to the roofs will be difficult and costly: especially of the high roofs. Ladders will have to be erected

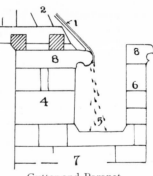

Gutter and Parapet.

from the ground to the top of the clerestory wall; the slaters or tilers engaged in repairing the high roofs may slip, and life be lost. Nor is it possible, in order to inspect the condition of the roofs, to walk round on the top of the walls of the clerestory or the aisles; for, with dripping eaves, the tiles or lead of the roof project over and beyond it.

To remedy all this inconvenience, the two or three upper courses of the walls were no longer built solid, but were built in three parts; an inner wall, an open channel, an outer wall.†

In the diagram, 3 is part of a tie-beam; 2 of a rafter, covered with lead, 1, from which the rain is dripping; 4 is the inner wall; 5 the gutter; 6 the

---

* Choisy's *Histoire*, ii. 371.

† This construction is clearly seen above; and the foot of Shottesbrooke spire, 395. The outer wall and part of the channel are seen at Heckington and Winchelsea, 388; Beverley St Mary and Lavenham, 387; Fountains, Netley, St Mary's York, and Bridlington, 385. In England a simpler arrangement than that shown above is usual; the coping, 8, of the inner wall, 4, being omitted; and the lead, 1, being brought down to the gutter. See Pugin's *Examples*, i. 4, Merton; and *A. A. Sketch Book*, New Series, xi. 18, Westminster.

parapet ; 7 the solid wall ; 8 the " larmier," or " coping," so designed as to prevent the rain from dripping down the wall-face. Supposing that the solid wall is 6 feet thick, it may become at the top an inner wall, say 3 feet thick ; a hollow or channel, 2 feet broad ; and an outer wall or parapet, 1 foot thick. Over the inner wall, which may be 2 or 3 feet high, are dripping eaves ; the lead or tiles no longer drip over the outer face of the solid wall, but over the inner wall only, and into the channel, which thus becomes a longitudinal gutter running the whole length of the wall. This gutter is carefully constructed ; sometimes of a hard, non-porous stone ; and to prevent infiltration, is covered with lead at the bottom and at the sides.

In later Gothic the walls become thinner (at Wells, c. 1175, the aisle-walls are 5 feet 3 inches thick) ; and there was hardly room on the top of the wall for inner wall (French, *bahut*), gutter, and parapet. Therefore it was usual to build the parapet, not in the plane of the outer face of the wall beneath, but projecting beyond it.* To support such an overhanging parapet, corbels or arches might be employed ; but usually sufficient projection was got by using long projecting blocks for the bottom course of the parapet ; the lower edge of these blocks was then molded. So a parapet, when it projects, is but an enlarged edition of the ancient corbel-table ; with this essential difference, that it no longer carries the lead or tiles. And this is the form the earliest parapets take ; *e.g.* in FOUNTAINS NAVE (385.6), 1135 or 1147 ; Whitby choir ; NETLEY CHOIR AISLE (385.7) ; SALISBURY (458.4) ; Ely presbytery, 1140, and Lincoln presbytery, 1160, in both of which a plain solid parapet rests on trefoiled arches, like those of ROMSEY (385) and Beverley nave, c. 1340, a very late example.†

In many cases, *e.g.* in the western bays of WELLS CHOIR (373), the old system of dripping eaves has been converted into the new one ; a four-teenth-century parapet having been superposed on the corbels of 1175, both in the aisle and clerestory. So also in BEVERLEY CHOIR (386.1), the corbel-table containing tooth ornament is thirteenth-century work ; the parapet is a century later. In LINCOLN NAVE at present the walls are crowned with a fourteenth-century parapet ; their original condition is shown in Mr Sharpe's restoration (115).

The transition from one system to the other is well seen at SOUTHWELL (390) ; where the Norman transept has a corbel-table ; the Gothic clerestory of the choir a corbel-table and parapet, both of the same date ; and the Gothic aisle a parapet ‡ without corbels.

Where, however, as in the diagram, the parapet did not project, a horizontal string, 9, commonly called a " cornice," was usually constructed at the level where the solid wall ended and the parapet began. This upper string was molded ; and in its hollow are often found the ball-flower, as in the clerestory of

---

* This is well seen in the sections of parapets on 385.6 ; *e.g.* FOUNTAINS NAVE. The parapet of NETLEY (385.7) is a remarkable example of *porte-à-faux*.

† The choir of Canterbury has an enriched lead parapet. The most ancient example of the parapet in existence seems to be that of the eastern aisle and clerestory walls of the Norman north transept of Ely, where a small molded parapet rests on a corbel table ; illustrated in Stewart's *Ely*, Plates 9, 10.

‡ This parapet may be not original.

WELLS CHOIR (396), square-leaved flowers, masks, and grotesques, as at GRANTHAM (385.4), ENSHAM (385.5), HECKINGTON (388.1), WINCHELSEA (388.2), LAVENHAM (387.4), ST MARY REDCLIFFE, BRISTOL (386.4), Mold, Gresford, Wrexham, TIVERTON, and BRIDLINGTON (390, 124).

It is interesting to note that the same causes which in the end almost universally replaced the system of corbel-table and dripping eaves by that of parapet and gutter, led also to the building of parapet spires, *e.g.* SHOTTES-BROOKE and LOUTH (611), instead of the earlier broach spire.

The gutter system of roof drainage was in constant employment in the Greek and Roman temples. But it does not follow that the Romanesque builders owed it to the survival of Roman building traditions. The break is too long. From Roman times it seems to have disappeared from use till the twelfth century. The chief exceptions are in the south-west of France; where at Poitiers Notre Dame, and Chauvigny, there are parapets which may be of the eleventh century.* Neither in France nor England did the parapet and

Shottesbrooke.

gutter system come into general use till the days of Gothic, *i.e.* till the thirteenth century. With us it appears first at Ely; then in the Cistercian churches; *e.g.* the naves of FOUNTAINS (385.6) and Kirkstall; Roche choir, Byland nave.

We may suggest that in its origin it was not due at all to drainage difficulties. For military reasons every castle wall and every tower wall had a parapet, with a path at the back of it, by which the defenders could pass along, sheltered by the parapet, to reinforce any spot where attack was imminent. The advantages of the continuous and protected path may well have struck the church builders, especially where, as in many districts of South-western France, the churches became fortresses. It was only necessary to add the "bahut" or inner wall, to solve completely the problem of roof drainage. At any rate, the earliest Romanesque parapets, *e.g.* those of Notre Dame, Poitiers, are so very lofty that it is plain they were motived by military reasons. As to the embattled parapet of England, there can be no doubt that it was military in origin.

At first, *e.g.* in Fountains nave and Lincoln choir, the parapet was regarded simply as something of practical value, and it did not occur to make it a decorative element of the exterior, except so far that its cornice and coping were molded. These plain parapets are in use at later periods also; *e.g.* HEDON (359); and Patrington, fourteenth century.

But, as with the buttress and the flying buttress, what engineering skill had invented, artistic instinct soon proceeded to beautify. In some of the earlier examples of the decorated parapet, the parapet remains solid, but is ornamented, *e.g.* at BEVERLEY MINSTER (386.1), with a diaper of square-leaved flowers, or as

* Choisy's *Histoire*, ii. 173, 204.

in ST MARY'S CHURCH, BEVERLEY (387.1), with quatrefoils studded with pellets (the beauty of the moldings of the cornice should be noticed): or in the north nave of Lichfield, with foliage. Both the Beverley parapets are of the fourteenth century. At this time tiny figures, or groups of figures, are sometimes perched on the parapet, as on that of the chapter house of York; Beverley nave; and SELBY CHOIR (86). Howden choir also had a decorated solid parapet, with ball-flower in the cornice.

But, obviously, a parapet tells much more against the sky-line when it is perforated. Of these pierced parapets one favourite design is constructed with undulatory curves, taken as it were out of the favourite window of the fourteenth century, that with reticulated tracery (618). Exceedingly beautiful is the flow and counterflow of curves thus produced. SELBY CHOIR (86) HECKINGTON (388.1) BISHOPSTONE, WILTS (387.3), have fine parapets of this type.

In France the tracery of parapets and windows corresponds invariably; period to period.* It was not always so in England. As we have seen, it was not till late, not indeed till the fourteenth century was well advanced, that the practice became general among us of decorating the parapet. But by that time we had discarded, or nearly so, the geometrical window tracery which had come into vogue about 1240, and had remained in vogue till about 1315. By the latter date flowing curves had largely supplanted rigid geometrical curves in our window tracery. To be consistent, therefore, we ought to have perforated our fourteenth-century parapets with fourteenth-century patterns, as in Selby clerestory, and with nothing else. But we chose to be inconsistent. We did not like to leave, unused in the parapet, the wealth of beautiful geometrical design which had been wrought out in thirteenth-century windows. And so, in spite of architectural propriety, the fourteenth-century parapet was more often designed after the fashion of the late thirteenth than of the fourteenth century, as in the transept of St Mary Redcliffe. A special favourite among the pierced parapets was a triangle containing trefoils. It is seen in WELLS PRESBYTERY (373); west of which it is superposed on a twelfth-century corbel-table, as above. Tewkesbury apse and MALMESBURY NAVE (375) have charming examples of the same character. So has the fifteenth-century choir of ST MARY REDCLIFFE, BRISTOL (376); borrowing its design from the fourteenth-century transept (386.4). The liking for geometrical patterns never wore out; though they are often combined with vertical lines, as in window tracery of the

Wells.

* Choisy's *Histoire*, ii. 396.

same date : *e.g.* the clerestory of St George's, Windsor ; and the Lady Chapel of St Mary Redcliffe. Fine examples of late pierced parapets are common in the West of England ; *e.g.* Bridgwater and Taunton St Mary's.

It should be added that the pierced parapet sometimes found its way into the interior also to protect the clerestory passage ; artistically, it was valuable where the triforium arcade was insignificant, as at Exeter or BRIDLINGTON (125) ; or was non-existent, as in Lichfield presbytery and SELBY CHOIR (390). It is omitted, and is missed, in TEWKESBURY CHOIR (165).

The artistic value of the parapet to the exterior can hardly be overestimated. For the exterior it performs precisely the same function as the longitudinal ridge rib of the vault (336) for the interior. It stands for unity. Buttresses, flying buttresses, pinnacles cut up the building into so many blocks, independent of each other. This independence of the several blocks of nave, choir, transept, menaced by the longitudinal expanse of ground-course and string, is finally checked by the powerful horizontal summit-line of parapet or battlement : above all, when the parapet or battlement is pierced. The predominance of the vertical line in a Gothic design is largely sub-

Side View of Cross

Section on Line A B.

SCALE OF 12 6 0 1 2 3 4 5 6 7 8 FEET

Louth, East Gable.

dued by strength of ground-course, string, and parapet ; it is only when it breaks loose into tower and spire, that it succeeds in overpowering the long horizontal lines of parapetted nave and choir and transept. Much has been written of the principle of " verticality " as the characteristic feature of Gothic design. Too much has been made of it. It is sure that even in Early Gothic, as at SALISBURY (458), the builders saw the danger of the undue predominance of the vertical line ; and scored the building from east to west, and from north to south, with the most powerful horizontal lines of ground-course, string, and parapet that they could devise. Of these horizontal lines the parapet was the most useful; for it gave not one horizontal line, but three; the molded coping, the molded cornice, and the broad band between them. And when that broad band was pierced, a strength of horizontal line was devised that no eye, viewing the exterior, could neglect. And so, in the first fervour of enjoyment of the new design, many a church received a beautiful fourteenth-century parapet; pierced sometimes with flowing, more often with geometrical patterns. The nave of Lincoln Minster has a fine example, with niched pinnacles.

Particularly beautiful was the parapet as applied to the slopes of the gables of the roof; *e.g.* the east front of LOUTH (397); the south transept of Lincoln; and the unique parapet of the east front of CARLISLE (128).

BATTLEMENT.

This form of parapet was clearly borrowed from fortified walls and towers. In it merlons alternate with embrasures or crenels. Through the lower part, the embrasure, the soldier got a view of the besiegers; behind the merlon he

Selby Choir.

stood for shelter. The merlon was pierced with arrow-slits (loopholes or eyelets). In a fortification these loopholes were splayed internally to give wider range to the defender's arrows. In ecclesiastical battlements loopholes occasionally occur, as in Ripon choir; but they are merely ornamental, being usually cut square.*

The battlement was in use among the Greeks and Romans; it is rare in our church-work till the fourteenth century; after that date, to a large extent, it ousted the horizontal parapet. It is a special feature of Late English as opposed to French Gothic. It gives a sharp and effective outline against the sky; but its contour is harsh and angular; and it interferes, every few feet, with the flow of the main horizontal line of the building. Nevertheless there was a craze for it: and much trouble was taken with its ornamentation. In its simplest and earliest forms only the horizontal lines of merlon and embrasure were molded; *e.g.* in the porch of ST MARY, BEVERLEY (365). Often the sides of each were molded also; as at TIVERTON (390) and Gresford. Sometimes the upper surfaces and sides were chamfered; and both the upper and

* Not always; in Oundle and Kettering towers they are splayed.—R. P. B.

the lower edge of the chamfer were molded, as in ST ERASMUS' CHAPEL, WESTMINSTER (386.5). Usually the face was left plain; but in late work it was often panelled; *e.g.* in the clerestory of NORWICH CHOIR (160). In East Anglia, the battlements are very frequently panelled in patterns of black flint; as at STRATFORD ST MARY'S, SUFFOLK (353). A still richer example is seen at LAVENHAM (387.4). Sometimes both merlon and embrasure were perforated in very unsubstantial fashion; as in YORK CHOIR (199); KING'S COLLEGE CHAPEL (199); and BATH ABBEY (373). Rarely, the faces were covered with carving; as at TIVERTON (390), with the arms and emblems of John Green, clothier, who founded a chantry and rebuilt the church at the end of the fifteenth century. Most gorgeous of all were the combinations of enriched parapet, battlement, and pinnacle which crowned the lordly towers of Somerset; *e.g.* TAUNTON ST MARY (607). In these miles of plain battlements there is great monotony; seldom, as in the eastern chapels of Peterborough, and KING'S COLLEGE CHAPEL (199) is trial made of a change of form. Elsewhere several other forms of battlement occur; *e.g.* in Scotland; and at Verona.

And having in the end monopolised to a very large extent the cresting of the walls, the battlement found its way into the interior also as a decorative ornament, wherever a horizontal line could be crowned with it; in the cornice of a monument or of a screen; and with great inappropriateness, in the transoms of the windows and even the capitals of piers; as at King's Cliffe.

Woodford.

In France the battlement occurs, for military reasons, in cathedrals of the south, like Béziers, where the wars of the religious made every church a fortress. It is very rarely used decoratively; the cathedrals of Châlons-sur-Marne and Troyes are the only important exceptions. It was tried and rejected.

GARGOYLE.

The gutter, gargoyle, and "larmier" or coping were all in use in Greek and Roman work; but were re-invented by the Gothic architects of the thirteenth century.

When such a gutter as that shown on page 393 has been constructed on the top of a wall, it is necessary to pierce the foot of the parapet at intervals to let off the water that collects in the gutter. It is desirable to throw the water as far away as possible from the face of the wall and the windows; therefore these openings are often made through buttresses. But it is necessary to protect the faces of the buttresses also from the falling water. So in the opening a perforated block is fixed, of as much projection as is safe. (Moreover, in fourteenth-century work, the buttresses are sometimes constructed more vertically than before, in order to escape, as much as possible, damage from the falling water.) These long projecting blocks are usually carved in grotesque shapes; *e.g.* bats, monsters, men baling out a boat, occur in SELBY CHOIR (398). Sometimes only a lead spout is used, as at WOODFORD; sometimes a gargoyle with a lead spout in its mouth. In some cases no doubt the grotesques may have been symbolical ; the idea being that the Church overcomes and converts to good uses even the most monstrous forms of evil.

One difficulty still remained. It was that the fall of the water from the gargoyles of the clerestory down on to the aisle-roof far below in time must damage that roof, if it were covered with tiles. One remedy was to cover the aisle-roof with lead. Another remedy, where flying buttresses existed, was to utilise each as an aqueduct. This is well seen in the flying buttress added *c.* 1337 to the thirteenth-century choir of SOUTHWELL MINSTER ; originally a spout or gargoyle projected from the foot of the pinnacle. Such a flying aqueduct ought to rise to the level of the gutter, as in the Southwell example. But the vaulting thrust, which it is the function of the flying buttress to transmit, is mainly felt at a considerably lower level. The head of the flying buttress, therefore, ought to be placed about the level of the one at Southwell on the right ; otherwise great damage may result. Indeed at Famagusta in Cyprus, flying

Southwell Choir.

buttresses, set too high, in order that they might act as aqueducts, did actually ruin the church ; and they would have done so in Evreux nave, if they had not been reconstructed.* In Chichester nave the flying buttresses serve as aqueducts, yet are placed at the proper level to transmit the thrusts of the high vault. It follows that the head of each is considerably below the level of the clerestory gutter. Vertical pipes, therefore, are passed through the wall at intervals from the gutter to the head of the flying buttress. Such pipes, however, are easily choked, and in such a case great damage may be quickly done to the masonry by infiltration. In the presbytery of Ely the upper flying buttress served as an aqueduct, and the rain from it originally passed through a hole made in the centre of each buttress just below the pinnacle.

But when the presbytery was remodelled in the fourteenth century, a gargoyle was constructed at the side of the buttress, so as to do away with the risk of infiltration into the inner masonry of the pinnacle.† But on the whole this utilisation of the flying buttress did not find much favour in England. In France, on the other hand, it was worked out to a complete solution. At first two flying buttresses were superposed ; compare those of WESTMINSTER ABBEY (379) ; the upper one forming the aqueduct, with its head at the level of the clerestory gutter. Later, as at Amiens nave, Auxerre, Bordeaux, Nicosia, Famagusta, Cologne, Eu, Abbeville, there was placed on the flying buttress proper a balustrade, and on the balustrade an inclined bar, the upper surface of which was hollowed as a channel for the rain. A flying buttress of this type, but of decorative origin only, and with a double bar, is seen in LOUTH SPIRE (611). In England the clerestories were usually some 50 feet

* Enlart's *Histoire*, 516.   † See section in Stewart's *Ely*, 4.

lower than those of France; and so the fall of water from the upper gargoyles was less dangerous; we were therefore satisfied usually to cover the aisle-roofs with lead, and leave the flying buttresses to their proper function.

SPOUTS.

But, it may be asked, why did not the builders save themselves all these complications by employing spouts, horizontal and vertical? One reason was that they could not cast iron spouts. But as a matter of fact they did try vertical spouts of lead to carry off the rain in the gutter; *e.g.* in the fifteenth-century work at KETTER-ING CHURCH and in King's College Chapel, Cambridge. Earlier still, in 1241, an order was given that lead spouts should be put up from the top to the bottom of the White Tower of London, which had been newly whitewashed, that the whitewashed walls might not be injured. Lydgate, in his poem, "Troy," 1555, speaks of houses

Kettering.

> "With spoutes thorough and pipes as they ought
> From the stone worke to the canell raught." *

It was not then that they were unacquainted with spouts, but probably because they knew the mischief of choked spouts and preferred an open system under observation and easily kept in order, that they adhered to the system of gutter, parapet, and gargoyle, or else of dripping eaves.

* Willis' *Architectural Nomenclature*, 38.

Chapter XXVI.

THE PROTECTION OF THE WALLS FROM RAIN.

Ground-Courses—Strings—Dripstones—Hood-Molds—Labels.

So far we have spoken of the methods adopted to drain the roofs. But it is necessary to protect from the drip of the rain the walls also, especially at their foot, and the heads of windows and doorways. For these was contrived a system of ground-courses, string-courses, dripstones, and hood-molds.

Ground or Basement Course.

For the real stability of a building, as well as for the satisfaction of the eye, which demands something to soften the abrupt transition from the horizontal ground to the vertical wall, the walls require a spreading base. In a Greek temple this took the form of steps. In early Romanesque work the projecting basement was usually composed of one or more projecting rectangular courses. But rain dripping from the eaves on to the level top of these soon wore down a hollow, and moreover bespattered and injured the surface of the wall adjacent. To get rid of this inconvenience, therefore, a 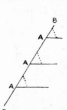 straight chamfer or chamfers was employed; e.g. in FOUNTAINS NAVE (679.1). But care had to be taken in the use of this chamfer. If a joint occurs in the chamfer-plane, it will be seen, e.g. at A, A, A, that it will be what is technically called "feather-edged"; * the dotted triangles will disintegrate early. It will be seen that in WHITBY (679.3) and FOUNTAINS (679.4) choirs a feather-edged joint occurs: but not in the other examples. Secondly, still further to prevent the rain from getting into the joints, as many of them as possible are placed under a projecting member. This practice was long in coming to maturity. In Fountains nave every joint is exposed; but protection is given to two joints at HEXHAM (679.2), to one at Whitby and Fountains choir; to five at RIEVAULX (5), to eight at BRIDLINGTON (6). So also, except in the two lowest courses, every joint is protected in the fourteenth-century ground-course of WELBOURNE (7), and the fifteenth-century one of KETTERING (8). The great amount of projection given in a fourteenth-century basement is well seen at TIDESWELL opposite. Care also had to be taken against excessive undercutting and excessive projection of the protecting members. The fragile upper course of the Whitby basement should be contrasted with those of Welbourne, which have the "scroll-molding." Basement-courses are exposed to an exceptional

* Pugin's *True Principles*, 15.

amount of wet ; that of Whitby, in a rainy district, is not good construction.
Again, no hollows should be provided where the rain can lodge ; there are two,
however, at Whitby ; and at Hexham, a particularly bad example, there are no
less than four.   Especially is it important that the rain should not be allowed
to trickle down from one member to another till it reaches the ground.   It
does so in Fountains nave, in the two upper courses at Hexham, in the four
lower courses at Whitby.   But at Rievaulx two of the projecting rolls, and at
Bridlington four, are so designed beneath that the drip is cut off by a hollow
(*coupe-larme* or " throat "), and is compelled to leave the face of the stone.

Then there was the question what projection a basement ought to have,
and what height, in proportion to the height and solidity of the walls.   In the
thirteenth century and onwards the basements grew greatly in height and bulk.

Tideswell.   Cawston.

Then came in artistic considerations ; how best to contrast vertical line, chamfer,
and curve ; and how to get beauty of curve.   In the fourteenth century the
straight chamfer gave way greatly to the subtle ogee curve ; *e.g.* at TIDESWELL.
Especially was it sought more and more to get nice gradation of high light,
half light, and shadow.   The ground-course of Fountains nave is shadowless ;
there is little shadow at Whitby or Fountains choir ; but there are two broad
bands of shadow at Rievaulx and Welbourne, and three at Bridlington and
Kettering.   In these protected recesses panelling might be introduced ; *e.g.* in
Cawston tower.   In the last fifty years of English Gothic bands of quatrefoils were often introduced ; as in the DIVINITY SCHOOL, OXFORD (492), and
KETTERING (95).   Sir G. Scott* was of opinion that the English basement-

* *Lectures*, i. 164.

molds of the thirteenth century were peculiarly excellent. " I have never seen any in France to equal many of our own in the quality of appearing eminently fitted to support the whole structure, or in the artistic arrangement of their parts." Mr E. Sharpe says,* perhaps with more justice, " in the use and design of the moldings of the basement-course the Curvilinear period (1315-1360) surpasses all others in England. Here, as well as in the set-offs of the buttresses, the ogee comes in, with its fine sweep, with great effect. The smallest churches of this period derive a dignity from this bold spreading external feature." But grand examples of fifteenth and sixteenth century basement-molds also occur ; especially in the towers of Norfolk and Suffolk. For other illustrations of basement-courses, see LINCOLN, SALISBURY, and SOUTHWELL (115, 458, 359).

The moldings of the basement of the buttress were usually the same as those of the basement of the wall. See plates of buttresses (352-357).

STRING.

A string or string-course is a projecting course of masonry, usually horizontal, whether external or internal. In thin Anglo-Saxon walls of rubble,† the horizontal strings are probably bonding-courses, used to strengthen the weak and bad masonry of the wall ; and may be derived from surviving traditions of Roman craftsmanship, or from observation of the bonding-courses of long tiles in existing Roman walls at Leicester, Pevensey, Richborough, and elsewhere.

In the earliest large Norman churches, Bernay and Jumièges,‡ string-courses may be seen just coming into existence again. At Jumièges there is no external string at all ; and in the interiors of both there is no string to separate triforium and clerestory ; while in Bernay and WINCHESTER (261) transepts there is no string to separate pier-arcade and triforium. After this the different stories, external and internal, were carefully marked by strings. But very soon, even in the Abbaye-aux-Hommes, Caen, and NORWICH (31), before the eleventh century was out, strings were introduced which did not demarcate vertical stages of the building, but were purely decorative.§ In the twelfth-century aisles of Rochester, Romsey, Peterborough, Northampton St Peter's, Southwell porch, the external abaci of the window shafts were continued to form additional strings. In the Abbaye-aux-Hommes and Norwich an additional string was got by continuing horizontally the dripstone of the lower window of the aisle. At Cérisy, Winchester, and Durham, the external abaci of the clerestory windows became strings, as they did internally at Winchester and Dunfermline. The importance given to the string at Norwich, begun 1096, is very remarkable. It is employed in greatest abundance and richness in the west front of Ely. The great artistic value of the string is perhaps only realised when it is absent, as in Malvern nave and GRESFORD (214); without it the wall is bare and desolate.

* *Lincoln Excursion*, 133.   † Baldwin Brown, 296.
‡ Illustrated in Ruprich-Robert, Plates 11, 12, 13.
§ A string which separates stories is called in French a *bandeau ;* one which does not is a *cordon.*

In Gothic, after *c.* 1260, the decorative string or *cordon* is of less importance ; for the simple reason that the windows of aisle and clerestory extend nearly or quite from buttress to buttress. In the façades it is especially useful in emphasising their stages. The beautiful eastern transept of BEVERLEY MINSTER (176), instead of being naturally divided by the windows into three or four stages, is divided by four strings into five stages, and gains greatly in apparent height ; for who can imagine that a building five stages high is not lofty? The east front of ELY (464), which is divided into four stages only, looks low in comparison. The west tower of WYMONDHAM (589) has six strings and seven stages. The eastern transept of Canterbury has eight strings.

Romanesque strings are often carved ; *e.g.* with zigzag or billet, as at Norwich ; the Southwell strings are exceedingly rich. In Gothic the string is generally molded.

Like parapet and basement-course, the string has great value in binding into one whole the disconnected units of the building, severed externally by buttress, flying buttress, and pinnacle, and internally by pier and vaulting shaft. Still further to reduce the disuniting power of the buttress the string is often, especially in the thirteenth century, carried round it. At Salisbury the greatest possible emphasis is given to string, basement-course, and parapet, to curb as much as possible the aspiring verticality of the design ; nowhere are the buttresses scored so deep and broad with horizontal lines.

One main use of the string is to act as a drip-course. Indeed in such an example as NORWICH (160), the string is but a horizontal continuation of the dripstone of the window ; or, to put it the other way, the dripstone is but the arched form of the string. String and dripstone, therefore, are very frequently the same in profile. So also a string is often but a continuation of the abacus ; and may be identical in form. Indeed very similar conditions dictate the form of the coping of the parapet, the string, the dripstone of the window, the hood-mold of the doorway, the set-offs of the buttress, and the basement-course ; and all naturally tend to take similar profiles.

What has been said, therefore, above of the molding of the basement-course is largely applicable to the string. It is undesirable that its upper surface should be horizontal ; for that, in an exterior, affords lodgment for snow, and in the interior to dust ; and if an external string be flat-topped, the face of the wall near is bespattered with rain. Such strings, therefore, as that of FURNESS (681.3) are objectionable. Yet, strange to say, the flat top was now and then reverted to in later Gothic ; *e.g.* 683.17. Again, the string should not project so much or be undercut so much as to be fragile : as at NETLEY (681.16), BRIDLINGTON (681.18), and ST MARY'S, YORK (683.3). And if it is an external string, it should be undercut to cut off the drip. The "throat" is usually present in thirteenth-century work, as at Netley, BRIDLINGTON (683.1), and HOWDEN (683.5) ; but is often absent from fourteenth-century and later strings : it appears, however, in examples 683.10, 12, 17, 18. Finally, if a black band of shadow is desired beneath it, it must be deeply undercut, as at Netley ; but if the hollow is to be filled with foliage, it should be broad ; deep enough to protect the foliage, but not so deep as to hide it from sight ; as it does at Tiverton ; a hollow "casement" strikes the happy mean.

Norman strings are commonly square or semi-hexagonal. The strings of FOUNTAINS and FURNESS (681) are of mid-twelfth century. A little later, *c.* 1170, the ROCHE string (4) is a pointed "bowtell," instead of being semicircular; and that of BYLAND (6) ceases to be flat-topped. JERVAULX (9), a few years later, has a filleted bowtell. WHITBY (11), NETLEY (16), BRIDLINGTON (18), TINTERN (683.2), and ST MARY'S, YORK (3) strings have the characteristic narrow, deep, semicircular hollow, and date from the middle to the end of the thirteenth century. Throughout the whole century the scroll-molding came more and more into fashion; in the fourteenth century the scroll or some variant of it was still more common (*e.g.* AUSTREY, 683.12), and its lower curve was an ogee. Sometimes, as in 683.17, the *coupe-larme* is retained; but the special feature is the presence of ogee curves or "wave-moldings." In later Gothic strings also the ogee or wave curve or the double ogee is rarely absent; but the special characteristic is that they are usually flat-topped, and that the hollow becomes a broad shallow "casement," as in 683.15 and 13.*

Dripstone, Hood-mold, Label.

These terms are often used indiscriminately of the strings which surmount openings, whether windows, doorways, or pier-arches. When the opening is the outer side of a window or doorway, the term *dripstone* is appropriate. But if the opening is within the building, where there is no rain to drip, it is better to call the string a *hood-mold,* not a dripstone. The term *label* may be dispensed with altogether; strictly it is applicable only to a rectangular dripstone over a doorway or window.† *Weather-mold* and *water-table* are synonymous with dripstone; and may also be dispensed with.

Just as strings are desirable to keep the drip of the rain off the walls, so dripstones are necessary, and to a much higher degree, to prevent the rain from dripping into the moldings of the window-arch and its tracery and the leading of its panes; or on to the moldings of a door-arch and the door itself. The main function, therefore, of string and dripstone being identical, and string and dripstone frequently being continuous, they are often similar in profile. The dripstones, strings, and abaci at Binham, WEST WALTON (432), and Netley are of much projection: at Binham and West Walton, in the thirteenth century, the excellent Barnack stone was employed. Two dripstones are given from AUSTREY (683.11, 12), fourteenth century: the second has the scroll molding, the first is a filleted scroll; both have an ogee curve beneath; they should be compared with strings 10 and 9. 18 is a late fourteenth-century hood-mold from COTTINGHAM.

Sometimes, in early work, carved dripstones and hood-molds occur: *e.g.* in Norman work in a window in St John's, Chester; and in the eastern arch of LLANDAFF CHOIR (580). Hood-molds of billet, zigzag, &c., are seen over the windows of Ely, Peterborough, and Norwich; over IFFLEY WEST DOORWAY

---

* For a fuller treatment of the moldings of strings, dripstones, and hood-molds, see Paley's *Manual of Gothic Moldings*, Section 11 and Plate 16. In studying strings, and indeed moldings in general, it must be borne in mind that each architectural province, *e.g.* that of Northants and the surrounding districts, has its special characteristics; some molds are exceedingly frequent; others, common elsewhere, hardly occur at all.

† *Cf.* Brandon's *Analysis*, ii. 35, note.

(574); over the pier-arches of Waltham, Steyning, and St. Margaret at Cliffe. The practice continues into the thirteenth century; the clerestory windows of Lichfield nave, *c.* 1270, having dripstones with the tooth ornament.

Usually the dripstone follows the curve, if any, of the opening. But from the fourteenth century an ogee dripstone, usually crocketed and terminating in a finial, frequently surmounts the pointed arch of a doorway, as at ST MARY BEVERLEY (365) and CLEY (85); and occasionally of a window, as in the Lady Chapel of Lichfield, and in LEVERINGTON PORCH (84); in Llandaff aisle both the head of the window and the dripstone are ogee arches. In the fifteenth century and onward the dripstone (*label*) of the doorway is often horizontal; as at SALL (575) and KETTERING (95).

In Early Norman work, *e.g.* at WINCHESTER (261) and Malvern, both dripstone and hood-mold are often omitted. So also over the pier-arches of the thirteenth-century church at Yarmouth; and often, at all periods, in small churches. In many of the latest and finest churches also it is omitted; *e.g.* at Wrexham and GRESFORD (214); and in large Norfolk churches such as CAWSTON (552), Worsted, Trunch, and St Andrew's, Norwich. These Norfolk churches are built of flint and rubble; and it may be that it was desired to economise freestone, which had to be brought from a distance.* But as the clerestory string is also omitted, and all the arches are chamfered but not molded, it may well be that the builders purposely designed the interiors with a plain base as a foil, omitting dripstone and string and molding of arch, that nothing might arrest or detain the gaze upward to the magnificent open roofs which all the above churches possess.

Both dripstone and hood-mold require some kind of finish. In early work this is sometimes bungled, as in the chapels of Kirkstall transept and the doorways of Glastonbury Lady Chapel. In Early Norman work, *e.g.* Chester St John's, the abacus is sometimes prolonged for the purpose. Later the ends of the dripstone die into the buttress on either side; as in the cloisters of Salisbury, WESTMINSTER (489), and NORWICH (506). Or one hood-mold meets another, and mitres into it; somewhat artlessly at St Mary's, Shrewsbury; late twelfth century. Frequently, when the windows are small, the dripstone "returns," *i.e.* is continued as a string, but at right angles. This treatment is naturally most common in the twelfth and thirteenth century; *e.g.* Southwell porch and WELLS CHOIR (373). But it may be seen also in late work; *e.g.* in the clerestory of Gloucester nave, and the Lady Chapel of St Mary Redcliffe. In the fourteenth century this treatment is less common; at this time the dripstone very commonly terminates in a couple of heads.†

But, far more frequently, both hood-mold and dripstone terminate in some kind of corbel; it is called a "stop." Much ingenuity and fancy is put into these "stops," and they should be specially noted. Their variety is so great that they hardly admit of classification.‡ A Norman example from Malmes-

---

* But the omission of internal strings and hood-molds is just as common in the Late Gothic of Somerset, where good stone was plentiful.

† See Rickman, 203, 266; and Paley's *Gothic Architecture*, 176.5.

‡ The "buckle" is worth note; a corbel producing by its shadows a reminiscence of the human face.

bury* also appears above the windows of Southwell porch. Leaf-scrolls are common in the Early English work ; *e.g.* at Stanwick ; † and on a piscina in Strumpshaw Church.‡   Heads, animals, and grotesques occur at all periods ; the example from Merton College § is *c.* 1280.   In fourteenth and fifteenth century work, instead of being continued into a string, the dripstone has often but a short return ; a truncated string ; as at St Martin's, Canterbury. ‖   Or this bit of string is curled up to form a circle, or extended so as to form a square, rhombus, or hexagon ; as at Chippenham.¶   When heads are employed here or elsewhere, they are often a clue to date ; each period having its characteristic headdress ; *e.g.* in the reign of Edward I. a common stop of the dripstone is the wimpled headdress.**

It has been pointed out above that a dripstone is necessary for practical reasons outside, but not inside a building.   In strict logic, therefore, it should not be employed as a hood-mold over pier-arches.   The French, more faithful to the logic of Gothic construction than ourselves, almost always omit it.   But the eye greatly desiderates that the demarcation between support and load shall be emphasised.††   It would seem that if it is right to mark off the supporting pier from the supported arch by a capital, it is just as right to mark off the supporting arch from the supported wall by a hood-mold.

* *Glossary*, 98.   † *Glossary*, 98.   ‡ Colling's *Details*, i., E.E., 2.
§ Colling's *Details*, i., E.E., 2.   ‖ *Glossary*, Text, p. 188.
¶ *Glossary*, 98, and Brandon's *Analysis*, ii., *Perp.*, 26, 29.
** " *Corbels, date of headdress.*   This is worth noticing, because the date of a church may thus sometimes be ascertained.   The principal varieties appear to be these :—
" About the year 1300, the *wimple* or handkerchief round the neck and chin.
" 1350. The *net*, confining the hair back from the forehead.
" 1380. The hair itself is braided in a square plait on each side the forehead.
" 1410. The *crespine*, resembling the latter style, but covered with a veil, which reaches to the shoulders. This, towards
" 1430, takes a lunar or horned shape, which grows more and more outrageous till about 1470.
" 1480. The *butterfly ;* where the hair is worn in a net behind, with pinners, on wire, like wings.
" 1500. The *kennel*, or triangular forehead dress.
" Maidens wear their hair loose, without any headdress ; and widows, in late times, have a *gorge* at the chin " (*Handbook of English Ecclesiology*, p. 119).
†† An arch without a hood-mold is as a fair face without eyebrows.—R. P. B.

CHAPTER XXVII.

ROMANESQUE CAPITALS.

Function of Capitals—Cubical and Scalloped Capitals—Interlacing, Figure, and Storied
Capitals—Semi-Naturalistic Capitals.

THE main function of the abacus and capital is to provide for the springing
of the arch a surface of greater area than is provided by the pier.

In Byzantine work, when the supports were but slender columns, it was
sometimes the practice, *e.g.* in S. Vitale, Ravenna, to superpose another cap
(French, *dosseret*). In Romanesque and Gothic this additional upper capital
is not found.

The depth of the capital is or should be proportionate to the diameter
of the shaft or column. This is well seen in the capitals of Lincoln choir;
and earlier still, in those of CHICHESTER RETROCHOIR (245).

From an artistic point of view, capitals are valuable in two ways. First,
they mask the awkward junction where the curving lines of the arch meet
the vertical lines of the pier. Secondly, where the plan of the pier is different
from the section of the arch, the junction of the two different sets of moldings
would be most unpleasant. But, where, as often in late work, *e.g.* at TENBY
(410), pier and arch have the same moldings, the capitals may be omitted;
the moldings running continuously and uninterruptedly from the base of one
pier up to and round the arch and down to the base of the next pier.* Or,
sometimes in late work, as in CHIPPING NORTON (548), the inner order of
the arch alone is supported by a capital: the outer order of the arch runs down
to the ground. These two methods of procedure may be right logically;
both are nevertheless objectionable. If there is what Willis calls a "dis-
continuous impost," then, as he says, "the arches appear ready to slip down
the sides of the pier, having nothing to rest upon." The capitals are omitted
in the thirteenth-century vestibule of the chapter house of Chester Cathedral;
it is rare to find so early an example. It is very common abroad in Late
Gothic; *e.g.* the cathedrals of Orleans, Louvain, and Antwerp.

CUBICAL OR CUSHION CAPS.

In Norman and Lombardic work the two chief capitals employed are the
Corinthian and the cubical. The latter, seen in Ernulph's work at CANTER-
BURY (430), is often asserted to be the earlier; but both in Normandy and

---

* In the Lady Chapel of LONG MELFORD (665.12), though the moldings of pier and
arch are identical, capitals are employed.

Tenby.
Ickleton.

England the Corinthian is more often found till *c.* 1090. Of the Romanesque provinces of Europe, those of Lombardy, Germany, Normandy, and England use the cubical capital most. In Lombardy the abacus is often very massive, and practically becomes a dosseret. Examples in the Brera Museum from the destroyed Church of Aurona have been attributed by De Dartein to the eighth century. At any rate in the eleventh century they may be seen in abundance, *e.g.* in S. Stefano, Bologna, and the adjoining cloister; in the crypt of S. Miniato, Florence; at Aquileia (1019-1025); in S. Abbondio, Como; in S. Theodore, Bologna, 1190; in Pavia they are not seldom executed in bricks. In Germany they are very common; *e.g.* at Speyer, Augsburg, Bamberg, Ratisbon. They are common in Normandy, and not infrequent in Anjou and Saintonge; they occur also in the Primitive Romanesque crypt of Nevers Cathedral.

As to the origin of the cubical capital there has been much controversy. It is very common, executed in wood, in the Romanesque churches of Norway;* which is natural enough, as it is a form easily obtained from wood. And as the Normans came from Scandinavia, Ruprich-Robert

* Several of these are illustrated by Ruprich-Robert, vol. ii.

predicates a Scandinavian origin for the cubical cap. On the other hand we may urge that Scandinavia did not receive Christianity till the time of Olaf Trygvason, *c.* 1000; and that consequently any church architecture there must be considerably later than the time when the Normans conquered and settled in Normandy. Again, the existing timber churches of Norway, from the richness and character of their ornament, would seem not to have been built till well into the twelfth century. Also, the stone cubical capital of Normandy is broader than the column or shaft: and is moreover executed in a separate block. But in the Scandinavian examples capital and post are all in one piece; the capital is formed in the simplest way by squaring the upper part of the round post into four faces; thus the four flat sides of the capital do not project, but are "in retreat." And even if the Scandinavian theory explained the Normandy capitals, it would still fail to explain the great multitude of cubical capitals in Lombardy, Germany, Anjou, Saintonge, where no Scandinavian influence can be predicated.*

Another theory is that these capitals are of Byzantine origin. They occur at S. Vitale, Ravenna; and this church was imitated by southern workmen, whom Charlemagne had sent for, at the end of the ninth century at Aix-la-Chapelle. Other examples occur in St Mark's, Venice, commenced in 1063. Examples occur as early as the seventh century, at Parenzo,† on the Adriatic; where the fact that the capital bears a dosseret, may point to Byzantine influence.‡ From Ravenna also it may well have passed to Lombardy, and from Lombardy to France.

But it is quite as probable that this capital was not borrowed at all in Northern Europe, but was a result of a peculiar process of craftsmanship. The Romans themselves used the lathe in turning shafts; and the lathe was in constant use among our own Anglo-Saxon builders, as it was from the eleventh century in France; § *e.g.* the monolithic columns of the choir of St Etienne Nevers, dedicated in 1099; monoliths turned in the lathe are in great use also in the choirs of the Romanesque churches of Auvergne. In Berry and Poitou also they are common; and sometimes there may still be seen the horizontal grooves produced by the lathe. Now the shape of a cubical capital, the penetration of a cube and a sphere, is precisely what would suggest itself to craftsmen using lathes.‖ It is probable then that in districts where the lathe was in use for turning shafts, the cubical capital was reinvented; and that from these districts it spread to their neighbours.¶

Where the face of the cubical capital was left plain, it seems to have been common to paint it; painted capitals survive at Jumièges and St Georges de

* See Brutails, 45. † Dehio, Plate 33.

‡ It should be mentioned, however, that the dosseret also occurs in S. Stefano Rotondo, Rome, consecrated 467, where no Byzantine influence can be suspected.

§ Viollet-le-Duc, *Architecture*, iii. 495.

‖ Or it may be regarded as the natural way—which would occur to many districts independently—of accommodating a square to a circle. "If a cubical block of stone be placed on a round shaft the diameter of which is less than a side of the square, and if now all the surface material be cut away at the bottom, so that the large square above gradually changes and diminishes into the circle beneath, we get the form of the new impost-capitals" (Lethaby's *Mediæval Art*, 39).

¶ See Brutails, 81.

1. Ely Transept.
2. Malmesbury Nave.
3. Lessay Nave.
4. Steyning Nave.

5. St David's Nave.
6. Wells Nave.
7. Steyning Nave.
8. Dore Choir.

Boscherville.* In the eastern aisle of the Norman transept of ELY (412.1) cubical caps may be seen with painted foliage : and others where painted foliage has been rendered, later on, in stone. In very many cases plain cushion caps have been carved later on ; specimens in all stages of development may be seen in the crypts of CANTERBURY (193) and WESTMINSTER (415.1). Also capitals rudely carved in the eleventh century were sometimes recut in the twelfth ; to the great confusion of archæologists ; † e.g. in Romsey choir and Porchester Church. ‡

SCALLOPED CAPS, *or Subdivided Cushions.* More often, instead of painting or carving the flat faces of a cubical capital, another process was adopted, which was to be very fertile in results. It was to subdivide each face into two, three, or more cushions. When the cushion cap is much subdivided, as at MALMESBURY (412.2), it is usually well advanced in the twelfth century. But this is not always so. Fully developed scalloped capitals, possibly imitations of Norman work, occur in the Anglo-Saxon belfries of Clee and Bracebridge ; and at Branston § in an arcade on the west wall of the tower, side by side with Corinthian and cubical capitals. In Normandy, according to Ruprich-Robert, the oldest examples go back to the last years of the eleventh century. Those of Lessay are not necessarily much later. They occur also in St Georges de Boscherville, as well as in the Abbaye-aux-Dames.‖ In Norwich Cathedral, begun 1096, capitals similar to those of LESSAY (412.3) occur in the triforium of the apse, and in the eastern bay of that of the south nave.¶

Winchester Lady Chapel.

By the middle of the twelfth century the scallops had become so numerous that the whole capital often became a fringe of tiny cones. These have been termed by Mr Sharpe *coniferous* capitals. The spaces between the cones were filled up with inverted cones, beads, &c. ; and thus a very rich and beautiful capital was elaborated out of the heavy, unsightly cushion ; *e.g.* STEYNING ** (412.4). Very fine scalloped and coniferous capitals occur at Ramsey Abbey, Sutton St Mary, Tilney All Saints, and Walsoken.†† By

* Dehio, Plate 312.
† See Anthyme St Paul's pamphlet on the subject.
‡ In WINCHESTER LADY CHAPEL is a cubical Norman capital carved into a mask ; probably in the fifteenth century.
§ Illustrated in Baldwin's Brown's *Arts in Early England,* ii. 161.
‖ Ruprich-Robert, Plate 93.   ¶ Illustrated in Rickman, 88.
** For other illustrations see Sharpe's *Ornamentation of the Transitional Period;* and Sharpe's *Lincoln Excursion.* A beautiful variant is one in which the cones imitate the folds of drapery.
†† Those of Walsoken are illustrated in Colling's *Details,* Norman, i. 6.

analogy with those of Sutton St Mary, the date of which is definite, probably none of the above are earlier than 1180.

Towards the end of the period, *e.g.* at ST DAVID'S (412.5), begun 1180, and specially in those churches which were put up in the West of England Gothic, a pretty modification was adopted ; the pier looks like the stump of a willow tree that has been pollarded. The cones now are incurved and seen to be growing out of the pier; and the upper ends are cut off sharp, as it were by a knife. The capital with incurved cones ; * *e.g.* in the west nave of Worcester, the east transept of Hereford, the arch leading into the north aisle of Lichfield choir, under the tower of Cheltenham, and in several churches of the Welsh border ; is specially characteristic of the late Transitional or Early Gothic of the twelfth-century school of the west country.†

The next step, as in several examples at ST DAVID'S (412.5) and WELLS (412.6), is for the cone to become a little hollow trumpet ; to bud and blossom and bring forth leaf and flower. Exquisitely beautiful and consummate in execution as is this capital from the western bays of the nave of Wells—nothing better was ever done in English art than the capitals of Wells—there is good reason to believe that it is not later than the year 1206.

The next capital is from STEYNING (412.7). Here the carver has retained the filling-in between the cones, but has omitted the cones. This capital is seen also at Icklesham, near Hastings.

INTERLACING CAPITALS.

The richer eleventh and twelfth century capitals, *e.g.* those of ELY TRANSEPT (412.1), ST PETER'S, NORTHAMPTON (415.6), OXFORD CATHEDRAL (417.1), and ABBEY DORE (412.8), often contain interlacings ; sometimes of flat bands, sometimes of pipes, sometimes of foliage, sometimes monsters or human beings intertwined after the fashion of those on the shafts of the doorways of IFFLEY (256), NORTHAMPTON (256), SHOBDON (415.3) and Kilpeck. As interlacings are very common in the Early Irish missals and crosses, and also in those of the Anglo-Saxons, some have attributed to these a Celtic, and others an Anglo-Saxon origin. But as they occur also very frequently in Byzantine work of the sixth century, *e.g.* in the screens of S. Vitale, Ravenna, and again in the eighth century,‡ both the Irish and Anglo-Saxons may have got their interlacing patterns in the way of patterned stuffs and ivories imported from Constantinople. It is hardly necessary, however, to fetch in the Byzantines ; for interlacings are particularly common in the Roman mosaic pavements which existed in every province of the Roman Empire, and undoubtedly furnished patterns largely for Early Christian art throughout Europe. If we take a broader survey, we shall find interlacings in many a savage tribe which never heard either of Byzantium or of Rome. It is one of the oldest and most widely-spread patterns in decorative art. Its motif is evidently the plaited basket. Wherever basket work was in

---

* Mr Sharpe in *Transitional Ornament* illustrates the incurved cone from Ely Infirmary, Llanthony, Worcester west nave, triforium of Romsey nave, Bibury.

† See on the triple shafting of the same school, page 245.

‡ Numerous examples are illustrated by Cattaneo.

1, 2. Westminster.
3. Shobdon.
4. Winchester Crypt.
5. Oxford Cathedral.
6. Northampton St Peter.

use, and some peoples have been so skilled in the art of plaiting that even their drinking vessels are made of basket work, pretty patterns consonant with the material have arisen, and have been transferred from the plaited vessel to decorative art generally.

The capital from Oxford, with interlacing pipings, is one of those to which an impossible Anglo-Saxon origin has been attributed; it is *c.* 1170: a very similar one may be seen in the southern clerestory of the nave of the Abbaye-aux-Hommes.* In the twelfth-century Gothic capitals of the West of England capitals of intertwining leafage were in great favour; *e.g.* in Wells nave.

Figure Capitals.

In Continental Romanesque it is not uncommon to find capitals composed of writhing and intertwining monsters; a fine example is seen in S. Zeno, Verona. In our Norman work, *e.g.* at Shobdon,† masks and grotesques occur; and occasionally, even in Gothic, a capital may be found composed, inartistically enough, of heads or grotesques; *e.g.* Hampton Poyle‡ and Oakham. In ST MARY MAGDALENE, TAUNTON (417.4) all the capitals are composed of angels with outspread wings. In France what are called "storied capitals" are by no means rare; a fine set of the twelfth century is seen in St Denis, Amboise; and others in the Cluny Museum, illustrating the fall of Adam and Eve, and other scriptural subjects. Here, however, except at Wells, we were not very successful in figure-sculpture; in the north porch of Wells is a complete set of "storied" capitals, now unfortunately much decayed.

Semi-Naturalistic Capitals of the Transitional Period.

Of these the most important is the so-called WATER-LEAF (*feuille d'eau*); it is a broad, thick, smooth leaf terminating in a very small volute; and this volute curls inward instead of outward. It is well seen at WALSOKEN (417.2), near Wisbech. It was astonishingly fashionable throughout Europe in the middle and latter part of the twelfth century; in England its vogue was limited to a quarter of a century; from *c.* 1165 to *c.* 1190; therefore, like the flattened lower roll of the base, 451, it is a valuable criterion of chronology.§ It was

* Another at Kirkton, *c.* 1165, illustrated in Sharpe's *Transitional Ornament.*

† Shobdon Church, near Leominster, was founded 1141 to 1150 by Oliver de Merlemond (see Norman-French charter in *Monasticon Anglicanum*, vi. 345), on his return from a pilgrimage to St James of Compostella in Spain. It is recorded that on his way back he stayed at the monastery of St Victor in Paris; and when his church was finished, he sent for two monks from that monastery to serve it. In going and returning on the pilgrimage he probably passed through Souillac; for the same intertwining monsters and human beings are found there on capitals and shafts as at Shobdon and Kilpeck, near Hereford. Such work is so exceptional in England that it may be that he brought or sent for carvers from the west of France for his church; and perhaps the same men executed the work at Kilpeck. Casts of both may be seen in the South Kensington Museum and the Crystal Palace. Shobdon Church is pulled down; the doorway is re-erected in the park (Rickman, 98).

‡ *Glossary*, i., Plate 51.

§ E. Sharpe in *Lincoln Excursion*, 113; he calls it the "Transitional volute." It is fully illustrated in his *Ornamentation of the Transitional Period.*

1. Oxford Cathedral Choir.
2. Walsoken Nave.
3. Le Puy Cloister.

4. Taunton Nave.
6. Steyning Nave.
7. Canterbury Crypt.

5. Dore Choir.

especially a favourite with the Cistercians; *e.g.* the pier-arcades of Furness and Byland. By the principles of their Order, they were debarred from the richly carved capitals of the later Romanesque: and at first confined themselves almost wholly to scalloped and coniferous capitals, as at Kirkstall, Fountains, and Buildwas, or to the water-leaf: perhaps justifying themselves in the employment of the latter by the fact that it was "good construction," as indeed it was. For the cubical capital of Norman work, with its convex curve, was replaced in the Transitional period by one with a hollow, concave curve; and as the abacus still remained square in plan, its four corners overlapped the circular bell below, and were dangerously unsupported. The water-leaf form gave support just at the point where it was needed, and that with the minimum waste of stone. A grand example of the water-leaf supports the refectory pulpit of Rievaulx. The same reason that adapts the water-leaf for use as a capital makes it equally serviceable as a "griffe" or spur; *e.g.* at BARNACK (695.9): so also at Laon, Troyes, and Paris cathedrals.*

Its origin is obscure. It may be but the lower band of leafage, seen in the capitals of the crypts of the Abbaye-aux-Dames and CANTERBURY (417.7), with the addition of the Ionic volute, incurved for the constructional reasons given above; themselves reminiscences of such Corinthian capitals as that of the Choragic monument of Lysicrates at Athens.

The only other leaf form in common use during the Transitional period was the *plantain*. Viollet-le-Duc, in his illustrations, v. 490, shows how closely the curves of young leaves of plantain are rendered in capitals at Notre Dame, Paris, and Montreale, Yonne. They occur, however, even in Norman work; *e.g.* at EASINGTON, DURHAM (428); and the analogy in form and position between these and the leafage of the upper band of the Tower of the Winds at Athens is so striking, that in spite of chronology and geography one can hardly doubt that this is a case of survival of ornamental detail. Nothing seems to have more persistent vitality than a decorative form.

The *fern leaf*, uncurling just as it protrudes from the ground in spring, now and then occurs; *e.g.* in York crypt; choir aisle of Abbey Dore; OXFORD CATHEDRAL (415.5); Canterbury choir; all Transitional examples.† On the remarkable capital from STEYNING (417.6), on the right, may be seen three fern leaves, separated by incurved cones. Occasionally the leaf of the common *arum* (*Arum maculatum*) with berries occurs; as in the west doorway of Ledbury,‡ and in the spandrels of Wells triforium. In the Ledbury example the berries are surrounded by a spathe as in nature, and overhung by a kind of foliated hood.

The most beautiful examples of Transitional foliage occur in the superb capitals of the eastern work of CANTERBURY CHOIR § (428); unsurpassed in this or any other country; the only parallels we have are those at Broad-

---

* Illustrated in Viollet-le-Duc, *Architecture*, vi. 51.

† A fine fern cap from Soissons Cathedral is illustrated in Parker's *Glossary*, Plate 48. One occurs in the cloister of Le Puy Cathedral, probably eleventh century. See also illustration in Viollet-le-Duc, *Architecture*, vol. v. 486.

‡ Illustrated in Colling's *Mediæval Foliage*, Plates 7, 24.

§ On the leafage of Canterbury choir, see Colling's *Mediæval Foliage*, pp. 32, 33, 34.

water Church * and Oakham Castle, and one or two in Oxford Cathedral nave.   Great was the promise of the Transitional capital, *c.* 1180 ; leaf after leaf, blossom and fruit were being experimented with ; we bade fair to have foliated capitals varied in design as nature herself.   But all came suddenly to an end.   All were abandoned, in the end, for a non-naturalistic capital ; the famous Early Gothic capital, which was elaborated into such forms of utmost beauty as we cannot but admire at Wells, Lincoln, Salisbury ; but a poor exchange for the infinite diversity of vegetative form that grew beneath the chisels of the craftsmen of Broadwater and CANTERBURY (423.7).†

* Capitals from Broadwater are illustrated in the *Building News*, Oct. 1, 1869. They differ from the Oxford and Canterbury capitals in admitting animal forms into the foliage ; animal forms are very plentiful also in the eastern bays of Wells nave.

† Equally grand are the Transitional capitals of the cathedrals of Paris, Lisieux, Senlis, and Vézelay choir, illustrated in Viollet-le-Duc's articles on *Chapiteau* and *Sculpture ;* and of St Laumer, Blois, illustrated in *Building News*, March 27, 1868.

Chapter XXVIII.

FOLIATED CAPITALS.

Roman Corinthian and Composite Capitals, and Norman Versions of them—Welding of
the Volute and the Scroll Capital in the Early Gothic Capital of Stalked Conventional Foliage—Naturalistic Capitals—Undulatory Foliage.

OF the three capitals in use in ancient Greece, the Doric was seldom employed
in the early Christian churches at Rome, and the Ionic far more rarely than
the Corinthian or its variant, the Composite. These two, the Corinthian and
the Composite, were produced by thousands in every province of the Roman
Empire, even in remote Britain. In some provinces Roman work survived in
great abundance, and in a high state of preservation, *e.g.* in Provence and
Languedoc, and in Burgundy; and in these districts, naturally, Corinthian
capitals were rendered with great fidelity; and indeed sometimes, in the schools
of Provence, Toulouse, and Burgundy, quite equalled or even surpassed their
prototypes. In Normandy and Britain it was otherwise; Roman work had never
been so abundant as in the highly civilised provinces of Southern Gaul; and
the destruction of what there was of it had been far more complete. Therefore
the Corinthian capital, as it appears in Norman and English hands in the
eleventh and twelfth centuries, is necessarily but archaic and rude. Nevertheless
this capital, which we may call the Corinthianesque, is of very considerable
interest not only for its high and ancient lineage, but from the predominating
influence which it will be found to have exerted over the development of carved
foliage, which is to a large extent but the history of the decomposition and
recomposition of the ancient Corinthian capital.

But, first of all, it must be borne in mind that the Corinthian capital of
Greece was not one, but diverse. That of the TEMPLE OF ZEUS (425) at
Athens may be regarded as the normal type; nevertheless such capitals as
those of the Choragic monument of Lysicrates and the TEMPLE OF THE WINDS
(425) at Athens have also to be taken into account. But our mediæval builders
knew nothing of Greek capitals; only Roman work; and the Romans had not
hesitated to bend to their purposes the Greek forms. In the first century of our
era, on the whole they adhered to the type of the Temple of Zeus; *e.g.* in the
portico of the Pantheon; the chief exception being that since the Corinthian
volutes looked, and were, too small and weak to support the angles of the
abacus, they often enlarged them; changing the Corinthian into what is called
the Composite capital: one in which the upper half is Ionic, the lower half
Corinthian.* Of these Composite capitals those in the BATHS OF DIOCLETIAN

* On early types of Composite capitals in Egypt and Phrygia see Anderson and Spiers,
98 and 154.

1. Newport St Woolos.
2. St Nicholas, Caen.
3. Dore Choir.
4. Youlgreave.

5. Newport St Woolos.
6. Oxford Cathedral.
7. Oxford Cathedral.
8. New Shoreham.

1. West Walton.
2. Lincoln Choir.
3. West Walton.
4. Llanidloes.
5. Llanidloes.

6. Llanidloes.
7. Llanidloes.
8. Dore Retrochoir.
9. Dore Retrochoir.
10. Dore Retrochoir.

1. New Shoreham.
2. New Shoreham.
3. Whaplode.
4. Tilney All Saints'.

5. Yarmouth.
6. Lincoln, St Mary-le-Wigford.
7. Canterbury, Saint's Chapel.
8. Oxford Cathedral Transept.

9. Lincoln Choir.

424

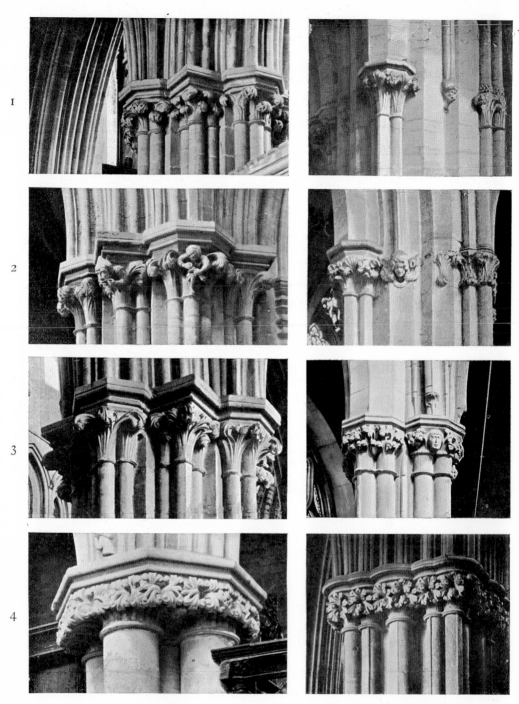

1. Wells Choir.
2. Wells Transept.
3. Wells Nave.
4. St Margaret's, Lynn.

5. Llandaff Nave.
6. Llandaff Nave.
7. St Mary's, Shrewsbury, Nave.
8. Lichfield Nave.

below may be regarded as typical; they occur in great numbers throughout Italy and the south of France (Anderson and Spiers, 150).

Now if we decompose these Greek and Roman Corinthian capitals, we find the following elements. (1.) Supporting the abacus are the geometrical spirals or volutes. These may be greatly enlarged; and they may be covered with

SCALE OF 6 3 0   6   12 INCHES

SCALE OF 1 0 1 2 3 4 5 FEET

SCALE OF 3 0 3 6 9 12 INCHES

SCALE OF 1 0 1 2 3 FEET

Temple of the Winds, Athens.
Choragic Monument of Lysicrates, Athens.

Temple of Zeus, Athens.
Baths of Diocletian, Rome.

foliated ornament. (2.) Midway between the volutes, on the same or on a higher level, may be a rose. This is reproduced exactly in a granite capital, probably Roman, in the eleventh century cloister of LE PUY CATHEDRAL (417.3). (3.) More often, instead of a rose, there is symmetrical leafage, as in the Choragic monument. This is sometimes called the *anthemion* or *honeysuckle*; but it is just as much like palm-leaves, and may be called a *palmette*. (4.) The volutes issue from scrolls. These scrolls may be spirals, repeating on a smaller scale the volutes above, as in the Choragic monument ; or scrolls of foliage, as in the Temple of Zeus. These leaf-scrolls are much emphasised in many Norman capitals, and are of great importance as one of the origins of the Gothic foliated capital. (5.) Then comes one band or more of acanthus. (6.) Below the acanthus, in the Choragic monument, is the so-called water-leaf. (7.) In the Temple of the Winds, an exceptional example, there are no volutes : the upper part of the capital consists entirely of a row of simple pointed leaves. These remind one strongly of the lotus caps of Egypt, and the leaf may be that of the lotus. It is often assumed to be that of the plantain.

The most striking part of the capital is the band of acanthus. As to this, it is by no means certain that it is acanthus at all ; in Greek capitals, where it has sharply pointed leaves, it has been assumed to be the *Acanthus spinosus ;* but it is just as much like the sea-holly, *Eryngium maritimum ;* and still more like the leaves of the common artichoke. But it is so much conventionalised that it does not resemble any known leaf exactly. In Roman examples, *e.g.* at Tivoli and Preneste, up to about the end of the first century of our era, the acanthus was carved, as in the Choragic monument, with sharply pointed lobes and angular notches between the lobes, and with " eyes " between each group of

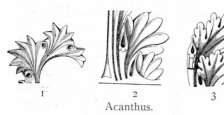

Acanthus.

lobes. And it was this Greek form of the acanthus which was employed in Byzantine work ; *e.g.* in St Sophia, Constantinople ; in the Syrian churches ; in the Golden Gate at Jerusalem ; in St Mark's, Venice. It has been assumed, therefore,* that wherever the pointed form of acan-thus occurs, there we must admit the influence of the patterns of Byzantine stuffs and ivories. Sir G. Scott recognises this form at St Front, Périgueux, *c.* 1130 ; St Denis, 1140 ; St Germain-les-Prés, Paris ; in England only in the work of William of Sens at Canterbury, and the north-west doorway of the west front of Lincoln. In both these, however, the acanthus is decidedly of the blunted type ; and no evidence of Byzantine influence in England.

In Roman work the acanthus is supposed to be the *Acanthus mollis ;* but there is really very little likeness between the two. In some instances, as in the arch of SEPTIMIUS SEVERUS (426.3), with which compare the Canterbury capital (428), it is very much like the oak leaf. When formed as at the PANTHEON (426.2), it is asserted by Sir William Chambers and Mr R. N. Wornum to be simply a bunch of olive or laurel leaves. There seems to be only one common characteristic of all the varieties of the Roman acanthus ; viz. that the tip of the lobe is never acutely pointed, as it is in Greek work.†

After the second century the Roman carvers, weary of monotonous correct-ness, altered the Corinthian and Composite capitals in the most fantastic fashion. The volutes become crouching dragons ; or eagles take the place of rose or

---

* See Sir G. Scott in *Archæological Journal*, 32, 360 ; and the numerous illustrations in his *Lectures*, i. 85.

† On the varieties of acanthus employed, see Anderson and Spiers, 149.

palmette ; or the whole capital, if for some temple of Bellona or Mars Ultor, may be composed of greaves, lances, cuirasses, and helmets ; as in the capitals re-used in S. Lorenzo, Rome. And it was this, the late and debased Corinthian-esque capital, which was being produced in every province of the Roman Empire, when the first Christian churches were built ; and which was most imitated in Northern Europe, the last provinces to be conquered ; where Corinthian capitals of the best period were few or non-existent. That being so, we need not be surprised at the vagaries of the Corinthianesque capital in Normandy and England.

It occurs in the midst of undoubted Anglo-Saxon work ; *e.g.* at Scartho, Great Hale, and Branston ; in the belfry windows of St Peter-at-Gowts and St Mary-le-Wigford, Lincoln ; in Sompting tower, where unfortunately the artist has got the volutes on one capital, and the acanthus on the other. Where such work occurs, it seems to be late ; due to contact with and direct imitation of Norman Romanesque.*

Barton-le-Street.

In the eleventh century in Normandy there is no attempt to render the intricacies of the acanthus band, with the exception of the capitals of Bernay, Bayeux, and Rucqueville, which are so exceptional that they must be by the hand of craftsmen from outside Normandy.† In the normal capital the volutes are present ; the bell is convex ; and between the volutes is usually a sort of "console" ; *e.g.* in the arches of the central tower of ST NICHOLAS, CAEN (421.2), *c.* 1083. In St John's Chapel in the Tower of London, the console takes the form of a tau. In the twelfth century the console hardly ever appears. Usually the bottom part of the capital is bare ; but sometimes, as in the crypts of the Abbaye-aux-Dames and CANTERBURY (193), and in the doorway of ST WOOLOS (421.1), Newport, Monmouth, there is a band of leafage. This may represent the lower leaves seen in the Choragic monument of Lysicrates ; but, more probably, it is acanthus leafage cut as well as the carver knew how ; not serrated, and usually without the veining. In Rome itself, in an upper story of the COLOSSEUM (430), the very same type of foliage occurs ; and here also, it is probably acanthus, roughly blocked out because it was to be seen only from a distance. Such rude caps are common in our early crypts ; there are especially fine ones at Lastingham.‡ In those portions of our Norman churches which were built in the eleventh century these Corinthianesque capitals are common ;

* See, however, Baldwin Brown's *Arts in Early England*, 161, 180.
† Ruprich-Robert, pp. 245, 65, 116.
‡ Illustrated in Britton's *Arch. Ant.*, vol. v., Plate 6.

Easington.

e.g., in the eastern limbs of Norwich and Chichester and the transept of Ely. It was not till the twelfth century that the cubical capital predominated.* The two photographs from BARTON - LE-STREET (427) and EASINGTON illustrate very well the fantasies of Norman work, as seen in many a remote village church. The latter, with its laurel or plantain† leafage, appears to be a direct descendant of the capital of the Tower of the Winds.‡ In Barton-le-Street both capitals have interlacing ornament ; one contains a mask, the other the favourite beak-head. In the capital on the left the anthemion appears below, and a symmetrical leaf-scroll above.§

After the middle of the twelfth century such rude work becomes rare ; but classical reminiscences still abound ; *e.g.* the capital from ABBEY DORE ‖ (421.3) has a small anthemion below, and a large symmetrical leaf-scroll above. The capital from OXFORD CATHEDRAL CHOIR (421.6), 1154-1180, also has the anthemion ; the large volutes at the angle are foliated ; and what is very important, the rest of the bell is ringed round

Canterbury, Capital of Saint's Chapel.

with a row of smaller volutes. The next step is seen in the capital from the NAVE (421.7) ; where the discovery has been made that a capital can be

---

* It is not intended to assert that the cubical capital was not largely employed in the eleventh century also ; it is the predominant cap in the eleventh-century work of Winchester and Durham.

† Capitals of plantain or laurel leaf occur at Battle, Tillington, Hurstmonceaux, Irthington, Fountains, and Abbey Dore.

‡ Illustrated in Sharpe's *Transitional Ornament*.

§ *Cf.* Pugin's *Gothic Ornaments*, Plate 76.

‖ *Cf.* Northorpe and Laughton in Sharpe's *Transitional Ornament*.

composed with volutes only.* These foliated volutes go by the name of crockets. All sorts of experiments with them may be watched in NEW SHOREHAM CHOIR (421.8). The cap of the cylinder is very artless; below is a symmetrical classical ornament; above is a band of crockets, all turned sideways, as if whirled round by a current of air. This "wind-blown" capital was a great favourite in the latter days of the twelfth century; *e.g.* in St Leonard's, Stamford. The capital of the OCTAGONAL PIER (423.1) has quite a Gothic appearance; nevertheless there are two small examples of the anthemion below; and above each arris of the pier is an unmistakable foliated volute or crocket. The capitals of the eastern respond are CROCKETS (423.2) and nothing else. (The classical leaf-scroll in the arches should be noted.) From this last capital it is not a long step to those of the retrochoir of the neighbouring cathedral of CHICHESTER (245), *c.* 1186: or from these to the crocket capitals of GREAT YARMOUTH (423.5) and ST MARY-LE-WIGFORD, LINCOLN (423.6). Thus then there is a lineal descent to be made out from the geometrical volutes of the Corinthian capital † of ancient Rome to the famous thirteenth-century capital of Early English and French Gothic.‡ An example from CANTERBURY (428) is illustrated; it is a magnificent specimen of the French Transitional Composite capital; but no direct imitations of these are to be found; except only at Oakham,§ and perhaps Broadwater.

So far we have spoken of the foliage of the Early Gothic capital as derived from the foliated volute of the crocket. But there is a good deal of foliage into which the form of the volute does not enter at all; *e.g.* the lower band of the capital over the octagonal pier of NEW SHOREHAM (423.1); those from CWM HIR, now at Llanidloes (422.4, 5); three from ABBEY DORE (422); two from LINCOLN (422.2 and 423.9); one from WHAPLODE WEST NAVE (423.3). These contain leafage with three or five lobes; in early work usually of three only. This capital is held to be a conventionalisation of the *Herba benedicta* or clover;‖ but the resemblance is not very marked; and if it were, it is in the highest degree unlikely that all Western Europe should hit upon such a motif almost simultaneously. Whatever the motif was, it must have been something that was in the hands of everybody already. This we hold was the leaf-scroll of the ancient Corinthian capital, *e.g.* that of the TEMPLE OF ZEUS (425), which was still in full use in the last years of the twelfth century; *e.g.* all round the late Norman trefoiled doorway in ELY CLOISTER (430)

---

* Compare the Barnack capital (695.9), and those at Polebrook (*Nene Valley*, 12). All Saints', Stamford, and Lichfield nave have good specimens.

† So also Enlart's *Manuel*, 558: "Le crochet dérive directement des volutes du chapiteau corinthien."

‡ It should be added that though it is convenient to designate this the crocket capital, it is erroneous to suppose that it is derived from the Gothic crocket proper. For the latter hardly came into existence till *c.* 1192 in the piers of Lincoln choir transept; while we have seen crocket capitals occur earlier than this, and more highly developed, at Oxford and New Shoreham. There are also several large capitals of this type in the Trinity Chapel, Canterbury. In France the crocket capital received excessive development at times; *e.g.* in Le Mans choir and the Collegiate Church of Semur-en-Auxois.

§ Colling's *Mediæval Foliage*, Plate 19.

‖ Others, with Viollet-le-Duc, regard it as an abstraction of leaf-form in general. But that seems a somewhat metaphysical conception to exist in the brain of a stone-mason.

are scrolls of trilobed leafage. Still more instructive is the work in the arches of NEW SHOREHAM CHOIR (273); where the classical and Gothic scrolls may be seen side by side. These very scrolls reappear at TILNEY ALL SAINTS'

Ely Cloister.

(423.4), c. 1180. In the upper panel * at NEW SHORE-HAM the bottom scroll is, if anything, more classical than that of the Arch of Septimius Severus (426.3); while above is a seven-lobed leaf, which would be at home in any thirteenth-century capital. In the lower panel is a compound leaf composed of two trefoils; and even marked by the bold projecting midrib which is so characteristic of our Early Gothic foliage. With the New Shoreham scrolls should be compared the Early Gothic scrolls (431). On the whole we may conclude that the Early Gothic leaf capital is the result arrived at by a long series of modifications of the combination of a simplified form of the Roman acanthus scroll, with a foliated form of the Roman Composite volute.

In some cases the leaf-scroll, in others the volute predominates; e.g. in OXFORD TRANSEPT (423.8), as in St Leonard's and All Saints', Stamford, there are two bands of small leaf-scrolls, and the volute type is hardly perceptible at the corners. In the two small capitals from the arcading of St Hugh's work at LINCOLN (422.2, 423.9) there is no trace at all of the volute; while in the capitals from the chancel arch of WEST WALTON (432) and the chapter house of Salisbury, and that from the arch leading into the Lincoln choir aisle, c. 1240, the volute is predominant. In Ely galilee, the two forms occur side by side, as they do in Auxerre choir; the volutes on the right, the scrolls on the left capital.

New Shoreham.   Canterbury Choir.
                             Rome, Colosseum.

All these capitals are usually designated "stiff-leaved capitals." And in the early examples they are stiff indeed; e.g. at NEW SHOREHAM, Whaplode, and Cwm Hir. But nothing can surpass the

* For the classical scroll see Brandon's *Analysis*, Semi-Norman, 2

free flow of curve and abandon of the later capitals ; *e.g.* those of the Chapel of the Nine Altars, Durham. In all the special characteristics are (1) that the foliage is conventional ; (2) that the stalks are always present. The object was that the foliage should seem to grow out of the shaft as naturally as the branches grow out of a tree trunk.

As to the treatment of the stalks, considerable differences prevail. Sometimes the stalk has a broad base ; and may indeed be the plantain leaf again, expanding above into a volute. This is well seen in volute caps in the Ely galilee ; so also in the tower arch of St Mary's, Stamford.* Somewhat similar are the sturdy stalks of the Durham capitals. There can be no doubt that

1. Salisbury. 2, 3. Stone. 4. Wells.

massiveness of stalk greatly adds, both in reality and to the eye, to the adequacy of the volutes to perform their functions as corbels to the abacus. It is far more common in French than in English Gothic. More often, our stalks are somewhat flat and characterless ; and in early work, especially in west country Gothic, as at Cwm Hir, Abbey Dore, Llandaff, they are often mere slender pipings or ribs, barely perceptible on the bell.

The extent of projection given to the volutes is a mark of the amount of skill reached by the carvers ; foliage of great projection does not occur in early work ; though the reverse is not necessarily true ; *e.g.* compare the capitals of

* Illustrated in *Nene Valley*, Plate 73.

Wells choir with those of the transept and nave which were built later. So again the little capitals (1190) from Lincoln cling lovingly to the bell ; great is the advance in such a capital as that of WEST WALTON (422.1). From their small projection the capitals of Cwm Hir and Abbey Dore may well have been executed before the twelfth century was complete.

The direction which the foliage takes should be noted. In the twelfth-century capitals and a little later it usually tends to be vertical ; *e.g.* the Lincoln arcading ; Cwm Hir ; Abbey Dore ; Wells ; Llandaff. But the early foliage sometimes swirls round ; *e.g.* at NEW SHOREHAM (421.8) ; ABBEY DORE (422.8) ; St Leonard's, Stamford ; Jedburgh ; Moulton ; and the porch of St Mary Redcliffe, Bristol ; * less often in later work, *e.g.* Southwell choir, Lichfield nave. In Lincoln presbytery it runs round both ways. In the end the favourite design was for the foliage to rise up to support the abacus, and then to fall over in heavy clusters, as at West Walton and the doorway of Lincoln choir aisle.

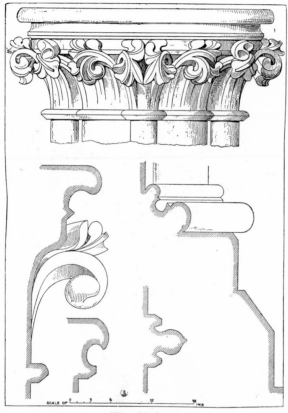

West Walton.

So again, the character of the scrolls employed is significant. It is only in early work that such small stiff trefoils, quatrefoils, and cinquefoils are employed as those of Cwm Hir ; Holyrood ; Lincoln arcading ; Whaplode ; Haverfordwest doorway ; Abbey Dore ; the corbels of Ryland, Rievaulx, and WHITBY (433) choirs ; the vaulting shafts in the south aisle of New Shoreham ; south doorway of Valle Crucis nave ; Oxford Cathedral ; † Lichfield choir ; Deerhurst ; Broadwater. ‡

Again, in early work, if the stalks are slender, they are often allowed to intersect ; as in the New Shoreham vaulting shafts ; the corbels of WHITBY CHOIR (433) ; § Valle Crucis, south doorway ; Jervaulx chapter house. ‖ So also, where the early carvers have enough skill, the foliage itself twists and interlaces ; *e.g.* at St John's, Chester ; Whitchurch ; Shrewsbury St Mary's ; New

* Illustrated in Sharpe's *Transitional Ornament.*   † Illustrated in Prior, *Gothic Art*, 148, 149.
‡ Illustrated in Colling's *Mediæval Foliage*, 20.   § Illustrated in Sharpe's *Parallels*, Plate 118.
‖ Illustrated in Prior, *Gothic Art*, 110.

Shoreham; Chichester; Wycombe, Hospital of St John; Byland.* Especially wonderful are the capitals in the west nave of WELLS (412.6); never were capitals tangled into such exquisite grace.

THE WEST OF ENGLAND CAPITALS deserve separate notice. Till recently the importance of the early and remarkable school of the west had not been recognised.† The earliest capitals probably are those in the south nave of St Mary's, Shrewsbury, and the western bays of Worcester nave, which may be as early as 1160-1170: in both of these they are still mixed up with Romanesque motifs. Then come a most remarkable group in the very middle of Wales, in the CHURCH OF LLANIDLOES (552). Here wall-pieces of the roof rest on broken bits of vaulting-shaft; capitals, piers, and arches have been largely transposed; the piers are designed to carry an aisle-vault, which is not there; it is plain that the whole arcade was not built on the spot, but was transferred from some other building. This can hardly be other than Cwm Hir, some 20 miles distant. It was probably the largest Cistercian monastery in England or Wales, with a nave 250 feet long; even surpassing Byland. Capitals found *in situ* at Cwm Hir are precisely the same in type as those at Llanidloes. The abbey was dissolved in 1536; and the Llanidloes roof, as the shields at the ends of the beams record, was put up in 1542. Probably, the Llanidloes people, wishing to add a north aisle to their nave, transferred one bodily, except the vault, from Cwm Hir.‡

Whitby.

The work at ABBEY DORE (151.4) is of two dates: the original short choir, and its subsequent eastern extension; 412.8, 417.5, 421.3 are from the choir; the rest are from the ambulatory. The early capitals in Wells Cathedral are nearly all of the volute type. They fall into four groups: first, those of the choir, *c.* 1175, where tall volutes are mingled with short knobby ones (424.1); secondly, those of the transept, where human figures are introduced, admirably carved (424.2); thirdly, those in the east nave, where animal forms abound; fourthly, those in the west nave (412.6), where animal forms are rare; some of these last are early in type, *e.g.* 424.3; others are of most intricate design, and difficult

* Prior, 142, 146.
† See account of Wells Cathedral in *English Cathedrals Illustrated.* It is one of the special features of Mr Prior's *History of Gothic Art in England* that he has insisted on the recognition of this as a distinct school of Early English Gothic.
‡ See *Montgomeryshire Collections,* xxiv. 395-417. Giraldus Cambrensis says that Cwm Hir was founded by "Robert, son of Stephen." This was the Robert Fitzstephen who commanded the first English invasion of Ireland in 1170; he was uncle to Henry II.

execution.*   Both in Wells and Llandaff Cathedrals the capitals are unusually tall and slender.   Another common characteristic, not a pleasant one, is that the necking or astragal is sometimes omitted, as in Glastonbury choir, Hereford east transept, ST DAVID'S (412.5).   Another characteristic of the LLANDAFF CAPITALS (424.5, 6) is the great height of the stalks and the smallness of the space allotted to the foliage ; and the fact that the stalks are so diminutive. To the Llandaff type belong the beautiful capitals of the north arcade of ST MARY'S, SHREWSBURY (424.7).

NATURALISTIC CAPITALS.—The reign of conventional foliage was long. Commencing about 1170 in such examples as New Shoreham and Wells, its vogue lasted till about 1280.†   By the middle of that time it had on the

Southwell Chapter House.

whole, with such exceptions as the capitals of Durham eastern transept, settled into a fairly uniform type.   And with uniformity came monotony.   After c. 1220 it was superseded to a considerable extent, e.g. at Salisbury, Beverley, Westminster, and the Temple choir, London, by the molded capital.

As we have seen above, experiments had been made with capitals of more or less naturalistic type in the last half of the twelfth century ; e.g. the campanula and ground ivy are carved in Canterbury choir.   So again ‡ in one of the western

* Capitals from Whitchurch, Dorset, are illustrated by Mr Prior.   The interior of Whitchurch is drawn in the *Spring Gardens Sketch Book*, vi. 65.

† Naturalistic foliage occurs in abundance in the diapered spandrels of the arcade round the chapter house of Westminster ; illustrated in *John of Gaunt Sketch Book*, i. 72.

‡ Colling's *Mediæval Foliage*, Plate 15, p. 33.

capitals from CWM HIR (422.7), one knot of foliage may be seen expanding into a lily bloom. A thoroughly naturalistic capital occurs in the Lincoln chapter house, c. 1225, which it is difficult to reconcile with the thoroughly conventional foliage round it.* In the Angel triforium of the presbytery the two forms may be seen side by side again and again; here conventional, there real leafage; c. 1260. But when the east side of the cloister was built, c. 1296, the capitals become reproductions of natural foliage. EXETER CATHEDRAL (241), commenced c. 1280, is a treasure-house of beautiful naturalistic foliage, especially the corbels of the vaulting-shafts, and the bosses of the vaults (297). LICHFIELD NAVE (424.8), like Lincoln presbytery and ST MARGARET'S, LYNN (424.4), has admirable specimens both of conventional and naturalistic leafage: the latter of more advanced character than at Lincoln: a cap of lilies is shown. Early lilies, of charming type, are seen in the north porch of

Southwell Chapter House.

Bridlington and at Warmington. Later on, all kinds of leaves and berries are copied. Perhaps the most beautiful work is the leafage of the shrines of St Frideswide and ST THOMAS CANTELUPE (187) in the cathedrals of Oxford and Hereford: the former contains maple, columbine, the greater celandine, oak, sycamore, ivy, vine, fig, hawthorn, and bryony. SOUTHWELL CHAPTER HOUSE (434) is richest of all in this work. Here the skill of the craftsmanship is wonderful. If a finger be placed at the back of the leaves, it will be found that they are finished off quite smooth behind. In one instance there is an animal behind the leaves, which can only be seen by looking up from underneath.

> " In the elder days of Art
>   Builders wrought with greatest care
> Each minute and unseen part ;
>   For the gods see everywhere."

* Colling's *Mediæval Foliage*, p. 40, Plate 33, 8.

No two capitals or bosses or spandrels are alike. In the middle order of the arch of the doorway the foliage stands quite free of the hollows, and is attached only to their edges ; and the hollows themselves are as cleanly chiselled as any of exposed moldings.* Another fine set of capitals representing the Seasons, *c.* 1310, may be seen in the pier-arcade of Carlisle choir. †

Another characteristic of these capitals is that the idea of growth out of the shaft or column is no longer present. The stalks which the thirteenth-century craftsmen had been so careful to insert were now usually omitted. This had begun in the previous period. Instead of stalks, branches were carved ; branches cut off by the knife from some neighbouring tree, as may be seen in the SOUTHWELL SPANDRELS (435), and then transmuted into stone. But more often it was rather tendrils than branches that were carved ; the capital or the boss became a globular mass of interlacing tendrils and leafage like a bunch of mistletoe. That being so, the outline of the capital was changed. The thirteenth century had been careful to follow the graceful curve of an inverted bell ; now the foliage became a globular mass, all beauty of outline lost : *e.g.* the capitals of Selby choir.

UNDULATORY FOLIAGE.—After a time the fashion changed once more. Such work as that at Southwell must have been tedious and costly in the extreme. What was worse, every one had learnt the trick. So the *tours de force* of undercut foliage were abandoned, except here and there, as in the capitals of Selby and Wells choirs, and the wonderful work at the back of the reredos of Beverley Minster. ‡ And a curious change set in as regarded the contour of the leaves. Ogee curves and ogee arches had invaded the windows, the parapets, and the moldings ; it was left to introduce them into every carved leaf ; to give each curve its just counter-curve.

First of all, the undulatory movement had caught the crockets and finials ; then it appears in the diapers of the stone screens of Lincoln and Southwell Minsters ; then the capitals caught the infection. It was as if the craftsmen had grown weary of copying healthy foliage ; and picking up some leaf stung by a fly, had set to work to reproduce diseased foliage for the sake of the bulbous swellings that gave the admired ogee curve.

At first the difference was slight. All sorts of leaves are treated naturalisti-cally in the Lincoln diaper, *c.* 1325 ; but each has the undulatory curve. Still naturalistic, but more undulatory, are the misericordes of the stalls of Wells ; a little later in date. Hardly naturalistic at all, but undulatory in the extreme, are the corbels of St Stephen's Chapel, Westminster, 1348. The tendency was henceforth to restrict the reproduction to those leaves which naturally assume an undulatory form ; *e.g.* the maple, the oak, but above all, the vine leaf. Indeed, as time went on, carved leafage was limited almost wholly to running patterns of grape and leaf ; hundreds of examples of which are to be seen beneath the cornices of stone monuments and wooden screens in the work of the fifteenth and sixteenth centuries.

Frequently neither branch nor tendrils occur ; the capital consisting of nothing but isolated leaves without any visible connection with the bell ;

* Livett's *Southwell*, 111.   † They were much restored in 1803.
‡ Illustrated in Colling's *Foliage*, Plates 52, 53.

gummed on, as it were. Not infrequently, as in the capitals of the lofty piers of
Hull nave, the foliage consists of quite small, isolated leaves studded on the
bell. On the whole, the tendency was towards larger leafage. Minute work
occurs in Chester nave; and in the beautiful rose capital of PATRINGTON
below, but in the other two capitals of PATRINGTON larger leaves are employed. In the capitals from WELLS RETROCHOIR both large and small
leafage occur side by side. Even in York nave, *c.* 1300, large-leaved capitals

1. Patrington Tower Pier.
2. Patrington Nave.
3. Patrington Transept.
4. Wells Retrochoir.
5. Salhouse.
6. Tiverton.

were already employed. The Berkeley Chapel in Bristol Cathedral, *c.* 1330, is
particularly remarkable for the large size of the leafage. The capital from
SALHOUSE above well illustrates a common type of large-leaved capital;
similar capitals occur to the end of the Gothic period. In a small village church,
such as Salhouse, such large leaves are out of scale; but they are very properly
employed in the soaring pier-arcades of the greater churches of the Perpendicular period. On the whole, however, the tendency in the late parish churches

was to prefer the molded capital; good specimens of foliated capitals are rare, except in Somerset and Devon.* The example from TIVERTON (437.6) contains the passion-flower. The later examples, in most cases, show a great degeneration from the wonderful work that had been wrought in the thirteenth and fourteenth century. Somewhat monotonous, doubtless, fourteenth-century work is (and from its uniformity and monotony valuable as a chronological criterion); but criticism is dumb before the exquisite design and consummate execution of such works as the Beverley reredos; the Heckington sedilia; and that superb treasure-house of fourteenth-century craftsmanship, the LADY CHAPEL OF ELY (269). All this wealth of beauty perished in one moment, on the awful advent of the Black Death in 1349. When we began to build and carve again, it was in very different fashion, in sober Perpendicular. What English art might have developed into may be seen in the exuberance and riot of French Flamboyant.

The reign of purely naturalistic foliage was short; and being peculiarly characteristic of the period c. 1280 to c. 1315, it is often a useful criterion of chronology. As specimens of craftsmanship these carvings are simply consummate. Every capital, corbel, spandrel, boss, is a masterpiece. Nevertheless it was a mistake, and stands on a far lower level than the conventional designs which it superseded. It was a mistake to attempt to compete with nature :† man's best efforts can be no more than a coarse reminiscence of nature; the humblest herb that grows in the cranny of a wall has a beauty that man cannot emulate. The more successful he is, the more faithful, true, and exact his reproduction of leaf, berry, or bloom, the more he invites comparison with nature, and must suffer from the comparison. The more painting and sculpture resemble camera work, the less artistic they are. In all this work, workmanship had gone ahead of design. Design indeed there was none. What credit there was belonged to the mason; and to nature, who fashioned the leaf, the fruit, and the bloom.

* In Devon a wreath of flowers and foliage, sometimes with ribbons, is common round the piers in place of capitals.

† *Cf.* Barry's *Lectures*, 104.

Chapter XXIX.

THE MOLDED CAPITAL.

Part I.—The Abacus.

THE abacus is the projecting slab which rests on the capital. It was made to project for two reasons; sometimes to enable a small capital and pier to support the springings of two broad arches; sometimes that its projection might give supports for the planks or centering, while the arches were being built.

In plan the Early Norman abaci were square. But soon after 1089 cylindrical piers of the West of England have circular abaci; *e.g.* Malvern, TEWKESBURY (297), Gloucester, Shrewsbury. At DURHAM (239), in 1093, cylindrical piers have octagonal abaci; so also at Buildwas. In the eastern aisle of ELY TRANSEPT (412.1), soon after 1090, the abacus is cruciform; so also in Peterborough choir and Melbourne. Good examples of the subdivided abacus occur also in Norwich* (commenced in 1096), in the eastern pier of the triforium arcade, and in the piers of the nave arcade. It is remarkable to find abacus and capital subdivided so early, each part having its own special function. At Peterborough one part carries the roofing shaft; another the transverse rib of the aisle-vault; two more its two diagonal ribs; the remaining four carry the two orders of each pier-arch.†

The upper surface of the Norman and Transitional abacus, up to *c.* 1180, was always horizontal, and its face was vertical; *i.e.* it was square-edged, not rounded. In Normandy in the eleventh century the under surface was always either a straight or a hollow chamfer.‡ The hollow chamfer occurs in our Anglo-Saxon abaci; *e.g.* Wing nave and Deerhurst. Good examples of both forms of chamfer occur in the west front of Lincoln. Not very much was done by the Normans § in molding the abacus; molded capitals they did not employ at all in their Romanesque. The molded capitals of the Gloucester type are rather imposts than capitals.

The use of an abacus square in plan differentiates not only English Romanesque from English Gothic; but also English from French Gothic. The circular abacus is no doubt more in harmony with the general elimination

---

* Both are illustrated in Britton's *Norwich*, Plate 21.

† "These Peterborough vaults are, for the epoch, designed and executed with more science and precision than those of the Domaine Royal of France or of Champagne or of Burgundy or of Central France. When this construction is compared with the contemporary work in France, one is astonished at the science and experience of the Anglo-Norman builders; who already, at the beginning of the twelfth century, were in a position to construct vaults with diagonal ribs, and who divided their capitals into as many parts as there were arches to receive" (Viollet-le-Duc, *Architecture*, iv. 101, 103).

‡ Ruprich-Robert, i. 124.   § Advanced specimens are seen at NEWPORT (421.1, 5).

1. Canterbury East Crypt.
2. Ketton.
3. Wisbech.

4. Shrewsbury Abbey.
5. Trunch.
6. Etchingham.

of rectangular forms from Gothic generally. And in some situations, *e.g.* in a re-entering angle over an angle shaft, the square abacus looks awkward, and room can hardly be found for it. On the other hand, it is useful, when set obliquely, to point out the direction of the diagonal ribs of a vault; it allows what is sometimes desirable, the retention of square with circular moldings in the arch; or, as at Wells, in the pier; and its square form presents a much more vigorous and emphatic stop to the moldings of arch above and pier below. Our abolition of the square abacus was by no means an unmitigated gain.*

The history of the English molded capital commences about the middle of the twelfth century: and as the earliest examples seem to occur in Cistercian abbeys—Buildwas, Fountains, Kirkstall, Furness, Byland, Jervaulx, in which the Cistercian objections to carving were at first carefully respected—it may well be due in part to the efforts of the English Cistercians to find a simple and effective substitute for the enriched Norman capitals which were being carved elsewhere. Outside these abbeys it seems not to occur till it is employed between 1154 and 1181 by the Secular Canons of Ripon, who had the Fountains capitals hard by to study; and by the Benedictines of Canterbury. In CAN-TERBURY (334) it occurs chiefly in the eastern part of the crypt, which was not commenced till the departure of the French architect, William of Sens, in 1179.

In Norman days the early abacus was square-edged, as at CANWICK (685.1), with a deep vertical face. The first step to lighten this clumsy form was to cut an angular nook (*quirk*) at the bottom of the face: as at HARMSTON (2). So also at WHAPLODE (3), where the depth of the face is further reduced by cutting a larger quirk.† But the Norman abacus often had beneath it a hollow chamfer instead of a straight slope; introduce this, and we arrive at the abacus of BUILDWAS, FOUNTAINS, KIRKSTALL (20, 21, 22). Add a small roll (*bead*) beneath the hollow, and we have the fully developed Transitional abacus, as it appears at ASWARBY, FURNESS, and BYLAND (5, 23, 24). The next step was to round off the upper edge of the abacus; and, secondly, to undercut it with a small hollow to get a narrow band of intense shadow: these two steps were probably taken in some districts just before 1190: *e.g.* at HORBLING and WHAPLODE (9, 8). Finally, lighten the upper member and give it more projection, and we arrive at the simplest type of Early Gothic abacus, that of LINCOLN (12).

The final emergence of the Early Gothic type of abacus, *c.* 1190, is marked by another very important change; its plan was changed, not merely its profile. Hitherto, most eleventh and twelfth century abaci had been square on plan; now, for a long period, except over octagonal piers, the Early Gothic abacus was to be circular on plan. This then is the outcome of the evolution; a light abacus, circular in plan, with its edge rounded, *i.e.* molded; and deeply undercut.

* See Sir G. Scott's *Lectures*, i. 156.
† This quirk is often useful in distinguishing true Norman work from later forms. The square-edged abacus *may* be late; the quirked abacus not.—R. P. B.

PART II.—MOLDED CAPITALS.

Below the semi-Norman abacus came the capital, which, as in Norman work, was cut in a separate block; see DEEPING ST JAMES (685). At the foot of this block, at its junction with the shaft, was the astragal or necking. This was usually semi-hexagonal, as at Deeping St James; or semicircular, as at FURNESS (23). Between the abacus and astragal there was usually a bare hollow chamfer. So that, starting from the top, in Transitional work, the usual order is abacus, side-hollow, necking. These hollow-necked capitals are of very ancient date outside England. They occur in the nave of St Etienne, Nevers (choir dedicated in 1099);[*] they are common quite early among the Mendicant Orders, who had taken them from the Cistercians.[†] English examples are seen at Ripon, Byland, Furness, Holme, Cultram, Old Malton, Darlington, Roche, Hartlepool, in the North of England; Navenby, Deeping St James, and Market Deeping, in Lincolnshire; and even in the Early Gothic work of Rochester Cathedral. In the Deeping caps only the lower part of the bell has the hollow chamfer. It is possible that the bare hollow bell may have been intended to be painted, as were some of the Norman cushion capitals.[‡]

THIRTEENTH-CENTURY CAPITALS.—I. As we saw above, these capitals, on plan, are usually circular. This distinguishes them from the earlier capitals, Norman and Transitional, which are usually square on plan. Of the later capitals, those of the fourteenth century are generally circular; the later ones circular or octagonal. II. Again, up to *c.* 1180, the upper edge of the abacus is always square; but from *c.* 1180 to *c.* 1360, it is nearly always rounded;[§] after *c.* 1360 it has often a straight chamfer. III. As for the profile of the Early Gothic abacus, it varies immensely, as in the Lincolnshire examples: more than a score forms might be described. Nevertheless it is quite distinct from the fourteenth-century capitals: in which the abacus nearly always has a scroll molding whose inner surface is an oblique ogee curve, and beneath this a small roll. The nearest approach to this is such a cap as that of Stickney and Lincoln;[‖] where, however, the ogee curve lies horizontally, not obliquely, and below it is not a roll, but a hollow.[¶] IV. The one mark of marks, however, is the presence of a *hollow* cut beneath the abacus to give a narrow band of shadow. In the later capitals this hollow is replaced by a small roll. In this respect capital and base to some extent reflect one another. The undercut abacus of the thirteenth century answers to the waterholding base; and the fourteenth-century capital to the base with triple roll.[**] In some cases, however, the hollow is not marked very decisively; sometimes it may even be absent, or

---

* Illustrated in Dehio, Plates 309 and 460.   † Dehio, ii. 579.

‡ The abaci in the south doorway of Barnack have red painted chevrons, still clearly visible.—R. P. B.

§ The fourteenth-century capitals at Oakham have square-edged abaci.—R. P. B.

‖ Illustrated in Paley's *Moldings*, x. 9, 12.

¶ There is, however, one among the capitals of Threckingham south doorway, *c.* 1250, which is of fourteenth-century type; illustrated in Bowman and Crowther, Plate 8.

** These last, however, are not quite contemporaneous; the triple roll of the base came into general use some time before the fourteenth-century capital.

its place may be supplied by a quirk.*   And it must be remembered that the hollow beneath the abacus occurs, not infrequently, in the fourteenth century; *e.g.* in the dated examples of Hingham and Harleston; and even in later work, at Lowick.†   V. Since the hollow is set under the abacus, a large space intervenes between it and the necking, *e.g.* in DURHAM EAST TRANSEPT (689.3).   Not infrequently, therefore, two projecting members are set in this space; and thus what is called a double capital is formed, *e.g.* WARMINGTON and WIGGENHALL ST MARY (689.6, 8).   In later capitals the hollow does not commence till much lower down, and therefore the double cap becomes rare.   VI. The *midroll* or rolls vary in form; but the most common is a roll with a fillet or fillets: as at Warmington and Wiggenhall.   VII. The astragal or necking is almost as protean as the abacus: it was evidently a time of experiment; the builders were trying all sorts of experiments in light and shade.   VIII. A band of carved ornament was often inserted; either nail-bead, as at KETTON (440.2), or tooth.

FOURTEENTH-CENTURY CAPITALS (*c.* 1315 to *c.* 1360).—A great gulf separates the early from the late molded capitals.‡   In the first place the double capital of the thirteenth century becomes rarer; but a dated example, 1325, occurs at Harleston,§ at Yaxley, Harringworth,‖ and elsewhere.   In late examples the tendency is to reduce the number of projecting members to two.   Secondly, the capitals have less spread than before; that from TILTEY (691.13) is notably narrow.   Thirdly, the upper member is no longer an abacus, cut out of a separate block; and separated from the midroll by a deeply upward cut hollow; though there are exceptions; *e.g.* Hingham, 1316-1359.   As the upper member is no longer an abacus, it is better to give it a distinct name—"upper roll."   Fourthly, the position and direction of the upper hollow is changed.   Apparently it was thought better to begin it lower down, so as to make the upper band of shadow more central; moreover it was cut sideways instead of upward.   Thus the "upper roll" becomes a much broader member than the thirteenth-century abacus had been.

Normally, the typical capital, shown diagrammatically in the example from CHIPPING HILL (444), consists of five parts, viz. three projecting members, separated by two hollows.   (1.) Almost always the upper edge, as in all the thirteen capitals illustrated, has the scroll-molding.   Beneath the scroll, as in all the thirteen examples, is almost always an ogee curve running obliquely. Beneath this is usually a small semicircular roll; HECKINGTON TOWER (691.5), exceptionally, replaces the ogee and roll by a double ogee.   Beneath this is generally a vertical fillet, in a plane with the arch above, as in all the thirteen examples.   (2.) Then comes the small upper hollow, cut sideways.   TILTEY (13) is an exception.   (3.) Then comes the midroll; which takes all sorts of

* Paley's *Moldings*, x. 16, 17, 34; and Bowman and Crowther's *Churches*, Frampton, 5.
† *Nene Valley*, Plate 60.
‡ Only the first thirteen capitals on page 691 belong to this period.   The three Rushden capitals, 14, 15, 16, are transitional in character, and were probably executed after 1360. They diverge in several respects from the typical fourteenth-century capital, and may be left out of account for the present.
§ Illustrated in *Churches of Northants*, 270.
‖ Illustrated in Paley's *Moldings*, 78.

eccentric shapes; but most often consists of a scroll with a fillet beneath, as, *e.g.* in Swayton, Sleaford, Heckington nave, Leadenham, Asgarby, Holbeach; or of some form of ogee roll with central fillet, as in Heckington chancel. (4.) Then comes the bell; a long shallow hollow, sometimes undercut above, to hold shadow. (5.) Finally, the astragal or necking also is almost always a scroll; as in all the thirteen examples, except LEADENHAM (8). It will be seen that the characteristic *par excellence* is the scroll-molding; in the capitals at Swayton, Sleaford, Heckington nave, Chipping Hill, Asgarby, and Holbeach, it occurs thrice. Three examples of double capitals are illustrated from Rushden; their general effect is similar to that of the TRUNCH CAPITAL (440.5). The characteristic of the fourteenth-century caps is their remarkable uniformity; at this period alone there was one normal standard design of molded capital.

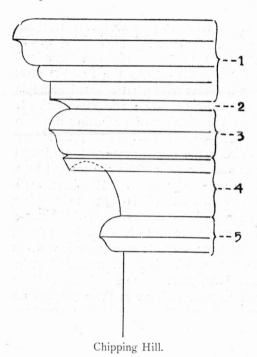

Chipping Hill.

FIFTEENTH AND SIXTEENTH CENTURY CAPITALS.—These, on the other hand, vary so much that it is difficult to characterise any one as a normal type. I. One great difference is in their *plan*. Hitherto most Norman capitals had been square in plan, and Gothic capitals circular; unless the pier itself was octagonal, when it usually had an octagonal cap. The chief exceptions occur when the shafts are small; as in arcading; *e.g.* octagonal caps occur over semi-circular shafts in the Gothic arcading of Peterborough west front, and of the walls of Fountains choir and Histon transept, near Cambridge.* When, however, an octagonal capital occurs over a cylindrical pier or column, the presumption is that it is of the fifteenth or sixteenth, or at any rate late in the fourteenth century. II. Also the number of projecting members in the capital tends to diminish. In the thirteenth century there were three, and not unusually four rolls; in the fourteenth century usually three; but in late work, as at TERLING (693.1) and CHELMSFORD PORCH (3), often only two. Out of thirty-four late capitals figured in Paley's *Moldings*, about one-half have two; one-half three rolls. III. The top edge of the upper roll, in the fourteenth century, *e.g.* at CHIPPING HILL, had been almost invariably a scroll. This hardly ever occurs afterwards. If the upper rolls of Terling and Chipping Hill be compared, it will be seen that each has an inverted ogee on a small roll on a vertical fillet on a hollow; but there is one important difference. It is that, *e.g.* at TERLING (1) and INGATESTONE (6), the curved top edge has been straightened. Probably 50 per cent. of Perpendicular capitals

* Paley's *Moldings*, 79.

start with this straight slope.* A second type, seen at ST MARY'S, OXFORD (693.2), and in CHELMSFORD PORCH (3), resembles a keel-mold whose point has either been rounded off or replaced by a fillet; in this capital the upper slope has the ogee curve instead of being straight. In the third type the upper member is a roll; and beneath it is a fillet set obliquely; e.g. BOCKING (7) and CHELMSFORD CHANCEL (4). Fourthly, the profile of the upper member may even be square, like that of a Norman abacus: and various other forms occur. IV. The midroll, where it occurs, varies greatly. V. (1) The astragal is often a simple semicircular roll, as in thirteenth-century work; e.g. Terling and ST ALPHEGE, CANTERBURY (446). Another early type, the semi-hexagon, or a variation of it, may occur.† Or it may be a repetition of the second type of upper roll; e.g. in Chelmsford porch, upper roll and astragal are

identical; so also at ELTHAM (5). Or the upper edge of the last type may have a straight chamfer, as at Bocking; or a hollow chamfer, as in CHELMSFORD CHANCEL (4). VI. Very often Perpendicular capitals are narrower and smaller than their predecessors.

ORIGIN OF MOLDED CAPITALS. — The molded capital is probably of composite origin. It was not uncommon to leave the detail of Romanesque capitals to be painted; as may be seen in the eastern aisle of Ely transept. And the reaction against sculptured imagery and artistic extravagance in church work which was pro-

Wells.

moted among the Cistercians by St Bernard led his Order to abandon foliated capitals, and to replace them either by a simple scalloped capital, as at Kirkstall, or by a naked bell, as at Fountains. It was, however, a considerable step further to mold this bell; especially when, as in Canterbury choir, it was of hard marble from Bethersden, Petworth, or Purbeck. But William of Sens "had lathes (torneumata) constructed very scientifically to shape stones" at Canterbury; they could be utilised not merely to round the smaller marble shafts, but to mold the capitals. We may, then, probably attribute the origin of moldings on a hollow-necked capital to the use of lathes.‡ In some

* The same chamfered edge occurs c. 1195 at Barnack and Orpington.

† So far as I have observed, the semihexagon is equilateral in Norman, but not in late Gothic.—R. P. B.

‡ These had been used in England long before the Conquest. The balusters of Jarrow, St Albans, Worcester, &c., could not have been molded except by lathes.

cases indeed the marks left by the counterpoint in the process of turning may be detected.* Suggestions came no doubt also from molded abacus, molded band, and molded base. In Lincoln choir the molded bands of the vaulting-shafts are in immediate juxtaposition to the molded abaci of the capitals. And the upward appeal of the molded base is for a molded, not for a foliated capital.

VALUE OF MOLDED CAPITALS.—These are almost wholly wanting in French architecture, except when the shafts are very small, as in the mullions of windows. Here, on the other hand, we have many great interiors in which the capitals of all the piers are molded: Rochester is perhaps the earliest example; Rievaulx; Beverley; Salisbury; Boxgrove; the Temple choir; St Saviour's, Southwark; Southwell; Westminster; Bridlington. The Cistercians revenged

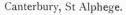

Canterbury, St Alphege.   Lavenham.

themselves in Rievaulx choir for the prohibition of foliated capitals by the unusual refinement of their moldings. The molded is, architecturally, more logical than the foliated capital. The vertical lines of a molded pier demand to be stopped above by the transverse lines of a molded capital and abacus, as they are stopped below by the transverse lines of a molded base, and midway often by those of a molded band. It may be urged also that if the capital is foliated, so also should the base. And indeed, while the "griffe" was yet in use, it frequently took the form of the same leafage as was employed in the capital; e.g. in Transitional piers both capital and plinth may be found with the characteristic water-leaf; in thirteenth-century piers, e.g. in Romsey nave, with leaf-scrolls.

* Paley's *Moldings*, 76; and his *Gothic Architecture*, 98. *Cf.* Prior, *Gothic Art*, 156.

CHAPTER XXX.

THE BASE, PLINTH, SPUR.

THE BASE.

NO member of a Gothic building perhaps obtains so little notice as the base. But of all molded members it is the most important to the archæologist; for every period has its own favourite, strongly marked, and characteristic form. At first, indeed, it received little attention from the Norman builders; but even before the eleventh century was complete, they may be seen experimenting with their bases, especially those of the smaller shafts, molding them and carving them; *e.g.* in the apses and apsidal chapels of Gloucester, Norwich, and Lessay. And indeed the base was worth attention; for it is near the eye, and every detail can be seen close at hand and fully appreciated. When this was recognised, the base rapidly grew in dimensions and importance. At DURHAM (239), in GLOUCESTER NAVE (99), even so late as the middle of the twelfth century in ST JOHN'S, CHESTER (448.1), the base is so insignificant that at a distance it is hardly noticeable. But by the middle of the thirteenth century the base had received much spread, *e.g.* at Ripon and TINTERN (697.7); indeed, had reached its maximum. For a practical objection to this far-spreading base could not but be felt; it occupied far too much floor space. So by the end of the thirteenth century it begins to retreat inward; and in the fifteenth and sixteenth century it reaches a minimum of projection, as in the nave piers of BEVERLEY ST MARY (697.20). On the other hand, in late work, by compensation, it is glorified in height; it rises in the fourteenth century, and in the fifteenth and sixteenth still more; set base upon base, plinth upon plinth, as in the five last bases (697). No doubt also a practical reason contributed very largely to the heightening of the later bases; it was that fixed seats had become common; there are great numbers of them left in the East Anglian churches, *e.g.* Tuddenham; Dennington; Wiggenhall St Mary the Virgin and St Germans; KILKHAMPTON, CORNWALL (568); in these the base could not be seen, unless it was set on a tall plinth so as to overtop the benches.* The height then of the base is not controlled by the dimensions of the pillar, as in Greek, Roman, and Renaissance work; however high and massive the pillar of a Gothic arcade may be, its base does not rise higher

* When Sir Christopher Wren built his London churches after the Great Fire, he followed the same principle. The pews of the day were exceedingly high; but he kept his bases above their tops. Where the pews have been cut down, as at St Stephen's, Walbrook, and his naked plinths have been exposed, the result is disastrous.

1. St John's, Chester.
2. Southwell Choir.
3. Louth Chancel.

4. Tewkesbury Porch.
5. Ash.
6. Cirencester Nave.

than the tops of the benches. In classical work, however, where the piers are of great size, the bases have to be raised proportionately; so that very logically, but inartistically, they are sometimes above the heads of the observer; *e.g.* at St Peter's, Rome. Such gigantic bases could be appreciated only if there were giants about. An exceptionally early example of a tall Gothic base is figured from the TEMPLE CHOIR, *c.* 1240 (689.4).

A great amount of thought was put into this humble member of the building. In the first place, it was necessary that the base should have some relation to the capital. The first Norman caps were immensely heavy and clumsy; *e.g.* PETERBOROUGH (318); and the bases ridiculously small. In logic, since the base has more to carry than the capital, it ought to be at least as large. But a big base is an awkward obstruction to an interior, and so the cap was usually larger than the base; this is well seen in the cap and base from the Temple, and those from St Mary's, Oxford, *c.* 1492. That raises another question. Ought a molded base to reflect the design of that of the molded capital, or *vice versâ?* It certainly does in the two examples cited above. Occasionally indeed the base is simply the cubical cap inverted. No doubt also facility of execution had a great deal to do with determining the profile of a base. Viollet-le-Duc (695) illustrates the successive steps by which an early molded base may be got out of two square blocks. In all the five diagrams, AB is supposed to be left square, to serve as a plinth. First, a cylinder is formed out of the upper square block; and then the upper part of it is cut back so as to form the smaller cylinder DE. Second, the groove F is cut back all round the small cylinder. Third, the angles at G and H are chamfered off.* Fourth, the nicks I, K, L, M are cut round the two cylinders. Fifth, IK, KL, LM are rounded off; so that KL forms a hollow or "scotia"; while IK, LM are rolls or "bowtells." Evidently, such bases as those of BOXGROVE NAVE (3, 4) might easily be obtained by such a process; so also the characteristic Early Gothic bases, *e.g.* at Fountains. And a base, that could be obtained so simply, would be preferred to one more difficult to work.† Moreover, the knowledge of how to produce such a base would be a workshop secret or recipe. The mediæval masons, no doubt, had a large number of trade secrets of this sort pertaining to their craft, which they guarded as jealously as a modern workman does. And, like a modern workman again, having got with some trouble into the habit of doing a thing in a particular way, the natural indolence of human nature would cause them to persist in that way. Traditions of craftsmanship are not lightly broken with. They pass on from one generation to another; from father to son and grandson. So there is nothing surprising in the fact, *e.g.* that the WATERHOLDING BASE (2) which came into use *c.* 1150 was still not wholly discarded *c.* 1260; *i.e.* it was the heritage of more than three generations of craftsmen.

There was still the artistic side of the question; beauty of form, good proportion, and above all, play of light and shade had to be secured. The last—the production of shadow effects—must have been a great worry. If

---

* Sometimes the upper roll, as in the second Boxgrove example (4), sometimes the lower roll, sometimes both, are left chamfered, not rounded off.

† This is true, of course, not only of bases, but of all molded work.

you look up at a molded cap or abacus or string or rib or arch, the shadows are on the underneath side ; and as you are looking from the underneath side, you can see and enjoy them. In a molded base or in a ground-course, the shadows are also on the underneath side of the rolls ; but unless you lie on your back on the pavement, you cannot see them. It was distinctly a puzzle then, how to make base-shadows visible from above. For about a hundred years, as above, the problem was solved by the waterholding base. A bad solution it was from every point of view but the artistic. If such a base is placed outside a building, *e.g.* under the shafts of a doorway, the hollow fills with rain and snow ; and the base soon must disintegrate ; indeed few of these external bases have survived. While, if the base be inside the church, it fills up with dust and dirt, and where then are the shadow effects? It is very seldom indeed that one finds the mediæval builder putting art in front of construction ; and the fact that he did so in the case of the water-holding base, is a witness to the great importance that he attached to play of light and shadow. By the middle of the thirteenth century, however, the hollow fills up ; and for about a century the base is often comparatively shadow-less, *e.g.* at Southwell and TINTERN (697.7). But before this a new idea had struck the builder. It was to let the base oversail the plinth ; as at TINTERN (8); then the base shadows the plinth below ; and most of the shadow can be seen from above. Here again the builder prefers art to construction ; for it is not good construction to make the plinth narrower than the base. An early ex-ample of this treatment is seen in SALISBURY CLOISTER (1); in late work the narrow octagonal plinth beneath the overhanging lower roll of the base is exceedingly common. It is well seen at LOUTH (23), BEVERLEY ST MARY (20), ARUNDEL (22), and COLCHESTER (24).

The plinth or pedestal too has its special history, dictated partly by practical, partly by artistic reasons. In Norman work it is generally square. Next, the edges were chamfered off, and the square plinth became octagonal. The octagonal plinth grew more and more common till about 1250; it is still retained in Westminster nave. For about another century the plinth more often follows the outline of the pier, in order to take up as little floor space as possible. In the following period, *c.* 1315 to *c.* 1360, the octagonal plinth comes into general use again ; the slenderness of these late plinths causing the octagon to waste but little space. In later work the plinth is almost always octagonal ; *e.g.* at LOUTH and CIRENCESTER (448.3, 6).

We may now attempt to follow out the history of the base in chronological order :—

BASES OF THE ELEVENTH AND TWELFTH CENTURIES.—In Early Norman work the moldings of the base are often but mere surface scratches; *e.g.* Hereford choir aisles. Sometimes there is nothing but a straight chamfer, as in the Caen abbeys ; or chamfers and a roll. More often the chamfer is hollow ; and there may be two hollow chamfers superposed ; as at Jumièges. Or there may be a hollow chamfer on a roll, as in Peterborough nave and at CASTLE HEDINGHAM (695.5). Rarely the "pudding-base," a single clumsy roll, is found ; it may possibly be a survival of the Tuscan base of Rome ; it occurs in Oxford Cathedral south transept, and is not uncommon as a base or a capital in Anglo-Saxon work; *e.g.* in Worcester slype. Insignificant as the Norman bases usually are, it is evident that in some places a good deal of attention was being given to them even in the eleventh century. There are many varieties of base in the crypts of Rochester and Worcester;* in CANTERBURY CRYPT (193) many of Lanfranc's bases were recut and improved in the twelfth century.

The most interesting base of all, and one that is by far the most common on the Continent in Romanesque, owing to the greater survival there of Roman examples, is the famous ATTIC BASE (695.1) of ancient Greece; which consists in the main of two rolls, the bottom one having the greater projection, separated by a hollow or *scotia*. The examples from TEWKESBURY PORCH (448.4) are grotesque enough; nevertheless, they are, as far as the mason knew how, Attic bases. But in the later Norman examples from CASTLE HEDINGHAM (695.5) and BOXGROVE (3, 4), the resemblance is very close. Then comes an important change. In the brilliant sun of Greece, the side-hollow gave an adequate shadow effect. Here it was ineffective. So the hollow begins to be cut more downward than sideways. It only remains to undercut deeply, and the Attic is transformed into the Early Gothic "water-holding" base.

This waterholding base occurs at Kirkstall † *c.* 1155, and continued in vogue for more than a century. But one curious difference is almost always present between the bases of *c.* 1155 to *c.* 1190 and later ones; it is that in the earlier work the lower roll is generally elliptical in section; it is somewhat flattened, as if it felt and partially succumbed under the heavy weight it has to bear. This is well seen in the base from ST JOHN'S, CHESTER (448.1); and in the profiles of those from JERVAULX and FURNESS (695.8, 6). The flattening of the lower

Canterbury Choir.

roll is very well marked in many bases of Canterbury Choir, as in those of Sens. A good example is illustrated from BARNACK (695.9), where the foot-ornament or *griffe* consists of the water-leaf which occurs within the same limits of time as the flattened lower roll (416).

BASES OF THE THIRTEENTH CENTURY.—From *c.* 1190 till it disappears towards the end of the thirteenth century, the waterholding base usually has lower rolls of semicircular instead of elliptical section; *e.g.* at WEST WALTON (432), Whitby, Fountains, Netley, Bridlington. The great spread of these bases is seen in the example from WHITBY (687.1). At this period both a double-molded capital and a double-molded base is not uncommon; as in ASH CHURCH, KENT (448.5), where the plinth is not octagonal, but follows the plan of the base and pier. In CANTERBURY CHOIR the deep bands of shadow are emphasised; base and plinth are doubled; and the plinths are concentric with the bases and shafts. It should be noticed that, almost invariably, the large spreading lower roll is worked out of the block (with which it usually stands

* Six from Worcester are illustrated in Rickman, 85. See Ruprich-Robert, Plates 220-226, for the variety of bases in the Abbaye-aux-Dames, Caen.

† Illustrated in Sharpe's *Arch. Parallels*, Plate 99.

flush, *i.e.* in the same plane) by a *quirk, i.e.* an angular nook ; * *e.g.* at Whitby, Fountains, Netley, Bridlington.

About the year 1240 the waterholding base begins to be largely supplanted by the base with double or triple roll, which is well seen in SOUTHWELL CHOIR (448.2) ; it abounds in Westminster. It is still in great vogue in the first half of the fourteenth century : *e.g.* at BOTTISHAM (697.19). An early example is seen in the TEMPLE CHURCH, *c.* 1240 (689.4), where it has a triple roll. The same type appears in the massive piers, *c.* 1290, of the tower of Merton College Chapel, Oxford. Less often, there are two, not three rolls, as in WINCHELSEA SEDILIA (697.3). The practical objections to the waterholding base and the difficulty and cost of working it probably led to its disuse ; and the new base may be regarded as an improved version of it ; the two rolls being brought close together, as in 3, or the hollow being filled up with an intermediate roll, making three in all. Or it may be of a more ancient descent ; for there is a Romanesque triple roll base, which occurs sporadically ; *e.g.* in the ninth-century tower of S. Satiro, Milan ; † in the crypt of St Benoît-sur-Loire ; ‡ in the crypts of Rochester and Worcester ; and the western doorways of Lincoln. Other peculiarities connected with the triple or double roll base are its great projection ; early examples are often as broad as they are high ; that it usually stands on a concentric and not on an octagonal plinth : *e.g.* Merton ; and that in later examples it often oversails the plinth.

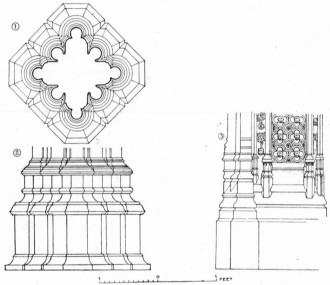

1, 2. Beverley Minster, Back of Reredos.
3. Rochester, Doorway to Chapter House.

BASES OF THE FOURTEENTH CENTURY.—The following century is characterised by ogee arches and ogee curves all over the church. For a time the triple roll base held its ground, as at BOTTISHAM (697.19) ; but in the end the contours of the base of this period came to consist almost entirely of reversed ogees ; or wave-moldings, of which there are two in the Bottisham example. Moreover, it began to contract ; and as it contracted in breadth, it rose in height. Thirdly, the octagonal plan of plinth was reverted to. All these three characteristics are retained in fifteenth-century work, but with certain additions. The bases of the fourteenth-century period may be regarded as transitional between

---

* Paley's *Moldings*, 86.   † Illustrated in Rivoira, i. 276.
‡ Illustrated in Enlart's *Manuel*, 368.

the triple roll base and the later base; *i.e.* they are but imperfect specimens of the latter;* so long as they retain the triple roll, and have considerable spread, they attach themselves to the earlier type; but when they abandon the triple roll, when they introduce ogee or undulatory curves, when they become narrow and tall, when they rise from octagonal plinths, when the base oversails the octagonal plinth, they are tending fast to the later type. In the example from the back of BEVERLEY REREDOS (452) it is only necessary to elongate base and plinth, diminishing the spread, to have a close approximation to the typical late base. An example of the ogee curve occurs at LEADENHAM (697.14); and of the wave-molding at SLEAFORD (17) and BOTTISHAM (19); all these have considerable spread. The bases from the doorway to the CHAPTER HOUSE, ROCHESTER (452), are thoroughly late in type; they are generally attributed to Bishop Hamo de Hythe, who died in 1352. Caveler assigns them to his successor, John de Sheppey (1352-1360).

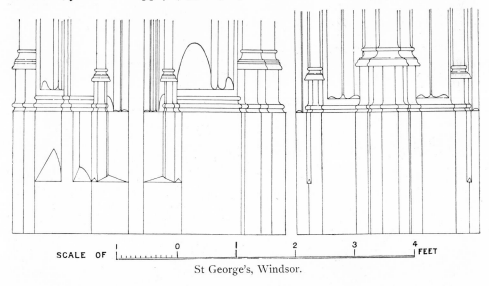

SCALE OF 0 1 2 3 4 FEET

St George's, Windsor.

FIFTEENTH AND SIXTEENTH CENTURY BASES.—With these, as with their ground-courses, the later builders were peculiarly successful; the best examples are exquisite in proportion; and have a delightful flow of curve, gradation of shadow, and nice contrast of octagon and circle. Their tall and slender proportions distinguish them from most of their fourteenth-century brethren. The base of the nave of BEVERLEY ST MARY (697.20) may be regarded as fairly typical. There are four members—A, the base; B, the upper octagonal plinth; C, the molded plinth, separated from B by a hollow chamfer, *d*, and from D by a quirk, *f*; and D, the lower octagonal plinth, the lower part of which is omitted in the diagram. The base A oversails the upper plinth, B. The roll of the molded plinth, C, is flush with the lower octagonal plinth, D. The base, A, has a roll, *a*, at the top; the isolation of this annular roll is very characteristic of the style. Usually, as at Beverley, it is semicircular; but it may be a debased form of

* On the other hand, the later molded caps are degenerate specimens of the perfect ones of the fourteenth century.

the scroll-molding; or, as at COLCHESTER (697.24), a debased roll and fillet. At
the bottom of the base A is another roll, *c*. The space between is usually filled
in, if there is room, with a "bracket" (double ogee), or some modification of
a bracket, *b*. As a whole, the base is bell-shaped. Some such profile,
contracted in small examples, heightened in large ones, is the normal one.
Sometimes, as in ARUNDEL NAVE (22), the molded plinth, C, is omitted.
In a tall example, such as the bases of the piers of LOUTH STEEPLE (23), an
additional octagonal plinth, E, may be added. With the Beverley base should be
compared the bases of LOUTH CHANCEL (448.3), ROCHESTER DOORWAY (452),
and ST MARY'S, OXFORD (693.2).

As was pointed out above (244), some of the Late Gothic piers contain

Base and Capital of Pier, Aldeburgh, Suffolk.

a large number of columns and shafts, and the builders took much pleasure
in composing for each, however small, a fully developed base; each strictly
proportioned in breadth to the diameter of the shaft or column which it supported. An elaborate and early example occurs in Gloucester south transept,
1330-1337. Sometimes, as in St Mary's, Oxford, and St Mary Redcliffe, Bristol,
all these bases, big and little alike, are on the same level. More often, as at
ST GEORGE'S, WINDSOR (453)* and the ROCHESTER DOORWAY (452), their
height as well as their breadth is proportioned to their load; and thus they
become of several different heights. In such a case the upper member of all—

---

* The CIRENCESTER piers and bases are illustrated on 544.

what we have called the necking—may be on the same level, and the plinths therefore descend to different levels ; and the builders found much amusement in providing for them supports at different heights (see especially the Rochester example). At Fotheringhay,* less happily, the smallest bases occur at the lowest level. In Flamboyant work, all over Europe, complicated bases occur ; care being often taken in them to give independent support to every rib of the vault, and even to the moldings of the rib.†

SPUR.—This is variously styled the spur, claw, foot ornament ; French *griffe*. It is used to fill up the unoccupied corners of a square plinth on which rests a circular base. When the plinth became octagonal, or concentric with the base, the spur naturally soon disappeared, as there was no longer room for it. Griffes are found in Roman work in a similar position ; the griffes at Spalato‡ are very similar to those of ST PETER'S, NORTHAMPTON (663.1), being geometrical in form. Pliny describes griffes of lizards and frogs ; with which may be compared those in the crypt of St Peter's, Oxford. They are common in Lombardic Romanesque ; *e.g.* in S. Ambrogio, Milan.§ In our Romanesque they increase in number with the general enrichment of Norman work towards the middle of the twelfth century. Transitional examples may be seen at BARNACK (695.9) ; and York crypt ; thirteenth-century examples at Stockbury ; ST CROSS, WINCHESTER (695) ; Romsey west nave ; and Salisbury ; in the last they even occur on a circular plinth. In France griffes occur at Sens Cathedral in the fourteenth century ; || in the fifteenth century at Pont-sur-Yonne ; and in the sixteenth at St Martin d'Auxerre and Chatel-Censoir. Griffes were especially favoured in Burgundy. ¶

* Plate 59 in *Nene Valley*.

† See illustrations of piers of St Severin, Paris ; St Lambert, Munster ; and S. Juan de los Reyes, Toledo ; in Dehio, Plate 567.

‡ Illustrated in Choisy's *Histoire*, i. 546.   § Ruprich-Robert, Plate 187.

|| Illustrated in Viollet-le-Duc, *Architecture*, vi. 52.   ¶ Enlart's *Gothique en Italie*, 279.

CHAPTER XXXI.

THE ORIGIN OF WINDOW TRACERY.

On Windows—Balustered Windows—Norman Windows—Dimensions of Opening—Early Glazing—Lancet Windows, Single and Grouped—Origin of Plate Tracery—Early Bar Tracery—Disuse of Lancets.

ROMANESQUE WINDOWS.

ONE of the earliest types of window is that in which two or more lights are separated by shafts or balusters. It is very common in the Campanili of Rome and Ravenna, and in Northern Italy; it is equally common in the Primitive Romanesque of Germany; in Anglo-Saxon and in Norman work. It occurs almost wholly in towers, e.g. ST MARY BISHOP HILL JUNIOR, YORK (457.1); the baluster not being well adapted for glazing. In all these windows the difficulty arises that the tower-wall is thick; and that when two arches are pierced through it, it is difficult to support their inner springing on the abacus of a shaft. The favourite Anglo-Saxon way out of the difficulty was to place on the shaft a long impost running the whole thickness of the wall, as at St Mary Bishop Hill Junior, York. This was not good construction, as the projecting ends of the impost were without support, and might snap off. So the Normans usually constructed a recessed arch under each of the arches, and if necessary another; i.e. they built the two window arches in two or more recessed orders; and thus the thickness of arch to be supported was little greater than that of the shaft.

From the Anglo-Saxon method of construction it followed that the shaft was placed centrally in the wall; it is designated a *midwall* shaft. In the Norman method, it was possible, according to the way the recessing was managed, either to place the shaft centrally or not. Almost always, it was placed towards the outer face of the wall; probably because it could thus be seen better, and become an effective architectural feature.*

The normal Romanesque window, however, is that which had been in use both in Roman and Byzantine work; an oblong opening, under a semicircular arch. Usually the glass was set rather close to the face of the wall; and, in order to admit as much light as possible, the opening had a broad internal splay. So that, though the window arch was small, the rear-arch was large. But the external reveal was soon increased in depth, e.g. at NORWICH (160), partly for decorative purposes; in order to admit a recessed order and jamb shafts; partly, perhaps, to protect the glass. So again at STEYNING (458) it will be seen that in the clerestory the glass is set well back from the face

* Both methods are illustrated in Baldwin Brown's *Arts in Early England*, ii. 64.

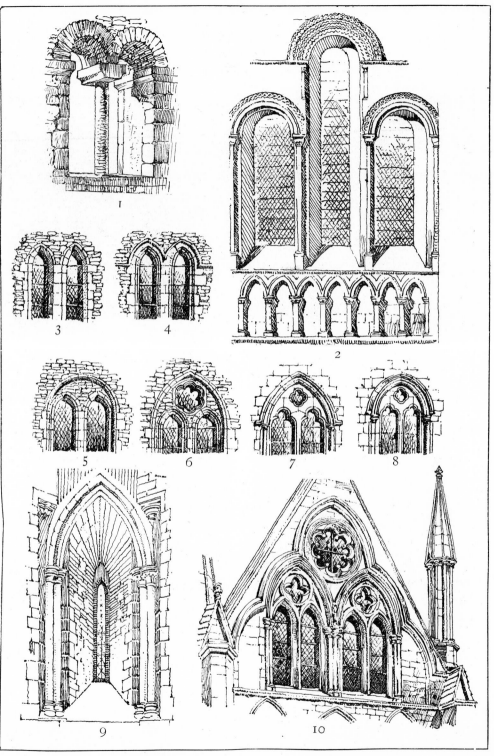

1. St Mary Bishop Hill Junior, York.
2. Romsey.
3, 4. Oxford St Giles.
5, 6. Netley.

7. Winchester Castle Hall.
8. Winchester St Cross.
9. Stanwick Tower.
10. Salisbury Cathedral Transept.

of the wall.   And occasionally well-marked instances of Norman windows occur, splayed both internally and externally; *e.g.* in the south cloister wall of Hereford, and the west cloister wall of Norwich.

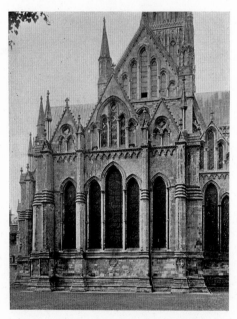
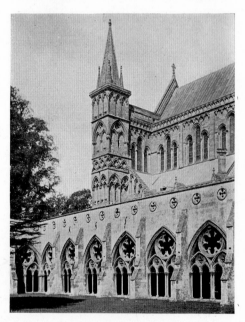

Steyning from N.E.   Towyn Nave.
Salisbury from E.   Salisbury from S.E.

The size of Romanesque windows varies curiously.   Originally they were large, as in the early Christian basilicas, and at St Généroux and the Basse Œuvre, Beauvais; and at Brixworth, which is probably seventh century.   Later, however, in many countries they become mere arrow-slits.   Perhaps the earliest examples of these are the windows of the Ravenna mausoleums of Galla Placidia, *c.* 440, and Theodoric, sixth century; where the size of aperture is evidently reduced for the sake of security. Isolated examples occur in the churches of S. Victor and S. Agatha, Ravenna, and of Bagnacavallo. An early example of the small window is at Alliata, ninth century.* In Norman work, some of these openings, *e.g.* at Nateley, Hants, and Stow, Norfolk, do not exceed a few inches in breadth, though 2 or 3 feet high. In many cases the aisle-windows are small, the clerestory windows large; *e.g.* at Secqueville in Normandy; † St Margaret at Cliffe; STEYNING (458); at Steyning the former are 1 foot broad, the latter 2 feet 9 inches. At TOWYN, NORTH WALES (458), the clerestory windows also are diminutive. Where the aisles are lofty, as in cathedrals, *e.g.* Norwich, Ely, Peterborough, the aisle-windows can be set high and therefore can be large. From these facts we would suppose that where the aisles were low, the windows were made diminutive in order to prevent pirates or thieves in general from scrambling through. It was for the same reason perhaps that Anglo-Saxon windows in general were set so very high in the wall; *e.g.* at Wing and Worth.

But it may be that peculiarities or difficulties of glazing had something to do with the diminution of the window area. It is difficult to say when glazing came into ordinary use. It was much used in the sixth century, in Byzantine churches; Wilfrid is said by Eddius and William of Malmesbury to have "provided with glass the windows of York Minster, which formerly derived their light from the transparency of linen or of boards pierced with many holes." ‡ Bede tells us that Benedict Biscop, founder of the monastery of Wearmouth, sent to Gaul in 675 for workers in glass. But it does not follow that, even in the eleventh and twelfth and thirteenth centuries, every church, great or small, glazed its windows. Indeed we know that it was not so. At Waltham and Darenth no provision was made originally for fixing panels of glass. A shutter probably was designed to close upon the rebate, which some-times may be seen worked externally in the masonry, as at Southease, Sussex.§ In the thirteenth-century chancel of Clymping, Sussex, all the windows, including the triplet of lancets in the east end, are rebated externally, and retain the hooks on which the shutters hung.‖ At the end of the twelfth century glass was still expensive. Even in the great Norman abbey of Peterborough, after the nave was finished in 1190, forty of the windows remained filled with reeds and straw to keep out the rain for another twenty

---

* Cattaneo, 239, 240.   † Ruprich-Robert, Plate 37, *bis*.   ‡ Willis' *York*, 3.

§ "At the restoration of Great Yarmouth Church in 1870 the transept windows were found never to have been glazed, but only provided with shutters" (A. W. Morant in *Norfolk and Norwich Arch. Soc.*, vii. 215). It must be borne in mind, however, that the absence of a glazing groove or *rebate* does not necessarily mean that a window was not glazed. We know that in houses, till quite a late date, the glass was often inserted in wooden frames, which were carried about by the rich from house to house. In Ely transept the glass was originally fixed in wooden frames, which were wedged into the window openings (Stewart's *Ely*, 44).

‖ Brandon's *Analysis*, 12. The great church of Constantine at Tyre, described by Bishop Eusebius, had not glass, but pierced wooden panels (Scott's *Essay*, 11). S. Miniato, Florence, eleventh century, has transparent slabs of alabaster. In Anglo-Saxon windows "the actual opening for light is at times cut in a thin slab of stone or a plank of wood built into the wall at the centre of its thickness" (Baldwin Brown's *Arts in Early England*, ii. 93).

years.* It may be, therefore, that sometimes the windows were reduced in area in the poorer churches because of the expense of glazing.

De Dartein, ii. 475, points out that in Lombardy the smallest windows are those of the twelfth century ; whereas in the Byzantine and Basilican churches the breadth is about one-half of the height, in these it is one-third, one-fifth, or even one-tenth. He suggests another explanation ; viz. that the difference in size of the windows is due to a difference in the methods of glazing ; that in the early windows a wooden or stone framework was placed to contain the glass, and therefore they had to be broad ; whereas in the later windows the glass was fixed with iron and lead directly in the stone jambs. Cattaneo objects to this ; and suggests that the builders designedly plunged the churches into gloom to produce effects of mystery and awe ; but that is to look at mediæval building through the spectacles of a modern æsthete, and to ignore the fact that the old men at all periods strove above all things to make their churches bright and cheerful.

LANCET WINDOWS.—For hundreds of years the heads of windows remained semicircular ; at last the heads were pointed, producing the "Lancet" type of window. The pointed arch had been in use for some time in constructional arches ; but there was a considerable reluctance and delay in employing it where the construction did not demand it, as in a window or doorway, or where the arch was merely a decorative one, as in the arcading of an aisle ; e.g. at FOUNTAINS (101), RIPON (102), and New Shoreham the arches of the pier-arcade were pointed, to facilitate the vaulting ; but the arches of the windows of Fountains and Ripon are semicircular, as are those of the aisle arcading of New Shoreham. Indeed to eyes that were habituated to the consecrated semicircle, so repugnant was the new pointed arch, that in the aisle of Glastonbury nave, though the window-arch is pointed, its rear-arch remains semicircular. But the desire for harmony in the end proved too strong ; not merely harmony with the pointed arches of the pier-arcade, but with the pointed arches which spanned the aisle, and above all with the pointed wall-arches of the aisle-vault. Indeed the immediate juxtaposition of wall-arch and window-head made identity of shape inevitable.†

As regards the proportions of the lancet window, there was at first a considerable diversity of treatment. Those of Canterbury choir, designed by William of Sens, naturally were of the French type ; somewhat broad in proportion to their height. A still greater excess in width is seen in the contemporary windows of Glastonbury and Wells. Those of Wells are no less than 5 feet 4 inches broad, with a height of only 13 feet 5 inches. Usually the precedent neither of Wells nor of Canterbury was followed. Everywhere in the thirteenth century the English lancet tended to differentiate itself from the French by its great loftiness and narrowness. And being slender, any single lancet was a thing of beauty in itself : while any single lancet of Canterbury or Wells or France was without grace. At Bottesford is a lancet 15½ feet high and only 8 inches broad. It has been said, indeed, that the breadth of the

---

* Craddock's *Peterborough*, 52.

† Nevertheless, for a time, as at Byland and elsewhere, round-headed windows were set under the pointed wall-arches of the aisle vault. See Plate 21 in Sharpe's *Arch. Parallels*.

Warmington Aisle.

Oundle Aisle.

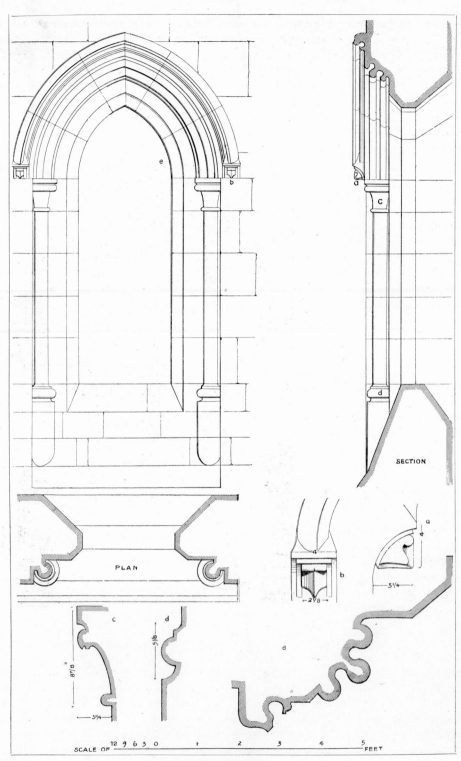

SECTION

PLAN

SCALE OF 12 9 6 3 0   1   2   3   4   5 FEET

Temple Choir.

English lancet varies inversely with its height.* In England, therefore, it was seen that the graceful single lancet could be composed into even yet more graceful groups of lancets : and that group could be contrasted with group. And so the history of the window passed in England through a whole stage of development which was summarily shortened in France. France arrived at window-tracery rather earlier than we; on the other hand, they experienced less of the delights of Lancet-grouping.

In BOXGROVE CLERESTORY (373) single lancets appear in the clerestory; in the aisles of LINCOLN (110) and in the chapter house the lancets are arranged in pairs; in the CLERE-STORY OF LINCOLN (115) and SALIS-BURY (458) they are in triplets. And as an odd number of lights was better adapted for filling up a gable, three, five, or seven lancets in a group are more common than four or six. Southwell choir, however, has a fine example of two sets of four lancets superposed ; and six occur in Repton Church. So again, the five gigantic lancets of the NORTH TRANSEPT OF YORK (11), the famous Five

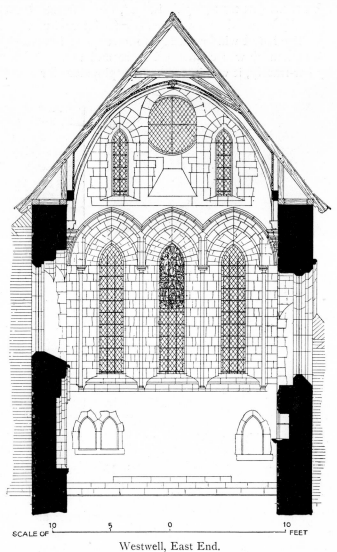

Westwell, East End.

Sisters, are not gradated in height. And these groups were nicely contrasted ; e.g. in ELY EAST FRONT (464) a quintet of gradated lancets has above and beneath it a triplet uniform in height. In BEVERLEY TRANSEPT (176) a gradated is superposed on a non-gradated triplet.†

* Brandon's *Analysis*, 18.

† Perhaps the most beautiful groups of all are those of the lancets of the choir of Brecon Priory Church, illustrated in Scott's *Lectures*, i. 285.

As in Norman windows, the glass was usually placed near the external face of the wall. Outside, therefore, there was little room for ornament. But there was all the more room inside ; and windows plain externally like those of the aisles of Worcester and CARLISLE (498) are often glorious within. The contrast is well seen in many a window on the chalk of Kent or Sussex, *e.g.* STONE CHURCH (513). Indeed, where freestone was scarce or dear, it was naturally reserved as far as possible for internal use.

The lancet window seems to have come into use about 1170 ; and though its supremacy was challenged more and more, first by plate-tracery, and then by bar-tracery, it was in constant employment for something like a century.*

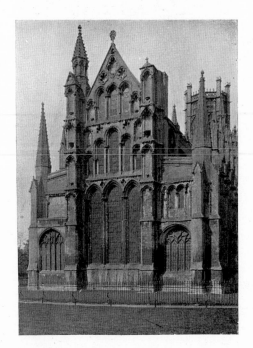

Ely East Front.   Hereford Lady Chapel.

TRACERIED WINDOWS.—Both Norman and lancet windows were at first employed singly on the flanks of the church, but in groups in the end walls. We find pairs of lancets in ST GILES', OXFORD (457.3, 4) ; and again in the aisles of Lincoln choir and nave, where they are separated by a minor buttress (115). At WILEY (466) two advances are seen. Three instead of two lancets are put side by side. Secondly, the central lancet is made higher than the two side lancets : this is an important step ; it is to introduce the principle of grouping. The same principle is recognised in a different way in Lincoln clerestory ; by the central lancet being made the broadest of the three. A remarkably early example of this treatment occurs in the west wall of ROMSEY

* Here and there it occurs much later ; *e.g.* in the fourteenth century at Ottery St Mary and in the south clerestory of St Albans nave. In the latter it is assimilated to the thirteenth-century work in the west of the nave.

SOUTH TRANSEPT * (457.2); which, even if not part of the original work, can hardly be later than the middle of the twelfth century. Another is in the west front of GLASTONBURY LADY CHAPEL, 1185. Both are round-headed.

Such a combination was inevitable after the treatment, so very frequent, of the inner arcade of the Norman clerestories, *e.g.* at ELY (57), Waltham, and PETERBOROUGH (161).

But it was usual to protect the windows from the drip of the rain by a dripstone. Sometimes each window has its own independent dripstone; but in one of the St Giles' windows, and in the Lincoln clerestory, though each window has still its own dripstone, all the dripstones are linked up. This goes far to diminish the independence of each window of the group. The next step is still more important. It is to supply the several windows of the group with a common dripstone. Sometimes, as in the aisle-window of WARMINGTON (461), each window has its independent dripstone and a share in a common dripstone. More often, as at NETLEY (457.5, 6), and WINCHESTER (457.7, 8), they lose their independent dripstone, and have only the common one.

Glastonbury Lady Chapel, W. Front.

But the result is a blank space of masonry; at Netley a blank spandrel. To ornament this, an aperture is pierced through; a circle, a quatrefoil, or the like. And so in this gradual but inevitable way arises what is called Plate-Tracery. The evolution may be well seen by comparing the two WARMINGTON WINDOWS (461); that of the aisle, which was built first; and that of the BELFRY (467). At SALISBURY (170) best of all one can watch the transition from the grouped lancets of the lower parts of the church to the plate-tracery of the gables of the transepts.

The above is the main origin of English Plate-Tracery; nevertheless it is a mistake to regard it as the only origin. Even in the Anglo-Saxon towers of Northumberland it was by no means uncommon to pierce the spandrel of the baluster windows of the belfry with a quatrefoil or some such aperture; *e.g.* at Billingham.† But these remote examples of Anglo-Saxon plate-tracery seem to have escaped recognition or to have been ignored. Again, in two bays of PETER-BOROUGH CHOIR (468), 1117-1140, the spandrels of the triforium arcade are pierced with little circles. When such a triforium arcade as that of Rievaulx or WHITBY (114) was designed, *c.* 1200, plate-tracery was inevitable. Again, when two lancets were set in the same bay of an aisle, *e.g.* at CARLISLE (498). it was only natural to pierce the spandrel between the tops of the lancets and

* *Cf.* the west front of PATRIXBOURNE (218).

† See illustrated paper by Mr C. C. Hodges in *Reliquary*, Jan. 1894, on the *Pre-Conquest Churches of Northumbria.*

2 G

SECTION OF SILL

SECTION ON LINE A.B

SCALE OF 12 9 6 3 0   1   2   3   4   5 FEET

Wiley, Wilts.

SCALE 0 1 2 3 4 5 OF FEET

Warmington Tower.

the wall-arch. A very early example of this is seen in the south transept of Kirkstall, where each bay is lighted by a pair of windows with a circle above them.*

Again, many an early west or east front had a wheel window in its gable; *e.g.* Barfreston, PATRIXBOURNE (218), Iffley, Castle Hedingham; above two or three of the usual type of oblong round-headed or lancet windows. To turn

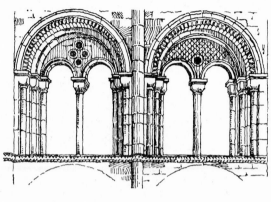

such a combination into a great plate-tracery window all that was necessary was to frame the combination under a common arch.† If the end walls of Chartres, with a circular window resting immediately on a group of lancets, be examined, it will be seen that here certainly is the origin of the early and remarkable plate-tracery windows of Chartres aisles and clerestory.‡ So also the superposition of a big circular window on a pair of pointed arches in the cloister of Laon§ was sure to lead to plate-tracery. ||

Of plate-tracery windows the earliest we possess is the Norman window of ST MAURICE, YORK, which may be *c.* 1160, and the Transitional one of the porch of ST MARY'S, SHREWSBURY, *c.* 1180; next come those of the Bishop's Hall at Lincoln, begun before 1200 and finished before 1224; those of the Winchester Castle Hall,¶ finished in 1234; and those of the

Peterborough Triforium.　Peterborough Triforium.
York, St Maurice.　Shrewsbury, Porch of
　　　　　　St Mary's Church.

Bishop's Hall at Wells, not later than 1239. Other examples of plate-tracery are illustrated from the belfry of OXFORD CATHEDRAL (512); from the aisle

---

* The same thing occurs at Notre Dame de la Coûture, Mans; where the aisleless nave is vaulted in great squares, and two lancets are set in each bay, and the spandrel above them is pierced with a circle. *Cf.* Dehio, ii. 9, 580.

† At Sporle, near Swaffam, a triplet lancet is seen under a foliated circle (Paley's *Gothic Architecture*, 158).

‡ So also Dehio, *loc. cit.*; and Lethaby's *Med. Art*, 171.

§ Illustrated in Viollet-le-Duc, *Architecture*, iii. 429.

|| In each side gable of SALISBURY LADY CHAPEL (458) a cusped circle occurs over a pair of lancets. The Lady Chapel was commenced in 1220 and finished in 1225. A good illustration of these windows is given in Parker's *Glossary*, Plate 231.

¶ Illustrated in Rickman, 165.

of STONE CHURCH, KENT (513); from BEELEIGH CHAPTER HOUSE; and from ST JAMES', BRISTOL (516).

In France plate-tracery windows of great size and complexity were designed at Laon *c.* 1170; at Chartres *c.* 1194. These windows, filled with rich twelfth-century stained glass, must have made a great impression on the French builders elsewhere. But it was not everywhere that such quarries could be found as those near Laon and Chartres and in Burgundy, producing slabs that were neither brittle nor difficult to work. Still there was a desire to have the new windows; and the question would arise, how to obtain the circles, jewelled in ruby and azure, of Laon and Chartres, without possessing the materials requisite for the production of plate-tracery. In France and in England the same and even better effects were got by substituting Bar for Plate Tracery. Hitherto the geometrical patterns had been got out of slabs of freestone, almost as if one were cutting patterns out of a board with a fret-saw. Now the stone was first worked into curved bars; which, when put together, gave the circle, the triangle, or what not. This great revolution followed fast on the Chartres plate-tracery of 1194. Orbais is said to have had bar-tracery by 1200;* the eastern chapels of Rheims Cathedral had it *c.* 1212.

SCALE OF 12   6   0   1   2 FEET

Beeleigh Chapter House.

[In England bar-tracery did not arise quite so early; we were engrossed in composing triplets, quintets, sextets of lancets. It is usually said that our first bar-tracery is that of Westminster choir, begun 1245; which, with the large circles in the window heads, may be admitted to be of French origin. But the important windows in the west front of BINHAM (471) must not be overlooked. They are now much dilapidated, but may be restored with certainty from the drawing by John Coney in Dugdale's *Monasticon.* The central window is one of eight lights: divided into pairs; each pair is contained by a detached pointed arch, with a quatrefoil in its head. Each pair of these arches is again included in a detached pointed arch, which has in its head a sexfoliated circle. Finally, these carry a centrepiece consisting of an octofoliated circle. Now Matthew Paris† expressly says that "Prior Richard de Parco built the front of the church from the foundation to the roof." He was Prior from 1226 to 1244. Consequently it would appear that we have at Binham large windows of bar-tracery which are anterior to those of Westminster. The early date assigned to the Binham work is borne out by comparison with other examples. Of all our early bar-tracery windows the most important is the east window of LINCOLN PRESBYTERY (177), which was begun soon after 1256 and consecrated in 1288. So great and magnificent a window must have had predecessors; and

* By Demaison.   † I am indebted for the reference to Mr W. H. St John Hope.

its prototype may well be the west window of Binham ; the number of lights is the same, the skeleton framework of the tracery is the same, practically every detail is the same except that the circle in the window arch is not octofoliated, but contains nine foliated smaller circles. Another important early example is the east window of the choir of NETLEY (471), which was begun in 1239 by the executors of Peter de Roche, Bishop of Winchester, with funds bequeathed by him for the purpose. This window has but four lights ; otherwise the design is precisely the same as that of Binham. Finally, we know that the presbytery of St Paul's, London, was consecrated, wholly or in part, in 1240, in the presence of King and Legate ; and that here also were windows of fully developed bar-tracery. Putting the evidence together, we may fairly come to the conclusion that large bar-tracery windows were in use in England not later than the year 1240. A drawing of one of the aisle-windows also of BINHAM WEST FRONT is given ; the lower half lighted the vaulted aisle, the upper half the triforium.* The bar-tracery windows of the west front of the abbey of Valle Crucis, near Llangollen, also appear to be of very early date.† The abbey is said by Dugdale to have been founded c. 1200.

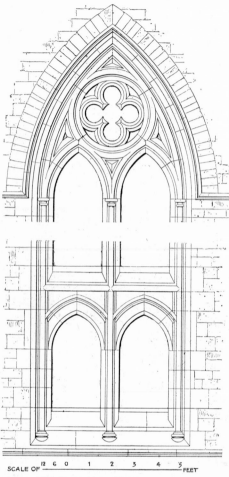

SCALE OF 12 6 0   1   2   3   4   5 FEET

Binham Aisle, West Window.

So far we have traced the change from grouped lancets to plate-tracery, and from plate to bar tracery. But it may be asked, why did we abandon the combinations of lancets, so beautiful and effective in Salisbury and else-where? The chief reason doubtless was that we wanted bigger windows, so as to make the churches less gloomy ; the stained glass of the period being as yet thick and opaque. Another, it may be, was the desire for harmony in bay design.

* The ruins of Binham Abbey are 4 miles from New Walsingham, Norfolk. The façade is built in admirable stone, and is of consummate design. For drawings and plan see Britton's *Architectural Antiquities*, iii. 72 ; Colling's *Details*, i. 23, 24, and ii. 34 ; Parker's *Glossary*, Plates 123 and 146. The whole of the work is very similar to that of West Walton Church, near Wisbech, which may be by the same builders, where is an exquisite Early Geometrical window of the Binham type ; *cf.* also the tooth ornament in Colling's *Details*, i. 22 and 24. West Walton is illustrated in Colling's *Details*, i., Plates 9 to 22.

† The exterior and interior of the west front of Valle Crucis are illustrated by H. H. Hughes in the *Architectural Association Sketch Book*, New Series, viii. 35.

With one bay and two windows, as in Salisbury aisles, or three as in Salisbury clerestory, there was a lack of harmony. What was wanted was one bay, one window. Here and there, too, the builders may have been feeling their way to the realisation of the ideal of the Gothic building, as one whose vault could be made to stand without support of walls : an ideal realised early in such chapter

Binham, West End.

Netley, East End.

houses as those of Westminster and Salisbury. In such a building it was un-necessary to confine the glass within the jambs of narrow lancet windows; the whole space from buttress to buttress could, if desired, be glazed. But if glazed, the glass must have mullions and bars of stone to support it; in other words, there must be tracery. From one cause or other the traceried window was inevitable.

CHAPTER XXXII.

GEOMETRICAL TRACERY.

WE now come to what is to most the outward and visible sign of Gothic architecture, the traceried window. Traceried windows were divided by Rickman into Decorated and Perpendicular, and the division still stands in the text-books. It is thoroughly misleading, however. A threefold division is necessary. The so-called Decorated needs to be subdivided into Geometrical, and what Mr Sharpe calls Curvilinear, Professor Freeman Flowing Tracery.* In practice this has always been admitted. Brandon, Bloxam, Bowman and Crowther, Parker, Sir G. G. Scott, constantly subdivide Decorated tracery. Geometrical tracery they variously style Early Decorated, or Early Middle Pointed, or Early Geometric Pointed; Curvilinear tracery they style Late Decorated, or Pure Decorated, or Flowing Middle Pointed. All these clumsy periphrases are avoided by adopting the terms Geometrical and Curvilinear.

The former came into use in windows of the former rank not later than 1240 in Binham, Netley, and Old St Paul's. It remained in vogue, according to Mr Sharpe, till about 1315. But many windows of purely Geometrical character, *e.g.* those with Kentish tracery or the ball-flower, were constructed for another generation or so. It should be borne in mind also that though Geometrical patterns without admixture of Flowing or Rectilinear patterns are rare after 1315; yet in such admixtures they are common to the last. In fact in Tudor days there was quite a strong reaction in favour of the employment of purely Geometrical patterns into window-tracery, basement-courses, parapets, &c.; especially the quatrefoil; *e.g.* KING'S COLLEGE, CAMBRIDGE (473).

EARLY GEOMETRICAL TRACERY.—But we can go further. We can subdivide Geometrical tracery into Early and Late work.† The first is seen in the BINHAM (470), NETLEY (471), and RUDSTON (508) windows, in SALISBURY CLOISTER (458); in SELBY CHOIR AISLE (86); in all these the main centrepiece consists of a foliated circle. So it does in WESTMINSTER CHOIR (63) and chapter house.‡ In other windows the main centrepiece is still a circle; but instead of being merely foliated, it contains a ring of smaller circles; *e.g.* the east windows of LINCOLN PRESBYTERY (177) and TINTERN CHOIR (475); this choir was finished in 1287.

LATE GEOMETRICAL TRACERY.—Of this there are three marks. First, the Geometrical figures employed—trefoils, quatrefoils, &c.—are not always bounded by circles, as in the earlier tracery; but the lines of the foliations

---

* Unfortunately Freeman added another, quite unnecessary, division; Flamboyant.
† To all these divisions and subdivisions exceptions occur.
‡ Canvas was bought for the windows of the chapter house in 1253.

King's College Chapel.
North Creake.

Exeter Lady Chapel.
Merton College Chapel.

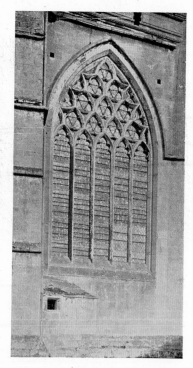

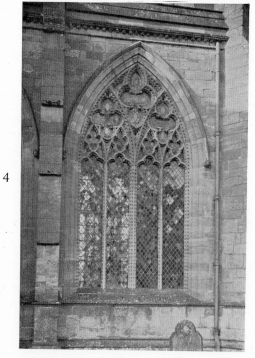

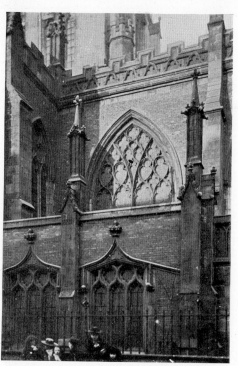

1. Gedney Chancel.　　　　2. Ledbury Nave.
4. Ledbury, St Catherine's Chapel.
3. Wells Lady Chapel.
5. Hull, S. Chancel (Curvilinear).

form the main lines of the figures, *e.g.* in the clerestory of HOWDEN NAVE (546), the aisles of York nave ; at Easby, GUISBOROUGH (476), Exeter.* Secondly, not only circles, but other Geometrical patterns are employed ; *e.g.* trefoils, quatrefoils, lozenges, spherical triangles, and spherical squares. Thirdly, in the spandrels of Late Lancet arcades, *e.g.* at Binham, a long-lobed, *pointed* trefoil had been common. This was introduced into the tracery *c.* 1290 ; and, where present, is an infallible sign of Late Geometrical work ; *e.g.* it appears in the great east windows of Ripon and GUISBOROUGH (476), *c.* 1290 to *c.* 1300, and in the west windows of Tintern and HOWDEN (72). The Guisborough window, the drawing of which is from a restoration by Mr Sharpe, was 63 feet high ; taller even than the Curvilinear windows of York and Carlisle. A Late Geometrical window of singular beauty remains in what was formerly the chapel of the Bishop of Ely, in Ely Place near the Holborn Viaduct, London, 1290-1300. The choir of EXETER (473) is 1308 to 1327. The window in the Lady Chapel, like all windows with five, seven, or nine lights, was difficult to design. It has seven lights: the central one being taller and broader, and independent of the other six. These six are under detached arches. Each pair of these arches is contained in two intersecting and detached arches ; these two arches are placed under an en-

SCALE OF 1 2 3 4 5 ⋯ 10 ⋯ 15 FEET

Tintern Choir.

gaged pointed arch, in the head of which is a circle. The centrepiece is a large circle, in which are six trefoils, three round-lobed and inverted, three pointed and normal in position.

We may again subdivide the Late Geometrical windows ; first, into those with centrepieces ; secondly, into those without. Of those with centrepieces we

* See illustrations in Sharpe's *Windows*, pp. 77, 78, 82, and Plates 17 and 24.

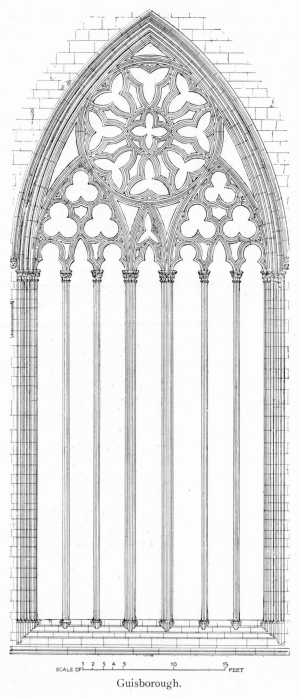

SCALE OF 1 2 3 4 5   10   15 FEET

Guisborough.

have *first*, those in which the centrepiece is a circle; *e.g.* GUISBOROUGH and WELLS CHAPTER HOUSE (123). There is an elaborate specimen in the chapel of MERTON COLLEGE, OXFORD (473), *c.* 1290. It has seven lower lights, of which the central light is treated independently. On each side of it are three pointed arches; these are set beneath two intersecting pointed arches, the outer one of which is engaged. These two intersecting arches are again set under an engaged pointed arch. The centrepiece is a wheel.

Secondly, the centrepiece may be some other Geometrical figure; not a circle. At NORTH CREAKE (473) it is a round-headed trefoil. In the west window of HOWDEN (72)—the transom is not original—it is a cusped quatrefoil inscribed in a spherical square, of which the two upper sides are formed by the window arch. In ST CATHERINE'S CHAPEL, LEDBURY (474.4), it is a quatrefoil studded with ball-flower.

Thirdly, the centrepiece may have what is called Kentish Tracery. It appears in all the chancel windows of CHARTHAM CHURCH (477), Kent, near Canterbury; and in the Infirmary Chapel and St Anselm's Chapel in Canterbury Cathedral; also in Whitby Nave; Billingborough; Great Bedwyn, Wilts; Lyddington, Berks; Capel St Mary, Suffolk. It has been variously described. Really it is nothing but a cusped quatrefoil or trefoil with straight or curving spikes projecting from between the lobes. But, if a quatrefoil, instead of its normal position, it lies diagonally. It is strong in construction, and handsome and unusual in design. It occurs so often in connection with ogee arches that probably it is usually *later* than 1315.

Then, there are several interesting types of Late Geometrical windows *without* centrepieces. The *first* contains two or more lights, whose pointed arches are continued to the main arch of the window so that they intersect. This intersecting tracery, when without cusps, as at Barholme, is not graceful. From its cheapness many windows which had fallen out of repair were rebuilt by the churchwardens in this fashion during the seventeenth and eighteenth centuries, *e.g.* in Leominster aisle and Chichester choir aisle.

More often it is cusped as at Dorchester and LEDBURY (474.2), and the interstices also may be filled in with small trefoils, quatrefoils, and circles: as at GEDNEY (474.1), DURHAM (514), and SOLIHULL (626).

The *second* is a group of gradated lancets, with bar-tracery. It is seen in its simplest form in the clerestory of the choir of St Albans,* begun *c.* 1257; and in ST MICHAEL'S, OXFORD (478). It is more common in Late than in Early Geometrical work; in Late work it is generally cusped, as in the choir of MILTON ABBEY, DORSET (478); begun after the fire of 1309. Naturally these windows are triplets, or quintets, as the great window of the north transept of Wimborne,† which, like that of Milton Abbey, contains the long-lobed pointed trefoil. At Ottery, however, the east window has eight lights.

A variant of this, with elongated mullions, was in use well into the middle of the fourteenth century in the West of England; *e.g.* in Tewkesbury choir;‡ Berkeley; Portbury; Somerset; LEDBURY (474.2); and Ottery St Mary. All these types persist well into the fourteenth century.

Chartham.

A *third* type, without centrepiece, is one whose tracery is entirely formed of foliated patterns; trefoils, quatrefoils, and the like. It seems usually to be late; for it is found surmounted with an ogee dripstone in Lichfield Lady Chapel, and in proximity to undoubted Curvilinear work in the LADY CHAPEL OF WELLS (474.3), which was finished in 1326. So again in HEDON WEST NAVE (359), it appears next to an undoubted CURVILINEAR WINDOW (480.3). Good examples are the four-light windows of Chester choir, and the three-light ones of the aisle of GLOUCESTER NAVE (360).

Fourthly, yet another set of windows seems to have been in use till well into

* Illustrated in Scott's *Essay*, Plate 23.
† Illustrated in Freeman's *Windows*, Plate 11, 52.   ‡ Illustrated in *Glossary*, Plate 239.

the fourteenth century ; those studded with ball-flower.   These also are characteristic of the West of England.   The most remarkable are the Leominster
windows ; * each of which contains 820 ball-flowers ;
while in the GLOUCESTER WINDOWS (360), 1318-1329,
if a horizontal line be drawn below the spring of
the arch of each window it cuts through 32 bands of
ball-flower ; and there are no less than 1,400 ball-
flowers in each window.   Most beautiful of all windows
of this type are those of ST CATHERINE'S CHAPEL,
LEDBURY (474.4).

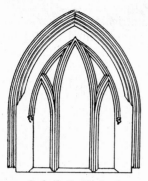

Oxford, St Michael.

The above classification by no means exhausts the
variety of Late Geometrical tracery, and its chrono-
logies must only be taken to be true in a general way ;
but at any rate it may serve to characterise the leading
types.   The great treasure-house of it is the Cathedral
of Exeter ; begun *c.* 1270 and finished *c.* 1350 ; with the later tracery largely
assimilated to the earlier.

It is curious that though the French commenced to produce bar-tracery
somewhat before ourselves, indeed at the very begin-
ning of the thirteenth century, they did not develop
its later Geometrical forms any sooner than we did,
nor to anything like the same extent.   It was not till
the last quarter of the thirteenth century,† that in
addition to circles they began to employ other forms
such as triangles and lozenges.   It is plain that the
development of Geometrical window-tracery went on
pari passu in the two countries ; neither ‡ borrowing
of the other.   We may add that the French to the
very last retained their liking for the simpler and
earlier types of tracery, viz., those with circular centrepieces.   In France they occur frequently in the fourteenth century ; *e.g.* in the choir chapels of Notre
Dame, Paris, 1320 ; § and of St Ouen, Rouen.   The
chief difference was that the fourteenth-century tracery
was made excessively exiguous ; a triumph of skill on
the part of the mason.   The chief centrepiece, other than a circular, in large use
in France was one of a pair of spherical triangles, supporting a third.

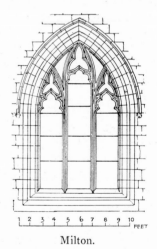

Milton.

* Illustrated in Sharpe's *Windows*, Plate 21.   † Enlart's *Manuel*, 528.
‡ Except probably at Westminster ; whose tracery, however, made no disciples.
§ Illustrated in Viollet-le-Duc, *Architecture*, vi. 338.

CHAPTER XXXIII.

CURVILINEAR TRACERY.

THE next species of bar-tracery is characterised by the presence of flowing curves and ogee arches; and occurs chiefly between 1315 and 1360. They may be arranged in three classes.

CLASS I.—In these the main arch of the window is subdivided into two *detached* sub-arches; *i.e.* the outer sides of which are not the same as the sides of the main arch of the window. These detached sub-arches are usually *ogee* arches. If it be a large window with 4, 6, or 8 lights, the ogee sub-arches are usually placed side by side; *e.g.* in the west window of YORK (82), where the ogee sub-arches each contain four lower lights. In such a window there is abundance of room for a centrepiece, which is usually large; at York it is unusually important, being double; it consists of a heart-shaped figure, carrying a vesica. These contain three leafed stems, which are repeated on either side of the heart. No centrepiece is so successful as the leafed stem; its beauty is well seen in the "Bishop's Eye" of LINCOLN (484); and, somewhat confused, in the east window of CARLISLE (128).

But if there are 5, 7, or 9 lights the ogee sub-arches intersect in very charming fashion, as in the east window of HULL (81), thus binding together the otherwise disconnected lateral compartments. The intersecting ogee arch became one of the favourite motives of our Late Gothic; it occurs constantly in the woodwork of the screens; and is employed not unsuccessfully so late as A.D. 1636 in the window of Jesus College Chapel, Oxford.

It should be noted that there is always a difficulty in designing tracery for 5, 7, or 9 lower lights. The easiest way out of the difficulty is to treat the central lower light independently, as in the seven-light windows of EXETER and MERTON COLLEGE, Oxford (473). So at Carlisle the separate treatment of the central light leaves four lights on each side, which admit of symmetrical treatment. But sometimes instead of dividing a window, say of seven lights, into 3, 1, 3; it was divided into 2, 3, 2. Almost always trouble followed, *e.g.* in the Late Geometrical west window of Tintern, which has seven lights, the central sub-arch rose higher than the other two, and had to be truncated to make room for the circular centrepiece.* So it was also in Curvilinear work. The great windows of Heckington, HAWTON (483) and Selby have seven lights arranged as at Tintern; but the unfortunate corollary is that the great ogee intersecting sub-arches have each one short and one long leg.

* Illustrated in Sharpe's *Arch. Parallels*, Plate 53.

1. Haverfordwest.
4. Hunstanton Porch.
2. Merton Vestry.
5. Old Walsingham.
3. Hedon Nave.
6. Tideswell Transept.

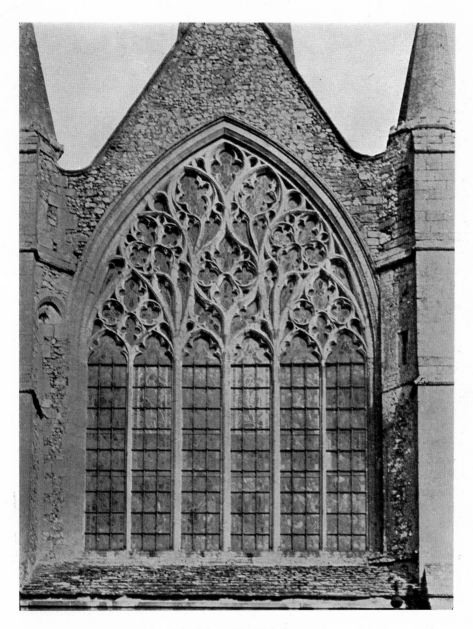

Snettisham West Window.

Detached *pointed* sub-arches are much less common in this class; but fine examples occur at Chipping Norton; Thurnham; Plympton St Mary's; Exeter west nave; and St Saviour's, York.*

CLASS II.—In these the main arch of the window is divided into two *engaged* sub-arches; *i.e.* of which the outer sides coincide with those of the main arch. As the main arch is pointed, it follows that the sub-arches also will be pointed, and not ogee arches.

If the window has an even number of lights, the engaged sub-arches are generally placed side by side: as in HULL CHANCEL (474.5). In that case there is not much room for a centrepiece, which therefore becomes small and uninteresting; *e.g.* in the south of the chancel of Hull it consists merely of foliations: so also in the south transept of ST MARY REDCLIFFE, BRISTOL (376).

If the window has an odd number of lights, the central light is usually treated independently, as at Carlisle. In such a case there is room for a large centrepiece. The east windows of the aisle of Hull chancel on the other hand,

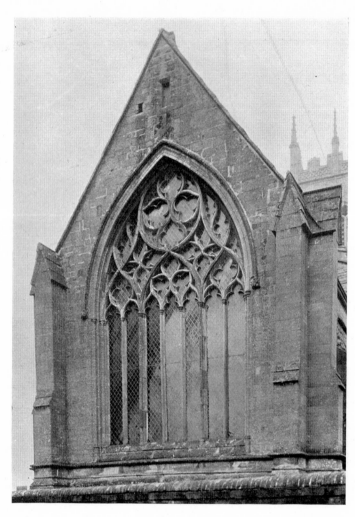

Hawton.

have five lights without a centrepiece; for which is substituted a collection of uninteresting foliations.†

CLASS III.—This is a miscellaneous collection of all windows whose skeleton does *not* contain two detached or engaged sub-arches; *e.g.* in TIDESWELL

* Illustrated in Freeman's *Window Tracery*, 59, 65, 66, 67, 105.
† Illustrated in Sharpe's *Windows*, Plate 52.

TRANSEPT (480.6), the five bottom pointed arches are united into four inter-secting pointed arches, and the two central of these into one ogee arch. At HEDON and OLD WALSINGHAM (480), SALFORD (487), HINGHAM (489), the three lower arches retain their independence altogether; so do the four lower arches in WESTMINSTER cloister (489).

I. Of this class the most common window is the *Reticulated;* so called from the net-like appearance of its tracery. It is probably the earliest of all Curvilinear tracery. For it appears in the vestry of MERTON COLLEGE CHAPEL, OXFORD (480.2), the foundations for which the College accounts show to have been dug in 1310.* And indeed if a window have three or more lights whose heads are ogee arches, and these ogee curves be continued till they meet the window arch, Reticulated tracery results inevitably. And each pattern, moreover, except the uppermost one, has two ogee arches, one right way up, the other inverted. Naturally, in the mania prevailing in the fourteenth century for the ogee arch, Reticulated tracery came early into favour. There is a superb specimen in WESTMINSTER CLOISTER (489);† in this every ogee pattern contains Kentish tracery.

Lincoln South Transept.

II. *Flamboyant* tracery developed in a very simple way out of Reticulated. The first thing necessary to change a Reticulated into a Flamboyant window is to give an acuter point to the ogee heads of the lower lights. As a corollary, the wavy curves of these ogee arches will prolong themselves up to the window arch much more vertically than before: which is very satisfactory. For the more the curves of flowing tracery tend to the horizontal, as in the east window of Shottesbrooke, ‡ the weaker they

* See Rickman, 237.   † A Reticulated window is shown at FRAMPTON (618).
‡ Illustrated in Butterfield's *Shottesbrooke.*

are to the eye, and the weaker they are in reality. The more vertical, the stronger and the more satisfactory.* The French saw this clearly ; and flowing curve and countercurve, always essaying the vertical, are the note of their later tracery. A good Flamboyant window is in essence the same as a Perpendicular one ; except that the tracery, instead of rising in straight supermullions, flickers to right and left. Secondly, in the best windows, the upper flow of curve is not a mere " repeat " of the ogee curves of the arches of the lower lights ; all sorts of subtle curves occur, as in the Beverley reredos : so that the patterns cease to be symmetrical ogees.

Of Flamboyant windows that from CHIPPING NORTON (487.4) is of typically English type.† In the window from the south aisle of the nave of HEDON (480.3), the aspiring effort of the curves is somewhat retarded by the depressed ogee arches beneath. At SALFORD, WARWICKSHIRE (487.2), the pointed arches of the outer lower lights are a blemish ; for the flow of their inner curves is suddenly cut short.

The finest examples of our Flamboyant tracery are to be found in arcadings and doors : e.g. in the stone screens of Selby choir, probably copied from woodwork ;‡ and of BEVERLEY MINSTER (486) ; where it will be seen that only the central pattern is a symmetrical ogee.

It has been the fashion to include the few examples we possess in England of Flamboyant tracery in the sweeping condemnation of the magnificent Flamboyant windows of France. This is the merest Chauvinism. They are both beautiful and practical. No other Flowing window equals them in beauty of curve, except perhaps the leafed stem windows of the south aisle of Beverley nave ; while their design in some cases, e.g. in the aisle-windows of Alençon, is almost as well adapted for the reception of stained glass as in the best of our late Perpendicular windows, such as that of the DIVINITY SCHOOL, OXFORD (492).

CLASS IV.—The rest, like the TIDESWELL WINDOW (480.6), defy classification. Many of them are hybrids ; half-curvilinear ; half-geometrical; or exceptional forms, such as the roue tournante of HUNSTANTON PORCH (480.4).

ORIGIN OF CURVILINEAR TRACERY.—It may not be uninteresting to turn back to some of the beautiful Geometrical tracery, such as that of Guisborough, Exeter Lady Chapel, and Merton College Chapel ; and endeavour to see whether there is any practical or artistic defect in it ; or whether it was merely abandoned from a desire for freshness and novelty. There can be little doubt that the latter motive was not without weight ; for great as is the variety of simple Geometrical forms, it is not infinite ; one comes at last to an end of the combinations of circles, trefoils, quatrefoils, spherical triangles and squares, and the like ; repeats occur ; monotony sets in. So, no doubt, it had been some seventy years before, when the beautiful Lancet groups were abandoned for Geometrical tracery. Another reason, however, is suggested by Mr Sharpe ; viz., that these rigid Geometrical forms left awkward interspaces (spandrels) between themselves

* That is why the leafed stem centrepiece is so satisfactory.

† Others are illustrated in Freeman's Window Tracery, Plates 44, 45, from Jersey ; Southwell ; Bolton Priory ; St Mary Magdalen, Oxford ; Etchingham ; Hawton.

‡ Prior, Gothic Art, 393.

Beverley Minster Reredos.

SCALE OF 12 9 6 3 0   1   2   3   4   5 FEET

and the window arch, and between one another. In such a window as that of Exeter Lady Chapel these spandrels are very numerous ; they are of all sorts of shapes, difficult in foliation and difficult to glaze. There is no doubt some truth in this ; in many of the later Curvilinear windows ; *e.g.* those of Tideswell and Selby, and especially in Flamboyant windows, such as those of Chipping Norton and Salford, the difficulties of the treatment of the spandrels are reduced to a minimum, or even are triumphantly surmounted. But in others, as in OLD WALSINGHAM (480.5) and Westminster cloister, the spandrels are even more

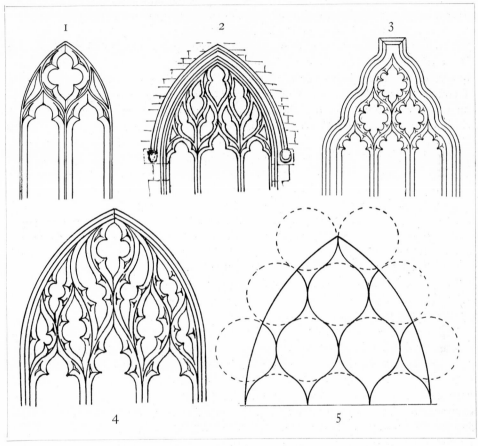

1. Little Addington. 2. Salford. 3. Caldicott.
4. Chipping Norton. *Flembos.* 5. Reticulated Tracery.

awkwardly treated than even in the Geometrical period. Indeed every Reticulated window is fringed with the scraps and fragments of patterns cut off by the window arch. This was felt at the time ; for we find several Geometrical windows of the type of that of HAVERFORDWEST (480.1), and Curvilinear ones as at CALDICOTT, Monmouth ; in which the scraps and fragments are got rid of by omitting the window arch altogether, or by making it conform to the curves of the ogee pattern. But another practical consideration may be suggested. These windows were meant to tell the story of saints and angels. But neither saints nor angels are known to be triangular or circular or square, or in any way geometrical in shape. Such a window, then, as that of the Exeter Lady Chapel is largely wasted, as a means of preaching Scripture History; practically the whole head of the window is useless to the glassman. If, however, we turn to a later type, such as that of Selby or York; or still better to the Flamboyant windows of Hedon, Salford, and Chipping Norton, we shall see how much better the glass craftsman can now utilise the tracery lights; they almost seem to invite the hierarchy of heaven to tabernacle in their niches with outstretched wings. From the point of view of the glass craftsman—and he was beginning to be a bigger person than the architect—the best Flowing tracery was a great improvement on the best Geometrical.

Nor can it be denied that Flowing tracery is in itself far superior to Geometrical. Who would care to gaze day after day into combinations of square, circle, triangle, rather than graceful intertwining flowing curves? And of course, artistically the Flowing tracery is on an altogether higher plane; in the window of Exeter Lady Chapel there is rule and compass, in the Carlisle window human brain. We may add, too, that in Geometrical tracery, unity

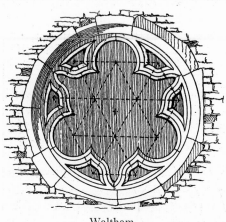

Waltham.

cannot be reached in the design: the sub-arches maintain their independence of the centrepiece, and the centrepiece of the sub-arches; they do not fuse. But in a good Curvilinear window, especially if it have Flamboyant tracery, mullion fuses into tracery without the slightest breach of continuity. Not that all the windows by any means reach this high standard, e.g. at TIDESWELL (480.6) the pointed arches and the Flamboyant tracery are discordant. In WESTMINSTER CLOISTER (489) there is an awkward break between the pointed arches of the lower lights and the Reticulated tracery above. The same awkwardness occurs at the same place in the CARLISLE WINDOW (128); and, in addition, five Geometrical patterns, quatrefoiled circles, are intruded; arresting the flow of curve: as also in the BEVERLEY REREDOS (486). There was many a divagation in directions where no road was. Nevertheless in many a Curvilinear window mullions and tracery at last touched and fused. "The trunks of the mullions, all springing from one soil, rose up to a certain height, and then shot themselves out into ramifications of the most intricate and delicate network, exhibiting a variety of combinations which baffles enumeration; the branches climbing and twisting one into the other in a maze full of entanglement, yet without confusion; the whole composition nevertheless, in its utmost license and seeming extravagance of fancy, subjected to the strict and inviolable laws of primary truth." *

SETTING OUT OF FLOWING TRACERY.—So far we have spoken of Flowing

* *English Review*, iv. 417.

as opposed to Geometrical tracery. As a matter of fact, both are Geometrical; in both the curves are drawn by a pair of compasses. The difference is that the curves of the former are simple, and of the latter compound. One reason, no doubt, why the Reticulated variety appeared so early was that though all its curves are ogee curves, and therefore compound, yet they can be set out in the simplest possible way. For example (487), in such a window as that of Merton vestry, if the base be taken as a radius, the window-arches are obtained. Then on the base set three semicircles, and let these be made to support four circles, and the four to support three circles, and the three to support two circles, all circles of the same size; then Reticulated tracery results at once. Even quite complicated tracery is easy to draw, if you know how; e.g. the circular windows at WAL-THAM ABBEY (488): to obtain centres for the curves, all that is necessary is to construct a hexagon with long and short sides alternating; each long side twice as long as each short one. So again in the windows at OLD WALSINGHAM (480.5), and the door at HOLBEACH (583), a pretty pattern common in East Anglia is got by intersecting hexagons. But, as time went on, in the subtle curves of Flamboyant, as in the Beverley reredos and the west window of SNETTISHAM (481), the draughtsman perhaps trusted to eye and wrist more than to rule and compass.

HYBRID WINDOWS. — Geometrical and Curvilinear patterns are often mixed; unskilfully, as in the case

Westminster Cloister.
Hingham S. Aisle.

of the five circles in the Carlisle window, and the six in the Beverley reredos ; or skilfully, as in the window at HINGHAM (489) and the south transept of Hull.*   In both these the skeleton of the window is purely Geometrical ; and the Geometrical patterns are filled up with flowing lines : but the two elements are kept entirely distinct, and are on different planes of tracery.   If the sub-arches consist of two ogee arches, the centrepiece may consist of a great circle ; as at MINCHINHAMPTON (286), in TEWKESBURY CHOIR (165), Nantwich and Exeter,† and in a great window of six lights at Chipping Norton ; the inner upper curves of the ogee arches forming part of the circumference of the circle.   An unhappy jumble of Geometrical and Curvilinear tracery is seen at Mildenhall,‡ the east window of Bristol Cathedral, and the south transept windows of St Mary Redcliffe.

ALTERNATION.—Both in the Geometrical and Curvilinear periods a range of windows in aisle or clerestory was usually of one uniform design ; *e.g.* in Lincoln presbytery, Beverley nave ; SELBY CHOIR (86).   Sometimes, however, while uniform in dimensions and in the number of their lower lights, the tracery was diversified.   This is especially the case at Exeter, where the windows differ all the way down the church, though each corresponds to a window on the opposite side of the church ;§ passing from Late Geometrical tracery in the east choir to assimilated Curvilinear in the western nave.   Instances of alternation occur also in purely Curvilinear work ; *e.g.* the four windows on the side of Patrington chancel are of two patterns.   The clerestory windows of Tewkesbury are much diversified.   All four in the Latin Chapel of Oxford Cathedral are different.   So also in the clerestory of Norwich choir windows of Perpendicular alternate with windows of Flowing design.

SIZE OF WINDOWS.—The side windows of the Gothic cathedrals soon grew to their full dimensions, practically occupying the whole space from buttress to buttress ; *e.g.* in Lincoln presbytery, *c.* 1260, and Exeter choir, *c.* 1280.   Perhaps the greatest amplitude was given to the window first in the chapter houses, *e.g.* Westminster and Salisbury.   In the latter, as in Amiens nave and in most of the Gothic of the Ile de France, the wall arch of the vault and the rear arch of the windows are fused together ; and Gothic construction is carried out to its logical issue ; the vault plainly resting not on walls but on detached piers. Fortunately we were not often so ultra-logical ; exceedingly unsatisfactory within and without is such an excessive attenuation of the supports ; indeed the preponderance of the voids over the solids is the crying sin of Late Gothic architecture.   Equally objectionable is the failure to provide the beautiful window tracery with a foil of blank stone around it.   How disastrous it would be to the design of SELBY CHOIR (86) to extend the windows from buttress to buttress !

* Illustrated in Sharpe's *Windows*, Plate 29.
† Sharpe's *Windows*, Plates 48 and 36.
‡ Illustrated in Paley's *Gothic Architecture*, 178.
§ For twelve of these windows see Britton's *Exeter*, Plate 12.

CHAPTER XXXIV.

RECTILINEAR TRACERY.

Reasonableness of Rectilinear Tracery — Transitional Types — Premature Rectilinear
and Belated Curvilinear Tracery—Characteristics of Rectilinear Tracery.

FROM the graceful tangles of flowing tracery we pass to the Rectilinear
"gridiron"; from poetic fancy to plain prose. It is an extraordinarily sudden
and complete revolution in the formation of window tracery; it is, moreover,
one into which none of the Continental Gothic styles passed, but is wholly
English. What brought it about? It has usually been held sufficient to say
that in later English art a degradation and debasement in taste set in; and
that this is its most conspicuous outward and visible sign. We humbly venture
to doubt it. Who that is an Englishman can regard the parish churches of East
Anglia, the choirs of Gloucester, York, and Norwich, the nave of Winchester,
the three Royal Chapels, but as a most precious heritage of mediæval art, to
be treasured among the greatest artistic triumphs of our race? Yet in all these
beauty of window tracery is almost wholly sacrificed and abandoned. Nevertheless it was not sacrificed and abandoned without a very sufficient reason.
Beauty of tracery was sacrificed for something which in the later days of Gothic
was treasured more and more, and for which there was nothing which clerk and
craftsman were not content and glad to sacrifice. And that was Stained Glass.
Ever will our later English art be misunderstood and unappreciated so long
as we refuse to visualise to ourselves what was that art's ideal. That ideal
was to build no more the House of God in stone, but to transmute the stone
into glass; to rear to the honour of God a spiritual house of coloured light;
fusing the very window jambs and mullions in the spreading effulgence
radiating from the multi-coloured stainings of the glass. To get the glory of
the lantern church there was nothing that our later builders were unwilling to
sacrifice; and the first thing to go was Flowing tracery.

It was in Gloucester Abbey that this great artistic revolution was initiated
and consummated. At Gloucester the glass,* the window tracery, the vault, all
received a special English character which was to differentiate them for ever
from the art of the Continent.

First, a great change was made in the glass.† It had been thick and

---

* Winston in his memoir on the east window of the choir minimises the importance of the
change made in glass at Gloucester; as is pointed out by Mr Lewis Day, p. 178.

† From the middle of the fourteenth to the later years of the fifteenth century the tendency
was more and more in the direction of light; "until our later Gothic windows become, in many

Gloucester Choir.
Oxford Divinity School.

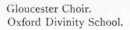

St George's, Windsor, Nave.
Sall, East Window.

opaque; now it was made thin and translucent. It had been a mass of colour; now colour was reduced to a minimum; a splash of ruby here, of azure there, a little purple or green, some golden stain, that was all; the greater part of the glass was uncoloured; a silvery white. The pictures too were harmonised with their architectural home; each figure was set in a tall canopy of silver glass, itself fitted into a stone niche of tracery. It is only necessary to compare the heavily coloured glass in the clerestory of the choir of Tewkesbury with the contemporary glass in the clerestory and east window of the neighbouring choir of Gloucester to realise how great the change was. It became possible now to use glass with the utmost freedom; it no longer dimmed and obscured. The light of Gloucester choir was as far from the dim, religious gloom that the modern ecclesiologist adores as from the light of common day.*

For the new glass there seems to have been a consuming enthusiasm. Lincoln, Ripon, Guisborough had led the way with great windows in their eastern fronts. In Carlisle and York we have seen the windows grow yet further in area. But Gloucester outdid all; she took out all her four end walls; first that of the SOUTH TRANSEPT (495), then that of the CHOIR (496), then that of the north transept, then that of the nave; and replaced all four by glass. This began while everybody else in England was putting in Flowing tracery; and indeed when Gloucester herself was erecting the monument, of thoroughly fourteenth-century type, to Edward II., which still stands in her choir. For the remodelling of the south transept took place between 1330 and 1337; and the vaulting of the choir and the glazing of its great east window seem to have been finished by 1350.†

But certain corollaries were inevitable. It is not possible to construct a window arch of the vast height and breadth of the east window of GLOUCESTER (496)—one, moreover, that has to take its share in supporting the weight of the

instances, not so much coloured windows as windows of white and stain enclosing panels or pictures in colour. Even in these pictures very often not more than one-third of the glass was in rich colour. And not only was more white glass used; but the white itself was purer and more silvery, lighter, and at the same time thinner" (p. 53). "The gradual dilution of the deep, rich, early colour is noticeable throughout the fourteenth century. Towards its close the glass craftsman halts no longer between two opinions, between light and colour. He conceives his window pretty generally as a field of white, into which to introduce a certain amount of rich colour; not often a very large amount. As a rule, perhaps, not more than one-fourth of the area of a fifteenth-century window was colour; for, in addition to the white of the canopy, there was commonly a fair amount of white in the draperies; and the flesh was now always represented by white. The typical Perpendicular window, then, is filled with shrine work in white; enclosing figures, or figure subjects, into which white enters largely (the flesh, and some of the drapery, often a good deal, is sure to be white), upon a background of colour" (p. 181). *Windows, a Book about Stained and Painted Glass*, by Lewis F. Day. Later, however, *e.g.* in the windows of Fairford Church, rebuilt *c.* 1490, and in those of King's College, Cambridge, contracted for in 1516 and 1526, the English tradition disappears, probably owing to Flemish influence; an immense amount of colour is used; enamelling is resorted to; the windows become opaque once more, and the interiors dark. See the photograph of King's College Chapel; it was taken in bright sunshine at mid-day in August. The invasion of Flemish glass is seen just as much in France; *e.g.* at Brou-en-Bresse.

* To see the new glass at its best, one should visit the ante-chapel of All Souls' College, Oxford, and St Martin's, York.

† See Willis' paper on *Gloucester*, and Winston on the east window.

vault and the roof—without taking precautions to ensure its stability. In the first place, lest the mullions bulge in, horizontal bars (*transoms*) have to be inserted from side to side. Secondly, instead of the tracery being independent of the window arch, as it is in the CARLISLE WINDOW (507), it must be so designed as to support the window arch, so that it may not be crushed in. For such support Flowing tracery, with its flickering ogee curves, is inadequate. The mullions, instead of curving, must be straight; as many of them as possible must rise straight up to the window arch. Nay, even secondary mullions (*supermullions*) must rise from the apex of every arch in the tracery, as in the window of the DIVINITY SCHOOL, OXFORD (492), to give yet additional vertical support. If that is not enough, secondary transoms may be introduced even into the tracery of the window head. The result is, a stone gridiron. But the stone gridiron is inevitable if, instead of the eight lights of York or the nine of Carlisle, Gloucester insists on having fourteen, ST GEORGE'S, WINDSOR (492), fifteen lower lights.

And whatever the artistic demerits of a gridiron, one may venture to imagine that it would not be without practical merits in the eyes of the draughtsman and the mason. How easy to draw! And how easy to execute, with its frequent repetitions of identical parts! Think of the Carlisle window, the curves of which required the plotting out of 263 different circles; and of its jointing, so complicated and artificial; while in the Gloucester and Windsor windows nearly all the joints are horizontal or vertical! Such a window was as easy to execute as it was to design. No doubt it appealed powerfully to the practical mind of the Englishman that so very much more window could now be had for the same money.

But what of the glassman, now most important of craftsmen? He must simply have been delighted with Gloucester's new east window. Instead of the circles and triangles of Geometrical tracery, and the writhing quatrefoils and ogees of Curvilinear, he had got now precisely what was wanted; (for every little figure in his stained glass there was a little rectangular niche. And here we may perhaps believe the new type of tracery reacted on the design of the glass. Rectilinear tracery lends itself readily to tier upon tier of priest and prophet and king; martyr, saint, and angel, one in each niche; it does not lend itself so well to story-telling, to picture-groups. And so design in glass grew much more simple; very much for the better of the art; for only the very simplest pictorial treatment is right in glass; glass should not try to be canvas. And so our best late windows, *e.g.* those at Gloucester and All Souls', become not as it were national picture galleries, but national portrait galleries.* And how much better the portraits are hung in such windows than in the Flowing windows! Imagine a portrait gallery with half the portraits hanging askew; some to the right, some to the left; a pain to the eyes. So it was with pictured saint and martyr; in the west window of York they flopped some to right, some to left. All this indecorum was subdued by putting them in rectangular niches, row upon row, each standing upright decorously on his

---

* It is not to be denied, however, that the picture-group still found admirers; *e.g.* the windows of Malvern, the east window of York Minster, and several windows in the parish churches of York.

Gloucester, South Transept and Crossing.

GLOUCESTER CATHEDRAL, THE PRESBYTERY.

feet.* Such an arrangement could not but find approval with canon, monk, craftsman, and devout layman alike.

May we not even go further, and argue that Geometrical and Flowing tracery was hardly worth the trouble and money it cost? The windows of Lincoln presbytery and Beverley nave are beautiful indeed from without. But are they beautiful from within? Mr Ruskin has drawn† specimens of Geometrical tracery, illustrating how exquisite is its beauty. So it is. But it is only under the conditions shown in Mr Ruskin's drawing that this or any other tracery is beautiful. Those conditions are that it be silhouetted either against a dark background or against the sky. Standing outside a church before its windows are glazed, the white stone of the tracery is projected against a dark background. See how beautiful under such a condition are the cloister windows of SALISBURY and NORWICH (458, 506). Even Rectilinear tracery looks lovely against the darkness. But if we stand inside a church, the tracery is only projected against a bright sky when the church is a ruin or when it is building; *i.e.* when the glass has been knocked out of the window or before it has been put in. What can be more beautiful than the tracery, albeit Rectilinear, of the ruined east window of Melrose, or than that of St Lawrence, Evesham, as it was when Britton drew it?‡ There are indeed three distinct stages in the inner history of the tracery of every window. It looks its best before it is glazed at all; it retains some of its beauty when glazed in transparent white glass; it loses it almost wholly when filled with stained glass, and viewed from within. If that be so §—it is only necessary to stand within a church with stained windows and good tracery to test the truth of it—may we not say that the old men were not altogether ill-advised to concentrate their attention on the inside rather than on the outside of the churches; not on the tracery which was effective externally, but ineffective within, but on the stained glass; which, ineffective externally, was, within, a sea of glory?

GLOUCESTER (59) did not confine her innovations to her end walls. She took down also the Norman clerestory of her choir, with its ineffective, small, isolated single windows, and replaced it by a towering clerestory that was practically one continuous sheet of glass: a clerestory that is to be regarded not so much as a series of independent windows, as a single choir-long continuous window with piers for mullions. The precedent of the Gloucester clerestory was followed soon after, timidly, at WINCHESTER and CANTERBURY (90); boldly at York, Malvern, Norwich. And what Gloucester had done with its clerestory, other churches hastened to do with their aisles; these also soon became sheets of glass. So that the end walls were glass, the clerestory walls glass, the aisle walls glass.

It was not, however, for a whole generation that the new art came to its throne. While Gloucester choir was building, the people at Tewkesbury, Beverley, Carlisle, Ely, Lichfield, Malmesbury, St David's, Selby, Wells, Worcester, developed into ever-growing splendour fourteenth-century art. But

---

* Equally indecorous is the disposition of the saints round the archivolts of the great French doorways.

† *Seven Lamps*, Plate 3, p. 105.   ‡ *Architectural Antiquities*, v. Plate 68.

§ Mr Ruskin elsewhere admits that "glass spoils all traceries" (*Seven Lamps*, 170).

Carlisle Choir Aisle.

in 1349 came the Black Death: after that there was neither the money nor the heart for another Ely Lady Chapel and Ely choir.   The simplicity of Gloucester stone-craft, the superiority of Gloucester glass, made their appeal at the right moment to a sobered England.   The new art spread like wildfire through the length and breadth of England; for the future the architecture of England was to be conditioned by glass and not by stone.   Cathedral church and abbey church were content to sit at the feet of Gloucester.   Above all, Gloucester set the fashion to all the later *parish* churches of England; in particular to Norfolk and Suffolk * and the glorious churches of the Fenland.

In 1327 Edward II. had been murdered at Berkeley.   The Bristol Augustinians dared not risk the animosity of the Court party by giving harbour to his corpse.   Brave Abbot Thokey conveyed it to Gloucester and buried it in the old Norman choir.   Miracles were wrought; pilgrims came by thousands from every part of the realm; so vast were their offerings that the Gloucester monks, so the chronicler tells us, might have rebuilt, had they willed, the whole abbey church.   They contented themselves at first with remodelling the south transept and the choir.   The works were commenced soon after 1330.   Round and above the new shrine of the King and Saint the works proceeded, till *c.* 1350 the vaults were up, and the windows glazed.   The scaffoldings were removed, and the world saw at last the revelation of a new art world; the glories of Gloucester choir.   And so it was that Gloucester choir, being in the fourteenth century so great a centre of English Christianity, was visited and inspected more than any other church in the country; and when the new glass and the new vaults were at length revealed to view, the fame of them passed at once to the furthest ends of the land.   Every pilgrim's tale, *c.* 1350, would be of the new vision in English art, the choir of Gloucester.

TRANSITIONAL WINDOWS.—It was not everywhere, however, that the conditions of the new style were accepted without demur, as they were in the east window of Gloucester and the west window of Winchester; where the tracery is almost wholly Rectilinear; *i.e.* composed of two sets of straight lines, vertical and horizontal, perpendicular to one another.   In a considerable number of the earlier windows, the greater part of the tracery is still composed of curves. A charming example is seen at Houghton-le-Dale; † and at St Michael's, Cambridge. ‡   Other well-known examples are the east windows of the choirs of Bristol § and WELLS (127).   Perhaps the finest example is the east window of the fourteenth-century chancel of HULL (81).   At first sight, with its two great intersecting ogee arches and ogeed lower lights, it looks as thoroughly Curvilinear as its rival, the west window of York.   But on closer inspection it will be seen that the vertical lines are there in abundance; and that in many cases these spring from the apices of arches, which are then said to be supermullioned.   (The transoms are probably not original.)   In the NAVE (96),

---

* At LONG MELFORD (547) there are no less than 74 traceried windows in the church proper.   Including the chapels, the vestries and the porch, but excluding the Lady Chapel, there are 97 (Lauriston Conder's monograph, 26).

   † Illustrated in Rickman, 223.   ‡ Illustrated in Freeman, 209.

   § A five-light geometrical window with its sub-arches supermullioned is illustrated in Freeman, 82, 94.

which is not much later and is but a Rectilinear version of the chancel, the principles of Rectilinear tracery are fully accepted, except that there are no transoms in the bottom lights.

JUXTAPOSITION OF CURVILINEAR AND RECTILINEAR TRACERY.—We now come to three puzzling sets of windows which appear to break the rules of chronological sequence that have been set forth hitherto. The first set comprises those which occur in a fourteenth-century building, the construction of which was postponed; so that when they were put up, a change of style had come about in window tracery, and the new window was given Rectilinear tracery. A curious early example of this is the east window of Evington, which has supermullions and transoms in the tracery; * i.e. it is a Rectilinear window; nevertheless the windows near it are of early Curvilinear design. It will be found that a large number of Rectilinear east windows, e.g. that of PAT-RINGTON (133), and some west windows also, e.g. in Ely Lady Chapel, occur in buildings of undoubtedly Curvilinear date. It would seem that the end windows were sometimes built later than the side windows.† We may suggest that in these cases, when all was complete except the end window, the Black Death may have arrived, 1349,‡ and stopped the works: and that when they were resumed the style had changed, and the window was filled in with Rectilinear tracery. Whether this be the true explanation or not, there must be some reason for the common occurrence in end windows of Rectilinear tracery in jambs and arches which have Curvilinear moldings; as at Patrington. So also in the fine Curvilinear church of Nantwich§ the end windows of the chancel and of one transept are Rectilinear.

A second set comprises examples of what we may call PREMATURE RECTILINEAR TRACERY.‖ Though Mr Sharpe gives c. 1360 as the commencing date for Rectilinear tracery, we have seen that it was evolved in the south transept of Gloucester between 1330 and 1337, and fully developed in the choir by c. 1350. At Gloucester, therefore, Rectilinear tracery did not follow on Curvilinear tracery. The Rectilinear tracery of the south transept followed on the heels of the Late Geometrical windows of the south aisle of the nave; built by Abbot Thokey, 1318 to 1329. At Gloucester¶ the Curvilinear period of tracery is largely missing. What was done at Gloucester would certainly be copied here and there elsewhere; e.g. in Cheltenham Church, where windows Rectilinear and Curvilinear in character occur side by side, and where the former have been erroneously supposed to be some thirty years later than the latter. And no doubt the same was the case elsewhere. For in the fourteenth century Gloucester was the greatest centre of pilgrimage in England; and its architectural doings could not fail to be reported far and wide, and here and there to be copied. In cases, therefore, where we see a Rectilinear and

* Illustrated in Brandon's *Analysis*, 252.

† Perhaps the end wall was left open for the removal of scaffolding, &c.

‡ Ely Lady Chapel is said to have been finished in 1349; but the east window was not inserted till 1373; the west window later still (Stubbs' *Ely*, 147).

§ Illustrated in Bowman and Crowther.

‖ A five-light window at the east end of the south aisle of Warmington has no tracery; the mullions rise straight up to the head. Its date is not later than c. 1280.—R. P. B.

¶ Beautiful Flowing tracery occurs, however, in the upper aisle of the choir.

a Curvilinear window side by side, they may be absolutely contemporaneous; the former having been executed between 1330 and 1360 on the lines of the work at Gloucester.

But there is an important and very large set of windows which are to be explained on other lines, and which we may call BELATED CURVILINEAR. It is usually assumed that c. 1360 all the world unanimously set to work to produce Rectilinear window tracery. This was certainly not so. In some districts, especially in those far distant from Gloucester, Flowing tracery held its own to the end of the fourteenth and probably well into the fifteenth century. Not everybody was willing to sacrifice the exquisite curves of Flowing tracery for the glassman's gridiron. This was especially the case in Norfolk and Suffolk; which at that time were hardly an integral part of England; but severed from the mainland by rivers and fens more completely than Ireland is now from England. East Anglia was an island, with insular and independent architectural traditions. There fourteenth-century grace found its last refuge. Thus at Ely, Bishop Barnet, 1367 to 1373, made three windows on the south side and two on the north side of the presbytery;* and these are of Flowing design.† So in Wimmington, Bedford, the brass of the founder gives 1391 as the date of his death; but "the details are remarkably pure Curvilinear."‡ So also the beautiful tomb in Durham Cathedral of Bishop Hatfield, who died in 1381, is of fine Curvilinear design. So also the Church of Etchingham, Sussex, built in 1386, is mainly Curvilinear.§ In East Anglia the retention of Curvilinear work is so common as to be characteristic. Thus in North Walsham Church, which was rebuilt after the destruction caused by the Norfolk rising of 1381, the east windows are thoroughly Curvilinear; and in the porch, which is probably later still, Curvilinear and Perpendicular windows alternate. So they do in the clerestory of the choir of Norwich Cathedral, 1361. The two Wiggenhalls, St Mary Magdalen, and St Mary the Virgin, are Curvilinear churches; so also is Walpole St Peter's; but all three have Perpendicular tracery in their windows.|| So also the windows of Terrington St Clement's have Rectilinear tracery; but the piers and arches are Curvilinear; it seems unlikely that the arcade was built in the fourteenth century without a clerestory; or that, if it had a clerestory, a new one was substituted for it in the fifteenth century. The same combination of Curvilinear arcade with Rectilinear windows is seen at Bacton¶ and Fresingfield, Suffolk; and Worstead, Norfolk. At Worstead, the hammerbeam roof and clerestory seem to

* *Anglia Sacra*, i. 664.

† In nearly all the aisle windows of Ely presbytery the masons copied the tracery without disguise from that which they found in one of the windows of Bishop Hotham's time, 1316-1337 (Stewart's *Ely*, 122).

‡ Brandon's *Parish Churches*, 93.

§ In the Battlefield Church, built after the battle of Shrewsbury in 1406, three of the windows have Curvilinear tracery (Mr W. A. Webb).

|| They are illustrated on pages 101, 107 of *Parish Churches*, by Mr Brandon, who assumes that the Walpole clerestory was originally Curvilinear, but rebuilt in Rectilinear style. He acknowledges, however, that it is very improbable that a fourteenth-century clerestory can have become ruinous in so short a time, so as to require renewal.

¶ Illustrated in Brandon's *Parish Churches*, 124, 118, 36.

have been built in 1378 with timber granted by the Prior of Norwich; here also it is easier to suppose that the Curvilinear arcade was built at the same time than to imagine that the arcade was put up *c.* 1340 and roofed; and that in 1378 this roof, which would still be sound, was pulled down and replaced by the present hammerbeam roof. So also at Rickenhall, Suffolk, a Rectilinear east window is "identical in date and workmanship" * with the other windows,

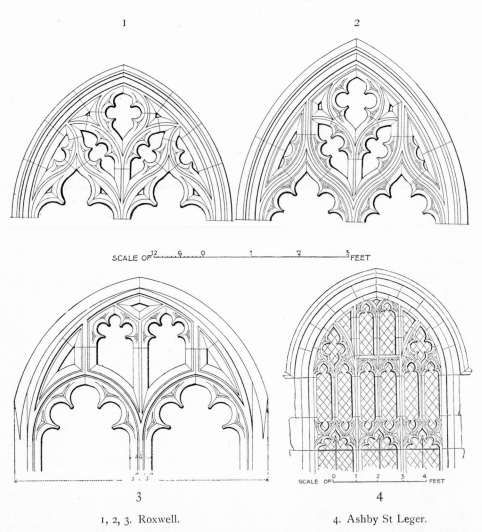

SCALE OF 12 6 0   1   2   3 FEET

SCALE OF 0 1 2 3 4 FEET

3

4

1, 2, 3. Roxwell.   4. Ashby St Leger.

which are of early fourteenth-century type: it seems more natural to accept the latter as Belated than with Mr Brandon to regard the former as Premature. For anticipations of style are rare, and require to be supported by the most positive documentary evidence; but survivals must always be a common result of the conservatism, indolence, and obstinacy of the average human

* Brandon's *Parish Churches*, 45.

mind.* The existence of "survivals" rises to a certainty in such an example as ROXWELL CHURCH (502), near Chelmsford. Here there are three windows, of which one would say that 1 is Curvilinear, 2 Transitional to Rectilinear, 3 Rectilinear. But the stones of all three windows come from the same layer in the same quarry. Also they were wrought at the same time; for if 3 were as much later than 1 as it appears to be, some sixty years, the stones in it would be in a higher state of preservation than those of 1; but after a minute examination of every stone, both inside and out, no difference can be detected.†

CHARACTERISTICS OF RECTILINEAR TRACERY.—As has been pointed out above, *transoms* were a necessity in windows of the vast span of the east window of Gloucester. In this they occur in the lower lights. But they occur also in the tracery, *e.g.* SALL (492), HULL (96), and CARLISLE (498); this is especially common in later work. At first the transom was a mere molded horizontal brace; but it was soon ornamented; in later work usually with miniature battlements or a cresting of Tudor flower. Or it was cusped in a very beautiful way, as in the ruined east window of Melrose and in Prince Arthur's chantry at Worcester and at ASHBY ST LEGER (502).

Transoms had been in common use in domestic work from the thirteenth century, *e.g.* in the halls of the Bishops of Lincoln and Wells, and in the Winchester Castle Hall. The object of them was to enable a casement to be inserted in that part of the lower light which was below the transoms. So also in a chancel the lower part of a side window was sometimes transomed, in order to permit the insertion of a shutter (page 517).

Transoms were frequently inserted later to strengthen the long mullions of earlier windows; *e.g.* the west window of HOWDEN (72) and the east window of HULL (81).

Another characteristic of Rectilinear windows is that the heads of the lower lights are almost always *cinquefoiled;* whereas in earlier windows the trefoiled head was common.

The quatrefoil also, which in the thirteenth century had had four equal arms, was to go through one more metamorphosis. In Curvilinear tracery it had had to take the form of a curved scimitar; in Rectilinear work the blade is straightened, and we get the form of the *dagger.*‡ Two examples of this are seen in the window from Ashby St Leger. In an early and simple form four examples occur in the west window of Hull; *cf.* William of Wykeham's work at Winchester; Edington Church; Headcorn Church; Merton College Chapel, and St Mary's Church, Oxford.§

As has been pointed out above, the primary motive of the design of Rectilinear windows was the provision of suitable accommodation for stained glass: beauty of tracery had become but secondary. Nevertheless artistic instinct did not cease to work; and in spite of the limitations imposed by the

---

* Flowing tracery is particularly common in windows of fifteenth-century towers. On the retention of fourteenth-century design in East Anglia, see Mr J. L. André in *Archæological Journal*, xlvi. 377, 389.

† Hadfield, 4.

‡ But this straight dagger appears also in late Geometrical tracery, *e.g.* SOLIHULL (626).

§ *Glossary*, Plates 252, 253, 254.

dominance of Rectilinear patterns, many of the windows have a distinct charm of their own. Among the most successful may be mentioned the west windows of BEVERLEY ST MARY (366), Shrewsbury Abbey, and HULL (96), all early examples, and reminiscent of the great traditions of fourteenth-century design, and of the north porches of Spalding and HEREFORD CATHEDRAL (203); both late work. The most disastrous change was the multiplication of the transom in the lower lights; which is as common in large early windows such as the east window of Gloucester and the west window of Winchester as in large late examples such as St George's, Windsor, and Henry the Seventh's Chapel, Westminster. It is only necessary to turn to the west window of Hull nave to see how much a window gains by the absence of transoms in the lower lights. Again, when arches occur in the tracery, they should not be cut through by straight lines. This occurs in the east window of SALL (492); but it is carefully avoided at Hull, and also in Sall transept.* The fewer curves there are in a Rectilinear window, the less is the risk of awkward collisions between the straight line and curve. Another objectionable practice, especially common in Tudor work, was the introduction of geometrical patterns in the middle of the rectilinear bars. It is seen at its worst, perhaps, in the lower windows of KING'S COLLEGE CHAPEL, CAMBRIDGE (473).

* Note in the DIVINITY SCHOOL, OXFORD (492), how well adapted for stained glass figures are the batement lights between the mullions, supermullions, and jambs ; cf. the Hull window ; also that the tracery does not commence at the spring of the arch, as it usually does in Geometrical and Curvilinear windows, and in the Hull window, but considerably below it : this is almost unavoidable when the window is set under a depressed four-centred arch. To this is given the name of Drop Tracery.

CHAPTER XXXV.

WINDOW CONSTRUCTION.

Functions of Tracery—Planes of Tracery—Cusping and Foliation—Scoinson Arch—
Inner Arcade—Mullions—Circular Windows—Sound Holes—Low Side Windows.

SO far we have traced the evolution of Gothic tracery from combinations of
lancets to the intermixture of rectilinear and geometrical patterns in Tudor
days. It remains still to deal with the functions and planes of tracery, cusping,
the rear-arch, moldings, and circular windows.

FUNCTIONS OF TRACERY.—The functions of tracery are partly constructional, partly decorative. Its chief constructional function is, with the aid of
the iron bars fixed in the sills and jambs, to enable the glass to withstand
wind pressure. In early work the weight of superincumbent wall is carried
by the window-arch without the aid of the tracery ; which indeed in early
windows almost invariably was constructed only after the window-arch was
complete,* and might be removed and has often been removed without endangering the stability of the arch. When, however, the arch is of a weak
form, e.g. when it is an ogee arch, the construction would be unsafe but for
the presence of the tracery. In large Rectilinear windows also, as has been
pointed out in 494, the mullions have real constructional value in strengthening the window-arch. In these the main mullions almost become piers, as
in the east windows of Gloucester, Sherborne, Warwick, and the west window
of Leominster ; and are sometimes strengthened outside by a buttress. But
even when it is not employed constructionally, the eye desiderates that the
tracery shall at any rate *appear* adequate to support the arch. This is all the
more so because from within the mullions are thinned to a surprising extent
by the irradiation of the light. Hence under no circumstances is attenuated,
wiry tracery, such as that of the east window of Shottesbrooke, endurable.

PLANES OF TRACERY.—But because it should be massive, it does not
follow that the whole of the tracery of the window need be equally massive.
One of the most beautiful features of the more highly developed mediæval
windows is the alternation of tracery of two, three, four, or even five † thick-
nesses, to which the name of *orders* has been given. It is necessary that leg,
arm, and backbone should be thick ; but not toes, fingers, ribs. So in the
window of NORWICH CLOISTER (506) the main skeleton is carefully differentiated from the minor work, the filling in of quatrefoils. The principle of subordination and recessing of orders had been worked out long before, even in
Norman days, in the arch (272) ; it produced equally beautiful results when

---

* Sharpe's *Windows*, 39.   † *I.e.* if the orders of the foliation be included.

applied to window tracery.* The west window of HOWDEN (72) may be taken as a characteristic example of subordination of orders. In this the window-arch, the tracery bars, and the centrepiece each contain two orders of moldings ; the foliation also contains two orders, the first of which is identical with the second order of the tracery, and the second of which is formed by soffit-cusps. Still more elaborate is the great east window at CARLISLE (128). The choir of Carlisle Cathedral was lengthened eastward after the great fire of 1292. The jamb shafts and the moldings of the jambs and the window-arch are of earlier date than the tracery ; the former, therefore, may be c. 1300, the latter considerably later ; indeed the tracery was not glazed till 1380-1384, as the arms remaining in the glass show. Both this and the west window of YORK (82)

Norwich Cloister. Ely Transept.

are 26 feet wide in the clear ; the Carlisle window is 51 feet high from the sill to the top of the tracery, while the York window is 2 or 3 feet lower ; on the other hand the tracery of the York window is more than 2 feet higher than that of Carlisle. It is a curious fact that in the Carlisle window more than half of the internal tracery was left unfinished. As is seen in 507, the tracery consists of 86 pieces ; some of these, e.g. 20 to 26, are very large, being between 4 and 5 feet long. They are beautifully jointed, and are arranged in such a way that any single stone can be removed for repairs without endangering the stability of

* It should be noted that the nomenclature is reversed. In an arch the innermost and narrowest order is spoken of as the first order ; in tracery the outermost and thickest order is the first. Also it should be remembered that the orders of the window-arch are one thing, and the orders of the tracery another ; students should describe the two sets of orders separately.

the tracery, except such as 1, 7, 26 to 20. The tracery, unlike that of York west window, is nowhere supported by the window-arch.

Fig. 2 shows the disposition of the three orders of tracery. The principal or outer order is confined to the window-arch, the sides of the sub-arches and the centrepiece, and the head of the circle in the lower part of the centrepiece. The middle order comprises all the lines in the centrepiece, except the head of the circle below and the three openings in the apex of the arch; also all the lines shown in the left sub-arch, and the corresponding lines in the right sub-arch. The inner order comprises the three openings in the apex of the arch at the top of the centrepiece; the tracery in the spandrels; and the whole of the tracery shown in the right sub-arch except that which has been specified as being of the middle order; also the corresponding lines in the left sub-arch.

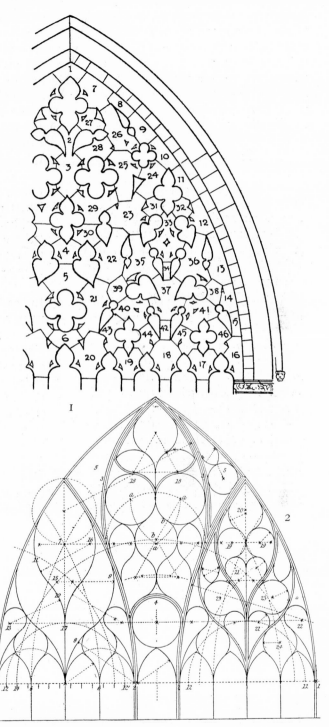

Carlisle East Window.

The curves of the window are struck from 263 centres.*

In the richer thirteenth and early fourteenth century work not only the jambs but the mullions were often faced with tiny shafts, provided with proper shaft and base; and these were continued as roll moldings in the curving bars which were the prolongation of the mullions upward. This roll is seen at RUDSTON, and in the aisle of the choir at Selby;† in the aisle of the nave it is omitted. But charming as this roll molding always is, it is in practice objectionable; for in horizontal lower portions of it, *e.g.* of the great circle in GUISBOROUGH WINDOW (476), the rain lodges, and, if frost supervenes, serious damage is done. Often, therefore, *e.g.* at LITTLE ADDINGTON (487.1), the roll molding is omitted, and the tracery is chamfered so as not to retain the wet. The same change took place in France.‡

Rudston.

CUSPING AND FOLIATION.— In such a window as that of RUDSTON, the four lower lights are set under pointed arches. The projecting points high up on either side of these four arches are called *cusps*, and the arcs on either side of the cusps are called *foils* (Latin, *folia*; French, *feuilles*).§ In each of these four lower lights there are two cusps and three foils. Each, therefore, is a trifoliated pointed arch.‖ On page 510 there are illustrated both a quatrefoil and a quatrefoiled circle. Each pair of lower lights is included in a detached pointed arch, in the head of which is a circle containing four cusps and four foils or lobes; it is therefore a quatrefoliated circle. The two great detached pointed arches carry a circle which has six cusps and six foils, and is therefore called a sexfoliated circle.

The origin of the foliated or cusped arch has been held to be arcading composed of trefoiled arches.¶ If a trefoiled arch be included within a pointed

---

* Billing's *Carlisle*, Plates 18, 19; text, 59 to 64.   † See Plate on page 86.

‡ Compare the window in Amiens choir figured in Dehio, Plate 577, 3, and text 2, 580, and that of St Gervais in Choisy's *Histoire*, ii. 383, 379.

§ What Rickman called *foils* are really cusps. In Parker's *Glossary*, also, 157, *cusp* is erroneously given as the equivalent of *feuille*.

‖ Such an arch is *pointed*, and must therefore be distinguished from a *trefoiled* arch. So also a quatrefoil by itself is nothing but a quatrefoil; but a circle containing a quatrefoil is a quatrefoiled circle, as in the small circles of the Rudston window.

¶ Willis' *Middle Ages*, 41; Sharpe's *Windows*, 32; Paley's *Gothic Architecture*, 160.

arch, a trifoliated pointed arch is produced. But there is no evidence whatever that such a combination was in common use.* Moreover, the trefoiled arch only appears in arcades in the second half of the twelfth century; whereas a cusped window is already seen in the Norman work of the ruins of Castle Rising; it is distinctly cusped by pendent knobs projecting out of the arch. Late Norman doorways also were sometimes trefoiled: *e.g.* the so-called Prior's doorway at ELY (39); and the Transitional doorway of the north transept of Ripon.† The function of cusps is asserted to be that of thickening and strengthening a curved bar at the point where pressure is concentrated.‡ It may be doubted, however, whether cusps are not mainly, perhaps wholly, inserted for decorative reasons. Certainly many cusps are set where they can be of no constructional value.

Cusping was in use earlier than tracery. It is common in lancet windows of the second quarter of the thirteenth century; *e.g.* at WINNAL MAGDALEN, HAMPSHIRE. When, therefore, in the Early Geometrical de-signs two or more lancets were put together into one window, it was natural to cusp both these lower lights, and the circular centrepiece which they carried.

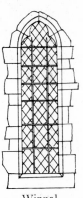

Winnal
Magdalen.

Cusps are of much importance as chronological § evidence. In the first place, early cusps spring from the soffit, and not as the later cusps do, from the chamfer plane of the arch, *i.e.* from the slope of the side. Soffit-cusps are seen clearly at Little Addington, Winnal Hampden, Rudston. It is usually asserted that the soffit-cusp is invariably early, and the chamfer-cusp invariably late. ‖ But this is to exaggerate. The west window of HOWDEN (72), which can hardly be earlier than 1300, has soffit-cusps; probably, however, they hardly ever occur after the first quarter of the fourteenth century. On the other hand, chamfer-cusps are sometimes found in the first half of the thirteenth century.¶ Secondly, as in 510.8, in early examples of cusped circles, a circle may be drawn passing through the points of all the cusps; *e.g.* inside the centrepiece and small circles of RUDSTON (508): whereas in later examples, the various foils are arcs not of one but of several circles. Thirdly, in early examples all the foils or lobes of a trefoil, quatrefoil, &c., are parts of equal circles disposed in a ring.** Fourthly, early thirteenth-century cusps are plain;

---

* Paley, *loc. cit.*, instances a lancet window in the tower of Clipsham, Rutland; and the windows of Stanton St John, illustrated in *Glossary*, Plate 226, as formed in this way.

† In France cusped doorways commenced early, especially in the South of France; from which they spread to Spain; where they had a great vogue. *Cf.* the doorways at Dorat and Rosiers, illustrated in Enlart's *Manuel*, 361, 305, 311.

‡ Garbett's *Principles*, 176. So also Choisy's *Histoire*, ii. 380, 381, 382. So essential a member did Mr Ruskin regard the cusp in Gothic construction that he defined Gothic as "Foliated Architecture"; which is much as if one should define man as a being which hath buttons.

§ It must be borne in mind that such minute distinctions as the following are only true in a general way.

‖ Rickman; Brandon; Paley; *Glossary*.   ¶ Sharpe's *Windows*, 34.

** Brandon's *Analysis*, 21.

late cusps are sometimes molded, as in LINCOLN PRESBYTERY. Fifthly, the easiest way of constructing a soffit-cusp was to cut a block to shape and to insert it in a groove made in the arch or circle for its reception. Sir G. Scott notes that at Westminster nearly all the windows of the church and cloister had detached cusps. In a circle a set of cusps so fixed would often keep one another in position. But if placed in the arch of a lower light, they would drop out, if the frost found its way in. So the cusps of the lower lights were sometimes cut out of the solid : while the cusps of the circles were detached blocks fixed in a groove. In the end moisture and frost generally penetrated

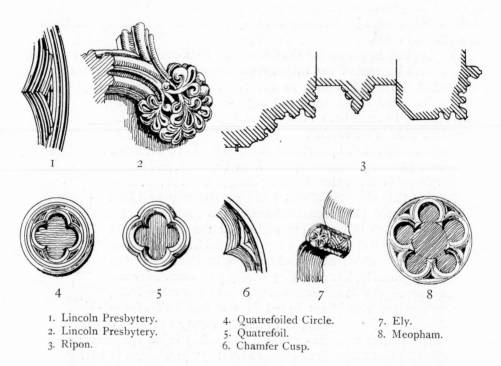

I   2   3

4   5   6   7   8

1. Lincoln Presbytery.   4. Quatrefoiled Circle.   7. Ely.
2. Lincoln Presbytery.   5. Quatrefoil.   8. Meopham.
3. Ripon.   6. Chamfer Cusp.

the groove, and the cusps of the circles also dropped out. Thus at Raunds * the solid cusps of the lower lights survive, whereas the detached cusps of the circles dropped out ; as also from the circles of the windows of the north aisle of Chichester nave.† In many late thirteenth-century windows circles which now are uncusped were formerly cusped ; cusps, which had dropped out, not having been renewed by the churchwardens, because of the expense or because they increased the difficulty of glazing. In some examples, however, there are no signs of grooves, and it is possible that the circles were always uncusped ; *e.g.* in the west window of Grantham north aisle.‡ Sixthly, the earliest cusps ended in a point, as in the lower lights of Rudston, or in a blunt square tip, as in the centrepiece, or in a round knob, as in Westminster chapter house. But this tip was very often ornamented ; *e.g.* with conventional foliage, as in LINCOLN

* Illustrated in Sharpe's *Windows*, Plate 9.   † They have been restored.
‡ Illustrated in Sharpe's *Windows*, Plate 10.

PRESBYTERY (510.2), and WARMINGTON (467); * or, later on, with masks, grotesques, and angels.

Cusp design reached its highest development in the fourteenth century. Cusps were now themselves cusped ; *i.e.* compound replaced simple cusping ; *e.g.* in the choir screen of Exeter. Exquisite effects were thus gained in the rich work of the fourteenth century ; *e.g.* in the cusping of the shrine of St Etheldreda, ELY, and the PERCY SHRINE,† BEVERLEY (269), where the tips of the cusps are carved into figures of the angelic choir, playing on instruments of music. In Rectilinear work this exuberance of fancy died away, except here

Ely, Pedestal of Shrine.

and there, as in HOWDEN CHAPTER HOUSE (137), and in some of the rich work of the Tudor period, such as Bishop West's Chapel at ELY (143). There is much beautiful cusping in woodwork of all periods ; *e.g.* in the Winchester choir stalls ;‡ and the Rectilinear rood-screens of Dickleburgh and Ranworth, Norfolk. §

* The great west window of Binham on page 471 should be shown with foliated cusps.

† Really this is the tomb of Lady Eleanor Fitz Alan, wife of Henry, first Lord Percy of Alnwick ; she died in 1328. Mr Longstaffe has pointed out that the canopy cannot have been finished before 1340 ; for a shield of France and England quarterly occurs on the south side.

‡ Illustrated in Colling's *Gothic Ornaments*, i., Plate 77.

§ Illustrated in Colling's *Gothic Ornaments*, ii. 19.

REAR-ARCH AND INNER ARCADE.—In the eleventh and twelfth centuries
the walls were often of poor construction, the inner and outer facings only
being of dressed stone (*ashlar*), while the middle was filled in with rubble.
Walls so constructed had necessarily to be thick.   And in order to get
as much light as possible through such thick walls, the early windows, *e.g.*
RIPON AISLE (102), TINTERN, and STANWICK (457.9), were given a very broad
internal splay, so that the inner arch of the window was usually four or
five times as broad as the outer.   But the splay was often not so extensive
above as at the sides ; * for it was not desired to project the light upward into
the roof, but downwards to the congregation.   While, therefore, the window-
arch in the Lancet period was acutely pointed, the rear-arch might be
obtusely pointed or segmental.   Sometimes, indeed, as in the south aisle of
St Albans, the rear-arch was actually lower than the window arch.   Such a
window consists of three parts : the outer or window-arch, the inner or rear-arch

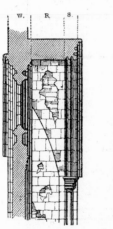

Tintern Aisle.   Oxford Cathedral Belfry.

(Professor Willis' *Scoinson* arch), and the space between, the rear-vault : all
three parts are well seen in the Tintern window.   Obviously the great thickness of the wall, and the consequent breadth of the rear-vault and its supporting
walls, offered great scope to the designer.   And so long as windows were built in
this fashion, with the glass near the external face of the thick wall, they could be
set in magnificent frames, as seen from within the church.   Sometimes, but not
often, the rear-vault itself was vaulted with diagonal ribs ; or it was molded,
as in the east window of Ripon ; and most elaborately of all, in the east
window of NETLEY (699.4) ; most often, it was left plain, as at Stanwick.   Its
jambs, as at Netley, might be beautified with detached shafts in correspond-
ence with the orders of the molded rear-vault above.   Much care was given
also to the rear-arch.   Sometimes, as at Stanwick, it was chamfered ; often it
was richly molded, as at Rievaulx, Guisborough, Netley, and TINTERN.†   These

* York transept is an exception ; here the window and rear arches are concentric.
† Here W = window ; R = rear-vault ; S = Scoinson arch.

moldings sometimes die into the jambs; sometimes they descend to the sill; sometimes they are stopped by a corbel; sometimes, as at Tintern and Netley, they are carried to the sill by a shaft or shafts. In later examples, *e.g.* in a fourteenth-century window in the triforium of Gloucester, and in the north aisle of the choir of Worcester, in thirteenth-century work, the arch may be cusped.

But there was a still more delightful way of turning the plain splay into a thing of beauty; this was to construct minor arches beneath the rear-arch. This had been done long before in many a clerestory; *e.g.* in Norman work at Winchester and ELY (506); and in the thirteenth century at Boxgrove. So also, for the sake of strength, belfry windows in towers, *e.g.* at OXFORD (512), had been at times built double. So arose a fashion of constructing two windows; the outer one glazed, the inner one unglazed. Charming examples remain in Salisbury transept, Worcester choir aisle, and Stone, Kent. In the late thirteenth century the inner arcade to the window was still employed in rich examples, as in Lincoln presbytery, and Durham eastern transept. And in the best work, both here and in France, *e.g.* at Stone, DURHAM (514), and the glazed triforium of St Ouen, Rouen, care was taken that the inner and outer tracery should be different in pattern.* One of the latest examples of the double window is in the presbytery of YORK (199). But here the whole arrangement is reversed; it is the outer tracery that is unglazed, the inner that is

Stone.

glazed. The result is that the window proper is in a line with the inner face of the clerestory wall, and from within the effect is flat and shadowless. Therefore,

---

* So those ingenious decorators, the Arabs, wishing to combine the beauties of two kinds of ornament, often do so without inconsistency by placing them on the same surface, but giving them different degrees of relief, or different colours, so that one appears superposed in front of the other, without interfering with it. The eye can follow each separately, as the ear follows the bass or treble of a complex piece of music (Garbett's *Principles*, 47).

2 K

when the choir was built a few years later, the outer unglazed arcade was abandoned, and the clerestory windows were set further away from the inner face of the wall. A similar change of design occurs in St Urbain de Troyes, where the windows both of choir and nave have double arcades of tracery; but in the choir the inner arcade is glazed, in the nave the outer.

So far we have spoken as if the custom of setting the window close to the outer face of the wall was universal. This was not so. There were many exceptions; *e.g.* at Glastonbury and Wells, and at Byland, Whitby, Lincoln, SOUTHWELL (390), the windows were considerably recessed externally. Such an exterior gains greatly by the shadowy recesses of its fenestration. But the reason for the

Durham Eastern Transept.

arrangement was probably not an æsthetic one. It was no doubt simply the practical reason that the glass, when recessed, was better protected from the rain. And as usual, in all good Gothic, the practical reason prevailed; and the windows were more and more recessed externally. In Curvilinear windows, as at SLEAFORD (701.3), the glass is usually placed exactly in the centre of the wall, and the moldings of the inner and outer arch are usually the same; in Geometrical windows this is rarely the case. In some Perpendicular windows, *e.g.* in the tower of LOUTH (611), the window is recessed very deeply externally, and very fine shadow effects are produced. But what such windows gained externally, they lost internally; especially now that the walls were less thick than they had been in the thirteenth century. The loss, however, of internal moldings such as those of Ripon and Netley may have been a matter of indifference to the fifteenth-century designer; who seems to have thoroughly appreciated the fact that black-and-white work would be thrown away in the blaze of colour of his windows; just as an etching is killed by juxtaposition with an oil painting.

MULLIONS (Monials).—In moldings of the mullions one practical improvement was made. Some of the earlier mullions were nearly equally broad both ways; *e.g.* in the east windows of Lincoln and Guisborough. But to resist wind pressure they needed to be longest in a direction perpendicular to the walls. The later ones are generally so designed; *e.g.* BERE (515.13-15). Artistically

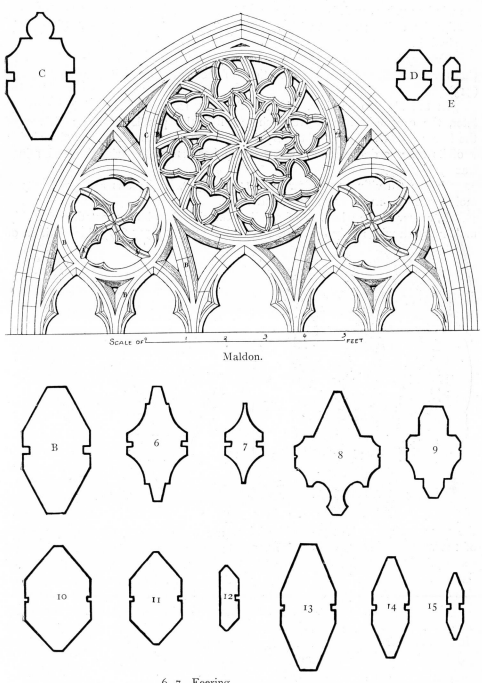

SCALE OF 0 1 2 3 4 5 FEET

Maldon.

6, 7. Feering.
8, 9. George Inn, Glastonbury.
10, 11, 12. White Colne.
13, 14, 15. Bere.

the window gains much by depth of mullion. For the glass cuts off half of each mullion from view ; so that with mullions of the earlier type there is little room for shadow.

Tracery bars are continuations of mullions ; and their moldings are sometimes repetitions, sometimes elaborations of those of the mullions, as at MALDON (515).

In the Maldon window, which is dated *c.* 1276 by Hadfield but appears later, the centrepiece is a great circle ; B is the profile of the mullions of the lower lights and of the tracery bars ; C of the outer order of the circle ; F of its inner order and of the curved spokes ; E of the triangles and minor tracery.

In the Curvilinear window of TILTEY (699), half plans are given of the moldings of the mullions, tracery, and cusps.

If, however, the windows of small plain churches be inspected, such richly molded work will rarely be found ; *e.g.* at FEERING (515.6, 7), though it is of

St James', Bristol.

Boyton.

the same period as Tiltey. Still plainer are the mullions, tracery, and cusps of the WHITE COLNE window (515.10-12); though it also is of the fourteenth century. At all periods merely straight chamfers may occur, as in the Rectilinear east window of BERE (515.13-15); the moldings of the south window of this chancel are of a type common in Late Gothic.

CIRCULAR WINDOWS.—A small circular window or *oculus* was a natural ornament to set in a gable, and occurs in Early Christian basilicas, and in our Norman and Transitional work ; *e.g.* Darenth ; Iffley ; and St Cross, Winchester. (1.) The smaller examples, and even the large circle in Canterbury south transept, are without tracery. (2.) Sometimes, however, as at Barfreston, PATRIXBOURNE (218), PETERBOROUGH WEST FRONT (112), and BEVERLEY MINSTER (176), tracery is inserted in the form of diminutive shafts, each with capital and base ; a window with such shafts or spokes is called a *wheel* window. (3.) Or *plate-tracery* may be inserted, as in ST JAMES', BRISTOL, and Beverley transept.   In England the example on the largest scale is in LINCOLN NORTH TRANSEPT (69), the *Dean's Eye* (it faces the Deanery). We have nothing, however, to compare with the immense plate-tracery circles of Laon and Chartres. (4.) Later come those with Geometrical bar-tracery, as at BOYTON, WILTS (516). (5.) Next come Curvilinear windows, with Flowing tracery, of which we illustrate examples at WALTHAM (488) and at LINCOLN (484), the *Bishop's Eye*, facing the Bishop's Palace. (6.) Rectilinear examples are rare : one is the east window of St Margaret, Lynn.

The rose window was not developed to the same extent as in France. Nor as a rule did we put it in so conspicuous a position ; employing it usually in the transepts only. In the west front of Byland, however, there is a ruined rose of great span ; and a vast rose, as big as the largest of France, those of the transepts of Notre Dame, Paris, seems to have occupied the east front of Old St Paul's.

In France the rose was first put under a circular arch ; as at Laon, Chartres, Paris west rose, Braisne, Mantes, Abbaye d'Ardenne. Then it was set under a pointed arch, as at Reims. Then it was inscribed in a square, and the spandrels were pierced, as in Paris and Sées transepts. This was the stage apparently reached in Old St Paul's.* Then the French set it on a tier of lower windows, so that the rose ceases to be pre-dominant, and becomes merely the centrepiece of a vast window-composition covering the whole end of such transepts as those of Rouen and Sens Cathedrals.

Circular windows occasionally occur in the clere-story ; *e.g.* in Southwell nave and Ledbury chancel ; and frequently in East Anglian parish churches ; more rarely in the triforium, as in Waltham Abbey, WEST-MINSTER (379), Hereford north transept.

Other forms of window occur. Especially common is the Vesica Piscis, *e.g.* in the gable of the south

Huish Episcopi.

transept of BEVERLEY (176). The clerestory windows of Lichfield nave are spherical triangles.

BELFRY WINDOWS.—In Somerset it is common to fill in the lower part of belfry windows with perforated stonework instead of louvre boards ; as at HUISH EPISCOPI and ILE ABBOT (591). In the next stage lower, rectangular openings called "sound holes," are usually employed in the towers of Norfolk ; they are generally filled with flowing tracery,† *e.g.* Worstead ; HOLME (591). Really they are not sound holes ; for they light the ringers' chamber ; not the belfry.

LOW SIDE WINDOW.—This occurs usually on one of the sides of a chancel : its lower part, or the whole of it, closed with a shutter ; *e.g.* GEDNEY (474.1). Its ritualistic use is still uncertain. The chief theories are these—(1.) It may be a Leper's window ; this is highly improbable. (2.) A lamp may have been placed within to scare away ghosts. (3.) Confessions may have been heard

* See Hollar's print in Prior, 345.
† A collection of " sound holes " was illustrated in the *Builder*, Aug. 18, 1900.

through it of persons not allowed to enter the church.   (4.) A small sanctus bell may have been rung from it, to apprise the neighbourhood of the Elevation of the Host.   See illustrated articles by J. H. Parker in *Archæological Journal*, vol. iv., Dec. 1847 ; J. Piggott in *Reliquary*, 1868, vol. ix. 9 ; P. M. Johnston in *Transactions of St Paul's Ecclesiological Society*, vol. iv. 263 ; J. J. Cole in *Journal of Archæological Institute*, March 1848 ; Rev. J. P. Hodgson in *Archæologia Aeliana*, 1901.

CHAPTER XXXVI.

THE TRIFORIUM.

Definition—Sham Triforium—Four-storied Interiors—Windowed Triforium—Blindstory —Walled Triforium—Absorption of the Triforium into the Pier Arcade or the Clerestory—The Transparent Triforium—Use of the Triforium.

DEFINITION.—The term *triforium* strictly applies only to the arcade which is seen in many vaulted churches below the clerestory and above the pier-arches. But it is often used, not of the arcade, but of the space at the back of the arcade. So that it means sometimes the triforium arcade, sometimes the triforium chamber.* We will speak first of the triforium chamber; secondly, of the triforium arcade.

TRIFORIUM CHAMBER.—This is the space between the vault of the aisles and a lean-to roof of sharp pitch which is constructed in order to protect the masonry of the vault from the weather. If, however, the vault of the aisle be a half barrel (284), as in St Trophime, Arles, there will be no space between the half barrel and the roof, and consequently no triforium chamber.† We have no example of an aisle so vaulted.

In SOUTHWELL NAVE (520) is seen the exterior of the north aisle of the nave with a lean-to roof. Below is shown the vaulting of this Norman aisle, which has diagonal ribs. In the interior of the nave one looks through the triforium-arcade, which consists of one semicircular arch in each bay, and has a glimpse of the lean-to roof of the aisle. In the example from CHICHESTER NAVE (520), the whole of the triforium-chamber of the south aisle is seen from end to end, from the distant east end where it opens into the south transept to the west end where it opens into the south-west tower. The interior of a lofty triforium-chamber is illustrated from NORWICH NAVE (371).

SHAM TRIFORIUMS.—Before going further, we may clear the ground of

---

* The etymology of the word is obscure. It has been derived from *trinæ fores*, "a triple opening." But the triforium has usually a single, double, or quadruple opening; very seldom a triple one. Mr Edward Bell, however, notes that Gervase, who first uses the term, applies it at Canterbury not only to the triforium proper, but to any passages in the thickness of the wall, *e.g.* in front of the clerestory. Now the arcade of a Norman clerestory is often a triple one; *e.g.* at Chichester and Ely. He therefore suggests that triforium was originally applied to the triple arcades of the clerestory passage, and was afterwards extended to any wall passages or thoroughfares. Willis, however (*Nomenclature*, 61, 3, and 70, 4), points out that *opus triforiatum* was applied to perforated work in lock plates, brass fenders, &c., in which figures of plants and animals were produced by piercing plates of metal. So also Enlart's *Manuel*, 255 : "*Triforium* vient de l'adjectif français *trifore* ou *trifoire*, sorti du latin *transforatum* et qui signifie repercé ou ajouré (fréquent dans les inventaires de joyaux). Le triforium est, en effet, un chemin de ronde dont la paroi est ajourée." So that originally it means any passage in the thickness of the wall as well as the passage provided by a triforium chamber.

† See *Classification of Romanesque*, 278.

Southwell from N.W.
Southwell, N. Aisle of Nave.

Southwell Nave from S.W.
Chichester, Triforium of Nave.

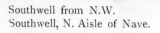

Waltham Abbey.
Cérisy Nave.

Shrewsbury Abbey.
St Saviour's, Southwark, Choir.

Chester Cathedral Cloister.
Malmesbury Nave.

Norwich Cathedral from S.W.
Ely Choir from S.W.

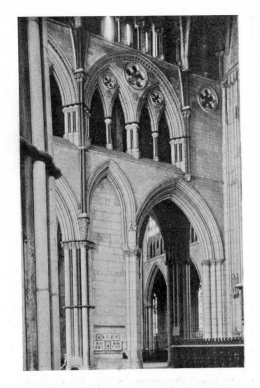

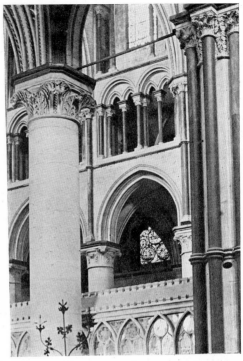

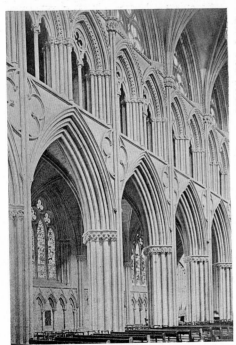

York S. Transept
Lichfield Nave.

Canterbury Choir.
Hereford N. Transept.

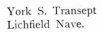

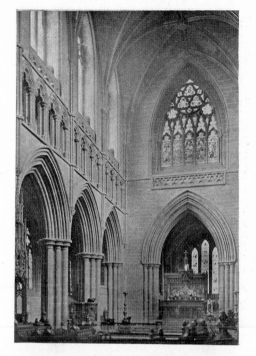

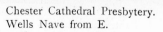

Chester Cathedral Presbytery.
Wells Nave from E.

Chester Cathedral N. Transept.
Tintern from N.E.

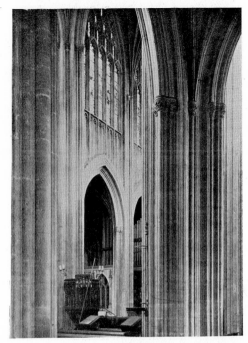

Bayeux Choir from S.W.
Oxford Cathedral Transept.

Bristol St Mary Redcliffe.
St David's Nave.

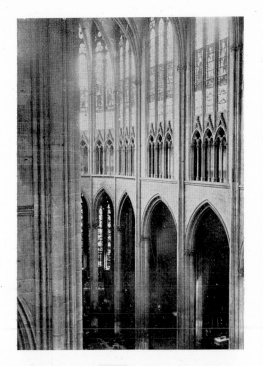

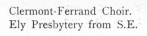

Clermont-Ferrand Choir.
Ely Presbytery from S.E.

Shrewsbury Abbey.
Ely Presbytery from S.W.

certain so-called triforiums,* which lack either the vault below, or the lean-to roof above, or both. Of the first, that of Rochester nave is an example; it has the triforium-arcade, but the aisles are unvaulted. It was never intended to have a triforium-chamber, for a passage is provided from bay to bay in the thickness of the wall. The nave of WALTHAM (521) also, c. 1130, has no aisle to the vault, as appears from the foreground, and therefore no triforium-chamber. But at the back of each pier and on the aisle wall opposite to each pier are the marks left by supports for a vault which have been torn away. So that originally there was a genuine triforium here. A French example of a sham triforium is seen in the archaic nave of Vignory.

To a second class belong those triforiums which have above them not a lean-to roof, but a vault. Of this second class we have two examples. One is ST JOHN'S CHAPEL (283) in the Tower of London, c. 1080; where above the groined lower aisle is a longitudinal barrel vault. The other is in GLOU-CESTER CHOIR (282), where above a groined lower aisle is a half barrel † vault. In the Romanesque and Gothic of the twelfth century in France the so-called triforium was frequently covered with a groined or with a ribbed vault. This occurs even in the eleventh century at Jumièges. Considerable confusion has been caused in French and English text-books by speaking of these as triforiums; they are both upper vaulted aisles. ‡

A third class includes those which have neither lean-to roof nor vaulted aisle, but a triforium-arcade; e.g. Malton, Dunstable, Tutbury, and SHREWSBURY ABBEY (521). This has come about accidentally. Originally there was a clerestory. When this became ruinous it was pulled down; the lean-to roof of the aisle was lowered, and the triforium-arcade was glazed; e.g. the triforium-arcade of SHREWSBURY ABBEY (526) was glazed after it had lost its clerestory; recently the clerestory has been rebuilt. At Binham it was the aisle that became ruinous and was pulled down; leaving a triforium-arcade, but no triforium-chamber. At PONT AUDEMER (131), in Normandy, a charming example of Flamboyant, it seems to have been found impossible to erect a clerestory; and so what was meant to be a triforium-arcade was utilised as a clerestory.

FOUR-STORIED INTERIORS.—Of this we have but an imperfect example in the south transept of Westminster. What would normally be occupied by a western aisle is here represented by one of the walks of the vaulted cloister; and above that is the muniment room; above which are triforium-chamber and clerestory; four vertical compartments in all. There was hardly room for four stories in English interiors. Our churches are much lower than those of France; our highest vaulted interior (excepting Westminster, the unusual height of which is no doubt due to French influence), that of Salisbury, is but 84 feet high. From the beginning the French interiors were very lofty; in the end Amiens reached 144 feet, Beauvais 150 feet, Cologne 155 feet. In the twelfth

---

* " Certaines eglises ont de fausses tribunes " (Enlart's *Manuel*, 256).

† Gloucester choir, with groined vault to its lower aisles and demi-berceau to its upper aisles, may possibly reproduce the original dispositions of the nave of the Abbaye-aux-Hommes, at Caen.

‡ " Les tribunes laterales ne sont autre chose qu'un second étage des bas-côtés " (Enlart's *Manuel*, 254).

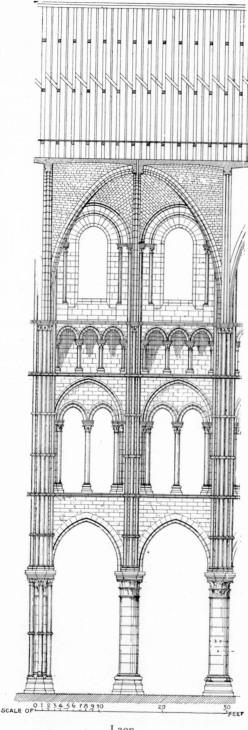

Laon.

century it seems to have been thought in France that clerestory walls so lofty and loaded with vaults required to be steadied; and so aisles were built up in two stories; both of them vaulted, and the upper vaulted aisle giving valuable abutment to the clerestory wall.* Jumièges, consecrated 1067, has superposed aisles; here, however, the nave was not vaulted, and the upper vaulted aisle was therefore hardly necessary; it does not appear again in the remaining churches of Anglo-Norman Romanesque. Tournay nave is a fine example; also Romanesque. Such an internal elevation found great favour in the last half of the twelfth century in the Transitional and Early Gothic of the Ile de France and Champagne; but seldom elsewhere; *e.g.* St Germer, near Beauvais; Montier-en-Der; Notre Dame, Chalons-sur-Marne; LAON nave; Noyon; Senlis; Soissons south transept; Mantes; Meaux, originally; Notre Dame, Paris, now only in the bays adjoining the transept. These are some of the most impressive interiors in Gothic architecture; multiplicity and complexity of parts, so effective in increasing the apparent length of the Gothic churches, was equally successful in magnifying their apparent height; nothing later ever surpassed the choir of St Remi, Reims; or its probable prototype, Notre Dame, Chalons-sur-Marne.† But for this

* "If the walls of the tribunes have themselves vaults or transverse arches, the tribunes provide abutment to the transverse arches or to the vaults of the central aisle. . . . The principal use of the tribunes is to provide abutment by their vault to the central vault" (Enlart's *Manuel*, 255, 256).

† Parts of Notre Dame, Chalons-sur-Marne, are 1157-1183; parts of S. Remi are 1170-1190 (Enlart's *Manuel*, 628).

a heavy price had been paid. The cost of giving the aisles additional height and an extra set of vaults must have been enormous. Moreover the pier-arcade was usually so curtailed as to be low and squat. So also was the clerestory. This perhaps was the most serious defect of all; for it meant to cut off much of the main source of light from the Early Gothic church, already plunged in gloom with its few insulated exiguous windows obscured by the opaque stained glass of the day. This objection was taken seriously to heart. Hardly was Notre Dame, Paris, finished, when the pitch of the aisle roofs was lowered, thus abolishing the triforium chamber and its arcade of circular apertures; and the clerestory windows were brought down lower to increase the amount of light; only the bays near the transepts being left unaltered, for fear of endangering the stability of the great arches of the transept. And so the greater part of Notre Dame now has a curious three-story elevation; viz. lower vaulted aisle, flat-roofed upper vaulted aisle, clerestory; without any triforium at all. While at Meaux, extensive repairs being necessary, the vault of the lower aisle was pulled out, without endangering the stability of the church; leaving the aisle covered with what had originally been the vault of the upper aisle.* At Eu, near Dieppe, the authorities evidently were halting between two opinions; for some of the bays are three, others four stories high internally.† Still more undecided was the state of mind of the architect of Rouen Cathedral; for he built up the nave wall in four stories; pier-arcade of the lower aisle, arcade of the upper aisle, triforium-arcade, and clerestory. But as a matter of fact there is only one aisle; not two aisles superposed; the lower vault never having been built, though the supports for it are there.‡ This period of hesitancy ended in the adoption by everybody of a three-story interior. In Gothic architecture Sens had already led the way in 1140; Lisieux, c. 1160-1188, set the fashion to Normandy, with the one exception of Rouen Cathedral; Soissons and Chartres were both designed by the end of the twelfth century with three stories only. In England, as we have seen, three stories had always been the normal arrangement. This now became universal throughout Western Christendom in churches whose aisles were covered with ribbed vaults.

HEIGHT OF TRIFORIUM.—As regards, however, the relative proportions of these three stories, and especially as to the prominence to be given to the triforium, considerable differences in practice prevailed. We may suggest that these differences arose mainly out of the difficulties of lighting the Norman interiors. To get more window-area, some preferred to increase the dimensions of the aisle-windows; others, to introduce an entirely new row of windows in the triforium chamber, immediately above the windows of the aisles. Where the latter course was preferred, it became necessary to make the triforium-arcade lofty, so as to obstruct the new source of light as little as possible. This meant a lofty triforium-arcade, and a corresponding low pier-arcade. In England many of our Norman churches, e.g. WINCHESTER (261), Waltham, ELY (57), Peter-

---

* Viollet-le-Duc, *Architecture*, i. 198.   † Section in Choisy's *Histoire*, ii. 434.

‡ One curious result was that in order to provide a passage, where the floor of the upper aisle ought to have been, between the different bays of the intended upper aisle, he had to construct a pathway at the back of each pier on shafts resting on the capitals which had been intended to support a vault of a lower aisle. Illustrated in Viollet-le-Duc, *Architecture*, vi. 18, 9.

borough, Wymondham, Binham, NORWICH (330), following the precedents of the ABBAYE-AUX-HOMMES and CÉRISY LA FORÊT * (319, 521), made the three stories nearly equal in height, assigning to each about one-third of the internal elevation. Even where the Norman church has passed away, the Norman proportions may sometimes still be recognised in the Gothic work which supplanted it; *e.g.* at ELY (522), the fourteenth-century choir has a tall triforium, to harmonise with the thirteenth-century presbytery east of it; and this presbytery again has a tall triforium to harmonise with that of the Norman choir which originally existed to the west of it (117, 526). So in Worcester nave we may conjecture that in the westernmost Transitional bays of the nave the triforium was built tall, because the triforium was tall in the eastern bays of the Norman nave then standing. Then in the thirteenth century the proportions of the Norman and Transitional nave were retained in the Gothic presbytery and choir; while in rebuilding the western bays of the nave in the fourteenth century, these were made to agree fairly as to proportions with those of the choir to the east and the Transitional bays to the west of them. So also in Romsey nave. But even in Gothic churches that were built *de novo* the tradition of the tall Norman triforium here and there lingered long; *e.g.* at ST SAVIOUR'S, SOUTHWARK (521). An elevation, however, so proportioned is never quite satisfactory; for a successful interior it is essential that the pier-arcade shall be lofty and dignified. To gain height for the ground story, and still more for the clerestory, became more and more the object of the mediæval builders.

But in the churches of the Benedictine, Cluniac, and Cistercian monks, and of the Augustinian and Premonstratensian canons, there was a special cause which seriously affected the proportions of the interiors; at any rate of the nave. It was that, attached to one wall of the nave, generally the south wall, as at Worcester, but sometimes, as at Gloucester and Chester, the north wall, was one of the covered walks of the cloister. Aisle-windows, therefore, pierced in this wall would look into the cloister and not into the open air; the light obtained would be but borrowed light and of very little service. At Chester, therefore, it was not thought worth while to pierce this wall at all; and this, the north-west corner of the nave, remains to this day plunged in perpetual gloom. At Worcester the monks could not resign themselves to gloom. They raised the aisle-walls, and inserted their windows high up so as just to clear the cloister roof. In Gothic days the same course was taken at CHESTER † (522). But still this half of the nave was but imperfectly lighted. The most drastic remedies for this defect were adopted by the monks of Tewkesbury and Gloucester. They had designed their choirs with low pier-arcades. But they designed their naves with positively Brobdingnagian piers. ‡ A similar design

* The vault of Cérisy is modern; lath and plaster. The balustrade in front of the Caen triforium is not part of the early work.

† One of these later inserted windows may be seen on the left of the photograph of the interior of Chester nave, ineffectually lighting the north aisle. At Leominster windows were built, one in stone, the rest in wood, so high above the cloister and the roof of the north aisle as to be half dormers.

‡ See illustrations (26) and (297).

is seen in the great abbey church of Tournus, where also there is a cloister walk alongside of the nave.* With aisles so lofty as these, tall windows could be had, which would be able to clear the cloister walk ; † and at the same time north and south aisles could be designed, if desired, symmetrically. Nevertheless, even with these lofty pier-arches, the naves of Tewkesbury and Gloucester, and those of Durham, St Georges de Boscherville, the Abbaye-aux-Dames, where also the piers are of considerable altitude, are badly lighted ; and this bold attempt at a solution of the lighting problem found little favour for a long time. It had, however, its importance in familiarising people even in the eleventh century with tallness of ground story ; and no doubt had its share in bringing about the ultimate improvement of side-lighting in lofty Gothic aisles, such as those of Bristol and Canterbury.

THE WINDOWED TRIFORIUM.—In such churches as the above neither side-lighting across the aisles nor top-lighting from the clerestory was at all adequate. In Gothic days, especially in Gloucester choir and its imitators, it was clerestory lighting that was to be developed ; in Norman days the builders were always intending to vault their naves, though they very seldom accomplished it ; and they may well have been unwilling to pierce their clerestory walls with bigger windows or more windows, weakened as they were already by having a clerestory passage (545) constructed in their thickness. But for the numerous windows in their end walls, *e.g.* in the apse of CÉRISY (161), and the transept of PETERBOROUGH (161), they would have been but imperfectly lighted. But there was yet one other method of illumining the central darkness beside the employment of end windows ; and this method in Norman and English Romanesque was in constant employment from the first. This was to insert windows at the back of the triforium. The object of these was not so much to light the triforium chamber, as to transmit light *across* the triforium chamber into the central area. ‡ To get these windows, of course, it was necessary to raise the aisle-walls considerably ; but so important was it considered to get an additional source of light, that the builders did not shrink from the great additional expense involved. § At NORWICH (522), so late as the fifteenth century, the triforium light was still considered to be of great value ; and to obtain more of it, the whole of the aisle-walls were raised, in order to allow the insertion of large Gothic windows on the top of the original Norman windows. In the choir triforium the new windows are exceptionally large (160).

In foreign churches where there was an upper vaulted aisle, this was lighted by windows in its outer wall ; *e.g.* in Lombardy at S. Ambrogio, Milan, and S. Michele, Pavia ; in Normandy at Jumièges in the eleventh century ; and in the twelfth century at Laon ; St Germer ; Paris Cathedral ; Soissons south

---

* Illustrated in *Classification of Romanesque*, p. 275. Tewkesbury nave was dedicated in 1123. Gloucester nave is apparently later than that of Tewkesbury.

† One of them, filled with later tracery, is seen on the left in the photograph of GLOUCESTER NAVE (160).

‡ So also at Notre Dame, Paris, the vault of the upper aisle was tilted up, " *comme une sorte d'entonnoir, par où la lumière plongeait jusque au centre de la grande nef* " (Choisy's *Histoire*, ii. 430).

§ This must have been very great ; calculate what it cost to raise all the aisle-walls of Ely, say 1,500 feet long, by 15 feet in height.

transept, and others.   Though this was well lighted, it was accessible only by narrow staircases in the thickness of the wall, and was therefore not intended for worship.   So it was also in the three-storied Norman churches ;   *e.g.* the triforiums of the Abbaye-aux-Hommes and CÉRISY (160) have windows of considerable size at the back.   This was the arrangement in the upper aisle of the choir of GLOUCESTER (135), and probably of Tewkesbury ;   also at St Albans, Winchester, Peterborough, and ELY (34.1, 57), Dunfermline, NORWICH (31).* In NORWICH NAVE (522), indeed, light from the triforium was judged so valuable that the back wall was raised still higher, and a range of large traceried windows was inserted.   So that in the external elevation of this nave, counting from the top, one sees, first, the clerestory windows ;   second, the Gothic windows ; and, under them, third, the Norman windows, now blocked, of the triforium ; fourthly, blank arcading, in which one broad low window has been inserted, on the left ;   fifthly, the upper windows of the cloister ;   sixthly, its lower unglazed windows.   In such naves as those of Ely and Peterborough, the lighting problem indeed is completely solved.   Nowadays they are over-lighted ;   but when they had their stained glass the lighting must have been admirable.

To get this source of light, however, as far as possible, in its entirety, it was necessary that the triforium-arcade should consist of single cavernous arches. And this, which we may call the logical arrangement, is what we do find in many examples ;   *e.g.* in the ABBAYE-AUX-HOMMES (319) ;   at NORWICH (330), where it is by no means so unsightly as usual ;   at Binham ;   at Wymondham ; at Blyth ;   at Carlisle ;   at Dunfermline ;   in GLOUCESTER CHOIR (47) ;   Selby nave, in part.   At ST ALBANS (14) the single cavernous arch occurs in the nave ;   but not in the transepts, where there was plenty of light from the end windows.   Where, however, as in some few of the above, there is no back window, the rationale of the single cavernous arch does not exist.

THE DARK TRIFORIUM OR BLINDSTORY.—So far we have dealt with the triforium as it was affected by the lighting problem.   But there was another and a very important problem that the Norman builders had to solve.   They were anxious to light their churches well ;   they were also anxious to vault them.   So it was all over Romanesque Europe ;   everywhere the same two problems.   Sometimes, in a sunny clime, the builders cared less for the lighting ;   and vaulted their churches after the fashion of Poitou or Auvergne.† Under the grey sky of Normandy and England, for a considerable time, vaulting was subordinated to lighting.   When the Abbaye-aux-Hommes and Norwich were built, the lighting difficulty was thoroughly overcome.   But the more thorough the success in triforium-lighting, the harder the vaulting problem became.   For in such churches as these, the nave-vaults they desired

---

* At Bernay, Caen St Nicholas, Mt. St Michel, St Georges de Boscherville, Lessay, Ber-nières, St Gabriel, the Abbaye-aux-Dames, Ouistreham, Romsey, Rochester, and elsewhere, the windowed triforium was not adopted, perhaps because of its great expense.   It is common to find the Norman windows at the back of the triforium enlarged and filled with tracery in Gothic days ;   *e.g.* in Peterborough transept, and in NORWICH TRANSEPT and CHOIR (160), where the square-headed window on the left lights the triforium.

† See *Classification of Romanesque.*

so much to have, would have to spring from between the great cavernous arches of the triforium ; which may have seemed unsound construction. So we may well believe that there was an opposition school who insisted on filling up these single arches more or less with minor arches, which should act as straining-arches * to keep the supports of the vaults from bulging inwardly or outwardly. The naves of Cérisy and Ely represent a compromise. Both have back windows to the triforium ; but the front arch is filled in with two minor arches. These, however, are so lofty, and the shaft between them so slender, that little obstruction was caused to the light (521, 57). At Romsey the tympanum above the minor arches is pierced ; but as there is no back window, the arrangement is objectless. At SOUTHWELL NAVE (520), the Romsey arrangement was intended ; here there are back windows ; so small, however, that they can barely be distinguished in the photograph of the exterior (520). Most often the tympanum is solid, and the shaft substantial ; some-times, as in Hereford choir, quite massive. With the subdivision of the triforium-arcade, logically, there should go the omission of the back windows.†

Of these subdivided triforium arches we may distinguish two main classes : first, those triforiums in which there are one or two containing-arches in each bay ; secondly, those in which there is no containing-arch.

Single Containing-arch.—Of this species of triforium-arcade, Durham, Rochester, Ely, Chichester, and originally Waltham Abbey, are Romanesque examples (8, 57, 521), also MALMESBURY (522) and St Bartholomew's, Smithfield. Beautiful Gothic parallels are seen in the presbytery and CHOIR OF ELY (117, 522), whose triforium should be compared with that of the NORMAN TRANSEPT (506). But there is a practical objection to the use of a single containing-arch ; viz. that it causes the triforium to take up too much space, at the expense of clerestory lighting ; as is plainly seen in Ely choir and presbytery, and at Hexham and Whitby and Bridlington. This was ingeniously obviated in the nave of RIPON, by allowing the arcade to occupy only the central part of the bay (102). Still more objectionable is the design of Salis-bury, YORK TRANSEPT (523), and the north side of the nave of BRIDLINGTON (125) ; where there are three sets of arches ; the outer containing-arch, two intermediate arches, and four lower arches ; this takes up far too much room ; the result is a truncated clerestory. At Pont Audemer there is an exquisite Flamboyant triforium of this character (131) ; but no clerestory at all. At Salisbury the clerestory retains reasonable height ; but the triforium suffers greatly ; being so squeezed together that its outer arches are of an unpleasant segmental form.

Two Containing-arches.—If, however, instead of one, there are two containing-arches, the height of the triforium can be greatly reduced, as is

* " Reste à prevenir la flexion qui se tend a se produire dans le sens transversal (*i.e.* from pier to pier). La solution consiste à rendre les piles solidaires deux à deux à l'aide d'arceaux ou de traverses d'entretoisement " (Choisy's *Histoire*, 313).

† In speaking of the back windows of the triforium, one excludes those which are so small that they were plainly intended not to light the nave, but merely to throw sufficient light on the aisle-vault to facilitate the execution of any necessary repairs ; *e.g.* those of Lincoln nave and presbytery ; and of Waltham nave.

seen in GLOUCESTER NAVE (26). This it was that became the favourite design of the English Gothic triforium. It is seen in the CHOIR OF CANTER-
BURY (106), as in that of Sens; it takes exquisite form in Rievaulx choir, in
LICHFIELD NAVE (523), in Lincoln presbytery, in WESTMINSTER (119). In
Westminster the triforium, like the vault, is purely English; no Frenchman
would have designed that black belt of shadow.* In an unusual form, two
containing-arches above *six* lower arches, it appears in that beautiful architectural freak, the NORTH TRANSEPT OF HEREFORD (523).

No Containing-arch.—Several Norman churches, *e.g.* the Abbaye-aux-
Dames, have simply an arcade of several small round-headed arches in each bay
of the triforium. Translated into Gothic, this gives the pointed arcades of the
triforiums of Byland, St David's, New Shoreham, Canterbury Trinity Chapel;
and the trefoiled arcades of that of Guisborough.† With the addition of a wall
behind the arches, the Byland design appears in St John's, Chester, and ST
SAVIOUR'S, SOUTHWARK (521); and that of Guisborough in the PRESBYTERY
OF CHESTER CATHEDRAL (524). The merit of this form of triforium is that
there being no containing-arches at all, it is greatly curtailed in height; and
the space thus gained can be added to the clerestory, to the great improvement
of the lighting.

Continuous Arcade.—In all of the last class vertical lines are drawn
between the bays in the form of vaulting shafts or roofing shafts. But in the
Early Norman TRANSEPT OF CHESTER CATHEDRAL (524), and still more at
WELLS (524), no distinction is made between the bays. At Wells the vaulting
shafts are stopped abruptly, and the arrangement of the arches of the triforium
does not correspond either with that of the pier-arcade or of the clerestory. The
object may have been by the uninterrupted flow eastward of small arches passing
count to give the appearance of length to this short nave: certainly it looks far
longer than it is.

WALLED TRIFORIUM.—There was yet one other treatment of the triforium;
for which something was to be said. If, as in the examples recently cited, the
triforium was an open blindstory, being unlighted it was of no ritualistic use.
Moreover, when its roof was covered with tiles, cold air was introduced, and there
were down draughts on to the heads of monk or canon in the stalls below. Also
it became a receptacle of dust; and this was blown into the church. But the
most serious objection to an open triforium was a constructional one: its
openings weakened the supports of the vault and roof. To the early Cistercians
in particular these objections must have seemed very serious; they loved sound
construction and they hated decorative extravagance. So in their twelfth-century
churches, *e.g.* FOUNTAINS (101) and Kirkstall naves, and even in thirteenth-
century TINTERN (524), the triforium had no arcade in front of it, but simply
a plain, solid wall.‡ BOXGROVE (318) is a curious example of this treatment;
owing to the presence of the big containing-arch over every pair of bays, one

---

* Perhaps he would not have wished to expose the roof timbers of the aisle, which at
times, as in Lincoln presbytery, are unpleasantly conspicuous.

† Illustrated in Sharpe's *Parallels.*

‡ This plain wall occurs also in the fine sixteenth-century church of St Pierre, Auxerre;
there it may have been intended to be frescoed.

forgets that there is a triforium at all.   In our late churches, too, the triforium is out of sight and out of mind ; merely a solid wall panelled, as in ST MARY REDCLIFFE (525), and ST GEORGE'S, WINDSOR (330).   In those early churches, on the other hand, which walled in the triforium chamber, the wall was decorated with single or with superposed arcades.   In St John's, Chester ; St Saviour's, Southwark ; Chester and St Albans choirs, the arcade is single ; and the blank wall makes its presence painfully felt.   But in Worcester and Beverley choirs there are two arcades, and the wall ceases to be obtrusive.   At Worcester both arcades are pointed ; at Beverley, on the other hand, a delightful contrast is obtained by constructing the back arcade low and pointed, while the front arcade is tall and trefoiled.*   But neither the triforiums of Beverley and Worcester nor of Amiens nave and Clermont Ferrand can compare with the blindstories of the Gothic of England and Normandy : e.g. BAYEUX (525) and Pont Audemer.   Those of our interiors which possess a blindstory have a charm unknown to French interiors with the walled triforium.   In such a nave as Westminster or Lichfield, above is the dazzling light of the clerestory ; below is the subdued light of the lower nave ; between the two, separating them, and contrasting with them, is the black band of triforium gloom.   No such gradations and contrasts of light and gloom are to be had in the characteristic French interiors.   In BEVERLEY CHOIR (51) alone, the masterpiece of thirteenth century Gothic, one hardly misses the shadowy blindstory ; so profuse is the employment of dark Purbeck shafting.

ABSORPTION OF THE TRIFORIUM INTO THE PIER-ARCADE.—Not even yet had all the possibilities of triforium design been exhausted.   In the Priory of St Frideswide, now the Cathedral, of OXFORD (525, 27), the whole height of the nave wall is under 42 feet.   Now if this height had been divided up into three equal stories, the ground story would have been only 14 feet high, and the whole internal elevation would have been crushingly low and squat.   But by heightening the piers so that their capitals are on a level with the floor of the triforium, and by constructing the arches † from these capitals above instead of under the triforium-arcade, a pier-arcade has been got which occupies not one-third, but nearly two-thirds of the total height, and which is really dignified and effective ; so much so that this low church appears quite lofty and imposing. The first example we have of this ingenious design, with triforium as it were suspended from the inside of the pier-arcade, is seen in the easternmost bay of Romsey nave.‡   This design was also adopted at Dunstable Priory ; also at Jedburgh,§ where it is employed much less clumsily.   In the great church of GLASTONBURY (536), c. 1185, it produced an interior of real grandeur.

ABSORPTION OF THE TRIFORIUM INTO THE CLERESTORY.—The Glastonbury design was an artistic triumph ; in practice it had one fatal defect ; viz. that the height of the real pier-arcade was cramped and curtailed : whereas it was

* The Beverley design is plainly inspired by the aisle arcading in St Hugh's work at Lincoln.

† Of course the real pier-arch is the plain lower arch corbelled into the piers half-way up.

‡ It is amusing to see the number of experiments in triforium design in Romsey transept and nave.

§ Illustrated in Fergusson, ii. 421.

desirable to have the pier-arches as lofty as possible. For this the reason was not primarily an artistic one ; everything essential in Gothic design was dictated primarily by a religious or constructional motive, only secondarily by artistic considerations. It was the practical reason that if the pier-arches were high, the aisle-walls could be built high, and lofty windows could be inserted in them, and

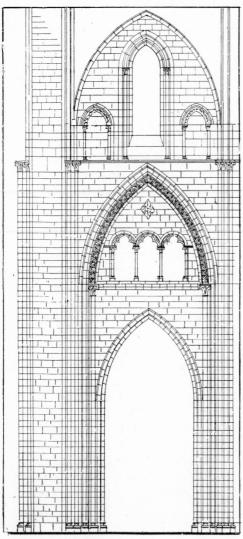

Glastonbury.

so one of the main sources of light, the side-lighting, could be vastly improved. The remedy for this was to make room for the heightened pier-arches by crushing the triforium and clerestory together into one story. Of the two the triforium suffered most ; for the clerestory was another very important source of light, and its height was by no means to be curtailed. A Norman example of this blend of triforium and clerestory was to be seen in St Botolph's, Colchester ;* founded in 1102 ; where, however, advantage was not taken of the design to heighten the piers. The next example is seen at ST DAVID'S (525), c. 1190; designed for sexpartite vaulting ; with which may be compared the twelfth-century church of Ouistreham, near Caen. This arrangement seems to have been particularly popular in our Western Gothic. It appears at Llanthony ; Christ Church, Dublin, and Pershore ;† and at Dore. Outside the western district it is seen in Southwell choir. Ultimately it greatly influenced English design ; such interiors as those of Chester and BRIDLINGTON (125) naves; the presbyteries of Wells and Lichfield, York and SELBY (390) choirs ; Winchester and Canterbury naves, are all attempts to reduce the triforium to a minimum in order to magnify the pier-arcade and clerestory. It is particularly interesting at Winchester to see how vastly the nave has gained by the transformation of a low into a tall pier-arcade (261, 90) ; and of course the lighting has been improved also. An interesting foreign parallel is seen

* Illustrated in Britton's *Arch. Ant.*, vol. i.
† Both illustrated in Prior, *Gothic Art*, 184, 5.

at Semur-en-Auxois, where the transept is three stories high, but in the nave triforium and clerestory are blended together.

TRANSPARENT TRIFORIUM.—In France the development of the triforium took an entirely different direction. Here also there was the same desire to utilise the triforium by causing it to provide an additional source of light. But whereas we had been putting windows at the back of the triforium, the French succeeded in putting them in front. The older and normal triforium design is seen in CLERMONT FERRAND (526), Auvergne. In this choir there is in front an open arcade; and, as is usual in French churches, a solid wall behind it. If this wall were removed or pierced, no light would be got; for behind it there is but the darkness of the triforium chamber beneath the lean-to roof. If, however, the upper part of the rafters be omitted, as shown in the drawing of ST DENIS, the roof can be reconstructed as a double or span roof; *i.e.* with two slopes instead of one. In that case if openings are made in the front wall of the triforium, they will look into the open air. These openings can now be filled with tracery and can be glazed; and there will now be in front of the triforium two sets of traceried arches, one unglazed, the other glazed. The change is seen in ST DENIS NAVE, which was rebuilt 1231-1280.* But there was a serious objection to the new span roof over the aisle. Its inner side sloped towards the clerestory wall at C; and it was difficult to arrange for the drainage of this lengthy longitudinal gutter. Two methods found favour. One, which was

St Denis Nave.

adopted about the same time in Amiens choir, 1240-1269, was to construct the new span roof of the aisles, not longitudinally, *i.e.* parallel to the length of the nave or choir, but in separate hipped roofs over each bay. Each of these roofs is called a *pavillon*. Transverse gutters were provided between the pavillons; and being short, were easily kept in order. Very many of the later French churches have aisles roofed in this fashion. The nearest approach we have to it is in the nave of SHREWSBURY

* Enlart's *Manuel*, 642.

ABBEY * (526). The second method was much simpler. It was to retain the lean-to roof, but to make it nearly flat; covering it with lead; or, as at Narbonne and Limoges, with stone slabs. Of the depressed roof we have an interesting example in BRIDLINGTON NAVE (124); where the north aisle has an acute, the south aisle a flattened roof. In RIPON CHOIR (540) the aisles originally had lean-to roofs of sharp pitch. Later, perhaps early in the fourteenth century, these roofs were flattened, as shown in the photograph; and the triforium-arcade was glazed. So also in the aisles of the choir of ST CROSS, Winchester (104), the roofs have been flattened. Two bays also of ELY PRESBYTERY (117) have been treated in similar fashion. The presbytery is dark; and the shrine of St Etheldreda, a great resort of pilgrims, was badly lighted. The original appearance of the triforium is illustrated on 526. Now two bays on either side of the presbytery are glazed. The thirteenth-century triforium of the presbytery had windows at the back : the windows and parapet of these two bays of the triforium are still there, but the windows have lost their glass. The roof has been flattened, and what was formerly an open arcade in front of these two bays of the triforium is now glazed.

These, however, are exceptions. It was in the Ile de France and in those districts which copied its architecture that the glazed triforium reached its highest development; e.g. in the choirs of Amiens, 1240-1269; Beauvais, 1247-1272; St Urbain, Troyes, 1262-1369; St Ouen, Rouen, 1318-1339; Sées, c. 1353; girdling their interiors round with an additional band of gleaming, sparkling stained glass. Burgundy, however, refused the transparent triforium ; Auxerre and Nevers Cathedrals, Semur and Notre Dame, Dijon, remained faithful to the blindstory; as to a large extent did the Normandy churches also.

Then came in the passion which attacked the Gothic architects as much in France as in England; the passion for harmonising and simplifying. The French architect when he looked up in his beautiful church, St Denis, Amiens choir, EVREUX (539), saw at its greatest height a magnificent range of stained glass windows lighting the clerestory, and below them another range, with similar tracery and similar glass, the new transparent triforium ; window above and window below ; comparing with one another, contrasting, both of them, with the pier-arcade below. Evidently the internal elevation was throwing itself into a tremendous contrast ; a contrast between light and shade; between the upper blaze of colour and the shadowed choir beneath. Artistically the elevation had arranged itself; it was become an elevation of two instead of three stories. It was simply pier-arcade versus window system. The triforium constructionally and artistically had effaced itself. The progress of effacement, once commenced, went on with rapid stride. The first step to recognise the essential unity of the two upper members of the internal elevation was to run the mullions of the clerestory window, as had been done already in Amiens nave and Clermont Ferrand, down to the sill of the triforium. This was to recognise that the clerestory and triforium were no longer two distinct members but one. And so the builders gradually became familiar with the idea of regarding triforium and clerestory windows as being but one window. And it was not long before they perforated the spandrels of the triforium windows and removed

* Here, however, the transverse roofs over the aisles are a modern addition.

all traces of solid wall between triforium and clerestory, as at Sées ; * making the whole one lofty window, descending from the ridge of the vault all the way to what had been the sill of the triforium arcade. This disastrous plunge into logic was first taken by the architect of St Urbain de Troyes ; the harbinger and precursor of the developments of Flamboyant Gothic. For a long time no one followed his lead : the triforium glazed or unglazed is the greatest glory of a Gothic interior ; and many a triforium was still erected even in the fifteenth and sixteenth centuries ; *e.g.* in Evreux choir, PONT AUDEMER (131), and Abbeville nave. But in the end logic prevailed. Late in the fifteenth and in the sixteenth century, *e.g.* at St Gervais and St Riquier, the members of the internal ele-vation dwindle down to two ; there is practically nothing left but tall clerestory and tall pier-arcade : of the tri-forium nothing remains but here and there a balustrade.

SINGLE - STORY IN-TERIOR.—One step more re-mained to work out the logic of the triforium design. It was taken with reluctance. We saw above the gradual upward leap of the pier. In Gloucester and Tewkesbury naves it rose to vast height in order to allow a win-dowed aisle high above the cloister roof. At Romsey, Oxford, Dunstable, Jedburgh, Glastonbury, it rose to the sill of the clerestory. But one step remained. It was to convert the wall-arch or *formerets* of the high vault into the arch of the pier.

Evreux.

This meant that the primary object of the piers was to support, not the arches below, but the high vault. The pier-arcade was to be subsidiary ; the vault-arcade was to be the main feature of the interior. And this was right. For the dominant factor in a Gothic building is or ought to be the vault ; plinth, base, pier, capital, abacus, buttress, flying buttress, pinnacle, all are con-ditioned by the vaults. All these had become subservient to the vault long ago ; the pier had remained recalcitrant. Now its turn had come. So far as it was a support of the arches of the ground story, it was to be made unobtrusive ; so far as it was a support of the vault, it was to be given the utmost emphasis. Few, however, learnt the new lesson thoroughly. In

* Illustrated in Viollet-le-Duc, *Architecture*, 9, 258, 11.

LICHFIELD NAVE (523), the vault-arch is there, in the clerestory; but it has no supports. In ST MARY REDCLIFFE, BRISTOL (525), the arch of the ground story is allowed to cut into the high pier (we will call it the *vault-pier*): and it is given capitals; *i.e.* an independent existence. At Winchester, the wall-arch of the vault is carried, not by a vault-pier, but by the ancient Norman vaulting-shafts retained in William of Wykeham's transformation of the nave (90). In CANTERBURY NAVE (90), the supports of the diagonal and transverse arches are strongly differentiated from those of the wall-arches of the vault, one does not see why; their upward flow is broken by bands; and

Ripon Choir and Transept.

the piers of the ground story are emphasised by capitals and bands: it is a bungled version of Winchester nave. GLOUCESTER (59), however, the cradle of our later Gothic, even in 1350, has the vault-pier fully developed, though one desiderates greater emphasis of the wall-arch of the vault. The lesson taught by Gloucester in her choir, and, still more perfectly, in her fan-vaulted CLOISTER (344), was more or less elaborated in the three Royal Tudor Chapels; King's College, Cambridge; Henry the Seventh's Chapel, Westminster; best of all in ST GEORGE'S, WINDSOR (330). Here there is no question that the piers belong to the vault and not to the ground story; they bring the vault right down to the ground; the elevation is no longer one of three or two stories, but of one. And so a magnificent unity was attained at last in the English interiors, whether vaulted like the Royal Chapels, or covered with wooden roofs, as at Worstead, Cawston; St Andrew's, and ST STEPHEN'S, NORWICH (228); and, most effectually of all, at CHIPPING NORTON (548).

TRIFORIUM ROOFS.—So far we have been regarding the rise, decline, and fall of the triforium from inside the church. Let us go outside. As we have seen, there was a widespread desire to diminish the height of the triforium-chamber. This was often done, as at Ripon, Ely, and Narbonne, by partly lowering the slope of the aisle-roof as in B, *e.g.* the south aisle of Bridlington; and St Ouen, Rouen;

or as in C, Ripon and Narbonne (558.1). From this followed a whole train of consequences more or less unexpected. First, a roof, flattened so much, must be covered with lead, and no longer with tiles. Secondly, there is incongruity between the flat pitch of the aisles and the steep pitch of the double or span roof of the nave; *e.g.* in SELBY CHOIR (86). Here steps in the principle of harmony. This suggests that the steep roofs in the centre should be lowered to correspond with the depressed roofs of the aisles. In many wood-roofed churches, where the roof was of the late tie-beam type, *e.g.* GRESFORD (214), the high roof had been flattened to the angle of a cambered tie-beam (562); so that there was precedent for the change. Moreover, when once the depressed four-centred transverse-arch had been adopted in vaults instead of the acutely pointed transverse-arch, it had been found possible to construct the vaults nearly flat; *e.g.* in the fourteenth century in Ely Lady Chapel, and in the sixteenth century in St George's, Windsor. The result was that in many a late church, whether unvaulted as in HULL CHANCEL and NAVE (96), or vaulted as in BATH ABBEY (373) and St George's, Windsor, both the high roof of the central aisle and the low roofs of the side aisles were constructed nearly flat, and covered with lead. But a roof so depressed disappears from view. The interior of the church is represented simply by a series of holes between some high and low walls. So that, all to get rid of the triforium, we have sacrificed what were the crowning glories of a Gothic exterior, the lofty gables of its end walls and the skyline of its acutely pointed roofs. The Gothic church has sunk down to the level of a Greek temple. And just as the Greeks had found it necessary to concentrate attention on the cresting of the temple, elaborating it into architrave, frieze, and cornice, so the Gothic builders tried to divert attention from the disappearance of roof and gable and the loss of skyline, by elaborating, more than ever before, the cresting of their walls with parapet, battlement, and pinnacle; as at ST GEORGE'S, WINDSOR * (492); KING'S COLLEGE CHAPEL, CAMBRIDGE (199); and above all, in HENRY THE SEVENTH'S CHAPEL, WESTMINSTER (378); by way of compensation. So that the florid exterior of a Tudor church is not without its meaning and apology.

USE OF TRIFORIUM.—As we have seen, the primary origin of the triforium chamber lay in the fact that a ribbed vault over an aisle was originally protected from the weather by a lean-to roof of sharp pitch. But being there, it may be asked, was no use made of it? In most cases it was not used at all. It cannot have been used, if it was a triforium with a wall in front, as in Tintern or Beverley; or if there was no wooden floor on the vaults, as at Lincoln; or if there were no large windows at the back to light it, as in Gloucester nave; or if the newel staircase leading to it was so narrow that only one person could ascend at a time. Sometimes, however, it was turned to practical account. It provided a passage all round the church at mid-height; which would be convenient, *e.g.* when tapestry † was to be hung down over the nave arches on festal days. Then again an open triforium-arcade diminished the weight resting on the pier-arches below.

---

* Probably the pinnacles originally supported beasts rampant in metal.

† In Winchester nave the hooks may still be seen from which was hung the tapestry at the wedding of Philip of Spain and Queen Mary.

But there is evidence that occasionally ritualistic use was made of the triforium chamber. This was certainly the case in the upper aisle of the choir and transept of Gloucester. Here there are broad staircases; and, before its eastern apse was lopped off in the fourteenth century, there was a broad chamber all round the apse on the first floor. Moreover this upper aisle is spacious; is floored; is open to the choir in front, and well lighted by windows at the back. At Gloucester its ritualistic use is quite clear. The eastern apses of its transept and the tangential apses of the choir are each three stories high. To the lowest chapel in each apse access is gained from the crypt; to the intermediate chapel from the ground floor of the church; but to the uppermost chapel only from the upper aisle. Here then the object of the upper aisle clearly is to provide access to chapels on the first floor, and a road from one chapel to another; as well as space for a congregation, the altared apse itself serving as sanctuary to the priest and his acolytes. In the transepts of CÉRISY-LA-FORÊT (199), the Abbaye-aux-Hommes, St Georges de Boscherville, Winchester, and originally Ely, return aisles run across each transept end, providing again a nave for a congregation gathered in front of the eastern apse of the transept. In WESTMINSTER ABBEY (119), the triforium chamber is unusually spacious and well lighted; and was perhaps designed to accommodate numerous spectators on grand occasions, such as coronations and royal funerals.* We have one more bit of evidence about a ritualistic use of the triforium. At Winchester, by way of protest against the heavy contribution imposed by the bishop on the monastery to recoup himself for the sums exacted from him by the king, the monks went round the triforium with banners and cross reversed; from which we may perhaps argue that they sometimes went round the triforium in procession with banners and cross in normal position.

* Scott's *Gleanings*, 25.

CHAPTER XXXVII.

THE CLERESTORY.

Growth of the Clerestory—The Clerestory Passage—The Wall Passage.

DEFINITION.—The term was formerly applied to any window or to any traceried opening* in a church; *e.g.* in an aisle, tower, cloister, or screen. It is now restricted to the high windows in an aisled nave; or to the range of wall in which the high windows are set.

GROWTH OF THE CLERESTORY.—Up to the end of the twelfth century the clerestory received little development. In the greater Norman churches the clerestory walls were almost always hollow, and there may well have been some reluctance to weaken the inner and outer shells of the wall more than necessary by windows. Secondly, where vaulting was contemplated, it was desirable to keep the clerestory wall as solid as possible. So in all the Norman churches, and even as late as Wells nave, and WHITBY CHOIR, *c.* 1210 (114), there is but a single window in each bay of the clerestory wall. But in Byland, *c.* 1170, in Wenlock, *c.* 1180, Rievaulx choir, *c.* 1230, and Southwell choir, *c.* 1230, there are two clerestory windows in each bay. Also triplets of lancets appear; first, three lancets graduated in breadth in LINCOLN CHOIR (110), begun 1192; then graduated in height, in SALISBURY (458); and Netley. Then comes the invention of bar-tracery, *c.* 1240; enabling clerestory windows to be immensely enlarged. Of the big broad clerestory window LINCOLN PRESBYTERY (56) offers an early example, 1256-1280; then come Bridlington, Guisborough, Exeter, and York nave. The lesson of the broadening of the window had been learnt in the chapter houses; *e.g.* of Westminster, Salisbury, Southwell, York, Wells. Having made the clerestory windows stretch from buttress to buttress, all that remained for the builders was to give them a vast increase in height. Here, as usual, GLOUCESTER CHOIR (59) led the way (492). Gloucester clerestory was copied in Norwich choir after the fall of the spire in 1360. WINCHESTER and CANTERBURY followed Gloucester with timidity (90); York choir with less reserve. Finally came the vast clerestories of ST GEORGE'S, WINDSOR (330); and BATH ABBEY (373). As we have seen above, expansion of the clerestory windows was necessary to get more light; but it was carried yet further, and beyond all architectural bounds, by the furore for stained glass. In some instances, however, artistic instinct rebelled against the undue predominance of the voids over the solids; the windows were not extended from buttress to buttress; the restraint which had been so beautiful in the Tintern of 1269, still made itself felt in the designs, so much more solid and satis-

* It follows that it is incorrect to say that it means a window *clear* of, *i.e.* above, the aisles.

Chichester Nave.
Cirencester Nave.

Peterborough Nave.
Hedon Nave.

factory, of the choirs of Selby and Howden and the nave of Beverley; and here and there in fifteenth-century work also. On the whole, however, the glass had its way.

CLERESTORY PASSAGE.—One of the things particularly desirable was the provision of means of getting at the clerestory windows without the trouble and expense of putting up ladders and scaffolding on each occasion when repairs were needed. In France it seems to have been more usual to construct a passage for this purpose outside the windows. This was rarely done in England. York presbytery is a late exception; in the choir, added immediately afterwards, the passage was made internal.* In Normandy and England the rule was to construct the clerestory passage inside the church.†

NO CLERESTORY PASSAGE.—The practice, however, was not universal, even in England. There is no clerestory passage at Blyth or Leominster. The early Cistercians, sticklers for sound building construction above everything, built their clerestory walls solid, i.e. without an internal passage, e.g. in the naves of FOUNTAINS (101), Kirkstall, and Buildwas; which is the more noteworthy, because none of them were intended to be vaulted. At Dore‡ also, c. 1190, and Tintern, 1269, which were vaulted throughout, the clerestory walls are solid. But even with the Cistercians the English practice in the end prevailed; e.g. at Byland, 1170, which was unvaulted; and in Rievaulx choir, which was vaulted. New Shoreham, c. 1200, follows the early Cistercian practice.§ Later on, the nave of Lichfield and the north transept of Hereford, owing to the peculiar shape of their clerestories, have to dispense with an internal passage (523). In our Late Gothic the clerestory passage is, with some exceptions, abandoned; e.g. in GLOUCESTER CHOIR (492); Winchester and Canterbury naves; St Mary Redcliffe, Bristol; St George's, Windsor; and Bath Abbey.

CLERESTORIES OF THE LESSER CHURCHES.—From the descriptions that have come down to us, it would seem likely that the greater Anglo-Saxon churches had clerestory lighting; but all such churches have perished. It was

---

* In the illustration on 199, the passage is external on the right of the transept, internal on the left.

† E.g. in the eleventh and twelfth centuries the Abbaye-aux-Hommes; Cérisy; Lessay; St Georges de Boscherville; St Albans; Winchester transept; CHICHESTER (313); ELY (273); Durham; Norwich; Christchurch, Hants; Selby nave; PETERBOROUGH (161); GLOUCESTER (26); MELBOURNE (203); Carlisle nave; Romsey; Southwell nave. Late in the twelfth century clerestory passages are seen at ST DAVID'S (525); Wells; Glastonbury; Llandaff; CANTERBURY CHOIR (106); Ripon transept; Malmesbury; St John's, Chester; Wenlock; Oxford Cathedral; Byland. In the first half of the thirteenth century they occur at Lincoln; Ely presbytery; St Saviour's, Southwark; Beverley Minster; Boxgrove; Christ Church, Dublin; Rochester; Rievaulx; Southwell; Pershore; in the second half in the north transept of Hereford and the presbyteries of Lincoln and Chester; at Exeter; Bridlington; Carlisle. In the fourteenth century in Ely, Selby, Tewkesbury choirs; and Chester nave. In later Gothic in York choir; Ripon nave, c. 1502; Winchester presbytery, 1500-1528. More instances might be added; but enough have been adduced to show how widespread was the practice, and that it was not altogether abandoned even in the last days of Gothic architecture.

‡ Dore choir seems not to have received a high vault till the fourteenth century.

§ The solid was of course far more ancient than the hollow clerestory wall; it appears at Bernay and Jumièges in the second quarter of the eleventh century.

not till the fourteenth century was well advanced that it became normal for the parish churches, first in the towns, and then in the villages, to have clerestories.* Nevertheless there never was a time when some few parish churches were not built with clerestories cathedral-fashion. Of these none can be more rude and archaic than Towyn, where the windows are mere slits in the wall (458). Well on in the twelfth century, at STEYNING (458), the aisle windows are

Howden Nave.

mere slits, probably for defensive reasons; but those of the clerestory are large; as also are those of St Margaret at Cliffe, St Woolos, Newport, and St Peter's, Northampton. In the thirteenth century clerestories become more common; e.g. Darlington. HEDON (544), late in the same century, has a clerestory still moderate in size; so also Warmington and Barnwell St Andrew's. In the fourteenth-century church of Hingham also the clerestory is moderate in size. Then the same cause which brought about the upward leap of the clerestory of the vaulted choir of Gloucester, came into play in the parish churches; e.g. in the collegiate nave of Howden, and that most magnificent of all our parish churches, BOSTON (222), whose foundations were laid in 1309. In Boston and at HOLBEACH (133), the design of which is very similar to that of Boston, two windows, instead of one, are inserted in each bay of the clerestory, which thus becomes an almost unbroken sheet of glass. And it is this, the Howden double window, which is seen in

* In Herefordshire, however, clerestories are the rule rather than the exception; and few are so late as the fourteenth century.—R. A. D.

many of the noblest churches of East Anglia, such as Snettisham; St Nicholas, Lynn; St Peter Mancroft and ST STEPHEN'S, NORWICH (228); and far away, as at Leighton Buzzard; and Southam, Warwick; though the single window remains to the end the more common; *e.g.* at LOUTH (139) and CIRENCESTER (544). In this last church such was the passion for light and stained glass that an additional clerestory was constructed over the north aisle as well as a great window above the chancel arch; the latter one more reminiscence of Gloucester choir; *cf.* CHIPPING NORTON (548).*

Moreover, vast numbers of churches constructed clerestories above ancient pier-arcades, and rebuilt their end walls in glass, making themselves Gloucesters as far as in them lay. Stratford-on-Avon is a fine example; with great Perpendicular west window, and with Perpendicular clerestory on the top of thirteenth-century pier-arcade.

In comparison with these brilliantly illuminated interiors, churches without a clerestory must have seemed indeed gloomy and old-fashioned. Nevertheless important examples occur; *e.g.* the great thirteenth-century churches of Yarmouth and Grantham; the fourteenth-century churches of PATRINGTON (133), Nantwich, and NORTH WALSHAM (562). The absence of the clerestory at North Walsham is due to the peculiar form of roof adopted.

In but few parish churches a wall passage occurs. At Rye, *c.*

Long Melford.

1200, there are wall passages both in the clerestory and in the aisle walls. At Deeping St James, originally a Benedictine church, there is on each side a continuous passage inside the clerestory windows, opening into the nave by thirteen

* Rather the window or windows over the chancel arch is one of the characteristics of West of England Gothic; a pair of small windows is common in Herefordshire in the thirteenth century.

Chipping Norton.

lancet arches.*   In the conventual unaisled chapel of Nun Monkton there is a continuous passage all round in front of the northern, western, and southern windows.†   There was a similar passage at Ripon in the thickness of the lower part of the twelfth-century unaisled nave.   At St Margaret's, Lynn, the thirteenth-century choir had a continuous passage in front of the clerestory windows.   In the fifteenth century the inner arcade of this was raised in order to insert taller windows; but several of the old shafts and foliated capitals were re-used.

* This is fully illustrated in *Nene Valley*, Plates 13, 14.
† Illustrated in *Churches of Yorkshire*.

CHAPTER XXXVIII.

ROOFS.

Roofs and Vaults—Trussed Rafter Roofs—Steep Roofs with Tie Beams—King and
Queen Posts—Depressed Roofs with Tie Beams—Arch Braced Roofs—Hammerbeam Roofs—Aisle Roofs—Wooden Vaults—Material and Construction.

ROOFS OVER VAULTS.—In the vaulted buildings of ancient Rome, whether
the vault took the form of a dome, a barrel, or a groined vault, *e.g.* the Pantheon
and the BASILICA OF MAXENTIUS (290), the vault was of brick or concrete;
and was so thick and massive, that the only external covering employed was
plates of bronze or lead. And this substantial method of construction was at
first imitated in the Romanesque dome and barrel-churches of Périgueux and
Auvergne.* But when, in order to lessen the thrust, the vaults were constructed
in thin shells, as in S. Vitale, Ravenna, in Cluny, and in Gothic-ribbed vaults, it
was usual to protect them from the weather by timber roofs. These external
roofs seem at first to have rested on the vaults,† as they now do in part in
Wells choir; thus imposing on the vault a dangerous weight, which it was not
intended to bear. As Gothic construction improved, however, care was generally taken to prevent any of the weight of the roof from falling on the vault.‡
Such external roofs are, of course, hidden by the vault; and so their form was
regulated by constructional motives only.

ROOFS OF UNVAULTED CHURCHES.—But both here and in France the vast
majority of churches were not vaulted at all. In France most of the smaller
churches, even those which were built with exceptional care and finish, were constructed without vaults even in the middle of the thirteenth century; this was
especially the case in Northern France, and still more in the Netherlands.§
Even in French parish churches that were vaulted, those parts were rarely
vaulted which had aisles, and which therefore would have required flying buttresses.‖ The vaulting was usually confined to the unaisled choir, and to the
central tower if there was one. This was the case in England also; where in
the twelfth century there was a marked tendency, afterwards largely abandoned,
to vault the chancel; *e.g.* Tickencote, Lastingham, Darenth, CASSINGTON (215.5),
Hemel Hempstead. The great majority of English parish churches, however,

* *Classification of Romanesque*, 279.

† The roofs still rest on the vaults in the Baptistery of Alliata, and at St Thomas near
Almenno (De Dartein, page 466).

‡ Not always. In Winchester nave parts of the vault were actually built in the fourteenth century round the ancient tie-beams. See Colson's account of the restoration of
this roof.

§ Enlart's *Manuel*, 496.   ‖ Choisy's *Histoire*, ii. 478.

Woodbastwick Nave.   Gedney Nave.
Paston Nave.   Sall Nave.

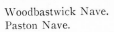

Llanidloes from S.W.
Paston Barn.

Trunch from W.
Cawston from W.

553

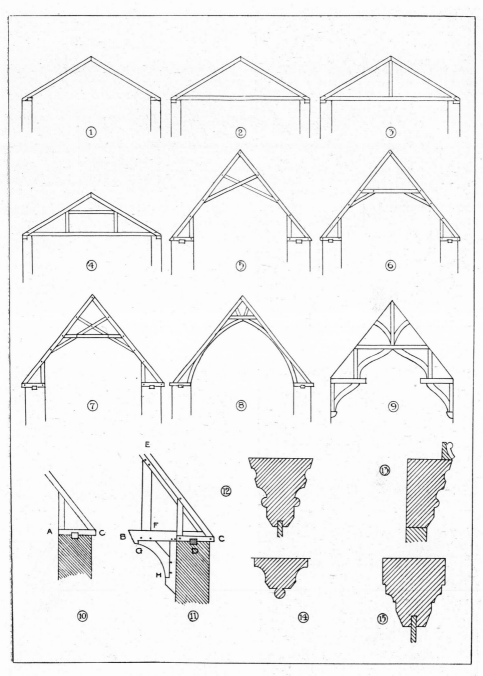

ROOFS.

8. Patrington.
13. Trunch, Cornice.
15. Trunch, Principal.

12. Trunch, Hammerbeam.
14. Trunch, Purlin.

SPAN OF ROOF 17 FEET.

Stuston.
Lympenhoe.

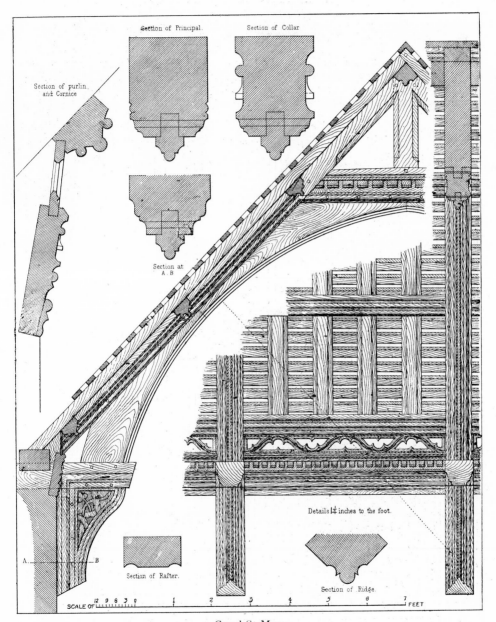

Section of Principal.

Section of Collar

Section of purlin, and Cornice

Section at A.B

A. ——————— B

Section of Rafter.

Details 1¼ inches to the foot.

Section of Ridge.

SCALE OF 12 9 6 3 0   1   2   3   4   5   6   7   FEET

Capel St Mary.

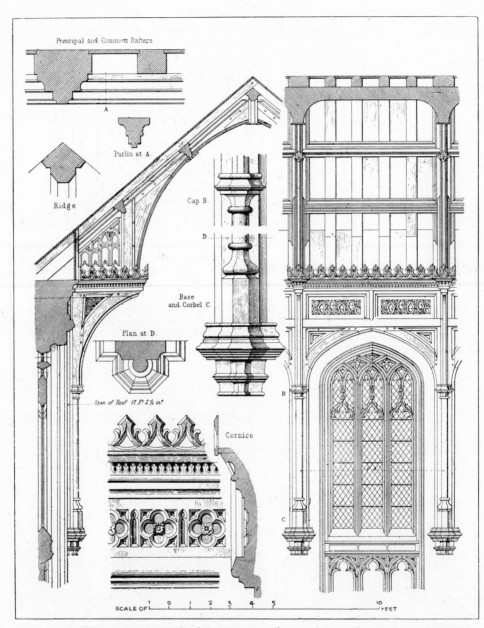

Principal and Common Rafters

A

Purlin at A.

Ridge

Cap B.

D

Base
and Corbel C.

Plan at D.

Span of Roof 17 Ft 2½ in.

Cornice

B

C

SCALE OF 1 0 1 2 3 4 5   10 FEET

SCALE OF DETAILS 12 9 6 3 0   1   2   3   4   5 FEET

Norwich St Stephen.

Westminster Hall.

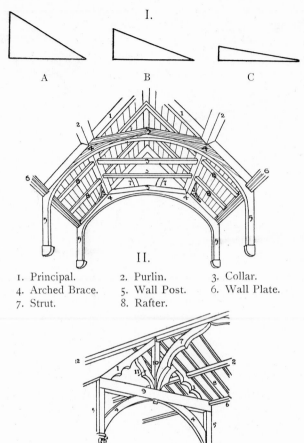

I.

A   B   C

II.

1. Principal.	2. Purlin.	3. Collar.
4. Arched Brace.	5. Wall Post.	6. Wall Plate.
7. Strut.	8. Rafter.	

III.

1. Principal.	2. Purlin.	4. Arched Brace.
5. Wall Post.	6. Wall Plate.	
7. Longitudinal Strut.	8. Rafter.	
9. Tie Beam.	10. King Post.	
11. Strut.	12. Ridge Piece.	

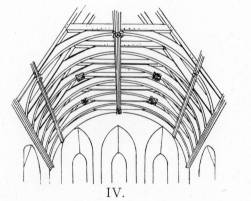

IV.

| I. Lowering of Roof. | II. Leicester St Mary. |
| III. Adderbury. | IV. Faringdon. |

were altogether without vaults.* Moreover, very few of the cathedral or abbey churches had high vaults till late in the twelfth century; some, like Peterborough,† have remained without high vaults to this day. Therefore it was a matter of primary necessity in England to work out a system of ornamental roof construction. At first, as in all our mediæval architecture, the problem was approached only from the engineering side. It was probably not till the beginning of the fourteenth century that the builders, having made their roofs satisfactory from the point of view of building construction, found themselves at liberty to develop the roof from the artistic side. An early example of the new type of roofs may be that of the barn of Easby Abbey;‡ other examples *c.* 1300 are to be seen at Polebrook, Sparsholt, Kiddington,§ ADDERBURY, and St Martin's, Leicester.‖

PITCH OF ROOFS.— The pitch of a roof depends

* In later days it was common to vault the western tower: and in East Anglia the porches also; *e.g.* the north and south porches of Sall church.

† With the exception of the eastern chapels added afterwards, and probably its Norman apse.

‡ G. E. Street in Prior, 355.

§ *Glossary*, Plates 173 and 176.

‖ Illustrated in Brandon's *Roofs*.

partly on climate, partly on roof-covering. In a climate like Norway, where the snowfall is excessive, the most essential thing is to get the snow away at once before it consolidate and break down the roof by its weight ; the pitch, therefore, of the roofs of Borgund and Hitterdal is excessively sharp. The pitch of an English roof is chiefly governed by the nature of the roof-covering. While tiles or thatch were chiefly employed, the pitch of the roofs was moderately sharp. But as lead came more and more into use, it became possible to reduce the pitch more and more, till indeed many later roofs are nearly flat. Though the Norman roofs have nearly all disappeared, we can recover their pitch from the weatherings of many an old roof, left on a western or central tower, as at TEWKESBURY (390) ; from these it would appear that an angle of 90 degrees was usual. Early Gothic roofs are usually steep, at Lincoln remarkably so ; but they are rarely equilateral ; *i.e.* with an angle of 60 degrees. Roofs of low pitch are most common in late work ; but they occur late in the thirteenth century at Warmington and Polebrook ; and soon after at St Martin's, Leicester, and at Wymington. At no period, however, was the roof of steep pitch disused.*

ROOF CONSTRUCTION.—The simplest form of roof is that in which the rafters are not supported by a framework of more massive timbers ; these are the trussed rafter or unframed roofs. But in large roofs the rafters are usually supported by a framework or truss of more substantial character ; comprising principal rafters and purlins ; and usually tie-beams or collars or both, to which various other members may be added. In the present chapter all the roofs except the trussed rafter roofs are framed or trussed roofs ; *i.e.* roofs with framed trusses.

TRUSSED RAFTER ROOFS.—The earliest large roofs probably had tie-beams ; and when they received the full apparatus of wall-piece, arched brace struts, principals, and ridge-piece, as at Gedney, they were very heavy. More-over, in many districts no doubt timber of sufficient scantling for big tie-beams was not to be had. What was wanted was a roof that could be constructed of small timber. This was got by constructing a roof of common rafters only ; to prevent these from spreading diagonal ties (553.5) were added ; all the timbers being halved and pegged together with wooden pins. The common rafters were placed from $1\frac{1}{2}$ to 2 feet apart ; their scantling averages 5 by 4 inches. Such a roof was comparatively inexpensive. It probably was in early use over barrel vaults ; for which it gave greater headway than a tie-beam roof. The foot of the rafter often projected beyond the outer face of the wall, especially in East Anglia, in order to give good "dripping eaves" (393) ; and therefore could not be fixed to a central wall-plate. Therefore, as in STUSTON PORCH (554), other short pieces of timber, *Sole-pieces*, are laid on the wall-plate at right angles to it ; and the rafters are pegged to their projecting ends. Still further to attach the rafters to the sole-pieces, and to prevent the former from spreading, upright struts (553.10), are inserted ; pegged to the rafter and to the inner end of the sole-piece. Such a roof has six sides, and may be distinguished as a six-sided rafter roof. It will be seen that it is much simpler in construction than the tie-beam roof ; dispensing as it does with ridge-piece, purlins, principals, and tie-beam. The defect of it is the absence of longitudinal ties ; when not

* Brandon's *Roofs*, 12.

boarded, the couples are generally out of the vertical, inclining, in a nave, either to east or west.   At Ely it was found that the trussed rafter roof of the presbytery, an exact counterpart of that of the nave, had pushed out the east wall so much that it overhung its base two feet; the wall was got back into position by means of screws.

In the above six-sided rafter roofs, in spite of the four ties (553.5), there is still much risk of spreading, and they are not fit for use over wide spans. Usually, therefore, they are strengthened by an upper beam called a collar beam,[*]

Wimbotsham.

or *Collar;* which is most commonly placed above the diagonal ties (553.6). Such a roof may be called a seven-sided rafter roof, *e.g.* PASTON (551).   Owing to the additional strength given by the collar, this roof was sometimes used over wide spans; *e.g.* in Reedham Church, 31 feet span; and Ely nave.   To keep out draughts, this roof also was often boarded over, as in Ely nave and WIMBOTSHAM.   Sometimes, as at Heckington, the chancel had boarded, the nave open rafters.

* This is also called a Wind-beam; because another of its functions is to resist wind pressure.   There may be two or more collars, as at Wimbotsham.

More rarely, the diagonal ties intersect the collar beam, as at LYMPENHOE (554), and FILBY,* Norfolk (553.7).

Large numbers of trussed rafter roofs of the above three types still remain ; they are an interesting feature in the Canterbury parish churches. They are said not to have been used till the thirteenth century. They never afterwards went entirely out of use.

STEEP ROOFS WITH TIE-BEAMS.—The earliest roofs of considerable span probably had tie-beams. A small roof might be constructed as in 553.1, with rafters only. But such a roof would tend to spread. To prevent this, two precautions were taken. One was to lay on or build into each wall a longitudinal *wall-plate* (553.2) ; into this the feet of the rafters were fastened. Secondly, across the nave, at right angles to the wall-plates, *tie-beams* were placed, and the ends of these tie-beams were pinned to the wall-plates. This prevented the wall-plate from being dislodged by the outward thrust of the rafters. Such a roof system stopped these thrusts. But there were serious objections to it, especially when employed over considerable spans. Beams of such length and scantlings as those of Winchester nave were difficult to obtain ; at Winchester they were obtained by a permission employed, not quite honestly, to cut down a royal forest.† With the bad roads and unbridged rivers of those days, the cost of transport also was excessive. And it must have been very difficult to raise them into position. Moreover, if it was wished to vault the church, the apex of the vault was prevented from rising higher than the tie-beam. But the worst of all was that a long tie-beam tends to sag or droop in the centre : a tendency which was aggravated in many roofs by the super-position of a king-post (553.3).

KING-POST ROOF.—We have said that there was a tendency of the rafters of a nave to spread outwardly ; *i.e.* north to south. But they also might rack from east to west. To prevent this, the tops of each pair were fastened to a longitudinal beam, called the *ridge-piece*.‡ To support this ridge-piece, upright posts, called *king-posts*, were sometimes set up in the centres of the tie-beams. Usually, to the upper part of the king-post were attached four struts ; two passing up to the ridge-piece, and two to a pair of rafters ; as at WOODBASTWICK§ (551). Such a construction made matters worse still ; additional weight from the roof being brought down on to the tie-beam just at its weakest point, the centre. Nowadays we should peg the king-post to the tie-beam as well as to the ridge-piece ‖ These king-post roofs were very common in Kent ; it will often be found that the king-post has been removed from the tie-beam ; probably because it made it sag.

QUEEN-POST ROOF.—A less objectionable roof is one in which there are two uprights (553.4). At NORTH WALSHAM (562), *c.* 1390, there is a king-post in the aisle roof, queen-posts in the nave roof. By a further extension of this

---

* Illustrated in Brandon's *Parish Churches*, 37.   † Britton's *Winchester*, 38.
‡ See ridge-piece in 564 ; and sections of ridge-pieces in 555, 556.
§ King-posts might also be placed on collar beams.
‖ That is, in mediæval construction the king-post was in *compression ;* in modern construction it would be in *tension*. A member is said to be in tension when a chain or wire can be substituted for it.

system, a row of uprights was sometimes set up on later tie-beams and collars ; as at ST NICHOLAS, LYNN (214) ; and LOUTH (213) ; harmonising very well with the tracery of the Perpendicular windows. A singularly beautiful roof of this type is to be seen in the Trinity Chapel, Cirencester Church.*

DEPRESSED ROOFS WITH TIE-BEAMS.—The more work was thrown on the tie-beam, the more it tended to sag. To stop this in later roofs, various remedies were adopted.

I. One was to *camber* † it ; *i.e.* so to cut it that it was slightly arched at the centre ; as at WOODBASTWICK (551), GEDNEY (551), LONG MELFORD (214). Almost all later tie-beams are more or less cambered. The camber may perhaps average 1 inch in every 5 feet ; in a modern roof perhaps 1 inch in 20 feet.

II. A second method was to construct arched braces under the tie-beam to support it. Sometimes the curved braces meet the tie-beam in the centre,

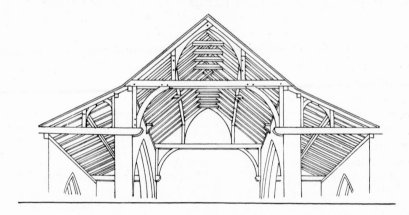

North Walsham.

and form a complete arch, as at ST MARY'S, LEICESTER ; ADDERBURY (558) ; LONG MELFORD ; ST NICHOLAS, LYNN (214) ; and Croydon Palace.‡ Sometimes they support the tie-beam only towards the extremities. In the latter case four-centred arches may be formed ; harmonising with the four-centred arches of doorways and windows ; see illustrations of LOUTH (213) ; GRESFORD (214) ; and MELBOURNE (203).

In some few examples, *e.g.* Morton Church, and Pulham,§ the arched braces are framed into, and look as if they pass through, the tie-beam, with very unpleasant effect.

III. But in later examples, such as Boston, Holbeach, St Peter Mancroft and St Stephen's, Norwich, the clerestories were perforated with numerous and large windows, between which little masonry or pier was left. To balance the

* In WESTMINSTER HALL great use is made of these upright struts (557).

† A cambered beam is defined as one whose upper surface has been cut to a slight slope from the middle towards each end.

‡ Illustrated in Pugin's *Examples*, i. 38.   § Illustrated in Brandon's *Roofs*, 13 and 21.

heavy tie-beam roofs on the tops of these slender piers would have been bad construction. So a corbel was inserted lower down in the wall, *e.g.* at LOUTH (213), and on this an upright post or *wall-post* (or *pendant post*) was placed, on which the end of the tie-beam rested. Then, by the insertion of a strut, the main weight of the roof was brought considerably lower down. Sometimes the wall-post is omitted; to the detriment of the construction and of artistic effect; as in HULL CHANCEL (81).

IV. Such a roof, however, was still very heavy, with its combination of tie-beam, struts, and principal rafters, as at GEDNEY (551). The remedy was to make the tie-beam serve also as principal rafter. This was a great economy of wood and of weight, dispensing as it did at once with principals and struts. The result was of course a very depressed roof, as at GRESFORD (214); Haverfordwest; St Mary's, Shrewsbury; Lavenham; Long Melford; Raunds and Rushden.* The gradual absorption of the principal rafter into the tie-beam is well seen in early examples; *e.g.* Kiddington and Sparsholt,† and the south aisle of St Martin, Leicester,‡ which are all early in the fourteenth century; in all of them the tie-beam is exceedingly massive.

PURLINS.—One more difficulty about roof construction remains to be noted. It is that the rafters, being slight, tended to bulge inward under wind pressure and the weight of the tiles or lead by which they were covered. To obviate this, the principal rafters or *Principals* over the tie-beams were made exceptionally strong; and into these one or more horizontal timbers were framed (555, 558). These are called *Purlins*. Then on the outside of the purlins were laid the outer rafters; which are called *Common Rafters*. Another service rendered by the purlins is that they prevent the rafters of a nave racking from east to west. In Leicester St Mary, Adderbury, North Walsham, Brinton, there is one purlin on each side of the roof; at Gresford there are three.

ARCH-BRACED ROOFS.—As we saw above, the later tie-beams were supported by arched braces; *e.g.* at Louth and Gresford, whose lower ends rested on the same corbels as the wall-posts. It was only necessary to support the collar instead of the tie-beam in this way, and a new and simple form of roof was obtained.§ At PATRINGTON (553.8), *c.* 1340, the principle is fully admitted; the collar being very small and set very high up.

In such an example as Patrington the collar is reduced to a minimum; the next step was to abolish it altogether. At Tenby it was felt a dangerous thing to do, the risk of spreading being great; so the arched braces were constructed exceedingly massive. Sometimes, however, little substance was put into them, as in UGGLESHALL (572) and BRINTON, NORFOLK (564). At Tenby and Outwell no precautions are taken against the spreading of the roof, which rests on the aisle wall. At Brinton, however, the arched brace is fastened to a wall-post; and the thrust of the rafters therefore cannot dislodge the wall-plate unless it also dislodges all the courses of wall against which the wall-post rests.

---

* Illustrated in *Churches of Northants*, 59, 185.

† *Glossary*, Plate 176.　　　　　　　　　　‡ Illustrated in Brandon's *Roofs*, Plate 8.

§ These roofs are styled by Mr Brandon *Collar-braced*. The term is objectionable; because not infrequently arch-braced roofs were constructed without collars; *e.g.* BRINTON (564).

Thus the wall-post not only serves to bring the weight of the whole roof lower down, as explained above, but also to stop the thrust of the rafters.* One of the most audacious roofs of this type is that of SALL, NORFOLK (551); in which the arched braces are minimised to a most dangerous extent.†

HAMMERBEAM ROOFS.—Arch-braced roofs are often assumed to be a simplification of hammerbeam roofs. Chronology seems to be against this.

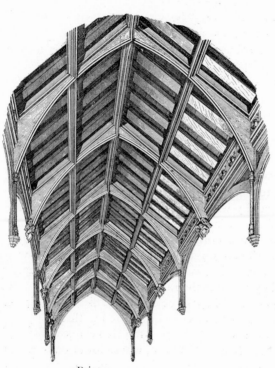

Brinton.

No hammerbeam roof is said to exist earlier than that of Westminster Hall, finished in 1399.‡ But arch-braced roofs existed more than half a century earlier than this. That of Patrington transept can hardly be later than 1340; earlier still was the arch-braced roof of the Worcester Guest Hall, now removed to Holy Trinity Church, near Shrub Hill Station; this roof was constructed in 1320. Hammerbeam roofs did not come into general use till late in the fifteenth century.§ The only real difference between an arch-braced roof and a hammerbeam roof is that in the former (553.10) the sole-piece does not project beyond the inner face of the wall; while in the latter (553.11) it is elongated, and may project considerably. If on page 553 a curved brace be made to spring, not from A, 10, but from B, 11, the end of the sole-piece elongated, the arch-braced roof will be converted to a hammerbeam. Another difference, but of minor importance, is that advantage is taken of the elongation of the sole-piece, CB, to erect a second upright or strut, EF, as shown

* That the wall-piece is not always put in to carry weight is clear from the fact that it sometimes is employed without any corbel to support it ; in such cases its object can only be to prevent spreading ; *e.g.* in the hammerbeam roofs of CAPEL ST MARY (555), Freslingfield, and Bacton ; and the arch-braced roofs of Pulham and Starston (illustrated in Brandon's *Roofs*, Plates 17, 31, 35, 27, 29) ; and UGGLESHALL (572).

† Vast spans, however, may be successfully roofed in this way. At Vicenza, the Basilica, built 1314, has a roof of the shape of a pointed arch, with a span of 70 feet. The great hall at Padua has a similar roof, with a span of about 85 feet ; the ribs have a scantling of about 13 inches square.

‡ But in Carlisle choir the hammerbeams remain of 1375 to 1400 ; see Billing's *Carlisle*, Plate 37 ; those of Boston must be still earlier ; the aisle of Hingham, 1316-1359, has a hammerbeam roof; but this may be contemporaneous with the nave roof of 1664, destroyed in a recent "restoration."

§ Brandon's *Roofs*, 21, note.

in 553.11, which still further prevents the rafters from spreading. The main feature of the hammerbeam roof is the elongation of the sole-piece: in fact the hammerbeam is nothing else than an elongated sole-piece.

This elongation may be seen slowly going on. In many cases it is not easy to say whether the roofs ought to be styled arch-braced or hammerbeam;

Wymondham Nave.

e.g. CAPEL ST MARY (555). If the hammerbeam be but of slight projection, as at Capel St Mary and LLANIDLOES (552), it is comparatively ineffective. It is only when it projects boldly some 5 or 6 feet, as at TRUNCH, CAWSTON (552), and KNAPTON (567), that full advantage can be taken of its decorative capacities.

Another unfounded assumption finds the origin of the hammerbeam in a tie-beam with the centre cut out.   For this there is nothing to be said except that occasionally tie-beam and hammerbeam do occur in alternation, as in PASTON BARN, NORFOLK (552); Weston Church, Lincolnshire; and elsewhere.   The real object of the elongation of the sole-piece is to provide a couple of curved braces (of which the upper brace descends either from the collar (555) or from the ridge (556) to the hammerbeam, and the lower from the hammerbeam to the wall-post) in order that the rafters may be prevented from spreading.   It will be seen also that while some of these roofs omit the collar, and others the struts, the hammerbeam and the curved brace are always present; evidently these are the essential elements.

We may arrange the hammerbeam roofs in order of complexity.*   First, some have neither collar nor struts; *e.g.* WYMONDHAM NAVE (565) and Palgrave; the upper part of the arched brace being strengthened so as to serve at once as collar and brace.†   Second, some have struts but no collar; *e.g.* CAWSTON (552), TRUNCH (552), and ST STEPHEN'S, NORWICH (556).   Thirdly, others have collar but no struts; *e.g.* CAPEL ST MARY (555); here the hammerbeam has little projection.‡   Fourthly, the single hammerbeam roof, with full complement of collar and struts; *e.g.* Freslingfield, Upwell, Blakeney, and Bury St Edmunds.   Fifthly, the double hammerbeam roof; in which the arched braces rise to the collar not in one, but in two flights.   In these the principal rafter is tenoned into the lower hammerbeam, but the upper hammerbeam into the principal; *e.g.* Bacton;§ Grundisburgh;‖ Woolpit;¶ Tostock; St Margaret's, Ipswich; Weatherden; Rattlesden; all the above in Suffolk; Swaffham, Tilney All Saints, and KNAPTON (567), in Norfolk;** MARCH (566), in Cambridge.

Outside East Anglia examples of single or double hammerbeams occur chiefly in or near London; *e.g.* Eltham Palace;†† Beddington Hall, near Croydon; Hampton Court Palace;‡‡ Westminster Hall;§§ Middle Temple Hall.‖‖   They occur but sporadically elsewhere; *e.g.* in the Law Library to the north of Exeter Cathedral; and at Llangollen and Gilgen, Denbighshire; and at Llanidloes.   They remained in use till the seventeenth century, well into the Renaissance period; *e.g.* Hampton Court, 1530; Middle Temple, 1570; Wollaton, 1580; Trinity College, Cambridge, 1604; and Wadham College, Oxford, 1612.¶¶

CORNICE.—In East Anglia the cornice is more developed than elsewhere. Owing to the local custom of dispensing with gutter and parapet, the rafters were set far back from the inner surface of the wall; *e.g.* in the trussed rafter

---

* Chronologically the simplest roofs may be the least ancient.

† Brandon's *Roofs*, Plates 20, 22.			‡ Brandon's *Roofs*, Plate 17.

§ Brandon's *Roofs*, Plate 35.			‖ Brandon's *Analysis*, Plate 26.

¶ Brandon's *Parish Churches*, 49.

** The latter retains much of its colour.   A reproduction of this roof in colour is given in Brandon's *Roofs*, Plate 38.

†† Pugin's *Examples*, i., Plate 46.			‡‡ Pugin's *Specimens*, ii., Plate 8.

§§ Pugin's *Specimens*, i., Plate 32 ; and Viollet-le-Duc, *Architecture*, iii. 32, 33, 34.

‖‖ Illustrated in Weale's *Quarterly Papers*, ii.

¶¶ Gotch's *English Renaissance*, 161.   A fine modern hammerbeam roof is illustrated at HOLBEACH (133).

MARCH, ROOF OF NAVE.

roof of STUSTON PORCH (554). This left a triangular space between the struts and the sloping rafters. It was easy to board over the front of this space; and in East Anglia a cornice of two or three parts is often thus formed in

Knapton.

different varieties of late roofs; sometimes carved, *e.g.* in the hammerbeam roof of KNAPTON with square flowers and angels with outspread wings, sometimes molded. The cornice, instead of being vertical, was often inclined

forward to be more directly opposite to the line of vision ; as in the cornice of
the roof of CAPEL ST MARY shown in section on 555.

Not only on the cornices, but at the ends of the hammerbeams, at the
foot of the wall-pieces, and erect on the collar beams, were often set angels
with outstretched wings, as at MARCH (566), Woolpit, Knapton, and Swaffham ;
some holding shields charged with the instruments of the Passion, others labels
with devout scriptures, others instruments of music ; spirits, as it were, arrested
midway in their heavenward flight ; hovering over, worshipping with the faithful
gathered below.

Kilkhampton.

ARCUATED
ROOFS.— Artisti-
cally, the note of
the later churches
was Unity. This
is just as clear at
March and Swaff-
ham as in ST
GEORGE'S, WIND-
SOR (330). Be-
low were the
arches of the
pier - arcade ;
above, those of
the clerestory
windows ; all set
longitudinally.
Now, set trans-
versely, arch rose
upon arch in
many a roof as
well. Such a roof
in form was be-
come arcuated
instead of tra-
beated ; roof and
church, wood and
stone, were ar-
cuated alike ; the
whole was indeed
"a house at one with itself." See the illustrations of TRUNCH (552), WYMOND-
HAM (565), GEDNEY (551), KILKHAMPTON, NEW WALSINGHAM (571).

LONGITUDINAL BRACES.—As we saw above (560), there was a tendency
of the rafters to deviate from a vertical plane. Except in trussed rafter roofs
this was partially guarded against by the provision of purlins and ridge-
pieces. But longitudinal arched braces are often inserted as well, even where
constructionally they are little needed. Thus at KNAPTON (567) they are inserted between the wall-pieces, and might be employed with perfect decorative

propriety in such a position as a repeat of the heads of the clerestory windows immediately below; as they are at TRUNCH (552) and ST STEPHEN'S, NORWICH (556). But they also occur between the principal rafters;* e.g. at Eltham, Worcester Guest Hall, Bury St Edmunds. Lastly, if the span from one tie-beam or collar to the next be considerable, a longitudinal arch may be erected from the centre of one beam to the centre of the next, in order to support the ridge-piece halfway ; as at ADDERBURY (558).

Sometimes a horizontal strut was provided between the collar beams ; as at Charney, Sutton Courtney,† WIGGENHALL ST MARY (571) ; where it passes below the collar and is supported by king-posts ; or as at FARINGDON (558), where it is unsupported from below. Cf. Kingsland and Horton Kirkby.

COLOUR.—Wherever windows contain fragments of ancient glass, there the roofs seem almost invariably to have been coloured. In Palgrave Church and Ely transepts the colours are chiefly black, white, and red. In Long Melford the rafters of the flat roofs are painted red ; the panels between them blue, powdered with gold stars. The gorgeous roof of the nave of Knapton is mainly yellow, green, and red. ‡

HYBRID ROOFS.—All the above—steep and depressed roofs with tie-beams, trussed rafter roofs with six or seven sides, arch-braced roofs without or with collars, hammerbeam roofs—are simple types. But frequently two or more forms of construction are combined in one roof. Thus Outwell aisle, Weston nave, and Paston barn have alternately hammerbeams and tie-beams. WOOD-BASTWICK (551) has a combination of king-post roof and boarded rafter roof with seven sides. Sandridge, Herts, has a trussed rafter roof with the addition of a tie-beam to each twelve rafters. Clymping, Sussex, has a similar roof.§ Pulham St Mary has an arched brace rising to the ridge-piece, and pinned into the tie-beam.‖ The roof of St Mary, Leicester, has arched brace and collar ; but, having no ridge-piece, it partakes also of the character of a trussed rafter roof.¶ The roof of Solihull, Warwick, is a combination of trussed rafter and arch-braced roof with collar. Inside the rafters and collar are fixed arched braces. When a roof of this sort is boarded over, it produces a type which from its frequency requires a special name. It is a *Barrel* roof. It occurs in Carlisle choir, instead of the hammerbeam roof originally planned. Barrel roofs are especially common in Somerset and Cornwall ; e.g. KILKHAMPTON (568). It will be noticed that in this church the aisles also have barrel roofs. A room at Charney, and the hall of Sutton Courtney, Berks, and the church of Wiggenhall St Mary, have a combination of king-post and seven-sided rafter roof. The tie-beams at Higham Ferrers have both king-post and queen-posts.** The roof of WESTMINSTER HALL †† (557), with the vast span of nearly 69

---

* Here they have value as against wind-pressure.   † See *Glossary*, Plates 171, 175.

‡ For coloured plates of the above, see Brandon's *Roofs;* Palgrave, Plate 22 ; Knapton, Plate 38 ; and Colling's *Gothic Ornaments ;* Long Melford, Plate 36 ; Bury St Edmunds, Plate 40.

§ Illustrated in Brandon's *Parish Churches*, 75.   ‖ Illustrated in Brandon's *Roofs*, 21.

¶ Illustrated in 558.2.   ** *Glossary*, Plate 174.

†† Westminster Hall is 68 feet wide internally ; the height of the walls is 42 feet, and of the roof 48 feet. Each truss is about 19 feet 10 inches apart, and has to carry, besides its own weight, the timber and slates necessary to roof 1,359 feet of floor. The pitch of the roof is 52°. It is of English oak, and was constructed in 1397. Professor Roger Smith in *Builder*, 48, 479.

feet, is a combination of hammerbeam roof and arched-brace and collar roof, with king and queen posts and numerous upright struts.

CEILINGS.—A few original ceilings remain. St Gregory's, Sudbury, has a flat molded ceiling in the chancel. The most elaborate of all is that of the nave of ST DAVID'S (525).

AISLE ROOFS.—If the aisle was broad, as at Wymondham, Outwell, and St Martin's, Leicester, it often had a roof of double slope; *i.e.* a *Span, Saddle, Gable,* or *Compass* roof. If the nave had a clerestory, the aisle roof was flattened in order not to interfere with the clerestory lighting. If there were no clerestory, all three span roofs might be equal in height ; *e.g.* at Old Basing, which may be seen on the left near the railway before entering Basingstoke from the east. A church so roofed corresponds in section with vaulted churches of the type of the choirs of the TEMPLE CHURCH (35.1).

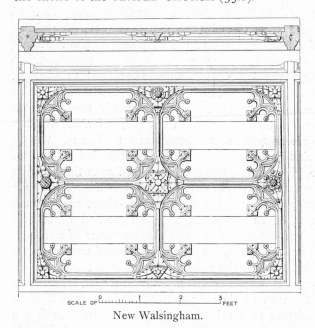

SCALE OF [0 ... 1 .... 2 .... 3] FEET

New Walsingham.

Usually the aisle had a lean-to roof; *i.e.* of one slope only. In many of the earlier thatched churches and barns the span roof of the naves was continued downward so as to shelter the aisles as well as the nave ; *e.g.* EAST-WOOD (224); TOOT BALDON (225).* This brought the eaves nearly down to the ground, and only the most diminutive aisle windows were possible. So in such examples the slope of the roof over the aisle is generally a little flatter than that of the nave ; in order to get more headway for the windows of the aisle. The principal rafters of the aisle roof were often strengthened with struts or with curved braces ; as at NEW WALSINGHAM (571).

Both in aisles and naves the rafters were often boarded over, and the spandrels of the trusses have traceried panels ; *e.g.* in the aisle of NEW WAL-SINGHAM and the chancel of Sall.

Hammerbeam roofs occur over the aisles of Upwell and Hingham.

WOOD VAULTS.—A considerable number of vaults were executed in wood. either through distrust or dislike of stone vaulting, or inability to find money for it ; especially in the North of England. At Selby and York heavy pinnacles had been erected to receive the thrust of stone vaults transmitted by flying buttresses ; but no stone vaults and no flying buttresses were ever erected (390, 10). Wood vaults appear *c.* 1300 in St Albans presbytery, and earlier still

* Compare Brandon's *Roofs*, Plate 2.

over Warmington Church. Winchester choir exemplifies their use as late as
1510 to 1528.

St Peter Mancroft, Norwich, has a hybrid roof.* The lower part is a ribbed
vault in wood ; the upper part an arch-braced roof ; so also at Framlingham.

Whether vaulted or semi-vaulted in wood, such roofs are objectionable as
being a reproduction in one material of forms which arose out of the nature of
another.

MATERIAL AND CONSTRUCTION.—These roofs appear to have been constructed of oak. It has often been asserted, *e.g.* by Evelyn and by Sir Christopher
Wren, that the sweet or edible Spanish chestnut was also employed. But papers
read before the Royal Institute of British Architects in 1858 by Mr Wyatt
Papworth and in 1878 by Mr Thomas Blashill show that the assumption is

Wiggenhall St Mary the Virgin.   New Walsingham.

doubtful. The sweet chestnut is not a common tree here ; and it is very unlikely that there were large forests of it in mediæval times. Neither Sir Gilbert
Scott nor Viollet-le-Duc came across any use of chestnut in the course of their
restorations. Mr Fowler, in a paper on Maulbronn Abbey, Wurtemberg, read
before the Institute, mentions that the south transept retains its original roof and
ceiling of fir.

The different timbers were always morticed and tenoned together, and fixed
with wooden pins ; no iron ties or straps, or even nails, being used in any part.†

According to Viollet-le-Duc,‡ none of the oak employed was of great
age ; sixty, eighty, or one hundred years at the most : it was cut before the heart

* Illustrated in Rickman, 280.   † Brandon's *Roofs*, 32.   ‡ *Architecture*, ii. 215.

had begun to decompose.   First the tree was barked, and then cut.   It was cut
in winter ; and then only during a certain moon.   It was squared and piled, well
ventilated, under cover ; and seasoned for several years.

Great care was taken to ventilate the roofs.   The tie-beams were laid on a
wall-plate ; not directly on the wall ; and as much of the surface of the timber
as possible was exposed to the air.   When well ventilated, and protected from
damp and from contact with stone, the duration of well-seasoned oak is almost
illimitable.

Uggleshall from E.

Southwold Nave.

OLDEST ROOFS.—Of the Norman roofs perhaps the best preserved is that
above the Bishop's Palace at Hereford.   At Winchester that of the south transept
is the original eleventh-century roof; and in the nave some of the Norman tie-
beams and rafters seem to have been re-used by Wykeham and his successors ; *
the length of the tie-beams in the nave was 45 feet; they were 12 inches thick
and 20 inches deep.   The ceiling of Peterborough nave is said, improbably, to be
Norman.   The roof of Adel Church is described as Norman.†   To the thirteenth
century belong the tie-beams of Old Shoreham ; which have tooth ornament. ‡

* Colson, 8, 14, 16.   † *Assoc. Soc. Reports*, xix. 110.
‡ Illustrated in *Glossary*, text 278.

CHAPTER XXXIX.

THE DOORWAY AND PORCH.

Lintel—Tympanum—Single and Double Doorways—Norman and Gothic Doorways—
Western Doorway—Priest's Doorway—Porch—Parvise—Doors—Rear Arch.

TRABEATED DOORWAYS.—The form of a doorway is in a measure controlled
by that of the door. And since it is as easy to construct an oblong door as
it is difficult to construct one with an arched head; and since also there is
a difficulty about opening a door with an arched head (584), the doorways
of the Greek temple and the modern tenement are alike square-headed. This
square-headed opening may be bridged by a beam (Latin, *trabs*) of wood or by
a lintel of stone.

But a long block so used will crack in the middle if the superimposed
weight is great. To protect the lintel, therefore, by carrying off as much
weight as possible to the right and left, the Romans turned over it what is called
a *discharging* or *relieving* arch; which, however, they usually concealed under
the plaster or marble veneering of the wall.* So also in the fifth-century
Baptistery of Ravenna the lintel of the square-headed doorway is protected by
a discharging arch of brick, hardly visible in the wall. In S. ETIENNE, NEVERS
(574), consecrated in 1099, a doorway of this simple type survives. The next
step is seen in the tenth century at the Baptistery of Biella; where a single
slab is introduced between the lintel and discharging arch.† So that now the
doorhead consists of three elements—lintel, tympanum, arch. The tympanum
offered an excellent field of sculpture; and became very popular in some districts. Many of our Norman doorways have carved tympanums; often Our
Lord is represented in majesty, with hand uplifted in the act of benediction of
all who enter the church; as at Malmesbury, North Newbald, in the so-called
monks' doorway in Ely nave; and the west doorway of ROCHESTER (574).
In French Gothic, *e.g.* at Chartres, the sculptured treatment of the doorway
received marvellous development. With us the art of sculpture, which in Wells
west front had shown equal promise with that of Chartres, fell more and more
into the background. With the exception of the Last Resurrection sculptured
on the south doorway of Lincoln presbytery, England, like Italy, abandoned the
French form of doorway, with tympanum peopled with statuary.‡

---

* Willis' *Nomenclature*, 115. The accentuation of the Roman relieving-arch over a lintel
is found in the second century A.D. in Asia Minor and Syria (Anderson and Spiers, 259).

† Illustrated in Cattaneo and Rivoira.

‡ Dehio, ii. 584, is of opinion that the design of these doorways is non-architectural, and
moreover does injustice to the statuary; but that, though disagreeable, it is very rich and
grand; and was based not on artistic, but on religious motives.

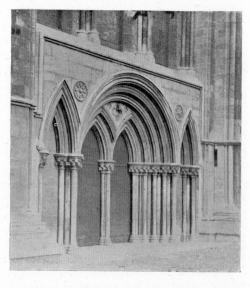

Iffley, W. Doorway.
Nevers, St Etienne.

Rochester, W. Doorway.
Beverley Transept.

Hales.
Binham.

Sall.
Trunch Chancel.

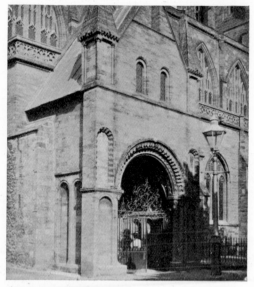

Gimingham.   Sherborne.
Tiverton.   Lavenham.

In all these doorways, as has been pointed out, there was risk of fracture of the lintel. Sometimes this was guarded against, as at St Etienne de Nevers, by making the lintel thicker in the centre. Or a horizontal arch was constructed; *i.e.* a coursed lintel; sometimes with joggled joints. Or the span of the opening was reduced by inserting corbels under the ends of the lintel; this expedient is not employed in Normandy till the twelfth century, except at Ducy.*

The most obvious way out of the difficulty was to put a pillar (*trumeau*) under the centre of the doorway, as was done in the west doorway of Vézelay; forming a double doorway. A later treatment of the door deserves mention; it is characteristic of Champagne; and consists in glazing the tympanum; *e.g.* Reims Cathedral.

SINGLE AND DOUBLE DOORWAYS. —But from the first it seems to have been not uncommon to omit both lintel and tympanum, as at IFFLEY (574). It is curious that Poitou and Saintonge, although sculpture was very advanced, and the tympanum offered a fine field for it, largely abandoned the lintel and tympanum type of doorway.†

Iffley South Doorway.

In the thirteenth century a central pillar or trumeau is sometimes introduced and a doorway with double arch is for the first time produced. Fine examples appear at Higham Ferrers and St Cross, Winchester. These double doorways are particularly characteristic of the chapter houses; *e.g.* Lincoln, Southwell, Wells, York. Fine double doorways lead into the transepts of Lichfield; in the west front the inner doorway is double, the outer single.

* Ruprich-Robert, 124. † Viollet-le-Duc, *Architecture*, vii. 408.

2 O

In France the trumeaux of great numbers of these doorways were removed in the eighteenth century; probably because they were serious obstructions, *e.g.* to carrying the shrine of a local saint, or to holding the baldachino over the head of the bishop in processions. For similar reasons probably they went more and more out of fashion in England after the thirteenth century.

SCALE OF FEET

Warmington West Doorway.

NORMAN DOORWAYS.—On their doorways the Romanesque builders lavished all their resources; especially valuable to them was the principle of recessing the orders. Arch was built upon arch to gain strength; and when all the strength required was gained, they still went on building more arches, as a field for decorative carving; till sometimes, as in the doorways of Malmesbury and S. Fermo, Verona, the arch consisted of no less than eight orders. Even in the thick Norman walls there was not always room for arches of such great breadth. So frequently the wall was built additionally thick all round the doorway; *e.g.* at Iffley. This projecting space of wall was sometimes carried up to a gable; as at SEMPRINGHAM (40) and Kirkstall.* But the gabled doorway never received here the great development given to it in France. We have nothing comparable with the five solid gables of the western doors of Bayeux; with those of Bourges, pierced with plate-tracery; still less with the gables of open-work tracery of the Porte de la Calende, Rouen Cathedral. Even more superb are the fifteenth and sixteenth century gabled doorways of Abbeville and Tours; of the transepts of Sens, Beauvais, and Senlis; of St Maclou, Rouen; and the sculptured gables of the cathedral of Troyes.

Of Norman doorways very numerous examples survive. Windows of the eleventh, twelfth, and thirteenth centuries had to be taken out to insert larger ones. But the doorways were generally large enough. At Birkin, when an aisle was added in the fourteenth century, the Norman doorway was taken down and reset; so also at Kenilworth. In the same way thirteenth-century doorways were reset at Louth and Leominster when the aisles were widened. The doorway described by William of Worcester as on the north side of St Stephen's, Bristol, is now on the south side.†

The doorway of the last half of the twelfth century usually has a semi-circular head; but in the larger examples, *e.g.*, Ketton, it may be flanked by a blank arcade of pointed arches.

GOTHIC DOORWAYS.—In the first half of the thirteenth century full advantage is taken of the recessing of the orders, just as much as in Norman work; *e.g.* at Elgin. This was the period that took most delight in shafting and in wealth of marble monoliths. Now, too, the double doorway had its vogue. Aided by profusion of tooth ornament and of small, deep, delicate moldings, and by exquisite foliage, as at West Walton, SKELTON (78), and WARMINGTON (578), the doorways have surpassing charm. No more beautiful examples exist than the doorways and arcading of the west front of BINHAM (575); executed in an admirable stone.

Later in the century doorways are more commonly single than double. In the richer examples, *e.g.* the west doorway of York, the pointed arch is usually surmounted by a straight-sided gable.

Doorways of the fourteenth century often employ an ogee instead of a straight-sided hood-mold; *e.g.* at CLEY, NORFOLK (85). In this rich example crockets are used profusely, and the hold-mold rises into a floriated finial; the cusping is compound; the foliage bulbous. ‡

In later Gothic a special characteristic of the doorways is that the arch is

---

* Late in the thirteenth century this straight-sided gable plays a very important part, appearing not only over doorways but over windows, niches, and arcades; *e.g.* in York nave and chapter house, and HOWDEN west front (72).

† See Willis' *Nomenclature*, 6.

‡ A rich doorway, of somewhat unusual type, at Heckington, is illustrated in Bowman and Crowther, *Churches*, Plate 31.

Tenby.
Llandaff Choir Arch.

often framed in a rectangular hood-mold (*i.e.* a *label*); *e.g.* at KETTERING (95), WILBY (270), Cawston, Tiverton, Sall. BEVERLEY ST MARY (365) is an exception; but it is very early in the period.* In the spandrels at SALL (575) are censing angels; the door is original.

FORM OF DOORWAY ARCH. —In Norman work this is usually semicircular, but other forms may occur; *e.g.* for want of space the semicircular arch becomes segmental in the south transept of Southwell. So also in the thirteenth century, where a doorway has to be placed under a window, it often becomes semicircular instead of pointed; *e.g.* in the transept of BEVERLEY (574). Even in the fourteenth century, semicircular arches may occur; *e.g.* at Badgeworth, Gloucester, where the doorway is ornamented with ball-flower.

Doorways with pointed arch occur till the end of Gothic, *e.g.* at Tiverton, Sall, Kettering; though in late work a depressed four-centred arch is frequent.

Trefoiled arches occur in Norman doorways; *e.g.* the so-called Prior's doorway at Ely; Mathon, Hereford; and Nately, Hants. About 1170, in Ripon north transept and Byland west front. About 1250, at WARMINGTON (578); it is rare in later work. In and after the fourteenth century the doorway sometimes has an ogee arch; *e.g.* the west doorway of TENBY. In some districts, *e.g.* Northants, it is extremely common.

* A rich example from LAVENHAM (576) is illustrated in Brandon's *Analysis*, Perpendicular, Plates 6 and 7.

WEST DOORWAYS.—
The side entrance for the
laity was in one of the
western bays of the nave.
In most churches there were
doorways both on the north
and the south side of the
nave. Probably this was
for processional * purposes.
In most of the smaller and
earlier parish churches there
was no western doorway ;
e.g. in none of the eighteen
Lincolnshire churches visited
by Mr Sharpe in 1870 was
there a western doorway ;
except at Helpringham.
But almost all the larger
churches† had a large
western doorway. This was
the great ceremonial door of
the church, and in many
churches remains so to this
day ; only opened on some
great function, as the visit
of the sovereign or the bishop
or for a wedding or a funeral.
In mediæval days it took a
leading part in the important
ceremonies of Palm Sunday,
which may still be seen
abroad ; *e.g.* at Troyes. On
that day half the choir is
outside the west door, and
sings the "Attollite Portas"
—"Open ye the gates that
the King of Glory may come
in." Then comes the ques-
tion from the choir within,
"Who is the King of Glory?"
Finally the great doors are
opened, and the procession
enters, symbolising Christ's
entry into Jerusalem.

Whissendine.

* A recess for a tall processional cross is found in many churches of East Suffolk, usually in
the thickness of one of the walls of the western tower ; *e.g.* at St Margaret, Lowestoft, and at Cromer.

† Romsey is an exception ; but it was a nunnery church.

In later days nearly all the larger parish churches seem to have had western doorways. This led to difficulties. For the later builders built usually their western windows as large as possible, to get all the western light they could for the nave.* The result was that there was no room for a doorway of scale proportionate to the magnitude of the west front or west tower in which it was placed. Attempts to cope with this difficulty may, however, occasionally be seen, *e.g.* at WHISSENDINE (581), Hickling, and Ingham.

PRIEST'S DOORWAY.—On one side of the chancel, usually the south, was placed a doorway, usually small and simple, but sometimes, as at Simonburn, highly ornate, to give the priest independent access to the chancel ; *e.g.* TRUNCH (575) ; where in curious fashion its porch is formed of a split buttress.

PORCH.—Just as the nave was more secular than the chancel, so the porch was more secular than the nave ; *e.g.* at Patrington "forty pounds was to be paid on March 25, 1613, within the south porch of the church" † (215.11).

Boxford.

A considerable number of Norman porches remain ; *e.g.* Castle Ashby, Durham, Kelso, Southwell, Malmesbury, SHERBORNE (576), Adel, Witney, Morwenstow, Balderton. Beautiful examples occur in all the Gothic periods. ‡ The porch at LEVERINGTON (84) shows fourteenth-century design at its best. In East Anglia especially, when everything had been done to make church and tower as glorious as possible, the parishioners set to work to build a porch : *e.g.* GIMINGHAM (576) and LAVENHAM (576). And as this was, comparatively, a small expense, it was often built more sumptuously than the church itself ; *e.g.* while the church walls might be of undressed or of split flints, the porch walls were of squared flints ; and sometimes, as at North Walsham, Norfolk, the flints were carefully arranged in zones of different colours ; often also the porch was traceried with patterns of different coloured flints. And while the church was roofed in wood, the porch was often vaulted, as in both the porches of Sall.

---

* Wellingborough, illustrated in *Nene Valley*, Plate 104, is an exception ; the west window being a small traceried circle.

† *Mem. of Patrington Manor Court.*

‡ See especially the E.E. porch of West Walton (illustrated in Colling's *Details*, i. 14).

BEVERLEY ST MARY'S (365) has a comparatively simple, TIVERTON a late and florid porch (576). HEREFORD indulged in the luxury of a double north porch; the inner porch built *c.* 1288, the outer *c.* 1520 (203).

In the churches of the monks and of the Regular Canons there was a cloister on one side of the nave; and their entrance into the church was from the cloister. Consequently in these churches the doorway of the laity was on the opposite side to the cloister. Now the normal position of the cloister was south of the nave. Therefore the majority of the doorways of the laity are on the north side; *e.g.* at Bayham, Bolton, Durham, Lanercost, Malvern, Peterborough, Romsey, Selby, Tewkesbury, Waltham, Westminster, Whitby, Worcester. On the other hand the cloister sometimes had to be placed on the north side; in these cases the lay doorway is on the south; *e.g.* Canterbury, Chester, Dorchester, Gloucester, Malmesbury, Monkton, Sherborne. Some, however, of the monastic churches had a narthex or western porch; *e.g.* Fountains, Byland, Glastonbury, Ely, St Albans, Winchester; others

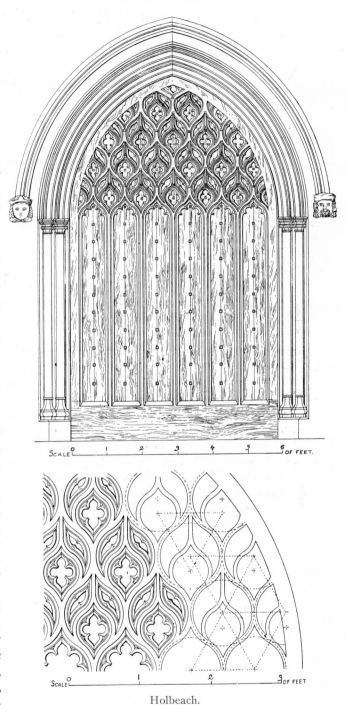

Holbeach.

had merely western doorways; *e.g.* Norwich, Rochester, Netley. But some of the cathedrals served by Secular Canons also indulged in the luxury of a cloister; in such cases the side doorway again was on the side opposite to the cloister; at Salisbury, Wells, Hereford, Lincoln; in all of which it takes the form of magnificent porches; at Lincoln* on the south side, the other three porches on the north. Turning to the other greater churches of the Secular Canons, we find the entrance on the north side; *e.g.* Beverley; Christchurch; Chester St John's; Southwell; Wimborne; Ripon; all of which, except Ripon, have north porches. Exceptional are Chichester, which has three porches, south, north, and west; Lichfield, which has doorways to the north and south transepts; and York, the side entrance to which is in the south transept; while in Benedictine Westminster it is in the north transept.

　　As to the porches of the parish churches, if the church was large or a town church, or if there were habitations on both sides of the church, there were often both north and south doorways, as at Louth and Sall. If the village was to the south of the church,† as for some mysterious reason it seems more often to have been, the doorway would be on the southern side of the nave; otherwise, on the northern.

Sutton.　　　　　　Higham Ferrers.

　　The porch was often two stories high. At Wedmore, Bruton, and Cirencester the porch is three stories high; at Cirencester it was the property of the trade gilds. This upper room is sometimes called a parvise. It was used for various purposes. At Southwell it has a chimney. In such cases it may have been the room of the sacristan, who was bound in some cases, *e.g.* at Southwell, to be on guard all night in the church. Sometimes it has a piscina; and then may have been an altared chapel; as at Fotheringhay and Sall. Sometimes there is a squint; blocked up or still left open. At Warwick the south porch had a room built over it in 1491 as a library.‡ After the Reformation it was often used as a church library. Or, as at Patrington, it became a registry of the parish books;§ but originally probably the sacristan's chamber.

---

　　* There seems to be no mediæval authority for the employment of the term Galilee for this Lincoln porch.

　　† The south aisle is generally of more importance than the north; more often it is broader; and therefore more often has a span roof; the porch is more often on the south; when there is but one porch, it is generally on the south; as also are the church-well or brook, the lych-gate, and the yew trees (Brandon's *Open Timber Roofs*, 30).

　　‡ Leland in *Glossary*, 343.　　　　　　　　§ *Churches of Yorkshire*, Patrington, 10.

WOODEN PORCHES.—In timber districts many charming examples of wooden porches and lichgates remain : *e.g.* at BOXFORD (582), Aldham, and Warblington.*

DOORS of all periods survive. The doors at Castor and SEMPRINGHAM (40) are Norman ; that of Castor retains the lock and key ; round the edge is an inscription that the Rector, Richard Beby, had it made ; that was about 1133.† The doors of Sempringham and of York chapter house are of deal. The great western doors of Peterborough are early thirteenth century ; and inside have tooth ornament. Late in the thirteenth century are the doors of York chapter house and St Margaret's Chapel, Herts. Fourteenth-century doors remain at Milton, Kent ; North Mimms, Herts ; Stoke, Suffolk ; Wells ; HOLBEACH, Lincolnshire, and CLEY, Norfolk, are illustrated in 583 and 85. Many fifteenth-century doors remain, *e.g.* at SALL (575). Doors at St Mary's Beverley, Helmingham, North Petherton, Stratford-on-Avon, and Tempsford, are illustrated in Colling's *Details ;* and an early example from St Albans in Brandon's *Analysis.*

HINGES survive of all periods ; *e.g.* Norman at Sempringham ; fourteenth-century at Cley. See especially J. Starkie Gardner's *Ironwork*, vol. i.

REAR-ARCH.—When a doorway with an arched head was set near the front of the wall, it was necessary to make the rear-arch segmental in form ; *e.g.* HIGHAM FERRERS (584) ; in order to allow the door to open.

* Illustrated in *Glossary*, Plate 164.   † Paley's *Gothic Architecture*, 197.

CHAPTER XL.

TOWERS.

Early Towers—Central Towers—Western Towers—Position of Towers—Tower Groups—
Plan of Towers—Round Towers—Tower Construction—Tower Roofs—Tower
Design.

ANTIQUITY OF TOWERS.—Both among the Greeks and the Romans towers were
in use. In the south of the Peloponnesus at Messena, at Phigalia, in the isle of
Andros, and at Paestum, there are well-constructed towers, both square and
round, several of which are in a fair state of preservation.* Many Roman
towers remain; *e.g.* a round tower at Périgueux; a square tower outside
Autun; the Pharos at Dover. It has been supposed, however, that bells of large
dimensions and belfries to carry them were not employed in Western Europe till
late. This, however, is a mistake. Fleury† has proved definitely from documents
that bells of very large dimensions, and towers to hold them, were in use in the
sixth century. To that century perhaps‡ belong several of the towers of
Ravenna; most of them round, some square. A mosaic of 432 to 440 in S.
Maria Maggiore, Rome, shows two churches near which are round towers. On
the doors of S. Sabina, Rome, which are early in the fifth century, is shown a
church with two western towers.§ Two low western towers were built in the
Syrian churches of Tourmanin‖ and Qualb Louzeh.

Of Romanesque towers one of the oldest is that of S. Satiro, Milan, A.D.
879; of campanile type; of four stories, with central-balustered window, pilaster
strips at the angles by way of buttresses, and a rudimentary kind of nebule
corbel table under each of the three strings.¶ There are many fine campaniles
in Rome; they have been given early dates;** but are so highly developed in
design that none of them are likely to be earlier than the eleventh century, not
even their lowest stages.†† The Irish round towers also are usually greatly
over-dated. Their date is practically certain; viz. from 890 to 1238.‡‡ In
France we have documentary evidence of the existence of church towers in very
early times; *e.g.* at St Martin, Tours, consecrated 477; one of grandiose design
at Nantes, consecrated by St Felix, 550 to 600; one at Narbonne, so lofty that

---

* See illustrations in Laloux's *L'Architecture grecque*, 263, 266.

† *La Messe.*   ‡ Cattaneo, 235.

§ Enlart's *Manuel*, 124.   ‖ Illustrated in Fergusson, i. 427.

¶ Illustrated in Cattaneo, 236. Rivoira, 51, regards Viterbo and San Ambrogio, Milan, as
possessing the earliest examples of church towers; both of the ninth century.

** Mr J. Tavernor Perry in a fully illustrated paper in the *Journal of the R.I.B.A.*, Feb. 21,
1898, dates them from the beginning of the ninth to the end of the eleventh century.

†† Cattaneo, 157.   ‡‡ See Miss Stokes' *Ecclesiastical Architecture of Ireland.*

Oxford St Michael.
Manorbier.

Ely Cathedral from S.W.
Hereford Cathedral from N.W.

Magdalen College, Oxford.
Glastonbury St John.

Canterbury Cathedral.
Wells Cathedral.

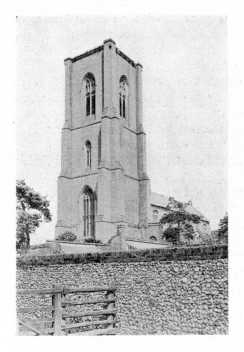

Cawston.
Merton College, Oxford.

Lavenham.
Wymondham.

Alaric II. had the upper stage demolished because it blocked the view from his palace; two others, one at Bordeaux, built *c.* 550; the other at Notre Dame, Paris, appear to be indicated by the descriptions of the poet Fortunatus.* Pope Stephen II., 752 to 757, built a tower at the Vatican, expressly for bells.

Of Anglo-Saxon towers we possess a great number; a few of which incline to the tall and slender campanile type; *e.g.* ST MICHAEL'S, OXFORD (587); and several in Lincolnshire and the North of England; *e.g.* Monkwearmouth. At Brixworth only the lowest stage of the Anglo-Saxon tower appears to be contemporaneous with the nave, *i.e. c.* 680. It seems probable that no Anglo-Saxon tower is earlier than the end of the ninth century; † and that Anglo-Saxon central towers, such as that of St Mary in the Castle, Dover, are but little anterior to the Norman Conquest.

CENTRAL TOWERS.—The central tower is a natural outcome of the cruciform plan; as facilitating the roofing of a church with transepts, especially when the transepts are lower than the nave and choir (see 196). At Clermont-Ferrand there was built in the year 510, in a church of secondary rank, a central tower "with a great luxury of materials and profiles." Several others of like date are described by Fortunatus of Poitiers. ‡ We possess an illustration of the primitive abbey of St Riquier; in which the central tower is crowned by an open pavilion or louvre. §

In Anglo-Saxon days it clearly existed at Ramsey Abbey, A.D. 969. ‖ And cruciform Anglo-Saxon churches with central towers still exist at St Mary's in the Castle, Dover; Norton; Stow; Breamore; and St Mary's, Guildford. Anglo-Saxon central towers also were built in churches without transepts; *e.g.* at Barton-on-Humber. In Normandy churches of this last type are rare, but there is one at Englesqueville.¶ In England Norman examples occur at Studland in Dorset; Basing, South Hayling, and Sopeley, Hants; Bredon and Iffley in Mid-England, and at Fairford, Kempsford, Tong. But a central tower is naturally more common over a cruciform church. In Normandy in the eleventh century there was hardly a cruciform church but had a central tower. In the twelfth century, in Normandy, there are a few examples of Norman western towers; the central tower was much more common. In England Norman central towers were less common.** In some cases perhaps a central tower fell, or threatening to fall was pulled down, *e.g.* at NEWARK (178). Often it seems not to have been rebuilt; †† but, instead, a western tower was built. Wherever aisles were being added or broadened, and an open arcade was substituted for a solid wall, the abutments of the central tower were rendered less stable; and there was risk of a collapse. Nevertheless, in the cathedrals and abbey churches with few exceptions, Llandaff is one, central towers con-

---

* Anthyme St Paul, *Histoire Monumentale*, 60, and M. De Rossi in *Revue de l'Art chrétien* 1890, page 5.

  † Baldwin Brown, *Arts in Early England*, 286, 246.

  ‡ A. St Paul in Planat's *Encyclopédie*, article *Architecture Romane*.

  § Illustrated in Enlart's *Manuel*, 173.

  ‖ See description quoted in Scott's *Lectures*, ii. 33.   ¶ Ruprich-Robert, 101.

  ** For list of towers which fell, see *Builder*, xix., 1861, April 13.

  †† At St Mary Redcliffe, Bristol, and at Great Wilbraham, Cambridge, the lower courses of the old central tower may still be seen beneath the roof of the crossing.

tinued to be employed; Bath Abbey has one of the latest.* In the parish churches, on the other hand, the central tower went more and more out of use; except in some of the greater churches, such as PATRINGTON (612), HULL (96), Nantwich, Doncaster, Rotherham.

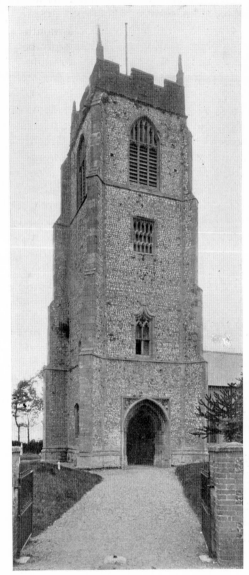

Holme.   Ile Abbot.

In Continental Romanesque the practice varied. Where it was insisted

* King's College Chapel, Cambridge; St George's, Windsor; Eton College Chapel; Henry the Seventh's Chapel, Westminster, were indeed built without towers; but they are all chapels; and the absence of a tower was at times a distinguishing mark of a chapel.

that the whole church should be made fireproof by vaulting, the broad space over the crossing was vaulted with a dome. But the dome itself required to be protected from the weather; and so on the same arches which supported the dome there was often run up a central tower; which not only protected the dome from the weather, but also weighted and steadied its haunches, as a pinnacle does a buttress. These towers over domes were sometimes square, as at Tournus; more often octagonal, and crowned with octagonal spires, as at Paray-le-Monial.* But we had no crossing-domes in England, till the present St Paul's; and consequently no such use of central tower. Spain developed a fine series of central domes, not masked by towers, at Salamanca, Zamora, and Toro.

In Normandy, however, a much earlier type of central tower was followed, that of St Riquier, surmounted by an open louvre. As to the object of this arrangement, there can be no doubt whatever. In the sixth century Gregory of Tours and Fortunatus of Poitiers, speaking of the central lantern towers of Clermont, Nantes, Narbonne, and Paris, designate them *turris domus altaris* or *domus arae: i.e.* the tower was placed over the high altar; and was pierced with windows, that on this, the most important spot in the whole church, a flood of light might pour from above, especially at the most sacred moment of the Mass, that the Elevated Host might be conspicuous afar, even to the remotest recesses of the nave. It has been urged that this central lantern of wood may be a survival of the tradition of the lanterned domes of S. Sophia, Constantinople, and S. Vitale, Ravenna; but chronology is against the hypothesis. These two Byzantine churches were built in the sixth century; but there was a central lantern at St Martin, Tours, as early as 477. Again, if the central lantern emanated from or through Ravenna, we should expect to find many early examples of it in Northern Italy. But it is just in Italy that they do not occur; except in the basilica of the Crucifix at Spoleto. In Romanesque times they became common in many districts; *e.g.* in Lombardy, Germany, Auvergne, Burgundy, Laonnais, Normandy, England, Germany, Spain. Early examples in France are Germigny-des-Prés, consecrated in 806; St Martin, Angers, which is variously dated at 819 or 1020; Querqueville in Normandy, and St Saturnin, tenth century.†

It is quite possible that the churches on which these louvred central towers were erected were in the shape of the *crux commissa* (195); *i.e.* with apse joined directly on to the central tower without the interposition of a choir. In such a church the clergy would be seated round the apse, and the altar would stand on the chord of the apse; as it still does at S. CLEMENTE, ROME (3). Such an interior, with the dramatic contrast of shadowy nave and brilliantly lighted crossing, would be exceedingly impressive; and we may be permitted to regret that it has passed out of mediæval and out of modern practice. Here and there, in Continental churches, such an interior has come about, somewhat fortuitously; *e.g.* at St Eusèbe, Auxerre, where the contrast between the brilliant Late Gothic choir with clerestory soaring out of sight and the low and dark nave is strikingly effective.

* *Classification of Romanesque*, 283.
† See Enlart's *Manuel*, 123, 124; and A. St Paul's *Histoire*, 60.

LINCOLN MINSTER, WEST FRONT.

But the lantern that was effective in a *crux commissa* was less effective in a *crux immissa, i.e.* where there was a choir east of the transept. At first, indeed, the Norman choirs were short; those of Cérisy, Lincoln, Selby, and Canterbury were but two bays long; and the central lantern was still of some service in illuminating the altar and the stalls in front of it. But most of the Anglo-Norman churches were planned, like Norwich and St Albans, with choirs four or more bays long. And in Gothic days these choirs were elongated still more, as at Ely, Lincoln, and Old St Paul's, till the altar was far away from the transept, and unapproachable by any light from a central lantern. This once recognised, we find monks and canons shutting up the central lanterns. In Gothic days indeed the fenestration of end walls and side walls had been increased to such a vast extent that supplementary lighting from a central lantern was supererogatory. Accordingly at Winchester the Norman lantern, in spite of its beautiful arcading, was shut off from view by a wooden vault; at Wells a fan vault was put under the late twelfth-century tower; at Gloucester the lierne vault of the choir was continued westward till not a vestige of central tower appears within the church. Beautiful as is the internal effect of a central tower, it seems to have been held of little account in later Gothic days. Not that the liking for a central tower, open to the transept, ever wholly disappeared; beautiful late examples remain; *e.g.* York Minster, Hedon, Howden, East Dereham.* And in many vaulted lanterns, care was taken to place the vault above, not below, the lantern; *e.g.* at LINCOLN (328), Coutances, Evreux, and Canterbury.

But for this feature, of supreme artistic value, even more externally than internally, a heavy price had to be paid. For its supports, the four isolated legs on which its arches rest, in such a cathedral as Winchester or Wells, it was necessary to have piers of enormous area, very largely obstructive to the chief use of the church; viz. the view of the elevation of the Host by the largest possible number of worshippers. Rather than have such huge obstructions the canons of Bourges and Llandaff dispensed with a transept altogether; while those of St Leu d'Esserent, Le Mans, Barcelona, EXETER (154.4), and Ottery St Mary,† instead of one central tower, built a couple of towers, one at the end of each transept. In most cases, however, the central tower was erected; by the cautious only so high as to provide a ring of windows; as at BEVERLEY MINSTER (176), WESTMINSTER (379), Winchester, and Bristol; by the bolder so as to be of imposing height and bulk; as at St Albans, St David's, NEW SHOREHAM (373), and TEWKESBURY (390); by the venturesome crowned with a wooden spire, as originally at Ripon, Hereford, and Lincoln; by the rash surmounted by a spire of stone, as at Norwich, Chichester, and Salisbury. Being built moreover with a thick core of rubble and mortar,‡ they were most unnecessarily heavy, exerting a pressure of from 5 to 20 tons to the square

---

* Both at Canterbury and York the original Norman central towers are still there, cased up in later towers. The original Norman arches of the crossing were taken out and replaced by the present Gothic arches without taking down the old towers resting on them.

† St Stephen's, Vienna, also has transeptal towers; but only one completed.

‡ This has often decomposed into a fluid powder. See Cottingham's report on the condition of the central piers at Hereford.

foot ; * yet sometimes with foundations of little depth or spread.   The result was that some, like Wells and York, tore away from nave, transept, and choir, burying themselves deeper into the ground ; some collapsed soon after they were built, *e.g.* the first Norman central tower of Winchester and the first Gothic tower of Lincoln ; from others their wooden spires had to be removed, as at Hereford, Lincoln, and Ripon ; Chichester central tower telescoped within the memory of living men ; † others, like those of St David's, Sherborne, Peterborough, St Albans, Hereford, Rochester, Salisbury, have had to be vastly strengthened and under-pinned or completely rebuilt.   The following is the diameter of some central tower piers :—

Canterbury	-	-	-	12 feet.	Worcester	-	-	-	9 feet.
York	-	-	-	10 „	Peterborough	-	-	-	7 „
Winchester	-	-	-	10 „	Salisbury	-	-	-	7 „
Norwich	-	-	-	10 „	Rochester	-	-	-	6 „

At Winchester, after the fall of their first tower, an area of 78½ feet was given to the piers of the new tower, which rests on arches of 30 feet span ; at Peterborough, the area was only 38½ feet, though the span of the arches was 35 feet. ‡   In France, in the Domaine Royale, all the constructional objections to a central tower existed in an aggravated form.   Their cathedrals were nearly twice as high as those of England ; any central tower, to dominate roofs so vast in height, must rise at least to 500 or 600 feet, like the new western spires of Cologne Cathedral.   That was to impose enormous weight on the arches and piers beneath.   The builders shrank from it.   So in the Domaine Royale they were satisfied, as at Amiens and Notre Dame, Paris, to crown the crossing with a light openwork spire of wood : a mere pinnacle in scale in comparison with the bulk of these enormous cathedrals.   At Beauvais, indeed, a spire was erected of the height of 486 feet ; but it fell down in 1573 after a life of but five years.

In some cases there was no western tower at all ; but simply a central tower.   When this is placed midway, as at Worcester, the effect is not quite happy.   Where the nave is considerably longer than the choir, as at Gloucester and Bath, the tower groups much better.   But, even at Salisbury, the effect is somewhat parochial ; from association one distinguishes a cathedral from a parish church by its plenitude of towers.   Contrariwise, when one comes across a parish church with two or three towers ; as St Margaret's, Lynn ; Ottery ; Beverley Minster ; Melbourne ; one expects them to be something more than parochial ; usually they are or have been collegiate. §

* See paper by Mr S. B. Beale in *Builder*, Jan. 11, 1890. The tower of St David's is estimated to weigh 4,000 tons.

† At Gloucester the S.W. tower fell between 1164 and 1175 ; at Worcester the "nova turris" fell in 1175 ; at Evesham the central tower fell in 1213 ; at Dunstable two western towers fell in 1221 ; at Worcester two small towers were blown down in 1222 ; the tower of St Radegund, Cambridge, fell in 1270 ; the central tower of Ely in 1321 ; the central tower of Selby in 1690 ; the single western tower of Hereford in 1806" (see Willis' *Chichester*, p. ii.).

‡ Craddock's *Peterborough*, 131.

§ Examples of churches which now at any rate have only a central tower are Bath, Cartmel, Gloucester, Hexham, Malvern, Milton, New Shoreham, Norwich, St Asaph, St David's Salisbury, Sherborne, Tewkesbury, Winchester, Worcester.

WESTERN TOWER.—In England the majority of our churches have now and always have had a western tower. The list of central towers of Anglo-Saxon date now surviving is very short; though it must be remembered that a central

Taunton St Mary Magdalen.

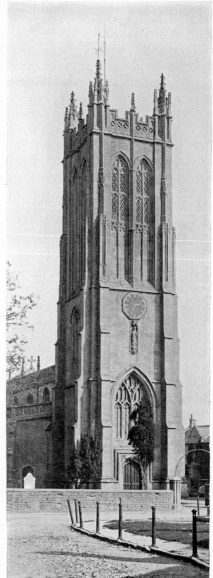

Evercreech.

tower may have formed a characteristic feature of their greater churches, now all destroyed. But of Anglo-Saxon western towers over eighty still remain; of which about fifty are in East Anglia, Lincolnshire, Yorkshire, Durham, and

Northumberland.* In the Romanesque of Normandy, on the other hand, a western tower is quite exceptional.† But of the Romanesque churches built in England a very large number have western towers. Whence came it? Not from Normandy, for there it was little employed. It must be a continuation of the tradition of Anglo-Saxon building; one of the very few instances in which Anglo-Saxon Romanesque may be held to have influenced that of Norman England. And as time went on, and as central towers fell into disrepair or collapsed, the tendency was ever, more and more, in all except the largest churches, to construct the tower westward.

The origin of the Anglo-Saxon western tower has been much disputed. It may be but an upward development of the fore-porch or narthex,‡ as at Corbridge, Monkwearmouth, South Elmham, Boarhunt, and Daglingworth. It has been derived from Germany, where the western tower is characteristic. But immense tower-groups are much more characteristic of German Romanesque than the single western tower; and we have none of the former. It is hardly likely that the latter should have had immense influence, the former none. Moreover, here and there outside Germany, where German influence did not exist, square western towers are common; e.g. in Western France. On the whole there seems to be little likelihood that the Anglo-Saxon western tower was borrowed from Germany.

By far the most common position of the western tower is central; i.e. at the end of the nave. Sometimes the aisles are continued along its northern and southern sides; sometimes only its eastern side is engaged; in either case much of the light of the western window is lost. Externally, as at Louth, Grantham, and NEWARK (627), where the former and more objectionable position is adopted, and at LAVENHAM (589) and Boston, where the tower is clear, it makes the nave appear low, while it crushes the aisles into insignificance. Much better is the effect when it is placed unsymmetrically.§ Singularly effective is the north-west position of the towers of St Mary Redcliffe, Bristol, and of TERRINGTON ST CLEMENT (92); in the latter of which the dignity of the façade is greatly enhanced by the increase of breadth; the tower in this instance being detached from the aisle. More often, as in Herne, Kent,‖ where also the tower is north-west, it forms the west end of the aisle. Here also it is very effective. Fleet Church, Lincolnshire,¶ has a south-western tower, clear of the aisles. At Donington, Lincolnshire,** and at All Saints, Maidstone, the south-west tower is added to the second bay from the west of the south aisle, and forms a most dignified porch to the church. But there is hardly any position in which a tower does not occur; e.g. south of the chancel; or south of the crossing, as at Whaplode; or serving as a south transept; or as a lichgate, as at WEST WALTON (597).

* Baldwin Brown, *Arts in Early England*, ii. 158.   † Ruprich-Robert, 97.

‡ See Peers in *Archæological Journal*, Dec. 1901, p. 429.

§ So also Dehio, ii. 562, who instances St Pierre, Rouen. On the other hand Mr James Cubitt wrote that a north-west or south-west position is the worst of all.

‖ Illustrated in Brandon's *Parish Churches*, 7.

¶ Illustrated in Brandon's *Parish Churches*, 51, 53.

** Illustrated in Brandon's *Parish Churches*, 51, 53.

West Walton.

Occasionally, the tower is detached altogether, as at Beccles, West Walton, Ledbury, and a good many churches in Gloucestershire and Herefordshire.* Wooden campaniles also are not infrequent in well-timbered districts such as Essex and the West of England.

Where the towers were central, as at Worcester and Salisbury, or much pierced with openings, as at Chichester, it was not uncommon to have an additional tower, detached, serving as campanile. Thus East Dereham has a central lantern tower and a detached campanile. Chichester preserves its campanile; those of Salisbury and Worcester have been destroyed.

A few Continental examples of eastern towers have been noted; *e.g.* the great church of the Jesuits at Antwerp; and some at Namur. There is one at Polesworth.

TWIN TOWERS.—In the larger Romanesque churches north of the Alps, in spite of numerous exceptions,† a common arrangement was to have two western towers. Of these one was intended to hold bells. Two western towers are shown in an Exeter seal of 1133, and may be those of the Anglo-Saxon cathedral restored *c.* 1020.‡ In the larger Romanesque churches both of Normandy and England, two western towers are common; *e.g.* the Abbayes aux-Hommes and aux-Dames; SOUTHWELL (520); Melbourne; Canterbury; DURHAM (28); LINCOLN (592). But it not seldom happened that the completion of the nave to the west was postponed; and when at length it was taken in hand again, no towers were erected in the façade. Whatever be the cause, it is a fact that many churches of great magnitude are without western towers. Some, however, which formerly possessed them, may have lost them. This may have been the case at Winchester, Gloucester, and Norwich; where great changes were made in the façades in the fourteenth and fifteenth centuries. Such façades have a parochial appearance, unworthy of churches of cathedral rank. Omission of western towers is, however, frequent; *e.g.* Binham, Chester Cathedral, Gloucester, Malvern, Rochester, Romsey, Tewkesbury, Worcester, Bolton, St David's, St Saviour's Southwark, Salisbury, Glastonbury, Whitby, Howden, Wenlock. The case of Byland, Buildwas, Fountains, Furness, Jervaulx, Kirkstall, Netley, Rievaulx, Roche, Tintern, Valle Crucis, is different. Like the great church of PONTIGNY (599), near Auxerre, which still exists complete, they were all Cistercian, and therefore omitted towers in conformity with the austere statutes of the Order.§

In most cases, if there are two towers, they are placed at the west end of the aisles. In that position they have decided constructional value. For if there be a central tower, its pressure tends to thrust the arcades of the nave out of the vertical. Against the western towers these thrusts are powerless. Nevertheless, in a considerable number of cases the towers were so placed as to flank the aisles and not the nave; *e.g.* Bury St Edmunds and Wells. This was the arrangement intended

* In the fine Fenland churches the tower very frequently is isolated from the church; *e.g.* Sutton St Mary; Fleet; Whaplode; Terrington St Clement and St John; West Walton.

† In Lombardy the typical Romanesque façade, such as that of S. Michele, Pavia, has no towers at all.

‡ Illustrated in Baldwin Brown, ii. 243.

§ A statute of 1154 says: "Let there be no stone towers for bells; nor yet wooden ones of inordinate height, such as to disgrace the simplicity of the Order."

at St Albans. (Ripon, too, had flanking towers to its unaisled nave; when aisles were added in the sixteenth century, the towers became axial to the aisles.)

Where there was a western transept (see 204), this was a natural arrangement. At ELY (587), where there is a western transept, its end towers become mere turrets owing to the presence of a big central western tower.

It would seem that in the tenth and eleventh centuries a common position was to the north and south of the choir; *e.g.* S. Ambrogio, Milan, and S. Abbondio, Como. This tradition may survive in Ernulph's Canterbury, which had towered chapels, on one side that of St Anselm, on the other side that of St Andrew. And again in the twelfth-century YORK Minster; on the foundations of whose choir-towers are built the eastern transepts illustrated on 199.

WESTERN AND CENTRAL TOWER.— We possess a considerable number of churches in which a central tower is combined with a single western tower occupying the centre of the

Beverley Minster from S.W.
Pontigny from S.W.

façade; *e.g.* ELY (587); WYMONDHAM (589); Wimborne; Christ Church, Hants; Shrewsbury Abbey; Waltham; Malmesbury; Bangor; Lewes.* They

* Mr St John Hope's paper, read to Royal Arch. Institute, August 1883. The western tower of Hereford, which fell in 1786, is said to have been added in the fourteenth century.

are not uncommon abroad ; *e.g.* St Martin, Tours ; St Benoît-sur-Loire ; Poissy ; St Germain des Prés ; Roeskilde. They are so common in the Romanesque of the school of Auvergne ; *e.g.* Notre Dame du Port, Clermont ; Issoire ; Brioude ; Le Dorat ; Le Puy ; St Savin ; that one is tempted to try to connect our English examples with that early and important school. But the monk Reginald, writing in the twelfth century, says that the Durham Cathedral of 999 had one central and one western tower ; and we have an equally clear statement about the Ramsey Abbey of 970.* Here then, as in the case of the western tower without central tower, the planning may be simply a continuation of indigenous Anglo-Saxon tradition.

TOWER GROUPS.—Where all three towers have been carried up, as at LINCOLN (44), SOUTHWELL (520), Wells, Canterbury, York, DURHAM (28), one

Thorington.

obtains masses, in their grouping as impressive as ever man wrought ; impressive even among the works of nature. LICHFIELD (frontispiece) alone retains its spires ; in Lichfield alone we see the glory complete of the English Gothic exterior as it was designed to be. The glorification of the tower went even further abroad. In Germany there are many instances of four towers ; *e.g.* Paulinzelle ; St Castor, Coblentz ; the Apostle's Church, Cologne ; in France Vézelay ; St Benoît-sur-Loire ; St Martin de Tours. There were five towers designed at Angoulême Cathedral, and Déols, Indre. At Cluny, Tournai, Limburg, Speyer, Worms, Laach, there were six. Rouen, Reims, and Laon Cathedrals were intended for seven towers ; five of them, like those still surviving at Tournai, were to be central. Chartres was designed for eight. Except at Peterborough, we were less ambitious.

PLAN OF TOWERS.—The most usual form is the square. But since the transepts are sometimes narrower than nave and choir, the central tower is often oblong ; at St John, Devizes, and BATH (373), it is markedly so.

Towers with eight † sides are not uncommon ; *e.g.* Uffington ; Coxwold. Sometimes an octagon is superposed on a square ; *e.g.* Ely west tower ; Fotheringhay ; Boston ; Irthlingborough ; Lowick. At Cartmel a square is set diagonally on a square. All Saints', Maldon, has a triangular tower.

Round towers are common in Norfolk and Suffolk ; and several examples

* See Scott's *Essay*, 105 ; and Baldwin Brown, *Arts in Early England*, ii. 242.

† An octagonal tower occurs in the eleventh century at Tordouet, Calvados ; Caumont, *Statistique Monumentale*, v. 809 ; Ruprich-Robert mentions five examples of the twelfth century in Normandy, i. 164.

occur in Essex, Cambridge, and Sussex.*   They have been regarded as survivals of Roman forms ; such as that of the Roman Pharos at St Mary in the Castle, Dover, which however is octagonal ; Roman lighthouses were still common in the time of Bede.   Round towers of the sixth century still remain at Ravenna ; † *e.g.* S. Apollinare in Classe.   In a mosaic of the fifth century in S. Maria Maggiore, Rome, round towers are shown in the neighbourhood of two churches.   In the ninth-century plan of St Gall round towers are shown.   From the end of the ninth to the beginning of the thirteenth century the Irish were building round towers.

We may indicate another source.   Newel staircases (*vis* or *vice*), circular staircases winding round a central column, were employed by the Romans, and still survive inside the Columns of Trajan and Antoninus at Rome and of Theodosius at Constantinople.   A tenth-century example exists in the Palatine Chapel, Aix.‡   Numerous examples of slender, round towers, containing staircases, exist all over Europe ; *e.g.* BECKLEY.   In Anglo-Saxon work a newel staircase is constructed in the thickness of the wall of the tower of Great Hale ; while at Brixworth, Brigstock, Houghton-on-the-Hill, and Broughton a half or three-quarter round turret is built for it in front of the west wall of the tower.   A similar turret seems to have existed at North Elmham.§   The resemblance between such staircase turrets as that of Beckley, and such towers as those of S. Giovanni, Ravenna, St Maurice, Epinal, ‖ and the Irish round towers, is so close that a causal connection seems possible.¶

Beckley, Oxford.

But for the broader English round towers a simpler explanation suffices.   They occur almost wholly in chalk districts, where for outer facing nothing is available but flint.   It was easier to construct flint-cased towers circular.   So the towers were made round.   If they had been made square, it would have been necessary to import freestone quoins from a distance.

TOWER CONSTRUCTION.—In the Romanesque and in the earlier Gothic towers there was an enormous waste of material.   It has been estimated that in the western towers of Coutances there is an excess of some 1,000 tons.   Still more remarkable is the case of the Leaning Tower of Pisa.**   In this the wall of the lower story is 13½ feet thick, that of the upper stories 9 feet.   With this we

* See illustrated paper in *Archæologia*, vol. 23.
† Rivoira denies the existence of any church towers anterior to the ninth century.
‡ Enlart's *Manuel*, 19.
§ Baldwin Brown, ii. 175, 211.   In Normandy also Romanesque staircase turrets occur, some in the thickness of the wall, some in turrets.   Ruprich-Robert, 163.
‖ Illustrated in Miss Stokes' *Early Christian Art in Ireland*, ii. 54.
¶ Minarets are but a decorative treatment of the staircase turret.
** For the calculations see paper by Mr S. B. Beale, in *Builder*, Jan. 18, 1890.

may compare the tower of St Mary Redcliffe, Bristol, A.D. 1292, which, according to William of Worcester, tapers from 7 to 5 feet; and that of Louth, which is 7 feet thick at the bottom; 6 feet 2 inches at the lower windows; 3 feet 9 inches at the belfry chamber; it is 20 feet 11 inches square inside. The whole steeple is 300 feet high above the street. It is estimated that the Leaning Tower brings a pressure of $7\frac{1}{4}$ tons to the square foot on soil which is only capable of sustaining $4\frac{1}{5}$ tons.* Had the tower been bonded into the cathedral, the latter must have been dragged down.† It is perhaps because they feared this, that the Italian architects usually detached their heavy campaniles from the churches.‡ In England and France, as masoncraft improved, it was felt to be as unnecessary as it was dangerous to build towers with walls so thick. In some cases the builders went further still. Anticipating the methods of construction of the domes of Florence Cathedral and St Peter's, Rome, the tower walls were built in two thin shells with a hollow space between; *e.g.* the central towers of Lincoln and Salisbury.§ While at Hereford and WELLS (588), where the fourteenth-century tower was built on weak Norman piers, the inner skin of the tower was constructed, girder-fashion, of vertical and horizontal stone beams. Similar construction occurs in the central towers of Coutances and St Etienne le Vieux, Caen.

TOWER ROOFS.—Norman tower roofs were apparently often hipped to a point; *i.e.* were low square spires, as at Priestholm ‖ or Puffin Island, and at Thaon in Normandy. Sometimes saddle-back roofs occur; as at Wadenhoe; Claydon; Little Claydon; Icomb; Tinwell; and along the coast of South Wales.¶ These are more common in Normandy than in England. We did not adopt the fashion common in late French Gothic of a roof hipped to a ridge. A few examples of stone roofs occur on towers.

TOWER DESIGN.—Occasionally an English tower is slender and tall; *e.g.* MANORBIER (587); but unless it be detached, like most Italian campaniles, it challenges disastrous comparison with the bulk of the church. On the other hand, provided that it have breadth, mass, bulk, it need not be tall. Indeed the characteristic tower of the smaller village-churches of England is one broad and low;** but little overtopping the nave roof: *e.g.* those of Gresford, ST MARY'S, BEVERLEY (603), TERRINGTON ST CLEMENT (92). The contrast is well seen at Oxford; where the slender tower of MAGDALEN (588) is satisfactory because it is detached; while the short, massive, engaged tower of MERTON (589) is equally effective. In a tower what is most desiderated is not grace, but strength. The central towers of York, HEREFORD (587), and WELLS (602) are all impressive; but it is not by their height. So also it is mainly to their bulk that the satisfactory effect is due

* On the weight-bearing capacities of soils see "Foundation" in R. Sturgis' *Dictionary of Architecture and Building.*

† Louth steeple, which is admirably built, has sunk 7 inches.

‡ So also in the oozy soil of the Fenland the towers are very often detached; see list in 598, note.

§ Sir Charles Anderson's *Lincoln*, 120.   ‖ Illustrated in Baldwin Brown, ii. 163.

¶ A fourteenth-century example, with spirelet rising from the saddle, occurs at Brentingby, Leicester.

** A tower for eight bells would have to be broad.

WELLS CATHEDRAL FROM S.E.

of such Norman towers as TEWKESBURY (390), Exeter, St Albans. But if with bulk there be combined height, the tower reaches the maximum of impressiveness ; as at NEW SHOREHAM (373); Fountains; GLOUCESTER (132); LAVENHAM (589) ;* Wymondham ; Cawston ; Cromer ; Southwold ; Hedon ; above all, in the king of towers, the Victoria Tower of the Houses of Parliament.

As regards central towers, the most important factor internally is not height, but breadth and illumination. If a central tower be high and narrow, like that of CANTERBURY (588), however graceful externally, its interior cannot be seen except with the sensation of looking up from the bottom of a well. If it be badly lighted, like that of LINCOLN (328), then its interior, being barely visible, cannot tell. The value of breadth and illumination are well

Trunch.   Beverley St Mary's, from S.E.

seen in York crossing. At ELY (45) the breadth of the central octagon is even greater than at York ; and floods of light stream down from its many-windowed flanks. Nowhere are there contrasts so sharp, so dramatic, of light and darkness as at Ely. The low, brilliantly lighted lantern of Dereham also deserves study.

Externally, the fenestration of towers, whether central or not, is of the highest importance. Unless the windows be deeply recessed, there is no adequate play of light and shadow : the windows do not look windows, being indistinguishable from the panelling. Many of our towers fail to tell at a moderate distance owing to the shallowness of the fenestration ; *e.g.* the central tower of Wells.

* Lavenham tower is just three times as high as the clerestory wall of the nave.

When a block of masonry has been raised high in the air, one's first anxiety is as to its stability. One's anxiety is roused if the voids, *i.e.* the windows, are numerous and large, as at Howden and HULL (96); more still, if one side of the tower has a huge hole in the wall, as at Shrewsbury Abbey. One is reassured if the solids greatly preponderate; and one does not object in the least if the ground story, as at Magdalen College and Manorbier, is plain solid wall. It may be doubted whether the richest towers of Somersetshire are more impressive than the gaunt mountain masses of East Anglia, four-square to the winds; such as HOLME (591) and CAWSTON (589); or than the fortress donjons of Kent and Bedford, with slits for windows; *e.g.* SOUTHFLEET.

It is in the towers of the west country that most attention is paid to the fenestration; *e.g.* ST MARY MAGDALEN, TAUNTON (595); Bishop's Lydiard; Huish Episcopi; ST JOHN'S, GLASTONBURY (588); Wrington; St Stephen's,

Southfleet.

Bristol; St John's, Cardiff. These bell towers naturally fall into three divisions; the ground story, which contains both state doorway and west window; the first floor containing the windows of the ringers' chamber; and the second floor containing the belfry windows. But many of the towers are so lofty; *e.g.* St Mary Magdalen, Taunton; that an additional mid-story has to be inserted. This additional story is usually a duplicate of that of the ringers' chamber. In some of the best examples, *e.g.* ST JOHN'S, GLASTON-BURY (588), and EVERCREECH (595), it seems to have been felt that the voids were in superabundance; and the intermediate story or stories has been kept solid or nearly so. All these towers are crowned with magnificent combinations of panelled or pierced parapets, battlements, and pinnacles (607). All were built in what used to be styled the "debased" period of English architecture.

In that masterpiece of Late Gothic, the steeple of LOUTH (611), great depth of shadow is gained in the windows by setting them back towards the inner face of the tower wall. How great is the gain may be seen by contrasting this steeple with the tower of BOSTON (222).

Midway in many Norfolk towers; *e.g.* North Walsham, Fakenham, Cromer, HOLME (591); square openings filled with Curvilinear or Rectilinear tracery occur; erroneously called "sound holes."

In several Somersetshire towers the upper windows are filled with perforated stone tracery; *e.g.* ILE ABBOT (591) and HUISH EPISCOPI (517). Elsewhere it is more usual to employ sloping louvre boards set horizontally. The treatment of these boards profoundly affects the character of a tower. In little village churches in France the louvre boards are few, broad, and have great projection; consequently there is a depth of shadow rare with us.

Very greatly, too, the character of a tower depends on the treatment of the angles. How they shall be treated depends on what is wanted. If it is to overawe, the tower may rise in sheer verticality from pavement to cornice, like the campanile in the piazza of St Mark's, Venice, and that of Manorbier.* What Mr Ruskin said of the transept wall of Beauvais, that there are few such lofty precipices even in the Alps, is still more true of the unbuttressed type of tower. But the corners are the weak points of towers. We did not like to lose the help of buttresses. So, here and there, we built buttresses, but built them practically vertical; *e.g.* in Magdalen College, Oxford; the Angel Tower of Lincoln; Whissendine, Rutland; Wymondham. If that was not enough, if we hankered after "the solemn frown of projection," corbel table and cornice could be built out, and on these over-sailing parapet, battlement, and pinnacles could be poised; as in the west towers of YORK (82); Dundry and St Stephen's, Bristol; and, above all, in the Kreisker at St Pol de Léon, Brittany.†

But we may wish, not to overawe, but to reassure. Nothing reassures so much as appearance of stability. And that appearance is given by the pyramidal form. So sometimes the walls of the tower "batter," *i.e.* slope backward; as in the lowest stage of many church towers of Herefordshire. In Gothic design each stage is usually vertical, but each stage may be drawn back a little from the stage below; *e.g.* Bishop's Lydiard, Somerset; Kettering, North Hants; Moulton, Lincolnshire; Ingatestone, Essex.‡ Or, as at TRUNCH, NORFOLK (603), both expedients may be resorted to. Such a tower, tapering upward, seems to be vertical, unless the process is overdone, as at Trunch and St Peter's, Oxford. An absolutely vertical tower appears to the faulty lenses of our eyes actually to overhang; just as do Flamborough cliffs, seen from a boat below. The Greeks, aware of this, sloped backward the columns of their temples.

We may set the tower buttresses diagonally, as at Trunch; one buttress doing the work of two. But the effect is not satisfactory unless the projection of the buttresses be slight, as at Chipping Campden and Gloucester Cathedral; or unless the tower has an octagonal spire, as at St Sepulchre's, Northampton, and Edenbridge, Kent; in which case the diagonal buttresses carry down the oblique sides of the spire. In later work, as in the central towers of Ashford, Cricklade, BATH (373), and CANTERBURY (588), and at WYMONDHAM (589) the buttresses may be hexagonal or octagonal; but nothing equals the older arrangement, as seen at ST JOHN'S, GLASTONBURY (588), and in the Somerset churches generally. In these last a fine effect is got sometimes by setting the two corner buttresses some little distance from the corner; thus the quoins peer through and present gratis an additional strong vertical line;

---

* In chalk districts there was naturally a tendency to omit buttresses; *e.g.* SOUTHFLEET (604), Kent; because of the expense of freestone quoins brought from a distance.

† Illustrated in Enlart's *Manuel*, 570.

‡ Described by Sharpe in *Lincoln Excursion*, 144; and Buckler in *Churches of Essex*, 100.

e.g. St Stephen's, Bristol; Dundry; Evesham; Wisbech; Titchmarsh.*
Whatever the form of buttress employed, undue spread must be guarded
against; otherwise to the horizontal line of nave and choir we shall have
opposed in the outline of the tower, not a vertical, but a sloping line. The
buttresses must not be developed so far as to destroy or impair the verticality
of the tower.

Another critical point is the relation of the buttress to the pinnacle. A
solution which is as easy as it is satisfactory is to make buttress and pinnacle
one; as in Auxerre Cathedral; Bath; Canterbury, Wells and York central
towers; Whiston; St Cuthbert, Wells; Ashford; Cricklade; Magdalen
College, Oxford. Another method, not so satisfactory, is to bring the tower
design to an end at the cornice; then to commence a fresh design for pinnacles
and battlements independent of all below; as in GLOUCESTER (132) and
HEREFORD (587) central towers; and ST MARY MAGDALEN, TAUNTON (607).
A similar fault is failure to carry the buttress, as at TRUNCH (603), or the
buttresses, as at CAWSTON (589), up to the cornice; they are pulled up with
a jerk, as it were. It is common in the Somerset churches; *e.g.* St Mary
Magdalen, Taunton; where an attempt at compensation is made in the
form of a flimsy little buttress hanging on to the corner of the pinnacle. This
weakness, however, is less observable in perspective than in elevation.

The different stories of the tower are usually marked off by strings. Should
they pass round the buttresses? As to that the practice varied, even in the same
district. Thus at Wrington no strings pass round the buttresses; *cf.* Moulton.
At St Mary Magdalen, Taunton, only the string beneath the belfry stage passes
round; severing in rather unfortunate fashion the belfry story and pinnacles
from the rest of the tower below. At Dundry and St Stephen's, Bristol, all the
strings pass round.

But buttresses themselves are usually divided into stages by set-offs.
Should these stages and set-offs correspond with the stories and strings of
the tower? Sometimes they correspond exactly; *e.g.* at St Mary Magdalen, Taunton; where notice, however, the difference in the treatment of the
quoins; and still more minutely at Wisbech; where even the hood-molds
of the windows become strings, each running into its own set-off. At
KETTERING (623) every other set-off corresponds with a string. On the other
hand, at St Neots, the set-offs are studiously independent of the strings; *cf.*
Moulton.†

But the most important question is the treatment of the skyline. Shall we
be satisfied with a strong horizontal line, as in Giotto's tower at Florence;
Trunch; Cawston;‡ Howden; Lavenham; St Nicholas at Wade; Wymondham;
New Shoreham; emphasising it to the utmost by projection of cornice; or
above the cornice subdivide the single huge vertical mass of the tower into four,
eight, or sixteen spirelets; cresting and crowning the tower with a galaxy of

---

* For Towers and Spires consult Wickes' three folios of illustrations.

† Of the seven stages of the western towers of SOUTHWELL (520), the four lowest are
determined by the strings and roof of the nave.

‡ In some cases it may be that the tower has a horizontal skyline only because it is
unfinished; *e.g.* York central tower and Wells western towers.

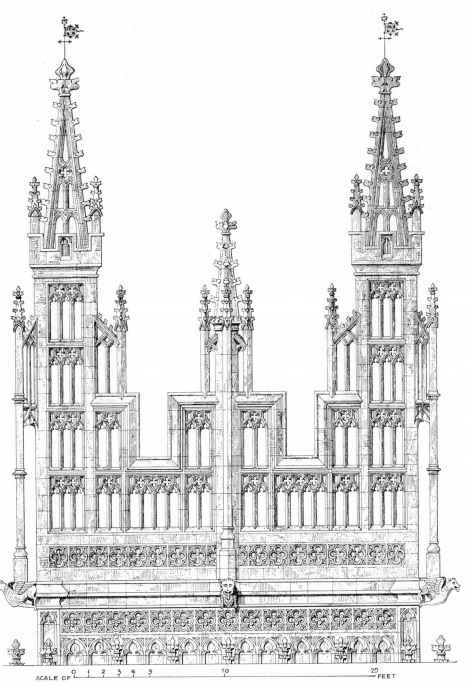

0 1 2 3 4 5   10   20 FEET

Taunton St Mary Magdalen.

pinnacles, parapets, and battlements.   Of the two types the pinnacled type had by far most admirers.

But as to pinnacles also there are rival schools; some adopting a tall, some a small pinnacle.   If the tower be tall and slender, as at Magdalen College; Ashford; Cricklade; Tideswell; Canterbury; a tall pinnacle sits well.   If it be short and bulky, short pinnacles are more usual; *e.g.* St Mary's, Beverley; Hull; Gresford; Chipping Campden; Terrington St Clement's.   On the whole the tendency is to a rather small pinnacle; the less the pinnacle is emphasised, the more important looks the belfry stage.   In Somersetshire the schools are equally divided; *e.g.* at Taunton the pinnacles of St James are insignificant, while those of St Mary Magdalen are large and important.*

As to the application of ornament, we may discriminate four types of tower; one, without ornament; a second, with equally diffused ornament; a third, with ornament concentrated in the ground story and the belfry story; a fourth, with ornament concentrated at the summit.   Of the first, Manorbier, Wymondham, and Southfleet are examples.   Where freestone is costly and the church is cased in flint, there will naturally be little or no ornament. Even when built, like Cawston, in an admirable freestone, it will follow the local tradition in its sparing of ornament.   To the second type belong the towers of the eleventh century in Normandy, and of the twelfth and thirteenth in England, covered with bands of arcading in the same fashion as the façades of Ely and Lincoln; *e.g.* ELY (587), DURHAM (28), Castor, LINCOLN (592), NORWICH (522), TEWKESBURY (390), EXETER (377), St Albans, of the twelfth century; and of the thirteenth century Whaplode, WEST WALTON (597), Raunds, SUTTON ST MARY (613); and St Mary, Stamford.   These are large and enriched examples; there are also simple and effective designs of smaller thirteenth-century towers, such as Madley, Herefordshire. Several of the greater towers of the fourteenth century also are smothered, in ornament; *e.g.* the central towers of Hereford and WELLS (602).   And in the fifteenth and sixteenth centuries many a great tower drips with panelled tracery from top to bottom; *e.g.* Evesham; Gloucester; Canterbury; WREXHAM (609); St Peter Mancroft, Norwich; most of all, perhaps, Eye Church, Suffolk, which is panelled in flint; ornament is everywhere; not a quiet spot anywhere to rest the eye; for want of which, window tracery, parapet, and pinnacle fail to tell.   In the Somersetshire towers generally a far higher level of design is reached.   At St John's, Glastonbury; North Petherton; Chewton Mendip; the Taunton churches; and many a fine tower elsewhere; *e.g.* at St Neots, Huntingdon; Whissendine; Wrexham; and at Terrington St Clement's; the intermediate story or stories is treated more simply; the main body of ornament being concentrated on the ground story and the belfry story.   Of these two the belfry story is usually the more decorated; and its richness is enhanced yet further by elaboration of pinnacle, parapet, and battlement.   The fourth type is seen in its simplest elements in the Italian campaniles; the ornament is reserved for the summit; or if there be any below the cornice, it rises in

* The original form of the pinnacles has often been departed from in "restorations"; *e.g.* the present pinnacles of Worstead tower, Norfolk, are far taller than those shown in Neale's *Churches of Great Britain*, 1824, vol. i.   So also those of Bath Abbey, now being removed.

Wrexham.

2 Q

richness as it nears the summit. This is the principle of design in the towers of St Stephen's, Bristol, and Magdalen College, Oxford. In these the glories of the summit are all in all; nothing is allowed to detain the gaze in its upward flight. Truly these late builders knew how to design. Nor had they said their last word in towers; there were Louth and Coventry spires to come. Their very success with the tower nevertheless curtailed the building of spires. In the thirteenth and fourteenth centuries it almost seems as if every tower was designed for a spire. The fifteenth-century tower needed no spire; and spires grew infrequent, except in certain districts, *e.g.* Northants; while towers were erected by hundreds.

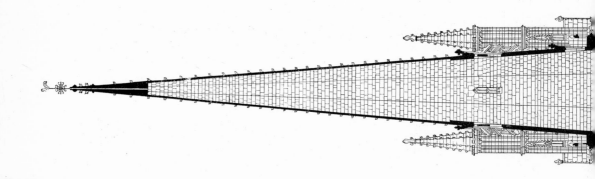

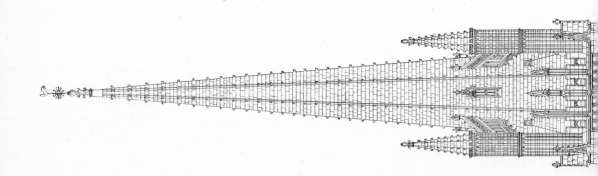

SECTION LOOKING EAST

WEST ELEVATION

LOUTH.

50 FEET 40 30 20 10 5 0 5 10

[*Between pages 610 and 611.*]

CHAPTER XLI.

THE SPIRE.

Origin and Classification of Spires—Spire Angles—Bands—Plate and Bar Tracery —Fenestration—Plan—Height—Proportions—Entasis—Spire Design—Spire Construction.

ORIGIN OF THE SPIRE.—Of all the members of a Gothic building the spire is the most original, the most religious, and the least essential. The pier, the arch, the capital, the base, the vault, the dome, all find their ancestry in a distant past. The spire was something new, that Greek and Roman knew not of. Not till the twelfth century was well advanced in France, not till it had neared its close in England, did the low pyramidal roof rise to that " sky-y-pointing pyramid," the spire. It was a concession, the chief concession in Gothic architecture, to religious symbolism. To Wordsworth, its lines, all converging upward and heavenward, were a reminder of the direction that his thoughts and prayers and life should take—

> " Watching with upward eye the tall spire grow
> And mount at every step—with living wiles
> Instinct—to rouse the heart and lead the will
> By a bright ladder to the world above."

Or, as he puts it in one of his sonnets—

> " Spires whose silent finger points to heaven."

Artistically, its special value lies in the strength of contrast which is afforded between the vertical lines of the spire and the prolonged horizontal lines of nave and chancel. Equally effective is it whether central, as at Patrington and Salisbury, converting all the projected masses of the buildings into one converging pyramid ; detached, as at Fleet, Ledbury, and St Mary Redcliffe ; * or giving the noblest of façades to the parish church, as at Grantham, Newark, and Louth.

In respect of the spire Gothic architecture abandoned one of its leading principles ; and perpetrated a piece of " constructed decoration." The spire has been defended as being a necessary roof to the tower. At first indeed it was but a tower roof ; either in timber ; or else in stone corbelled inwards, as at Priestholme. But it soon became much more than a roof ; and in the openwork spires of the Continent, Freiburg, Strasburg, Antwerp, it forgot to be a roof altogether.

Something of the character of the spire existed doubtless in quite early times. The earliest representations of French churches, *e.g.* that of the abbey

* To the eye the Bristol steeple is detached : though really it is engaged in the north aisle.

Ledbury.
Tilney All Saints'.

Bridgwater.
Patrington from S.E.

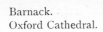

Barnack.
Oxford Cathedral.

Sutton St Mary.
North Luffenham.

Southam.   Denford.

King's Sutton.   Holbeach.

Bingham.   Desborough.

church of St Riquier, show us central towers with superposed louvres. And in various Anglo-Saxon manuscripts; *e.g.* in Caedmon's metrical paraphrase of Scripture history * the exact form of a spire is represented. But all those probably were in wood. It is not till the latter half of the eleventh century that a low spire appears in masonry. This is at Thaon, Calvados.† In England early examples are seen at Penmon ‡ and Priestholm or Puffin Island, Anglesea. A spire is shown in the conventual seal of Kenilworth.§ Turner's *Liber Studiorum* has a careful drawing of the western spires of SOUTHWELL (520); they have lately been restored. All these, however, are still roofs; not spires. Thaon spire is quite low; the interior is still tied with wooden beams. In France, however, the stone roof of the tower leaped almost at once into a spire; and by the middle of the twelfth century probably, great spires had been constructed; *e.g.* at St Germain, Auxerre, and at La Trinité de Vendôme;‖ the latter of which rises 262 feet from the ground. In England it is possible that the spire of BARNACK ¶ (613) may have been built in the last years of the twelfth century. Another early spire is that of OXFORD CATHEDRAL (613). This also is a spire of obtuse angle; and it is of a type somewhat rare in England, but common in France, *e.g.* in the south-west spire of Chartres; viz. without parapet, but with pinnacles and dormers: in this there may be French influence, and the date may be early. The New Romney spire also was designed for pinnacles. Another early spire, hardly clear of Transitional detail, is that of SUTTON ST MARY ** (613), Lincolnshire. This, however, is a timber spire, covered with lead.

The above spires, however, did not produce schools. It was not till the first half of the thirteenth century that indigenous schools of English spire builders arose. One built in timber, not in Sutton fashion, but as at NEWHAVEN (17); or else, as at ETTON (620), they copied in stone the forms which had arisen out of timber technique. The second school arose in Northamptonshire and the neighbouring districts, wherever that beautiful freestone, the Oolitic limestone, was found on or just below the surface of the ground. Its spire was of stone; the angle of the spire, at first, was obtuse; it had numerous windows; these, at first, were large; it had no parapets, and it had broaches; *e.g.* Sleaford, Rauceby, Warmington, Polebrook, FRAMPTON (618), NORTH LUFFENHAM (613). This long was the premier school in England. The third school, which in the end ousted the rest, was that of the parapetted spire, usually with pinnacles; and sometimes with flying buttresses.

It was not till the fourteenth century that spire building was fully developed. Then it was first that great spires were erected; *e.g.* Salisbury; Grantham and its imitator Newark; St Mary's, Oxford; St Mary's, Stamford.†† By this time

---

* *Archæologia*, xxiv., Plate 83.　　　　† Illustrated in Pugin's *Normandy*, Plate 22.
‡ Illustrated in Parker's *Introduction*, 81.　§ Illustrated in Bloxam, 103.
‖ Illustrated in Viollet-le-Duc, *Architecture*, iii. 357, 56.
¶ Prior, p. 370; who suggests a late twelfth-century date also for the spires of Oxford Cathedral and Sutton St Mary's; and the base of New Romney spire.
** See measured drawings in *Spring Gardens Sketch Book*.
†† The towers of Ketton, Melton Mowbray, and St Mary, Stamford, are very similar, and are probably by the same hand. The spires of Ketton and St Mary, Stamford, are a century later in date than their towers, and show an even greater similarity to one another.—R. P. B.

Frampton.

many a chancel had been lengthened (225); and the tower, which had been dominant before, had become inadequate.

Still more was this the case in the fifteenth century, when the passion raged for elevating clerestories; to many a tower was added a spire, because the nave had received a clerestory; *e.g.* Burton Latimer, Northants. And these later spires, *e.g.* Coventry and Louth, were as noble as any.

But as in its beginning, so to the end, spire building was curiously sporadic and local. Pass by rail from Spalding to Lincoln, or down the Nene valley, and spires cut the horizon far as the eye can reach. In other districts, *e.g.* Norfolk and Somersetshire, the tower is equally predominant. On the whole, as was natural, spire building was in vogue most where there was the best craftmanship, *i.e.* just where there was the best and most abundant freestone; or where there was the cheapest transport; all places, whose rivers or drains put them within reach of Barnack, Ketton, and Ancaster quarries, could afford to build spires.

CLASSIFICATION OF SPIRES.—English spires are very varied in design; nevertheless they may be reduced to a few main types. One feature distinguishes them from a large class of Continental designs; viz. that our builders kept in view the sound Gothic principle, that the load should be distinct from the support. They did not mix up pier and arch, except in a few late examples, *e.g.* TENBY (410); and they did not mix up tower and spire. Abroad, however, it is frequently quite impossible to say where the tower ends and the spire begins; *e.g.* at Le Puy, Senlis, Freiburg, Antwerp, and St Stephen's, Vienna. In England there is seldom any such difficulty; there is a distinct line of demarcation between tower and spire, and on that line we can base a simple system of classification. It is this. Some spires have no path round their foot; we may call them *Pathless* spires. The rest have a path round; we might call them footpath spires; but as the path is always guarded by a parapet or a battlement, we may as well avoid a barbarism, and call them *Parapetted* spires.

PATHLESS SPIRES: CLASS I.—Of these the first division consists of timber spires; which are of course plentiful where oak was abundant and stone scarce; *e.g.* in the Sussex Weald and much of Kent and Essex. These are without windows; *e.g.* at Shere, Tangmere, Merstham, NEWHAVEN (17), Plumpton, Southwick, Bourn, Walsingham, Wickham Market, Ryton, Chesterfield, Harrow, Hemel Hempstead, Godalming. The normal type is well seen at Newhaven. Another type, less common, is that which, as at Irchester, starts as a square spire, but almost immediately becomes octagonal. The Chesterfield spire is curiously warped; probably it was built of unseasoned timber, and has twisted round on the sunny side.* Many wooden spires have perished by fire, lightning, or decay; or have had to be pulled down; *e.g.* the triplets of Lincoln and Ripon. The wooden spire on the central tower of Lincoln was 523 feet high, a landmark far out at sea: that of Old St Paul's was probably 500 feet high. Ely had one western spire of wood; Durham two: Hereford a central spire. Worcester, Rochester, Finchall Abbey, Malmesbury, Tewkesbury, also had spires.

The curious form which is characteristic of most timber spires is due to the fact that some distance above the base of the spire there is a timber collar, which

* See paper read at the R.I.B.A. by Mr Coldwell; and *Builder*, 1855, 13, 40.

is upheld by timbers sloping up to it from the four angles of the tower : on this collar much of the upper part of the spire rests. A similar construction pre-

Etton.

vailed in the wooden spires of France ; *e.g.* the central spire of Notre Dame, Paris.

The second division consists of those which imitated in stone the characteristic form of a timber spire ; *e.g.* ETTON ; Crick ;* Bythorne ; and Lostwithiel.† This curious nonlithic design was infrequent.

CLASS II.—The next type, the broach spire, was common in the thirteenth and still more in the fourteenth century. In its native district, in and near Northants, it lingered till the fifteenth century ; *e.g.* at Brampton, Barrowden, and Stanion. At first the broach—the pyramidal mass of masonry, covering a squinch, and leaning against an oblique side of the spire—was low or of moderate size ; *e.g.* at NORTH LUFFENHAM (613). Strictly, however, the broach ought to have a slope intermediate between the vertical line of the tower and the inclination of the spire ; and very soon the broach was made much taller to the great improvement of the general effect ; *e.g.* at KETTON (621), at Aumsby ; Walcot ; Anwick ;‡ Aldwinkle ;§ Threckingham ;§ and above all, at EWERBY ‖ (630). Late broaches, however, are often exceedingly small and low ; especially in the typical spire of Gloucestershire ; *e.g.* Leckhampton. Outlying examples of broach spires are Hemingborough, Yorkshire ; Kidwelly, Carmarthen ; St Cuthbert's, Cornwall. In France the broach occurs detached ; *e.g.* at Nesle ; and St Leu d'Esserent. At NORWICH (622), instead of broaches, the spire has buttresses ; with somewhat unhappy effect. Just as the timber spire-form was copied in stone ; so the stone broach was copied in wood ; *e.g.* at Braunton, Devon.¶ In the broach spire the window plays a prominent part. It should be added that in mediæval documents the term *broach* is usually applied to a whole spire of any type.

Sometimes, by way of variation, these spires substitute a pinnacle for the

* Johnson's *Reliques*, Plate 76.　　　　† Wickes' *Spires*, Plates 21, 23.
‡ Johnson's *Reliques*, Plates 15, 13, 22.　§ Brandon's *Parish Churches*, 59.
‖ Bowman and Crowther.　　　　　　　　¶ Illustrated in Prior, 372.

broach. The earliest example is probably that of OXFORD CATHEDRAL (613). While the broach spire has two or more tiers of windows, this type has but one. This window is large and is placed between the pinnacles. Just as the broach or pinnacle stops the thrust of the oblique sides of the spire, so the big gabled windows bring down more vertically the thrusts of the cardinal sides. It is a type of spire somewhat infrequent in England; but common in early French work; *e.g.* at St Germain, Auxerre; Chartres; the Abbaye-aux-Hommes, and St Pierre, Caen; Bayeux; Bernières; Vernouillet; Limay;* Migneville;* Plessis-le-charmant;* Beaulieu.* It is the typical Normandy spire of the thirteenth century; and was probably the earliest type of French spire.

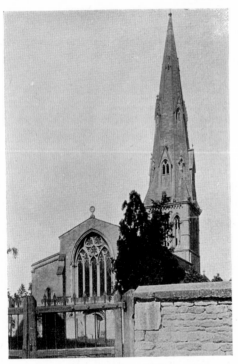

Ketton from S.W.

Witney from S.

In a few broach spires the experiment was made of allowing the pinnacle to grow up out of the broach, like a pin out of a pincushion; *e.g.* WITNEY,† Wollaston, SOUTHAM (614), Wellingborough. The same design occurs at Bayeux.

CLASS III. PARAPETTED SPIRES—To all the above spires, however, there is one grave objection. It is that they are difficult to repair. But if a space round the edge of the tower wall be kept clear, it can be used for hauling up material from the ground; and if it be protected by a parapet, ladders set up

* Illustrated in Johnson's *Specimens of Early French Architecture.*
† That of Witney is similar to, and probably not much later than, the neighbouring spire of Oxford Cathedral.

against the sides of a spire in construction or under repair cannot slip at the foot. So a pathway was left round the spire. And to get as much breadth as possible for this pathway, it was sometimes set on a corbel table or on a cornice ; so that the parapet overhung the face of the tower. Such an oversailing parapet is well seen in the fourteenth-century spire of SHOTTESBROOKE (395) ; still better in the spire of Autun Cathedral and at the Kreisker in St Pol-de-Léon, Finisterre.*

(i.) Of the varieties of parapetted spires the first comprises those which have neither pinnacle nor broach ; *e.g.* WINGHAM, near Canterbury ; LEDBURY ; BRIDGWATER (612). Simple as it is, the sharp contrast between tower and spire is very effective. It is exceedingly common in the village churches.

Norwich Cathedral.

Wingham.

An early example of the parapetted spire is the south-western spire of PETER-BOROUGH (112), which is probably *c.* 1330.† Good examples are seen at Donington, Lincoln ; Bredon, Worcester ; Bramford, Suffolk.‡

Then we have variants in which the timber type of spire, the broach spire, and the pinnacle spire are surrounded by a parapet.

(ii.) The timber type of spire, worked in masonry, with a parapet, occurs at St Sepulchre's, Northampton ; and DENFORD, NORTHANTS (614) ; but is not common.

* Illustrated in Enlart's *Manuel*, 570.

† Deene in Northants has a parapetted spire of the second half of the thirteenth century.— R. P. B.

‡ Illustrated in Brandon's *Parish Churches*, 53, 109, 125.

(iii.) To this division belongs the parapetted spire which has broaches, but not pinnacles. At BINGHAM (616), the broach is emphasised ; the parapet is unimportant. At HOLBEACH (615) the parapet is emphasised ; the broach is less important. Naturally this design is rare ; for the broaches, unless small, obstruct the pathway.

(iv.) This hybrid form combines broach, pinnacle, and parapet. Here again the broach obstructs the pathway ; moreover pinnacle and broach harmonise ill. Nevertheless it occurs in a few early and important spires ; *e.g.* Grantham and NEWARK (627), *c.* 1340 ; and in the fifteenth century at All Saints', Stamford.

(v.) Still less common and less successful is the parapetted spire in which the pinnacle sticks up out of the broach ; *e.g.* at DESBOROUGH (616). This has a parapet ; but no passage round.

(vi.) In the end the broach disappeared. The way was then clear for the final development of the English spire with pinnacles, simple or compound.

Many shapes of pinnacle were experimented with. In the Abbaye-aux-Hommes the pinnacles are triangular. At Newark they are hexagonal. At Shipton they are circular. All these are exceptional. Most often they are square or octagonal ; square in harmony with the tower ; or octagonal in harmony with the spire. In and near Northants there was a special local cult of pinnacles in the form of a polygonal turret embattled in harmony with the battlemented parapets below ; *e.g.* KETTERING ; Exton ; Byfield ; Oundle ; All Saints', Stamford ; Leverington.

Kettering.

The position of the pinnacle or the turret varies. Sometimes it is a continuation of the buttresses of the tower. Or it was set at the corner of the tower, as at Witney. Less often, as at Adderbury ; St Nicholas, Gloucester ; and Leverington, it nestles up to the spire.

But when the tower was high, and its walls consequently thick, there was

Newcastle.

more room at the angles, and the builders could indulge in pairs of pinnacles; a lower pinnacle at the angle or over the buttress, a taller pinnacle behind, leading the eye up to the spire.* At Peterborough the outer pinnacle is a square set diagonally; the inner a triangle. At Chichester there are two octagons. At Salisbury the outer pinnacle is octagonal, the inner square. At ST MARY'S, OXFORD † (631), there is the richest cluster of all.

(vii.) At St Mary's, Oxford, we saw the inner pinnacles climbing up the tower. More easily to lead the eye "by a bright ladder" to the spire above, there was substituted for the inner pinnacle a flying buttress. This, however, involved the builders in much trouble. The eye demanded that the flying buttress should be massive; to abut the spire. But the builders seem to have thought that if it were massive and heavy, it would push out the pinnacle on which its foot rested. ‡ So they made the flying buttress almost always light and flimsy; often designed with weak curves; and usually set at too flat an angle. Unsatisfactory examples are only too plentiful; e.g. COVENTRY (635); PATRINGTON (612), where the pinnacle straddles

---

* Plans of pinnacles are given in Mr James Cubitt's paper on "Spires"; *Building News*, May 29, 1885.

† For plan of the springing of this spire see monograph on St Mary's, Oxford, by Mr T. G. Jackson, 84.

‡ It has done so at Higham Ferrers.

on two ridiculously weak legs; Rushden; Moulton; Billingborough; Higham Ferrers; Fleet; Loughton-en-le-Morthen; Thaxted; Helpringham; Hanslope. At WILBY (629) the steeple has an octagonal drum; and both spire and drum have flying buttresses; these are set at a proper angle. At KING'S SUTTON (615) and Patrington the inner pinnacle is retained. In the former spire there is a double flight of flying buttresses; from the outer to the inner pinnacle, and from the latter to the spire. At Patrington the inner pinnacles are grouped into a coronal for the spire; it may have been to maintain the importance of this coronal that the outer pinnacles were made so insignificant. At LOUTH (611) alone was the difficulty of the flying buttress design completely surmounted. Here the architect, on the one hand, strengthened his pinnacles, and on the other perforated his flying buttresses; getting in them the appearance of mass without weight.

(viii.) The flying buttresses once introduced, the next step was to let them converge; thus crushing the spire proper out of existence; the new composition consisting simply of four flying buttresses converging to a centre, on which was poised a pinnacle. It was a *chef-d'œuvre* of building construction if not of art. It occurs in NEWCASTLE CATHEDRAL (624). In Scotland it is seen in the Cross Steeple, Glasgow; King's College, Aberdeen; and St Giles', Edinburgh,* and formerly existed at Haddington and Linlithgow. It was repeated by Sir Christopher Wren in St Dunstan-in-the-East, London.

Spire-Crocket, Rushden.

SUMMARY.—Setting aside the less frequent or exceptional or hybrid forms, we arrive at the conclusion that there are three chief types of English spire. The first is the timber type, whether executed in wood or in stone; the second is the broach spire. Both are without pathway and parapet; both occur mainly in the thirteenth and fourteenth centuries. The third is the parapetted spire without pinnacles; or with pinnacles, and with or without flying buttresses. It is the parapetted spires that are most characteristic of the later Gothic of England.

SPIRE ANGLES.—In many cases the builders were quite satisfied to leave the spire to tell its own tale; *e.g.* at North Luffenham and Barnack. But at a distance the sharp edges or arrises of an octagonal spire hardly tell sufficiently; instead of being octagonal, the spire appears to be circular. Now it had been customary early in the thirteenth century to decorate the sides of turrets with slender shafts; *e.g.* at Peterborough; and to continue these shafts up the converging arrises of the pinnacle which crowned the turret. In imitation of this, many spires were built with their edges emphasised by a slender roll; *e.g.* Witney; Peterborough; St Mary's, Oxford; Wingham; Ketton; Bridgwater; Ledbury; Coventry. For this roll there was substituted in some fourteenth century spires a band of the ballflower characteristic of the period; *e.g.* at Salisbury and the western spires of Lichfield. The crocket was also greatly in vogue during and after the fourteenth century: and many a spire employed this beautiful ornament to emphasise its edges; *e.g.* Higham Ferrers, Walcot, Wimmington, King's Sutton, Oundle, Moulton, Louth, Norwich. It was especially

* For measured drawings see *Building News*, Sept. 7, 1877.

commended to the builders in that it afforded ready access to all parts of the spire in case repairs were needed, without the expense of putting up scaffolding ;

Solihull.

a function which it performs to the present day. At RUSHDEN (625) there can be no doubt that the crockets were purposely designed to give foothold to the steeplejack.

STRINGS AND BANDS.—In many cases the sides of the spire also were ornamented ; sometimes with strings or bands, sometimes with spire-lights. The western spires of LICHFIELD and that of SOLIHULL are notable instances of multiplicity of strings ; with these we may compare the central spire of Sémur-en-Auxois. Other examples, where they are used less emphatically, are Denford, Southam, and St Sepulchre's, Northampton. Sometimes, instead of a string, there was a broad band of carved ornament ; King's Sutton has one small band ; Salisbury and the rebuilt spire of St Mary Redcliffe, Bristol, have three. It may be doubted whether these horizontal lines do not lessen the apparent height of the spires ; that may be the reason why they were not employed more frequently.

PLATE-TRACERY. — Rarely with us, e.g. SOLIHULL, Warwickshire ; Fleet, Lincolnshire ; but frequently in France ; e.g. St Pierre and St Sauveur, Caen ; the sides of the spire were perforated with bands of quatrefoils. It has been asserted * that the object of these quatrefoils, as of spire windows, is to lessen wind pressure, by allowing the wind to pass through the spire. The reverse is the case. Openings in the sides

* Paley's *Gothic Architecture*, 259.

of the spire give the wind a better grip.

SPIRE WINDOWS or Spire-lights or Lucarnes. So far as openings in the sides of a spire have practical value, it is to light the interior,* thus facilitating repairs. But their value is mainly decorative. In many spires they were eschewed; *e.g.* Barnack, Ledbury, Bridgwater, Patrington. In spires of the type of that of Oxford Cathedral there was usually but one tier of large windows; set at the foot of the spire; so also at Bloxham and St Mary's, Oxford.

The earliest fenestrated spires had two or three tiers of windows; *e.g.* Rauceby, Warmington, Sleaford, Polebrook, Anwick, North Luffenham. There was quite a furore for windows in the district of the Northamptonshire broach spire; at first they could hardly be too numerous or too large. The windows were sometimes elaborated to the detriment of the spire. All the above examples, and many more, have the windows so large that their vertical lines seriously break up the converging lines of the spire. In the florid western spires of LICHFIELD (frontispiece) windows are in excess. But at NEWARK and in later spires, such as Louth and Coventry, better design came in. The number and the dimensions of the windows were greatly curtailed. At Moulton and Coventry the upper windows are quite small; at Louth windows play a still less important part. In the later spires too, *e.g.* at Moulton, the upper windows

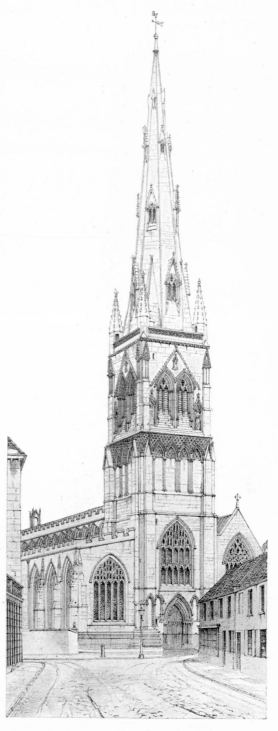

Newark.

* Rarely, as at Weobley Herefordshire, and Ringstead, Northants, the belfry windows are in the spire.

were still further curtailed in order that their rapid diminution upward might make the spire look taller; even the crockets diminish in size upward at Moulton, for the same reason.

Sometimes, as at LICHFIELD, King's Norton, Grantham, the windows were set in tiers, not alternating, on every face; but this was rare. More often, especially in broach spires, *e.g.* Ketton, EWERBY (630), Wollaston, Threckingham, Bingham, Newark, Walcot, Anwick, Holbeach, North Rauceby, St Mary Stamford, Billingborough, Moulton, the windows are set alternately; the lowest and upper four occupying the cardinal sides of the spire, and the intermediate tier the oblique sides. Usually the oblique sides are without windows; all the windows being set on the cardinal sides of the spire; as at Kettering, Whittlesea, Rushden, Market Harborough, Bythorne, Desborough, Oakham, Denford, Barnwell, Luddington, Ringstead, Warmington, Higham Ferrers, FRAMPTON (618).

BAR-TRACERY SPIRES.—Abroad, with marvellous skill, the spire was sometimes composed wholly, or nearly so, of bar-tracery; *e.g.* at Chartres; Antwerp; Strasburg; Freiburg; St Marie de l'Epine, Chalons-sur-Marne; St Stephen's, Vienna; Batalha; Burgos. It might perhaps be pleaded in extenuation of this treatment of stone as if it were wood or metal, that in these openwork spires wind pressure is reduced, and less burden imposed on the supports.

Stanwick.

PLAN OF SPIRES.—A spire may be the same on plan as its tower. Thus the Irish Round Towers and Southese Church, Sussex, have a conical capping or spire. The early square Norman towers, *e.g.* Thaon and Priestholme, had low square spires; which also appear later in many Sussex churches, *e.g.* Rodmell and Slaugham. In the Early Gothic of France * square spires, either hipped to a point or to a ridge, had a much greater vogue; especially in Normandy and the South, where more than twenty examples survive, some mounting to the fifteenth century. So again an octagonal tower may support an octagonal spire, as at STANWICK (628) and Wickham Market.

Wilby.

But in spire design contrast was found more telling than harmony. So the round tower of Piddinghoe, Sussex, carries an octagonal spire. But experiment proved that by far the best combination was that of an octagonal spire and a square tower: and to this type nearly all our steeples conform.

A sort of compromise, however —and like most compromises, not very satisfactory—was to introduce the octagonal form in the upper part of the tower; so that the steeple consisted of three stories; the square tower, the octagonal drum, and the octagonal spire. It appears at Barnack and Exton,† Rutland; WILBY, Northants; Graftham, Hunts; Bloxham, Oxfordshire; Masham, York; Patrington; Norwich; Coventry. In the greater number of these the drum fails to extricate itself sufficiently from the tower; making it difficult to see where the tower ends and the spire begins; or else it is so smothered in panelling and pinnacles, that its presence is hardly perceptible.

A more important consideration is the height the tower should have in proportion to that of the spire. As to this, great diversity of practice prevailed. On the whole, we seem to have got our towers too squat. How far superior is the effect of a tall spire, when seated on a tall tower, is seen at once by inspecting such examples as Louth, Coventry, Salisbury, Patrington, which are among the finest steeples

* *E.g.* Tournai Cathedral and St Gille, Caen.   † Illustrated in Wickes' *Spires*, 24.

SCALE OF 10 5 0 10 20 30 40 50 FEET

Ewerby.

in England. It was in Normandy that this principle was most fully recognised ; it is to the height, slenderness, and lightness of their towers that such steeples as Bernières and Vernouillet owe their surpassing charm. Sometimes our towers were crushingly squat in proportion to the needle-like spires which they carried ; *e.g.* BRIDGWATER (612) ; Hemingborough, York ; Walcot, Lincoln. While at Louth, Newark, Kettering, and Ketton, tower and spire are about equal in height,* at Hemingborough the spire is twice as high as the tower. But just as the spire may be too tall for the tower, so the tower may be too tall for the spire. This was naturally the case with many of the earlier spires ; *e.g.* Oxford Cathedral, Barnack, Sleaford ; and with several later spires in the Norfolk and Lincolnshire marshland ; *e.g.* Walsoken, Fleet, and TILNEY ALL SAINTS' (612). But almost at once the spire soared upward at a sharp angle ; *e.g.* at Ketton and Salisbury ; and earlier still in France ; *e.g.* St Germain, Auxerre. The change from a somewhat obtuse to a sharp angle was so rapid that there must have been some other than æsthetic reasons for it. Probably the builders calculated that the acuter the angle of the spire, the less it tends to thrust out the corners of the tower on which it rests; moreover an acute spire is less affected by wind pressure. The later spires on the whole vary from an angle of fifteen degrees, *e.g.* Chichester, to one of ten degrees, *e.g.* Louth and Moulton : in later Gothic they were generally slender.

* In the best *broach* spires of Northants the spire and tower seem to be generally equal in height, and the tower is generally from 3 to 3¼ squares high from the ground to the corbeltable. Louth steeple is 300 feet high from the street ; 294 feet from the floor ; the tower and spire are each 147 feet high. At St Mary's, Oxford, the tower is 87 feet 5 inches from the floor ; the spire is 101 feet 1 inch high.

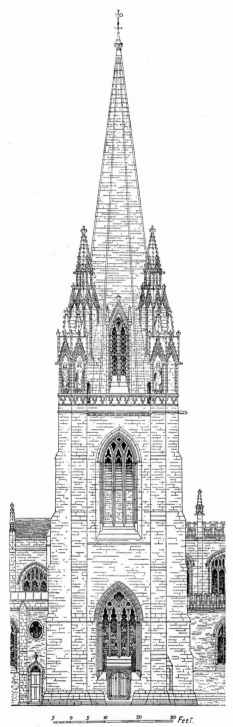

Oxford St Mary.

ENTASIS.—In some spires the sides are straight ; *e.g.* Kettering ; St Mary's, Oxford ; and Salisbury ; several have been shortened * at the top after damage from storm or lightning, and have thus accidentally lost their straight outlines, *e.g.* Grantham ; a few were built with slightly convex outline, like the Greek columns. This entasis, as it is called, was given because a long upright line appears hollow at or about the centre. The entasis † corrects this optical illusion. It is quite slight in a spire, probably not amounting to more than 1 inch in 60 feet in the best examples. This is greatly exceeded, however, in the circular spires of the district of the Charentè ; *e.g.* Saintes ; and in a few of our own spires ; *e.g.* the Lincolnshire spires of Caythorpe, Welbourn, and Glinton ; which have been opprobriously designated "sugarloaf" spires. It occurs in the twelfth-century spire of St Germain, Auxerre ; and in the Normandy spire of Bretteville. Other English examples are Gedling and Wittering. At Louth the necessary correction is obtained by increasing the projection of the crockets about one-third of the way up.

UNITY OF TOWER AND SPIRE.—In many cases the tower was completed some considerable time before the spire was built ; *e.g.* Norwich ; Salisbury ; St Mary's, Stamford ; Gedney ; Walsoken. This may have familiarised the builders with the idea of designing the tower without reference to the spire. It might chance that funds for adding a spire might never be forthcoming. It was well therefore to design a tower which should be complete in itself : *e.g.* St Martin's, Stamford, has an excellent Perpendicular tower ; but it has squinches ; so that a spire was evidently intended.

But with some exceptions—Salisbury is one—the best spires were those which were designed not from the tower upwards, but from the weathercock downward ; *e.g.* Louth, Bingham, and Kettering are spires all the way to the ground. ‡ We may indeed go so far as to lay down that where we find a bad tower produced by the removal of the spire, the presumption is that the steeple is a success. This is true of Patrington ; St Mary's, Oxford ; Louth ; Bloxham ; Heckington ; Billingborough ; § St Mary Redcliffe, Bristol ; and more especially of the broach spires ; *e.g.* Bingham ; Aumsby ; Barnwell ; Threckingham ; Walcot ; Wollaston. Nevertheless it must be admitted that there are some steeples which would remain excellent as towers, if the spires were removed ; *e.g.* Newark ; Coventry ; Moulton ; Whittlesea.

DISTRIBUTION OF ORNAMENT.—Some of the earlier spires tended to be florid. At Grantham the architect has given the spire double the usual number of windows ; together with parapet, pinnacles, broaches, and crockets. Newark is better ; there are not so many windows ; and rolls are substituted for crockets. For a lesson in the use, not the misuse, of ornament we must study

---

* Others have been heightened at "restorations," *e.g.* Oundle.—R. P. B.

† The entasis of a spire may be due to a curious bit of masoncraft. "The stone-masons who put up a tall pole in the axis of the spire they were building, and who diminished the height of this pole from day to day, building always so that the slope of the spire was directed towards the upper end of the pole, were giving the same entasis to the slope that a Greek artist gave to his columns" (Sturgis' *Dictionary of Architecture and Building*, iii. 267).

‡ But this may be overdone ; as at St Sepulchre's, Northampton ; where the vast projection of its diagonal buttresses makes the tower a mere annexe to the spire.

§ Johnson's *Reliques*, 34.

the composition of such spires as Patrington ; St Mary's, Oxford ; Louth ; and Coventry.

PATRINGTON STEEPLE (634) is practically a three-storied elevation. The lower story, *i.e.* the lower stage of the tower, is absolutely plain. So is the spire. All this to show off better the ornament of the intermediate story, which includes the upper stage of the tower and the pinnacled drum. In this steeple all the ornament is concentrated at the mid-zone.

In ST MARY'S, OXFORD (631), the mid-zone is the pinnacled base of the spire. Owing to the wealth of ornament here, it is possible to give more ornament to the tower than at Patrington, and to provide the spire with rolls.

At LOUTH (611) again the ornament grows in richness upward till it culminates at the base of the spire. For the great west window is substituted a pair of windows ; in the next story the windows have crocketted ogee dripstones ; then comes a galaxy of panelled pinnacles, big and little, battlements, windows, and flying buttresses. Finally this wealth of ornament dies away in the crockets converging to the summit. Louth is beyond compare. One of the most remarkable of its characteristics is the vast height to which it seems to soar ; therein surpassing every spire. It is moderately high ; 300 feet ; but it seems lofty beyond finite measurement.

If any prefer a more florid type, what can surpass ST MICHAEL'S, COVENTRY ? (635). As the eight string-courses show, it is an elevation of nine stories. These continually increase in richness and beauty from the doorway to the battlements which crown the tower. From that point the decoration gradually dies away. The sixth story, the octagonal drum, is a little less rich. The seventh and eighth have panelling and windows ; the ninth has windows only. Again, the nine stories are arranged in triplets ; the highest of the three lower stories being the richest of the three. In the spire, which also has three stories, this is reversed ; the lowest story being the richest. The three middle stories are the richest of all ; and of these the central one has tiers of statuettes to give it predominance over the other two. In the presence of such design as that of Louth and Coventry, it is futile indeed to speak of our late Gothic as " debased." *

ELEVATION AND PERSPECTIVE.—A special difficulty which confronted the builders was that a square tower looks different, but an octagonal spire the same, whether seen from a cardinal point or obliquely. A square tower is half as wide again when seen diagonally as it is when seen full-face. Therefore a spire, in relation to its tower, if right when seen full-face, is wrong when viewed diagonally ; and *vice versa ;* it cannot be right both ways. The point of view from which a square tower is seen therefore affects the aspect of the spire. Seen from north, south, east, or west, a spire seems more massive ; seen from the intermediate points, it seems more slender.† This seems occasionally to have been recognised ; *e.g.* Helpringham Church is approached by a long road leading straight eastward to the spire ; which, like Threckingham spire, from this point

---

* For an appreciation of Moulton steeple, see Sharpe's *Lincoln Excursion*, 99, 147.

† This is most so with a parapetted spire ; especially if it has turrets instead of pinnacles. If it has pinnacles, and these nestle up to the spire, it looks equally well at an angle or seen straight on ; *e.g.* Nassington.—R. P. B. See Mr T. G. Jackson on St Mary's, Oxford, 86.

Patrington from W.

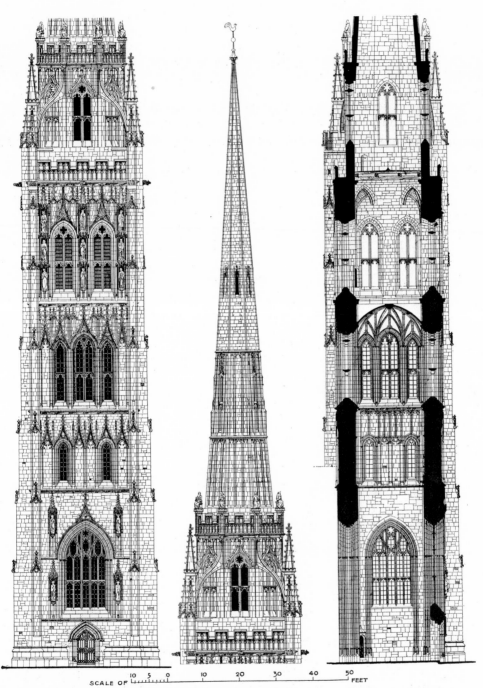

Coventry St Michael.

of view is seen to much greater advantage than when seen diagonally.* The slender spire of Louth also looks adequate when approached from the only point from which it was intended to be seen ; viz. the west.

SPIRE CONSTRUCTION.—When the spire superposed on a square tower is octagonal, only the cardinal sides rest on the walls of the tower. For the oblique sides therefore some support has to be devised. This support is obtained by building concentric arches receding towards each angle of the tower ; as is seen at Oxford Cathedral ; an early spire, where the squinches are rude and archaic ; at SALISBURY ; SHOTTESBROOKE (395) ; COVENTRY (635) ; and LOUTH (611).

Special precautions were sometimes taken to prevent the capstone being dislodged by the movements of the vane. The interior of Salisbury spire is filled with a timber frame, consisting of a central piece with arms and braces. This entire frame, the arms of which were made to support floors which served as scaffolds whilst the spire was building, is hung to the capstone of the spire by iron cross bars, and by the iron standard of the vane, which is fixed to the upper part of the central piece.†

Salisbury Cathedral Spire.

To diminish the weight on the tower as much as possible, the later spires were built very thin. The south-west spire of Chartres, an Early Gothic cathedral of exceptionally massive construction throughout, is $31\frac{1}{2}$ inches thick at the bottom and $11\frac{3}{4}$ inches at the top. That of Salisbury is 9 inches thick at the bottom and 7 inches at the top. But in the two great spire-building districts—the Caen stone district of Normandy, and the Oolitic limestone districts of England—these dimensions were considerably reduced. The first $9\frac{1}{2}$ feet of Kettering spire are 14 inches thick ; above, it is 6 inches. The Normandy spires of the thirteenth century are very often only from 5 to 6 inches.‡ The thickness of the spire of St Mary's, Oxford, is about 14 inches, clear of the spire lights and pinnacles ; and at the top, before it becomes solid, from 6 to 7 inches. Oundle spire, after the first 9 or 10 inches, is about 7 inches

* Sharpe's *Lincoln Excursion*, 77.   † Murray's *English Cathedrals*, 87.
‡ Ruprich-Robert, 163.

thick. Louth * spire is 10 inches thick below ; 5 inches thick above. The spire of Moulton, Lincolnshire, is not more than 5 inches thick.

The courses of a spire might be laid horizontally ; or with the joints at right angles to the slope of the spire. In the latter case the spire is a genuine vault ; simply a tall elongated vault.† But being a vault, it has a decided outward thrust, diminished indeed by the acuteness of the angle of most spires, but still present, and needing to be guarded against. Moreover it is easy for the rain to penetrate into its inclined joints. For these reasons the builders seem to have preferred to build the spires in horizontal courses ; *i.e.* corbelled inwardly.

* For Louth Church and spire see paper by Mr James Fowler in the *Transactions of the Lincoln Diocesan Arch. Society*, 1873. The Churchwardens' accounts of the building of the spire have been printed in *Archæologia*, x. 70-98 ; see also Britton's *Archit. Antiq.*, iv. 1-7. The spire cost £279. 10s. 5d.

† Indeed in the French example of Loches, it is difficult to say whether the nave is roofed with a couple of domed vaults or a couple of spires. *Classification of Romanesque*, 273.

Winchester.

CHAPTER XLII.

CHRONOLOGY OF ENGLISH CHURCHES.

[In the following list are included most of the larger churches ; and of the smaller churches those for whose date documentary evidence exists. Where no authority is quoted, the date is fixed by architectural evidence only, and must be regarded with suspicion. The documentary evidence also must be received with caution ; see paper by the author in the *Journal of the R.I.B.A.*, 26th November 1898, on *The Comparative Value of Documentary and Architectural Evidence in Establishing the Chronology of the English Cathedrals.* Fuller quotation of authorities will be found in the seventh edition of Rickman's *Gothic Architecture.* Additions to the list and corrections will be welcomed.]

ARLINGHAM, Gloucestershire. PARISH CHURCH. 1373. *Bloxam*, 227.

ARUNDEL, Sussex. Made Collegiate in 1380.

ASHBOURNE, Derbyshire. PARISH CHURCH. Parts are 1235-1241. Inscription on brass plate : facsimile in *Rickman*, 170.

ASHFORD, Kent. PARISH CHURCH. Rebuilt 1461-1490. *Rickman*, 308.

AUGHTON, Yorkshire. PARISH CHURCH. *Steeple*, 1536. *Rickman*, 318.

AVENING, Gloucestershire. PARISH CHURCH. *c.* 1125. Messrs Carpenter and Ingelow in *Transactions of Bristol and Gloucester Archæological Society*, xiv. 5.

BALSHAM, Cambridgeshire. PARISH CHURCH. *Chancel*—1390-1400. Inscription on brass plate : facsimile in *Rickman*, 293.

BANGOR CATHEDRAL, Carnarvonshire. SECULAR CANONS. Built, except the *Choir*, 1509-1532. *Rickman*, 315.

BARTON-UNDER-NEEDWOOD, Stafford. PARISH CHURCH. 1517. *Rickman*, 316.

BATH, Somerset. PARISH CHURCH. Formerly Abbey Church of Benedictine Monks. Begun *c.* 1500 ; nearly finished in 1539. *Rickman*, 313.

BATTLE ABBEY, Sussex. BENEDICTINE MONKS. Founded 1067. *Refectory*—First half of XIII. Cent. *Gatehouse*—License to crenellate granted 1339. *Rickman*, 240.

BEAULIEU ABBEY, Hampshire. CISTERCIAN MONKS. Founded 1204; Church hallowed 1246 ; Frater, now Parish Church, between these dates. *Mr Harold Brakspear.*

BERKHAMSTED, Hertfordshire. PARISH CHURCH. First half of XIII. Cent.

BEVERLEY MINSTER (St John's), Yorkshire. SECULAR CANONS. *Choir and Transepts* —*c.* 1225—*c.* 1245. *Nave*—*c.* 1320—*c.* 1349. *West Front*—*c.* 1380—*c.* 1430. Mr John Bilson in *Architectural Review*, iii. 199.

BEVERLEY ST MARY, Yorkshire. PARISH CHURCH. Originally aisleless Church of second quarter of XII. Cent. Aisles added to nave in second quarter of XIII. Cent. Chapel on east side of north transept, east aisle of south transept, and south aisle of chancel, of end of XIII. and beginning of XIV. Cent. North arcade of chancel and north chapel, of second quarter of XIV. Cent. Nave clerestory and west end, early XV. Cent., followed by chancel clerestory and reconstruction of transepts, to middle of XV. Cent. Nave and tower reconstructed after fall of tower in 1520. *Mr John Bilson.*

BINHAM PRIORY, Norfolk. BENEDICTINE MONKS. *Nave—c.* 1100. Was in existence 1093, but not fully endowed till 1101-1106. (Dugdale's *Monasticon*, iii. 341. *West Front*—Built by Richard de Parco, who was Prior 1226-1244. *Matthew Paris.*

BIRKIN, Yorkshire. PARISH CHURCH. Granted to the Templars in 1152.

BISHOP AUCKLAND, Durham. *Hall, now the Chapel—c.* 1190.

BLYTH PRIORY, Notts. BENEDICTINE MONKS. *Nave*—Founded, and probably begun, 1088. Monograph with measured drawings by Mr C. C. Hodges; Hexham, 1881.

BLYTHBURGH, Suffolk. PARISH CHURCH. 1442-1473. *Suffolk Arch. Institute*, iv. 233 and 422.

BOLTON PRIORY, Yorkshire. AUSTIN OR BLACK CANONS. *Parts of Nave, Transept, and Choir*—Begun *c.* 1151. *Parts of Nave, North Aisle, and Older Façade*—Early XIII. Cent. *Part of Choir*—Second quarter of XIV. Cent. *New Front and Tower*—Inscription has date 1520. *Builder*, 4th May 1895.

BOLTON PERCY, Yorkshire. PARISH CHURCH. Built by its Rector, 1411-1423.

BOSTON, Lincolnshire. PARISH CHURCH. Foundations laid in 1309. *Nave and West Chancel*—Before 1350. *Tower—c.* 1510. *Assoc. Soc. Reports*, x. 175.

BOURN ABBEY, Lincolnshire. AUSTIN CANONS. Founded 1138. *Assoc. Soc. Reports*, xx. 7.

BOXGROVE PRIORY, Sussex. BENEDICTINE MONKS. *Choir—c.* 1235. Same in carving and style as the south chapels of Chichester nave and east chapel of north side of nave. *Mr E. S. Prior.*

BRADSOLE, ST RADEGUND'S ABBEY, Kent. PREMONSTRATENSIAN OR WHITE CANONS. Founded in 1191. W. H. St John Hope in *Arch. Cant.*, xiv. 140.

BRAY, Berks. PARISH CHURCH. Partly rebuilt, 1293 *seq. Rickman*, 235.

BRECON PRIORY, Brecknock. BENEDICTINE MONKS. *Choir and Transepts*—Early XIII. Cent. *Alterations*—Second half of XIV. Cent.

BRIDLINGTON PRIORY, Yorkshire. AUSTIN CANONS. *North Aisle, North Porch and both Arcades of Nave, c.* 1250. *Upper Work, North Side, c.* 1270; *South Side, c.* 1290. *West End and S.W. of Nave, c.* 1480. *Assoc. Soc. Reports*, iii. 40.

BRINGTON, Northants. PARISH CHURCH. 1445-1457. *Churches of Northants*, 261.

BRINKBURN PRIORY, Northumberland. AUSTIN CANONS. Late XII. Cent.

BRISTOL ABBEY. AUSTIN CANONS. Became a Cathedral in 1542. *Chapter House*—Third quarter of XII. Cent. (*Rickman*, 99.) *Elder Lady Chapel*—Early XIII. Cent. Abbot David was buried in it in 1253. *Choir*—Built by Abbot Knowle, 1298-1332. (*Abbot Newland's Roll.*) *Central Tower—c.* 1450—*c.* 1470. *Mr G. E. Street.*

BRISTOL, ST MARY AT REDCLIFFE. PARISH CHURCH. *Inner Porch*—End of XII. Cent. *Porch and Tower*—Begun 1292. (*Rickman*, 234.) *South Transept*—Second quarter of XIV. Cent.; finished in 1376 by William Canynges the elder. The rest built chiefly by William Canynge the younger, who died in 1474. *William of Worcester* in Canon Norris' *Guide* to the Church.

BRISTOL, ST STEPHEN'S. PARISH CHURCH. 1455.

BUCKLAND, Herts. PARISH CHURCH. 1348. Inscription reproduced in *Rickman*, 241.

BUILDWAS ABBEY, Shropshire. Cistercian Monks. Founded 1135. Some of it is before 1148; but the greater part immediately after. *Mr Harold Brakspear.*

BURNHAM ABBEY, Bucks. Austin Canonesses. Was founded 1277 by Richard, King of the Romans, and the buildings are of this date, though there is no documentary evidence of their erection. *Mr Harold Brakspear.*

BURY ST EDMUNDS, Suffolk Abbey. Benedictine Monks. *Ruins*—Some part completed in 1095; consecration in 1096. (*Rickman*, 82.) *Tower Gateway*—1121-1130. (*Rickman*, 92.) *Gatehouse*—After 1327. (*Rickman*, 239.) Dr M. R. James in *Camb. Antiq. Soc. 8vo publications*, No. 28.

BURY ST EDMUNDS, St Mary's. Parish Church. 1424-1433. *Rickman*, 299.

BYLAND ABBEY, Yorkshire. Cistercian Monks. The monks removed to Byland in 1177 from a few miles away; probably had begun building some few years earlier.

CAMBRIDGE, Corpus Christi College. *Old Court*—1352-1377; practically no old work left.

CAMBRIDGE, Christ's College. *First Court*—Nearly finished in 1509; entirely refaced in the XVIII. Cent.

CAMBRIDGE, Holy Sepulchre. Probably 1120-1140.

CAMBRIDGE, Holy Trinity. Parish Church. *Tower-piers*—Late XIII. Cent. *Nave and Aisles*—Late XIV. Cent. *Transepts, North Porch, and Clerestory of Nave*—Late XV. Cent.

CAMBRIDGE, King's College. First stone of *Chapel* laid 1446. Parts in white stone (magnesian limestone) are 1446-1461. The rest by Henry VII. and his executors, 1508-1515. *Fan Vault*—Begun 1512.

CAMBRIDGE, Pembroke College. *First Court*—1346 *seq.*; but entirely altered.

CAMBRIDGE, Peterhouse. *Hall*—Partly *c.* 1286; two doorways (restored) left. *North Quadrangle*—1424. *West Quadrangle*—1431. *Kitchen*—1450. *Stone Parlour*—1460. Courts refaced in the XVIII. Cent.

CAMBRIDGE, Queen's College. *First Court and Far Side of Second Court*—1447 and 1465.

CAMBRIDGE, St Andrew the Less. The so-called "Abbey" Church. Early XIII. Cent.

CAMBRIDGE, St Benedict. Parish Church. *Tower and N.E. Angle of Nave*—Pre-Norman. *Nave*—XIII. Cent. *Aisles*—Rebuilt 1853 and 1872.

CAMBRIDGE, St Edward. Parish Church. Late XIV. Cent.; except *Tower*, some parts of which are XIII. Cent. *Aisles*—Added *c.* 1445.

CAMBRIDGE, St John's College. *Gatehouse*—*c.* 1511. *First Court*—1510-1520; refaced.

CAMBRIDGE, St Mary the Great. Parish Church. Begun 1478. *Nave Roof*—1506. *Tower*—1491; 1530. *Belfry Stage*—1593-1608.

CAMBRIDGE, St Mary the Less. Parish Church. 1340-1352.

CAMBRIDGE, St Michael. Parish Church. After 1323.

CAMBRIDGE, St Radegund. Benedictine Nuns. *Chapel of Jesus College*—Early XIII. Cent. A. Gray, *Camb. Antiq. Soc. 8vo publications*.

CAMBRIDGE, Stourbridge Chapel. Hospital of St Mary Magdalen.—*c.* 1125.

CAMBRIDGE, Trinity College. *Great Gate*—1518-1535. *Chapel*—*c.* 1564. *Great Quadrangle*—Mainly 1593-1615. The dates of buildings in Cambridge are taken from the *Architectural History of the University of Cambridge*, by Robert Willis and J. W. Clark.

CANTERBURY CATHEDRAL, Kent. BENEDICTINE MONKS. *Parts in West Crypt*—Rebuilt by Archbishop Lanfranc, 1070-1077. *Choir and Crypt*—Rebuilt by Ernulf, Prior 1096-1107, and Prior Conrad. Dedicated 1130. *Choir again rebuilt*—William of Sens, 1175-1178; and William the Englishman, 1179-1184. *Black Prince's Chantry*—1370-1379. *Western Bays of Nave*—1379-1381. *Rest of Nave and West Side of Transepts*—1382-1400. *Cloister*—1397-1412. *St Michael's, Somerset, or Warrior's Chapel*—Finished 1439 (*Hope*). *South-west Tower*—1440-1452. *Lady or Dean's Chapel*—*c.* 1448-1455 (*Hope*). *Central Tower*—1495-1503. *Christ Church Gateway*—1517. See Professor Willis' *Canterbury*.

CANTERBURY, ST AUGUSTINE'S ABBEY. BENEDICTINE MONKS. Founded *c.* 597. Begun by Abbot Scotland 1070-1087; his work finished in 1091. *St Augustine's Gateway*—1309. *Mr W. H. St John Hope.*

CANTERBURY, HOLY CROSS. PARISH CHURCH. Removed to present site, 1380. *Rickman*, 290.

CARLISLE CATHEDRAL, Cumberland. A house of Austin Canons was founded and endowed in 1101. *Nave and Transept*—Probably soon after 1101. Became a cathedral in 1133. *Choir*—Middle of XIII. Cent. *Choir-piers, Triforium, and Clerestory*—Rebuilt after fire of 1292; prolonged up to springing of arch of east window by 1322; east window glazed 1380-1384. C. J. Ferguson in *Builder*, 6th May 1893.

CARTMEL PRIORY, Lancashire. AUSTIN CANONS. Founded in 1188. *South Aisle of Presbytery*—Second quarter of XIV. Cent. *Nave*—Rebuilt later.

CASTLE ACRE, Norfolk. CLUNIAC MONKS. Founded before 1089 or in 1090. W. H. St John Hope in *N. and N. Arch Soc.*, 1894.

CASTOR, Northants. PARISH CHURCH. *Tower* and parts are 1124. Inscription over doorway: illustrated in *Rickman*, 93.

CATTERICK, Yorkshire. PARISH CHURCH. 1412. The contract for building was printed in 1834 by Rev. J. Raine.

CHATTERIS PRIORY, Cambridge. BENEDICTINE NUNS. Probably rebuilt after fire of 1310. Consecrated 1352. *Rickman*, 242.

CHELMSFORD, Essex. PARISH CHURCH. Repaired or rebuilt 1489 *seq. Rickman*, 312.

CHEPSTOW PRIORY, Monmouth. BENEDICTINE MONKS. Begun between 1135 and 1154, if not earlier.

CHESTER CATHEDRAL, Cheshire. BENEDICTINE MONKS. Founded and richly endowed by Hugh Lupus in 1093. *North Transept*—1093. *East Bay of Choir Aisle*—*c.* 1200. *Chapter House and Vestibule*—First half of XIII. Cent. *Choir*—Was rebuilding in 1283. *South Transept and South Nave*—Chiefly in the second quarter of the XIV. Cent. *Nave*—Finished in XV. Cent.

CHESTER, ST JOHN. SECULAR CANONS. Cathedral in 1075. *Fragments West of Nave*—Soon after 1075. *Nave*—Ground story, *c.* 1170; triforium, *c.* 1180; clerestory, *c.* 1200.

CHETWODE, Buckinghamshire. AUSTIN CANONS. Founded in 1244. *Chancel. Rickman*, 172.

CHICHESTER CATHEDRAL, Sussex. SECULAR CANONS. *Choir*—*c.* 1091; consecrated 1108. *Nave*—*c.* 1114-1123. *Lady Chapel*—Finished before 1175. *Retrochoir, Recasing and Vaulting*—After fire of 1186. *Eastern Chapels, Library, Vestry, South and North Porch*—First quarter of XIII. Cent. *South Chapels of Nave, East Chapels of North Side of Nave, and Doorway of South Porch*—

Second quarter of XIII. Cent. *West Chapels of North Side of Nave and West Porch*—Third quarter of XIII. Cent. *Lady Chapel*—1288-1304. *South Transept* —Remodelled 1305-1337. *Spire* (which fell down in 1860)—Begun *c.* 1370 ; finished *c.* 1470. *Campanile*—Begun *c.* 1370 ; still in progress in 1436. *Cloisters* —XV. Cent. Professor Willis on *Chichester*, and E. Sharpe on *New Shoreham*, Report by Mr Gordon M. Hills, and paper by Mr E. S. Prior on *Chichester Masoncraft* in *Proceedings of Harrow Architectural Club*, 1904.

CHICHESTER, St Mary's Hospital. *Hall and its Chapel*—*c.* 1290.

CHIPPING CAMPDEN, Gloucester. Parish Church. *Chancel*—1380-1401. *Rickman*, 290.

CHRIST CHURCH, Hampshire. Secular Canons ; replaced by Augustinian Canons in 1150. Probably commenced by Flambard *after* he became Bishop of Durham in 1099. (*Sir G. G. Scott.*) *Lady Chapel*—Completed before 1395 or 1406. *West Tower and Choir*—XV. Cent. ; choir vaulted between 1502 and 1520. Ferrey's *Memorials of Christ Church, Twynham.*

CIRENCESTER, Gloucester. Collegiate Church. *Nave*—Rebuilt *c.* 1515.

CIRENCESTER ABBEY, Gloucester. Austin Canons. *Foundations*—*Temp.* Henry II.

CLEE, Lincolnshire. Parish Church. *Chancel and Transepts*—Consecrated in 1192, according to inscription cut on an earlier pier : facsimile in *Rickman*, 158.

COLCHESTER PRIORY, St Botolph, Essex. Austin Canons. Founded 1102. *Rickman*, 89.

COLCHESTER ABBEY, Essex. Benedictine Monks. Consecration 1104.

COLLUMPTON, Devon. Parish Church. *Lane's Chantry and Fan Vault*—1510-1528. *Rickman*, 316.

COLMOUTH, Bedford. Parish Church. Finished 1396. *Rickman*, 294.

COVENTRY, St Michael, Warwick. Parish Church. *Tower*—Finished 1394. *Spire*—Begun 1432. *Nave*—Enlarged *c.* 1420. *Bloxam*, 268.

COVENTRY, Holy Trinity. Parish Church. *Chancel*—Rebuilt in 1391. East end rebuilt in 1786.

CROWLAND or CROYLAND ABBEY, Lincolnshire. Benedictine Monks. *Choir* —Commenced in 1113. *Façade*—Early and late XIII. Cent., and XV. Cent. *Nave*—Recast in XV. Cent. *Tower*—1427. *Builder*, 1st September 1894. *Rickman*, 307.

CROXDEN ABBEY, Stafford. Cistercian Monks. *South Transept*—First half of XIII. Cent.

CRUMWELL, Notts. Parish Church. *Tower*—1442. *Rickman*, 303.

CWM HIR ABBEY, Radnor. Cistercian Monks. Founded in 1143 by Robert Fitz Stephen, who commanded in the first invasion of Ireland, 1170. *Giraldus Cambrensis.* See "Llanidloes," and page 433.

DARLINGTON, Durham. Parish Church. Was building in 1192, and unfinished in 1195. *Arch. Aeliana*, xvii. 145.

DARTON, York. Parish Church. *Chancel*—Inscription, 1517, on wall-plate. *Rickman*, 316.

DAVINGTON PRIORY, Kent. Benedictine Nunnery. Founded 1153. *Arch. Cant.*, xxii. 275.

DEEPING ST JAMES PRIORY, Lincolnshire. Benedictine Monks. *c.* 1180. Sharpe's *Nene Valley.*

DEERHURST PRIORY, Gloucester. Benedictine Monks. *Nave*—Probably last years of XII. Cent.

DEVIZES ST MARY and DEVIZES ST JOHN, Wilts. Parish Churches. Built by Roger of Sarum. May be as late as 1139. *Mr Harold Brakspear.*

DONNINGTON, Lincolnshire. Parish Church. *Nave*—1351. *Rickman, 242.*

DORCHESTER ABBEY, Oxfordshire. Austin Canons. Parts of all periods, especially of the last half of the XIII. Cent. *Dorchester Abbey,* published by Parker.

DORE ABBEY, Hereford. Cistercian Monks. Founded 1147. *Choir*—Probably the last years of the XII. Cent. *East Portion of Choir—c.* 1200.

DOVER, St Martin. Austin Canons. *Choir*—Begun 1131; finished 1140. (*Rickman,* 96.) *Refectory,* 1131-1139. Plumptre in *Arch. Cantiana,* iv.

DUBLIN, Christ Church. Cathedral. Arrosian Canons. *Choir and Transepts*— Probably begun soon after 1171, when Henry II. landed. Strongbow was buried in it in 1176, and a stone altar was given to it in 1180. Monograph by G. E. Street. *Nave*—Completed in 1235. Sir T. Drew in *Builder,* 7th April 1894.

DUBLIN, St Patrick. Cathedral. Patent Roll of 1225 speaks of preachers going through Ireland to beg alms for the fabric. Bernard's *St Patrick's Cathedral,* 9.

DUCKLINGTON, Oxfordshire. Parish Church. *North Aisle—c.* 1335. *Rickman,* 238.

DUNFERMLINE ABBEY, Fife. Benedictine Monks. Probably built soon after the accession of David I. in 1124. Macgibbon and Ross's *Ecclesiastical Architecture of Scotland.*

DUNMOW PRIORY, Essex. Austin Canons. *Choir*—XIV. Cent.

DUNSTABLE PRIORY, Bedford. Austin Canons. *Choir*—Begun in 1122. *Rickman,* 96. *Nave*—Probably third quarter of XII. Cent. *West Front*—Probably after the fall of the central tower in 1222.

DUNSTER, Somerset. Priory Church. Documentary evidence gives 1419 as date of tower. Murray's *Somerset,* 475.

DURHAM CATHEDRAL. Benedictine Monks. *Choir*—Begun 1093; works had reached the nave in 1099; body of St Cuthbert translated to the choir in 1104. *Nave*—Completed by 1128; except its *Vault,* 1128-1133. *Chapter House*— 1133-1140. *Galilee—c.* 1170 to *c.* 1175. *Upper Part of West Towers*—Perhaps 1217-1226. *East Transept*—Begun 1242; finished 1280. *Reredos*—1380. *Central Tower*—Probably begun *c.* 1470. *Prior's Kitchen*—Begun in 1368. *Rickman,* 248. Mr J. Bilson's *Beginnings;* Canon Greenwell's *Durham Cathedral.*

EDINGTON, Wilts. Priory Church. Dedicated in 1361. *Rickman,* 243.

ELY CATHEDRAL, Cambridgeshire. Benedictine Monks. Begun 1083. Became a cathedral in 1109. *Choir*—Destroyed. *Ground Story of Transept*—Begun *c.* 1090. *Upper Stories of Transept and Nave—c.* 1100-1130. *Upper Part of West Transept, Façade, and Infirmary—c.* 1170-1200. (*E. Sharpe.*) *St Mary's Parish Church*—Ditto. *Galilee*—Built by Eustace, who was Bishop 1198-1215. (*Sir G. G. Scott.*) *Presbytery*—1235-1252. *Lady Chapel*—Commenced in 1321; unfinished in 1349. (*Monasticon Anglicanum,* i. 464.) *Central Tower*—Fell in 1322. *Octagon and Choir*—Begun 1322. *Prior Crauden's Chapel*—1325-6. *Choir Stalls*—Begun 1338. *Great Gatehouse*—Begun 1396-7. *Octagon of West Tower*—1401 or 1444. *Bishop Alcock's Chapel*—1488. *Bishop West's Chapel* —1534. *North-west Doorway of Transept*—1699. D. J. Stewart's *Arch. Hist. of Ely Cathedral,* 1868.

ETCHINGHAM, Sussex. PARISH CHURCH. Brass of the founder, who died in 1387. *Rickman*, 292.

ETON COLLEGE, Bucks. CHAPEL. Begun 1441; consecration 1443; unfinished in 1463; finished 1522. *Rickman*, 303.

EVESHAM ABBEY, Worcester. BENEDICTINE MONKS. *Tower*—1514-1539.

EWENNY PRIORY, Glamorgan. BENEDICTINE MONKS. Founded 1147; church mainly of this date, but crenulated in the XIV. Cent. *Mr Harold Brakspear.*

EXETER CATHEDRAL, Devon. SECULAR CANONS. *Towers*—1112-1136. (*Rickman*, 90.) The lower part of the Lady Chapel with its companion chapels and the retrochoir are certainly one work, *c.* 1270; the remodelling of the transepts is probably before 1280; the above is the work of Branscombe, who was Bishop 1257-1280. Quivil, who was Bishop 1280-1291, began the presbytery, which was ready for its roof in 1299 and was partly glazed in 1301; about the same time the Lady Chapel was completed. Bitton, who was Bishop 1292-1307, nearly finished the choir, and inserted a triforium arcade in the presbytery. Stapledon, who was Bishop 1308-1326, probably built the crossing and the eastern bay of the nave; the latter was not glazed till 1317 or 1318. To Stapledon also belong the Bishop's throne, the sedilia, and the choir screen. Grandisson, who was Bishop 1327-1369, finished the nave *c.* 1350. The east window is Brantingham's (1370-1394). The lower part of the screen of the west front is *c.* 1345-1369; the upper figures are 1377-1399. The screens to the three eastern chapels have the arms of Stafford, who was Bishop 1395-1419. The three chantries are later. Professor Lethaby in *Architectural Review*, March and May 1903.

FAIRFORD, Gloucester. PARISH CHURCH. *c.* 1490. Leland in Carbonell's *Fairford*, 2.

FINCHALE PRIORY, Durham. BENEDICTINE MONKS. Founded 1196. New church begun 1242, and probably finished *c.* 1265. *Rickman*, 171.

FORDINGTON, Dorset. PARISH CHURCH. Endowed in 1091. Sculptured lintel illustrated in *Bloxam*, 86.

FOTHERINGHAY, Northants. COLLEGIATE. *Chancel*—1415. *Nave*—1435 *seq. Rickman*, 301.

FOUNTAINS ABBEY, Yorkshire. CISTERCIAN MONKS. Founded 1132. *Nave*— Begun *c.* 1135. *Chapter House*—*c.* 1150-1160. *Presbytery*—Begun *c.* 1210; finished *c.* 1220. *Eastern Transept*—Built by John of Kent, abbot 1220-1247. *Great North Tower*—Built by Marmaduke Huby, abbot 1494-1526. *Infirmary and Cloister*—Built for the most part by Abbot John of Kent. *Mill*—Before 1147; with later additions. *Eastern Guest-house*—*c.* 1150. *Northern Half of Western Range, and Western Gatehouse*—*c.* 1160-1170. *Warming-house, Frater, Kitchen, Southern Half of Western Range, and Infirmary of Lay-brothers*—Late XII. and early XIII. Cent. W. H. St John Hope in *Yorkshire Arch. Journal*, xv., 1900.

FURNESS, Lancashire. CISTERCIAN MONKS. *Nave and Transepts*—Probably begun soon after the monks became Cistercian in 1148. *Crossing-piers*—Before 1148. *Presbytery*—Early XV. Cent. *Western Tower*—Late XV. Cent. *Chapter House, Northern Part of Dorter Range, and Abbot's House*—Early XIII. Cent. *Chapel without the Gates*—Late XIII. Cent. *Infirmary Hall, Chapel, &c.*—Early XIV. Cent. Mr W. H. St John Hope in *Transactions of Cumberland and Westmorland Archæological Society*, xvi.; and Mr Harold Brakspear in *Transactions of Lancashire and Cheshire Arch. Soc.*, xviii.

GLASTONBURY ABBEY, Somerset. BENEDICTINE MONKS. *Lady Chapel*—Begun after fire of 1184; dedicated 1186. (*Willis,* 13.) *Choir*—Commenced 1184. (*Willis,* 23.) *Choir*—Lengthened two bays by Walter Monington, abbot 1341-1374. (*Willis,* 31.)

GLASTONBURY ST JOHN, Somerset. PARISH CHURCH. 1485.

GLOUCESTER ABBEY. BENEDICTINE MONKS. Became Cathedral in 1541. *Choir*—Foundation stone laid in 1089; dedication in 1100. *Nave—c.* 1120. *Vault of Nave*—1245. *South Aisle of Nave*—1318-1329. *Shrine of Edward II.*—1329-1334. *Work in South Transept*—1331-1337. *Choir and North Transept*—Remodelled 1337-1377. *Choir Vault and Northern Stalls*—Were finished 1337-1357. The east window was probably glazed 1347-1350; according to Winston in *Archæological Journal,* xx. *North Transept*—Remodelled 1368-1374. *East Walk of Cloister up to Chapter House Doorway*—1351-1377. *Cloisters*—Completed 1381-1412. *West Front, two West Bays of Nave, and probably South Porch*—1421-1437. *Central Tower*—Begun 1450-1457; finished by the monk Tully, who became Bishop of St David's in 1460. *Lady Chapel*—Begun 1457-1472; finished 1472-1498. Mr W. H. St John Hope's *Notes on the Benedictine Abbey of St Peter at Gloucester,* and Professor Willis, *Arch. Institute,* 1860.

GREAT BOOKHAM, Surrey. PARISH CHURCH. *Chancel*—1341. *Rickman,* 240.

GREAT PONTON, Lincolnshire. PARISH CHURCH. *c.* 1519. *Rickman,* 317.

GUISBOROUGH PRIORY, Yorkshire. AUSTIN CANONS. *Choir*—After the fire of 1289; probably was building in 1309.

HARLESTON, Northants. PARISH CHURCH. *Chancel*—1320. *Nave*—1325. *Churches of Northants,* 266 *seq.*

HARTLEPOOL, Durham. PARISH CHURCH. *c.* 1190. *Arch. Aeliana,* xvii. 201.

HAVERFORDWEST PRIORY, Pembroke. AUGUSTINIAN CANONS. Probably *c.* 1220. *Rickman,* 162.

HAWTON, Notts. PARISH CHURCH. *Chancel*—Second quarter of XIV. Cent. *Tower*—*c.* 1483. *Rickman,* 310.

HAYLES, Gloucester. CISTERCIAN MONKS. Founded 1246. *Church,* with thirteen altars, hallowed 1251. *New Work,* in consequence of gift of the Holy Blood, begun 1270 and finished 1277. Mr Harold Brakspear in *Bristol and Gloucester Transactions,* xxiv. 126-135.

HEDON, Yorkshire. PARISH CHURCH. *South Transept*—End of XII. Cent. *Chancel and North Transept*—First half of XIII. Cent. *Nave*—Probably commenced in the last quarter of the XIII. Cent.; its western bay probably not earlier than 1325. *Central Tower*—1427-1437. *Hedon,* by Mr J. R. Boyle; and G. E. Street in *Archæologia,* xlviii.

HEREFORD CATHEDRAL. SECULAR CANONS. *Choir*—Begun 1079-1095; dedication 1110. (*William of Malmesbury.*) *East Wall of South Transept*—Ditto. *Nave*—Completed 1131-1148. (*William of Wycumbe.*) *East Transept*—1186-1199. (*Sir G. G. Scott.*) *Lady Chapel—c.* 1220. *Choir Clerestory—c.* 1250. *North Transept—c.* 1260. *Inner North Porch—c.* 1288-1300. *Remodelling of Aisles—c.* 1282-1350. *Central Tower*—1325-1352 (*Hills*); 1316-1327 (*Scott*). *Vaulting of South Transept—c.* 1400. *Vicar's Cloister—c.* 1490. *Bishop Audley's Chantry—c.* 1500. *Outer North Porch—c.* 1520-1530. *Cloisters—c.* 1520. *Fall of Western Tower, Shortening and Remodelling of Nave by Wyatt*—1786-1796. Gordon Hills in *Journal of British Archæological Institute,* 1871.

HEXHAM ABBEY, Northumberland. AUSTIN CANONS. *Choir*—Probably *c.* 1180— *c.* 1210. *Transept*—Probably *c.* 1215—*c.* 1230. Monograph by Mr C. C. Hodges, with measured drawings.

HIGHAM FERRERS, Northants. The College. 1422 *seq. Rickman*, 298.

HILLESDON, Bucks. PARISH CHURCH. 1493. *Rickman*, 313.

HINGHAM, Norfolk. PARISH CHURCH. Built by Remigius, who was rector 1316-1359.

HINTON CHARTERHOUSE, Somerset. CARTHUSIAN MONKS. Founded 1232. *Chapter House, with Treasury over, and Fragment of Church. Rickman*, 168.

HITCHIN, Hertford. PARISH CHURCH. *Pier Arcade*—Finished before 1302. *Rickman*, 235.

HOWDEN, Yorkshire. Became Collegiate in 1265. *Transepts, Nave, and West Front* —*c.* 1265—*c.* 1310. *Choir*—*c.* 1310—*c.* 1330. *Chapter House*—1380-1407. *Central Tower*—Middle stage, first quarter of XV. Cent.; upper stage, end of XV. Cent. *Mr John Bilson.*

HULL, HOLY TRINITY, Yorkshire. PARISH CHURCH. Chapel to Hessle Church till 1661. Said to have been begun in 1285. *Transept*, with crossing, built first. William Scale was buried "in the *New* Chapel" in 1327. *Choir*—Probably unfinished in 1350. Work was being done in the *Nave c.* 1389 and in 1395. *Tower*—Upper stages probably 1520-1529. See Mr J. R. Boyle's monograph (Brown, Hull, 1890).

HURLEY, Berks. BENEDICTINE PRIORY. 1082-1089. (*Rickman*, 86.) Present church not earlier than *c.* 1120. *Mr W. H. St John Hope.*

HYTHE, Kent. PARISH CHURCH. Early XIII. Cent. *Arch. Cant.*, xviii. 403.

IFFLEY, Oxford. PARISH CHURCH. Given to Kenilworth Priory *c.* 1160; probably built soon after. *Rickman*, 92.

ILMINSTER, Somerset. PARISH CHURCH. *c.* 1490.

INGOLDMELLS, Lincolnshire. PARISH CHURCH. *Aisles, South Porch, Tower, and Font*—1346. *Rickman*, 241.

IPSWICH, ST LAWRENCE, Suffolk. PARISH CHURCH. 1420-1431. *Rickman*, 297.

IRON ACTON, Gloucester. PARISH CHURCH. *Tower*—*c.* 1430. *Rickman*, 299.

JEDBURGH ABBEY, Roxburgh. AUSTIN CANONS. *c.* 1175—*c.* 1190. Mr C. C. Hodges' *Hexham.*

JERVAULX ABBEY, Yorkshire. CISTERCIAN MONKS. May be *c.* 1170—*c.* 1190.

KENILWORTH PRIORY, Warwick. AUSTIN CANONS. Founded in 1122. *Rickman*, 92.

KETTON, Rutland. PARISH CHURCH. Indulgence in 1232 to all who would contribute to the building or reparation. *Rickman*, 168.

KIRKHAM PRIORY, Yorkshire. AUSTIN CANONS. Founded 1121. *Outer Parlour* —*c.* 1190. *Presbytery*—*c.* 1240. *Gateway*—Finished 1296. Mr C. C. Hodges' *Hexham;* and *Rickman*, 92.

KIRKSTALL ABBEY, Yorkshire. CISTERCIAN MONKS. Removed to present site in 1152; the church and all the claustral buildings of the Abbey are recorded to have been finished by the first Abbot, Alexander.

LACOCK ABBEY, Wilts. AUSTIN CANONESSES. Was founded 1232 by Ela, Countess of Salisbury, and the buildings are of the date of the foundation. There was a large Lady Chapel being erected 1320, of which a building agreement exists, but the chapel is destroyed. *Mr Harold Brakspear.*

LAMBETH, Surrey. CHAPEL OF ARCHBISHOP'S PALACE. First half of XIII. Cent.

LANERCOST PRIORY, Cumberland. AUSTIN CANONS. Consecration in 1169; probably only of the ground story of the choir. The works progressed slowly, upwards and westwards, till the nave and west front were complete, *c.* 1250. Mr E. R. Tate in *Builder*, 1st October 1898.

LASTINGHAM, Yorkshire. BENEDICTINE MONKS. *Crypt—c.* 1080. The present Parish Church is but the Choir and Crossing of the Monastic Church contemplated. *Rickman*, 82.

LAVENHAM, Suffolk. PARISH CHURCH. *Vestry*—1470-1486. *Porch—c.* 1529. (*Rickman*, 308.) *Nave*—Early XVI. Cent. *Suffolk Archæological Institute*, vi. 114, and ix. 370.

LEEDS, ST JOHN, Yorkshire. PARISH CHURCH. Consecrated 1634.

LEOMINSTER PRIORY, Hereford. BENEDICTINE MONKS. Granted to Reading Abbey in 1121. *Nave*—A consecration in 1130. *Lower Part of Tower*—Late XII. Cent. *Inner Aisle; and South Doorway*, not *in situ*—Before the consecration of 1239. *Outer South Aisle*—First half of XIV. Cent. See *Archæological Journal*, x.

LEWES PRIORY, Sussex. CLUNIAC MONKS. Founded 1077. Enlarged 1091-1098, and again in 1142-1147. See paper by Mr W. H. St John Hope in *Archæological Journal*, vol. xl.

LICHFIELD CATHEDRAL, Stafford. SECULAR CANONS. *Choir, Ground Story—c.* 1195. (*Prior*, 119 and 157.) *South Transept—c.* 1220. (*Willis.*) *North Transept, Chapter House, and Vestibule—c.* 1240. (*Willis.*) *Nave*—Second half of XIII. Cent. *West Front and Towers*—Probably *c.* 1280-1330. *Lady Chapel*—Begun 1310; unfinished in 1331. (*Rickman*, 236.) *Presbytery and Upper Choir*—Second quarter of XIV. Cent. *South-west Spire*—Ditto. *North-west Spire and Upper Part of Tower* is a XV. Cent. copy of the south-west steeple. (*J. T. Irvine.*) *Choir Clerestory Repaired and Central Spire Rebuilt*—After 1661. See Willis in *Archæological Journal*, 1861.

LILLESHALL ABBEY, Shropshire. AUSTIN CANONS. The Abbey was founded in 1145. *Presbytery, Crossing,* and *South Transept* of this date remain, together with part of *Eastern Range. Mr Harold Brakspear.*

LINCOLN CATHEDRAL. SECULAR CANONS. *West Front*—Remigius' work, commenced between 1072 and 1075; consecrated 1092. *Lower Portions of West Towers and North and South Gables—c.* 1140. *West Doorways—c.* 1150. *Choir and Eastern Transepts*—1192—*c.* 1200. *Great Transept*—Probably followed choir. *Galilee Porch—c.* 1230. *Chapter House*—Is mentioned 1220-1235. *Nave* —Timber for roof was bequeathed in 1233. *Central Tower*—Fell in 1237-1239, and was rebuilt. *Presbytery*—1256—*c.* 1320; but St Hugh's body was translated to it in 1280. *Cloister, South Side*—1296. *Upper Stage of Central Tower*—1307. *South Transept End*—Probably after the death of Bishop Dalderby in 1319. *Upper Stories of Western Towers*—Before 1380. *Chantry Chapel of Bishop Fleming*, died 1430-1431. *Chantry Chapel of Bishop Russell*, died 1494. *Chantry Chapel of Bishop Longland*, died 1547. See Sharpe's *Lincoln Excursion;* and Venables in *Archæological Journal*, xl.

LINCOLN, ST MARY-LE-WIGFORD. PARISH CHURCH. Was building in 1228. *Rickman*, 168.

LINDISFARNE PRIORY, Northumberland. BENEDICTINE MONKS. Some part was finished before *c.* 1128, but the Church was probably not completed till *c.* 1150. Mr C. C. Hodges in *Builder*, 1st June 1895 ; and Mr John Bilson's *Beginnings*, 315, 316.

LITTLE KIMBLE, Bucks. PARISH CHURCH. Consecrated 1317. *Rickman*, 237.

LITTLE MALVERN PRIORY, Worcester. PARISH CHURCH. Built by Bishop Alcocke between 1476 and 1482. *Bloxam*, 273.

LLANDAFF CATHEDRAL, Glamorgan. SECULAR CANONS. *Remains of Norman Choir*—1120-1133. *Nave Arcades*—*c.* 1190. (*Prior*, 157.) *West Front*—Early XIII. Cent. *Chapter House*—1244-1265. *Lady Chapel*—*c.* 1280. *South-west Tower*—End of XV. Cent. See monograph by Mr J. H. James.

LLANIDLOES, Montgomery. PARISH CHURCH. Piers and arches probably brought from Cwm Hir in 1542 ; the Abbey was dissolved in 1536. These piers and arches appear to belong to the last years of the XII. Cent.

LLANTHONY PRIORY, Monmouth. AUSTIN CANONS. Last quarter of XII. Cent. See Freeman in *Archæologia Cambrensis*, Series I., vol. i. ; and *Prior*, 157.

LONDON, AUSTIN FRIARS. AUGUSTINIAN FRIARS ; now Dutch Church. Rebuilding 1354 ; again *c.* 1475. Mr A. S. Walker in *Builder*, 4th April 1896.

LONDON, ST ANDREW UNDERSHAFT. 1520-1532. *Stow.*

LONDON, ST BARTHOLOMEW'S PRIORY, Smithfield. AUSTIN CANONS. 1123-1133. *Clerestory*—Early XV. Cent. *Architectural Review*, i. 1.

LONDON, ST ETHELDREDA, Ely Place, Holborn. Chapel of the Palace of the Bishops of Ely. *c.* 1290—*c.* 1300. Sir G. G. Scott in *Lectures*, i. 184.

LONDON, ST HELEN, Bishopsgate. The North Aisle was the Chapel of the Benedictine Nunnery ; the South Aisle was Parochial. The screen between them was removed *c.* 1538. *Side Chapels*—Probably XIV. Cent. *Tall Arches of Nave*—Probably 1475.

LONDON, SAVOY CHAPEL. 1505 *seq. Rickman*, 313.

LONDON, CHURCH OF KNIGHTS TEMPLARS. *Nave*—Consecrated 1185. *Choir*— Consecrated 1240. *Rickman*, 111 and 171.

LONDON, Tower of London. ST JOHN'S CHAPEL. Last quarter of XI. Cent.

LONG MELFORD, Suffolk. PARISH CHURCH. *Chancel*—Finished 1479. The seven western bays of the *Nave* are inscribed 1481. *South Aisle*—*c.* 1484. *Lady Chapel*—Finished *c.* 1496. Monograph by Lauriston Conder.

LOUTH, Lincolnshire. PARISH CHURCH. *Chancel*—*c.* 1400-1445. *Tower*—*c.* 1445-1500. *Spire*—1501-1515. James Fowler in *Transactions of Lincoln Archæological Society*, 1873 ; and J. J. Creswell in do., 1897.

LOUTH PARK ABBEY, Lincolnshire. CISTERCIAN MONKS. Founded in 1139 ; the foundations have been excavated. The work varies from 1139 to the XIII. Cent. west front. *Assoc. Arch. Soc. Reports*, vol. xii.

LOW HAM, Somerset. PARISH CHURCH. Built by Sir Richard Hext, who died in 1624. Murray's *Somerset*, 444.

LUDLOW, Shropshire. Enlarged when it became Collegiate in the latter part of the XIV. Cent. *Tower* and much rebuilding in late XV. Cent. Mr Thomas Wright's *Guide to Ludlow*.

LUTON, Bedford. PARISH CHURCH. *Chancel*—1430-1440. *North Chapel*—*c.* 1460. *Rickman*, 299.

LYNN, CHAPEL OF RED MOUNT, Norfolk. 1484-1485. *Corporation Records.*

LYNN, ST MARGARET, Norfolk. *Earliest Work*—1091-1119. *North-west Tower*— Ordered to be built 1453. *South Aisle of Nave*—Before 1483. *North Aisle of Chancel*—Ordered to be rebuilt 1472. *Clerestories*—Rebuilt and new roofs, 1491.

South Aisle of Chancel—Nearly finished in 1494. *Spire* on south-west tower was blown down in 1741. Wooden central octagon, 132 feet high, was taken down, and *Nave* rebuilt by 1745. *Fen and Marshland Churches*, ii.

LYNN, St Nicholas, Norfolk. Chapel to St Margaret. Was being pulled down in 1413. Built entirely by voluntary contributions before 1419. See *Lynn St Nicholas*, by Mr E. M. Beloe, p. 151.

MAIDSTONE, All Saints', Kent. The Church was made Collegiate by Archbishop Courtenay, 1381-1396. The rebuilding was largely complete in 1395. Whichcord in Weale's *Quarterly Papers*, iv.

MALLING, Kent. St Leonard's Tower. Built by Gundulf, Bishop of Rochester from 1077 to 1108.

MALLING ABBEY, Kent. Benedictine Nuns. *Lower Part of West Front*—By Bishop Gundulf, *c.* 1077-1108. *Upper Part*—*c.* 1150. *Remains of Cloister*—*c.* 1190.

MALMESBURY ABBEY, Wiltshire. Benedictine Monks. *Nave*—The Church was not commenced by Roger, Bishop of Salisbury, who died 1139, but after the monastery regained its independence in 1140; for William of Malmesbury, whose History ends in 1142, does not mention building as going on in the Church. (Bilson's *Beginnings*, 309.) *Clerestory and Vault*—Second quarter of XIV. Cent.

MALTON PRIORY, OLD, Yorkshire. Gilbertine Canons. Last quarter of XII. Cent.

MALVERN PRIORY, Worcester. Benedictine Monks. Said to have been begun *c.* 1084. *Rebuilding* begun *c.* 1450; service resumed 1460. Completed between 1476 and 1486. Tiles have dates 1453 and 1456. *Builder*, 2nd January 1897.

MANCHESTER CATHEDRAL, Lancashire. Made Collegiate in 1422; Cathedral in 1847. *Choir and Chapter House*—1422-1458. *Nave*—Said to have been completed 1465-1481. *Chapel of Holy Trinity*—1498. *Jesus Chapel* (Vestry and Library)—1506. *St James' Chantry or Ducie Chapel; also the Choir Stalls; and St George's Chapel*—1508. *Derby and Ely Chapels*—*c.* 1515. *Lady Chapel*—Remodelled 1518-1535. Perkins' *Manchester Cathedral*, 6.

MELBOURNE, Derbyshire. Parish Church. First half of XII. Cent.

MEOPHAM, Kent. Parish Church. Built 1315 *seq.* Repaired 1381-1396. *Rickman*, 237 and 290.

MILTON ABBEY, Dorset. Benedictine Monks. *Choir and South Transept*—Commenced after fire of 1309. *Vaults of Tower and Transept*—1481. Roland Paul in *Builder*, 5th January 1901.

MINSTER, THANET, Kent. Benedictine Nuns. Early Norman vaulting remains; also Tudor work.

MINSTER, THANET, Kent. Nuns' Church. Also Parochial. *Nave*—Probably third quarter of XII. Cent. *Vaulted Chancel and Transept*—First half of XIII. Cent.

MONKTON, Pembroke. Benedictine Monks. Probably first half of XII. Cent.

NANTWICH, Cheshire. Collegiate. *Chancel*—1327-1333.

NETLEY ABBEY, Hants. Cistercian Monks. Begun in 1239. *Rickman*, 170.

NEW ROMNEY, Kent. Parish Church. *c.* 1190 and first half of XIV. Cent. *Arch. Cant.*, xiii. 466.

NEW SHOREHAM, Sussex. ? Collegiate. *Nave, Four Arches of Crossing, Lower Part of Tower*—*c.* 1130. *Choir, Pier-arcades, with North and South Aisles and their Vaults, and Upper Part of Tower—c.* 1175. *Upper Parts of Choir—c.* 1190, 1210. E. Sharpe's monograph; and *Arch. Aeliana*, xvii. 217.

NORTHAMPTON, St Peter. Parish Church. *c.* 1140-1160. *Proceedings of Soc. of Ant.*, 1902, 74.

NORTHAMPTON, St Sepulchre. Parish Church. *c.* 1100—*c.* 1110. *Cox and Serjeantson's Monograph.*

NORTHLEACH, Gloucester. Parish Church. *Nave*—1458. *Roof*—Soon after. *Rickman*, 306.

NORTH WALSHAM, Norfolk. Parish Church. Probably rebuilt after destruction in the rising of 1381. The heraldic bearings in the porch prove that this was built before 1405.

NORWICH CATHEDRAL, Norfolk. Benedictine Monks. *Choir, Transepts, East Nave as far west as the Altar of the Holy Cross*—Built by Herbert, who was Bishop 1096-1119. *Foundation Stone laid*—1096. *West Nave and Tower*—Built by Eborard, who was Bishop 1121-1145. *St Ethelbert's Gateway*—After riots of 1272. *Chapel of Charnel House*—1310-1325. *Presbytery Clerestory*—Probably after fall of spire, *c.* 1362. *Erpingham Gate*—1416-1425. *Vault of Nave*—After 1463-1472. *Vault of Presbytery and alteration of pier-arches*—1472-1499. *Vault of Transepts, and Chantry Chapel of Bishop Nykke*—1501-1536. *Chapter House*, begun 1289; *Cloister*, begun opposite chapter house, 1297; east and south alley, 1299-1325; west alley, 1416-1426; north alley finished, 1430. *W. H. St John Hope.*

OAKHAM, Rutland. Hall of King's Manor. 1165-1191. *Rickman*, 104.

OTTERY ST MARY, Devon. Collegiate. Bishop Grandisson's rebuilding began *c.* 1337.

OXFORD, All Souls' College. *South Quadrangle*—Foundation 1438. *Chapel*—Consecrated 1442.

OXFORD, Balliol College. *Library*—1431-1460.

OXFORD, Bodleian Library. *Older Portion*—1613.

OXFORD, Brasenose College. *Chapel*—Consecrated 1666.

OXFORD CATHEDRAL. 1154-1180. Confirmation of charters to the Austin Canons in 1158. A consecration in 1180. *Chapter House—c.* 1220. *Lady Chapel—c.* 1220. *Latin Chapel*—Built before 1355. *Choir Vault—c.* 1478-1503. (*Rickman*, 103, 244.) Became Cathedral 1546.

OXFORD, Christ Church. College. *Hall, Kitchen, and Part of Great Quadrangle*—1528-1530. *Staircase to Hall, Fan Vault*—1640. *Great Quadrangle*—Finished 1665.

OXFORD, Corpus Christi College. *Chief Buildings and Chapel*—1516-1520.

OXFORD, Divinity School. 1445-1480.

OXFORD, Exeter College. *Quadrangle, Hall, &c.*—1610-1618.

OXFORD, Jesus College. Founded 1571.

OXFORD, Kettel Hall, Broad Street. 1615.

OXFORD, Lincoln College. *Hall, Library and North Quadrangle*—1436-1438. *South Quadrangle*—1612. *Chapel*—Consecrated 1631.

OXFORD, Magdalen College. 1474-1480. *Chapel*—Consecrated 1480. *South Cloister*—1490. *Tower*—Completed 1505.

OXFORD, Merton College. *Chapel*—Probably commenced about 1277, soon after the founder's death. *Vestry of Chapel*—1310. *Library—c.* 1380. Transepts and crossing completed, except the top of the *Tower*, in 1424. *Tower*—Finished 1450. *Great Southern Quadrangle*—1610.

OXFORD, NEW COLLEGE. *Foundation Stone* laid 1380. *New Buildings* finished 1386. *Cloisters and Bell Tower* completed 1400.

OXFORD, ORIEL COLLEGE. *South and West Sides of Quadrangle*—1620-1637.

OXFORD, ST ALDATE. PARISH CHURCH. *South Aisle*—1335. *Rickman*, 238.

OXFORD, ST JOHN'S COLLEGE. *Gateway, Tower and Part of West Front*—1437. *Library and First Quadrangle*—1597. *Inner Quadrangle and Library*—1631-1635.

OXFORD, ST MARY'S CHURCH. *Tower*—1280-1290. *Spire*—First half of XIV. Cent. *Chancel*—Begun 1462. *Nave*—1490-1503. *Porch*—1637. *Mr T. G. Jackson's monograph.*

OXFORD, ST MARY MAGDALEN. PARISH CHURCH. *South Aisle*—1318-1337. *Tower* —Completed 1505.

OXFORD, ST MARY'S HALL. *Chapel, &c.*—1640.

OXFORD, ST PETER IN THE EAST. PARISH CHURCH. *Crypt and Chancel and Doorway* —*c.* 1170.

OXFORD, SCHOOLS' QUADRANGLE. 1610-1618.

OXFORD, UNIVERSITY COLLEGE. *West Quadrangle*—Begun 1634. *Hall*—Completed *c.* 1657.

OXFORD, WADHAM COLLEGE. 1610-1613.

The above chronology of Oxford buildings is taken from Parker's *Visitors' Guide to Oxford.*

PATRINGTON, Yorkshire. PARISH CHURCH. *Transepts*—Probably first quarter of XIV. Cent. *Choir, Nave, and Tower*—Second quarter of XIV. Cent. *Spire* —Probably early XV. Cent. See Mr J. T. Micklethwaite's paper in *Yorkshire Arch. Journal*, ix. 99.

PERSHORE ABBEY, Worcester. BENEDICTINE MONKS. *South Transept*—Probably late XI. Cent. *Choir*—The earlier work is 1223-1239. *Upper Choir and Central Tower*—After the fire of 1288. *Rickman*, 165; and *Arch. Soc. Reports*, iv. 355.

PETERBOROUGH ABBEY. BENEDICTINE MONKS. Became Cathedral in 1541. *Foundations* laid in 1117 or 1118. The monks entered the "nova ecclesia" in 1140 or 1143. The work done probably included the Pier-arcade and Triforium of the *Choir*; of part of the *Transepts*; of the two Eastern Bays of the *Nave*; and most of the South Aisle Wall. The *Choir* and *Transepts* were probably finished 1155-1175; also three stages of the *Central Tower* and the six Central Bays of the *Nave* except the Clerestory. The Clerestory of the *Nave*; the West Bays of the Nave; and the *Western Transept*—Probably 1177-1193. *West Front*—Probably built by Acharius, 1201-1214. (*Mr J. T. Irvine.*) *Bell Tower*—1274-1295. *South-west Spire*—Probably second half of XIV. Cent. *Bishop's Gateway* —1303. *Porch in West Front*—*c.* 1370. *Eastern Chapels*—Begun between 1438 and 1471; finished between 1496 and 1528. Mr J. T. Irvine and Craddock's *Peterborough Cathedral*; and *Journal of the R.I.B.A.*, 26th November 1898.

PORCHESTER, Hampshire. A Priory of Austin Canons was founded here in 1133.

PORTSMOUTH, ST THOMAS, Hampshire. AUSTIN CANONS. They settled here between 1180 and 1200, and before 1189 obtained the confirmation of a charter for the Chapel of St Thomas the Martyr, "which they had begun to build." *Rickman*, 109.

POYNINGS, Sussex. PARISH CHURCH. 1368 *seq. Rickman*, 247.

RAMSEY, Huntingdon. PARISH CHURCH, belonging to Benedictine Abbey. Last half of XII. Cent.

READING ABBEY, Berkshire. BENEDICTINE MONKS. Ruins. Founded 1121.

RIEVAULX ABBEY, Yorkshire. CISTERCIAN MONKS. *Fragments of Nave and Transept*—Built with stone brought by a canal cut *c.* 1145. *Frater, Transepts, and Choir* are of Hollins stone brought by a canal, the ground for which was acquired between 1193 and 1203. Mr H. A. Rye in *Archæological Journal*, March 1900.

RIPON MINSTER, Yorkshire. SECULAR CANONS. Became Cathedral in 1836. Built 1154-1181. *West Front—c.* 1233. *East Front*—Probably 1288-1300. *Nave*—Aisles begun in 1502 or 1503. Sir G. G. Scott in *Archæological Journal*, December 1874.

ROCHE ABBEY, Yorkshire. CISTERCIAN MONKS. Founded in 1147, and soon largely endowed with land. Probably third quarter of XII. Cent. Gordon Hills in *Archæological Journal*, xxx. 421; and *Assoc. Soc. Reports*, xvii. 39, xviii. 35, xix. 392.

ROCHESTER CATHEDRAL, Kent. BENEDICTINE MONKS. *Parts of Nave and Crypt*—Gundulf's work, 1077-1108. *Nave*—Chiefly 1115-1130. *Presbytery and Eastern Transept*—Begun *c.* 1200. *Choir*—Finished 1227. *North Transept*—*c.* 1240-1255. *South Transept—c.* 1280 *seq. Lady Chapel—c.* 1512. *Rochester Cathedral*, by Mr W. H. St John Hope.

ROMSEY ABBEY, Hampshire. BENEDICTINE NUNS. The *Eastern Parts* are probably not later than 1120. (Mr E. P. Loftus Brock in *Builder*, 5th October 1895.) Commenced *c.* 1110. (Mr Bilson's *Beginnings*, 307.) *Western Nave and Façade —c.* 1220.

ROTHERHAM, Yorkshire. COLLEGIATE. 1480-1501.

ROTHWELL, Northants. PARISH CHURCH. Last half of XII. Cent.

RYARSH, Kent. PARISH CHURCH. *Tower*—1450. *Rickman*, 305.

RYE, Sussex. PARISH CHURCH. *c.* 1195. *Prior*, 156.

ST ALBANS ABBEY, Hertfordshire. BENEDICTINE MONKS. Became a Cathedral in 1877. Earliest portions built 1077-1088. Dedicated and probably completed 1115. *West Front*—Commenced 1195-1214. *Completion of West Front, and Western Bays of Nave*—1214-1235. *Choir Clerestory*—Begun 1257. *Antechapel*—1260-1326. *Lady Chapel*—1291-1326. *St Alban's Shrine*—1302-1308. *Rebuilding of East Bays of South Nave*—After 1323. *Cloister*—1323, 1335, 1349, 1360. *Rood Screen*—1340-1350. *Gatehouse*—1349-1396. *Reredos*—1476-1484. *Monographs by Mr James Neale and Messrs Buckler.*

ST CROSS, Winchester, Hants. Hospital. Probably none of it is earlier than *c.* 1160, except the *Sacristy.*

ST DAVID'S CATHEDRAL, Pembroke. SECULAR CANONS. Begun 1180. Repairs after fall of Central Tower in 1220. *Lady Chapel*—1296-1328. *Rood Screen*—1324-1347. *Nave Roof*—1472-1509. *Bishop Vaughan's Chapel—c.* 1509. See Jones and Freeman's *St David's.*

SALISBURY CATHEDRAL, Wilts. SECULAR CANONS. Begun 1220. Consecration in 1225. Another consecration in 1258; finished 1266. *Chapter House and Cloister*—1263-1284. *West Front*—Probably late in XIII. Cent. *Upper Tower and Spire*—Second half of XIV. Cent. *Rickman*, 164, 175, 239.

SARUM, OLD, Wilts. CATHEDRAL. Consecrated 1092. Rebuilt 1115-1139. Britton's *Salisbury*, ii. *Rickman*, 90.

SANDWICH, St Bartholomew, Kent. Chapel of Hospital. Founded by Thomas Craythorn in 1190. *North Aisle*—Finished by Sir Humphrey Sandwich in 1230. *Rickman*, 172. *Archæologia Cantiana*, vol. xv. 7.

SCARBOROUGH, St Mary, Yorkshire. Parish Church. Given by Richard I. to the Abbey of Citeaux in 1198.

SEDGEFIELD, Durham. Parish Church. Probably 1242-1280. Mr C. C. Hodges in *Archæologia Aeliana*, xvi.

SELBY ABBEY, Yorkshire. Benedictine Monks. Founded 1069. *East Nave*— *c.* 1097-1123. *Central Nave*—*c.* 1123-1175. *West Nave, West Front, and North Porch*—*c.* 1175—*c.* 1190. *Parts of Upper Nave and West Front*—*c.* 1190— *c.* 1220. *Part of Choir Aisles and Sacristy*—*c.* 1280-1300. *Choir*—Completed in second quarter of XIV. Cent. Mr C. C. Hodges in *Yorkshire Archæological Journal*, xii. 340.

SHERBORNE ABBEY, Dorset. Benedictine Monks. Begun in 1107. *Choir*— Vaulted 1436-1459. *Nave*—Vaulted 1475-1504. R. H. Carpenter in *Journal of R.I.B.A.*, 19th March 1877.

SHOBDON, Hereford. Parish Church. Ruins. 1141-1150. *Rickman*, 98.

SHOTTESBROOKE, Berkshire. Collegiate. Founded 1337. Monograph by Mr Butterfield.

SHREWSBURY ABBEY, Shropshire. Benedictine Monks. *Choir*, now destroyed, begun 1083. *Builder*, xlviii. 740.

SKELTON, Yorkshire. Parish Church. Finished before 1247. Monograph by E. Christian.

SKIRLAUGH, Yorkshire. Chapel. Shortly before 1405. *Bloxam*, 270.

SLEAFORD, Lincolnshire. Parish Church. *Chancel*—1403. *Rickman*, 296.

SOUTHWARK, St Saviour or St Mary Overie. Austin Canons. Burnt in 1213. Rebuilt by Peter de Rupibus, Bishop of Winchester from 1204 to 1238—*East Limb*, probably up to crossing. *North Transept*, then *South Transept*—Probably after 1273. *Reredos*—By Bishop Fox, of Winchester, *c.* 1500. *Nave*—Demolished and rebuilt 1833; again demolished and rebuilt 1895. Monograph by F. T. Dollman (1881). Became a cathedral 1st May 1905.

SOUTHWELL MINSTER, Notts. Secular Canons. Became Cathedral in 1884. Commenced 1108-1114. *Nave*—Second quarter of XII. Cent. *Choir* was building in 1233; a *Chantry* was founded in it in 1241. *Chapter House*—*c.* 1294. (*Guide to Southwell*, by Rev. G. M. Livett.) In the glass are the arms of Eleanor of Castile, who died in 1290.

SOUTHWOLD, Suffolk. Parish Church. Said to have been finished 1460-1461. *Porch*—1488-1489. *Suffolk Arch. Institute*, viii. 413.

STAMFORD, St John. Parish Church. Finished in 1451. *Rickman*, 305.

STAMFORD, St Leonard's Priory, Lincolnshire. Benedictine Monks. End of XII. Cent.

STANTON HAROLD, Leicestershire. Parish Church. 1653.

STAVERDALE PRIORY, Somerset. Austin Canons. *Nave, Choir, and Chantry Chapel*—Consecrated 1443. *Rickman*, 303.

STEWKLEY, Bucks. Parish Church. Granted to Kenilworth Priory, *c.* 1150. *Rickman*, 92.

STEYNING, Sussex. Parish Church. *c.* 1160. *Mr E. Sharpe.*

STOKE GOLDINGHAM, Leicester. Parish Church. 1275-1290. Weale's *Quarterly Papers*, i.

STONE, Kent Parish Church. Probably 1251-1274. Monograph by G. E. Street.

STOW, Lincolnshire. PARISH CHURCH. *Chancel*—1123-1148. Mr Bilson's *Beginnings*.

STRATA FLORIDA ABBEY, Cardigan. CISTERCIAN MONKS. 1166-1203. *S. W. Williams' monograph.*

STRATFORD ON AVON, Warwick. COLLEGIATE. *Choir*—1465-1491. *Rickman,* 308.

SUTTON ASHFIELD, Notts. PARISH CHURCH. Soon after 1391. Bishop Buckingham's *Mem.,* 379.

SUTTON ST MARY, or LONG SUTTON, Lincolnshire. PARISH CHURCH. Site granted *c.* 1180. *Fen and Marshland Churches,* iii. 25.

SWAFFHAM, Norfolk. PARISH CHURCH. *Chancel*—1474. *Tower*—Finished 1510.

TATTERSHALL, Lincolnshire. Castle and Church. Both 1433-1455. *Rickman,* 299.

TENTERDEN, Kent. PARISH CHURCH. *Tower*—1462. *Rickman,* 308.

TERRINGTON ST CLEMENT, Norfolk. PARISH CHURCH. *c.* 1377-1399. *Fen and Marshland Churches,* i. 37. Dr Seccombe in *Norfolk Archæology,* xii. ; 1389-1425.

TEWKESBURY ABBEY, Gloucester. BENEDICTINE MONKS. The Lordship of Tewkesbury was granted in 1087 to Robert Fitz-Hamon, who founded the Abbey. The monks entered their new Church in 1102. In 1123 there was a consecration, probably of the whole Church, including the Nave. *Lady Chapel*—First half of XIII. Cent. *Remodelling of Choir*—Second quarter of XIV. Cent. *Rickman,* 89.

THORNEY ABBEY, Cambridge. BENEDICTINE MONKS. *Part of Nave*—1085-1108. *Rickman,* 85.

THORNTON ABBEY, Lincolnshire. AUSTIN CANONS. Became an Abbey in 1148. *Church*—Begun in 1263. *Chapter House*—Begun in 1282 ; paved in 1308. *Gatehouse*—1382. *Barbican*—Perhaps 1520. Mr C. C. Hodges in *Reliquary,* ii. 1.

TIDESWELL, Derbyshire. PARISH CHURCH. John Foljambe, who "did many good things in the building of the Church," died in 1358, and is buried in the Chancel.

TINTERN ABBEY, Monmouth. CISTERCIAN MONKS. Founded 1131. *Conventual Buildings*—Rebuilt middle of XIII. Cent. *Church*—Begun 1269 ; and *Presbytery, South Transept, Crossing,* and two bays of the *Nave* finished 1288, when Mass was said at the High Altar. Rest of *Nave* and part of *North Transept* not finished till middle of XIV. Cent. *Mr Harold Brakspear.*

TONG, Shropshire. COLLEGIATE. 1401-1411. *Rickman,* 295.

TUTBURY PRIORY, Stafford. BENEDICTINE MONKS. Founded in 1080 ; founder interred in it in 1090. Mr C. Lynam in *Archæological Journal,* New Series, iii. 148.

TUXFORD, Notts. PARISH CHURCH. *Building*—1473. *Chancel*—1495. *Rickman,* 309.

TYNEMOUTH PRIORY, Northumberland. BENEDICTINE MONKS. Last years of XII. Cent. *Lady Chapel*—*c.* 1400. *Arch. Aeliana,* 23, 29.

VALLE CRUCIS ABBEY, near Llangollen, Denbigh. CISTERCIAN MONKS. Said by Dugdale to have been founded *c.* 1200.

WALSBERSWICK, Suffolk. PARISH CHURCH. Dedicated 1493. Unroofed 1695. *Suffolk Arch. Institute,* viii. 418.

WALTHAM ABBEY, Essex. AUSTIN CANONS. *Nave*—Not the work of King Harold in 1062. The rebuilding of the Church was probably commenced after grants of Henry I. in 1120. Building operations were going on in 1125 and 1126. See *Builder,* 30th April and 21st May 1898.

WANBOROUGH, Wilts. PARISH CHURCH. *Tower*—1435. *Rickman,* 301.

WARKWORTH, Northumberland. PARISH CHURCH. *Vaulted Chancel—c.* 1125. Mr J. Bilson's *Beginnings*, 316.

WARWICK, ST MARY. COLLEGIATE. *Chancel*—1381-1391. *Beauchamp Chapel*— Begun 1439. *Nave*—1694-1706. *Rickman*, 290, 302.

WAVERLEY ABBEY, Surrey. CISTERCIAN MONKS. Founded 1128. *Monks' Infirmary with Chapel*—Before 1201, when the latter was hallowed. *New Church*—Begun 1203. Five eastern altars hallowed 1214. Three chapels in *North Transept* 1226. Three chapels in *South Transept* hallowed and *Choir* entered 1231. Completed and hallowed 1278. *Cott. MS. Vesp. A.*, xvi. 90B to 180. *Mr Harold Brakspear.*

WELLS CATHEDRAL, Somerset. SECULAR CANONS. (1.) Begun by Reginald de Bohun, who became Bishop in 1174; and made a large grant to a fabric fund prior to 1180. A charter referring to the "admirable structure of the rising Church" is attested by witnesses who appear elsewhere in 1206 and 1221. Probably he built the *Choir and East of the Transept*. (2.) The rest of the *Transept* and the *Nave* and *North Porch* seem to have been completed in two sections before 1206. (3.) *West Front*—1220 to consecration in 1239. *Undercroft to Chapter House*— *c.* 1270. *Staircase to Chapter House*—*c.* 1286-1300. *Chapter House*—Not finished before 1319. *Lady Chapel*—Finished before 1326. *Central Tower*—Raised and roofed *c.* 1321. *Retrochoir and Remodelling of Choir*—1329-1363. *South-west Tower*—After 1386. *North-west Tower*—After 1424. *Bishop's Palace*—1225-1239. *Ruined Hall of Palace*—1280-1292. *Gatehouse*—1340. Canon Church's *Chapters in the Early History of Wells*.

WENLOCK PRIORY, Shropshire. CLUNIAC MONKS. Last quarter of XII. Cent.

WESTENHANGER, Kent. PARISH CHURCH. 1520. *Rickman*, 317.

WESTMINSTER ABBEY. BENEDICTINE MONKS. Parts underground are the work of Edward the Confessor; begun 1050. *Choir*—Dedicated 1065. (1.) Present Church commenced 1245. In 1253 canvas was bought for the windows of the Chapter House. Choir, Transept, and one bay west of the Crossing, the Revestry, and so much of the Cloister as lay within the South Transept, with its east wall to beyond the doorway of the Chapter House—1245-1260. (2.) Second to fifth eastern bays of the Pier-arcade and Triforium, first to fourth bays in the Clerestory, also first to fourth bays in north walk of Cloister—1260-1269. The monks entered the choir in 1269. (3.) East walk of the Cloister carried to the corner—*c.* 1330-1350. The Cloister was nearly finished in 1352. (4.) West bays of the Nave probably commenced *c.* 1350, and went on slowly under Richard II. (1377-1399); almost stopped in Henry IV.'s time (1399-1413); and were nearly finished by Henry V. (1413-1422); except—(5.) The fifth and sixth bays from the east and the westernmost bay of the *Clerestory*, and the west front. In the vaulting Tudor badges appear—*c.* 1500. (6.) Henry the Seventh's Chapel —1500-1512. Mr J. T. Micklethwaite in *Archæological Journal*, li.

WESTMINSTER HALL. Built by William Rufus, and first used in 1099. Re-modelled and new roof, 1397-1399. *Rickman*, 294.

WESTWICK, Norfolk. PARISH CHURCH. *Tower*—1460 and 1473.

WHISTON, Northants. PARISH CHURCH. Built by Anthony Catesby, who died 1553. *Mr R. P. Brereton.*

WHITBY ABBEY, Yorkshire. BENEDICTINE MONKS. Destroyed by the Danes in 1175, and rebuilt at the beginning of the XIII. Cent.

WIMBORNE MINSTER, Dorset. SECULAR CANONS. *Crossing*—Early XII. Cent. *Central Tower and East Nave*—Third quarter of XII. Cent. *Presbytery—c.* 1220.

Lengthening of Transepts and Nave—XIV. Cent. *Clerestory and Western Tower* —1448-1464. Perkins' *Wimborne Minster.*

WINCHELSEA, Sussex. PARISH CHURCH. The earliest monument is that of Gervase Alard, who was living in 1306. The Chancel appears to be of the first quarter of the XIV. Cent.

WINCHESTER CASTLE. Shire or Great Hall. 1222-1235. *Rickman,* 165.

WINCHESTER CATHEDRAL, Hampshire. BENEDICTINE MONKS. *Crypt and Transept Ends*—Begun 1079, consecrated 1093. *Crossing and Inner Parts of Transept*—Built after the fall of the Central Tower in 1107. *Central Tower*— Probably second half of XII. Cent. *Eastern Part and Lady Chapel*—Begun 1202; the west part of the *Lady Chapel* may be a little later. *Presbytery*— Probably *temp.* Bishop Edington, 1345-1366. *Remodelling of the Nave*—Begun by William of Wykeham in 1371. Probably the *West Front* is of this date; Rest of Nave, 1394 to *c.* 1460. *Reredos*—*c.* 1480. *Remodelling of Lady Chapel*—After 1487 to *c.* 1500. Fox's work in *Presbytery*—1500-1528. *Choir Enclosure*— Dated 1525. *Mr W. H. St John Hope.*

WINCHESTER COLLEGE. 1387-1393. *Chantry Chapel and Library in Middle of Cloister*—1420. *Rickman,* 292.

WINCHCOMBE, Gloucester. PARISH CHURCH. 1456-1474. *Rickman,* 306.

WINDSOR CASTLE, Berkshire. ROYAL CHAPEL OF ST GEORGE. Begun by Edward IV. *c.* 1473; but little done. *South Transept*—1481-1502. *Choir Vault*—Begun in 1507; but unfinished in 1519. Mr Ambrose Poynter, on heraldic evidence, assigned the date of 1528 to the High Vault, and of 1537 to the Aisle Vaults of the *Nave. Rickman,* 314.

WITHAM CHARTERHOUSE, Somerset. CARTHUSIAN MONKS. Chapel of the Frary or House of the Lay Brothers; now Parish Church. 1176-1186. *Rickman,* 109.

WORCESTER CATHEDRAL. BENEDICTINE MONKS. *Crypt*—Begun 1084; Synod held in it in 1092. *West Bays of Nave*—Probably *c.* 1170. (See *Prior,* 91 and 121.) *Retrochoir*—Probably after the fire of 1202 and the canonisation of St Wolfstan in 1203: dedicated 1218. (*Prior,* 162, note.) Foundation stone of *Choir* laid 1224. *Five East Bays of North Nave*—1317-1324. *Guest Hall*—1320. *Frater and Cloister*—1372. *Sub-vault of Frater*—Early XII. Cent. *Tower*— Finished 1374. *Vault of Crossing*—1376. *Two Bays of North Nave and seven of South Nave*—May be *c.* 1350-1377. *Vault of two Western Bays of Nave*— 1377. Willis in *Arch. Journal,* xx.

WORKSOP PRIORY, Notts. AUSTIN CANONS. Probably *c.* 1175. *Assoc. Soc. Reports,* v. 219.

WYMINGTON, Bedford. PARISH CHURCH. Brass of founder, who died in 1391. Brandon's *Parish Churches,* 93.

WYMONDHAM ABBEY, Norfolk. BENEDICTINE MONKS. Founded as a Priory before 1107; became an Abbey in 1448. *Central Tower*—1390-1409. *Font*— *c.* 1410. *Nave and North Aisle, Clerestory and Roofs*—1432-1445. *West Tower* —1445-1478. *South Aisle*—1534. Rev. J. L. Petit's monograph.

YARMOUTH. PARISH CHURCH. Founded and built 1096-1119. *Nave Arcade*— Probably *c.* 1190. *Aisles and West Front*—Perhaps *c.* 1230. A. W. Morant in *Norfolk and Norwich Arch. Soc.,* vii. 215.

YATTON, Somerset. PARISH CHURCH. *Nave and Aisles*—*c.* 1375. Finished in 1475. *Rickman,* 309.

YORK CATHEDRAL. SECULAR CANONS. *Part of Crypt*—1154-1181. *South Transept*—1230—*c.* 1241. *North Transept*—1241-1260. *Nave*—1291-1324; except wooden vault of *c.* 1354. *Part of West Front*—West window glazed, 1338. *Chapter House*—" The glass was executed before 1307." *Vestibule*—After Chapter House. *Presbytery*—*c.* 1361-1370. *Choir*—*c.* 1380—*c.* 1400. *East Window Glazed* — 1405-1408. *Central Tower* — *c.* 1400-1423. *South-west Tower* — 1433-1447. *North-west Tower*—1470-1474. See *Guides to York*, by *A. Clutton Brock*, 20 ; by *G. Benson*, 84 ; and *Rickman*, 168, 173, 181, 185, 240, 215, 234, 241, 244, 246, 256, 296, 273, 292, 308 ; and Willis on *York Minster.**

YORK, ST MARY'S ABBEY. BENEDICTINE MONKS. The first stone was laid in 1271. The first stone of the columns was not laid till 1273. Finished before 1296. *Rickman*, 175.†

YORK, ST MARTIN-LE-GRAND. PARISH CHURCH. *Tower and Glass*—1437. *Rickman*, 302.

YORK, ST MICHAEL-LE-BELFRY. PARISH CHURCH. 1535-1545. *Bloxam*, 275.

* For the English Cathedrals, see the illustrated articles in the *Builder*, published in one volume in 1894 ; Britton's *English Cathedrals;* Browne Willis' *Survey of the Cathedrals*, 1727 ; and Carter's plans and drawings.

† For the English Abbeys, see the illustrated articles in the *Builder*, 1894 to 1901.

ROMANESQUE PIERS OF THE GREATER CHURCHES.

1. Durham Choir.

2. Ely North Transept, West Aisle.

3. Winchester Nave.

4. Winchester North Transept, West Aisle.

5. St Albans Nave.

6. Peterborough, Minor Pier in Nave.

7. Norwich Nave.

ROMANESQUE PIERS OF THE GREATER CHURCHES.

GOTHIC PIERS OF THE GREATER CHURCHES.

1. Kirkstall.

2. Roche.

3. Byland.

4. Wells.

5. York St Mary's.

6. Guisborough.

7. Bridlington.

8. Lichfield Choir.

9. Exeter Nave.

10. Canterbury Nave.

11. Bristol Choir.

12. St George's, Windsor (enlarged, page 255).

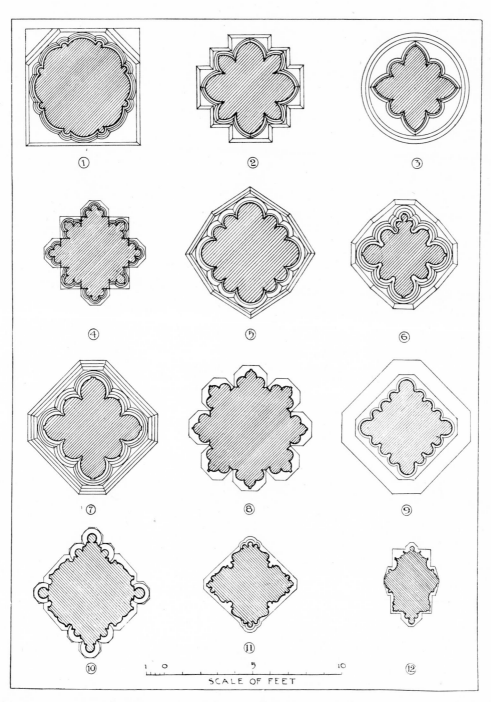

SCALE OF FEET

GOTHIC PIERS OF THE GREATER CHURCHES.

PIERS OF PARISH CHURCHES.

1. Northampton St Peter.

2. Market Deeping.

3. Skelton.

4. Higham Ferrers.

5. Northborough.

6. Bottisham.

7. Lavenham.

8. Coggeshall.

9. Long Melford Nave.

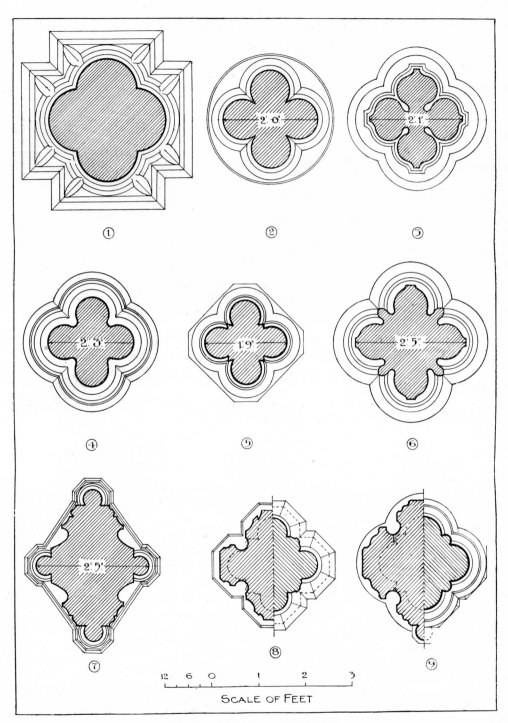

PIERS OF PARISH CHURCHES.

PIERS AND ARCHES.

1. Northampton St Peter.

2. Warmington.

3. Market Deeping.

4. Barnack.

5. Stamford All Saints Nave.

6. Stamford All Saints Nave.

7. Stone.

8. Stamford All Saints Chancel.

9. Finedon.

10. Stamford St Martin.

11. Hutton.

12. Long Melford Lady Chapel.

SCALE OF FEET

PIERS AND ARCHES.

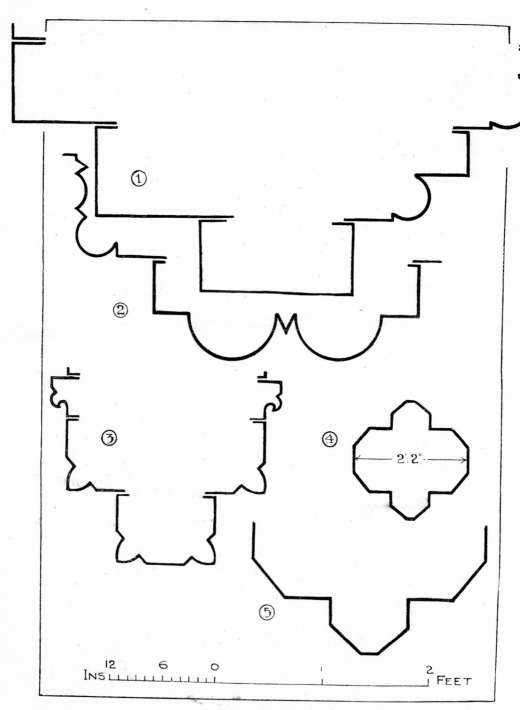

ARCHES—Sheet I.

1. Chichester Nave.
2. Hedingham.

3. Warmington.
4, 5. Wawne.

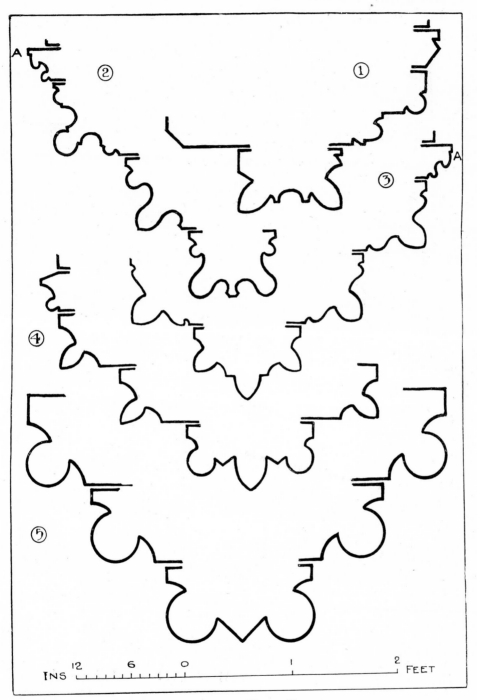

ARCHES—Sheet II.

1. Walsoken.
2. New Shoreham.
3. New Shoreham.
4. Byland.
5. Grimsby.

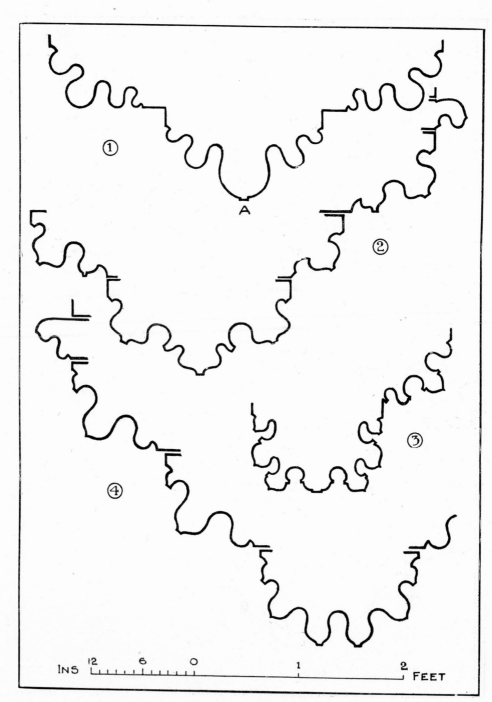

ARCHES—Sheet III.

1. Temple Choir.
2. Lincoln Nave.
3. Temple Choir.
4. St Mary's Abbey, York.

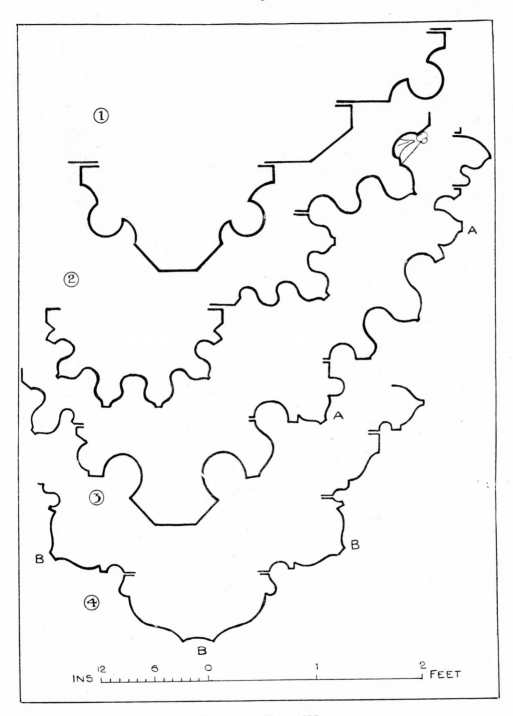

ARCHES—Sheet IV.

1. Bridlington.
2. Lincoln Presbytery.
3. Tintern Choir.
4. Winchelsea.

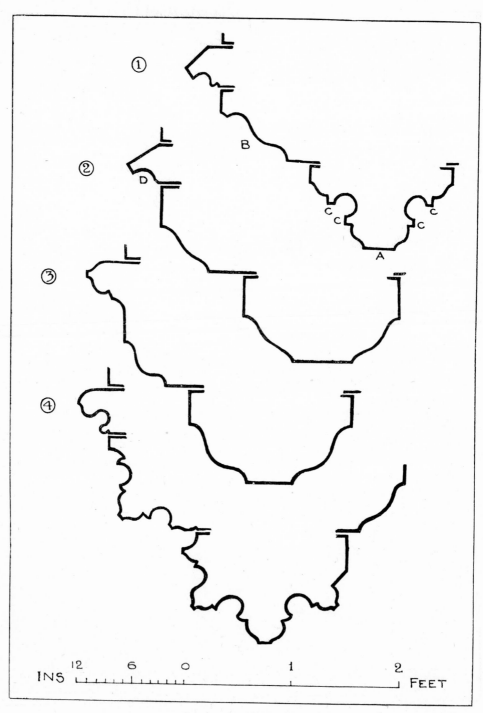

ARCHES—Sheet V.

1. Leadenham.

2. Helpringham.

3. Northborough.

4. Beverley St Mary Chancel.

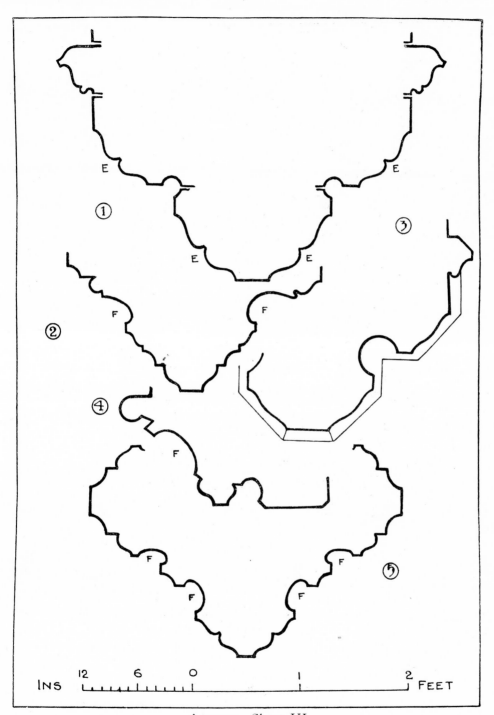

ARCHES—Sheet VI.

1. Bottisham.
2. Chelmsford.
5. St Mary, Oxford.
3. Kettering.
4. George Inn, Glastonbury.

Rib-Molds—Sheet I.

1. Gloucester Crypt.

2. Canterbury Treasury.

3. Birkin Apse.

4. Abbaye-aux-Hommes, Caen.

5. Kirkstall Nave Aisle, Transverse Rib.

6. Kirkstall Nave Aisle, Diagonal Rib.

7. Furness Nave Aisle, Transverse Rib.

8. Furness Nave Aisle, Diagonal Rib.

9. Furness Nave Aisle, Wall Rib.

10. Buildwas Chapter House, Transverse Rib.

11. Buildwas Chapter House, Diagonal Rib.

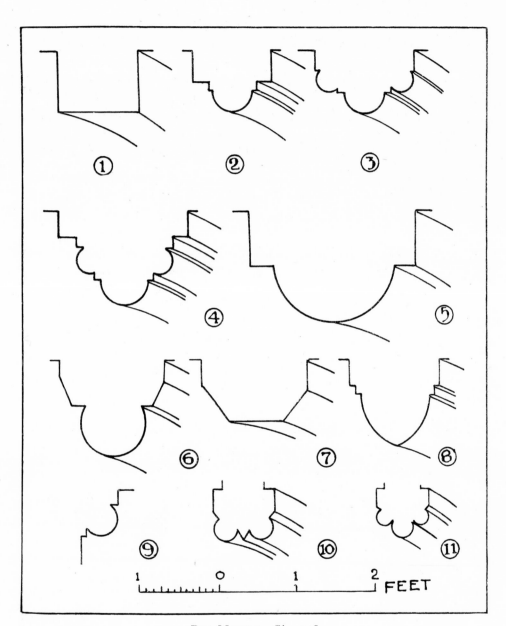

Rib-Molds—Sheet I.

Rib-Molds—Sheet II.

1. Roche, Transverse Rib.

2. Roche, Diagonal Rib.

3. Byland Aisle, Transverse and Diagonal Ribs.

4. Byland Aisle, Wall Rib.

5. Jervaulx Aisle, Transverse Rib.

6. London, Aisle of Nave of Temple Church.

7. London, Aisle of Nave of Temple Church.

8. London, Aisle of Nave of Temple Church.

9. London, Aisle of Nave of Temple Church.

10. London, Aisle of Nave of Temple Church.

11. London, Aisle of Nave of Temple Church.

12. Whitby Choir Aisle, Transverse and Diagonal Ribs.

13. Whitby Choir Aisle, Wall Rib.

14. Rievaulx Choir and Aisles, Transverse and Diagonal Ribs.

15. Rievaulx Choir and Aisles, Wall Rib.

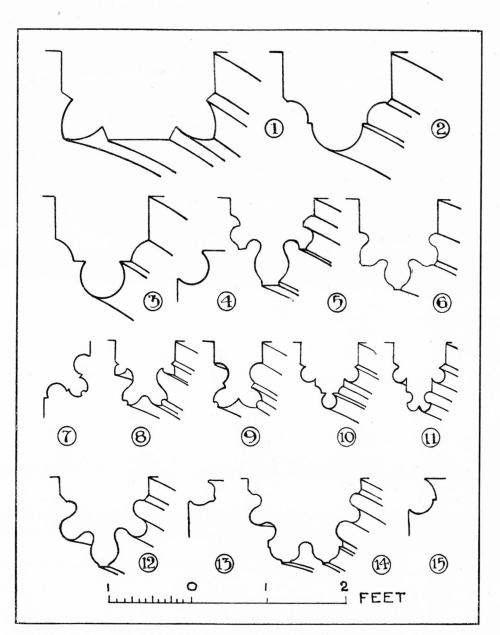

RIB-MOLDS—Sheet II.

Rib-Molds—Sheet III.

1. Fountains Choir Aisle, Transverse and Diagonal Ribs.

2. Fountains Choir Aisle, Wall Rib.

3. Lincoln Galilee.

4. Bridlington Nave Aisle, Transverse and Diagonal Ribs.

5. Tintern Aisles, Transverse and Diagonal Ribs.

6. Tintern Aisles, Wall Rib.

7. York, St Mary's Abbey ; Nave Aisle, Transverse Rib.

8. York, St Mary's Abbey ; Nave Aisle, Diagonal Rib.

9. York, St Mary's Abbey ; Nave Aisle, Wall Rib.

10. Howden Choir, Transverse and Diagonal Ribs.

11. Howden Choir, Wall Rib.

12. Selby Choir Aisle, Transverse and Diagonal Ribs.

13. Selby Choir Aisle, Wall Rib.

14. Wells, Porch of Staircase of Vicars' Close.

15. Great Chalfield, Wilts; Porch of Manor House.

16. Great Chalfield, Wilts; Porch of Manor House.

17. Kenilworth, Octagonal Lobby.

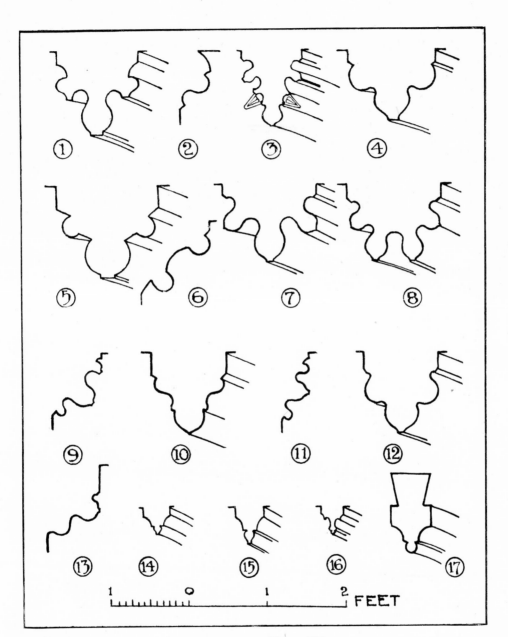

RIB-MOLDS — Sheet III.

Ground or Basement Courses.

1. Fountains Nave.

2. Hexham North Transept.

3. Whitby Choir.

4. Fountains Choir.

5. Rievaulx Choir.

6. Bridlington Nave.

7. Welbourne.

8. Kettering Tower.

9. Stoke Golding.

10. Merton College Chapel Transept, Oxford.

11. All Souls' College Chapel, Oxford.

12. Magdalen College Chapel, Oxford.

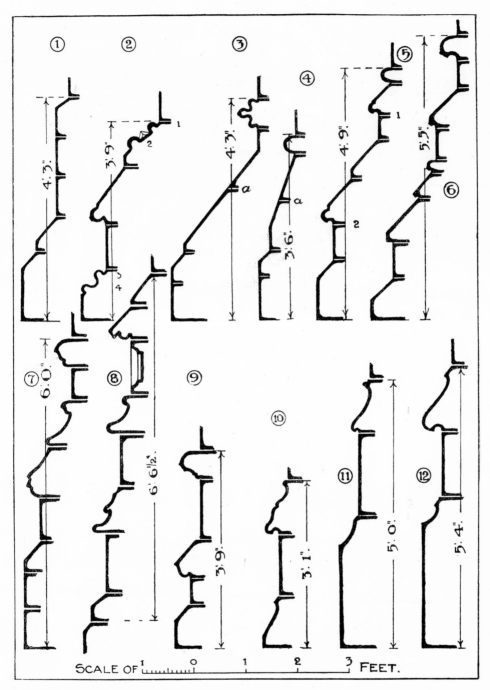

GROUND-COURSES.

Strings—Sheet I.

1. Fountains, Aisle of Nave.

2. Fountains, Clerestory of Nave.

3. Furness, Aisle of Nave.

4. Roche Triforium.

5. Roche Aisle.

6. Byland Triforium.

7. Hexham, Aisle of Choir.

8. Hexham, Triforium of Choir.

9. Jervaulx Aisle.

10. Jervaulx Aisle.

11. Whitby Triforium.

12. Whitby East End.

13. Whitby Aisle.

14. Fountains Aisle.

15. Rievaulx Triforium.

16. Netley Aisle.

17. Netley Aisle.

18. Bridlington Aisle.

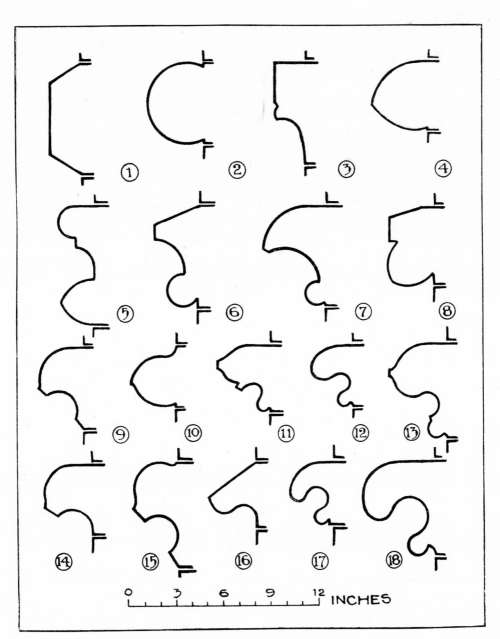

STRINGS—Sheet I.

Strings—Sheet II.

1. Bridlington Clerestory.

2. Tintern Clerestory.

3. St Mary, York, Aisle.

4. Guisborough Aisle.

5. Howden, Aisle of Choir.

6. Selby, Aisle of Choir.

7. Brandon's *Analysis*.

8. Brandon's *Analysis*.

9. Brandon's *Analysis*.

10. Brandon's *Analysis*.

11. Austrey Dripstone.

12. Austrey Dripstone.

13. Frampton, Dripstone.

14. Brandon's *Analysis*.

15. Brandon's *Analysis*.

16. Brandon's *Analysis*.

17. Brandon's *Analysis*.

18. Cottingham

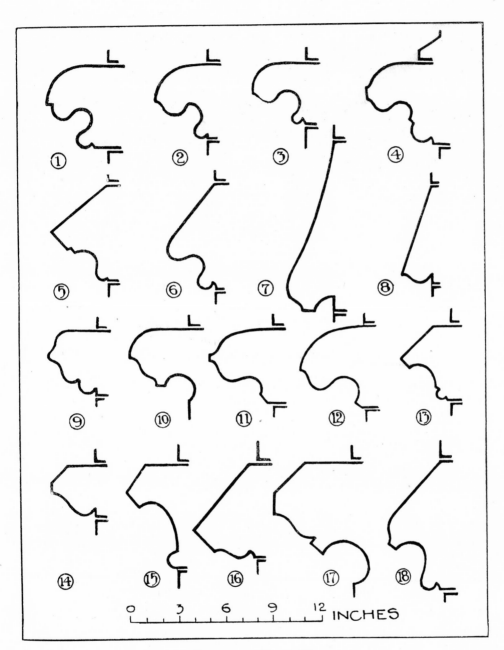

STRINGS—Sheet II.

MOLDINGS OF ABACI AND CAPITALS—Sheet I.

1. Canwick.

2. Harmston.

3. Whaplode.

4. Whaplode.

5. Aswarby.

6. Moulton.

7. Fulbeck.

8. Whaplode.

9. Horbling.

10. Weston.

11. Waddington.

12. Lincoln.

13. Lincoln.

14. Lincoln St Mary Wigford.

15. Threckingham.

16. Threckingham.

17. Lincoln.

18. Lincoln.

19. Lincoln.

20. Buildwas.

21. Fountains Nave.

22. Kirkstall.

23. Furness.

24. Byland

25. Deeping St James.

26. Deeping St James.

27. Deeping St James.

28. Market Deeping.

29. Northampton St Sepulchre.

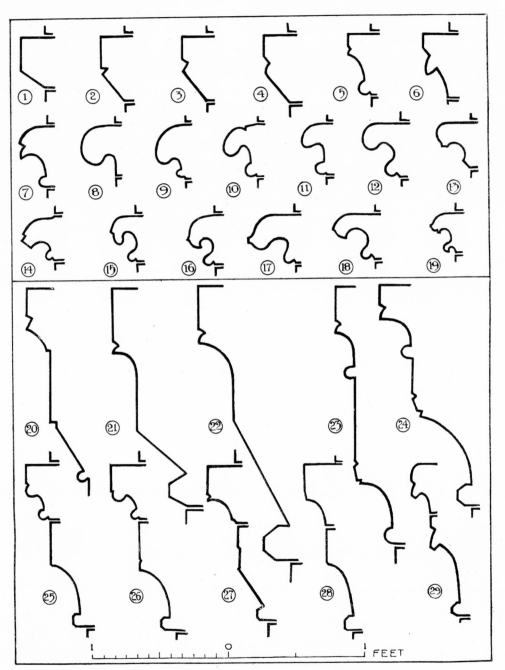

Abaci and Capitals—Sheet I.

MOLDED CAPITALS AND BASES—Sheet II.

1. Whitby.

2. Fountains.

3. Netley.

4. Bridlington.

5. Tintern.

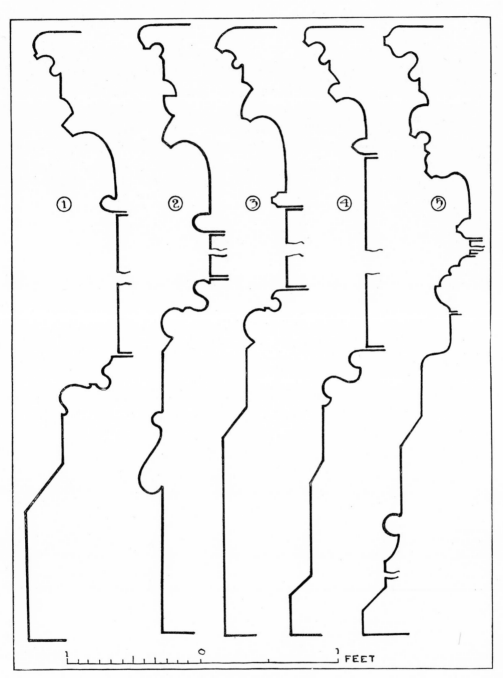

CAPITALS—Sheet II.

Molded Capitals—Sheet III.

1. Doddinghurst, Shaft in Doorway.

2. East Thorpe Sedilia.

3. Durham Eastern Transept.

4. London, Temple Choir.

5. Great Baddow Pier.

6. Warmington, Shaft in West Doorway.

7. Warmington, Shaft in West Doorway.

8. Wiggenhall St Mary the Virgin, Shaft in North Doorway.

9. Wiggenhall St Mary the Virgin, Shaft in North Doorway.

10. Fairstead Sedilia.

689

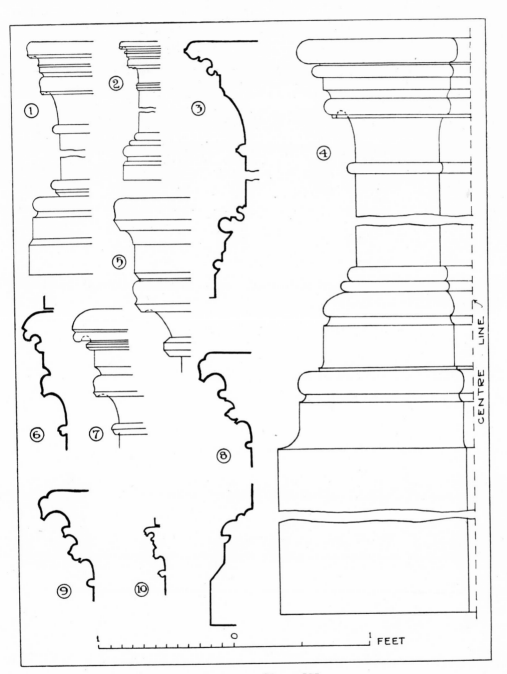

CAPITALS—Sheet III.

2 X

MOLDED CAPITALS—Sheet IV.

1. Swayton Nave.

2. Sleaford North Transept.

3. Sleaford North Transept.

4. Helpringham Nave.

5. Heckington Tower.

6. Heckington Chancel.

7. Heckington Nave.

8. Leadenham Nave.

9. Chipping Hill, Piers of Nave.

10. Asgarby Nave.

11. Aswarby Nave.

12. Holbeach Nave.

13. Tiltey Sedilia.

14. Rushden, Piers of North Side of Nave.

15. Rushden, Piers of North Side of Nave.

16. Rushden, Piers of North Side of Nave.

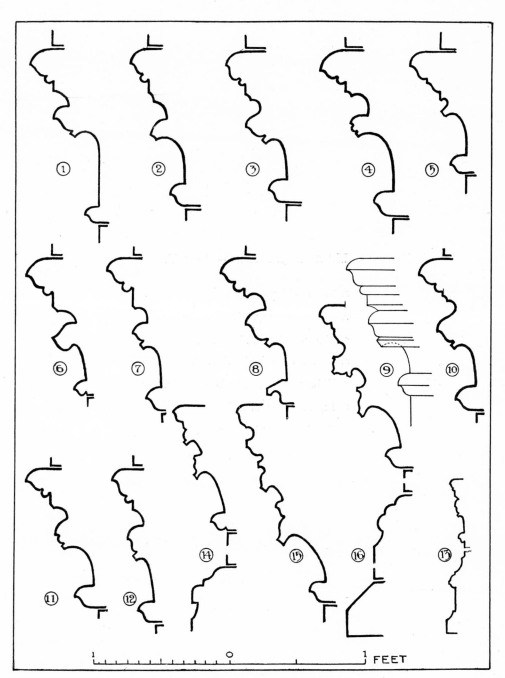

CAPITALS—Sheet IV.

MOLDED CAPITALS—Sheet V.

1. Terling, Pier of Nave.

2. Oxford St Mary, Pier in Nave.

3. Chelmsford, Shaft in Porch.

4. Chelmsford, Pier in Chancel.

5. Eltham Palace, Shaft in Doorway.

6. Ingatestone, Pier in Nave.

7. Bocking, Shaft in Doorway.

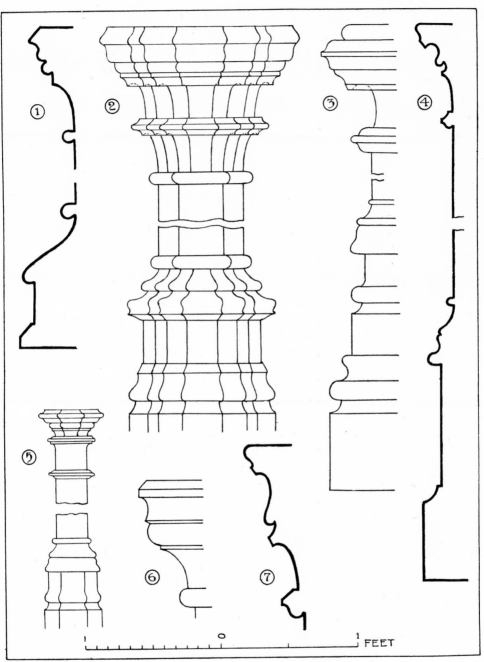

CAPITALS—Sheet V.

BASE-MOLDS—Sheet I.

1. Attic Base.

2. Waterholding Base.

3. Boxgrove Cloister.

4. Boxgrove Cloister.

5. Hedingham Castle, Window Shaft.

6. Furness.

7. Fountains.

8. Jervaulx.

9. Barnack.

10. Winchester St Cross.

11. Winchester St Cross.

695

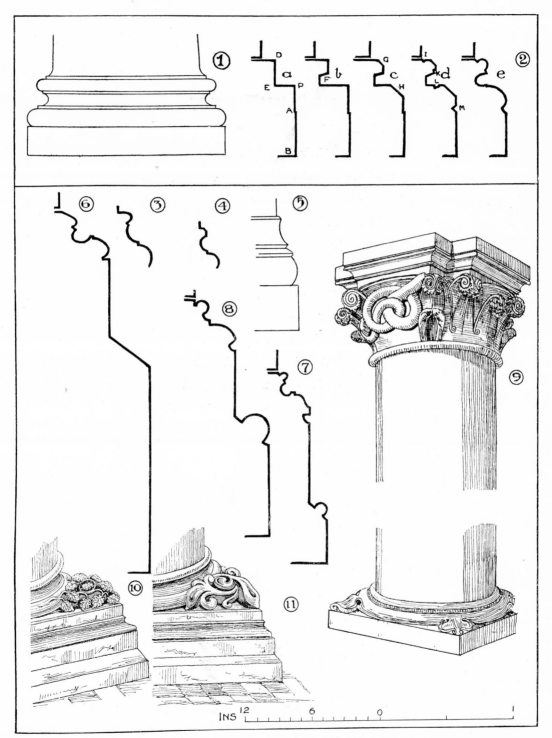

BASES—Sheet I.

BASE-MOLDS—Sheet II.

1. Salisbury Cloister.

2. Winchelsea Piscina.

3. Winchelsea Sedilia.

4. Winchelsea, Shaft of Window.

5. Winchelsea Pier.

6. Austrey Pier.

7. Tintern.

8. Tintern, Pier of Nave.

9. Great Gonerby Pier.

10. Wells Chapter House, Central Column.

11. Selby Choir, Arcading and Vaulting Shaft.

12. Guisborough, Arcading and Window Jamb.

13. Beverley St Mary, Shaft of Window in Flemish Chapel.

14. Leadenham Pier.

15. Billingborough Pier.

16. Osbournby Pier.

17. Sleaford Pier.

18. Holbeach Pier.

19. Bottisham Pier.

20. Beverley St Mary, North Side, Pier of Nave.

21. Bristol, Colston House, Shaft of Fireplace.

22. Arundel, Pier of Nave.

23. Louth, Respond of Tower Arch

24. Colchester Pier.

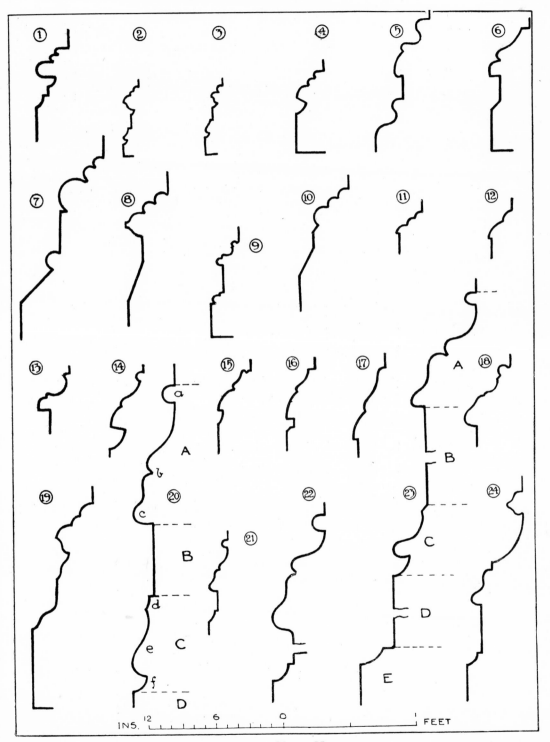

BASES—Sheet II.

WINDOW-MOLDS—Sheet I.

1. Rievaulx, Lower Triplet of East End, Jamb and Bases.

2. Rievaulx, Arch and Abaci.

3. Netley, East Window, Jamb and Bases.

4. Netley, Arch and Abaci.

5. Stone, both Jambs, Bases, and Mullion.

6. Stone, Arch.

6A. Stone, Arch Enlarged.

7. Guisborough, Aisle of Choir, Jamb and Bases.

8. Guisborough, Arch and Abaci.

9. Tiltey, Mullions.

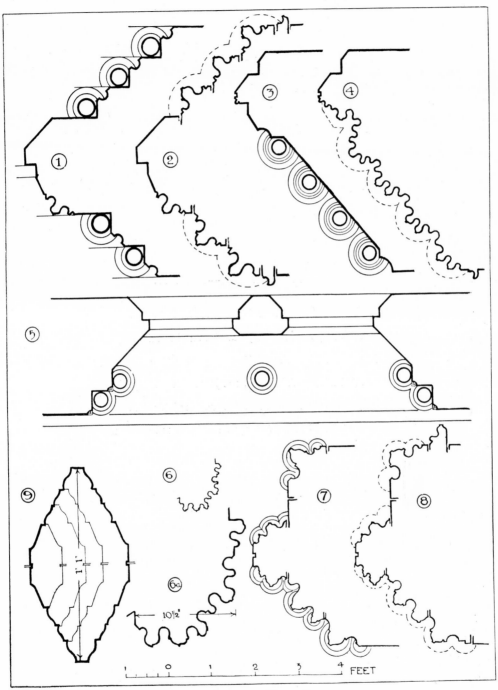

WINDOWS—Sheet I.

WINDOW-MOLDS.

Window-Molds—Sheet II.

1. Bishopstone, Wilts, both Jambs and Mullion.

2. Wells, Vicars' Close, one Jamb and Mullion.

3. Sleaford, Arch and Mullion.

4. Maidstone All Saints, one Jamb and Mullion.

5. Maidstone All Saints, one Jamb and Mullion.

6. Oxford All Souls' Chapel, one Jamb and Mullion.

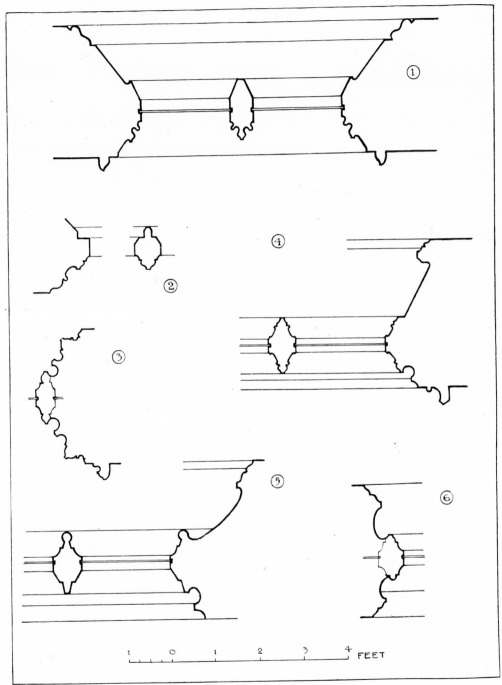

WINDOWS—Sheet II.

Molds of Doorways—Sheet I.

1. Rochester Cathedral, Jamb of West Doorway.

2. Arch of ditto.

3. Plan of ditto.

4. Codford St Mary, Wilts, Jamb and Arch of Chancel Arch.

5. Wenlock, Arch and Abaci of Doorway into Cloister.

6. Jamb and Bases of ditto.

7. Colchester Magdalen Chapel, Jamb and Base of Doorway.

8. Arch of ditto.

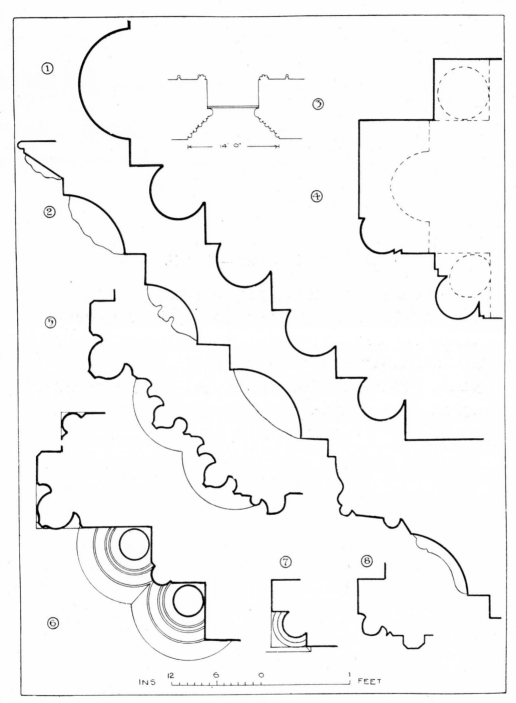

DOORWAYS—Sheet I.

MOLDS OF DOORWAYS—Sheet II.

1. Clare Church, Suffolk ; West Doorway; Jamb, Arch, and Abaci.

2. Wiggenhall St Mary the Virgin, Norfolk ; North Doorway ; Jamb, Arch, and Abaci.

3. Stamford, St Leonard's Priory ; West Doorway ; Jamb, Arch, and Abaci.

4. Middleton Cheney, Northants ; Doorway of South Porch.

5. London, St Etheldreda's, Holborn ; Arch of Doorway on South Side (*c.* 1380, Caveler).

6. Jamb, Bases and Abaci of ditto.

7. Warmington ; Doorway of South Porch ; Jamb, Arch, and Abaci.

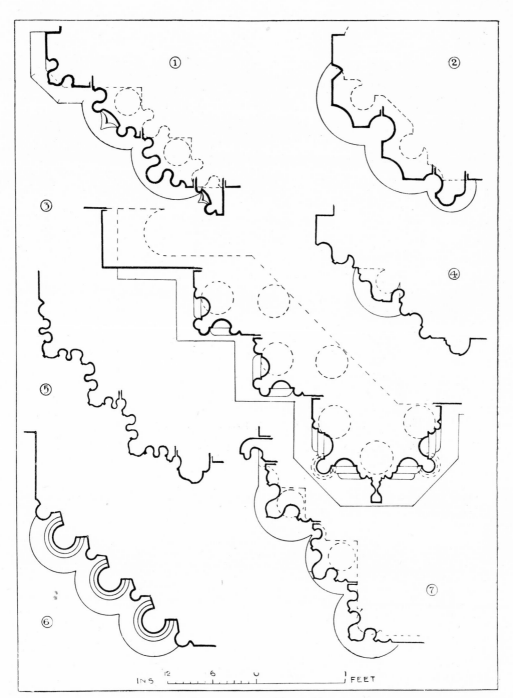

DOORWAYS—Sheet II.

2 Y

Doorways—Sheet III.

1. Houghton-le-Dale, Norfolk ; Jamb.

2. Oxford, Merton College Transept ; Plan of Moldings above Capitals.

3. Oxford, Merton College Transept ; Plan of Columns showing Capitals.

4. Oxford, Merton College Transept ; Plan of Columns showing Bases.

5. Oxford, Magdalen College Chapel ; West Doorway.

6. Fotheringhay ; West Doorway ; Arch and Abacus.

7. Fotheringhay ; West Doorway ; Jamb and Bases.

707

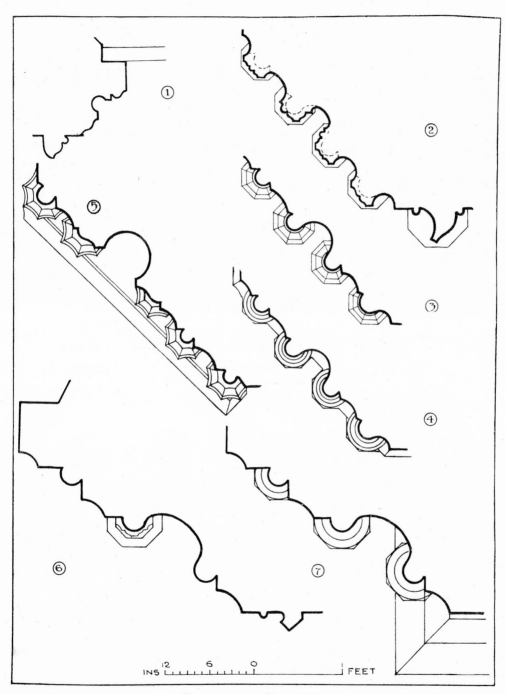

Doorways—Sheet III.

INDEX TO ILLUSTRATIONS.

NOTE.—The full titles and descriptions of the books referred to in this list will be found in the List of Authorities, pages xii-xvi. The illustrations to which no book is appended as authority are from photographs and drawings. Professional photographers are distinguished by the name of their town being given.

INDEX OF PLACES.

ABBAYE-AUX-HOMMES; AUX-DAMES. See CAEN.

ABBEVILLE. *Nave*, triforium, 539.

ABBEY CWM-HIR. *Capitals and foliage*, 429, 430, 431, 432, 435 : " Western " style of capitals, 433 and note, 435. *Gothic*, " Western school " of, 105. *Piers*, " Western," 245. *Roll molds*, 278. See also LLANIDLOES.

ABBEY DORE. *Aisles*, two eastern, 172. *Ambulatory*, rectangular, 106, 171. Capitals and foliage, 418, 428 and note, 429, 431, 432 : interlacings on capitals, 414 : " Western " style of capital, 433. *Chapels*, five eastern, 172 : low walls between, 200. *East front*, 68. *Flying buttresses*, absent, 372. *Gothic*, " Western school " of, 105. *Piers*, " Western," 245. *Screens and Woodwork*, Jacobean, 203, note. *Triforium*, absorbed into clerestory, 536. *Vault*, 545, note.

ABBOTSBURY. St Catherine's Chapel. *Stone roof*, 284.

ABERDEEN. King's College. *Spire lantern or crown*, 625.

ABINGDON. *Aisles*, 224.

ABINGER. *No buttresses*, 362.

ACHURCH. *Transepts*, 222.

ADDERBURY. *Roof*, 558 : arched braces of, 562 : longitudinal braces of, 569. *Spire*, pinnacles, 623.

ADEL, 220. *Norman porch*, 582. *Norman roof*, 572.

AGLIATE. Basilica, 232.

AIRAINES. *Vaulting*, ridge ribs, 335, 339.

AIX-LA-CHAPELLE. *Capitals*, cubical, 411. *Columns*, 232, note. *Vaults*, groined, 292, 295, note 3 : wall ribs, 300.

ALBI. Cathedral. *Hall plan*, 321 ; without aisles, 229. *Vault*, groined, 291.

ALLIATA. Baptistery. *Roof on vault*, 550, note. Church. *Apses*, three eastern, 163. *Vaults*, east bay of aisles and crypt, groined, 292. *Windows*, small Romanesque, 459.

ALMENNO. St Thomas. *Roof on vault*, 550, note.

ALPIRSBACH. Basilica, 232.

AMIENS. Cathedral. *Altitude and proportion*, 61. *Arches*, ogee, north chapel, 270. *Buttresses*, flying, aqueduct on, 400. *Chapels*, 131, note ; 170. *Chapels between buttresses*, 197, notes. *Flèche*, 594. *Height*, 527. *Piers*, illogical, 241, note. *Pinnacles*, 363, 377. *Porches*, western, 205. *Roofs of aisles*, 537. *Spire*, 594. *Transepts*, 197. *Triforium*, choir, 537 : nave, 535 : glazed, 537, 538. *Vaulting*, span of, 291 : ridge ribs, 335. *Windows*, 490 : choir, 508, note : clerestory, 57.

ANGERS. Cathedral. *Aisleless*, 228, 321. *Vault*, high, in squares, 321 : ridge ribs, 335. La Trinité. *Vault*, quasi-sexpartite, 321. St Martin. *Tower*, central lantern, 592.

ANGOULÊME. *Domes*, 13, 281.

ANJOU. Churches. *High aisles or parallel naves*, counter-thrusts of vaults, 282.

AQUILEIA. *Capitals and abaci*, 410.

ARBONA. *Vaulting*, ridge ribs, 335.

ARDENNE. *Aisled barn*, 225.

ARLES. Roman Amphitheatre. *Ceilings*, Roman, stone, 285. *Orders*, 274. St Trophime. *Arch*, pointed, 264. *Vault*, barrel, 13 : half barrel in aisles, 13, 519.

ARUNDEL. *Base*, 450.

ASGARBY. *Molded capital*, 444.

ASH. *Capitals and bases*, 451.

175, note. *Clerestory*, passage, nave, 545, note. *Crypt*, 191, 284. *Doorways*, trefoil headed, north transept, 580: transitional, 509. *Fronts*, east, 68; west, 71, 73 (see *Towers*). *Narthex*, 204. *Nave*, formerly unaisled, 16, 201. *Pulpitum*, 179, 381. *Roof*, flat, of aisle, 538, 540, 541. *Spires*, former, 593, 594, 619. *Stalls*, 179. *Transepts*, aisle, eastern, 198; western, 204. *Triforium*, choir, transparent, 538: transept, single containing arch, 533. *Towers*, western flanking, 73, 204, 599. *Vaulting*, Anglo-Saxon barrel, 284. Choir, wall ribs, 238. Transept aisle, ridge ribs, 335, 339; web, French method of filling, 335. *Windows*, east, 475: semicircular headed, 462: splays, 512. CHAPEL OF ST MARY MAGDALEN, 219.

ROCHE. *Advanced work*, "Northern school," vaulted throughout, 103, 106. *Sanctuary*, unaisled, 176. Strings, pointed bowtell, 406.

ROCHESTER. *Abacus strings*, 404. *Aisles*, unvaulted, 29. *Arch*, early pointed, 266. *Bases*, chapter house doorway, 444, 453: crypt, 451, 452. *Capitals*, molded, 446: pilaster strips, 358. *Choir*, raised, with high flight of steps, 191. *Crypt*, 189, 191. *Diaper work*, 84. *Flying buttress*, only one, 113, 372. *Fronts*, north transept, 68: west, 28. *Marble shafts*, 252. *Nave*, 527: unvaulted, 20. *Pier*, "Southern," crypt, 246. *Pilaster strips*, Norman, 358. *Pinnacles*, octagonal, west front, 362. *Pulpitum*, 179. *Sanctuary*, unaisled, 176. *Shrine*, 183, note, 189. *Spire*, 619. *Styles*, mélange of, 46. *Triforium*, 84, 266, 532, note, 527: single containing arch, 533. *Tower*, central, rebuilt, 594. *Transepts*, east, 189: north, front of, 68. *Tympanum*, sculptured, 573. *Vaulting*, fan, abandoned, Lady chapel, 346: groined, 292, 294: sexpartite, 320: spring, 307: vaulting shaft, 240.

RODA, ISLAND OF. NILOMETER. *Pointed arches*, 263.

RODMELL. *Spire*, plan of, 629.

ROMAINMOTIER. *Narthex*, 202.

ROME. ARCH OF CONSTANTINE, 230. ARCH OF SEPTIMUS SEVERUS. *Acanthus leaf*, 426. BASILICA OF JUNIUS BASSUS. *Roman corbel-table*, 392. BASILICA OF MAXENTIUS OR CONSTANTINE, 230. *But-*

tresses, internal, pierced with aisles, 362. *Roof* over vault, 550. *Vaults* and buttresses, 201. BASILICAS, FIVE PATRIARCHAL, 146. BASILICAS, SECULAR. *Atrium*, 201. BATHS OF CARACALLA. *Vaults*, external covering of, 384: material of, 303. BATHS OF DIOCLETIAN (*S. Maria degli Angeli*). *Composite capitals*, 420, 425. *Vault*, exterior of, 384: groined, 291. BATHS OF TITUS. *Vault material*, 303. CAMPANILES, 586. CHRISTIAN CHURCHES, 145. CLOACA MAXIMA. *Compound arch*, 272. COLOSSEUM. *Capitals*, 427. *Vault material*, 303. MONTE TESTACCIO. Formed from old broken wine jars, 303. PANTHEON. *Corinthian capitals*, 420. *Dome*, 281. *Roof* over vault, 550. S. AGNESE. 233. S. BALBINA. *Pilaster strip buttresses*, 351. S. CLEMENTE. *Altar*, 592. *Atrium*, 201. *Screen walls*, 183. S. LORENZO. *Capitals*, 427. *Columns*, 231, 233. S. MARIA DEGLI ANGELI (Baths of Diocletian). S. MARIA IN ARA CŒLI. *Columns*, 231, 233. S. MARIA IN COSMEDIN. *Apses*, three parallel eastern, 159. S. MARIA IN DOMINICA. *Apse*, early eastern triple, 159. S. MARIA MAGGIORE. *Columns*, 231, 233. *Ritualistic divisions*, 183. *Round tower*, in mosaic, 586. ST PAUL'S EXTRA MUROS. *Columns*, 231, 233. ST PETER'S. *Bases*, 449. *Confessio*, 191. ST PETER'S (OLD), 5. *Atrium*, 201. *Sacristy and library*, 159. S. PRASSEDE. *Columns*, 234: alternation of, 317. S. PUDENZIANA. *Arches*, orders in, 274. *Pilaster strip buttresses*, 351. S. SABINA. *Doors*, *towers*, church represented having two western, 586. SS. SIXTUS AND CÆCILIA, 145. S. STEFANO ROTONDO. *Dosseret*, 411. TEMPLE OF MINERVA MEDICA. *Apses* and *buttresses*, 351. *Vault material*, 303. VATICAN. *Tower*, 590. VAULT MATERIAL. 303.

ROMSEY. *Abacus string-course*, 404. *Aisle*, eastern, 171, 172. *Apses*, lateral eastern, 164: *Apsidal chapels*, transepts, 197. *Arches*, pier, square-edged with chevron, 33. *Capitals*, incurved cones, 414, note: leaf scroll, 446: re-carved, 413. *Corbeltables*, 392. *Doorway*, western, absent, 581, note. *Front*, west, 73. *Gothic*, slow growth, mélange of styles, 45, 46. *Griffes*, 446, 455. *Lady chapel*, eastern, 106. *Nave*, east, Romanesque, not Gothic, 45: internal elevation, 26, 530. *Transept*, apsidal chapels, 197. *Triforium*, 26, 530, 532, note: absorbed into pier arcade, 535:

INDEX OF SUBJECT MATTER & GLOSSARY.

(DEFINITIONS OF ARCHITECTURAL TERMS WILL BE FOUND ON THE PAGES WHICH ARE REFERRED TO IN CLARENDON TYPE.)